Cyberterrorism –

the use of the Internet for terrorist purposes

Council of Europe Publishing

Disclaimer

It should be noted that the views expressed in this publication do not necessarily reflect the position of individual States, the Committee of Experts on Terrorism (CODEXTER) or the Council of Europe as a whole with regard to the interpretation of the legislation and situations referred to.

The views expressed in the analytical report are those of the authors. The national contributions are those originally submitted by delegations, subject to editorial revision. The contributions originally submitted in French have been translated for the purposes of this publication.

For further information, please contact us:

Counter-Terrorism Task Force
Council of Europe
F-67075 Strasbourg Cedex (France)
Tel.: + 33 3 88 41 34 79 – Fax: + 33 3 90 21 51 31
E-mail: gmt@coe.int – Internet: http://www.coe.int/gmt

Council of Europe Publishing
F-67075 Strasbourg Cedex
http://book.coe.int

ISBN 978-92-871-6226-7
© Council of Europe, December 2007
Printed at the Council of Europe

Contents

Foreword

The threat of cyberterrorism and the misuse of the Internet for terrorist purposes is particularly alarming because our society is so dependent on computer systems and the Internet.

While it is true that the threat may be exaggerated, it cannot be denied or ignored. The increasing visibility of terrorism has led to these unconventional weapons being harnessed by a new computer-savvy generation of terrorists.

The Council of Europe's Cybercrime Convention (2001) and the Convention on the Prevention of Terrorism (2005) provide a legal response which is consistent with the protection of human rights and individual freedoms. These innovative and unique treaties have created a new dynamic at international level, fostered by the ever-increasing need for international co-operation.

This publication, which is the result of the work of the Council of Europe's Committee of Experts on Terrorism (CODEXTER) which has been studying this matter and surveying the situation in member states since 2006, is intended as a comprehensive overview of the issues at stake and the possible solutions.

Terry Davis
Secretary General
of the Council of Europe

Analytical report

**Cyberterrorism and Other Use of the
Internet for Terrorist Purposes –
Threat Analysis and Evaluation
of International Conventions**

Expert Report prepared by

Prof. Dr. Dr. h.c. Ulrich Sieber
and Phillip W. Brunst
Max Planck Institute for Foreign
and International Criminal Law
Freiburg, Germany

Executive Summary

1. Threat Assessment and Phenomenology

Cyberterrorism, whether targeting the Internet or conducted by means of the Internet, represents a serious threat, since many essential aspects of today's society are completely dependent upon the functioning of computer systems. When analysing this threat and evaluating legal responses, it is necessary to distinguish among three phenomena:

(a) *attacks via the Internet* that cause damage not only to essential electronic communication systems and the IT infrastructure but also to other infrastructures, systems, and legal interests, including human life;

(b) *dissemination of illegal content*, including threatening with terrorist attacks; inciting, advertising, and glorifying terrorism; fundraising for and financing of terrorism; training for terrorism; recruiting for terrorism; and dissemination of racist and xenophobic material; as well as

(c) *other logistical uses of IT systems* by terrorists, such as internal communication, information acquisition, and target analysis.

2. Applicability of Existing Conventions

The *existing international conventions* and other instruments that promote the harmonisation of national substantive and procedural law and international co-operation are applicable to these misuses of the Internet for terrorist purposes: The computer-specific provisions of the Council of Europe's Cybercrime Convention that address national substantive law, national procedural law, and international co-operation can be used in cases of terrorism. Furthermore, the substantive and procedural rules as well as the rules on international co-operation found in international instruments on terrorism, on money laundering and financing of terrorism, and on general mutual assistance and extradition are also applicable in the cyberterrorism context. As a result, the basic question to be addressed in this report – that of the existence of "terrorist-specific" gaps in "computer-specific" conventions and "computer-specific" gaps in "terrorist-specific" conventions – can be answered in the negative as far as the application of the conventions is concerned.

3. Evaluation and Recommendations

The confirmed applicability of existing international instruments in the cyberterrorism context thus limits future consideration to the second question to be addressed in this report, namely, whether the aforementioned "computer-specific" and "terror-specific" instruments have *general gaps*, i.e., gaps that are not specific to the use of the Internet for terrorist purposes. A comprehensive answer to this second question, which would require an in-depth analysis of all legal issues arising

11

both in the cybercrime as well as in the terrorism context, exceeds the scope of this report. However, an analysis of the main problems that arise in the context of cyberterrorism leads to the following evaluation and recommendations:

(a) A serious problem common to *all existing international instruments* is the insufficient number of states parties. This is especially true with respect to the Cybercrime Convention and the Convention on the Prevention of Terrorism, the two most important international instruments for fighting cyberterrorism and other terrorist use of the Internet. Therefore, signing, ratification, and implementation of these two conventions should be supported, and any additional courses of action undertaken in this context should be carried out in such a way as to avoid hindering or distracting from this process.

(b) The *Convention on the Prevention of Terrorism* – and its catalogue of offences, in particular – must be examined for provisions in need of amendment. At present, serious threats to commit terrorist acts are not adequately covered either by this Convention or by other Council of Europe conventions, and this deficit is not fully compensated by the instruments of other international organisations. Considering the effects of threats to commit terrorist acts, there is a need for action in this area – possibly in the form of a protocol to the Convention.

(c) The *Cybercrime Convention* should be evaluated with regard to its ability to cover newly emerging or newly discussed technical advances, particularly in the area of forensic investigative techniques (such as online searches or the use of key logger software). In the fast-paced, technical environment of cybercrime, such evaluations, which frequently lead to revisions and updates, are an absolutely normal process, especially when dealing with high risks such as those posed by terrorism. Should a decision be taken to supplement the Cybercrime Convention with a follow-up protocol addressing new investigative techniques, the possibility of excluding the political exception clause for some of the Convention's offences – especially in serious cases of data and system interference – might also be considered. An additional provision dealing with serious attacks on IT-based or general infrastructures is not essential. It would suffice for countries to make sure that their domestic statutes on data and system interference provide sanctions appropriate for cases involving terrorist attacks against computer systems. Indeed, such "effective, proportionate and dissuasive sanctions" are already required by the Cybercrime Convention, and it can be left to the national legislatures to achieve this result by means of sentencing rules, aggravated offences on data interference, or infrastructure offences.

(d) *New international efforts* should focus on the development of repressive and preventive measures that target the dissemination of illegal content on the Internet and that are both effective and respectful of civil liberties. This could be done either with a special focus on illegal terrorist content or in a more general way that would encompass other types of illegal content as well. As far as the substantive law is concerned, this would also require harmonised rules regarding the responsibility of Internet providers. These rules could then serve as the basis for international notice and takedown procedures. The necessary developments in the areas of criminal procedure and international co-operation will require specific regulations that are based on technical control mechanisms in the Internet and that do not unduly inhibit the free exchange of information. The Council of Europe, with its long tradition of balancing security interests in criminal matters with the protection of human rights, would be the ideal institution to tackle the difficult problems posed by the development of such international standards and procedures for regulating illegal content in computer networks. Due to the global nature of the Internet and its strong resistance to national control mechanisms, an initiative in this area could even lead to new forms of co-operation that might recognise the global cyberspace as a common heritage of mankind, a heritage in need of new mechanisms of governance implemented by new institutions.

Introduction

This report,[1] prepared for the Council of Europe, is designed to analyse the use of the Internet for cyberterrorism and for terrorist purposes.[2] It is divided into two main parts: The first part will explore the possible uses terrorists might be able to make of the Internet and other IT-systems (chapter I.). This part will not only cover IT-based attacks against infrastructure or human life, it will also investigate other terrorist forms of Internet use, such as the dissemination of terrorist content or the planning of conventional attacks. The second part will then present and evaluate legal responses taken by international institutions (chapter II.). In order to compare the various existing legal instruments, the chapter will differentiate between the harmonisation of national substantive as well as procedural criminal law and the improvements in international co-operation. A final chapter (chapter III.) will summarise the conclusions concerning the closure of possible gaps in international law or action.

I. Threat Analysis: Use of the Internet for Terrorist Purposes and Cyberterrorism[3]

The threat that is posed by terrorist use of the Internet is the subject of an ongoing controversial discussion. While some authors claim that, to date, not a single instance of cyberterrorism has been recorded, others argue that terrorists already routinely make use of the Internet. One reason for these differences in opinion is that neither terrorism[4] nor cyberterrorism[5] is a well-

---

[1] The report was prepared by Prof. Dr. Dr. h.c. Ulrich Sieber (chapters II. and III.), Director at the Max Planck Institute for Foreign and International Criminal Law, Freiburg, Germany, and Phillip W. Brunst (chapter I.), Head of Section 'Information Law' at the same Institute. Thanks are due to *Emily Silverman* and *Indira Tie* for invaluable translation and editing assistance.

[2] In this report, the term "terrorism" is understood in a broad sense in order to enable a comprehensive examination of possible use of the Internet for terrorist purposes. It includes the elements of violence or the threat of violence, psychological impact (such as the increase in fear), political goal(s), and the unlawfulness of the committed acts. For an analysis of definitions of terrorism, see *C. Tomuschat*, Council of Europe Committee of Experts on Terrorism (CODEXTER), Strasbourg, On the possible "added value" of a comprehensive Convention on Terrorism, 26 Human Rights Law Journal 2005, pp. 289-293 (paras. 8-20 and 21-35).

[3] Chapter I. prepared by *Phillip W. Brunst*, Head of Section 'Information Law' at the Max Planck Institute for Foreign and International Criminal Law.

[4] According to a 1988 study, more than 100 different definitions of terrorism with more than 20 definitional elements were in existence, see J. *Record,* Bounding the global war on terrorism, 2003, http://www.strategicstudiesinstitute.army.mil/pdffiles/PUB207.pdf [last visited: July 2007], p. 6. Also, neither states nor international organisations were able to establish a common definition of terrorism. For an overview, see *B. Golder/G. Williams,* What is 'terrorism'? University of New South Wales Law Journal 2004, Vol. 27, pp. 270-295, (273ff). In this report, "terrorism" is understood in a broad sense, see footnote 2.

defined term. Instead, definitions of cyberterrorism range from common use of the Internet by terrorists (e.g., sending emails) to real criminal cases involving either virtual or physical losses. This report will not be able to provide an extensive definition. Instead, based on a broad working hypothesis of terrorism,[6] it will give an overview of use that terrorists can make of the Internet.[7]

To achieve this goal, it is not sufficient merely to analyse current cases of cyberterrorism or terrorist use of the Internet. Instead, it is necessary to identify possible targets, risks, and other forms of terrorist Internet use. The threat analysis in this chapter is therefore based on an analysis of cybercrime- and cyberterrorism literature as well as on specialised security reports and everyday news reports. This broad approach was chosen to obtain an expanded view, not only of the real occurrences of cyberterrorism and other uses of the Internet, but also of possible future forms of utilisation.

The most commonly discussed use is a terrorist attack carried out via the Internet. Such an attack could be directed either at other IT-infrastructures, such as computers, servers, and routers or at objects in the "physical world," such as buildings, planes, trains, or even human life (part A.). Apart from such IT-based attacks, terrorists can use the Internet to disseminate content to the public. Since Internet connections are widely available and offer various advantages over conventional communication, terrorist organisations can put them to use: for example, to communicate with the public in order to present terrorist point of views or disseminate threats, to find new supporters, and/or to distribute information to followers (part B.).[8] Finally, the Internet can also be used for other purposes. Not only does it enable terrorists to engage in confidential communication among themselves, it also contains a multitude of information that was hard to obtain in former times. Satellite images and construction plans – even for complicated designs – are freely available through the Internet. Therefore, the Internet as a planning

---

[5] *B. Foltz*, Cyberterrorism, computer crime, and reality, Information Management & Computer Security, 15.03.2004, Vol. 12, No. 2, pp. 154-166; *M. Conway*, Reality Bytes: Cyberterrorism and Terrorist 'Use' of the Internet, First Monday, 04.11.2002, Vol. 7, No. 11, http://firstmonday.org/issues/issue7_11/conway/ [last visited: July 2007]; *M. Gercke*, "Cyberterrorismus" – Aktivitäten terroristischer Organisationen im Internet, CR 2007, pp. 62-68 (63).

[6] See footnote 2.

[7] The report, however, will not cover conventional attacks against IT-infrastructures which, in some cases, are also regarded as acts of cyberterrorism, see *C. Wilson*, Computer Attack and Cyberterrorism: Vulnerabilities and Policy Issues for Congress, Congressional Research Service Report for Congress (RL32114), updated 1 April 2005, p. 2f.

[8] However, this chapter will not evaluate whether the communication between terrorists and terrorist organisations or the communication with the public can (or should) be criminalised. The contents of such forms of communication can range from informal conversations containing private contents to collusive agreements on criminal acts.

instrument and as a tool for internal communication and preparation will be another focus in the following analysis of threats posed by terrorists and their use of the Internet (part C.).

A. Attacks via the Internet

The Internet is just as available for terrorists and terrorist organisations as it is for anybody else. In addition, cybercrime, i.e., criminal acts committed with the help of computer networks, has been common since the early days of computer technology. Therefore, the possibilities cybercrime has to offer can also be committed with a terrorist intent. Terrorists, however, have not yet claimed responsibility for any concrete acts.[9] Additionally, the digital traces often do not allow investigators to determine whether the reason for the breakdown of a system was a mere system failure or the result of a purposeful attack. Even if an attack seems highly likely, it is not possible to determine with certainty whether it was the result of the purposeful aggression of a terrorist group or an arbitrary experiment by a ten-year-old schoolgirl who tried out a program she found while browsing the Internet. For this reason, some authors have claimed that, up to now, not a single instance of cyberterrorism has been recorded.[10]

However, the threat of cyberterrorism and the other uses terrorists could make of the Internet do not remain either unreal or unrealistic. Since information on how to manipulate or misuse Internet services is widespread and often publicly available, not only security specialists but also terrorist organisations can gather such information and put it to use. Furthermore, the use of Internet-based attacks would seem to be highly attractive for terrorist purposes for the following reasons:

– Attacks can be launched from anywhere in the world. An Internet connection is available at most locations or can be initiated from most up-to-date mobile phones;

– Attacks are quick. Especially in cases of Distributed Denial-of-Service (DDoS) attacks, but also in many other scenarios, the attacker is not dependent on a fast Internet connection. Instead, he or she can exploit the connection speed of the victim. Worms and viruses can spread at the fastest possible rate without the need for any further involvement of the attacker;

– Since actions on the Internet can be disguised by anonymising services or using similar camouflage techniques, in many cases it is extremely difficult to trace evidence back to the true perpetrator;

---

[9] According to informal sources, cyberterrorist attacks have already taken place and are posing an actual threat to the security of important infrastructures. However, most cases are being kept confidential in order to protect the safety of the affected state and other similarly affected infrastructures. Accordingly, current literature often only contains potential or realistic scenarios. Whether these settings have actually taken place, however, is rarely known.

[10] U. Sieber, The Threat of Cybercrime, in: Council of Europe (ed.), Organised Crime in Europe, Strasbourg 2005, pp. 81-218 (173).

- Finally, use of the Internet is cheap. In most cases, only a small bandwidth connection is needed, which is highly affordable in most countries. Damage that can be caused via the Internet, however, an be very costly: IT-experts need to be involved constantly in order to fix newfound security flaws, and, if cases involve physical damage as well, these costs are additionally incurred.

In the following two parts, IT-based attacks will be analysed in more detail. Part 1 will cover attacks on IT-infrastructure. The aim of such assaults can either be to gather protected information or to sabotage the system or data contained within the attacked system. Another aim can be to manipulate a physical infrastructure whose operation is controlled by an IT-system. Part 2 will deal with IT-based attacks that threaten human life. As explained above, these scenarios are discussed in the literature as possible threats or have already become known to the public as actual incidents. However, in most – if not all – of these cases, it is not known whether *terrorists* have also made use of these possibilities. So, to a certain extent, it is necessary to speculate on which possibilities terrorist organisations would have if they were to accumulate knowledge themselves – or if they were able to hire security specialists to launch such attacks on their behalf.

1. Attacks on Infrastructure

The first group of attacks consists of those directed against infrastructure. In general, IT-based attacks are directed against other IT-infrastructures, resulting in a violation of IT-systems or -data. However, since an IT-infrastructure often controls other (physical) infrastructures, these digital attacks can have an effect on "real world objects" as well. These attacks are basically the same as those launched by "common" cybercriminals, but with a terrorist interest or intention. This part will therefore first address the terrorist objectives and aims behind attacks on IT-infrastructure (a). It will then analyse different types of IT-based attacks against infrastructure (b).

a) Aims and objectives

When looking at the aims pursued by terrorist attacks on an IT-infrastructure, various objectives can be distinguished:[11]
- By circumventing security measures, attackers can corrupt the *integrity* and *confidentiality* of computer systems and data;
- By rendering systems useless, a loss of *availability* can be caused. This can lead to serious results, especially if mission-critical IT-systems are affected;

---

[11] See *US Army*, Cyber Operations and Cyber Terrorism, DCSINT Handbook No. 1.02, 15 August 2005, http://www.fas.org/irp/threat/terrorism/sup2.pdf [last visited: July 2007], p. II-3.

  –   Finally, if IT-systems are connected to other critical infrastructures, such
       as transportation, power, or water facilities, *physical harm* apart from a
       loss of integrity of the system itself can be the result.

However, these are only primary objectives. In contrast to a common hacker
or cybercriminal, a terrorist typically takes a long-term perspective.[12] In order
to achieve his or her goals, a terrorist pursues an underlying agenda when
committing attacks on IT-systems. Upon a closer look, three different aims
can be identified: the causing of economic confusion, the discrimination of
the opponent, and the generation of monetary income for the terrorist
organisation. Economic confusion and the discrimination of the opponent
both aid in establishing the aforementioned long-term goal, whereas the
generation of monetary income is often needed to keep the organisation
running, to buy food for members, or to produce information materials for
followers.

The first two aims, economic confusion and the discrimination of the
opponent, are closely linked to one another. Both intend to show the
vulnerability of industry and state security and the lack of technical
knowledge of the other party. At the same time, successful attacks
demonstrate the competence of the attacker and thereby create fear on the
part of others who are also vulnerable to similar attacks.

However, as far as cybercriminals are concerned, such publicity is often
considered undesirable. This is especially true if attacks are launched with
the intent of gathering information rather then destroying resources.[13] In
these cases, terrorists might also prefer not to claim responsibility for a
successful attack. However, even in cases of destructive attacks, terrorists
might choose to remain incognito for two reasons. First, if it becomes known
that a certain incident was the result of a hacking attack by terrorists, pity
and solidarity for the victims might be the result. However, if the impression
arises that a breakdown was the result of technical incompetence, a lack of

---

[12] This (primarily political) goal is a common denominator for most definitions of
terrorism, see *C. Tomuschat,* Council of Europe Committee of Experts on Terrorism
(CODEXTER), Strasbourg, On the possible "added value" of a comprehensive
Convention on Terrorism, 26 Human Rights Law Journal 2005, pp. 287-306 (293).
[13] This becomes especially clear in cases where so-called spyware (i.e., software
created with the intent of gathering information and secretly sending it to the
software's owner) is implemented with a long-term strategy. The servers of the
mobile phone provider *Vodafone,* for example, were infected with a specialised
spyware that made it possible to monitor the calls of more than 40 high-ranking
persons in Greece between the Olympic Games in 2004 and March 2005. The attack
was only detected after *Vodafone* noticed an increase in customer complaints. It is
unknown who implemented the software. However, it is likely that only an intelligence
service would be able to carry out such an assault. See *F. Patalong/ H. Dambeck,*
Spiegel Online, 03 February 2006, Griechenlands Premier wurde abgehört,
http://www.spiegel.de/netzwelt/web/0,1518,398835,00.html [last visited: July 2007].

trust would be the outcome.[14] Therefore, terrorists – in some situations – might have an interest in not "showing their faces" when attacking digitally. A second aspect is that public knowledge of cyberterrorist attacks might result in an increased security level in many areas, making successful aggressions even more difficult to achieve. An unknown source of mysterious breakdowns, however, could instead lead to greater fear that could, in turn, be exploited by terrorist intents.[15]

According to some organisations, the fiscal losses resulting from cybercrime attacks are costing businesses $48 billion annually and cost consumers $680 million in 2005.[16] These numbers would increase rapidly if terrorist attacks aimed at causing maximum damage were to take place. However, in order to create economic confusion, more targeted aggressions are necessary. In a potential scenario, terrorists could combine the distribution of information to investors about an upcoming attack, e.g., against a company, with a targeted DDoS attack[17] against a few major banks or stock exchanges.[18] The rapid spread of false business information and even a temporary blockage of communication could seriously damage the economy and – furthermore – could result in long-lasting consequences and lack of

---

[14] Today, most computer-related problems are the result of human errors. Therefore, it is unknown whether evidence that points to a deliberate attack instead of the "usual problems" would be noticed at all. See *J. Dunnigan,* The next war zone, New York 2002, p. 219.

[15] Due to limited public knowledge of such cases, the distribution of cases cannot be evaluated. However, it can be assumed that incognito scenarios are only a small percentage of all cases. This is because a long-term goal of terrorist's is the creation of fear. This can be caused more efficiently if the target audience knows of the source of a breakdown – and expects additional incidents.

[16] http://www.darkreading.com/document.asp?doc_id=103809 [last visited: July 2007] quoting *Vincent Weafer,* who is responsible for the Security Response Global Research Center Teams at Symantec Corp. *Weafer,* in his speech to the United States House of Representatives, had referred to figures of the Federal Trade Commission that stated costs caused by identity theft alone were burdening businesses with $48 billion and consumers with $680 million each year. See http://www.symantec.com/content/en/us/about/media/Weafer_Telecomms_Internet_ Hearing_Testimony_9-13-06-Long.pdf [last visited: July 2007]. According to another survey conducted by IBM, the costs of cybercrime have already overtaken the costs of physical crime. See http://www-03.ibm.com/press/us/en/pressrelease/19367.wss [last visited: July 2007].

[17] A DDoS attack is a large-scale attack by many computers against one victim. See below for more details.

[18] *G. Giacomello,* Bangs for the Buck: A Cost-Benefit Analysis of Cyberterrorism, studies in conflict & terrorism, Vol. 27 (2005), p. 387-408 (392). How – and especially how fast – false information can spread was discovered in a cyberterrorism exercise held at a homeland security convention in 2006. In this exercise, electronic highway signs were manipulated to show a "bioterror evacuation warning." Additionally, the city's website was defaced with a similar alert. Consequently, the persons in charge evacuated the affected buildings – before realising that it was only a hoax. See *C. Suellentrop,* Sim City: Terrortown, Wired Issue 14.10, October 2006, http://www.wired.com/wired/archive/14.10/posts.html?pg=2 [last visited July 2007].

confidence in the reliability of financial services.[19] The results could be even more disastrous if they were to be combined with a classical physical attack on resources. Since institutions such as banks or stock exchanges are vital for the economic well-being of a country, they could be promising targets for terrorists.

This was already tested in 1999, when the group called "J18" invited people to plan individual actions focusing on disrupting "financial centres, banking districts and multinational corporate power bases."[20] The events were initiated as a protest against financial centres on the occasion of the meeting of the G8 in Cologne, Germany, and led to teams of hackers from Indonesia, Israel, Germany, and Canada attacking the computers of at least 20 companies, including a stock exchange and Barclays Bank.[21] Exposing the vulnerability of such institutions was also one of the outcomes of a war game of the U.S. Naval War College in 2002. It was discovered that the telecommunications infrastructure in the United States was hard to bring down because many redundancy measures had been implemented. However, this was not true for the financial system.[22] The financial funds transfer system (*Fedwire*) that exchanges money among U.S. banks and the electronic transactions network (*Fednet*), in particular, were found to have only one primary installation and three backups, all of which could easily be located with the help of the Internet – and therefore lend themselves to a targeted attack.

b) Types of attacks

Four different types of attacks that could be interesting to terrorists can be distinguished. The first makes use of so-called bot-nets that can be instructed to administer large-scale attacks against targets. Tools and know-how for the acquisition and use of such networks are widely available and

---

[19] However, threats by a radical Muslim group in December 2006 to attack financial websites were not taken seriously: the Dow Jones Index lost only 0.27%. Many claimed that they did not believe that such an attack was possible. See *A. Schröder*, Al Qaida droht US-Finanzbranche mit Hacker-Angriff, Spiegel Online, 01 December 2006, http://www.spiegel.de/wirtschaft/0,1518,451811,00.html [last visited: July 2007], *Süddeutsche Zeitung*, Die Heiligen Krieger drohen der Wall Street, Süddeutsche Zeitung Online, 01 December 2006, http://www.sueddeutsche.de/finanzen/artikel/352/93259/ [last visited: July 2007].

[20] See *D. Denning*, Activism, Hacktivism, and Cyberterrorism: The Internet as a Tool for Influencing Foreign Policy, http://www.totse.com/en/technology/cyberspace_the_new_frontier/cyberspc.html [last visited: July 2007].

[21] *D. Denning*, Activism, Hacktivism, and Cyberterrorism: The Internet as a Tool for Influencing Foreign Policy, http://www.totse.com/en/technology/ cyberspace_the_new_frontier/cyberspc.html [last visited: July 2007].

[22] See *C. Wilson*, Computer Attack and Cyberterrorism: Vulnerabilities and Policy Issues for Congress, Congressional Research Service Report for Congress (RL32114), updated 1 April 2005, p. 8 (esp. n.32).

can also be put to use by terrorist organisations (1). The second type of attack does not operate on a large scale but uses conventional hacking techniques to gain access to specific computers (2). A third type of attack combines one of the aforementioned two types with a conventional bomb attack, thereby effectively cumulating effects in the virtual and physical worlds (3). Finally, a fourth type of attack also aims at the physical world: it manipulates IT-systems that serve as control systems (e.g., for railway or airport traffic) and is thereby able to cause damage, especially to physical goods (4).

(1) Large-scale attacks

The first example of the use of computers to attack IT-infrastructure is the implementation of large-scale DDoS attacks[23] with the help of so-called bot-nets.[24] In these cases, viruses and Trojan horses are used to control other computers. These computers are turned into so-called "zombies" that are forced to report to a bot-net on a regular basis. These zombies are, in turn, controlled by a bot-master that instructs them, for instances, to send spam or forward thousands of requests to a particular site in order to make it inaccessible to its users.[25] Currently, bot-nets can also be being rented, that is, dubious companies can pay money to have spam sent by bot-nets. By doing so, these companies cover their tracks since the spam messages originate from thousands of different computers instead of from the company itself. In other cases, operators of bot-nets are paid to bring down competing businesses.[26] For a terrorist organisation, the operation of a bot-net could be highly interesting since, on the one hand, bot-nets can be rented to third parties as a source of income. On the other hand, they can also be used for their own terrorist purposes, e.g., sending emails with terrorist content (e.g., propaganda) or bringing down an opponent's (for example, government)

---

[23] For DoS-attacks, see *L. Janczewki/A. Colarik,* Managerial Guide for Handling Cyber-Terrorism and Information Warfare, London 2005, p. 85ff.
[24] A bot-net is the abbreviated term used for a *network of robots.* See also *C. Wilson,* Computer Attack and Cyberterrorism: Vulnerabilities and Policy Issues for Congress, Congressional Research Service Report for Congress (RL32114), updated 1 April 2005, p. 38.
[25] *Symantec Corp.,* Internet Security Threat Report XI (March 2007), http://www.symantec.com/enterprise/theme.jsp?themeid=threatreport [last visited: July 2007], pp. 16-17 reports that between 1 July 2006 and 31 December 2006 an average of 63,912 active bot-infected computers could be observed per day. Furthermore, 6,049,594 distinct bot-infected computers were detected in that period. These "zombies" were controlled by only 4,746 command-and-control servers. The authors therefore conclude that "organisations will have to deal with a well entrenched, experienced, and dedicated group of bot network owners instead of a population of hobby hackers."
[26] Prices for such attacks range from about 150 to 400 US-Dollar, depending on the target and the duration of the attack. Some operators even offer discounts for multiple orders. See *B. Bidder,* Angriff der Cyber-Söldner, Der Spiegel 31/2007, pp. 74-76.

sites.[27] Examples of this technique (executed either with bot-nets or by supporters) are the FloodNet attacks of pro-Israeli hackers that brought down Hezbollah's website[28] or the electronic attack carried out during the allied air strikes on Kosovo and Serbia in 2000 that completely disrupted the internal and external communications of NATO troops.[29] Even the thirteen root servers of the Internet domain name system (DNS) have been the targets of DDoS attacks.[30]

With a view to the legal problems that result from DDoS attacks, it is important to stress that – as already mentioned above – the *reason* for or the motivation behind a DDoS attack cannot be determined. In 2001, for example, an online demonstration was launched against the German airline "Lufthansa" to call attention to the involvement of the company in the deportation of illegal alien residents. Over 13,000 people took part in this demonstration and opened the web page of the company at the same time. The Lufthansa server was unable to reply to the sudden peak of requests so that the web page was unavailable to customers during this time-frame.[31]

---

[27] Today already 32% of all Denial-of-Service-attacks (DoS) are directed against the government sector, making it the Number 2 target of DoS-attacks. Only ISP suffer from even more aggressions (38%). Other sectors, such as telecommunications (8%), transportation (4%), or financial services (2%) currently seem to be less interesting targets for cyber-criminals. See *Symantec Corp.,* Internet Security Threat Report X (September 2006),
http://www.symantec.com/enterprise/theme.jsp?themeid=threatreport [last visited: July 2007], p. 39.
[28] Following this attack, six different Hizbollah sites were set up and brought down again by the FloodNet device that sent ping attacks to the respective servers. See *M. Conway,* Reality Bytes: Cyberterrorism and Terrorist 'Use' of the Internet, First Monday, 04.11.2002, Vol. 7, No. 11, http://firstmonday.org/issues/issue7_11/conway/ [last visited: July 2007]. See also *D. Denning,* Activism, Hacktivism, and Cyberterrorism: The Internet as a Tool for Influencing Foreign Policy,
http://www.totse.com/en/technology/cyberspace_the_new_frontier/cyberspc.html [last visited: July 2007].
[29] *B. Foltz,* Cyberterrorism, computer crime, and reality, Information Management & Security, 15.03.2004, Vol. 12, No. 2, p. 154-166.
[30] The attack was launched in October 2002 against the "heart of the Internet network." However, due to built-in safeguards, no slowdowns or outages were caused. See *G. Weimann,* Cyberterrorism. How real is the threat? United States Institute of Peace Special Report 119, December 2004,
http://www.usip.org/pubs/specialreports/sr119.pdf [last visited: July 2007], p. 5.
The same is true for the latest attack which took place in February 2007: even though the aggression lasted for almost twelve hours, the influence was hardly noticeable. See *C. Stöcker,* Delle im Datenstrom: Hacker attackieren Internet-Rootserver, Spiegel Online 07 February 2007,
http://www.spiegel.de/netzwelt/tech/0,1518,464926,00.html [last visited: July 2007]; *ICANN,* Factsheet on root server attacks on 6 February 2007, as of: 01 March 2007, http://icann.org/announcements/factsheet-dns-attack-08mar07.pdf [last visited: July 2007], esp. p. 1.
[31] Apart from this "human DDoS attack", other forms of "virtual sit-ins" and "virtual blockades" are also being discussed, see *D. Denning,* Activism, Hacktivism, and

Since – in this case – the company was informed about the campaign before it took place, it was aware of the reason for the downtime. However, Lufthansa customers not involved in the demonstration who attempted to access the web page could not know whether the error message was the result of a server problem, a (legitimate[32]) online demonstration, or a criminal DDoS attack.[33] Had the operator not been informed, they would have experienced the same uncertainty: whether the failure is due to a terrorist attack or mere sudden increase in interest on the part of customers (perhaps due to media coverage) cannot be determined by IP-packets.

(2) Hacking attacks

While the aforementioned large-scale attacks are a way to bring down a system and to suppress data flow, they do not enable access to protected data. If, however, a security weakness of a system can be exploited, access can be gained. This makes it possible either to shut down a computer or hinder its service in other ways, or to gain access to information that would otherwise be inaccessible. The hacking techniques used to access computers can also be used by terrorists to access and control government computers.[34] The hacking of web servers often results in so-called defacements,[35] in which the entry page of the website is replaced with another site that informs the user that the server has been hacked. Often, this replacement page is also used to give clues as to who the hacker was (by using nicknames), to send out greetings to fellow hackers, and also publicly to demonstrate how weak the security system of the attacked server

---

Cyberterrorism: The Internet as a Tool for Influencing Foreign Policy, http://www.totse.com/en/technology/cyberspace_the_new_frontier/cyberspc.html [last visited: July 2007].

[32] In 2006, the initiators of the online-demonstration were acquitted of coercion (OLG Frankfurt a.M. MMR 2006 pp. 547-552).

[33] For similar *swarming* attacks, see *G. Weimann,* Cyberterrorism. How real is the threat? United States Institute of Peace Special Report 119, December 2004, http://www.usip.org/pubs/specialreports/sr119.pdf [last visited: July 2007], pp. 4-5. With respect to the previously mentioned problem, in *D. Denning,* Activism, Hacktivism, and Cyberterrorism: The Internet as a Tool for Influencing Foreign Policy, http://www.totse.com/en/technology/cyberspace_the_new_frontier/cyberspc.html [last visited: July 2007], the differentiation is made between three different types of electronic activities: activism, a "normal, non-disruptive use of the Internet in support of an agenda or cause; hacktivism, the use of techniques with the intent of disrupting normal operations "but not causing serious damage"; and cyberterrorism, a "politically motivated hacking operation intended to cause grave harm such as loss of life or severe economic damage."

[34] *M. Pollitt,* Cyberterrorism – Fact or Fancy? http://www.cs.georgetown.edu/~denning/infosec/pollitt.html [last visited: July 2007], correctly points out that this risk exists independent of motive and perpetrator.

[35] *L. Janczewski/A. Colarik,* Managerial Guide for Handling Cyber-Terrorism and Information Warfare, London 2005, p. 46 and 97f. *M. Vatis,* Cyber attacks during the war on terrorism: a predictive analysis, 22.09.2001, http://www.ists.dartmouth.edu/analysis/cyber_a1.pdf [last visited: July 2007], pp. 5-6.

was.[36] Especially in cases in which the web server belongs to a security agency, the damage to the public's confidence in the trustworthiness and abilities of the affected agency is much higher than the monetary loss. For example, according to a recent study, 85% of IT-executives believe that U.S. government agencies are not adequately prepared for cyberterror attacks.[37] By hacking and defacing a governmental site, a terrorist group can prove its existence and also its dangerousness. Al-Qaeda, for example, hacked the website of Silicon Valley Landsurveying Inc. in order to deposit a video file showing the hijacked (and later beheaded) *Paul Marshal Johnson*.[38] By publishing the link to the stored video, the organisation could simultaneously demonstrate its technical as well as its conventional dangerousness. In another case, pro-Palestinian hackers used a co-ordinated attack to break into 80 Israel-related sites and deface them.[39]

Even though web servers are seldom connected to other security-relevant services, the general public does not know this. Therefore, the damage to the image of the respective agency is the same. Furthermore, if a hacking attack is successful on a server actually carrying relevant data, a terrorist could make use of such a situation. For example, terrorists could attempt to steal or irreversibly damage vital data, such as the Social Security database, financial institution's records, or even secret military documents.[40] Older[41]

---

[36] The group "Pentaguard", for example, demonstrated its capabilities in 2001 when it simultaneously defaced a multitude of government and military websites in the U.K., Australia, and the United States. The attack was evaluated as "well planned" and one of "the largest, most systematic defacements of worldwide government servers on the Web." See *J. Leyden*, Mass hack takes out govt sites, The Register, http://www.theregister.co.uk/2001/01/22/mass_hack_takes_out_govt/ [last visited: July 2007]. For an excerpt of websites defaced by the Pentaguard group, see http://www.attrition.org/mirror/attrition/pentaguard.html [last visited: July 2007].

[37] http://www.darkreading.com/document.asp?doc_id=103285 [last visited: July 2007] quoting a survey conducted by security vendor nCircle. According to this study, 86% of IT executives believed that their own organisation was sufficiently safe from cyberterror attacks. However, 85% did not believe that U.S. government agencies were adequately prepared for such assaults. The study was based on a poll of 395 IT executives.

[38] See *Y. Musharbash*, US-Firmen-Website für Qaida-Botschaft gehackt, Spiegel Online, 17.06.2004, http://service.spiegel.de/digas/find?DID=31237523 [last visited: July 2007].

[39] *M. Conway*, Cyberterrorism and Terrorist 'Use' of the Internet, First Monday, 04.11.2002, Vol. 7, No. 11, http://firstmonday.org/issues/issue7_11/conway/ [last visited: July 2007]. See *M. Vatis*, Cyber attacks during the war on terrorism: a predictive analysis. 22.09.2001, http://www.ists.dartmouth.edu/analysis/cyber_a1.pdf [last visited: July 2007], p. 6 for a graphical overview of political events and subsequent increases in defaced websites.

[40] *S. Berinato*, The Truth About Cyberterrorism, CIO Magazine 15.03.2002, http://www.cio.com/archive/031502/truth.html [last visited: July 2007].

[41] In 1997, the NSA launched an exercise under the codename "Eligible Receiver." A group of hackers was in essence challenged to use publicly available tools to try to break into the U.S. Pacific Command in Hawaii, which is responsible for all military contingencies and operations conducted in the Pacific. To the surprise of the military,

and even more recent attacks have shown that even top-secret military computers[42] and sensitive nuclear research centres[43] are not immune against all attacks. Therefore, such scenarios are threats that need to be considered.

However, those cases in which the attack does not become publicly known are even more dangerous. In the Internet, many tools that can be used to exploit known security vulnerabilities are freely available. If, for example, by means of a defacement, it becomes known that such a weakness has been exploited, the security hole can be fixed and another attack based on the same weakness prevented. If, however, a custom-made attack has been launched, it will not be detectable by any scanner available on the market. In one case, for example, a security company prepared USB sticks with a custom-designed, newly developed Trojan horse that could not be detected by virus scanners. Twenty of these sticks were "lost" on the premises of a credit union. Of these, 15 sticks were found by employees – and promptly connected to the company network where the Trojan started to collect passwords and other valuable information and emailed this data back to the creators.[44] Such an attack would be a powerful way for a terrorist organisation to start counterespionage. The same is true for so-called "Zero-Day exploits."[45] These are exploits that are not yet known to the manufacturer (or, in some cases, to anyone else). Therefore, neither patches nor bug fixes are available against these attacks, nor can virus scanners detect them.[46] In particular, the fact that it is not known at all that the security

---

the group gained access to the user account management and were able to reformat server hard drives, scramble data, and shut systems down. Even the disruption of telephone services and interception of emails did not pose a large challenge. See *G. Weimann,* Sum of All Fears?, Studies in Conflict & Terrorism, 28 (2005), pp. 129-149 (138).

[42] *C. Wilson,* Computer Attack and Cyberterrorism: Vulnerabilities and Policy Issues for Congress, Congressional Research Service Report for Congress (RL32114), updated 1 April 2005, p. 12 reports on viruses that have infiltrated two top-secret computer systems at the Army Space and Missile Defense Command.

[43] *M. Vatis,* Cyber attacks during the war on terrorism: a predictive analysis. 22.09.2001, http://www.ists.dartmouth.edu/analysis/cyber_a1.pdf [last visited: July 2007], p. 5.

[44] *S. Stasiukonis,* Social Engineering, the USB Way, Dark Reading, 07.06.2006, http://www.darkreading.com/document.asp?doc_id=95556&WT.svl=column1_1 [last visited: July 2007].

[45] See *C. Wilson,* Computer Attack and Cyberterrorism: Vulnerabilities and Policy Issues for Congress, Congressional Research Service Report for Congress (RL32114), updated 1 April 2005, p. 13; *Symantec Corp.,* Internet Security Threat Report, Vol. XI (March 2007), http://www.symantec.com/enterprise/theme.jsp?themeid=threatreport [last visited: July 2007], p. 47.

[46] For information on the time needed by vendors to develop patches against *known* security weaknesses and the resulting "window of exposure," see *Symantec Corp.,* Internet Security Threat Report, Vol. X (September 2006),

systems are being violated makes such an attack especially dangerous. Zero-Day exploits do not have to be developed by terrorists themselves. Instead, a black market has evolved that has the potential to put these dangerous instruments into the hands of all interested parties.[47] Finally, custom-made Trojan horses could also be implemented via legal channels. In the year 2000 for example, Japan's Metropolitan Police Department used a software system to track 150 police vehicles, including unmarked cars. It turned out that this software had been developed by the Aum Shinrikyo cult – the same group that gassed the Tokyo subway in 1995.[48] Additionally, members of this cult had developed software for at least eighty firms and ten government agencies. This was possible because the software developers were engaged as subcontractors, thus enabling personnel clearance of the subcontractor to be easily circumvented.

(3) Hybrid attacks

Apart from the "established" ways of rendering a system inaccessible, *hybrid attacks* are also being discussed as ways to cause the greatest possible damage. To carry out a hybrid attack, a classic bomb attack could be launched.[49] At the same time, however, the communication devices of police

---

http://www.symantec.com/enterprise/theme.jsp?themeid=threatreport [last visited: July 2007], pp. 58-62. According to this document, the windows of exposure have been cut down 50% compared to the year before. Nevertheless, exploits are still valid for about a month until a repair is possible.

[47] *Symantec Corp.,* Internet Security Threat Report, Vol. XI (March 2007), http://www.symantec.com/enterprise/theme.jsp?themeid=threatreport [last visited: July 2007], p. 47.

[48] *G. Weimann,* Sum of All Fears?, Studies in Conflict & Terrorism, 28 (2005), pp. 129-149 (139).

[49] Many conventional scenarios are possible that are directed against IT-infrastructures. For example, many transcontinental data connections rely on transatlantic cable connections between Europe and the United States. While European cable ends are widely spread between many different countries, they are often bundled on the American side (e.g., in New Jersey and Rhode Island). An attack on one or two of these connections could have a serious impact on Internet connections in general. In the past, this was observed when cables were damaged accidentally, see *A. Wilkens,* Kabelbruch im Atlantik koppelt Island vom Internet ab, Heise Online 18.12.2006, http://www.heise.de/newsticker/meldung/82700 [last visited: July 2007]; *C. Persson,* "Rückfall ins Telefonzeitalter" nach Erdbeben, Heise Online, 28.12.2006, http://www.heise.de/newsticker/meldung/83007 [last visited: July 2007]. Also, a conventional attack against one or more of the central so-called peeringpoints that interconnect different networks could lead to a great damage. The German peeringpoint DE-CIX in Frankfurt, for example, is said to handle 80% of the German and 35% of European Internet traffic. The London Internet Exchange LINX is the world's largest Internet peeringpoint. In 2006, it was at the center of a planned assault. However, Scotland Yard arrested suspects beforehand. An MI5-website is reported to have said that "without these services, the UK could suffer serious consequences, including severe economic damage, grave social disruption, or even large-scale loss of life." See *D. Leppard,* Al-Qaeda plot to bring down UK Internet, Times Online 11.03.2007,

or ambulances could be hindered by way of a DDoS attack, resulting in even greater losses and confusion.[50] Many security specialists agree that this would be a likely scenario.[51] The same idea is possible in another scenario that is aimed against national financial networks (such as *Fedwire* or *Fednet*). A hybrid attack against those networks or against transfer networks such as SWIFT would be able, it is said, to wreak havoc on the entire global economy.[52]

(4) Attacks resulting in physical damage

When a system is being attacked – either by a large-scale DDoS or a specialised hacking attack – usually only the system itself is affected. However, in some settings physical damage can also occur. This can be achieved mainly by a manipulation of SCADA systems.[53] SCADA is an acronym for "Supervisory Control And Data Acquisition." Basically, SCADA-systems are used to measure and control other systems. In many cases, these systems are connected to the Internet in one way or another.[54] Even though, for security reasons, this is not advisable, the need to cut costs and the ability to remotely control several SCADA-systems centrally instead of

---

http://www.timesonline.co.uk/tol/news/uk/crime/article1496831.ece [last visited: July 2007]. However, since this report focuses on the *use* of the Internet, these conventional attacks on infrastructure will be not covered.

[50] According to experts, even the voice communication systems of emergency services are vulnerable to software attacks, see *M. Vatis*, Cyber attacks during the war on terrorism: a predictive analysis. 22.09.2001,
http://www.ists.dartmouth.edu/analysis/cyber_a1.pdf [last visited: July 2007], p. 18.

[51] *C. Wilson*, Computer Attack and Cyberterrorism: Vulnerabilities and Policy Issues for Congress, Congressional Research Service Report for Congress (RL32114), updated 1 April 2005, p. 2. *M. Vatis*, Cyber attacks during the war on terrorism: a predictive analysis. 22.09.2001, http://www.ists.dartmouth.edu/analysis/cyber_a1.pdf [last visited: July 2007], p. 9 even claims that a close interrelation between physical attacks and cyber attacks can be proven.

[52] Phil Williams, Director of the Program on Terrorism and Trans-National Crime and the University of Pittsburgh as quoted by *C. Wilson*, Computer Attack and Cyberterrorism: Vulnerabilities and Policy Issues for Congress, Congressional Research Service Report for Congress (RL32114), updated 1 April 2005, p. 9.

[53] *F. Cohen*, Cyber-Risks and Critical Infrastructures, in: Alan O'Day (Ed.), Cyberterrorism, pp. 1-10 (2ff) criticises that many threats to critical infrastructures are exaggerated. In his opinion, cyber attacks are not of the same class as conventional attacks carried out with bombs. However, the United States, for example, launched a "national strategy to secure cyberspace" in part because "individuals, criminal cartels, terrorists, or nation states" could maliciously act in the Internet to exploit vulnerabilities, *White House,* The national strategy to secure cyberspace, http://www.whitehouse.gov/pcipb/cyberspace_strategy.pdf [last visited: July 2007], p. 27.

[54] According to a unpublished study of SCADA Security Specialist Company Wurldtech Research Inc., 17% of SCADA malfunctions are being caused by a direct Internet access to the SCADA system. Other possibilities include VPN-, modem- or trusted connections, e.g., for a remote access to allow maintenance work. However, 49% were caused by access through a corporate WAN or business network.

having one person control one system on-site increases the interconnectivity of such systems. However, each system that is accessible to legitimate users through the Internet is also the potential victim of an illegitimate hacker. Additionally, many control systems are based on the Windows- and Unix operating systems.[55] In this way, publicly known security weaknesses in these operating systems can be exploited in these control systems.[56] The power-down of energy systems in 2003[57] in the United States and Eastern Canada impressively demonstrated their dependence on SCADA systems and the hard-to-understand interdependency of linked computer systems.[58] Even though 21 power plants were brought down, the reason was not a terrorist or even purposeful attack. Instead – as far as is publicly known – it was a mere coincidence that these systems were shut down by the W32.Lovsan worm: this worm was using the same port to exploit a weakness on individual personal computers that was being used by the plants to communicate with each other. However, had this weakness been known to terrorists, the same result – 60 million households without electricity – could have been initiated by a criminal organisation. Finally, a combination of the above-mentioned DDoS attacks and SCADA systems of critical infrastructure could lead to considerable physical damage.[59]

(5) Result

According to current literature, *cybercriminals* can attack anything that is important to modern society and connected to the Internet or accessible via other communication lines.[60] Therefore, *terrorists* in general can also use the same techniques and acquire the same knowledge as other criminals. The telecommunications, energy, and financial services sectors would seem to make interesting targets for such attacks.

---

[55] See *D. Bachfeld,* War der Wurm drin? IT-Sicherheit in der US-Stromversorgung, http://www.heise.de/ct/03/18/034/default.shtml [last visited: July 2007].

[56] Some hackers therefore claim that it would take them only about a week to get into most of the existing control systems. See *R. Lenzner/N. Vardi,* The Next Threat, Forbes 20.09.2004,
https://www.mywire.com/Auth.do?extId=10022&uri=/archive/forbes/2004/0920/070.html [last visited: July 2007].

[57] The worm also affected other critically important institutions in the United States, including Edwards Air Force Base, the test center for B-2 and B-1 bombers, see *D. Bachfeld,* War der Wurm drin? IT-Sicherheit in der US-Stromversorgung, http://www.heise.de/ct/03/18/034/default.shtml [last visited: July 2007].

[58] See *C. Wilson,* Computer Attack and Cyberterrorism: Vulnerabilities and Policy Issues for Congress, Congressional Research Service Report for Congress (RL32114), updated 1 April 2005, p. 10; *M. Vatis,* Cyber attacks during the war on terrorism: a predictive analysis. 22.09.2001, http://www.ists.dartmouth.edu/analysis/cyber_a1.pdf [last visited: July 2007], p. 17.

[59] *G. Giacomello,* Bangs for the Buck: A Cost-Benfit Analysis of Cyberterrorism, Studies in Conflict & Terrorism, Vol. 27 (2004), pp. 387-408 (391).

[60] *U. Sieber,* The Threat of Cybercrime, in: Council of Europe (ed.), Organised Crime in Europe, Strasbourg 2005, pp. 81-218 (174).

2. Attacks on Human Life

The attacks described in the previous part can likely cause severe damage. However, in general, no human lives would be endangered. Therefore, it is questionable whether such attacks are an interesting option for terrorists. Even though the power cut of 2003 in the United States was caused by a computer worm, no panic erupted, there were only a few injuries, and hospitals and emergency services continued to function properly.[61] The security hole was subsequently fixed, so a second attack based on the same weakness is not likely. From a terrorist's point of view, attacks are more interesting and efficient if they cause fear in the public and the possibility of repeatability at any point in time seems highly likely. This is especially the case if human life can be endangered or the attack results in other kinds of physical harm.[62]

a) Attacks using control systems

The scenarios that are being discussed and that could directly result in lost lives have, for the most part, not yet taken place[63] (at least this has not become known to the public) and often involve an attack on SCADA systems. The results of such attacks could hamper the functioning of the affected industries. In the worst case, however, attacks could not only bring companies to a standstill or cause them to shut down for a longer period of time,[64] but also affect lives.[65] If, for example, hackers were to gain control over SCADA systems controlling hydroelectric dams, a surprise opening of

---

[61] G. Giacomello, Bangs for the Buck: A Cost-Benfit Analysis of Cyberterrorism, Studies in Conflict & Terrorism, Vol. 27 (2004), pp. 387-408 (400)

[62] For this reason, conventional attacks with only an electronic basis have created larger media coverage than entire digital attacks. For example, the idea that RFID-chips (radio-frequency identification) which are integrated in the new generation of many passports could trigger a bomb attack prompted many news articles. See G. Ou, RFID passports with improper shielding triggers bomb in simulation, ZDNet 09.08.2006, http://blogs.zdnet.com/Ou/?p=289 [last visited: July 2007]; H. Cheung, Blackhat 2006: Explosive risks in FRID-enabled passports? TG Daily 03.08.2006, http://www.tgdaily.com/content/view/27899/113/ [last visited: July 2007]; S. Koesch/ F. Magdanz/R. Stadler, Funkchip-Reisepass zündet Bombe, Spiegel Online 21.08.2006, http://www.spiegel.de/netzwelt/mobil/0,1518,432654,00.html [last visited: July 2007].

[63] B. Foltz, Cyberterrorism, computer crime, and reality, Information Management & Computer Security, 15.03.2004, Vol. 12, No. 2, pp. 154-166.

[64] U. Sieber, The Threat of Cybercrime, in: Council of Europe (ed.), Organised Crime in Europe, Strasbourg 2005, pp. 81-218 (174).

[65] In one scenario, hackers gained access to a computer system at an Antarctic research station. It was unclear whether this system was also responsible for controlling the life-support systems and whether researchers were in danger, K. Poulsen, South Pole 'cyberterrorist' hack wasn't the first, SecurityFocus 18.08.2004, http://www.securityfocus.com/print/news/9356 [last visited: July 2007]. Even if such a danger did not exist in this case, the scenario shows the general potential of hacking attacks.

the gates could cause flooding of the surrounding areas. Two cases are known in which attackers managed to enter such a system; however, they did not do any harm.[66] Additional cases have not been officially verified.[67] However, materials found in computers of captured terrorists show that these scenarios are actually being evaluated.[68] Furthermore, systems operated by private companies are often claimed to be less secure than those operated by the military – even though a dysfunction can cause severe harm in both areas.[69]

Apart from the manipulation of hydroelectric dams, the tampering of control systems for railway or air traffic is also being discussed. This tampering could, at the least, affect service (as in an incident in 1997)[70] or – in a worst case scenario – mean colliding trains or airplanes, which could possibly cost

---

[66] G. Giacomello, Bangs for the Buck: A Cost-Benfit Analysis of Cyberterrorism, Studies in Conflict & Terrorism, Vol. 27 (2004), pp. 387-408 (397) explains that, in one case, the attacker was a consultant who merely wanted to cause a problem so that he could get a better contract to fix it afterwards. A different case, however, indeed involved a hacker who was able to but obviously not willing to cause any harm.

[67] The security company Wurldtech Research Inc. maintains an "Industrial Security Incident Database" (ISID) to track incidents that directly impact industrial and SCADA operations. Even though not only malicious, but also accidental incidents are being tracked, 135 incidents were recorded by spring 2006. Ten to 15 new incidents are being added to the ISID quarterly. Currently, the ISID contains information stemming from only 22 companies in the U.S., Canada, U.K., France, and Australia (of these 22 companies, 14 are part of the U.S. Fortune500 companies) so the extrapolated overall sum should, in fact, be even higher.

[68] G. Weimann, How Modern Terrorism Uses the Internet, United States Institute of Peace Special Report 116, March 2004, http://www.usip.org/ pubs/specialreports/sr116.pdf [last visited: July 2007], p. 7 states that on one captured al-Qaeda computer, engineering and structural features of a dam were found that would allow engineers and planners to simulate catastrophic failures. In other computers, evidence was found that terrorists had spent time on digital switches that run power, water, transportation, and communications grids.

[69] M. Pollitt, Cyberterrorism – Fact or Fancy? http://www.cs.georgetown.edu/ ~denning/infosec/pollitt.html [last visited: July 2007] especially mentions power grids, oil pipelines, dams, and water systems as "less-protected secondary targets." Because they are in the private sector and not yet regarded as national security loopholes, they "tend to be less secure than government and military systems." Regarding the latest ratings from the Federal Information Security Management Act of 2002, however, this is questionable. Also, as C. Wilson, Computer Attack and Cyberterrorism: Vulnerabilities and Policy Issues for Congress, Congressional Research Service Report for Congress (RL32114), updated 1 April 2005, p. 1, points out, military services make increasing use of civilian technology, thereby opening additional loopholes.

[70] In 1997, a hacker shut down control tower services at the Worcester, Mass. Airport. Even though the incident did not cause any accidents, service was affected, see S. Berinato, The Truth About Cyberterrorism, CIO Magazine 15.03.2002, http://www.cio.com/archive/031502/truth.html [last visited: July 2007].

hundreds of lives.[71] The greatest risks would arise if the control systems of nuclear power plants were accessed (as has already happened).[72] In this case, a plant could either be powered down or an attacker could try to overheat the system. This – again in a worst case scenario – could result in a nuclear catastrophe. The same holds true for an electronic intrusion into a military control centre, possibly resulting in a missile launch.[73]

However, these situations rely on the failure of all other security measures at the same time,[74] a scenario which is not as realistic as other possible situations. Furthermore, military facilities that are able to launch missiles are often not connected to the Internet ("air-gapping"), making a remote launch simply impossible.[75] However, since the military also makes use of increased connectivity and remote controlling in order to save the lives of soldiers, it is not completely unlikely that this situation will change over time.[76] Furthermore, the military also uses civilian technology, thereby opening

---

[71] G. Giacomello, Bangs for the Buck: A Cost-Benfit Analysis of Cyberterrorism, Studies in Conflict & Terrorism, Vol. 27 (2004), pp. 387-408 (398); G. Weimann, Sum of All Fears?, Studies in Conflict & Terrorism, 28 (2005), pp. 129-149 (138).
[72] In 2003, the Slammer worm was able to corrupt the control systems at the Davis-Besse nuclear power plant located in Ohio. Even though the control room was protected by a firewall, this security measure was circumvented because the business network connecting the corporate offices was found to have multiple connections to the Internet. Nevertheless, the worm was not able to cause any damage to the plant because it was closed and offline when the attack occurred. See C. Wilson, Computer Attack and Cyberterrorism: Vulnerabilities and Policy Issues for Congress, Congressional Research Service Report for Congress (RL32114), updated 1 April 2005, p. 11; K. Poulsen, Slammer worm crashed Ohio nuke plant network, http://www.securityfocus.com/print/news/6767 [last visited: July 2007].
[73] B. Foltz, Cyberterrorism, computer crime, and reality, Information Management & Computer Security, 15.03.2004, Vol. 12, No. 2, pp. 154-166.
[74] M. Pollitt, Cyberterrorism – Fact or Fancy? http://www.cs.georgetown.edu/~denning/infosec/pollitt.html [last visited: July 2007], stresses the point that, especially in air traffic scenarios, controllers as well as pilots are trained on "situational awareness" and that computers only function as an aid. So, for a successful attack, it would be necessary to manipulate pilots and/or controllers as well as intrude the computer system.
[75] J. Green, The Myth of Cyberterrorism, Washington Monthly, November 2002. http://www.washingtonmonthly.com/features/2001/0211.green.html [last visited: July 2007], for example, writes that "nuclear weapons and other sensitive military systems enjoy the most basic form of Internet security: they're 'air-gapped', meaning that they're not physically connected to the Internet and are therefore inaccessible to outside hackers." See also B. Foltz, Cyberterrorism, computer crime, and reality, Information Management & Computer Security, 15.03.2004, Vol. 12, No. 2, pp. 154-166.
[76] For examples of successful attacks on military infrastructure, see US Army, Cyber Operations and Cyber Terrorism, DCSINT Handbook No. 1.02, 15 August 2005, http://www.fas.org/irp/threat/terrorism/sup2.pdf [last visited: July 2007], p. IV-2 ff.

additional loopholes for security risks.[77] Also, the human factor is often underrated: literature often distinguishes only between "computer only" and "human only" scenarios. The cases of hacking into a hydroelectric dam,[78] however, show that – especially with the help of an insider – many security measures which would normally prevent a computer attack can be circumvented and that the additional knowledge of an insider can also be extremely helpful, especially when it comes to an electronic attack.[79]

b) Long-term developments

Whereas the situations mentioned above can result in a one-time catastrophe, other ideas being discussed involve long-term scenarios that could be initiated by cyberterrorists. These scenarios include the manipulation of machinery, for example in the production of food[80] or medication.[81] If the alteration is not detected by internal quality-management, consumers could be contaminated or poisoned. Other possible targets include the weapons-production process, where manipulation could lead to useless ammunition. However, since these production areas are usually high-risk areas for other reasons as well, security measures are high, and production computers are seldom linked to public networks. However, if this were the case, risks would rise considerably.

c) Result

Since the attacks on human life require access to systems that not only control IT-infrastructure but that can also be abused to cause physical harm, a focus of such attacks is on the military production, energy services, and transport sectors. The latter is of particular interest since successful attacks can result in heavy losses of human life. Furthermore, fear – a terrorist constant – could be significantly heightened, even if such an attack was a one-time possibility that could not be repeated. Therefore, the great amount

---

[77] See, for example, *US Army,* Cyber Operations and Cyber Terrorism, DCSINT Handbook No. 1.02, 15 August 2005, http://www.fas.org/irp/threat/terrorism/sup2.pdf [last visited: July 2007], p. IV-2.

[78] See above and footnote 66.

[79] For example, the Audit Report "Safeguards Over Sensitive Technology" of the U.S. Department of Energy from January 2004 (DOE/IG-0635) contains cases involving foreign nationals from "sensitive countries." These were no terrorists, but indicate the danger and possibilities for attacks and misuse, even in high-security areas.

[80] *M. Pollitt,* Cyberterrorism – Fact or Fancy? http://www.cs.georgetown.edu/~denning/infosec/pollitt.html [last visited: July 2007], mentions a potential case involving a cereal manufacturing line. However, he correctly points out that the sudden increase in the use of different ingredients would likely draw attention. Furthermore, the taste of the altered product would likely change.

[81] *G. Weimann,* Sum of All Fears?, Studies in Conflict & Terrorism, 28 (2005), pp. 129-149 (138).

of time, knowledge, and (possibly) money that would need to be invested in a terrorist attack could "pay off" if it affected human lives.

B. Dissemination of Content

Internet use apart from attacks that are launched via the Internet may be of more interest for terrorist groups. Using the network to communicate with the public or with each other gives organisations new possibilities in a "war of ideas."[82] This part will therefore focus on the use of the Internet for the dissemination of terrorist content to the public. For terrorist organisations, this is an important way (1.) to explain the reasons and motivation behind the terrorists' struggle, (2.) to disseminate threats and propaganda, (3.) to recruit supporters and train new members, and (4.) – in some cases – also to finance further activities.

1. Presentation of Terrorist Views

When terrorist organisations want to communicate their points of view, aims, and ambitions, they are typically faced with the problem that they hardly have any possibility to do so because they have to work undercover. Of course, leaflets are a way to justify assaults, and "mouth-to-mouth" propaganda can be used to recruit new members. However, both alternatives are time-consuming and risky, and they do not reach a large group of people. Additionally, terrorists are faced with the problem of how to communicate with (and possibly influence) the media.

With the help of the Internet, though, this has changed. Almost every terrorist organisation of any importance has its own website.[83] Many of them contain detailed information on leaders, the history of the organisation, aims, or recent successes. Facts are put together for relevant target groups[84] and in

---

[82] G. Giacomello, Bangs for the Buck: A Cost-Benfit Analysis of Cyberterrorism, Studies in Conflict & Terrorism, Vol. 27 (2004), pp. 387-408 (387).
[83] G. Weimann, How Modern Terrorism Uses the Internet, United States Institute of Peace Special Report 116, March 2004, http://www.usip.org/pubs/specialreports/sr116.pdf [last visited: July 2007], p. 3; M. Conway, Cyberterrorism and Terrorist 'Use' of the Internet, First Monday, 04.11.2002, Vol. 7, No. 11, http://firstmonday.org/issues/issue7_11/conway/ [last visited: July 2007], states that, according to the United States Department of State, in 1999 already 12 of 30 deemed foreign terrorist organisations had their own websites. In 2005, more than 4,500 terrorist-related websites were known, see S. Coll/S. Glasser, Terrorists turn to the web as base of operations, The Washington Post 7 August 2005, Section A01. See also US Army, Cyber Operations and Cyber Terrorism, DCSINT Handbook No. 1.02, 15 August 2005, http://www.fas.org/irp/threat/terrorism/sup2.pdf [last visited: July 2007], p. I-3.
[84] G. Weimann, How Modern Terrorism Uses the Internet, United States Institute of Peace Special Report 116, March 2004, http://www.usip.org/pubs/specialreports/sr116.pdf [last visited: July 2007], p. 4f. distinguishes between three different audiences: supporters, international public

different languages[85] in order to ensure that even foreigners can compare media news with the views of the relevant organisation. The most popular terrorist sites attract tens of thousands of visitors each month[86] and make use of the "censorship resistance" of the Internet.[87]

2. Propaganda and Threats

The opportunities for a terrorist organisation offered by a website are manifold: everything is virtually possible, from a mere presentation of viewpoints, to a general glorification of terrorism or justification of recent acts of violence (or threatening to perform new acts), up to and including the incitement of further (also digital)[88] terrorist acts by the reading audience and recruits.[89] All of this information can be presented in an impressive way that

---

opinion, and enemy publics. See also *Y. Tsfati/G. Weimann,* www.terrorism.com: Terror on the Internet, Studies in Conflict & Terrorism 2002 (25), pp. 317-332 (326).

[85] The website of the Revolutionary Armed Forces of Colombia (FARC – http://www.farcep.org [last visited: July 2007]), for example, offers information in English, Italian, Portuguese, Russian, and German. For a (partly outdated) overview of terrorist websites and their languages of operation, see *M. Conway,* Cyberterrorism and Terrorist 'Use' of the Internet, First Monday, 04.11.2002, Vol. 7, No. 11, http://firstmonday.org/issues/issue7_11/conway/ [last visited: July 2007].

[86] *M. Conway,* Cyberterrorism and Terrorist 'Use' of the Internet, First Monday, 04.11.2002, Vol. 7, No. 11, http://firstmonday.org/issues/issue7_11/conway/ [last visited: July 2007].

[87] *D. Denning,* Activism, Hacktivism, and Cyberterrorism: The Internet as a Tool for Influencing Foreign Policy, http://www.totse.com/en/technology/cyberspace_the_new_frontier/cyberspc.html [last visited: July 2007], reports a case in which Jordanian officials removed an article from 40 print copies of The Economist on sale in Jordan. However, an online copy was printed, photocopied, and faxed to 1,000 Jordanians, thereby circumventing local censors.

[88] Recently, a software called "the electronic jihad program" has been discovered on jihadi websites. The program can be downloaded by interested followers and is designed as to allow followers to easily attack different websites over a windows-like interface. Usernames and hours spent for attacking websites are being collected on public "highscore"-lists to further encourage other users. The software-publishers hope that with a spreading use of the Internet continually more users engage in such a form of "electronic jihad". See *L. Greenemeier,* "Electronic Jihad" app offers cyberterrorism for the masses, IT News 3 July 2007, http://www.itnews.com.au/Tools/Print.aspx?CIID=85204 [last visited: July 2007] and *L. Greenemeier,* Cyberterrorism: by whatever name, it's on the increase, InformationWeek 7 July 2007, http://www.informationweek.com/story/showArticle.jhtml? articleID=200900812 [last visited: July 2007].

[89] The website alneda.com, for example, has published the names and home phone numbers of 84 al-Qaeda fighters that were captured. Presumably, the aim of this action was to allow sympathisers to contact their families and let them know that they were alive. See *T. Thomas,* Al Qaeda and the Internet: the danger of "cyberplanning", Parameters, Spring 2003, pp. 112-123 (117). Other websites contain obituaries of suicide bombers, effectively glorifying them and encouraging others to follow this

makes use of every available multimedia option. The assassination of *Daniel Pearl*, for example, showed the impact of psychological warfare conducted by these new means. Other messages, such as the latest threats against German and Austrian involvement in Afghanistan, are also no longer forwarded as mere text-messages. Instead, professional-looking videos with German subtitles are sent out – often directly to TV stations[90] that incorporate the material and broadcast it in their programs.[91] The Internet has therefore become the most important means by which terrorist organisations communicate with their supporters and other interested parties.[92]

Terrorist websites, however, have one big disadvantage: only those interested in the organisation itself will be able to find it among the millions of other websites. Even they can be seriously hindered by government organisations that strive to make websites of terrorist organisations inaccessible. Therefore, organisations try to find new possibilities for propaganda and advertising. A more decentralised approach also makes it harder for the government to control content and could also make propaganda available for those capable of being influenced or open to the views of the organisation but not actively looking for it. It is perhaps for this reason that many propaganda videos have shown up on video-sharing-platforms such as YouTube. These videos often depict terrorism in a glorious light. Frequently, assault scenes are accompanied by modern music and graphics with a fresh look. Apart from videos, Internet radio shows can be also launched.[93] These videos and radio shows allow organisations to spread their body of thought among young viewers who are vulnerable to influence and may stumble over such videos while looking for a new pop song.

---

path. See *Y. Musharbash*, The Cyber-Cemetery of the Mujahedeen, Spiegel Online 28.10.05,
http://www.spiegel.de/international/0,1518,382097,00.html [last visited: July 2007].
[90] The video message directed against Germany and Austria was sent to a website called "Global Islamic Mediafront (GIMF)." Intelligence services assume that the site is linked to al-Qaeda. See *A. Ramelsberger,* Krieger im Internet, Süddeutsche Zeitung 15 March 2007, p. 5.
[91] See, for example, *Süddeutsche Zeitung,* „Diesen Krieg könnt ihr Euch nicht leisten", Süddeutsche Zeitung Online 11 March 2007,
http://www.sueddeutsche.de/deutschland/artikel/189/105084/ [last visited: July 2007].
A. Ramelsberger, Krieger im Internet, Süddeutsche Zeitung 15 March 2007, p. 5, quotes a high-ranking member of the German Office for the Protection of the Constitution who said that the video is seen as a form of "psychological warfare" because it does not make direct threats but instead creates an atmosphere of unease.
[92] See *Bundesministerium des Inneren (Ed.),* Verfassungsschutzbericht 2005, Berlin 2006, p. 169.
[93] *M. Conway,* Cyberterrorism and Terrorist 'Use' of the Internet, First Monday, 04.11.2002, Vol. 7, No. 11, http://firstmonday.org/issues/issue7_11/conway/ [last visited: July 2007].

Apart from footage that has been introduced in video platforms such as YouTube, the anonymity of website operators is another factor that can be put to use by terrorist organisations. While in the past only a few well-established organisations were able to produce newspapers, magazines, or TV shows, the Internet makes it possible for virtually anyone to launch their own periodicals or otherwise use the power of the media.[94] Viewers are often unable to verify whether the news being broadcast is true or false. This again can be exploited by organisations that express their own views under the name of a seemingly neutral authority.[95] With the help of several well-styled and -prepared websites that claim a certain viewpoint, interested parties and even journalists may have difficulty distinguishing propaganda from fact. By means of the same technique, opinions can also be altered and influenced if a seemingly large proportion of news services suddenly criticise certain governmental actions where, in reality, these news services are in fact operated by one and the same organisation.[96] Finally, even traditional mass media make increasing use of the Internet as a source of stories and illustrated footage.[97] By attractively presenting viewpoints and opinions, terrorist organisations can increase their chances of introducing these opinions into products of the mass media.

---

[94] *D. Denning*, Activism, Hacktivism, and Cyberterrorism: The Internet as a Tool for Influencing Foreign Policy, http://www.totse.com/en/technology/cyberspace_the_new_frontier/cyberspc.html [last visited: July 2007], correctly points out that the cost advantage over traditional mass media also helps to promote such journals. Al-Qaeda has even launched a weekly bilingual news show containing world news from a terrorist point of view, Al-Qaeda launches a weekly news show, Spiegel Online, 07.10.2005, http://www.spiegel.de/international/0,1518,378633,00.html [last visited: July 2007]; *Bundesministerium des Inneren (Ed.)*, Verfassungsschutzbericht 2005, Berlin 2006, p. 207.

[95] However, also the opposite sometimes is true: due to the quick proliferation of fake communiqués it was for some time not easy to distinguish real terrorist messages from statements of non-existent groups. See the Statement of *Evan Kohlmann* on ZDNet Government 19 April 2006, http://government.zdnet.com/?p=2216 [last visited: July 2007].

[96] *T. Thomas,* Al Qaeda and the Internet: the danger of "cyberplanning", Parameters, Spring 2003, pp. 112-123 (118ff). In addition, *semantic attacks* against traditional news sites are being discussed. Such attacks change the content of a web page subtly, thus disseminating false information, *M. Vatis*, Cyber attacks during the war on terrorism: a predictive analysis. 22.09.2001, http://www.ists.dartmouth.edu/analysis/cyber_a1.pdf [last visited: July 2007], p. 14. See also *L. Janczewski/A. Colarik*, Managerial Guide for Handling Cyber-Terrorism and Information Warfare, London 2005, p. 97ff. However, it is doubtful whether these attacks would remain unnoticed.

[97] *G. Weimann,* How Modern Terrorism Uses the Internet, United States Institute of Peace Special Report 116, March 2004, http://www.usip.org/pubs/specialreports/sr116.pdf [last visited: July 2007], p. 3.

3. Recruitment and Training

When it comes to recruitment and training, the Internet again offers terrorists an excellent platform, as all contents can be easily deposited, mirrored between different locations in order to circumvent censorship or deletion, and anonymously gathered by those interested in this information. For example, special interests that might, in the past, have attracted a librarian's attention can now be pursued in the Internet, and information can be accessed without causing any suspicion. For some types of attacks, handpicked information has been already compiled, e.g., on bombs, poisons, or many other dangerous goods.[98] The "Mujahadeen Poisons Handbook," for example, contains various "recipes" for homemade poisons and poisonous gases for use in terrorist attacks.[99] Modern terrorists amend these handbooks by adding extra information on hostage taking,[100] guerrilla tactics, and special bombs. For example, al-Qaeda prepared the "Encyclopedia of Jihad," which runs to thousands of pages.[101] Young terrorists can gather such information from the Internet in order to prepare their assaults.[102] However, the danger that appears to originate from many of these compilations should not be overestimated: even though these documents are clearly labelled, many of them contain the same information that can be found in most standard chemistry books for university students. Even training materials for interested terrorists are available through the Internet.[103] Therefore, some authors claim that the Web has become "an

---

[98] For example, the "Terrorist's Handbook," the "Anarchist Cookbook," the "Mujahadeen Poisons Handbook," the "Encyclopedia of Jihad," the "Sabotage Handbook" and the famous "How to make Bombs," all of which are freely available.

[99] G. Weimann, How Modern Terrorism Uses the Internet, United States Institute of Peace Special Report 116, March 2004,
http://www.usip.org/pubs/specialreports/sr116.pdf [last visited: July 2007], p. 9.

[100] Al-Qaeda terrorists, for example, have compiled a handbook on hostage taking. Since 2004, this handbook is freely available at many websites. For excerpts of the handbook, see Y. Musharbash, Qaidas Leitfaden für Entführungen, Spiegel Online, 30.11.2005, http://www.spiegel.de/politik/ausland/0,1518,387691,00.html [last visited: July 2007].

[101] G. Weimann, How Modern Terrorism Uses the Internet, United States Institute of Peace Special Report 116, March 2004,
http://www.usip.org/pubs/specialreports/sr116.pdf [last visited: July 2007], p. 9.

[102] The German "suitcase bombers" of 2006, for example, gathered their knowledge from Internet sources. Only a small mistake in assembly prevented the detonation of the explosives. Experts stated that the explosion would have killed many. See J. Jüttner/Y. Musharbash, Kofferbomber wollten möglichst viele Menschen töten, Spiegel Online, 25.10.2006,
http://www.spiegel.de/panorama/justiz/0,1518,444715,00.html [last visited: July 2007].

[103] Al-Qaeda is said to run a "massive and dynamic online library of training materials" which is supported by experts who can answer questions either on message boards or in chatrooms. Topics covered in this database range from weapons and poisons to navigation instruments and even to camouflaging and masquerading. See Coll/Glasser, web-based operations.

open university for jihad."[104] Others agree and state that using the Internet for cyberplanning might be a more important and realistic option for terrorists than specialised cyber attacks.[105]

4. Fundraising and Financing

Some organisations use their websites as a source of financing or fundraising by selling CDs, DVDs, T-shirts, badges, flags, or books over the Internet.[106] Other websites give supporters the opportunity to donate money directly with their credit card, or they provide bank account details for contributions.[107] In doing so, organisations can also establish a link to supporters and candidates for possible recruitment. Apart from websites operated by the terrorist organisation itself, hundreds of support websites commonly appear and disappear. As with any other movement, they are often linked by web rings that allow visitors to quickly find similar websites. For example, Yahoo! has pulled dozens of sites in the Jihad Web Ring, a coalition of 55 Jihad-related sites.[108]

C. Use of the Internet for other Purposes

In addition to the use of the Internet for IT-based attacks and communication with the public, terrorists can also benefit from other possible uses that are seemingly "harmless," such as sending emails or visiting websites. The following two parts will cover the individual communication between terrorists

---

[104] S. Coll/S. Glasser, Terrorists turn to the web as base of operations, The Washington Post, 7 August 2005, Section A01.

[105] T. Thomas, Al Qaeda and the Internet: the danger of "cyberplanning", Parameters, Spring 2003, pp. 112-123 (112).

[106] G. Weimann, How Modern Terrorism Uses the Internet, United States Institute of Peace Special Report 116, March 2004,
http://www.usip.org/pubs/specialreports/sr116.pdf [last visited: July 2007], p. 5 describes this in relation to the website of al-Qaeda; M. Conway, Cyberterrorism and Terrorist 'Use' of the Internet, First Monday, 04.11.2002, Vol. 7, No. 11, http://firstmonday.org/issues/issue7_11/conway/ [last visited: July 2007], reports that the website of the Tamil Tigers sold books, pamphlets, videos, audio tapes, CDs, calendars, and flags in an online store. The current website (http://www.eelam.com [last visited: July 2007]) no longer offers this service. The author also describes a Taliban website that included instructions on how to make financial donations to the Afghan militia. See also T. Thomas, Al Qaeda and the Internet: the danger of "cyberplanning", Parameters, Spring 2003, pp. 112-123 (116); M. Gercke, "Cyberterrorismus" – Aktivitäten terroristischer Organisationen im Internet, CR 2007, pp. 62-68 (65).

[107] G. Weimann, How Modern Terrorism Uses the Internet, United States Institute of Peace Special Report 116, March 2004,
http://www.usip.org/pubs/specialreports/sr116.pdf [last visited: July 2007], p. 7.

[108] M. Conway, Cyberterrorism and Terrorist 'Use' of the Internet, First Monday, 04.11.2002, Vol. 7, No. 11, http://firstmonday.org/issues/issue7_11/conway/ [last visited: July 2007].

or terrorist groups (1.). Another focus is on the use of the Internet for preparatory purposes, e.g., to plan conventional attacks (2.).

1. Individual Communication

Many of the aforementioned advantages of the Internet are also applicable to IT-based communication: it is cheap, fast, often anonymous, and widely accessible. And, since encryption technologies are extensively available, it is also secure, even if messages have to be transported over public networks. Whereas the communication between a terrorist organisation and the public depends on good visibility, messages between terrorists or terrorist groups depend to a high degree on good camouflage and secure communication channels. Even though the Internet is basically an open network, its advantages predestine it for this communication task and make it an outstanding command and control mechanism.[109] Customary text-based techniques such as email, chat rooms, or mailing lists can be used, as can real speech by voice-over IP (VoIP).[110] Since many companies offer these services free of charge, no organisation has to operate its own service. Instead, many different and cost-free services can be used – alternatively or even simultaneously. The organisers of the 9/11-attacks, for example, had opened multiple accounts on largely anonymous email services such as "Hotmail."[111] Additionally, since the text-based techniques operate on the basis of process-and-store mechanism, new information can be gathered at any convenient point in time, so that terrorists neither have to be online all the time, nor do they have to entrust third-parties with the task of accepting personal messages for them. Additionally, with the help of modern mobile phones, the Internet can be accessed virtually everywhere.

In essence, the digital transportation of information enables loosely interconnected groups to maintain contact with one another.[112] This even goes so far as to allow terrorist groups that fight for different political goals

---

[109] *T. Thomas,* Al Qaeda and the Internet: the danger of "cyberplanning", Parameters, Spring 2003, pp. 112-123 (117); *Whine,* Cyberspace, p. 242.

[110] *C. Wilson,* Computer Attack and Cyberterrorism: Vulnerabilities and Policy Issues for Congress, Congressional Research Service Report for Congress (RL32114), updated 1 April 2005, p. 18 states that "Al Qaeda cells reportedly used new Internet-based telephone services to communicate with other terrorist cells overseas." *G. Weimann,* How Modern Terrorism Uses the Internet, United States Institute of Peace Special Report 116, March 2004, http://www.usip.org/pubs/specialreports/sr116.pdf [last visited: July 2007], p. 9 also reports on the use of "Pal Talk," a VoIP software used by al-Qaeda recruiters.

[111] *M. Conway,* Cyberterrorism and Terrorist 'Use' of the Internet, First Monday, 04.11.2002, Vol. 7, No. 11, http://firstmonday.org/issues/issue7_11/conway/ [last visited: July 2007].

[112] *G. Weimann,* Terrorists and Their Tools – Part II. Using the Internet to recruit, raise funds, and plan attacks, YaleGlobal, 26.04.2004, http://yaleglobal.yale.edu/article.print?id=3768 [last visited: July 2007].

and are located in different geographical areas to communicate with each other and exchange information, such as on weapons or tactics.[113]

Even if terrorists fear that their messages might be intercepted, they can take appropriate measures.[114] They can either disguise the message itself or use conventional encryption techniques. To hide messages, two techniques, in particular, are being discussed. For example, an organisation could hide messages in pictures with the help of steganography.[115] These pictures can be put on any public website, for example a classic photo site such as webshots.com. In turn, other members of the organisation could download the picture and decrypt the message. The entire process is concealed because no one (except for the terrorists) knows that the pictures contain a secret message. Furthermore, the course of action is completely inconspicuous because it is an everyday event that does not draw any attention to itself. The second technique involves the use of free mailer email accounts. However, the account is used in an unconventional way: instead of logging in, writing, and sending an email, the password is not just known to one person but to two – sender and recipient. The sender logs onto the account and writes but does not send the message. Instead, the message is saved as a draft. Later, the recipient logs onto the same account and reads the message in the draft folder. By means of this technique, the message never leaves the system, so that no traces of an email remain on any system – governmental filtering systems are successfully circumvented.[116]

---

[113] G. Weimann, Terrorists and Their Tools – Part II. Using the Internet to recruit, raise funds, and plan attacks, YaleGlobal, 26.04.2004,
http://yaleglobal.yale.edu/article.print?id=3768 [last visited: July 2007]. See also the next chapter on the Internet as a planning instrument for terrorists and terrorist organisations.

[114] However, this does not always to be the case: the organisers of the 9/11 attacks did use email, but did not see the need to encrypt their messages. See M. Conway, Cyberterrorism and Terrorist 'Use' of the Internet, First Monday, 04.11.2002, Vol. 7, No. 11, http://firstmonday.org/issues/issue7_11/conway/ [last visited: July 2007].

[115] G. Weimann, How Modern Terrorism Uses the Internet, United States Institute of Peace Special Report 116, March 2004,
http://www.usip.org/pubs/specialreports/sr116.pdf [last visited: July 2007], p. 10; S. Krempl, Terroristen verstecken Botschaften angeblich in IP-Headern, Heise News from 09.03.2003, http://www.heise.de/newsticker/meldung/35137 [last visited: July 2007]. Some authors, however, claim that the use of steganography is only a myth, M. Conway, Cyberterrorism and Terrorist 'Use' of the Internet, First Monday, 04.11.2002, Vol. 7, No. 11, http://firstmonday.org/issues/issue7_11/conway/ [last visited: July 2007]. Nevertheless, this is a possibility that could be used by terrorists, whether it has occurred already or not.

[116] See B. Wagner, Experts Downplay Imminent Threat of Cyberterrorism, National Defense Magazine, Issue July 2007,
http://nationaldefensemagazine.org/issues/2007/July/ExpertsDownplay.htm [last visited: July 2007].

However, even if the organisation decides to send messages as proper emails, it can do so because all of the messages can be encrypted.[117] Good encryption programs are available to the public as open-source software; thus, terrorists can be sure that no hidden backdoor is contained in the program. If the right encryption parameters are used, even up-to-date technology is not able to decrypt the message without the right key. Thousands of encrypted messages, for example, were found by federal officials on the computers of arrested al-Qaeda terrorists Abu Zubaydah[118] and Ramzi Yousef, who was tried for the previous bombing of the World Trade Center.[119] However, terrorists might also send unencrypted emails – if for example, they desire the content of their communication to become known. Since it is common knowledge that the surveillance of telecommunications is on the rise, such information could be purposefully disseminated in order to conceal other – real – attack plans that concentrate on other objects.[120]

2. The Internet as a Planning and Support Instrument

Apart from its function as an instrument of communication, the Internet also serves as a planning tool that can be used for real-world as well as for digital attacks.[121] Information, such as satellite maps, that was only available to experts until recently is now a common good.[122] These graphics are already being used by terrorists,[123] and they can easily be combined with other data, such as street names. As a result, for example escape routes can be planned with great precision even before a territory is inspected in person.[124]

---

[117] According to the President of the German Federal Police (*Bundeskriminalamt*) *Jörg Ziercke,* terrorists are using all possibilities that computers and networks offer, "starting from encryption techniques to password-protected repositories somewhere in the virtual world." See Der Spiegel, 9/2007, p. 36.

[118] G. Weimann, How Modern Terrorism Uses the Internet, United States Institute of Peace Special Report 116, March 2004, http://www.usip.org/pubs/specialreports/sr116.pdf [last visited: July 2007], p. 10.

[119] C. Wilson, Computer Attack and Cyberterrorism: Vulnerabilities and Policy Issues for Congress, Congressional Research Service Report for Congress (RL32114), updated 1 April 2005, p. 18.

[120] T. Thomas, Al Qaeda and the Internet: the danger of "cyberplanning", Parameters, Spring 2003, pp. 112-123 (122).

[121] G. Weimann, How Modern Terrorism Uses the Internet, United States Institute of Peace Special Report 116, March 2004, http://www.usip.org/pubs/specialreports/sr116.pdf [last visited: July 2007], p. 2 mentions the "everyday" use terrorists make of the Internet.

[122] For example, on Google Earth (http://earth.google.com, [last visited: July 2007]) or on Google maps (http://maps.google.com [last visited: July 2007]).

[123] J. Radü, Terroristen suchen Ziele mit Google Earth, Spiegel Online, 13.01.2007, http://www.spiegel.de/netzwelt/web/0,1518,459542,00.html [last visited: July 2007].

[124] The US Army, Cyber Operations and Cyber Terrorism, DCSINT Handbook No. 1.02, 15 August 2005, http://www.fas.org/irp/threat/terrorism/sup2.pdf [last visited: July 2007], p. I-2 lists an example where maps, a time schedule for shuttle busses, and a copy of the official telephone directory of a military base were available via the

This information can be combined with other information that is often freely available on the websites of companies, governmental institutions, and news services. For example, reports of security weaknesses in airports or transport companies could be gathered and used.[125] According to a terrorist training manual, such public sources can make up at least 80% of all information on the opponent that is required.[126] Actual findings on terrorists' computers show that these kinds of information are in fact downloaded and used for planning purposes.[127] Furthermore, according to some authors, terrorist organisations even use databases to gather, sort, and evaluate details of potential targets in the United States.[128] Against this background, it is reasonable that governments around the world have begun to ask providers of digital maps for disclosure of certain – security-relevant – information.[129]

---

official website. *B. Foltz*, Cyberterrorism, computer crime, and reality, Information Management & Computer Security, 15.03.2004, Vol. 12, No. 2, pp. 154-166, correctly points out, however, that these uses – like buying airline tickets or locating a possible target – are legitimate uses of the Internet, despite the underlying motivations and intentions. Nevertheless, these activities do fall within the definition of cyberterrorism according to some authors.

[125] *T. Thomas*, Al Qaeda and the Internet: the danger of "cyberplanning", Parameters, Spring 2003, pp. 112-123 (114).

[126] *G. Weimann*, How Modern Terrorism Uses the Internet, United States Institute of Peace Special Report 116, March 2004, http://www.usip.org/pubs/specialreports/sr116.pdf [last visited: July 2007], p. 7, quoting Secretary of Defense *Donald Rumsfeld* in 2003 who refers to an al-Qaeda training manual recovered in Afghanistan. This assessment was shared by *Richard Clark* who stated that the combination of all unclassified information available on the Internet "adds up to something that ought to be classified," see *US Army*, Cyber Operations and Cyber Terrorism, DCSINT Handbook No. 1.02, 15 August 2005, http://www.fas.org/irp/threat/terrorism/sup2.pdf [last visited: July 2007], p. I-1.

[127] *G. Weimann*, How Modern Terrorism Uses the Internet, United States Institute of Peace Special Report 116, March 2004, http://www.usip.org/pubs/specialreports/sr116.pdf [last visited: July 2007], p. 7; *T. Harding*, Terrorists 'use Google maps to hit UK troops', Telegraph 13 January 2007, http://www.telegraph.co.uk/news/main.jhtml?xml=/news/2007/01/13/wgoogle13.xml [last visited: July 2007]. In addition, the German "suitcase bombers" had gathered information for their bombs from the Internet. Even though the terrorists deleted this information from their laptops, German forensic experts were able to reconstruct this data, see *J. Kuri*, BKA-Forensiker entlöschen Bombenbaupläne, Heise News from 08.03.2007, http://www.heise.de/newsticker/meldung/86388 [last visited: July 2007].

[128] *G. Weimann*, How Modern Terrorism Uses the Internet, United States Institute of Peace Special Report 116, March 2004, http://www.usip.org/pubs/specialreports/sr116.pdf [last visited: July 2007], p. 7 quoting *Dan Verton* from his book Black Ice: The Invisible Threat of Cyberterrorism.

[129] See *F. Patalong*, Das zensierte Weltauge, http://www.spiegel.de/netzwelt/web/0,1518,464186,00.html [last visited: July 2007]; *A. Seith*, Google Earth verschleiert indische Verteidigungsanlagen, http://www.spiegel.de/netzwelt/web/0,1518,464178,00.html [last visited: July 2007].

Additionally, the compilations of specialised information mentioned above (such as the "Mujahadeen Poisons Handbook") are available for the planning and support of (mostly conventional) attacks. Therefore, the claims of some authors – that the Web has become "an open university for jihad"[130] and that cyberplanning might be a more important and realistic option for terrorists than specialised cyber attacks[131] – cannot be dismissed.

D. Conclusions

When looking at IT-based attacks, it is difficult to decide whether the phenomenon is just an exaggerated "cyber angst" or whether cyberterrorism is indeed an imminent threat. To identify what terrorists might do in the future, technical know-how combined with imagination is needed.[132] In the literature, this debate is fuelled by the many different definitions of cyberterrorism and terrorist use of the Internet, ranging from very narrow to very broad. A narrow definition is often followed by the assumption that cyberterrorism does not pose a threat, has never occurred, and cannot do any serious harm, whereas proponents of a broad definition take a more cautious point of view and claim that the threat is real.[133]

Realistically, one has to look at the possibilities and drawbacks of digital attacks and compare the necessary investments on the part of a terrorist organisation with the potential results. In addition, everything that *could* be done with the help of computers is often equated with what *will* be done.[134] For a rational evaluation, however, many different aspects have to be taken into account. An example of a real disadvantage of digital assault is that such attacks are often not repeatable since security flaws can and will be fixed once they are discovered. Therefore, terrorists have to assess carefully whether their investments in terms of time, personnel, and money are worth a one-time attack. Furthermore, apart from the attacks described above in which human lives are endangered, many scenarios result only in the unavailability of computer service, which is a common phenomenon even without terrorist attacks. Thus, neither public fear nor extensive media coverage can be expected from computer-related cyberterrorist attacks;

---

[130] *S. Coll/S. Glasser,* Terrorists turn to the web as base of operations, The Washington Post, 7 August 2005, Section A01.
[131] *T. Thomas,* Al Qaeda and the Internet: the danger of "cyberplanning", Parameters, Spring 2003, pp. 112-123 (112).
[132] Wired News from 25.05.2005: "CIA: Take That, Cyberterrorism!", http://www.wired.com/news/politics/0,1283,67644,00.html [last visited: July 2007] quoting Dorothy Denning: "You want to think about not just what you think may affect you, but about scenarios that might seem unlikely."
[133] *B. Foltz,* Cyberterrorism, computer crime, and reality, Information Management & Computer Security, 15.03.2004, Vol. 12, No. 2, pp. 154-166.
[134] *T. Thomas,* Al Qaeda and the Internet: the danger of "cyberplanning", Parameters, Spring 2003, pp. 112-123 (115).

cyberterrorism in this area is largely quiet.[135] Finally, attacks in security-relevant areas require highly developed computer skills and, very often, knowledge of exact circumstances. Therefore, experts claim that it could take from two to four years of preparation for a structured cyber attack against multiple systems and networks.[136] Also, the tremendous costs that accompany such a long preparation time might be a serious hindrance.

However, these disadvantages are no reason to underestimate the threat of cyberterrorism: the current generation of young terrorists has grown up in a digital world,[137] and specialised skills and information can also be acquired[138] on the free market.[139] When it comes to supporting and financing costly co-ordinated cyber attacks, several terrorist-sponsoring nations might

---

[135] S. Berinato, The Truth About Cyberterrorism, CIO Magazine 15.03.2002, http://www.cio.com/archive/031502/truth.html [last visited: July 2007].

[136] C. Wilson, Computer Attack and Cyberterrorism: Vulnerabilities and Policy Issues for Congress, Congressional Research Service Report for Congress (RL32114), updated 1 April 2005, p. 17. For a "complex co-ordinated cyber attack, causing mass disruption against integrated, heterogeneous systems" even six to ten years could be calculated.

[137] Seized computers of al-Qaeda, for example, show that young terrorists are becoming increasingly familiar with hacker tools that are freely available over the Internet, C. Wilson, Computer Attack and Cyberterrorism: Vulnerabilities and Policy Issues for Congress, Congressional Research Service Report for Congress (RL32114), updated 1 April 2005, p. 23

[138] G. Giacomello, Bangs for the Buck: A Cost-Benfit Analysis of Cyberterrorism, Studies in Conflict & Terrorism, Vol. 27 (2004), pp. 387-408 (395). Increased sophistication of skills has already been identified as a new trend in terrorism. Some authors even claim that it has become "a web directed phenomenon," see R. Perl, Trends in Terrorism: 2006, Congressional Research Service Report for Congress (RL33555), dated July 21, 2006, p. 5. According to other statements of officials, after a governmental test for a "Digital Pearl Harbor," however, terrorists would have to spend about $200 million for appropriate resources. See J. Green, The Myth of Cyberterrorism, Washington Monthly, November 2002. http://www.washingtonmonthly.com/features/2001/0211.green.html [last visited: July 2007].

[139] It is widely assumed that the capabilities of terrorists will increase if they employ hackers. See T. Espiner, Foreign powers are main cyberthreat, U.K. says, ZDNet 11/22/05, http://news.zdnet.com/2102-1009_22-5967532.html [last visited: July 2007]. According to C. Wilson, Computer Attack and Cyberterrorism: Vulnerabilities and Policy Issues for Congress, Congressional Research Service Report for Congress (RL32114), updated 1 April 2005, p. 20, the Islamic fundamentalist group "Harkat-ul-Ansar" attempted to buy cyber attack software from hackers in late 1998. The Japanese Aum Shinrikyo cult had contracted for an attack of 80 Japanese companies and 10 government agencies. Information on Zero-Day exploits is reportedly available from $1000 to $5000. Also Resources for Distributed Denial of Service Attacks can be bought. Prices are reported to range from $150 to $400, depending on the target and duration of the attack. Even discounts for multiple orders are being offered. See B. Bidder, Angriff der Cyber-Söldner, Der Spiegel 31/2007, pp. 74-76.

want to become involved.[140] Furthermore, the nature of the Internet makes cyber attacks interesting for terrorists: it guarantees a high level of anonymity; it makes attackers hard to trace; and it frees attackers from having physically to be at the place where the attacked object is located. Furthermore, since all attacks are digital, they can be scripted and launched on a large scale. For example, in a standard attempt, programs are sent out in order automatically to scan full networks. If they find possible victims for a known attack, they can be programmed either to infect or merely to report the exact address of the targeted computers. By doing so, an attacker can first evaluate which victims would be interesting targets and which ones would only be a waste of time. Also, by employing this technique, only a handful of perpetrators is needed to launch many attacks at the same time or over a longer period of time without the need constantly to monitor their systems. For this reason, digital assaults are highly attractive.

However, perhaps the one reason that makes a cyberterrorist aggression highly likely is the fact that there are so many potential targets in the Internet that are vulnerable.[141] In a recent study, for example, U.S. authorities were audited on the implementation of the Federal Information Security Management Act of 2002 (FISMA) that defines IT-security measures such as secure password management or access control. The overall rating for all government agencies was a school grade of "D$^+$".[142] Interestingly enough, the Department of Homeland Security, which is also responsible for the co-ordination of state cybersecurity, received an "F". Indeed, it failed the test

---

[140] As of October 2004, for example, seven designated state sponsors of terrorism were listed by the U.S. Department of State (Cuba, Iran, Iraq, Libya, North Korea, Syria, and Sudan). In 2003, Iraq was taken off the list, but only de facto, and some sanctions against Libya have been erased. See *C. Wilson*, Computer Attack and Cyberterrorism: Vulnerabilities and Policy Issues for Congress, Congressional Research Service Report for Congress (RL32114), updated 1 April 2005, p. 19. However, the mere existence of state sponsors for terrorist attacks poses a great risk. Also, since some of those countries also engage in their own activities in order to prepare for a cyberwar, not only financial resources but also technical help could be provided. For example, North Korea is said to be training more than 100 new computer hackers per year for national defense purposes. See *C. Wilson*, Computer Attack and Cyberterrorism: Vulnerabilities and Policy Issues for Congress, Congressional Research Service Report for Congress (RL32114), updated 1 April 2005, pp. 19-20. See also *T. Espiner*, Foreign powers are main cyberthreat, U.K. says, ZDNet 11/22/05, http://news.zdnet.com/2102-1009_22-5967532.html [last visited: July 2007] and *C. Wagner*, Countering Cyber Attacks, The Futurist Issue May/June 2007, p. 16 on the problems of terrorist cyber attacks by states.
[141] *G. Weimann*, Sum of All Fears?, Studies in Conflict & Terrorism, 28 (2005), pp. 129-149 (137).
[142] U.S. school grades, where "A" stands for "excellent", "B" for "above average", "C" for "average" and "D" for "below average, but passing." Grades of "F" (or "E") mean failure. http://en.wikipedia.org/wiki/Grade_(education)#United_States [last visited: July 2007].

three times in a row.[143] However, the private sector fares none the better. According to Richard Clarke, special adviser to the president of the United States for cyberspace security in 2001, a typical company devotes one quarter of one percent of its information technology budget to cybersecurity – "slightly less than they spend on coffee."[144] Apart from the question of technical security measures, however, the aspect of human control has to be kept in mind. In the case of the manipulated hydroelectric dam, for example,[145] the attacker needed 46 attempts to unleash millions of gallons of raw sewage. The people managing the critical infrastructure did not notice any of the unsuccessful 45 attempts.[146]

Apart from the risks of a cyber attack, it can be safely assumed that terrorists have begun to use the Internet not as a target but as a means for communicating or planning their attacks. By doing so, they can reach new groups of people that would typically not take notice of a terrorist group or its aims. Also, other people who are interested in contacting and contributing to a terrorist group (either financially or personally) might in the past have had problems in establishing a link to the organisation since the group previously had to work underground. With the help of the Internet, terrorist groups can now establish a "clean" link to information, possibilities for anonymous contact, and a wide range of material for the interested. Furthermore, it will prove technically impossible to hinder these websites or block communication between terrorists[147] – especially if they make use of encryption technology or other methods to obscure their communications. Therefore, it can also be assumed that terrorists might prefer using the Internet for non-violent acts since using it in this way is more effective for the achievement of their ultimate goals.

---

[143] *P.-M. Ziegler,* US-Behörden fallen bei IT-Sicherheit durch. Heise Security from 16.03.2006, http://www.heise.de/security/news/meldung/70946 [last visited: July 2007].
[144] *J. Green,* The Myth of Cyberterrorism, Washington Monthly, November 2002. http://www.washingtonmonthly.com/features/2001/0211.green.html [last visited: July 2007].
[145] See *B. Wagner,* Experts Downplay Imminent Threat of Cyberterrorism, National Defense Magazine, Issue July 2007,
http://nationaldefensemagazine.org/issues/2007/July/ExpertsDownplay.htm [last visited: July 2007].
[146] See *S. Berinato,* The Truth About Cyberterrorism, CIO Magazine 15.03.2002, http://www.cio.com/archive/031502/truth.html [last visited: July 2007].
[147] See *T. Thomas,* Al Qaeda and the Internet: the danger of "cyberplanning", Parameters, Spring 2003, pp. 112-123 (114).

II. Legal and Policy Evaluation: International Co-operation Against Terrorist Use of the Internet[148]

A. Overview

1. The Need for International Co-operation

Terrorism is a global phenomenon that transcends national borders. Computer networks and computer data, which also disregard physical boundaries, create a global cyberspace. In addition, computer networks such as the Internet allow for the development of new forms of technology that enable users to maintain their anonymity, to engage in hidden communication, and to make use of sophisticated encryption programs in the transfer and storage of data. Thus, the global cyber space provides a unique environment in which to carry out cyberterrorism and to pursue other international terrorist goals.[149]

As a result of these specific features of computer networks, three major areas for terrorist activities on the Internet have been identified in chapter I of this report: the commission of destructive attacks by means of the Internet; the mass dissemination of illegal content via the Internet; and the use of the Internet for individual communication and for the commission of traditional forms of crime. In the first area, *destructive attacks against computer systems carried out by means of the Internet* (cyberterrorism) can lead not only to the destruction, corruption, and rendering inaccessible of intangible computer data, thus blocking production processes, banking systems, or public administration. Internet-based attacks can also damage physical property and human life if, for example, the attacked computer systems are responsible for the administration of nuclear power stations, dams, flight control systems, hospital computers, or military weapon systems. Since many aspects of modern society are highly dependent on computer systems, the risks posed by this type of criminal activity are considerable. However, at this time, very few cases involving these kinds of attacks are known. In contrast, terrorist use of the Internet and other electronic communication systems in the second of these areas – the *public dissemination of illegal content* – is common. Here, the Internet and other communication systems are exploited by terrorists in order to threaten the commission of terrorist acts; to incite, advertise, and glorify terrorism; to engage in fundraising for and financing of terrorism; to provide training for terrorism; to recruit for terrorism; and to disseminate racist and xenophobic material. As a result, the Internet has become an important tool by means of which terrorists send their messages to a broad audience. Finally, the Internet and other computer

---

[148] Chapter II and III prepared by Prof. Dr. Dr. h.c. *Ulrich Sieber,* Director at the Max Planck Institute for Foreign and International Criminal Law in Freiburg,Germany.
[149] For a more detailed analysis of these problems see *U. Sieber*, The Threat of Cybercrime, in: Council of Europe (ed.), Organised Crime in Europe, Strasbourg 2005, pp. 81-218 (212-218).

systems play a significant role in the third area mentioned above, the *logistical preparation of terrorist offences*, including internal communication, acquisition of information (e.g., on bomb-building, hostage-taking, or hijacking), analysis of targets, and other forms of information gathering.[150]

The investigation and prosecution of most of these crimes is complex and challenging due to the technical nature of the Internet. Investigation and prosecution in this area require both adequate substantive criminal law provisions as well as adequate procedural capabilities, such as the authority and the technical ability to identify foreign attackers, preserve stored computer data, issue production orders requiring the submission of specified computer data, engage in search and seizure of computer systems, break encryption, engage in the real time collection of traffic data, and intercept content data. In many cases, these phenomena have an international dimension, which may require concerted investigation in numerous countries. As a consequence, the prosecution and prevention of terrorist activities on the Internet depend to a great extent on the existence of appropriate international conventions and other instruments of international co-operation. These instruments must address the specific legal and forensic challenges posed by the Internet, they must make use of new Internet-based investigation techniques, and, at the same time, they must balance the need for effective prosecution against the obligation to protect citizens' civil liberties.

2. Aim, Method, and Structure of the Following Analysis

The *aim of the following analysis* is to determine whether existing international conventions and other instruments of legal co-operation are adequate for the containment of cyberterrorism and other use of the Internet for terrorist purposes or whether the instruments should be amended. In light of this aim, the analysis focuses on the questions of whether the computer-specific international instruments are applicable with respect to terrorism and whether the terrorist-specific instruments are applicable in the IT environment. Furthermore, while this report is the result of a limited study and does not reflect a comprehensive evaluation of international instruments in general, it will provide an initial analysis with respect to the question of whether the various international instruments provide adequate coverage of crimes associated with the use of the Internet for terrorist purposes or whether the instruments exhibit gaps or other general problems regarding this kind of criminal activity that should be addressed in the future.[151] The

---

[150] For the phenomena of cyberterrorism and other use of the Internet for terrorist purposes see chapter I supra and *U. Sieber*, The Threat of Cybercrime, in: Council of Europe (ed.), Organised Crime in Europe, Strasbourg 2005, pp. 81-218 (173-175); *G. Weimann*, Cyberterrorism: The Sum of All Fears?, Studies in Conflict & Terrorism 28 (2005), pp. 129-149.

[151] For an analysis of deficits in the international conventions on terrorism, see *C. Tomuschat*, Council of Europe Committee of Experts on Terrorism (CODEXTER), Strasbourg, On the possible "added value" of a comprehensive Convention on

term "gap," it should be pointed out, is understood broadly: since the effects of the criminal law are felt both in the area of security as well as in the area of liberty, gaps can exist with respect to the effective prosecution of crime *and* with respect to the effective protection of human rights.[152]

The *method of the following study* involved the selection and analysis of international instruments. In this process, all relevant conventions of the Council of Europe concerning terrorist use of the Internet were included as well as those of other major organisations, such as the United Nations and the European Union. Non-CoE instruments are also examined in this analysis, which was prepared for the Council of Europe, because the existing instruments of some international institutions (such as the UN) can reduce the need for the Council of Europe to take action, and some other standards (such as standards of the EU) can provide guidance with regard to possibilities for closer co-operation among non-EU Member States. The relevant phenomena – criminal activities associated with terrorist use of the Internet – that should be covered by these conventions were identified in chapter I of this report and in a previous study conducted by the Max Planck Institute for Foreign and International Criminal Law on behalf of the Council of Europe.[153]

The following analysis encompasses all three areas of law that require international legal co-ordination as a prerequisite for effective transnational prosecution. Thus, the report addresses the development and harmonisation of national substantive criminal law (infra B.), national criminal procedure (infra C.), and the law of international co-operation (infra D.).

Terrorism, 26 Human Rights Law Journal 2005, pp. 287-306 (299 ff.), dealing with criminalisation of terrorist offences, appropriate penalties, jurisdiction, duty to investigate, denial of right of asylum, administrative measures, exchange of information, liability of entities, freezing and forfeiture of funds, protection of judicial personnel, assistance to victims of violent crime, direct contacts between national authorities, establishment of special anti-terrorist units, extradition procedures, administrative detention, and human rights, etc. *Tomuschat's* extensive enumeration shows the impracticability of addressing here all general problems associated with cybercrime and all problems of terrorism encountered in international instruments.

[152] The identification and elimination of any such gaps requires a normative evaluation that depends, to some extent, on subjective attitudes. Thus, the identification of gaps is understood as the identification of a situation that – based on the subjective consideration of the author – might benefit from changes in the international law of co-operation, either to improve efficiency or to enhance the protection of civil liberties.

[153] See chapter I supra and *U. Sieber*, The Threat of Cybercrime, in: Council of Europe (ed.), Organised Crime in Europe, Strasbourg 2005, pp. 81-218 (173-175); *G. Weimann*, Cyberterrorism: The Sum of All Fears?, Studies in Conflict & Terrorism 28 (2005), pp. 129-149.

B. Developing and Harmonising National Substantive Criminal Law

The basic requirement for the prosecution of cyberterrorism and other use of the Internet for terrorist purposes is the existence in all countries of adequate national substantive criminal law provisions that cover the various terrorist acts. Thus, this chapter analyses the relevant international standards that govern the three aforementioned types of exploitation of the Internet for terrorist purposes: (1) destructive attacks on computer systems carried out by means of the Internet, (2) computer-based communication of illegal content to the public, and (3) other computer-based planning and support.

1. Destructive Attacks Carried Out by Means of the Internet

a) Structural Analysis of the Relevant Attacks With Respect to the Existing Legal Framework

The analysis of destructive attacks on computer systems carried out by means of the Internet shows a wide variety of possible techniques: terrorists could circumvent the integrity, confidentiality, and availability of computer systems and data either by hacking computers, deceiving victims, or spreading viruses and worms, thus manipulating systems, or by bringing about mass queries and other large scale attacks on the victim's computer system (such as distributed denial of service attacks using bot nets).[154] If the attacked IT-systems are connected to other critical systems and infrastructures, both the disruption of services as well as physical harm and loss of life could result. Physical damage could be brought about, for example, by attacking the computers of electrical supply systems, hospitals, food production or pharmaceutical companies, air, railroad or other transport control systems, hydroelectric dams, military control systems, or nuclear power stations.[155] Thus, in order to respond to the question of whether international legal instruments have gaps with respect to the coverage of terrorist attacks on computer systems, a wide variety of abuses involving different attack techniques and different results must be considered.

The national substantive criminal law provisions and the various international standards in question are characterised by descriptions of acts, results, and intents. Thus, the investigation of the applicability of these provisions to terrorist attacks on computer systems carried out by means of the Internet requires a systematic analysis not only of the acts themselves but especially of the various results (actual and intended) of the attacks. This leads to the

---

[154] For a general overview on destructive attacks against computer systems via the Internet, see I.A. supra and *B. Foltz,* Cyberterrorism, computer crime, and reality, Information Management & Computer Security, 15.3.2004, Vol. 12, No. 2, pp. 154-166; *U. Sieber,* The Threat of Cybercrime, in: Council of Europe (ed.), Organised Crime in Europe, Strasbourg 2005, pp. 81-218 (173-175).

[155] This can be achieved by manipulating the "supervisory control and data acquisition" systems (SCADA systems) that measure and control other systems, if these systems are connected to the Internet. See I.A.2.a) supra.

following pattern, which is valid for the analysis of all destructive attacks on computer systems carried out by means of the Internet:

- The *primary result* of all destructive acts against computer systems carried out by means of the Internet must be *interference with data*, that is, destruction, alteration, suppression, or the rendering unavailable of data. This is simply because in the absence of such interference the perpetrator can neither influence an attacked computer system nor affect the accessibility or availability of the system.[156]

- *Secondary results* of this kind of interference with data can be seen in *two types of damage*: Digital (or intangible) damage may result if data are rendered unavailable or manipulated so that services can no longer be delivered or if the computer system of the victim is compromised. Physical (or tangible) damage may result if the attacked computer system is used in the administration of property (such as hydroelectric dams or power plants) or human life (such as medical records).

- In causing these primary and secondary results, the perpetrator *intends* to bring about a *third result*, namely, the effectuation of his or her *political goals* (such as intimidating a population, compelling a government to act in a certain way, or destabilising political structures).

The development and use of this analytical pattern for Internet-based attacks on computer systems offers the opportunity to understand better the different approaches and the relationship between the existing regulations that target cybercrime and those that target terrorism: Attacks on computer systems carried out by means of the Internet can be addressed by means of special IT-based statutes that focus on the first "result level" mentioned above, that is, the integrity, availability, and confidentiality of data and computer systems (as does the Cybercrime Convention). In cases of additional (proprietary and especially human) harm, attacks can also be addressed by means of offences that focus on the second "result level," namely, physical damage (as do the UN conventions on typical terrorist acts), possibly in combination with a specific terrorist intent on the third "result level" (as does the EU Framework Decision). In sum, cyberterrorism can be tackled with a "computer-specific" data approach (focusing on the intangible harm to data) and/or with a "terrorist-specific" tangible damage approach (focusing on the physical harm and – possibly – also on a certain political intent).

These two possible approaches will be analysed in more detail on the basis of the relevant international conventions, that is, the Convention on Cybercrime of the Council of Europe, the EU Council Framework Decision on attacks against information systems, the EU Council Framework Decision on combating terrorism, and the various UN conventions that obligate states to enact substantive criminal law provisions.

---

[156] Furthermore, if the attacked system is protected by security measures, the intrusion cannot be achieved without the application of additional technical manipulations or deceptions, such as hacking techniques or methods of social engineering.

b) Analysis of the Relevant Conventions

CoE Convention on Cybercrime

The Council of Europe's Convention on Cybercrime,[157] which takes the data approach described above, is the most comprehensive of the existing international instruments that address computer crime. It includes obligations with respect to substantive criminal law, criminal procedure, and international co-operation.

In the area of substantive criminal law (Chapter II Section 1), Articles 4 and 5 address the "damaging, deletion, deterioration, alteration or suppression of computer data" and the "serious hindering ... of the functioning of a computer system by inputting, transmitting, damaging, deleting, deteriorating, altering or suppressing computer data":

> *Art. 4: Data interference*
> 1. Each Party shall adopt such legislative and other measures as may be necessary to establish as criminal offences under its domestic law, when committed intentionally, the damaging, deletion, deterioration, alteration or suppression of computer data without right.
> 2. A Party may reserve the right to require that the conduct described in paragraph 1 result in serious harm.
>
> *Art. 5: System interference*
> Each Party shall adopt such legislative and other measures as may be necessary to establish as criminal offences under its domestic law, when committed intentionally, the serious hindering without right of the functioning of a computer system by inputting, transmitting, damaging, deleting, deteriorating, altering or suppressing computer data.

Thus, Articles 4 and 5 of the Cybercrime Convention cover all types of interference with data and computer systems that – as shown – are a prerequisite for terrorist attacks on computer systems carried out by means of the Internet. Since Article 4 is not limited to the deletion of data but also encompasses the alteration and suppression of data (and is extended to the hindering of a computer system by Article 5), such interference is not limited to IT-based attacks on computer systems but also occurs in the context of the aforementioned attacks on other infrastructures, on physical property, or on the life or well-being of persons.[158] This consequence of the underlying

---

[157] Convention on Cybercrime of the Council of Europe of 23.11.2001 (ETS No. 185).
[158] Convention on Cybercrime of the Council of Europe of 23.11.2001 (ETS No. 185), Explanatory Report, No. 65 interpreting Art. 5 states that "the protected

concept of the Cybercrime Convention on the comprehensive protection of the integrity and availability of computer systems is confirmed in the Explanatory Report of the Convention, which explains that Article 5 is formulated in "a neutral way so that all kinds of functions can be protected by it."[159] As a result, all types of terrorist attacks against computer systems fall under Articles 4 and 5.

In addition, Articles 2 and 3 of the Cybercrime Convention cover the intrusion techniques of hacking and interception of computer data (e.g., by means of technical manipulations or by misusing intercepted information), which in many cases must be engaged in order to overcome the security measures in place on the victim's computer system so that the intruder can interfere with and alter data:

Art. 2: Illegal access
Each Party shall adopt such legislative and other measures as may be necessary to establish as criminal offences under its domestic law, when committed intentionally, the access to the whole or any part of a computer system[160] without right. A Party may require that the offence be committed by infringing security measures, with the intent of obtaining computer data[161] or other dishonest intent, or in relation to a computer system that is connected to another computer system.

Art. 3: Illegal interception
Each Party shall adopt such legislative and other measures as may be necessary to establish as criminal offences under its domestic law, when committed intentionally, the interception without right, made by technical means, of non-public transmissions of computer data to, from or within a computer system, including electromagnetic emissions from a computer system carrying such computer data. A

---

legal interest is the interest of operators and users of computer or telecommunication systems being able to have them function properly."
[159] Convention on Cybercrime of the Council of Europe of 23.11.2001 (ETS No. 185), Explanatory Report, No. 65 interpreting Art. 5. See also Nos. 60 and 61 describing the concept of Art. 4 in protecting "the integrity and proper functioning or use of stored computer data or computer programs." The term "alteration" in Art. 4 means the modification of existing data covering "the input of malicious codes, such as viruses and Trojan horses." It is due to this broad concept of the Cybercrime Convention in protecting system integrity that the Convention can also cover all specific forms of terrorist attacks, such as invading a computer system and replacing official websites by websites containing terrorist propaganda.
[160] "Computer system" is defined in Art. 1a as "any device or group of interconnected or related devices, one or more of which, pursuant to a program, performs automatic processing of data."
[161] "Computer data" is defined in Art. 1b as "any representation of facts, information, or concepts in a form suitable for processing in a computer system, including a program suitable to cause a computer system to perform a function."

Party may require that the offence be committed with dishonest intent, or in relation to a computer system that is connected to another computer system.

These provisions are extended in scope by rules on attempt and aiding and abetting (Art. 11) and on corporate liability (Art. 12) and are supported by rules requiring effective, proportionate, and dissuasive sanctions, including the deprivation of liberty (Art. 13). In addition, Article 6 on the "misuse of devices" aims at the criminalisation of acts preparatory to intrusion, such as the illegal production, sale, procurement for use, or otherwise making available of "a device, including a computer program, designed or adapted primarily for the purpose of committing any of the offences established in accordance with Articles 2 through 5" or a "computer password, access code, or similar data by which the whole or any part of a computer system is capable of being accessed," with intent that the device or data be used for the purpose of committing any of the offences established in Articles 2 through 5. Article 6 also targets the possession of these items with intent that the item be used for the purpose of committing any of the offences established in the aforementioned articles.[162] Thus, with respect to terrorist attacks via the Internet, Articles 2, 3, and 6 give additional protection, allowing perpetrators to be prosecuted at an early stage.

As a consequence, the implementing requirements of the Cybercrime Convention in the area of substantive criminal law demand a broad criminalisation of IT-based terrorist attacks on computers and all other legal interests that depend on the functioning of computer systems. As shown above, physical harm to property or human life and well-being is not a prerequisite for punishment under the Cybercrime Convention, but leads to the applicability of additional "traditional" offences of national criminal law. Thus, the Cybercrime Convention achieves the criminalisation of attacks on computer systems by means of a "data approach" that does not require, consider, or evaluate physical damage or the (political) intent of the perpetrator.

EU Council Framework Decision on Attacks Against Information Systems

The EU Council Framework Decision on attacks against information systems[163] is based on the Cybercrime Convention of the Council of Europe and, like the Convention, requires Member States to ensure that illegally accessing information systems (Art. 2), illegally interfering with systems (Art. 3), and illegally interfering with data (Art. 4) are punishable as criminal offences.[164] In addition, it includes requirements concerning the

---

[162] Furthermore, there is a provision against computer-related forgery (Art. 7), which can apply to preparatory electronic falsifications that might also facilitate intrusion.
[163] Council Framework Decision 2005/222/JI of 24.2.2005 on attacks against information systems (OJ L 69/67 of 16.3.2005).
[164] The Framework Decision does not contain a provision on misuse of devices.

criminalisation of instigation, aiding and abetting, and attempt. As a consequence, it can also cover the necessary interference with data in IT-based cyberterrorism attacks.[165]

EU Council Framework Decision on Combating Terrorism

Cyberterrorism is also addressed in the EU Council Framework Decision on combating terrorism.[166] In contrast to the aforementioned instruments, this Framework Decision follows a "terrorist-specific," traditional corporeal damage approach (focusing on the physical or human corporeal harm). Unlike the Cybercrime Convention, the focus of the Framework Decision is not on the interference with data or on the IT-based forms of attack, but on the result of the perpetrator's action and on his or her intent with respect to the political aim of the attack. Article 1 of the Framework Decision reads as follows (emphasis added):

> Each Member State shall take the necessary measures to ensure that intentional acts referred to below [...] which, given their nature or context, may seriously damage a country or an international organisation where committed with the aim of:
> – seriously intimidating a population, or
> – unduly compelling a Government or international organisation to perform or abstain from performing any act, or
> – seriously destabilising or destroying the fundamental political, constitutional, economic or social structures of a country or an international organisation,
> shall be deemed to be terrorist offences:
> [...]
> (d) causing extensive destruction to a Government or public facility, a transport system, *an infrastructure facility, including, an information system*, a fixed platform located on the continental shelf, a public place or private property likely to endanger human life or *result in major economic loss* ...
> [...]
> (i) threatening to commit any of the acts listed in (a) to (h).

Articles 2 and 4 contain additional rules on participation (including supplying information, material resources, or funding) and on attempt. Thus, the Framework Decision applies a "corporeal damage approach" that focuses more specifically on terrorist attacks than do the data and system

---

[165] The Commission of the European Communities is currently preparing further actions that would prohibit spam, spyware, and malicious software. See Commission of the European Communities, Communication from the Commission to the European Parliament, the Council, the European Economic and Social Committee and the Committee of the Region on Fighting Spam, Spyware and Malicious Software, Brussels, 15.11.2006, COM (2006) 688 final.
[166] Council Framework Decision on Combating Terrorism (2002/475/ JHA of 13.6.2002), OJ L 164/3 of 22.6.2002.

interference provisions of the Cybercrime Convention. In contrast to the Cybercrime Convention, it takes into consideration the extent of the damage to a computer infrastructure, thus covering serious attacks on infrastructures and against a multitude of computers by large scale virus attacks or DDoS attacks and excluding minor attacks against individual computer systems. In addition, it takes into consideration the "terrorist" intent of the perpetrator, that is, whether he or she pursued specific political aims. As a consequence of these aggravating factors, Article 5 of the Framework Decision requires that such offences be punishable by custodial sentences longer than those that can be imposed under national law for offences committed without special intent. Since the means of attack are not specified, the EU Council Framework Decision on combating terrorism covers both traditional violent attacks as well as IT-based attacks. Thus, there are no gaps in criminalisation when the provision is applied to attacks via the Internet.

UN Conventions and Protocols Against Specific Acts of Terrorism

The UN has elaborated numerous multilateral conventions and protocols relating to states' instruments for combating violent acts and terrorism.[167] The focus of these instruments is on the enumeration of dangerous acts and results that are typical of terrorism:

- The Convention for the Suppression of Unlawful *Seizure of Aircraft*, the Convention for the Suppression of Unlawful Acts Against the Safety of *Civil Aviation*, and the Protocol for the Suppression of Unlawful Acts of Violence at *Airports Serving International Civil Aviation*[168] aim to criminalise certain acts of seizure of an aircraft, violence against a person on board an aircraft, destruction of aircraft or air navigation facilities, and other similar offences. Attempting to perform such an offence as well as serving as an accomplice to someone who performs or attempts to perform such an offence is also punishable. These provisions could be applied, for example, in cases of computer-based manipulation of flight control systems in airplanes or airports.

---

[167] See *C. Bassiouni,* International Terrorism: Multilateral Conventions (1937-2001), 3 vol., New York 2001/2002; *K. Nuotio,* Terrorism as a Catalyst for the Emergence, Harmonization and Reform of Law, Journal of International Criminal Justice 4 (2006), pp. 998-1016, 1002 ff. For the UN Conventions on the Suppression of the Financing of Terrorism of 1999, see II.C.2. and II.D.2. infra.

[168] Convention for the Suppression of Unlawful Seizure of Aircraft of 16.12.1970, UN Treaty Series Reg. No. 12325; Convention for the Suppression of Unlawful Acts Against Safety of Civil Aviation of 23.9.1971, UN Treaty Series Reg. No. 14118; Protocol for the Suppression of Unlawful Acts of Violence at Airports Serving International Civil Aviation of 24.2.1988 (http://www.unodc.org/unodc/terrorism_convention_airports.html [last visited: 1 July 2007]). In addition, the Convention on Offences and Certain Other Acts Committed on Board Aircraft of 14.9.1963, UN Treaty Series Reg. No. 10106, regulates the powers of the aircraft commander with respect to offences committed on board.

- The Convention on the Prevention and Punishment of *Crimes Against Internationally Protected Persons*[169] obligates the parties to criminalise certain acts against heads of state, heads of government, and other representatives of a State, such as murder, kidnapping, certain violent attacks, the threat and the attempt to commit any such act, as well as participation in such acts. Such an attack could be committed, for example, by manipulating a hospital computer system in order to kill a person protected by the Convention.

- The International Convention Against the *Taking of Hostages*[170] punishes "any person who seizes or detains and threatens to kill, to injure or to continue to detain another person ... in order to compel a third party ... to do or abstain from doing any act as an explicit or implicit condition for the release of the hostage." Attempt and participation are also punishable. The provisions required by this Convention could be applied, for example, in a case in which terrorists communicate demands for ransom via email.

- The Convention on the Physical *Protection of Nuclear Material*[171] aims to bring about the criminalisation of certain acts involving nuclear material. Article 7 covers "an act without lawful authority which constitutes the receipt, possession, use, transfer, alteration, disposal or dispersal of nuclear material and which causes or is likely to cause death or serious injury to any person or substantial damage to property." It also deals with "an act constituting a demand for nuclear material by threat or use of force or by any other form of intimidation" as well as "a threat ... to use nuclear material to cause death or serious injury to any person or substantial property damage." Attempt and participation are also covered by the Convention. Similarly, the new Convention for the Suppression of *Acts of Nuclear Terrorism* (not yet in force)[172] aims to prevent the illegal use of radioactive material. A person commits an offence if, for example, he or she unlawfully and intentionally possesses or uses radioactive material with the intent to cause death or seriously bodily injury or to cause substantial damage to property or to the environment. The Convention also includes threat, attempt and participation provisions. Convention offences could be committed, for example, by terrorists manipulating the computer system of a nuclear power plant with the intent to set free nuclear material.

- The Convention for the Suppression of Unlawful Acts Against the *Safety of Maritime Navigation*[173] establishes a legal regime applicable to acts

---

[169] Convention on the Prevention and Punishment of Crimes Against Internationally Protected Persons of 14.12.1973, UN Treaty Series Reg. No. 15410.

[170] Convention Against the Taking of Hostages of 17.12.1979, UN Treaty Series Reg. No. 21931.

[171] Convention on the Physical Protection of Nuclear Material of 3.3.1980, UN Treaty Series Reg. No. 37517.

[172] See http://untreaty.un.org/English/Terrorism/English_18_15.pdf [last visited: 1 July 2007].

[173] Convention for the Suppression of Unlawful Acts Against the Safety of Maritime Navigation of 10.3.1988, UN Treaty Series Reg. No. 29004.

threatening the safety of international maritime that is similar to the regimes applicable to acts threatening the safety of international aviation. It makes it an offence for a person unlawfully and intentionally to seize or exercise control over a ship by force, threat, or intimidation, to destroy a ship, or to perform certain acts of violence against a person on board a ship, or to engage in other acts against the safety of ships. The same applies if someone communicates information that he or she knows to be false, thereby endangering the safe navigation of a ship. Such action could be committed, for example, by manipulating an electronic ship control system. Attempting as well as abetting or otherwise serving as an accomplice in the commission of a listed offence are also punishable offences.

- The Protocol for the Suppression of Unlawful Acts Against the Safety of *Fixed Platforms Located on the Continental Shelf*[174] creates a legal regime for fixed platforms on the continental shelf that is similar to the regimes established to safeguard international aviation. According to Article 2, a person commits an offence if he or she unlawfully and intentionally seizes or exercises control over a fixed platform by force or threat thereof or any other form of intimidation. An offence is also committed by a person who destroys a fixed platform or who threatens, with or without a condition, aimed at compelling a physical or judicial person to do or refrain from doing any act, to commit such offences, if that threat is likely to endanger the safety of the fixed platform. Such destruction of a fixed platform could be achieved by electronic interference with the platform's security control system. Attempting as well as abetting or otherwise serving as an accomplice in the commission of a listed offence are also punishable offences.

- The International Convention for the Suppression of *Terrorist Bombings*[175] addresses the unlawful and intentional use of explosives and other lethal devices. According to Article 2, a person commits an offence "if that person unlawfully and intentionally delivers, places, discharges or detonates an explosive or other lethal device in, into or against a place of public use, a State or government facility, a public transportation system or an infrastructure facility: (a.) with the intent to cause death or serious bodily injury; or (b.) with the intent to cause extensive destruction of such a place, facility or system, where such destruction results in or is likely to result in major economic loss." According to the definition in Article 1, an "explosive or other lethal device" is "an explosive or incendiary weapon or device that is designed, or has the capability, to cause death, serious bodily injury or substantial

---

[174] Protocol for the Suppression of Unlawful Acts Against the Safety of Fixed Platforms Located on the Continental Shelf of 10.3.1988, UN Treaty Series Reg. No. 29004.

[175] Convention for the Suppression of Terrorist Bombings of 15.12.1997, UN Treaty Series Reg. No. 37517. In this connection, see also the Convention on the Marking of Plastic Explosives for the Purpose of Detection of 1991, UN Treaties Series Reg. No. 36984, which provides for chemical marking to facilitate detection of plastic explosives, e.g., to combat aircraft sabotage.

material damage" or "a weapon or device that is designed, or has the capability, to cause death, serious bodily injury or substantial material damage through the release, dissemination or impact of toxic chemicals, biological agents or toxins or similar substances or radiation or radioactive material." Attempt and participation in listed offences are also punishable. Thus, the criminal law provision demanded by the Convention could be applied in a case of cyberterrorism in which a bomb is triggered via the Internet. However, the definition of Article 1 and the aim of the Convention obviously do not allow an extension to "virtual bombs" (such as "mail bombs" or other destructive software tools) that cause only intangible damage.

The enumeration shows that the criminal provisions of the UN conventions follow the traditional "corporeal damage approach" mentioned above (focusing on physical or human corporeal harm) by protecting certain persons (e.g., senior representatives of States) or infrastructures (e.g., air and sea traffic or maritime platforms) or criminalising certain dangerous acts (e.g., bombing, uncontrolled transfer of nuclear material, and hostage-taking). Concentrating as they do on specific dangerous acts that are punishable per se, they do not contain a subjective requirement of political ("terrorist") intent. All of them have additional provisions that regulate attempt and participation.

With respect to cyberterrorism and the use of the Internet for terrorist purposes, it is important to note that all criminal provisions contained in the conventions and protocols discussed above are worded in general terms. They are applicable regardless of how the acts are committed, that is, whether the acts are committed by traditional means or by means of IT-based attacks. For example, the provisions demanded by the aforementioned UN Conventions are applicable if the Internet is used to take control over an airport or a ship navigation system, if a computer network is used to trigger a bomb or an attack on an aircraft, or if computer manipulations are undertaken in order to misroute the transfer of nuclear material. The non-applicability, mentioned above, of the Convention for the Suppression of Terrorist Bombings to "virtual bombs" is not an exception to this rule, but rather a desired result of the legal framework of the UN conventions on terrorism, which are directed at specific, enumerated acts only. Thus, the UN instruments are generally applicable and do not have gaps in criminalisation with respect to IT-based attacks. However, due to the system of the UN conventions on terrorism, these conventions do not cover all terrorist acts in a general way. Thus, the evaluation of existing international conventions raises the question of whether a new convention, one that would specifically address terrorist attacks on computer systems or computer infrastructures, is necessary.

c) Summary, Evaluation, and Consequences of Legal Policy

General Evaluation

The previous analysis has shown that international instruments promoting the harmonisation of criminal law take two complementary approaches to IT-based attacks against computer systems, infrastructures, and other legal interests:

- The "computer-specific" data approach taken by the Cybercrime Convention (which focuses, beyond the interception of and illegal access to computer systems, on the damage caused by such attacks to data) covers the interference with data that is the necessary prerequisite for any attack via the Internet. The provisions are broad and cover even the early stages of perpetrating (e.g., by means of provisions prohibiting the possession of illegal devices).
- In contrast, the traditional "corporeal damage" or "terrorist-specific" approach (which focuses on the physical or human corporeal damage caused by the attack and – possibly – also on the perpetrator's political intent) found in the EU Council Framework Decision on combating terrorism and in the various UN conventions covers many attacks with traditional corporeal results, even when these attacks are committed by means of information technology.

As a consequence, all serious attacks against computer systems, infrastructures, and other legal interests are covered by the international conventions and instruments discussed above, which require states parties to ensure the existence of criminal law sanctions.

Pros and Cons of an Additional Infrastructure Offence

Thus, the question remains as to whether IT-based terrorist attacks against computer systems and other infrastructures should be addressed by these provisions alone or whether they should also be addressed by a more specific provision that takes into account the fact that destructive attacks are committed against computer systems via the Internet, that destructive attacks are committed with terrorist intent, and/or that destructive attacks against IT-systems, other infrastructures, and other legal interests are potentially extremely dangerous. Technically, such special protection could be achieved by adopting one of the following approaches for the introduction of new criminal offences:

- The first approach would be to require states parties to create an aggravated "IT offence" – perhaps in an additional protocol to the Cybercrime Convention – whose elements would include and combine abuse of the Internet, terrorist intent, and – possibly – serious harm to an IT-system or IT-infrastructure.
- The second approach would be to require states parties to create an aggravated "infrastructure offence" for the protection of IT-infrastructures or – more generally – for the protection of various types of

infrastructures, either as such or in combination with a specific political (terrorist) intent (e.g., following the example of the specific UN resolutions against special acts of terrorism or following the example of the EU Council Framework Decision on combating terrorism of 2002 with its general infrastructure clause).

The practical advantages of such amendments would be relatively small: the new provisions could symbolise the seriousness of attacks on (IT) infrastructures and could provide for more serious sanctions and – possibly – for the exclusion of the political offence exception, a topic discussed in more detail later on in the text. On the other hand, there are substantial arguments against such provisions:

- Illegal destruction and alteration of computer data, without more, are already treated as punishable acts by the provisions of the Cybercrime Convention. Thus, the creation of new criminal offence definitions with additional offence elements is unnecessary, as special intent and special harm can be considered at the sentencing level (where significant differences exist among the various legal systems[176]).

- Terrorist intent, in particular, should not become a general aggravating factor for all types of traditional offences.[177] Defining and proving terrorist intent is difficult. This is particularly true for offences involving the Internet, where the majority of attacks against computer systems are carried out by hackers and malicious crackers and where – due to the difficulties in identifying the origin of the attack – the identity of the perpetrators and the nature of their intent may remain unknown for a long time during investigation. Because of its subjective nature, a terrorist intent-requirement in a criminal provision might afford law enforcement agents more latitude than desirable in the investigation and prosecution of suspects and might prove difficult to control. Thus, it is for good reason that many of the UN conventions discussed above focus on the actus reus elements of an offence (such as "bombing").

- Developing a definition of specifically protected infrastructures for the purpose of a new infrastructure offence would be less problematic. However, it might be difficult to achieve agreement at the international level as to which infrastructures (in addition to the obvious: power, water, and food supply) should be protected and/or to agree on the level of harm required to fulfil the aggravation requirement of a specific offence. In the terrorism context, the complex question of terrorist acts against tangible and intangible property would arise.[178] Establishing the level of harm necessary to satisfy the offence element would be difficult in cases

---

[176] See *U. Sieber*, Punishment of Serious Crimes, Vol. 1, Freiburg 2004, pp. 26 ff.

[177] See also Council of Europe, Parliamentary Assembly, No. 8 of the Recommendation 1644 (2004) on Terrorism: A Threat to Democracies (adopted 29.1.2004).

[178] See *C. Tomuschat*, Council of Europe Committee of Experts on Terrorism (CODEXTER), Strasbourg, On the possible "added value" of a comprehensive Convention on Terrorism, 26 Human Rights Law Journal 2005, pp. 287-306 (292 ff.).

involving attacks against computer systems on the Internet, since these attacks range from "online demonstrations" (flooding a server with queries), to denial-of-service attacks that make a server inaccessible to its users, to the damage (limited or serious) caused by viruses and worms, to the serious destruction of world-wide infrastructures. Thus, there are good reasons for countries to address the gradations of damage caused to tangible and intangible property by means of general sentencing rules or sentencing ranges rather than by creating new offences.

As a consequence, there is no strong justification for requesting new instruments on the international level to address aggravated IT-based attacks on computer systems. It is sufficient for countries to evaluate existing domestic statutes that address data and system interference and make sure that they provide sanctions appropriate for cases involving terrorist attacks against computer and other essential infrastructures and other legal interests. However, such "effective, proportionate and dissuasive sanctions" are already required by Article 13 of the Cybercrime Convention, and it can be left to the national legislatures to achieve this result by means of sentencing rules, aggravated offences involving data interference, or infrastructure offences.[179] Thus, in the view of the author, the lack of an infrastructure offence is not a serious gap requiring amendments to the existing Council of Europe conventions.

Insufficient Signing, Ratification, and Implementation of the Cybercrime Convention

A serious gap is apparent, however, with respect to the signing, ratification, and implementation of the various instruments: the Cybercrime Convention, for example, currently has only 43 signatures and has been ratified by only 19 states; full implementation is even rarer.[180] As a result, the goal of preventing computer crime havens by co-ordinating national rules on substantive, procedural, and co-operation law is still far being achieved. Thus, the signing, ratification, and implementation of the Convention should be a top priority, and care should be taken that additional efforts – both within and beyond the scope of the existing conventions – do not hinder or distract from this important process.

---

[179] See, e.g., the specific sentencing rule of sec. 303b subsection 4 No. 3 of the current German draft combating computer crime ("Entwurf eines Strafrechtsänderungsgesetzes zur Bekämpfung der Computerkriminalität"), BT-Drucksache 16/3656.
[180] See Treaty Office on http://conventions.coe.int/ [last visited: 1 July 2007]; M. Gercke, The Slow Wake of a Global Approach Against Cybercrime, Computer Law Review International 2006, pp. 140-145 (145).

2. Dissemination of Illegal Content

a) Structural Analysis of the Phenomena With Respect to the Legal Framework

As mentioned above, the second major use of the Internet for terrorist purposes consists in the dissemination of illegal content. In order to spread their messages of fear and terror, perpetrators use all types of media, systems, and content. As a result, websites, video-sharing platforms, and other media have become important tools of an "open university for jihad."[181] Thus, the identification of possible gaps in international instruments with respect to illegal content requires the identification of the various acts that correspond to the categories of conduct prohibited by the relevant national and international provisions.

In most national legal systems and in the international instruments under study, the applicability of these legal provisions no longer depends on the type of carrier used to disseminate the illegal content. In other words, the relevant criminal provisions found in international instruments and in most domestic legal orders do not distinguish between data that are distributed by means of traditional carriers (e.g., paper documents for traditional writings), data that are distributed by corporeal electronic data carriers (e.g., CDs), and data that are distributed by incorporeal transmitters such as the Internet, the radio, or television.[182]

Instead, domestic legal orders and international instruments differentiate with respect to the various kinds of illegal content and the types of harm they may cause to different legal interests. An analysis of terrorist communication leads to the identification of the following typologies and kinds of content:
* threatening to commit terrorist offences,
* inciting, advertising, glorifying, and justifying terrorism,
* training for terrorism,
* recruiting for terrorism,
* fundraising for and financing of terrorism,
* disseminating racist and xenophobic material and denying, approving, or justifying genocide.[183]

---

[181] See I.B. supra; *S. Coll/S.B. Glasser,* Terrorists turn to the web as base of operations, The Washington Post, 7 August 2005, Section A01.
[182] See the comparative legal analysis by *U. Sieber,* Jugendschutz und Providerverantwortlichkeit im Internet (ed. by the German Ministry of Justice in the series "recht"), Bonn 1999, p. 27.
[183] For general threats against Germany and Austria by a video message sent to a website called "Global Islamic Mediafront" (GIMF), see I.B.2. supra; *A. Ramelsberger,* Krieger im Internet, Süddeutsche Zeitung, 15 March 2007, p. 5, Online available at http://www.sueddeutsche.de/deutschland/artikel/695/105590/ [last visited: 1 July 2007].
For terrorist webpages, other forms of propaganda, psychological warfare as well as inciting, advertising, glorifying, and justifying terrorism, see I.B.1. and 2. supra;

A legal assessment of most of these phenomena exposes the difficulty in pinpointing the transition between illegality and legality while balancing underlying interests in security and freedom (especially freedom of the press[184]). This can be seen, for example, in the gradual transition between inciting, advertising, glorifying, justifying, explaining, and merely reporting terrorist offences (as illustrated by the publication of assassination videos set to music). The same applies to the publication of information on special weaponry: information that could be useful to terrorists but might also be found in common chemistry or physics textbooks. Similar difficulties also arise with respect to fundraising for charitable organisations that are connected to terrorist groups. Thus, it is obvious that not all of the above mentioned phenomena are or should be fully covered by the substantive criminal law provisions in international conventions.

Due to the difficulty of balancing security and human rights in the context of each of the aforementioned types of content, this analysis cannot judge in detail whether the balancing approach undertaken in international conventions with respect to each of these categories should be approved or reconsidered. Instead, the following sections examine whether the issue was recognised and whether it was taken into account in a reasonable way during the development of the various international instruments. Also with respect to the competent international institutions' possible chances to

---

D. Denning, Activism, Hacktivism, and Cyberterrorism: The Internet as a Tool for Influencing Foreign Policy, http://www.totse.com/en/technology/cyberspace_the_new_frontier/cyberspc.html [last visited: 1 July 2007]; U. Sieber, The Threat of Cybercrime, in: Council of Europe (ed.), Organised crime in Europe, Strasbourg 2005, pp. 81-218 (173-178); T.L. Thomas, Cyberplanning, Al Qaeda and the Internet: the danger of "cyberplanning", Parameters, Spring 2003, pp. 112-123 (117), Online available at http://www.carlisle.army.mil/usawc/Parameters/03spring/thomas.pdf [last visited: 1 July 2007]; U.S. Army Training and Doctrine Command, Cyber Operations and Cyber Terrorism, DCSINT Handbook No. 1.02, http://www.fas.org/irp/threat/terrorism/sup2.pdf [last visited: 1 July 2007], pp. 1-3; G. Weimann, www.terror.net, How Modern Terrorism Uses the Internet, United States Institute of Peace Special Report 116, March 2004, http://www.usip.org/pubs/specialreports/sr116.pdf [last visited: 1 July 2007].
For fundraising by selling books, videos, and CDs in online stores and by giving instructions for on-line donations, see I.B.4. supra; M. Gercke, "Cyberterrorismus" – Aktivitäten terroristischer Organisationen im Internet, Computer & Recht 2006, pp. 62-68 (65); T.L. Thomas, ibid., p. 116; U. Sieber, The Threat of Cybercrime, ibid., p. 178; G. Weimann, ibid., pp. 5-7.
For teaching and training manuals, such as the "Terrorist's Handbook," the "Anarchist Cookbook," the "Mujahadeen Poisons Handbook," the "Encyclopedia of Jihad," the "Sabotage Handbook" and the pamphlet "How to Make Bombs," see I.B.3. supra; S. Coll/S.B. Glasser, ibid; U. Sieber, The Threat of Cybercrime, ibid., 173-178, 179-180; G. Weimann, ibid., p. 9.
For recruiting for terrorism, see I.B.3. supra; U. Sieber, The Threat of Cybercrime, ibid., 178.
[184] See II.B.2.f) supra.

reconsider and change existing conventions , the aim of this analysis is not to judge the approach to the balancing of interests taken in the many specific solutions found in the various instruments but to identify gaps – or deficiencies – in the treatment of serious issues (both with respect to criminalisation and with respect to the protection of human rights).

Based on these considerations, the following analysis will be undertaken with respect to threats to commit terrorist offences; incitement, recruitment, and training for terrorism; fundraising for and financing of terrorism as well as dissemination of racist and xenophobic material. In addition, the relationship between these types of content and the liability of media representatives and Internet providers will be addressed.

b) Threatening to Commit Terrorist Offences

UN Conventions and Protocols Against Specific Acts of Terrorism

Some of the UN conventions against specific terrorist acts described above[185] contain provisions against terrorist threats that are also applicable to terrorist threats disseminated on the Internet: The Convention on the Prevention and Punishment of *Crimes Against Internationally Protected Persons* covers a threat to commit any of the listed acts against senior representatives of a State (Art. 2). The Convention on the Physical Protection of *Nuclear Material* refers to a threat "to use nuclear material to cause death or serious injury to any person or substantial property damage" or "to commit an offence described in sub-paragraph (b) in order to compel a natural or legal person, international organisation or State to do or to refrain from doing any act" (Art. 7). The Convention for the Suppression of Unlawful Acts Against the *Safety of Maritime Navigation* explicitly includes as separate offences certain threats related to the commission of some (but not all) listed offences against the safety of ships (Art. 3). The Protocol for the Suppression of Unlawful Acts Against the Safety of *Fixed Platforms Located on the Continental Shelf* explicitly includes as separate offences certain threats related to the commission of some (but not all) listed offences against the safety of fixed platforms (Art. 2). The International Convention for the Suppression of *Acts of Nuclear Terrorism* (not yet in force) also explicitly includes as an independent offence certain threats related to the commission of some (but not all) of its listed offences (Art. 2).[186]

In contrast, the Convention for the Suppression of *Unlawful Seizure of Aircraft*, the Convention for the Suppression of *Unlawful Acts Against the Safety of Civil Aviation,* the International Convention Against the *Taking of Hostages* and the International Convention for the Suppression of *Terrorist*

---

[185] See II.B.1.b) supra.
[186] See II.B.1.b) supra.

Bombings do not have such threat provisions.[187] Thus, there is no common systematic approach to this issue in the various conventions.

EU Council Framework Decision on Combating Terrorism

In contrast to the UN Conventions, the EU Council Framework Decision on combating terrorism[188] goes further with respect to the criminalisation of terrorist threats. Article 1, a comprehensive general provision dealing with terrorist offences based on objective and subjective criteria, contains a list of acts, such as attacks upon a person's life, attacks upon the physical integrity of a person, kidnapping or hostage taking, causing extensive destruction to certain infrastructures, attacks on aircrafts, ships or other means of public or goods transport, use of weapons, release of dangerous substances, etc. Article 1 requires that these acts be deemed terrorist offences under national law if they seriously damage a country or an international organisation where committed with the aim of:
- seriously intimidating a population, or
- unduly compelling a government or international organisation to perform or abstain from performing any act, or
- seriously destabilising or destroying the fundamental political, constitutional, economic or social structures of a country or an international organisation.

The advantage of this "uniform" approach can be seen with respect to the present question concerning the criminalisation of terrorist threats: Article 1 section 1(i) prohibits in a systematic and transparent way *"threatening to commit any of the acts listed."* Thus, all serious terrorist threats within the scope of Article 1 are covered, irrespective of whether they are directed at individual persons, at institutions, or at the public. It also does not matter whether the threat is communicated via traditional media or on the Internet.

c) Incitement, Recruitment, and Training for Terrorism

CoE Convention on the Prevention of Terrorism

The Council of Europe Convention on the Prevention of Terrorism[189] is the most specific instrument addressing the harmonisation of substantive criminal law in the area of terrorism and with related questions of victims, jurisdiction, international co-operation, etc. According to Article 1, the term "terrorist offence" means any of the offences within the scope of and as defined in one of the treaties listed in the Convention's appendix, which lists the major UN conventions against terrorism. In the field of substantive

---

[187] See II.B.1.b) supra.
[188] EU Council Framework Decision 2002/475/JHA of 13.6.2002 on combating terrorism (OJ L 164/3 of 22.6.2002).
[189] Council of Europe Convention on the Prevention of Terrorism of 16.5.2005 (CETS No. 196).

criminal law, the Convention requires each state party to adopt such measures as may be necessary to establish as criminal offences the following acts when committed unlawfully:

- *Art. 5: Public provocation to commit a terrorist offence*, i.e., "the distribution, or otherwise making available, of a message to the public, with the intent to incite the commission of a terrorist offence, where such conduct, whether or not directly advocating terrorist offences, causes a danger that one or more such offences may be committed."
- *Art. 6: Recruitment for terrorism,* i.e., the solicitation of another person "to commit or participate in the commission of a terrorist offence, or to join an association or group, for the purpose of contributing to the commission of one or more terrorist offences by the association or the group."
- *Art. 7: Training for terrorism,* i.e., the provision of "instruction in the making or use of explosives, firearms or other weapons or noxious or hazardous substances, or in other specific methods or techniques, for the purpose of carrying out or contributing to the commission of a terrorist offence, knowing that the skills provided are intended to be used for this purpose."
- *Art. 9: Ancillary offences,* i.e., the participation in, organising of others to commit, or contribution by a group of persons acting with a common purpose to an offence as set forth in Articles 5 to 7, as well as the attempt to commit an offence as set forth in Articles 6 and 7.

Due to these ancillary offences, the limitation of Article 5 to public provocation does not lead to a serious gap in criminalisation, as the (non-public) provocation of individual persons to commit a terrorist offence can often be covered by the provisions on participation (instigation, in particular). Glorification and justification of terrorism and terrorist acts are at least partly covered by Article 5 by the vague wording "distribution of a message to the public, with the intent to incite the commission of a terrorist offence, where such conduct, whether or not directly advocating terrorist offences, causes a danger that one or more such offences may be committed."[190]

These provisions do not require that the dissemination of the relevant material take place by means of traditional writings or documents (as was the case with some traditional offences against illegal content in national legislation).[191] Thus, they also apply to the incitement of terrorist offences, to the recruitment for terrorism, and to terrorist training on the Internet and in other electronic communication systems.

---

[190] For details, see the evaluation at II.B.2.g) infra.

[191] See the comparative legal analysis by *U. Sieber*, Kinderpornographie, Jugendschutz und Providerverantwortlichkeit im Internet (ed. by the German Ministry of Justice in the series "recht"), Bonn 1999, p. 27.

UN Security Council Resolution 1624

UN Security Council Resolution 1624[192] deals with the prohibition against incitement to terrorism. In number 1(a) of the Resolution, the Security Council "calls upon all States to adopt such measures as may be necessary and appropriate and in accordance with their obligations under international law to ... prohibit by law incitement to commit a terrorist act." This provision covers both traditional and IT-based incitement.

d) Fundraising for and Financing of Terrorism

UN International Convention for the Suppression of the Financing of Terrorism

The UN International Convention for the Suppression of the Financing of Terrorism[193] obligates parties to criminalise the financing of terrorism. According to the Convention, a person commits an offence if that person "unlawfully and wilfully, provides or collects funds with the intention that they should be used" in order to carry out an act that constitutes an offence within the scope of the annexed UN conventions "or any other act intended to cause death or serious bodily injury to a civilian ... when the purpose of such act ... is to intimidate a population, or to compel a government or an international organisation to do or abstain from doing any act."[194] Attempt as well as various forms of participation, contribution and organisation are also dealt with in the Convention.[195]

UN Security Council Resolution 1373

UN Security Council Resolution 1373, which was adopted on 28 September 2001,[196] shortly after the 9/11 attacks, contains a similar obligation. In the area of substantive criminal law, the Security Council decided that "all States shall ... criminalise the wilful provision or collection, by any means, directly or indirectly, of funds by their nationals or in their territories with the intention that the funds should be used, or in the knowledge that they are to be used, in order to carry out terrorist acts." Furthermore, "all States shall ... ensure that any person who participates in the financing, planning, preparation or

---

[192] UN Security Council Resolution 1624 (2005) of 14.9.2005.

[193] The UN International Convention for the Suppression of the Financing of Terrorism, UN Treaty Series Reg. No. 38349, adopted by the General Assembly of the United Nations inResolution 54/109 of 9.12.1999.

[194] Art. 2. For the definition of terrorist acts in this Convention, see S. *Oeter*, Terrorismus und Menschenrechte, 40 Archiv des Völkerrechts 2002, pp. 422-453 (428-432).

[195] With respect to the financing of terrorism, this Convention is more specific and far-reaching than the above-mentioned UN Convention against Transnational Organized Crime. See United Nations Convention against Transnational Organized Crime of 8.1.2001 (A/Res/55/25).

[196] UN Security Council Resolution 1373 (2001) of 28.9.2001.

perpetration of terrorist acts or in supporting terrorist acts is brought to justice and ensure that, in addition to any other measures against them, such terrorist acts are established as serious criminal offences in domestic laws and regulations and that the punishment duly reflects the seriousness of such terrorist acts." In contrast to UN Security Council Resolution 1624, which only "calls upon" States,[197] Resolution 1373 is intended to be binding (States "shall" criminalise). Like the other UN instruments, the resolution is applicable to acts involving terrorist motives committed online.

CoE Convention on Laundering, Search, Seizure and Confiscation of the Proceeds from Crime

The CoE Convention on Laundering, Search, Seizure and Confiscation of the Proceeds from Crime[198] also contains rules pertaining to the adoption of substantive criminal law provisions. The "laundering offences" defined in Article 6 include the various acts of conversion or transfer of property that is the proceeds of crime, the concealment or disguise of such property's true nature, the acquisition of such property, and the participation in such acts. However, in contrast to the above UN instruments, the convention does not cover the financing of crimes with legally obtained funds. For that reason, the substantive criminal law provisions of the convention as well as of other UN and EU money laundering instruments are not dealt with in detail here.

e) Dissemination of Racist and Xenophobic Material

Additional Protocol to CoE Convention on Cybercrime

During the process of drafting the Convention on Cybercrime, it was difficult to reach an agreement on the criminalisation of acts of a racist and xenophobic nature.[199] Thus, these acts were addressed in a separate additional protocol.[200] According to the Protocol, "each Party shall adopt such legislative and other measures as may be necessary to establish as criminal offences under its domestic law, when committed intentionally and without right, the following conduct":

- *Art. 3: Dissemination of racist and xenophobic material through computer systems,* i.e., "distributing, or otherwise making available, racist and xenophobic material to the public through a computer system."

---

[197] UN Security Council Resolution 1624 (2005) of 14.9.2005.

[198] Convention on Laundering, Search, Seizure and Confiscation of the Proceeds from Crime and on the Financing of Terrorism of 16.5.2005 (CETS No. 198).

[199] See *S.D. Murphy*, Contemporary Practice of the United States Relating to International Law, 96 American Journal of International Law 2002, pp. 956-983 (973-975); *M. Gercke*, The Slow Wake of a Global Approach Against Cybercrime, Computer Law Review International 2006, pp. 140-145 (144).

[200] Additional Protocol to the Convention on Cybercrime, concerning the criminalisation of acts of a racist and xenophobic nature committed through computer systems of 28.1.2003 (No. 189).

- *Art. 4: Racist and xenophobic motivated threat,* i.e., "threatening, through a computer system, with the commission of a serious criminal offence, as defined under its domestic law, (i) persons for the reason that they belong to a group distinguished by race, colour, descent or national or ethnic origin, as well as religion, if used as a pretext for any of these factors; or (ii) a group of persons which is distinguished by any of these characteristics."
- *Art. 5: Racist and xenophobic motivated insult,* i.e., "insulting publicly, through a computer system, (i) persons for the reason that they belong to a group distinguished by race, colour, descent or national or ethnic origin, as well as religion, if used as a pretext for any of these factors; or (ii) a group of persons which is distinguished by any of these characteristics."

In addition, Article 6 addresses the denial, gross minimisation, approval, or justification of genocide or crimes against humanity by "distributing or otherwise making available, through a computer system to the public, material which denies, grossly minimises, approves or justifies specific acts constituting genocide or crimes against humanity." According to Article 7, the substantive law provisions must be accompanied by rules concerning aiding and abetting.

With respect to terrorism, the provisions of this Protocol are relevant to threats and insults committed with the intent to incite conflicts and violence between groups distinguished by race, colour, or national or ethnic origin. The provisions are directed at IT-based content and are therefore also applicable to the use of the Internet for terrorist purposes.

European Union Council Framework Decision on combating racism and xenophobia

A similar proposal of the European Union for a Council Framework Decision on combating racism and xenophobia has not yet been enacted.[201]

f) Liability of the Media and of Internet Providers

The Media

As mentioned above, most of the offences that target illegal content have a critical relationship with freedom of expression, which is a basic element of democratic and pluralistic societies. This is especially important in the

---

[201] See COM (2001) 664 final of 28.11.2001, OJ C 75E/269 of 26.3.2002. The European Parliament gave its opinion on the initial draft proposal on 4 July 2002. On 19 April 2007, the Justice and Home Affairs Council reached a general agreement on this Framework Decision. However, the modifications made by the Council could justify a re-consultation of the Parliament. Furthermore, the Framework Decision is subject to parliamentary scrutiny reservations by various countries.

present context since the free and unhindered dissemination of information and ideas is a most effective means of promoting understanding and tolerance, which can, in turn, help prevent terrorism. These aspects are addressed by a multitude of international declarations that address the tension between fighting terrorism and protecting human rights.

The basic instrument of protection for this aim is the European Convention on Human Rights,[202] which guarantees the right to freedom of expression (Art. 10). This guarantee is taken up in the texts of many of the conventions discussed above, and the relevant case law of the European Court of Human Rights is cited in the Explanatory Report to the Council of Europe Convention on the Prevention of Terrorism.[203] Furthermore, there are other instruments besides the European Convention on Human Rights that deal more specifically with the conflict between preventing terrorism and protecting human rights.[204] In addition, there are special instruments that cover the specific aspect of preventing terrorism and protecting the freedom of the press. The CoE Declaration on freedom of expression and information in the media in the context of the fight against terrorism,[205] for example, calls on public authorities in Member States to refrain from adopting measures equating media reporting on terrorism with support for terrorism, but also recommends that the media be aware of their responsibility not to contribute to the aims of terrorists and to adopt self-regulatory measures. Similar recommendations can be found in the Council of Europe Parliamentary Assembly Recommendation 1706 on "Media and Terrorism,"[206] in Recommendation 1687 on "Combating terrorism through culture,"[207] and in many other international declarations.[208] The OSCE Ministerial Council Decision No.3/04 of 2004 on combating the use of the Internet for terrorist purposes also decided that "States will exchange information on the use of

---

[202] Convention for the Protection of Human Rights and Fundamental Freedoms of 4.11.1950 (ETS No. 5), as amended by Protocol No. 14 of 13.5.2004 (CETS No. 194).

[203] See, e.g., Council of Europe Convention on the Prevention of Terrorism of 16.5.2005 (CETS No. 196), Art. 12, and Explanatory Report, Nos. 30, 88-98, 143-152, 143-152.

[204] See, e.g., Council of Europe, Human Rights and the Fight Against Terrorism – The Council of Europe Guidelines, 2005; UN Resolution No. 60/158 of the UN General Assembly and the report of the Secretary-General pursuant to this resolution on "Protecting human rights and fundamental freedoms while countering terrorism" of 11.9.2006 (A/61/353).

[205] CoE Declaration on freedom of expression and information in the media in the context of the fight against terrorism adopted by the CoE Committee of Ministers on 2.3.2005 at the 917th meeting of the Ministers' Deputies.

[206] Council of Europe Parliamentary Assembly, Recommendation 1706 (2005) of 20.6.2005 on "Media and Terrorism."

[207] Council of Europe Parliamentary Assembly, Recommendation 1687 (2004) on "Combating terrorism through culture."

[208] E.g., Council of Europe Parliamentary Assembly, Media and Terrorism, of 20.5.2005, Doc. 10557, and the corresponding reply from the Committee of Ministers of 18.1.2006, Doc. 10791.

the Internet for terrorist purposes and identify possible strategies to combat this threat, while ensuring respect for international human rights obligations and standards, including those concerning the rights to privacy and freedom of opinion and expression."[209]

These declarations, recommendations, and reports show that the complex problem of balancing freedom and security, especially with respect to press publications on terrorism is discussed on the international level. An assessment of the appropriateness of the approaches taken in all these conventions and instruments is, however, beyond the scope of this report.

Internet Providers

Problems similar to those experienced in the traditional press context arise in the Internet context as well. Internet providers who transmit and store the illegal content of perpetrators – along with huge amounts of legal data –, generally do so without knowledge of the data and, in particular, without knowledge of the legality of the data according to the laws of the countries through which the data are being transmitted. Thus, with respect to the dissemination of illegal content fostering terrorism, the question arises as to the conditions under which host service providers on the Internet (storers of third-party content) as well as access and network providers (transmitters of third-party content) can be held responsible for such data. Similar questions regarding criminal responsibility for third-party content arise with respect to search engines and with respect to liability in general for Internet links.[210] Attempts in many countries to address these problems by means of the general criminal law rules of participation have shown that these rules are inadequate and that special legislation is required in order to ensure legal security. The analysis of the Explanatory Report to the Council of Europe Convention on the Prevention of Terrorism indicates that this central problem was not considered in the drafting process of the Convention.[211]

The EC Directive on electronic commerce[212] addresses these problems. It seeks to contribute to the proper functioning of the European internal market by ensuring the free movement of information society services between Member States: "Member States may not, for reasons falling within the co-

---

[209] Organization for Security and Co-operation in Europe (OSCE) Ministerial Council Decision No. 3/04 of 7.12.2004 on combating the use of the Internet for terrorist purposes.
[210] For details, see *U. Sieber*, in: Hoeren/Sieber (eds.), Handbuch des Multimediarechts, München 2007, Part 18.1.
[211] See Council of Europe Convention on the Prevention of Terrorism of 16.5.2005 (CETS No. 196), Explanatory Report, No. 102 mentioning "hyperlinks", and No. 132 mentioning a "service provider" without considering the limiting function of the rules of participation and respective special provisions.
[212] Directive 2000/31/EC of the European Parliament and the Council of 8.6.2000 on certain legal aspects of information services, in particular electronic commerce, in the Internal Market (Directive on electronic commerce), OJ L 178/1 of 17.7.2000.

ordinated field, restrict the freedom to provide information society services from another Member state" (Art. 3 Sec. 2). Only in situations covered by Article 3 Secs. 4 to 6 are Member States entitled to take measures in derogation of Article 3 Sec. 2 (e.g., when the measures are necessary for reasons of public policy, in particular the prevention, investigation, detection, and prosecution of criminal offences). Thus, the Directive aims to harmonise the liability of natural and legal persons who provide information society services: In certain cases involving the "mere conduit" of data, access providers are broadly exempt from civil and criminal liability (Art. 15). In certain cases involving the storing of data, host service providers are only liable if they have actual knowledge of illegal activity or information (Art. 14). Similar regulations exist with respect to caching functions of Internet providers (Art. 13).

This liability regime is important not only for ensuring free exchange of information and legal certainty for Internet providers, it is also important for the prosecution of past crimes and for the prevention of illegal content in the future as well. It provides the basis for "notice and takedown procedures", by which host service providers storing illegal content can be forced to erase or block illegal information after they have been given notice concerning the presence of the illegal content on their servers. The existence of "notice and takedown procedures" enables hotlines (services that collect tips from Internet users concerning illegal information from the public) and the police to force host service providers to take down illegal content so that this content can no longer be accessed by the public.[213] Such "notice and takedown procedures," hotlines, awareness-raising, industry self-regulation, and codes of conduct are the most important tools for the prevention of illegal content on the Internet.

g) Summary, Evaluation, and Consequences of Legal Policy

General Evaluation

The analysis undertaken here shows that the dissemination of the various types of illegal terrorist content is addressed by international instruments in an extensive and differentiated manner:

- *Threatening to commit a terrorist act* is covered by a number of UN conventions with respect to specific acts of terrorism and is addressed in a more comprehensive way by the EU Council Framework Decision on combating terrorism. However, with the exception of the efforts taken at the EU level, there is no systematic or general approach to the coverage of threats to commit terrorist acts.

---

[213] See Commission of the European Communities, Communication from the Commission to the Council, Final evaluation of the implementation of the multiannual community action plan on promoting safer use of the Internet by combating illegal and harmful content on global networks, Brussels 6.11.2006, COM (2006) 663 final.

- *Inciting, advertising, and glorifying terrorism* is dealt with by the CoE Convention on the Prevention of Terrorism. While the central aim of Article 5 of the Convention is to criminalise specific cases of distribution of a message to the public with the intent to incite the commission of a terrorist offence, this Article also covers some cases of advertising, glorifying, and justifying terrorism.[214]
- *Training for terrorism* is tackled by Article 7 of the CoE Convention on the Prevention of Terrorism.
- *Recruiting potential terrorists* by soliciting "another person" to commit a terrorist offence is central to Article 6 of the CoE Convention on the Prevention of Terrorism.
- *Fundraising for and financing of terrorism* is covered extensively in particular by the UN International Convention for the Suppression of the Financing of Terrorism of 1999 and UN Security Council Resolution 1373.
- *Dissemination of racist and xenophobic material* is dealt with by the CoE Additional Protocol to the Convention on Cybercrime.
- The international instruments also cover general aspects of these contents, especially with respect to the difficult balancing of freedom and security:
- *Freedom of the press with respect to terrorist content* is addressed in various instruments of the Council of Europe and the OSCE.
- *Responsibility of Internet providers* is (only) regulated in the EC Directive on Electronic Commerce of 2000.

In all areas covered by these conventions, one might argue either for more far-reaching or for more restrained solutions. However, this is a common situation for an area in which both a difficult balancing of interests and broad international agreement are required. Slightly different policy evaluations alone do not justify a possible revision of the substantive criminal law provisions of international conventions covering illegal content on the Internet. This can be illustrated with respect to glorifying and justifying terrorism and terrorist acts. These acts are only partly covered in Article 5 of the Convention on the Prevention of Terrorism by the vague wording "the distribution of a message to the public, with the intent to incite the commission of a terrorist offence, where such conduct, whether or not directly advocating terrorist offences, causes a danger that one or more such offences may be committed." However, a more extensive or a more precise wording with respect to glorifying and justifying terrorist acts might conflict with such rights as freedom of expression and freedom of the press.[215] Thus, in the context of this general overview of possible problems, the current regulation on glorifying and justifying terrorism cannot be considered a clear gap, neither with respect to criminalisation nor with respect to civil liberties. In addition, on the political level, reopening these issues for discussion only

---

[214] For more details, see below.

[215] See also Council of Europe Convention on the Prevention of Terrorism of 16.5.2005 (CETS No. 196), Explanatory Report, Nos. 30, 88-98.

two years after the adoption of the Convention is not a real option as such a discussion would hamper the process of signing and ratifying the Convention.

Gaps With Respect to Threatening to Commit Terrorist Offences

The situation of illegal content, however, is different as far as the special problems associated with threatening to commit terrorist offences are concerned. In some of the UN conventions dealing with specific terrorist offences, threatening to commit the described acts is not criminalised. The EU Council Framework Decision of 2002 goes further than the UN conventions in that it covers "threatening to commit any of the acts listed" in its broad catalogue of terrorist offences (including attacks on infrastructures): however, as the threat must be related to one of the specified acts, the Framework Decision does not cover general unspecified threats. The Council of Europe Convention on the Prevention of Terrorism does not contain a general threat provision with respect to terrorist offences, either. The Explanatory Report to the Convention and the underlying expert report do not address the issue of threats to commit terrorist acts.[216] This gap should be a topic for future reform discussions at the CoE or UN level. On the Council of Europe level, a general provision could be included in an additional protocol to the Convention on the Prevention of Terrorism. Another – more systematic – solution would be to create a comprehensive CoE Convention on Terrorism in which the various terrorist offences (including ancillary offences and general rules) would be systematised and consolidated.[217] The problem could also be dealt with on the UN level by systematically analysing the need to amend the specific terrorism conventions that currently do not cover the threat to commit the relevant offence. However, such an offence-specific approach could cause problems in the context of unspecified general threats that do not refer to an act enumerated in one of the UN conventions. In any event, the question of the form and content of threats to be covered would have to be carefully considered and limited, with a focus on destructive attacks and *not* on the "supporting offences" of glorifying terrorism, training for terrorism, recruiting for terrorism, and fundraising.

---

[216] See Council of Europe Convention on the Prevention of Terrorism of 16.5.2005 (CETS No. 196), Explanatory Report, Nos. 17, 26 in connection with No. 49; Council of Europe (ed.), "Apologie du terrorisme" and "incitement to terrorism," Strasbourg 2004, pp. 11 ff.

[217] For this proposal, see C. *Tomuschat*, Council of Europe Committee of Experts on Terrorism (CODEXTER), Strasbourg, On the possible "added value" of a comprehensive Convention on Terrorism, 26 Human Rights Law Journal 2005, pp. 287-306 (299 ff.); Council of Europe Convention on the Prevention of Terrorism of 16.5.2005 (CETS No. 196), Explanatory Report, Nos. 5-23.

Lack of Specific Regulations Regarding Responsibility of Internet Providers

An additional problem arising in this context is due to the fact that the Council of Europe and the UN conventions provide for liability as direct perpetrators and as aiders and abettors. Application of such general rules with respect to the liability of providers does not lead to clear results and legal certainty. In contrast, the EC Directive requires Member States to create provisions that specifically regulate the liability of various types of Internet providers. This is advantageous with respect to legal certainty. In addition, increased specificity and a broader harmonisation of rules establishing the responsibility of Internet providers could serve as the basis – at least for the aforementioned harmonised areas of illegal terrorist content – for specific "notice and takedown procedures"[218] on an international level. Such rules could then be the basis for improved practical co-operation and for international public-private partnerships (e.g., hotlines, codes of conducts for providers, joint international efforts to erase, to block, and/or to monitor illegal content).[219]

Given the amount of terrorist propaganda on the Internet, this issue is an important one. Open societies should not needlessly leave the Internet and other electronic communication systems vulnerable to abuse at the hands of their adversaries. On the other hand, they should also abstain from ineffective control methods of a purely symbolic nature, especially if these methods infringe information rights, contribute to the development of uncontrollable surveillance systems, and create high costs for the Internet industry. Thus, it is essential to investigate the possibilities, the dangers, and the limits of international efforts to prevent illegal content on the Internet and in other electronic information systems. The Council of Europe, with its long tradition in the development of criminal law and in the protection of civil liberties, would be the ideal institution to co-ordinate such efforts.

Furthermore, such rules and procedures are important not only in the context of the dissemination of illegal terrorist content but also with regard to the dissemination of other illegal content, such as child pornography. Thus, it would make sense to develop rules and procedures that would apply both to illegal terrorist content as well as to the many other types of illegal material for which an international consensus can be found.

---

[218] "Notice and takedown procedures" are based on liability rules establishing responsibility only if the provider has actual knowledge of illegal content. Thus, by giving notice to the provider he or she is forced to take down the illegal content in order to avoid responsibility.

[219] See *U. Sieber*, Responsibility of Internet Providers: Comparative Analysis of a Basic Question of Information Law, in: E. Lederman/R. Shapira (eds.), Law, Information and Information Technology, The Hague 2001, pp. 231-292; *U. Sieber* Legal Regulation, Law Enforcement and Self-Regulation – A New Alliance for Preventing Illegal Contents on the Internet, in: J. Waltermann/M. Machill (eds.), Protecting Our Children on the Internet, Gütersloh 2000, pp. 319-400, as well as the other contributions in this volume.

Insufficient Signing, Ratification, and Implementation of the Convention on the Prevention of Terrorism

Finally, a serious gap can again be identified with respect to the signing, ratification, and implementation of the various instruments: The most important international instrument against the illegal dissemination of illegal terrorist content, the Convention on the Prevention of Terrorism, has 39 signatures and six ratifications.[220] Thus, the goal of preventing safe terrorist harbours by co-ordinating national rules on substantive criminal law has not yet been achieved. As a consequence, future efforts should concentrate on the signing, ratification, and implementation of the Convention.

3. Use of the Internet for Other Purposes

a) Relevant Phenomena

Computer systems and the Internet are also used to support communication relating to planning of terrorist activities as well as to facilitate other preparatory acts for all types of terrorist cases. The perpetrators may send encrypted email or email containing hidden messages; they may acquire information online (e.g., tips on constructing bombs, on hostage-taking, or on hijacking). They may use the Internet to analyse targets by satellite maps available on the Internet, to gather other types of information such as reports of security weaknesses in airports, to pursue logistical planning, to engage in money laundering (e.g., by means of Internet banking), or to make money by selling pirated software and by other crimes using the Internet. The analysis of seized computer systems has confirmed that such acts already play a considerable role in practice.[221]

---

[220] See Treaty Office on http://conventions.coe.int/ [last visited: 1 July 2007]; *M. Gercke*, The Slow Wake of a Global Approach Against Cybercrime, Computer Law Review International 2006, pp. 140-145 (145).
[221] For the communication of terrorists on the Internet, see I.C. supra; *U. Sieber*, The Threat of Cybercrime, in: Council of Europe (ed.), Organised Crime in Europe, Strasbourg 2005, pp. 81-218 (179); *G. Weimann*, www.terror.net, How Modern Terrorism Uses the Internet. United States Institute of Peace Special Report 116, March 2004, http://www.usip.org/ pubs/specialreports/sr116.pdf [last visited: 1 July 2007], pp. 9 f.; *G. Weimann*, Terrorists and Their Tools – Part II. Using the Internet to recruit, raise funds, and plan attacks, YaleGlobal, 26.4.2004, http://yaleglobal.yale.edu/article.print?id=3768 [last visited: 1 July 2007]; *M. Whine*, Cyberspace – A New Medium for Communication, Command, and Control by Extremists, Studies in Conflict & Terrorism 1999 (22), pp. 231-245 (233 ff.); *C. Wilson*, Computer Attack and Cyberterrorism: Vulnerabilities and Policy Issues for Congress, Congressional Research Service Report for Congress (RL32114), updated 1 April 2005, p. 18.
For the use of the Internet by terrorists for logistical planninig see I.C. supra; *U. Sieber*, ibid., p. 180; *U.S. Army Training and Doctrine Command*, Cyber Operations and Cyber Terrorism, DCSINT Handbook No. 1.02, http://www.fas.org/irp/threat/terrorism/sup2.pdf [last visited: 1 July 2007], pp. 1-2;

b) Analysis of Relevant Conventions

The above-mentioned activities are addressed to a certain degree by the aforementioned conventions. As described, the criminal acts dealt with in these conventions are broadly defined and the definitions do not specifically address the question of (traditional or computer-based) means of commission. Most of the provisions in these conventions include adequate rules on participation as well as rules covering preparatory acts and attempt. Besides these rules of the general part of criminal law, there are additional statutes in the specific part of criminal law which already cover preparatory acts at an earlier stage and also extend the attribution of these acts to accessories. On the international level such respective rules on "conspiracy" and "participation in criminal organisations" are addressed in the following additional instruments.

UN Convention Against Transnational Organized Crime

The UN Convention Against Transnational Organized Crime[222] aims to criminalise participation in an *organised criminal group* (Art. 5), laundering of proceeds of crime (Art. 6), corruption (Art. 8) and obstruction of justice (Art. 23). Article 5.1.(a) reads as follows:

Art. 5: Criminalisation of participation in an organised criminal group

1.   Each State Party shall adopt such legislative and other measures as may be necessary to establish as criminal offences, when committed intentionally:
  (a) Either or both of the following as criminal offences distinct from those involving the attempt or completion of the criminal activity:
    (i) Agreeing with one or more other persons to commit a serious crime for a purpose relating directly or indirectly to the obtaining of a financial or other material benefit and, where required by domestic law, involving an act undertaken

---

G. *Weimann,* www.terror.net. How Modern Terrorism Uses the Internet. United States Institute of Peace Special Report 116, March 2004, http://www.usip.org/pubs/specialreports/sr116.pdf [last visited: 1 July 2007], p. 2.
For other patterns of terrorists seeking financial gains, see *U. Sieber,* The Threat of Cybercrime, ibid., pp. 180 f.
[222] United Nations Convention Against Transnational Organized Crime of 8.1.2001 (A/Res/55/25). See also the specific Protocols supplementing the United Nations Convention against Transnational Organized Crime, e.g., the Protocol to Prevent, Suppress and Punish Trafficking in Persons, Especially Women and Children (A/Res/55/25 of 8.1.2001, Annex II); the Protocol Against the Smuggling of Migrants by Land, Sea and Air (A/Res/55/25 of 8.1.2001, Annex III); and the Protocol Against the Illicit Manufacturing of and Trafficking in Firearms, Their Parts and Components and Ammunition (A/RES/55/255 of 8.6.2001).

by one of the participants in furtherance of the agreement or involving an organised criminal group;

(ii) Conduct by a person who, with knowledge of either the aim and general criminal activity of an organised criminal group or its intention to commit the crimes in question, takes an active part in:

    a. Criminal activities of the organised criminal group;

    b. Other activities of the organised criminal group in the knowledge that his or her participation will contribute to the achievement of the above-described criminal aim.

Article 2a defines an organised criminal group as "a structured group of three or more persons, existing for a period of time and acting in concert with the aim of committing one or more serious crimes or offences established in accordance with this Convention, in order to obtain, directly or indirectly, a financial or other material benefit." Thus, Article 5.1 (a) (ii) can be relevant, if terrorist groups, in addition to their destructive activities, commit crimes with a financial or other material benefit in order to finance the costs of their political crimes. However, the requirement of obtaining "a financial or other material benefit" (which is also contained in Article 5.1. (a) (i) offering an alternative "conspiracy approach") limits the application of the Convention in many cases of terrorism.[223]

EU Council Framework Decision on Combating Terrorism

Unlike Article 5.1 (a) of the EU Convention Against Transnational Organized Crime, Article 2 of the EU Council Framework Decision on combating terrorism[224] contains a more specific "offence relating to a terrorist group." It includes "participating in the activities of a *terrorist group*, including by supplying information or material resources, or by funding its activities in any way, with knowledge of the fact that such participation will contribute to the criminal activities of the terrorist group." This wording is not limited to recruiting and training for terrorism but covers broadly all types of IT-based support given to a terrorist group irrespective of its – political or financial – goals.[225]

c) Summary and Evaluation

The analysis shows that no computer-specific problems arise when treating communication activities as participation or when treating advanced planning

---

[223] For this reason, the Convention's provisions on procedural law and on law of international co-operation are not dealt with in the following chapters.

[224] EU Council Framework Decision 2002/475/JHA of 13.6.2002 on combating terrorism (OJ L 164/3 of 22.6.2002).

[225] For the activities of the EU, see also the Communication from the Commission to the European Parliament and the Council concerning terrorist recruitment: addressing the factors contributing to violent radicalisation, 21.9.2005, COM (2005) 313 final.

activities as attempt. Thus, just as *the general rules on attempt and participation* can be applied to traditional acts outside the IT-area, they can be used when terrorists communicate with each other online or prepare their attacks with the help of computer systems. As a consequence, there is no computer-specific gap with respect to terrorist use of the Internet.[226]

For that reason, one might only raise the question of whether the criminalisation of preparatory acts in support of *terrorist organisations* should be extended. As shown above,[227] Article 2 of the EU Council Framework Decision on combating terrorism[228] covers all acts of "participating in the activities of a *terrorist* group. In contrast, Article 5.1 (a) of the UN Convention Against Transnational Organized Crime[229] prohibits taking an active part in the criminal activities of an *organised criminal group* that – according to Article 2a – must have the aim of committing serious crimes "in order to obtain ... a financial or other material benefit." This difference between the "terrorist specific approach" of the EU (specifically directed at politically motivated terrorist groups) and the "organised crime approach" of the UN (limited to organised groups with serious financial benefit crimes) illustrates the question of whether the broader EU approach of criminalising support for a terrorist organisation should also be implemented on a more global level in a Convention of the Council of Europe or the UN.

However, this general question goes beyond the scope of the present analysis, with its focus on cyberterrorism and other terrorist use of the Internet. Dealing with the question of a terrorist specific group offence would cause difficulties relating to defining the respective terrorist act (e.g., by referring to the special UN conventions or by creating a general definition of terrorism) and would have to deal with the question on how legal uncertainty, over-criminalisation, and abuse of such a broad "material support provision" could be prevented. In addition, one would have to consider that many preparatory acts (such as public provocation of terrorism, recruitment, training, and financing) are already covered by the above-mentioned specific rules in the CoE Prevention of Terrorism Convention. Similar questions would arise with a possible extension of the "conspiracy approach" of Article 5.1 (a) (i) of the EU Council Framework Decision to the CoE- or UN-level. Thus, these questions should be analysed in a separate study.

---

[226] For an analysis of the various legislative techniques employed to provide for the early onset of criminal liability, see *U. Sieber*, Grenzen des Strafrechts, Zeitschrift für die gesamte Strafrechtswissenschaft (ZStW) 119 (2006), pp. 1-68 (27-40).

[227] II.B.1.b) supra.

[228] EU Council Framework Decision 2002/475/JHA of 13.6.2002 on combating terrorism (OJ L 164/3 of 22.6.2002).

[229] With respect to the financing of terrorism, this Convention is more specific and far-reaching than the aforementioned UN Convention against Transnational Organized Crime. See United Nations Convention against Transnational Organized Crime of 8.1.2001 (A/Res/55/25).

C. Developing and Harmonising National Criminal Procedure and Preventive Measures

New forms of cybercrime as well as the commission of traditional crimes in computer networks pose new, computer-specific problems not only with respect to substantive criminal law but also for the investigation, prosecution, and prevention of crime. These problems stem from a variety of sources: the complex technical environment of computer systems; the multitude and invisibility of computer data; the techniques of encryption and steganography; the difficulty of identifying perpetrators on the Internet; the fact that computer systems can be attacked from a distance; and the global nature of the Internet, which cannot be controlled by purely national measures. Thus, special procedures are essential for investigations of criminal activity on the Internet and in other IT environments.

Legal rules for these computer-specific investigations can be found on the international level in the CoE Cybercrime Convention. In addition, there are other instruments with special procedural rules addressing problems of international co-operation. In order to systemise the existing international standards, this chapter will analyse the international conventions for (1) computer-specific investigations, (2) financial investigations, and (3) investigations in terrorist and other cases.

1. Computer-Specific Investigations

CoE Convention on Cybercrime

The development of the CoE Convention on Cybercrime[230] was not only a success with respect to substantive criminal law but also a breakthrough in the international development of computer-specific investigations in computerised environments. Besides dealing with substantive criminal law, the Cybercrime Convention obliges parties to adopt a variety of legislative measures for computer-specific investigations. These measures are laid down in Articles 14 through 22 of the Convention. They cover, among other things, the expedited preservation of stored computer data, the expedited preservation and partial disclosure of traffic data (necessary for tracing attacks back to their origin), production orders to submit specified computer data, search and seizure of stored computer data, real-time collection of traffic data, interception of content data, conditions and safeguards for these measures, as well as jurisdictional rules.[231]

These specific investigation methods are keys for successful Internet investigations, both in general and specifically in terrorist cases. This is

---

[230] Convention on Cybercrime of the Council of Europe of 23.11.2001 (ETS No. 185).
[231] For details, see Convention on Cybercrime of the Council of Europe of 23.11.2001 (ETS No. 185), Explanatory Report, Nos. 131-239.

obvious, for example, if the perpetrators do not attack other computers directly but "jump" via a number of third-party computer systems that they hijack, control, and abuse as intermediaries in order to shield the identity of their own system. Using this technique, an attack from country A on country B can proceed via numerous computer systems in many jurisdictions. Since the victim can – at best – identify only the "direct" (ultimate) attacker, the process of tracing and identifying the perpetrator often depends on the analysis of the traffic data of many computer systems in numerous countries. Since these traffic data are often not stored by Internet providers – or not stored for a long period of time – the implementation of common traceback procedures requires rules for "quick freeze procedures" of data that would otherwise be erased and/or obligations on providers to retain traffic data for a certain period of time. The Council of Europe's Cybercrime Convention concentrates on such specific "quick freeze" provisions (differentiating between a fast "quick freeze" and the later transfer procedure). The corresponding procedure of expedited preservation of data is a completely new measure of criminal law.

Additional specific rules concern other specialised instruments, for example, with respect to search and seizure in connected computer systems (which might be located in different countries), or production orders to submit specified computer data (which are often difficult for the prosecution to access either due to the encryption of data or due to the technical problems of dealing with IT applications unfamiliar to the investigators). These examples show that the Cybercrime Convention is designed to address the special problems of investigations in the IT-environment and is the central instrument for procedural measures and for international co-operation in the area of cybercrime.

Consequently, it is necessary to ensure that the specialised procedural provisions of the Cybercrime Convention are applicable in cases involving the use of the Internet for terrorist purposes. The relevant scope of the procedural provisions of the Cybercrime Convention is regulated in Article 14: "Each Party shall apply the powers and procedures" of section 2 of the Convention (Arts. 14 through 21) to "(a) the criminal offences established in accordance with Articles 2 through 11 of this Convention; (b) other criminal offences committed by means of a computer system; and (c) the collection of evidence in electronic form of a criminal offence."

This leads to a clear result: Subsections (b) and (c) guarantee that – subject to two exceptions – the special investigation methods of the Cybercrime Convention can be applied to all kinds of criminal activities on the Internet.[232]

---

[232] For details, see Convention on Cybercrime of the Council of Europe of 23.11.2001 (ETS No. 185), Explanatory Report, Nos. 140-148. See also Art. 8 of the "Additional Protocol to the Convention on Cybercrime, concerning the criminalisation of acts of a racist and xenophobic nature committed through computer systems" of

As a consequence, it is safe to say that there are no gaps of coverage regarding the use of existing computer-specific procedural provisions of the Cybercrime Convention to investigate cyberterrorism and other forms of terrorist use of the Internet. Thus, the only question that arises is whether the instruments of the Convention are adequate and up-to-date (see infra C.4.).

EC Directive on Data Retention

Whereas the goal of the Cybercrime Convention is to address all procedural problems in a computerised environment, the EC Directive on the retention of data of publicly available electronic communication services[233] only deals with a specific issue that could not be agreed upon during the drafting of the Cybercrime Convention: as explained above, successful investigation on the Internet and in other electronic networks depends to a large degree on the ability to trace back perpetrators to their original computer system. Ordinary traceback procedures require that certain traffic data be stored so that they can be used in an investigation that in many cases may not take place until some time after the crime occurs. Thus, the EC Directive on the retention of data of publicly available electronic communication services obligates Member States to adopt measures providing that certain traffic data and location communication services be retained for periods of not less than six months and not more than two years from the date of the communication (with exceptions in Art. 12 of the Directive).

Such retention of data could be especially useful for the investigation of terrorist activity. It cannot fully be replaced by the "quick freezing" of traffic data provided for by the Cybercrime Convention, since quick freezing of traffic data cannot take place if the data are not stored. However it could allow for a shortening of the retention period, thus reducing the impact on the data protection interests of Internet users.

2. Financial Investigations

Specific investigative mechanisms and other measures beyond those contained in the Cybercrime Convention can be found in the context of special financial investigations with respect to money laundering and the financing of terrorism. Such measures are regulated in the instruments against the laundering of the proceeds from crime and against the financing of terrorism.

28.1.2003 (ETS No. 189) confirming that the relevant articles of the Cybercrime Convention are applied to the crimes defined in the Additional Protocol.
[233] Directive 2006/24/EC of the European Parliament and the Council of 15.3.2006 on the retention of data generated or processed in connection with the provision of publicly available electronic communication services of public communication networks and amending Directive 2002/58/EC, OJ L 105, 13.4.2006, pp. 54-63.

The CoE Convention on Laundering, Search, Seizure and Confiscation of the Proceeds from Crime[234] contains specific measures on confiscation, investigation, freezing, seizure and confiscation, preventive measures, as well as provisions establishing financial intelligence units (FIUs). According to Article 2 of the Convention, parties must ensure that the provisions are applicable to search, trace, identify, freeze, seize, and confiscate property used for the financing of terrorism or the proceeds of this offence.[235]

Similar measures are found in the UN International Convention for the Suppression of the Financing of Terrorism[236] or – with respect to organised crime – in the UN Convention against Transnational Organized Crime.[237] The same is true of UN Security Council Resolution 1373,[238] according to which all States must implement a variety of measures against terrorism, such as preventing and suppressing the financing of terrorist acts, freezing financial assets of terrorists, preventing acts of terrorism, affording measures of assistance, providing effective border controls, creating provisions of early warning, exchanging information, identifying the whereabouts and activities of persons, and conducting inquiries with respect to the movements of funds relating to the commission of such offences.

None of these instruments depends on whether the offences are committed with the assistance of IT-systems. Thus, there are no gaps in these instruments with respect to their applicability in an IT environment.

3. Terrorist-Specific Investigations

Other conventions on terrorism include either specific or general rules on investigation. For example, the Council of Europe Convention on the Prevention of Terrorism[239] not only creates obligations to criminalise illegal content but also contains general procedural provisions with respect to these offences. The same is true for the UN Convention against Transnational Organized Crime.[240] As far as national procedural law is concerned, these

---

[234] Convention on Laundering, Search, Seizure and Confiscation of the Proceeds from Crime and on the Financing of Terrorism of 16.5.2005 (CETS No. 198).

[235] "Financing of terrorism" means the acts set out in Article 2 of the UN International Convention for the Suppression of the Financing of Terrorism of 1999, UN Treaty Series Reg. No. 38349, adopted by the General Assembly of the United Nations in Resolution 54/109 on 9.12.1999.

[236] UN International Convention for the Suppression of the Financing of Terrorism of 1999, UN Treaty Series Reg. No. 38349, adopted by the General Assembly of the United Nations in resolution 54/109 on 9.12.1999.

[237] United Nations Convention against Transnational Organized Crime of 8.1.2001 (A/Res/55/25).

[238] UN Security Council Resolution 1373 (2001) of 28.9.2001.

[239] Council of Europe Convention on the Prevention of Terrorism of 16.5.2005 (CETS No. 196).

[240] United Nations Convention against Transnational Organized Crime of 8.1.2001 (A/Res/55/25).

obligations include the establishment of certain conditions and safeguards, the protection of victims of terrorism, the establishment of jurisdiction, and the duty to investigate. Additional regulations are contained in general instruments on mutual assistance and extradition, such as the European Convention on Mutual Assistance in Criminal Matters and its two additional protocols[241] as well as in the European Convention on Extradition and its two additional protocols.[242] Since these general rules on investigation are drafted broadly, it is not a problem to apply the provisions to cyberterrorism and to other use of the Internet for terrorist purposes.

4. Evaluation and Consequences for Legal Policy

a) General Evaluation

The analysis shows that – like the *rules of substantive criminal law* – the procedural rules of the Cybercrime Convention are also applicable with respect to all use of the Internet for terrorist purposes and that the main problems of national procedural law with respect to the terrorist use of the Internet are addressed by the Cybercrime Convention. This is primarily due to the fact that the computer-specific investigation measures contained in Article 14 of the Cybercrime Convention apply not only to computer-specific offences defined in the Convention but to all "other criminal offences committed by means of a computer system" and to the "collection of evidence in electronic form of a criminal offence" as well. This includes all types of terrorist use of the Internet and other computer systems. Furthermore, it is not a problem to apply the special investigation methods of the international instruments for financial and terrorist cases to the IT-environment. As a consequence, there are no gaps in the application of the existing international rules on national criminal procedure to cyberterrorism or to other terrorist use of the Internet.

b) Checking the Contemporariness of the Cybercrime Convention

The only questions that remain open are whether the procedural instruments of the Cybercrime Convention are adequate for the investigation of cases of suspected terrorism and whether they are up-to-date. Despite some criticism concerning the lack of transparency in the historical development of its provisions and a resulting lack of concrete safeguards for the protection of civil liberties,[243] it is widely acknowledged that the investigation methods

---

[241] European Convention on Mutual Assistance in Criminal Matters of 20.4.1959 (ETS No. 30); Additional Protocol on the European Convention on Mutual Assistance in Criminal Matters of 17.3.1978 (ETS No. 99); Second Additional Protocol to the European Convention on Mutual Assistance in Criminal Matters of 8.11.2001 (ETS No. 182).

[242] European Convention on Extradition of 13.12.1957 (ETS No. 24) and its additional protocols of 15.10.1975 (ETS No. 86) and of 17.3.1978 (ETS No. 98).

[243] See Art. 15 of the Convention and *P. Breyer,* Cyber-Crime-Konvention des Europarats, DuD 2001, pp. 592-600 (594); *A. Dix,* Regelungsdefizite der Cyber-

described in the Cybercrime Convention are well-designed and essential for the efficient investigation of computer systems. In addition, special procedural conditions and safeguards are taken into account by Article 15, which refers to the Council of Europe Convention for the Protection of Human Rights and Fundamental Freedoms.[244] As a consequence, and especially with a view to the difficult process of drafting international conventions, there are no grounds for jeopardising the signing and ratification of the Convention by reconsidering the regulated issues. Thus, in order to avoid safe havens for cybercriminals and terrorists, there should be a clear message to sign and ratify the *Cybercrime Convention*.

However, as the Cybercrime Convention was drafted between 1997 and 2000, as the technical environment and the available forensic investigation tools change rapidly, and as terrorism creates special risks, the necessity and possibility of updating the procedural tools in an *additional protocol* to the Cybercrime Convention should be explored. Such a protocol might address, for example, the clandestine use of hacking techniques employed by the police when searching computer systems online (so-called "clandestine online searches"): An effective international co-operation under traditional mutual assistance rules requires that *all* parties have similar provisions in these areas and that these measures also be taken up in the rules on international co-operation. If, for example, state A requests another state to conduct online searches, such measures must be possible in both state A and in the requested state. Similar problems arise with other types of forensic software, for example, the clandestine installation of a key logger program on the computer system of a suspect in order to circumvent his or her encryption (which should be discussed as an alternative to highly problematic solutions such as limitations on encryption or encryption key escrow procedures). Another controversial issue has to do with the period of time for which traffic data should be stored.[245] Even if these questions were discussed by the drafters of the Cybercrime Convention, they should be reconsidered in light of the new criminological, technical, and forensic developments and of the new risks posed by terrorism. Also, if specific solutions are rejected, this should be communicated to Member States so that they can avoid adopting the rejected approaches.

Crime-Konvention und der E-TKÜV, DuD 2001, pp. 588-591 (588 f.); *M. Gercke,* Cybercrime Konvention des Europarates, CR 2004, pp. 782-791 (783); *G. Taylor,* The Council of Europe Cybercrime Convention – A civil liberties perspective, http://www.crime-research.org/library/CoE_Cybercrime.html [last visited: 1 July 2007]. See also the comments of the American Civil Liberties Union, the Electronic Privacy Information Center and Privacy International on Draft 27 of the CoE Convention on Cybercrime at
http://www.privacyinternational.org/issues/cybercrime/coe/ngo_letter_601.htm [last visited: 1 July 2007].
[244] For details, see Convention on Cybercrime of the Council of Europe of 23.11.2001 (ETS No. 185), Explanatory Report, Nos. 145-148.
[245] Abuses of third-party computers for attacks involving mass queries raise the additional question of the necessity of creating obligatory security measures.

c) Preventive Procedures with respect to Illegal Content

An additional protocol to the Cybercrime Convention would also be a possibility with respect to preventive measures dealing with the blocking of illegal content. In the context of search and seizure, Article 19 of the Cybercrime Convention not only empowers competent authorities to seize or similarly secure a computer system but also permits the authorities to "render inaccessible or remove those computer data in the accessed computer system." However, the Convention does not say how this should be done with respect, for example, to data on the Internet, and the search and seizure provision of Article 19 cannot replace a general regulation for blocking Internet data.[246] Moreover, the legal, procedural, and technical questions of blocking illegal content on the Internet are highly complex and controversially discussed all over the world. Solution of these questions would require not only the participation of lawyers but also that of specialists in the field of computer systems and networks. Furthermore, the technical problems in this area are exacerbated since a possible control of illegal content cannot be limited to illegal websites on the Internet but should also be extended to content disseminated by other Internet services (such as Internet relay chat) or to media disseminated via mobile phones (such as video uploading). Any approach dealing with illegal content on the Internet will also require a difficult balancing of security interests and human rights, a task for which the Council of Europe, as an international institution, would be ideally suited.

As far as practical results are concerned, there is the risk that no perfect or even adequate solution can be found for blocking access to illegal content on the Internet in the future because of the extreme difficulty of controlling the Internet and the global cyberspace. However, in this case, even a rejection of possible solutions would be extremely helpful for reasons of legal certainty.[247] Rejection could also help prevent a situation in which states enact control mechanisms that are ineffective and doomed to failure and that create risks for the free flow of information and privacy rights. Thus, working on global solutions for the prevention of illegal content on the Internet could be a promising task for the Council of Europe, an institution dedicated both to the prevention of crime and to the protection of freedom.

However, an evaluation of the up-to-dateness of the procedural measures of the Cybercrime Convention as well as the development of preventive measures for illegal content is not a problem specific to cyberterrorism and

---

[246] For the interpretation of this clause, see Council of Europe, Convention on Cybercrime, Explanatory Report (ETS No. 185), Nos. 196-199 (especially the hint in No. 199: "seize or similarly secure data has two functions").

[247] See U. Sieber, Legal Regulation, Law Enforcement and Self-Regulation – A New Alliance for Preventing Illegal Contents on the Internet, in: J. Waltermann /M. Machill (eds.), Protecting Our Children on the Internet, Gütersloh 2000, pp. 319-400 (319 ff.).

other uses of the Internet by terrorists but rather is an issue that arises in the context of organised crime, economic crime, and all other forms of crime as well. Thus, as indicated above, a broader approach that would go beyond the scope of cyberterrorism and the use of the Internet for terrorist purposes should be considered.

D. Improving International Co-operation

1. Co-operation in Computer-Specific Cases

The special investigation problems encountered in computerised environments, especially in the global cyberspace, require not only computer-specific investigation measures but also require corresponding rules for international legal co-operation when dealing with these measures. Again, the most highly developed regime of rules of international legal co-operation is found in the *Cybercrime Convention of the Council of Europe* of 2001, specifically in Chapter III of the Convention.[248] Article 24, for example, consists of an extradition provision applicable in cases involving the computer-specific offences established in accordance with Articles 2 through 11, provided that they are punishable under the laws of both parties concerned (double criminality requirement). Chapter III also contains detailed computer-specific provisions for mutual assistance, including co-operation in the areas of expedited preservation of stored computer data, expedited disclosure of preserved traffic data, accessing of stored computer data, real-time collection of traffic data, and interception of content data. It also provides general principles relating to mutual assistance, confidentiality, and limitation on use, and addresses the issue of spontaneous information.[249] Article 27 subsection 4 allows a requested party to refuse assistance if the request concerns an offence that the requested party considers a political offence or if it considers it likely that execution of the request will prejudice its sovereignty, security, *ordre public*, or other essential interests.

The Cybercrime Convention also puts great emphasis on practical co-operation. It provides for the organisation of a "24/7 network" with contact available on a twenty-four hour, seven-day-a-week basis. Such contact is extremely important, for example, in cases where traceback procedures based on traffic data and quick freeze operations are required. Article 35 requires each party to designate "a point of contact available on a twenty-four hour, seven-day-a-week basis, in order to ensure the provision of immediate assistance for the purpose of investigations or proceedings concerning criminal offences related to computer systems and data, or for the collection of evidence in electronic form of a criminal offence." Such

---

[248] Convention on Cybercrime of the Council of Europe of 23.11.2001 (ETS No. 185).
[249] For details, see Convention on Cybercrime of the Council of Europe of 23.11.2001 (ETS No. 185), Explanatory Report, Nos. 240-302.

assistance includes the provision of technical advice, the preservation of data pursuant to Articles 29 and 30, the collection of evidence, the provision of legal information, and the locating of suspects.[250]

As in the case of procedural rules, the scope of the provisions on co-operation is broad, covering not only the specific offences of the Convention but all "criminal offences related to computer systems and data, or for the collection of evidence in electronic form of a criminal offence" (Art. 23). The obligation to co-operate as to this broad class of crimes was agreed upon because there is the same need for close international co-operation in all these cases. Only Articles 24 (extradition), 33 (mutual assistance regarding the real-time collection of traffic data), and 34 (mutual assistance regarding the interception of content data) permit the parties to provide for a different scope of application of these measures.[251] Thus, the special co-operation proceedings of the Cybercrime Convention can also be used for cyberterrorism and for all other types of terrorist activity on the Internet.

2. Co-operation in Cases of Money Laundering and the Financing of Terrorism

The special international instruments against money laundering and the financing of terrorism described above also provide for specific co-operation rules.

- The CoE Convention on Laundering, Search, Seizure and Confiscation of the Proceeds from Crime[252] contains specific rules of co-operation with respect to investigations of bank data, spontaneous information, provisional measures, confiscation, and co-operation between specialised financial investigation units. The Convention reserves broad grounds for refusal not only with respect to political offences but also with respect to the national *ordre public* and other reasons. Refusal for political offences is, however, excluded for the financing of terrorism (Art. 28).
- The UN International Convention for the Suppression of the Financing of Terrorism[253] also fosters international co-operation. According to Article 14, requests for co-operation may not be refused on political grounds.
- UN Security Council Resolution 1373 of 2001[254] ensures in paragraph 3 (g) that "claims of political motivation are not recognised as grounds for

---

[250] For details, see Convention on Cybercrime of the Council of Europe of 23.11.2001 (ETS No. 185), Explanatory Report, No. 297-302.
[251] For details, see Convention on Cybercrime of the Council of Europe of 23.11.2001 (ETS No. 185), Explanatory Report, Nos. 243, 245, 253.
[252] Convention on Laundering, Search, Seizure and Confiscation of the Proceeds from Crime and on the Financing of Terrorism of 16.5.2005 (CETS No. 198).
[253] UN International Convention for the Suppression of the Financing of Terrorism of 1999, UN Treaty Series Reg. No. 38349, adopted by the General Assembly of the United Nations in Resolution 54/109 on 9.12.1999.
[254] UN Security Council Resolution 1373 (2001) of 28.9.2001.

refusing requests for the extradition of alleged terrorists" and decides in paragraph 2 (f) that all States shall "afford one another the greatest measure of assistance in connection with criminal investigations or criminal proceedings relating to the financing or support of terrorist acts." At the time it adopted Resolution 1373, the Security Council also established the monitoring Counter-Terrorism Committee (CTC). Member States are required to report regularly to the Committee on the measures they have taken to implement Resolution 1373.

- UN Security Council Resolution 1535[255] creates among other things the Counter-Terrorism Committee Executive Directorate (CTED), which provides the CTC with expert advice on all areas covered by resolution 1373. The CTED was established also with the aim of facilitating technical assistance to countries as well as promoting closer co-operation and co-ordination both within the UN system of organisations and among regional and intergovernmental bodies.

The rules in these financial investigation instruments on co-operation apply regardless of whether or not the perpetrators made use of computer systems.

3. Co-operation in Terrorist Cases

Rules on co-operation are also provided in the various conventions, protocols, and decisions that address terrorism:

- The European Convention on the Suppression of Terrorism as amended by the Protocol of 2003[256] focuses on issues of extradition and specifically deals with extradition in "political cases." For the purpose of extradition, Article 1 excludes the political offence exception for a list of offences including, for example, the unlawful seizure of an aircraft, offences against internationally protected persons, kidnapping, and offences involving bombs. According to Article 2, the decision not to regard an offence as a political offence can be extended to other acts of violence and acts against property if the act created a collective danger for persons. According to Article 8, Contracting States may not refuse requests for mutual assistance based on the fact that the request concerns a political offence.
- The Council of Europe Convention on the Prevention of Terrorism[257] deals with international co-operation in prevention and in criminal matters. Article 20 excludes the political exception clause for extradition

---

[255] UN Security Council Resolution 1535 (2004) of 26.3.2004.

[256] The European Convention on the Suppression of Terrorism of 27.1.1977 (ETS No. 90) as amended by the Protocol of 15.5.2003 (ETS No. 190). The Additional Protocol to the Convention on the Suppression of Terrorism of 2003 addresses offences within the scope of the Convention for the Suppression of the Financing of Terrorism with new rules on reservations.

[257] Council of Europe Convention on the Prevention of Terrorism of 16.5.2005 (CETS No. 196).

and mutual assistance. However, any party may, in a reservation, declare that it reserves the right not to apply this paragraph.

- The European Union has additional, more specific rules on co-operation. For example, the EU Council Decision of 2005 on the exchange of information and co-operation concerning terrorist offences[258] is designed to improve co-operation in cases of terrorist offences by regulating practical measures. Each Member State must designate a specialised service within its police services that will have access to and collect all relevant information resulting from criminal investigation and prosecutions with respect to terrorist offences and that will send the information to Europol or Eurojust, respectively. The Decision also provides for the establishment of joint investigation teams.

- Most other instruments against terrorism also contain general provisions on international co-operation. This is true of the UN conventions and protocols against specific acts of terrorism (such as bombing) discussed above.[259] These conventions each contain a provision according to which the defined offences must be deemed extraditable offences in any existing treaty between States parties.[260] In addition, for purposes of extradition, offences shall be treated as if they had been committed not only in the place where they occurred but also in the territory of the states that have established jurisdiction under that convention. The conventions also contain special provisions that exclude the political offence exception, for example, Article 11 of the Convention for the Suppression of Terrorist Bombings, Article 15 of the Convention for the Suppression of Acts of Nuclear Terrorism, Article 16 No. 14 of the UN Convention against Transnational Organized Crime, and Article 9 Sec. 1a of the Hostages Convention.

For these provisions, again, it is irrelevant whether or not the perpetrator committed the defined acts with the support of a computer system. Thus, there are no computer-specific gaps in any of these instruments.

---

[258] EU Council Decision 2005/671/JHA of 20.9.2005 on the exchange of information and co-operation concerning terrorist offences. OJ L 253, 29.9.2005, pp. 22-24.
[259] See II.B.1.b) supra.
[260] E.g., Art 8 of the Convention for the Suppression of Unlawful Seizure of Aircraft of 16.12.1970, UN Treaty Series Reg. No. 12325; Art 8 of the Convention on the Prevention and Punishment of Crimes Against Internationally Protected Persons of 14.12.1973, UN Treaty Series Reg. No. 15410; Art 11 of the Convention on the Physical Protection of Nuclear Material of 3.3.1980, UN Treaty Series Reg. No. 37517; Art 11 of the Convention for the Suppression of Unlawful Acts Against the Safety of Maritime Navigation of 10.3.1988, UN Treaty Series Reg. No. 29004; Art 9 of the Convention for the Suppression of Terrorist Bombing of 15.12.1997, UN Treaty Series Reg. No. 37517; Extradition Exception Clause Art. 9 of the Convention Against the Taking of Hostages of 17.12.1979, UN Treaty Series Reg. No. 21931.

4. Co-operation in General Cases

Particularly in cases where there are no applicable specific co-operation agreements for cybercrime, terrorism, or money laundering, mutual assistance in criminal matters and extradition are regulated by general conventions and protocols. These instruments contain broad grounds for refusals to co-operate, such as for political offences or with respect to the *ordre public*. This is true of the European Convention on Mutual Assistance in Criminal Matters and its two additional protocols[261] as well as the European Convention on Extradition and its two additional protocols.[262] These conventions are applicable to both computer-specific and non-computer-specific crimes.

5. Evaluation and Consequences for Legal Policy

a) General Evaluation

The co-operation agreements that specifically address cybercrime are applicable to all kinds of cyberterrorism and other use of the Internet for terrorist purposes. Thus, the detailed co-operation procedures of the Cybercrime Convention are available in cases of terrorist use of the Internet. These procedures are the most important instruments for the identification and prosecution of terrorism on the Internet. Similarly, the instruments that address international co-operation in financial, terrorist, and other general investigations can be applied in an IT-environment, thereby also enabling investigations of all types of terrorist activities involving the use of computer systems.

b) Political Offence Exception Clause

The only question that remains open is whether the existing international instruments of co-operation should be amended or updated. This question is particularly relevant with respect to the fact that – unlike many of the existing conventions on terrorism – the Cybercrime Convention permits a refusal to co-operate for political reasons. Such a result could be changed by the introduction of a special provision on cyberterrorism committed by attacks against computer infrastructures to which the political offence exception would not apply (an option not favoured above). Another option would be to exclude the political offence exception for specific serious acts in the Cybercrime Convention. This would be beneficial to international co-operation. It would also be in accordance with the trend – described above –

---

[261] European Convention on Mutual Assistance in Criminal Matters of 20.4.1959 (ETS No. 30); Additional Protocol on the European Convention on Mutual Assistance in Criminal Matters of 17.3.1978 (ETS No. 99); Second Additional Protocol to the European Convention on Mutual Assistance in Criminal Matters of 8.11.2001 (ETS No. 182).

[262] European Convention on Extradition of 13.12.1957 (ETS No. 24) and its additional protocols of 15.10.1975 (ETS No. 86) and of 17.3.1978 (ETS No. 98).

towards abandoning the political offence exception in serious cases of terrorism. However, even conventions that exclude the political offence exception may allow states party to opt out of the exclusion by means of a reservation (Art. 20 of the CoE Convention on the Prevention of Terrorism, for example). Thus, international efforts with respect to the political offence exception in the Cybercrime Convention and in other conventions are not a priority. However, in the process – recommended above – of evaluating and updating the procedural provisions of the Cybercrime Convention, exclusion of the political offence exception should be considered for certain offences, such as data and system interference, in serious cases.

c) Specific Co-operation With Respect to the Prevention of Illegal Content

A more serious need for improving international co-operation, again, exists with respect to the prevention of illegal content on the Internet. As described above, it is obvious that specific international co-operation mechanisms are necessary for the establishment of the accessory liability of Internet providers, for "notice and takedown" procedures, for the development of new forms of self-regulation, for public-private "co-regulation," as well as for national instruments for removing and blocking illegal content. These efforts include, but are not limited to, improvements in the sharing of information and allocating of tasks in the control of the global cyberspace. Since purely national control and blocking mechanisms on the Internet are often doomed to failure, effective solutions depend to a great extent on close international co-operation or action on a supranational level. To the extent that the global co-operation of states is essential for such solutions, soft sanctions applicable to non-complying states would be useful, such as those found in the international system of money laundering of the Financial Action Task Force (FATF) of the OECD. Efforts with respect to these issues might lead to an increase in international co-operation with regard to the Internet. A deeper analysis of the new regulatory questions might even lead to the conclusion that the global cyberspace is a common heritage of mankind that – like the high seas – requires new mechanisms of supranational governance implemented by means of new institutions. Thus, in addition to the support for signing, ratification, and implementation of the Cybercrime Convention, these questions merit further efforts with respect to illegal terrorist content as well as other illegal content in a more general context.

III. Conclusions

A. Use of the Internet for Terrorist Purposes

Cyberterrorism against or by means of the Internet poses a significant risk since computer systems today are responsible for carrying out many essential functions of society. Such attacks via the Internet could cause damage not only to the IT-infrastructure and essential electronic communication systems but also to other infrastructures, systems, and legal interests, such as nuclear power stations, electrical supply systems, air control systems, medical computer systems, public administrations, and private companies, all of which depend on the functioning of IT. Interference with many of these systems can also cause harm to the life or well-being of persons. However, at this time, very few cases involving these kinds of attacks are known to the public.

Instead, a primary use of the Internet and of other electronic communication system consists in the public dissemination of illegal content. The Internet and other communication systems are abused by terrorists in order to threaten the commission of terrorist acts; to incite, advertise, and glorify terrorism; to engage in fundraising for and financing of terrorism; to provide training for terrorism; to recruit for terrorism; and to disseminate racist and xenophobic material. In sum, the Internet has become an important tool by which terrorists send their messages to a broad audience.

In addition, the Internet and other computer systems play a significant role in the logistical preparation of terrorist offences, including internal communication, acquisition of information (e.g., on bomb-building, hostage-taking, or hijacking), analysis of targets, and other forms of information gathering.

B. Applicability of Existing Conventions

The existing international conventions and other instruments for the harmonisation of national substantive and procedural law and for international co-operation are applicable to the prosecution of cyberterrorism and other use of the Internet for terrorist purposes. The computer-specific provisions of the Council of Europe's Cybercrime Convention on national substantive law, national procedural law and international co-operation can all be applied to the cases of terrorism analysed above. For computer-specific reasons, all destructive attacks via the Internet require interference with data, i.e., offences that fall under the substantive law provisions on data and system interference of the Cybercrime Convention. The applicability of the computer-specific procedural rules and the international co-operation law of the Cybercrime Convention to all types of terrorism is due to the fact that the application of the special provisions of the Cybercrime Convention that deal with procedural law and international co-operation law is defined broadly and is not limited to cybercrime. Similarly, the substantive, procedural, and co-operation rules of the international instruments on terrorism, on money laundering, on the financing of terrorism, and on mutual assistance or extradition are also applicable to cyberterrorism since they are worded generally and thus can apply in an IT-environment.

Consequently, the primary question posed in this report concerning the existence of "terrorist-specific" gaps in "computer-specific" conventions and "computer-specific gaps" in "terrorist-specific conventions" can be answered in the negative as far as the application of the Cybercrime Convention and other instruments is concerned. As a result, only the second question posed remains: whether these instruments have *general gaps*, i.e., gaps that are not specific for the use of the Internet for terrorist purposes. As explained above, this analysis cannot provide a general "super-evaluation" of all relevant international instruments on cybercrime and/or terrorism and their possible gaps with respect to the prosecution of crime and the protection of civil liberties. However, the report has analysed the major problems relevant for both cyberterrorism and for the use of the Internet for terrorist purposes.

C. General Problems of Existing Conventions

1. The major problem facing all existing international instruments is the lack of *signatures, ratifications, and implementations*. Broad acceptance is especially important for the Cybercrime Convention as well as for the Convention on the Prevention of Terrorism, which are the most important international instruments for fighting cyberterrorism and other terrorist use of the Internet. The role of the Cybercrime Convention is essential not only for substantive criminal law (with the Convention's important provisions on data interference and system interference) but also for criminal procedure and the law of international co-operation (with the Convention's highly specialised investigation and co-operation tools). The Convention on the Prevention of Terrorism is decisive with respect to the creation of adequate substantive criminal law provisions for illegal content. Thus, in the future, serious efforts should be made to promote the process of signing, ratifying, and implementing the Convention.

2. As a consequence, all additional efforts both within and beyond the present scope of the Cybercrime Convention should be pursued in such a way as not to hinder or distract from signature, ratification, and implementation.

Thus, the discussion of possible amendments and updates to the *Cybercrime Convention* in the quickly changing IT-environment should be undertaken only with the aim of a possible *additional protocol* to the Convention, which would recognise the Convention as its basic mother convention. In such a process, the *Cybercrime Convention* should be evaluated with regard to its ability to cover newly emerging technical advances, particularly new forensic investigative techniques (such as online searches or the use of key logger software). In the fast-paced technical environment of cybercrime, such evaluations, which frequently lead to revisions and updates, are an absolutely normal process, especially when dealing with high risks such as those posed by terrorism.

Should a decision be taken to supplement the Cybercrime Convention with a follow-up protocol addressing new investigative techniques, the possibility of excluding the political exception clause for some of its offences – especially in serious cases of data and system interference – could also be considered, thus following the trend of other co-operation instruments, particularly in clearly defined cases of terrorism.

In addition, the option of adopting a new provision prohibiting serious attacks on IT-based or general infrastructures could be discussed. The advantage of such a provision, however, would be limited and such a provision is not recommended by this report. It is sufficient for countries to evaluate existing domestic statutes on data and system interference and to make sure that they provide sanctions appropriate for cases involving terrorist attacks against computer and other essential infrastructures and other legal interests. However, such "effective, proportionate and dissuasive sanctions" are already required by the Cybercrime Convention, and it can be left to the national legislatures to achieve this result by means of sentencing rules, aggravated offences on data interference, or infrastructure offences.

3. An additional protocol to the *Convention for the Prevention of Terrorism* should also be considered in order to achieve full coverage of illegal terrorist content, particularly threats to commit terrorist acts. Currently, such threats are not adequately covered in the relevant Council of Europe conventions, and this deficit is not fully compensated by instruments of other international organisations. Considering the effects of threats to commit terrorist acts, a response is necessary. It would also be possible to cover this issue in a better and more systematic way in the specific UN conventions. However, such an approach would pose problems with respect to unspecified general threats, as it is difficult to deal with such threats by means of the sector-specific approach taken by the UN.[263] Considering possible amendments to the terrorist specific conventions, in a future study one might also analyse whether the EU approach of "participation in a terrorist organisation" should be transferred to a wider CoE- or UN level.

D. New Efforts With Respect to Illegal Content

Due to the frequent use of the Internet for the dissemination of illegal terrorist content, additional efforts should be made to develop repressive and preventive measures that are both effective and respectful of civil liberties. This could be done either with special regard to illegal terrorist content or – which is more advisable – in a more general way that would also cover other types of illegal content.

Effective standards for the prosecution and prevention of illegal content on the Internet could be achieved by means of an additional protocol to the Cybercrime Convention, which could contain new rules for national substantive law, national procedural law, law on international co-operation,

---

[263] See II.B.1.b) supra.

soft law, as well as rules establishing public-private partnerships.[264] In the area of substantive law, effective prevention of illegal content not only needs harmonised rules on illegal content in the special part of criminal law (as in the Convention for the Prevention of Terrorism or in the Protocol to the Cybercrime Convention), but also harmonised rules on the responsibility of Internet providers, which could be the basis of international notice and takedown procedures (as in the EC Directive on e-commerce). Such rules would require a difficult balancing of security interests and human rights, especially with respect to freedom of information rights. This is also true for the necessary provisions of procedural law and the law on international co-operation, both of which require specific regulations based on research on technical blocking and control mechanisms on the Internet and must take into consideration the consequences of such measures for the freedom of information. These questions are difficult but essential: Open societies should not leave the Internet and other electronic communication systems vulnerable to the abuse of their adversaries. They should also refrain from enacting ineffective control methods of a purely symbolic nature that seriously infringe freedom of information rights and can lead to the development of uncontrolled surveillance.

The Council of Europe, with its long tradition in balancing security interests in criminal matters with the protection of human rights, would be an ideal institution to tackle the difficult problems associated with international standards and procedures for illegal content in computer networks. Due to the global nature of the Internet and its strong resistance to national control measures, an initiative in this field could even lead to new forms of co-operation that might recognise the global cyberspace as a common heritage of mankind that requires new mechanisms of supranational governance implemented by new institutions.

---

[264] The need for international action to deal with illegal content has been shown in all three areas dealt with above: national substantive law, national procedural law, and international co-operation law. See II.B.2.g), II.C.4., and II.D. supra.

References

Bachfeld, Daniel, War der Wurm drin? IT-Sicherheit in der US-Stromversorgung, http://www.heise.de/ct/03/18/034/default.shtml [last visited: July 2007].

Bassiouni, Cherif, International Terrorism: Multilateral Conventions (1937-2001), 3 volumes, New York 2001/2002.

Berinato, Scott, The Truth About Cyberterrorism, CIO Magazine, 15.03.2002, http://www.cio.com/archive/031502/truth.html [last visited: July 2007].

Bidder, Benjamin, Angriff der Cyber-Söldner, Der Spiegel 31/2007, pp. 74-76.

Breyer, Patrick, Die Cyber-Crime-Konvention des Europarats, DuD 2001, pp. 592-600.

Bundesministerium des Innern (Ed.), Verfassungsschutzbericht 2005, Berlin, May 2006.

Cheung, Humphrey, Blackhat 2006: Explosive risks in RFID-enabled passports? TG Daily 03.08.2006, http://www.tgdaily.com/content/view/27899/113/ [last visited: July 2007].

Cohen, Fred, Cyber-Risks and Critical Infrastructures, In: Alan O'Day (Ed.), Cyberterrorism, pp. 1-10.

Coll, Steve/Glasser, Susan B., Terrorists turn to the web as base of operations, The Washington Post, 7 August 2005, Section A01.

Conway, Maura, Reality Bytes: Cyberterrorism and Terrorist 'Use' of the Internet, In: First Monday, 04.11.2002, Vol. 7, No. 11, http://firstmonday.org/issues/issue7_11/conway/ [last visited: July 2007].

Council of Europe (ed.), Human rights and the fight against terrorism – The Council of Europe Guidelines, Strasbourg 2005.

Council of Europe (ed.), "Apologie du terrorisme" and "incitement to terrorism", Strasbourg 2004.

Denning, Dorothy E., Activism, Hacktivism, and Cyberterrorism: The Internet as a Tool for Influencing Foreign Policy, http://www.totse.com/en/technology/cyberspace_the_new_frontier/cyberspc.html [last visited: July 2007].

Dix, Alexander, Regelungsdefizite der Cyber-Crime-Konvention und der E-TKÜV, DuD 2001, pp. 588-591.

Dunnigan, James F., The next war zone, New York 2002.

Espiner, Tom, Foreign powers are main cyberthreat, U.K. says, ZDNet 11/22/05, http://news.zdnet.com/2102-1009_22-5967532.html [last visited: July 2007].

Foltz, Bryan C., Cyberterrorism, computer crime, and reality, In: Information Management & Computer Security, 15.03.2004, Vol. 12, No. 2, pp. 154-166.

Gercke, Marco, "Cyberterrorismus" – Aktivitäten terroristischer Organisationen im Internet, CR 2007, pp. 62-68.

Gercke, Marco, The Slow Wake of a Global Approach Against Cybercrime, Computer Law Review International 2006, pp. 140-145.

Gercke, Marco, Die Cybercrime Konvention des Europarates, CR 2004, pp. 782-791.

Giacomello, Giampiero, Bangs for the Buck: A Cost-Benefit Analysis of Cyberterrorism, In: Studies in Conflict & Terrorism, Vol. 27 (2004), pp. 387-408.

Golder, Ben/Williams, George, What is 'terrorism'? Problems of legal definition, University of New South Wales Law Journal 2004, Vol. 27, pp. 270-295.

Green, Joshua, The Myth of Cyberterrorism. There are many ways terrorists can kill you – computers aren't one of them. Washington Monthly, November 2002. http://www.washingtonmonthly.com/features/2001/0211.green.html [last visited: July 2007].

Greenemeier, Larry, Cyberterrorism: By Whatever Name, It's On The Increase, InformationWeek 7 July 2007, http://www.informationweek.com/story/showArticle.jhtml?articleID=200900812 [last visited: July 2007].

Greenemeier, Larry, "Electronic Jihad" app offers cyberterrorism for the masses, ITNews 3 July 2007, www.itnews.com.au/Tools/Print.aspx?CIID=85204 [last visited: July 2007].

Harding, Thomas, Terrorists 'use Google maps to hit UK troops', Telegraph 13 January 2007, http://www.telegraph.co.uk/news/main.jhtml? xml=/news/2007/01/13/wgoogle13.xml [last visited: July 2007].

ICANN, Factsheet on root server attacks on 6 February 2007, as of: 01 March 2007, http://icann.org/announcements/factsheet-dns-attack-08mar07.pdf [last visited: July 2007].

Janczewski, Lech J./Colarik, Andrew M., Managerial Guide for Handling Cyber-Terrorism and Information Warfare, Hershey, London 2005.

Jüttner, Julia/Musharbash, Yassin, Kofferbomber wollten möglichst viele Menschen töten, Spiegel Online, 25.10.2006, http://www.spiegel.de/ panorama/justiz/ 0,1518,444715,00.html [last visited: July 2007].

Koesch, Sascha/Magdanz, Fee/Stadler, Robert, Funkchip-Reisepass zündet Bombe, Spiegel Online, 21.08.2006, http://www.spiegel.de/netzwelt/ mobil/0,1518,432654,00.html [last visited: July 2007].

Krempl, Stefan, Terroristen verstecken Botschaften angeblich in IP-Headern, Heise News from 09.03.2003, http://www.heise.de/newsticker/meldung/ 35137 [last visited: July 2007].

Kuri, Jürgen, BKA-Forensiker entlöschen Bombenbaupläne, Heise News from 08.03.2007, http://www.heise.de/newsticker/meldung/86388 [last visited: July 2007].

Lenzner, Robert/Vardi, Nathan, The Next Threat, www.forbes.com/forbes/ 2004/0920/070_print.html [last visited: July 2007].

Leppard, David, Al-Qaeda plot to bring down UK internet, Times Online, 11.03.2007, http://www.timesonline.co.uk/tol/news/uk/crime/article 1496831.ece [last visited: July 2007].

Leyden, John, Mass hack takes out govt sites, The Register, 22.01.2001, http://www.theregister.co.uk/2001/01/22/mass_hack_takes_out_govt/ [last visited: July 2007].

Murphy, Sean D., Contemporary Practice of the United States Relating to International Law, 96 American Journal of International Law 2002, pp. 956-983.

Musharbash, Yassin, Al-Qaida launches a weekly news show, Spiegel Online, 07.10.2005, http://www.spiegel.de/international/0,1518,378633, 00.html [last visited: July 2007].

Musharbash, Yassin, Qaidas Leitfaden für Entführungen, Spiegel Online, 30.11.2005, http://www.spiegel.de/politik/ausland/0,1518,387691,00.html [last visited: July 2007].

Musharbash, Yassin, The Cyber-Cemetery of the Mujahedeen, Spiegel Online, 28.10.2005, http://www.spiegel.de/international/0,1518,382097, 00.html [last visited: July 2007].

Musharbash, Yassin, US-Firmen-Website für Qaida-Botschaft gehackt, Spiegel Online, 17.06.2004, http://service.spiegel.de/digas/servlet/find/ON=spiegel-304473 [last visited: July 2007].

Nuotio, Kimmo, Terrorism as a Catalyst for the Emergence, Harmonization and Reform of Law, Journal of International Criminal Justice 4 (2006), pp. 998-1016.

Oeter, Stefan, Terrorismus und Menschenrechte, 40 Archiv des Völkerrechts 2002, pp. 422-453.

Ou, George, RFID passports with improper shielding triggers bomb in simulation, ZDNet 09.08.2006, http://blogs.zdnet.com/Ou/?p=289 [last visited: July 2007].

Patalong, Frank, Das zensierte Weltauge, http://www.spiegel.de/netzwelt/web/0,1518,464186,00.html [last visited: July 2007].

Patalong, Frank/Dambeck, Holger, Griechenlands Premier wurde abgehört. http://www.spiegel.de/netzwelt/web/0,1518,398835,00.html [last visited: July 2007].

Perl, Raphael, Trends in Terrorism: 2006, Congressional Research Service Report for Congress (RL33555), dated 21 July 2006.

Persson, Christian, "Rückfall ins Telefonzeitalter" nach Erdbeben, Heise News, 28.12.2006, http://www.heise.de/newsticker/meldung/83007 [last visited: July 2007].

Pollitt, Mark M., Cyberterrorism – Fact or Fancy? http://www.cs.georgetown.edu/ ~denning/infosec/pollitt.html [last visited: July 2007].

Poulsen, Kevin, Slammer worm crashed Ohio nuke plant network, http://www.securityfocus.com/print/news/6767 [last visited: July 2007].

Poulsen, Kevin, South Pole 'cyberterrorist' hack wasn't the first, http://www.securityfocus.com/print/news/9356 [last visited: July 2007].

Record, Jeffrey, Bounding the global war on terrorism. Strategic Studies Institute of the U.S. Army War College, http://www.strategicstudiesinstitute.army.mil/ pdffiles/PUB207.pdf [last visited: July 2007], December 2003.

Radü, Jens, Terroristen suchen Ziele mit Google Earth, Spiegel Online, 13.01.2007, http://www.spiegel.de/netzwelt/web/0,1518,459542,00.html [last visited: July 2007].

Ramelsberger, Annette, Krieger im Internet, Süddeutsche Zeitung, 15 March 2007, p. 5.

Schröder, Alwin, Al-Qaida droht US-Finanzbranche mit Hacker-Angriff, Spiegel Online, 01.12.2006, http://www.spiegel.de/wirtschaft/0,1518, 451811,00.html [last visited: July 2007].

Seith, Anne, Google Earth verschleiert indische Verteidigungsanlagen, http://www.spiegel.de/netzwelt/web/0,1518,464178,00.html [last visited: July 2007].

Sieber, Ulrich, The Threat of Cybercrime, In: Council of Europe (Ed.), Organised crime in Europe: the threat of cybercrime, Strasbourg 2005, pp. 81-218.

Sieber, Ulrich, The Punishment of Serious Crimes, Part 1, Freiburg 2004.

Sieber, Ulrich, Kinderpornographie, Jugendschutz und Providerverantwortlichkeit im Internet (ed. by the German Ministry of Justice in the series „recht"), Bonn 1999.

Sieber, Ulrich, Responsibility of Internet Providers: Comparative Analysis of a Basic Question of Information Law, In: Lederman, Eliezer/Shapira, Ron (eds.), Law, Information and Information Technology, The Hague 2001, pp. 231-292.

Sieber, Ulrich, Legal Regulation, Law Enforcement and Self-Regulation – A New Alliance for Preventing Illegal Contents on the Internet, In: Waltermann, Jens/Machill, Marcel (eds), Protecting our Children on the Internet, Gütersloh 2000, pp. 319-400.

Sieber, Ulrich, Grenzen des Strafrechts, Zeitschrift für die gesamte Strafrechtswissenschaft (ZStW) 119 (2006), pp. 1-68.

Sieber, Ulrich, Responsibility, in: Hoeren/Sieber (eds.), Handbuch des Multimediarechts, Part. 18.1, München 2007.

Stasiukonis, Steve, Social Engineering, the USB Way, http://www.dark reading.com/document.asp?doc_id=95556&WT.svl=column1_1 [last visited: July 2007].

Stöcker, Christian, Delle im Datenstrom: Hacker attackieren Internet-Rootserver, http://www.spiegel.de/netzwelt/tech/0,1518,464926,00.html [last visited: July 2007].

Süddeutsche Zeitung, Die Heiligen Krieger drohen der Wall Street, Süddeutsche Zeitung vom 01.12.2006, http://www.sueddeutsche.de/ finanzen/artikel/352/93259/ [last visited: July 2007].

Süddeutsche Zeitung, „Diesen Krieg könnt ihr Euch nicht leisten", Süddeutsche Zeitung vom 11.03.2007, http://www.sueddeutsche.de/ deutschland/artikel/189/105084/ [last visited: July 2007].

Suellentrop, Chris, Sim City: Terrortown. Wired 14.10, http://www.wired. com/wired/archive/14.10/posts.html?pg=2 [last visited: July 2007].

Symantec Corp., Internet Security Threat Report, Vol. X (September 2006), http://www.symantec.com/enterprise/theme.jsp?themeid=threatreport [last visited: July 2007].

Symantec Corp., Internet Security Threat Report, Vol. XI (March 2007), http://www.symantec.com/enterprise/theme.jsp?themeid=threatreport [last visited: July 2007].

Taylor, Greg, The Council of Europe Cybercrime Convention – A civil liberties perspective, http://www.crime-research.org/library/CoE_ Cybercrime.html [last visited: July 2007].

Thomas, Timothy L., Al Qaeda and the Internet: the danger of "cyberplanning", In: Parameters, Spring 2003. Online available at http://www.carlisle.army.mil/usawc/Parameters/03spring/thomas.pdf [last visited: July 2007].

Tomuschat, Christian, Council of Europe Committee of Experts on Terrorism (CODEXTER), Strasbourg, On the possible "added value" of a comprehensive Convention on Terrorism, 26 Human Rights Law Journal 2005, pp. 287-306.

Tsfati, Yariv/Weimann, Gabriel, www.terrorism.com: Terror on the Internet, In: Studies in Conflict & Terrorism 2002 (25), Pp.317-332.

U.S. Army Training and Doctrine Command, Cyber Operations and Cyber Terrorism, DCSINT Handbook No. 1.02, http://www.fas.org/irp/threat/ terrorism/sup2.pdf [last visited: July 2007].

Vatis, Michael A., Cyber attacks during the war on terrorism: a predictive analysis. 22.09.2001, http://www.ists.dartmouth.edu/analysis/cyber_a1.pdf [last visited: July 2007].

Wagner, Breanne, Experts Downplay Imminent Threat of Cyberterrorism, National Defense Magazine, Issue July 2007, http://www.nationaldefense magazine.org/issues/2007/July/ExpertsDownplay.htm [last visited: July 2007].

Wagner, Cynthia G., Countering Cyber Attacks, The Futurist, Issue May/June 2007, p. 16.

Weimann, Gabriel, Cyberterrorism. How real is the threat? United States Institute of Peace Special Report 119, December 2004, http://www.usip.org/pubs/specialreports/sr119.pdf [last visited: July 2007].

Weimann, Gabriel, Cyberterrorism: The Sum of All Fears? In: Studies in Conflict & Terrorism, 28 (2005), pp. 129-149.

Weimann, Gabriel, Terrorists and Their Tools – Part II. Using the Internet to recruit, raise funds, and plan attacks, YaleGlobal, 26.04.2004, http://yaleglobal.yale.edu/article.print?id=3768 [last visited: July 2007].

Weimann, Gabriel, www.terror.net. How Modern Terrorism Uses the Internet. United States Institute of Peace Special Report 116, March 2004, http://www.usip.org/ pubs/specialreports/sr116.pdf [last visited: July 2007].

Whine, Michael, Cyberspace – A New Medium for Communication, Command, and Control by Extremists, In: Studies in Conflict & Terrorism 1999 (22), pp. 231-245.

White House, The U.S., The national strategy to secure cyberspace, February 2003, http://www.whitehouse.gov/pcipb/cyberspace_strategy.pdf [last visited: July 2007].

Wilkens, Andreas, Heise News, 18.12.2006, http://www.heise.de/newsticker/ meldung/82700 [last visited: July 2007].

Wilson, Clay, Computer Attack and Cyberterrorism: Vulnerabilities and Policy Issues for Congress, Congressional Research Service Report for Congress (RL32114), Updated 1 April 2005.

Ziegler, Peter-Michael, US-Behörden fallen bei IT-Sicherheit durch. Heise Security from 16.03.2006, http://www.heise.de/security/news/meldung/70946 [last visited: July 2007].

National reports

Armenia

A. National policy

1. Is there a national policy regarding the analysis, detection, prosecution and prevention of cybercrime in general and the misuse of cyberspace for terrorist purposes in particular? If yes, please briefly describe it.

A national policy regarding the analysis, detection, prosecution and prevention of cybercrime and the misuse of cyberspace for terrorist purposes has not yet been worked out in the Republic of Armenia. There are several reasons for that: computer network technologies are not widely used in Armenia yet and so far no case of the misuse of cyberspace for terrorist purposes has been registered in Armenia.

The maintenance of the security of computer network technology, including the misuse of cyberspace for criminal purposes, is among the items included in the National Security Strategy of the Republic of Armenia (adopted in February 2007). One of the main directives of the Strategy is to participate in global security efforts, particularly in relation to the fight against terrorism.

B. Legal framework

2. Does your national legislation criminalise the misuse of cyberspace for terrorist purposes, and
a. are these offences specifically defined with regard to the terrorist nature or technical means of committing the crime, or
b. is the misuse covered by other, non-specific criminal offences? How are these offences defined and which sanctions (criminal, administrative, civil) are attached?

The misuse of cyberspace for terrorist purposes is not defined in the Criminal Code of the Republic of Armenia as a separate *corpus delicti*, but in case of such offences the misuse of cyberspace is defined with regard to the technical means used to commit the crime.

Chapter 24 of the Criminal Code of the Republic of Armenia, entitled Crimes against computer information security, criminalises actions such as accessing (penetrating) computer information systems without permission, changing computer information, computer sabotage, illegal appropriation of computer data, manufacture or sale of special devices for illegal penetration into computer systems or networks, manufacture, use and dissemination of hazardous software, breach of rules for operation of a computer system or network.

Article 217 of the Criminal Code of the Republic of Armenia defines the *corpus delicti* of "Terrorism"; Article 217.1 refers to the Financing of terrorism and Article 389 refers to International terrorism.

Sanctions for the misuse of cyberspace for terrorist purposes are applied with the aggregation of crimes, which incorporate articles on terrorist offences (Chapter 23 of the Criminal Code) and offences in the field of computer information security (Chapter 24 of the Criminal Code).

3. Do you plan to introduce new legislation to counter terrorist misuse of cyberspace? What are the basic concepts on these legislative initiatives?

The competent authorities of the Republic of Armenia are working now on a draft Law on Information Technologies and Information Security which contains provisions on the misuse of cyberspace for terrorist purposes.

4. What are the existing national practices in the field of detecting, monitoring and closing down websites used for terrorist purposes?

No cases of the detecting, monitoring and closing down of websites used for terrorist purposes have been registered in the Republic of Armenia.

5. Does your national legislation provide criteria for establishing jurisdiction over such offences? What are those criteria?

Since the national legislation of the Republic of Armenia does not define misuse of cyberspace for terrorist purposes as a separate *corpus delicti* there are no criteria for establishing jurisdiction over such offences.

6. Does your national legal system establish ancillary offences related to the misuse of cyberspace?

There are no ancillary offences related to the misuse of cyberspace in the national legal system of the Republic of Armenia.

7. What kind of national procedures do you have for submitting an application on the activities of Internet-providers and/or hosting companies, to deprive a user from a domain name or to cancel his/her/its registration license?

According to the national legislation of the Republic of Armenia, the illegal activities of Internet providers and/or hosting companies are cancelled by the Court on the basis of the grounded decision of an investigator who initiates an application to the Court.

8. **What non-legislative measures do you have in your country to prevent and counter terrorist misuse of cyberspace, including self-regulatory measures?**

No non-legislative measures to prevent and counter terrorist misuse of cyberspace are applied in Armenia.

C. **International co-operation**

9. **Please describe the general framework for international co-operation regarding the misuse of cyberspace for terrorist purposes.**

Taking into consideration that no cases have been registered in the field of detecting, monitoring and closing down websites (see question 4) the competent authorities of Armenia do not have any experience in the framework of international co-operation.

10. **What are the existing practices and experiences with regard to international co-operation, in particular in relation to the procedures described in question 4?**

-

D. **Institutional framework**

11. **Please list the institutions that are competent for countering terrorist misuse of cyberspace.**

According to the Law on Combating Terrorism, the National Security Service, the Police and the Ministry of Defence are directly involved in the fight against terrorism. Within their competencies, the other bodies of Executive Power are also involved in the activities related to the fight against terrorism.

12. **Are there any partnerships between the public and private sectors (Internet-service providers, hosting companies, etc.) to counter terrorist misuse of cyberspace?**

The private (Internet service providers, hosting companies, etc.) and public sectors of Armenia co-operate with each other to counter terrorist misuse of cyberspace.

E.   Statistical information

13. Please provide relevant statistics on offences relating to the misuse of cyberspace for terrorist purposes (including possibly: cases recorded, investigated, brought to court, convictions, victims etc).

There are no statistics on offences relating to the misuse of cyberspace for terrorist purposes.

14. Where possible, please describe briefly the profile of offenders typically involved in the misuse of cyberspace for terrorist purposes (professional background, gender, age nationality), and possible typical organisational characteristics, including trans-national links and links to other forms of organised crime.

The competent authorities of Armenia do not have any statistical information about offenders typically involved in the misuse of cyberspace for terrorist purposes.

Austria

A.   National policy

1.   Is there a national policy regarding the analysis, detection, prosecution and prevention of cybercrime in general and the misuse of cyberspace for terrorist purposes in particular? If yes, please briefly describe it.

Austrian counter-terrorism policy is guided by respect for human rights, effective law enforcement and full international co-operation. In the field of the prosecution and prevention of cybercrime in general, Austria has implemented the Convention on Cybercrime of the Council or Europe, and established a high level of protection against this kind of crime. Austria has no specific rules related to cyberterrorism, but an offender who commits a terrorist act by the misuse of cyberspace is punished in accordance with the general provisions on combating terrorism (see below).

B.   Legal framework

**2.   Does your national legislation criminalise the misuse of cyberspace for terrorist purposes, and
a. are these offences specifically defined with regard to the terrorist nature or technical   means of committing the crime, or
b. is the misuse covered by other, non-specific criminal offences? How are these offences defined and which sanctions (criminal, administrative, civil) are attached?**

Austrian legislation has no specifically defined cyberterrorism offences; the misuse of cyberspace for terrorist purposes is criminalised in an indirect manner. Austrian penal law criminalises terrorist activities and does not distinguish between terrorist acts committed via the misuse of cyberspace and those committed in a "common" way. The specific offences against cybercrime remain unaffected.

3.   Do you plan to introduce new legislation to counter terrorist misuse of cyberspace? What are the basic concepts of these legislative initiatives?

At present, no initiatives to expand the legislation are planned.

4.   What are the existing national practices in the field of detecting, monitoring and closing down websites used for illicit, in particular, terrorist purposes and what kind of national procedures allow the blocking of access to websites or pages considered illicit?

There will be no existing national practice in the field of cyberterrorism until there is a record of a concrete case of a terrorist activity. If there are

113

indications that a website may contain terrorist content, the Federal Bureau of State Protection and Counter-Terrorism monitors the website and if necessary, they report it to the office of the public prosecutor.

5.   What are the existing national practices in the field of interception of, or infiltration to, the electronic correspondence (e.g. e-mail, forum, instantaneous message service, voice over IP-skype, etc).

Austrian procedural rules provide for the possibility of listening in on, intercepting, controlling, recording and monitoring telecommunications and for the audiovisual monitoring of individuals. It is also possible to establish the location of the premises where a final device being characterised by a certain subscriber's line is situated or has been situated and what the subscriber's lines are or have been and the origin or the destination of a telecommunication. These methods require a judicial order issued by an investigation judge or a chamber of three judges ("Ratskammer"). However, more intrusive methods like the monitoring of a telecommunication, the audio-visual monitoring of individuals by technical means and computer-aided data cross-referencing require a judicial order issued by a chamber of three judges.

6.   Does your national legislation provide criteria for establishing jurisdiction over the misuse of cyberspace for terrorist purposes? What are those criteria?

Basically jurisdiction is established over all offences committed on Austrian territory. Under certain conditions, Austrian jurisdiction is also existent, when terrorist criminal offences are committed outside Austrian territory (for example, when the perpetrator is an Austrian at the time of the offence or he/she gained Austrian citizenship afterwards and is still in its possession at the time of the institution of penal proceedings, or the perpetrator has his/her domicile or general residence in Austria; the offence is committed on behalf of a legal entity which has its seat in Austria; the offence is committed against the National Parliament, the Federal Parliament, the Federal Assembly, the Federal Government, a Provincial Parliament, a Provincial Government, the Constitutional Court, the Administrative Court, the Supreme Court, any other court or administrative authority or against the people of the Republic of Austria; the offence is committed against an authority of the European Union or against an entity under the treaties for the institution of the European Communities or the treaty on the European Union, having its seat in the Republic of Austria; or the perpetrator was a foreigner at the time of the offence, but is now in Austria and cannot be extradited).

7. **Does your national legal system establish additional offences related to attempts at, or complicity in, the commission of the misuse of cyberspace for terrorist purposes (ancillary offences)?**

Austria has no ancillary offences related to the misuse of cyberspace for terrorist purposes.

8. **What kind of national procedures do you have for submitting an application on the activities of Internet-providers and/or hosting companies or other entities, to deprive a user from a domain name or to cancel his/her/its registration or licence?**

According to the Austrian Telecommunications Act 2003, providers are obliged to provide all the facilities which are required for the interception of telecommunications according to the provisions of the Code of Criminal Procedure (on the basis of a judicial order).

9. **What non-legislative measures do you have in your country to prevent and counter terrorist misuse of cyberspace, including self-regulatory measures?**

The association of service providers in Austria has established hotlines, to which users can report the detection of illicit content. In reaction, the Internet provider closes access to this website. Currently it is only possible to report websites containing child pornography or national socialistic ideas. Hotlines for reporting cases of cyberterrorism are currently not arranged by the Association of Service Provider.

C. **International co-operation**

10. **Please describe your country's general framework for international co-operation regarding the misuse of cyberspace for terrorist purposes.**

Austria is a party to several bi- and multilateral treaties in the field of mutual legal assistance in criminal matters and extradition. Among others, it has signed and ratified the European Convention on Mutual Assistance in Criminal Matters and its First Additional Protocol, as well as the European Convention on the Suppression of Terrorism and twelve United Nations anti-terrorism-conventions. Furthermore, Austria has signed, ratified and implemented the Convention on Mutual Assistance in Criminal Matters between the member states of the European Union and its Protocol and has implemented other relevant EU instruments such as the EU Framework Decision on combating Terrorism and the Framework Decision on the European Arrest Warrant and the surrender procedures between member states.

11. What are the existing practices and experiences with regard to international co-operation, in particular in relation to the procedures described in question 4?

See the answer to question 4.

D. Institutional framework

12. Please list the institutions that are competent for countering terrorist misuse of cyberspace.

The Federal Ministries with most responsibility are those of the Interior and Justice. In addition to the organisational system of public prosecutor's offices and courts, the federal agencies to be mentioned in this context are the Federal Bureau of Criminal Investigation and the Federal Agency of State Protection and Counter-Terrorism.

13. In order to counter terrorist misuse of cyberspace are there any partnerships between the public and private sectors or legal obligations for operators of electronic communication (Internet-service providers, hosting companies, etc.) as well as persons providing the public with access to systems which allow on-line communication via access to the network (cybercafe, WiFi hotspot)?

-

14. Are there any hotlines regulated by the public or private sectors permitting denouncement of those websites which could be of a terrorist character / nature?

See the answer to question 9.

E. Statistical information

15. Please provide relevant statistics on offences relating to the misuse of cyberspace for terrorist purposes (including possibly: cases recorded, investigated, brought to court, convictions, victims etc.).

There are no specific statistics on such offences in Austria. The Constitution Guard Report for 2007 of the Federal Agency of State Protection and Counter-Terrorism does not mention any cases of cyberterrorism.

16. Where possible, please describe briefly the profile of offenders typically involved in the misuse of cyberspace for terrorist purposes (professional background, gender, age, nationality), and possible typical organisational characteristics, including trans-national links and links to other forms of organised crime.

-

Belgium

A. National policy

1. Is there a national policy regarding the analysis, detection, prosecution and prevention of cybercrime in general and the misuse of cyberspace for terrorist purposes in particular? If yes, please briefly describe it.

A working group on cyberterrorism was set up under the Action Plan against Radicalism, adopted by the Ministerial Intelligence and Security Committee on 25 March 2005. It includes representatives of the State Security Department, the Intelligence and Security Department, the co-ordinating body responsible for analysing the threat (OCAM) and the Federal Computer Crime Unit of the Federal Police. It is chaired by the Central Terrorism Department of the Federal Police.

B. Legal framework

2. Does your national legislation criminalise the misuse of cyberspace for terrorist purposes, and
a. are these offences specifically defined with regard to the terrorist nature or technical means of committing the crime, or
b. is the misuse covered by other, non-specific criminal offences? How are these offences defined and which sanctions (criminal, administrative, civil) are attached?

In Belgium these offences are generally covered by the Cybercrime Act of 28 November 2000 (Official Gazette 03/02/2001), under which new provisions were added to the Belgian Criminal Code, covering computer forgery, computer fraud and offences against the confidentiality, integrity and availability of computer systems and data stored in or processed or transmitted by them.

These latest provisions, Articles 550bis and 550ter of the Criminal Code, also cover the use of cyberspace for terrorist purposes. They read as follows:

Article 550bis

§1. Anyone who, knowingly and without authorisation, gains access to or remains in a computer system shall be punished by three months' to one year's imprisonment and/or a fine of 26 francs to 25 000 francs.
If the offence provided for in paragraph 1 is committed with fraudulent intent, the prison sentence shall be from six months to two years.

§2. Anyone who, with fraudulent or malicious intent, misuses his or her authority to gain access to a computer system shall be punished by six months' to two years' imprisonment and/or a fine of 26 francs to 25 000 francs.

§3. Anyone in one of the situations provided for in §§1 and 2 who:

1. re-uses, in any way, data stored in or processed or transmitted by the computer system;

2. or makes use in any way of a computer system belonging to a third party or uses the computer system to obtain access to the computer system of a third party;

3. or causes any damage, even unintentionally, to the computer system or data stored in or processed or transmitted by the system or to the computer system of a third party or data stored in or processed or transmitted by that system

shall be punished by one to three years' imprisonment and/or a fine of 26 Belgian francs to 50 000 Belgian francs.

§4. An attempt to commit one of the offences provided for in §§1 and 2 shall carry the same penalties.

§5. Anyone who unlawfully possesses, produces, sells, obtains with a view to using it, imports, disseminates or makes available in another form any device, including computerised data, principally designed or adapted to make it possible to commit the offences provided for in §§1 to 4 shall be punished by six months' to three years' imprisonment and/or a fine of €26 to €100 000.

§6. Anyone who orders or incites the commission of any of the offences provided for in §§1 to 5 shall be punished by six months' to five years' imprisonment and/or a fine of 100 francs to 200 000 francs.

§7. Anyone who, knowing that data have been obtained by means of one of the offences provided for in §§1 to 3, possesses them, discloses them to another person or divulges them, or makes any use whatsoever of data thus obtained shall be punished by six months' to three years' imprisonment and/or a fine of 26 francs to 100 000 francs.

§8. The penalties provided for in §§1 to 7 shall be doubled if an offence under one of these provisions is committed within five years of a conviction for one of these offences or one of the offences provided for in Articles 210bis, 259bis, 314bis, 504quater or 550ter.

Article 550ter

§1. Anyone who, knowingly and without authorisation, directly or indirectly inserts in a computer system, modifies or deletes data, or modifies by any technological means the normal use of data in a computer system shall be punished by six months' to three years' imprisonment and/or a fine of €26 to €25 000.

If the offence provided for in §1 is committed with fraudulent or malicious intent, the prison sentence shall be six months to five years.

§2. Anyone who, as a result of committing an offence under §1, damages data in the computer system concerned or in any other computer system shall be punished by six months' to five years' imprisonment and/or fine of 26 francs to 75 000 francs

§3. Anyone who, as a result of committing an offence under §1, completely or partially prevents the computer system concerned or any other computer system from functioning properly shall be punishable by one to five years' imprisonment and/or a fine of 26 francs to 100 000 francs.

§4. Anyone who unlawfully possesses, produces, sells, obtains with a view to using it, imports, disseminates or makes available in another form any device, including computerised data, principally designed or adapted to make it possible to commit the offences provided for in §§1 to 3 in the knowledge that the data may be used to damage data or completely or partially prevent a computer system from functioning properly shall be punished by six months' to three years' imprisonment and/or a fine of €26 to €100 000.

§5. The penalties provided for in §§1 to 4 shall be doubled if an offence under one of these provisions is committed within five years of a conviction for one of these offences or one of the offences provided for in Articles 210bis, 259bis, 314bis, 504quater or 550bis.

§6. An attempt to commit the offence provided for in §1 shall carry the same penalties.

In addition, Article 137, paragraph 2, of the Criminal Code, which concerns terrorist offences, explicitly states that the offences provided for in Article 550bis, §3.3 constitute terrorist offences under the conditions provided for in §1. This explicit reference to part of Article 550bis does not, however, mean that the other offences in Articles 550bis and 550ter may not be classified as terrorist offences: indeed, Article 137, §3, provides that other offences may also, under the conditions laid down in §1, constitute terrorist offences. These include destruction of, massive damage to or flooding of a transport system or public or private property which endangers human life or causes substantial economic loss, other than the offences provided for in § 2.

3. Do you plan to introduce new legislation to counter terrorist misuse of cyberspace? What are the basic concepts of these legislative initiatives?

For the time being, Belgium has no plans to introduce new statutory provisions specifically designed to combat the misuse of cyberspace for terrorist purposes.

A Bill approving the Council of Europe Convention on Cybercrime, which was signed in Budapest on 23 November 2001, and the Additional Protocol to the Convention on Cybercrime, concerning the criminalisation of acts of a racist and xenophobic nature committed through computer systems, signed in Strasbourg on 28 January 2003, has been drafted, but the last government was unable to adopt it. The draft should be adopted by the next government and, once it has been approved by the Cabinet, tabled in Parliament.

4. What are the existing national practices in the field of detecting, monitoring and closing down websites used for illicit, in particular, terrorist purposes and what kind of national procedures allow the blocking of access to websites or pages considered illicit?

Article 25 of the Belgian Constitution prohibits censorship and Article 19 safeguards the freedom to express one's opinions, without prejudice to the punishment of offences committed when use is made of this freedom.

The investigative powers of the Public Prosecution Department and investigating judges allow them to seize property such as computer equipment and documents, which may subsequently be confiscated by the courts - for example, property that is the object of an offence, has served or is intended to serve to commit an offence or has been produced as a result of the offence. They may also seize property that may serve to elicit the truth. When computerised data are seized, if the data constituting the object or product of the offence are contrary to public policy, the Public Prosecutor is required to use all appropriate technical means to prevent access to the contentious data.

With regard, more particularly, to blocking access to websites, several situations may arise:
- if the website is hosted in Belgium, it is possible to take action on its content directly, on the basis of a court decision or request from the FCCU (Federal Computer Crime Unit of the Federal Police). When illicit content is found, the ISPA (Internet Service Providers' Association) may act as a "contact point" for the purpose of restricting or blocking access to the contentious website.
- If the website is hosted in an EU member state, the Directive on Electronic Commerce applies. It is the "Mediation and Supervision"

Directorate General of the Federal Department of Economic Affairs that is responsible for calling for action by the member state concerned.
-   If the website is hosted in another country, it is the legislation of the country concerned that applies, and everything depends on the co-operation agreements that Belgium has signed with that country.

5.   What are the existing national practices in the field of interception of, or infiltration to, the electronic correspondence (e.g. e-mail, forum, instantaneous message service, voice over IP-skype, etc).

The interception of electronic correspondence is covered by Articles 90ter et seq. of the Criminal Investigation Code.

As regards infiltration, it is necessary to observe the rules introduced by the Special Research Methods Act, and more specifically Articles 47octies and 47nonies of the Criminal Investigation Code.

6.   Does your national legislation provide criteria for establishing jurisdiction over the misuse of cyberspace for terrorist purposes? What are those criteria?

The general rules in the introduction to the Code of Criminal Procedure apply, and there are therefore no specific criteria concerning the misuse of cyberspace for terrorist purposes.

The relevant articles are as follows:
Article 6.1ter provides that *any Belgian or other person whose main residence is on Belgian territory who is guilty, outside the territory of the Kingdom, of a terrorist offence provided for in Book II, Part Iter, of the Criminal Code may be prosecuted in Belgium.*

The general rule is set forth in Article 7: *Any Belgian or other person whose main residence is on Belgian territory who is guilty, outside the territory of the Kingdom, of an offence under Belgian law may be prosecuted in Belgium if the offence is punishable under the law of the country in which it was committed.*

If the offence was perpetrated against a foreigner, prosecution may take place only with a writ of execution from the Public Prosecutor's Office and subsequent to a complaint by the injured party or his or her family or official notice to the Belgian authorities from the authorities of the country in which the offence was committed.

Lastly, Article 10.6 provides for a form of extra-territorial jurisdiction in respect of foreigners who have committed, outside the territory of the Kingdom, an offence covered by Article 2 of the European Convention on the Suppression of Terrorism, signed in Strasbourg on 27 January 1977, where the offence has been committed on the territory of a State Party to the

Convention, if the presumed perpetrator is on Belgian territory and the Belgian Government has refused to extradite the foreigner to that State for one of the reasons mentioned in Article 2 or Article 5 of the above-mentioned convention or Article 11 of the European Convention on Extradition, signed in Paris on 13 December 1957, or because extradition is likely to have exceptionally serious consequences for the person in question, particularly on account of his or her age or state of health.

7. Does your national legal system establish additional offences related to attempts at, or complicity in, the commission of the misuse of cyberspace for terrorist purposes (ancillary offences)?

Yes. As regards attempts, the relevant articles provide that attempts to commit certain offences provided for in the articles in question are punishable.

Under Article 550bis, §4, attempts to commit one of the offences provided for in §§ 1 and 2 carry the same penalties.

Under Article 550ter, §6, attempts to commit one of the offences provided for in §1 carry the same penalties.

As regards complicity, the general rules in Book1 of the Criminal Code (Articles 66-69) apply. These articles read as follows:

Article 66

The following shall be punished as perpetrators of an offence:
Persons who carried out the offence or directly co-operated in its commission;
Persons who in any way provided assistance with the commission of the offence such that it could not have been committed without their help;
Persons who, through gifts, promises, threats, misuse of authority, conspiracy or reprehensible procedures, directly incited the commission of the offence;
Persons who, either through speeches made at meetings or in public places or through written material, printed matter, images or emblems of any kind that were put up, distributed or sold, offered for sale or put on public display, directly incited the commission of the offence, without prejudice to the statutory penalties applicable to persons guilty of incitement to commit offences, even where such incitement had no effect.

Article 67

The following shall be punished as accessories to an offence:
Persons who gave instructions to commit it;

Persons who procured weapons, instruments or any other means used to commit the offence in the knowledge that they were to be used for that purpose;

Persons who, except in the case provided for in Article 66, §3, knowingly aided or abetted the perpetrator(s) of the offence in their preparations or efforts to facilitate the commission of the offence or in its commission.

Article 68

Persons who, being aware of the criminal conduct of criminals engaging in armed robbery or violent offences against State security, law and order, persons or property, regularly provided them with accommodation, hideouts or meeting places, shall be punished as accessories.

Article 69

Accessories to an offence shall be punished by the sentence immediately below that which they would have incurred if they had been the perpetrators of the offence, in accordance with Articles 80 and 81 of this Code.

The sentence handed down to accessories to an offence shall not exceed two-thirds of that which would have been applied to them if they had been the perpetrators of the offence.

8. **What kind of national procedures do you have for submitting an application on the activities of Internet-providers and/or hosting companies or other entities, to deprive a user from a domain name or to cancel his/her/its registration or licence?**

A Co-operation Protocol designed to combat cybercrime was signed by the Federal Government (the Ministers for Justice and Telecommunications) and the ISPA (Internet Service Providers' Association) on 28 May 1999. The Protocol is available on the ISPA website: www.ispa.be. It covers only the monitoring of the provision of public information via the Internet (and not private communications such as e-mail, chat lines and restricted-access websites). Co-operation has been established with the judicial authorities via a central judicial contact point, which is responsible for checking whether suspect content (which may be reported either by an Internet Service Provider or by a user) is in fact illegal. The ISPA undertakes to abide by instructions issued by this judicial contact point (as to whether or not to block access to the illicit content, etc).

9. **What non-legislative measures do you have in your country to prevent and counter terrorist misuse of cyberspace, including self-regulatory measures?**

A Federal Government contact point has been set up to combat misuse of the Internet (including the misuse of cyberspace for terrorist purposes, but not only that). Anyone may report offences committed on or via the Internet on the following website www.ecops.be.

C. International co-operation

10. **Please describe your country's general framework for international co-operation regarding the misuse of cyberspace for terrorist purposes.**

As part of its efforts to prevent the misuse of cyberspace for terrorist purposes, Belgium is actively involved in the European Union "Check the Web" scheme, which is designed to improve co-operation and the exchange of Internet surveillance information.

11. **What are the existing practices and experiences with regard to international co-operation, in particular in relation to the procedures described in question 4?**

International co-operation in connection with efforts to combat cybercrime and terrorism takes place through the "classic" channels: via Interpol, Europol and Eurojust and by means of the various multilateral and bilateral mutual assistance and extradition agreements to which Belgium is party.

D. Institutional framework

12. **Please list the institutions that are competent for countering terrorist misuse of cyberspace.**

As a general rule, the following institutions play a role in countering terrorist misuse of cyberspace:
–   the Central Terrorism Department of the Federal Police;
–   the Federal Computer Crime Unit (FCCU) of the Federal Police;
–   the State Security Department;
–   the General Intelligence and Security Department;
–   the co-ordinating body responsible for analysing the threat (OCAM);
–   the Federal Prosecution Department.

13. **In order to counter terrorist misuse of cyberspace are there any partnerships between the public and private sectors or legal obligations for operators of electronic communication (Internet-service providers, hosting companies, etc.) as well as persons providing the public with access to systems which allow on-line communication via access to the network (cybercafe, WiFi hotspot)?**

See the reply to question 8.

14. **Are there any hotlines regulated by the public or private sectors permitting denouncement of those websites which could be of a terrorist character / nature?**

See the reply to question 9. There is no hotline, but there is a public sector website: www.ecops.be

E. **Statistical information**

15. **Please provide relevant statistics on offences relating to the misuse of cyberspace for terrorist purposes (including possibly: cases recorded, investigated, brought to court, convictions, victims etc.).**

No statistics for offences relating to the misuse of cyberspace can be provided because it is very difficult to distinguish between the misuse of cyberspace for terrorist purposes, terrorist offences and cybercrime offences.

16. **Where possible, please describe briefly the profile of offenders typically involved in the misuse of cyberspace for terrorist purposes (professional background, gender, age, nationality), and possible typical organisational characteristics, including trans-national links and links to other forms of organised crime.**

Belgium does not have a profile of offenders typically involved in the misuse of cyberspace for terrorist purposes.

Bosnia and Herzegovina[1]

A. National policy

1. Is there a national policy regarding the analysis, detection, prosecution and prevention of cybercrime in general and the misuse of cyberspace for terrorist purposes in particular? If yes, please briefly describe it.

National policy regarding the analysis, detection, prosecution and prevention of cybercrime is regulated by the Bosnia and Herzegovina (BiH) Strategy for Combating Organised Crime and Corruption (adopted by the BiH Council of Ministers in June 2006.) which is based on the Council of Europe Convention on Cybercrime, signed on 9 February 2005 and ratified on 19 May 2006. The Criminal Codes (of the Federation of Bosnia and Herzegovina (FbiH), Republika Srpska (RS), and Brcko District (BD)) criminalise offences against electronic data processing systems (computer and network systems).

B. Legal framework

2. Does your national legislation criminalise the misuse of cyberspace for terrorist purposes, and
a. are these offences specifically defined with regard to the terrorist nature or technical means of committing the crime, or
b. is the misuse covered by other, non-specific criminal offences? How are these offences defined and which sanctions (criminal, administrative, civil) are attached?

BiH legislation does not specifically define cyberterrorism offences. The misuse of cyberspace is covered by the criminal offences against electronic data processing systems.

3. Do you plan to introduce new legislation to counter terrorist misuse of cyberspace? What are the basic concepts on these legislative initiatives?

BiH will take into consideration the criminalisation of the misuse of cyberspace offence for terrorist purposes within the scheduled process for the amendment of the Criminal Code. However, at previous consultations at expert level, the opinion prevailed that any amendment in this sense would not be necessary. Nevertheless, steps are to be taken in order to harmonise the Criminal Codes of the entities (CCFBiH, CCRS, and CCBDBiH) and to fully implement the Cybercrime Convention.

---

[1] See also Bosnia and Herzegovina's Country profile on counter-terrorist capacity, criminal codes and criminal procedure codes (of BiH, FBiH, RS, BDBiH) at http://www.coe.int/gmt.

4. **What are the existing national practices in the field of detecting, monitoring and closing down websites used for terrorist purposes?**

So far there have not been any cases involving the misuse of cyberspace for terrorist purposes.

Generally, websites can be closed down and offenders prosecuted. Websites are closed down pursuant to the BiH Law on Communications, its by-laws and other relevant regulations.

5. **Does your national legislation provide criteria for establishing jurisdiction over such offences? What are those criteria?**

The criteria for establishing jurisdiction are the same as for any other criminal offence (see BiH Country Profile and attached Crime and Criminal Procedure Codes).

6. **Does your national legal system establish ancillary offences related to the misuse of cyberspace?**

There are general provisions in the Criminal Code that criminalise ancillary activities. The above-mentioned provisions can also be applied in cases involving the misuse of cyberspace (see BiH CT Profile).

7. **What kind of national procedures do you have for submitting an application on the activities of Internet-providers and/or hosting companies, to deprive a user from a domain name or to cancel his/her/its registration license?**

The regulations on the requirements for holders of .ba domain names (the national domain) also set out control mechanisms. BiH Communications Regulatory Agency has jurisdiction over the above-mentioned issues.

8. **What non-legislative measures do you have in your country to prevent and counter terrorist misuse of cyberspace, including self-regulatory measures?**

-

C. **International co-operation**

9. **Please describe the general framework for international co-operation regarding the misuse of cyberspace for terrorist purposes.**

The legal framework for international co-operation regarding the misuse of cyberspace for terrorist purposes is the same as for all other criminal offences and is regulated by the Criminal Procedure Code, as well as by the bilateral and multilateral agreements which BiH has concluded with other states.

10. What are the existing practices and experiences with regard to international co-operation, in particular in relation to the procedures described in question 4?

So far, there are no existing practices or experiences with regard to international co-operation in the field of the misuse of cyberspace for terrorist purposes.

D. Institutional framework

11. Please list the institutions that are competent for countering terrorist misuse of cyberspace.

The Prosecutor's Office, Ministry of Security of BiH, BiH Intelligence Agency, Ministries of the Interior of FBiH, RS and the Police of Brcko District, BiH Communications Regulatory Agency.

12. Are there any partnerships between the public and private sectors (Internet-service providers, hosting companies, etc.) to counter terrorist misuse of cyberspace?

There are agreements, contracts and licences between the public sector (BiH authorities) and the private sector (Internet service providers), for example: licences for Internet service providers, which are based on the BiH Law on Communications, are issued by the BiH Communications Regulatory Agency. These documents regulate, *inter alia*, the measures to be taken in the case of the misuse of cyberspace.

E. Statistical information

13. Please provide relevant statistics on offences relating to the misuse of cyberspace for terrorist purposes (including possibly: cases recorded, investigated, brought to court, convictions, victims etc).

and

14. Where possible, please describe briefly the profile of offenders typically involved in the misuse of cyberspace for terrorist purposes (professional background, gender, age nationality), and possible typical organisational characteristics, including transnational links and links to other forms of organised crime.

Since there are no officially recorded cases of terrorist misuse of the Internet in BiH, no statistics or offender profiles are available at the moment.

Croatia

A. National policy

1. Is there a national policy regarding the analysis, detection, prosecution and prevention of cybercrime in general and the misuse of cyberspace for terrorist purposes in particular? If yes, please briefly describe it.

The possible misuse of the Internet for terrorist purposes is a topic that will be covered in more detail in the National Strategy for Suppression of Terrorism which is expected to be adopted in the near future. Various acts of terrorism are proscribed within the Croatian Penal Code, as has already been stated in Croatia's Country Profile.[1]

B. Legal framework

2. Does your national legislation criminalise the misuse of cyberspace for terrorist purposes, and
a. are these offences specifically defined with regard to the terrorist nature or technical means of committing the crime, or
b. is the misuse covered by other, non-specific criminal offences?
How are these offences defined and which sanctions (criminal, administrative, civil) are attached?

Croatian legislation has no specifically defined cyberterrorism offences. Moreover, the means used to commit terrorist acts or terrorism-related actions, including possible misuse of the Internet or computer systems, are not influential in the prosecution of criminal offences related to terrorism.

3. Do you plan to introduce new legislation to counter terrorist misuse of cyberspace? What are the basic concepts of these legislative initiatives?

The planned drafting of amendments to the Penal Code may take into consideration this specific phenomenon.

4. What are the existing national practices in the field of detecting, monitoring and closing down websites used for terrorist purposes?

There are no existing national practices in this field since thus far there is no record of a concrete case of a website supporting terrorism appearing on the Internet in Croatia. However, tools and mechanisms for blocking such sites and/or providing additional surveillance of Internet users who visit suspected websites are already in place and can be used after obtaining a warrant from the competent court.

---

[1] Country profiles are available at www.coe.int/gmt.

5. Does your national legislation provide criteria for establishing jurisdiction over such offences? What are those criteria?

As in the answer to question 2, the relevant part of Croatia's national legislation is available in its Country Profile (under the chapter on Jurisdiction and Criminal Proceedings).

6. Does your national legal system establish ancillary offences related to the misuse of cyberspace?

All of the offences proscribed in the Cybercrime Convention (to which Croatia is a State Party and which has been in force in Croatia since 1 July 2004), with the exception of offences that can generally be described as cyberterrorism, are incorporated into the domestic legal framework.

7. What kind of national procedures do you have for submitting an application on the activities of Internet-providers and/or hosting companies, to deprive a user from a domain name or to cancel his/her/its registration or licence?

To obtain information on a website user/owner and his/her IP address from Internet providers and/or hosting companies, the only requirement is an official request by the Ministry of the Interior (a court order is not necessary).

8. What non-legislative measures do your have in your country to prevent and counter terrorist misuse of cyberspace, including self-regulatory measures?

-

C. International co-operation

9. Please describe the general framework for international co-operation regarding the misuse of cyberspace for terrorist purposes.

International co-operation, at police level, is efficiently conducted within the framework of Interpol and Europol and on the basis of signed bilateral agreements. Moreover, mutual legal co-operation is under the competence of the Ministry of Justice and is covered by the international legal instruments to which the Republic of Croatia is a State Party and through domestic legislation – the Penal Code, the Criminal Procedures Act and, most notably, the Act on International Legal Assistance in Criminal Matters.

10. What are the existing practices and experiences with regard to international co-operation, in particular in relation to the procedures described in question 4?

There are no official records of such co-operation.

D. Institutional framework

11. Please list the institutions that are competent for countering terrorist misuse of cyberspace.

The Ministry of the Interior of the Republic of Croatia.

12. Are there any partnerships between the public and private sectors (Internet-service providers, hosting companies, etc.) to counter terrorist misuse of cyberspace?

With regard to preventing misuse of the Internet, the competent Croatian authorities find there is an excellent working relationship with the Internet providers and hosting companies, as well as with other civilian Internet users, in mutual exchanges of information on illegal use of Internet. There is nothing to suggest that there would not be the same excellent co-operation if a case of cyberterrorism was uncovered.

E. Statistical information

13. Please provide relevant statistics on offences relating to the misuse of cyberspace for terrorist purposes (including possibly: cases recorded, investigated, brought to court, convictions, victims etc.).

-

14. Where possible, please describe briefly the profile of offenders typically involved in the misuse of cyberspace for terrorist purposes (professional background, gender, age, nationality), and possible typical organisational characteristics, including trans-national links and links to other forms of organised crime.

Since no cases of terrorist misuse of the Internet have been officially recorded in the Republic of Croatia, no statistics or offenders' profiles are available at this moment.

Cyprus

A. National policy

1. **Is there a national policy regarding the analysis, detection, prosecution and prevention of cybercrime in general and the misuse of cyberspace for terrorist purposes in particular? If yes, please briefly describe it.**

Currently there is no legislation in force which directly addresses the issue of the misuse of cyberspace for terrorist purposes in particular. However the new antiterrorism law, which is currently awaiting ratification by Cyprus' Parliament, contains a provision which criminalises the incitement of terrorism including attempts at or complicity in the commission of the misuse of cyberspace for terrorist purposes. A special task force is under establishment at Cyprus' Police Headquarters, the members of which are being specially trained for the purpose of detecting and combating child pornography and paedophiles who use the Internet as a tool for committing these crimes. This same task force will also have powers of investigation with respect to cases involving cyberterrorism.

B. Legal framework

2. **Does your national legislation criminalise the misuse of cyberspace for terrorist purposes, and**
    a. are these offences specifically defined with regard to the terrorist nature or technical means of committing the crime, or
    b. is the misuse covered by other, non specific criminal offences? How are these offences defined and which sanctions (criminal, administrative, civil) are attached?

See the answer to question 1.

3. **Do you plan to introduce new legislation to counter terrorist misuse of cyberspace? What are the basic concepts of these legislative initiatives?**

See the answer to question 1.

4. **What are the existing national practices in the field of detecting, monitoring and closing down websites used for illicit, in particular, terrorist purposes and what kind of national procedures allow the blocking of access to websites or pages considered illicit?**

Such practices and procedures have not yet been defined.

5. **What are the existing national practices in the field of interception of, or infiltration to, the electronic correspondence (e.g. e-mail, forum, instantaneous message service, voice over IP-skype,etc).**

The interception of telecommunications or telephone tapping and therefore the surveillance of the Internet, is not permitted in Cyprus, according to Cyprus' Constitution except in very restricted circumstances, provided by Article 17 and the Law Providing for the Protection of the Secrecy of Private Communications (Interception of Communications) Law 92 (1) / 96. Interception is permitted only in cases of convicted prisoners and/or accused persons held in custody or where the communication is conducted by unlawful means and after a court order.

6. **Does your national legislation provide criteria for establishing jurisdiction over the misuse of cyberspace for terrorist purposes? What are those criteria?**

Currently there is no legislation in place. However, once the antiterrorism law comes into force (which criminalises cyberterrorism), then according to the Criminal Code, Cyprus' courts will have jurisdiction to try cybercrime offences committed on the territory of the Republic or in any foreign territory where the offence is committed by a citizen of the Republic of Cyprus subject to the condition that the offence is punishable by imprisonment which exceeds two years and that the offence is also considered as a criminal offence in the territory where it was committed.

7. **Does your national legal system establish additional offences related to attempts at, or complicity in, the commission of the misuse of cyberspace for terrorist purposes (ancillary offences)?**

Once the new anti-terrorism law comes into force, a new criminal offence of cyberterrorism will be created and will criminalise as offences attempts to commit an offence and complicity in the commission of an offence. Therefore attempts at or the commission of the misuse of cyberspace for terrorist purposes will be established as additional offences.

8. **What kind of national procedures do you have for submitting an application on the activities of Internet-providers and/or hosting companies or other entities, to deprive a user from a domain name or to cancel his/her/its registration or licence?**

There is no defined procedure. However there is a procedure for notifying an Internet provider to remove a webpage if it is illicit.

9. **What non legislative measures do you have in your country to prevent and counter terrorist misuse of cyberspace, including self-regulatory measures?**

The Counter-Terrorism Office co-operates closely with the other agencies and ministries, as well as with other member states, Europol and Interpol, in order to prevent and counter the terrorist misuse of cyberspace.

C. **International co-operation**

10. **Please describe your country's general framework for international co-operation regarding the misuse of cyberspace for terrorist purposes.**

The Counter-Terrorism Office co-operates closely with Europol, Interpol and other EU institutions towards this objective.

11. **What are the existing practices and experiences with regard to international co-operation, in particular in relation to the procedures described in question 4?**

The competent agencies and ministries are in contact with the relevant institutions and organisations in order to establish these procedures.

D. **Institutional framework**

12. **Please list the institutions that are competent for countering terrorist misuse of cyberspace.**

In the Republic of Cyprus there is no institution competent for countering terrorist misuse of cyberspace yet, but it is being established.

13. **In order to counter terrorist misuse of cyberspace are there any partnerships between the public and private sectors or legal obligations for operators of electronic communication (Internet-service providers, hosting companies, etc.) as well as persons providing the public with access to systems which allow on-line communication via access to the network (cyber café, WiFi hotspot)?**

There are partnerships between the public and private sectors only to the extent that this does not violate Personal Data Processing Law 138 (I)2001. Furthermore there are persons providing the public with access to systems which allow on-line communication via access to the network, though their functions are not covered by the existing legislation.

14. **Are there any hotlines regulated by the public or private sectors permitting denouncement of those websites which could be of a terrorist character/nature?**

No hotlines exist for this specific purpose (permitting denouncement of those websites which could be of a terrorist character/nature). However there is a general hotline: Cyberethics-Cyprus Safer Internet Awareness Node.

E.   Statistical information

15. **Please provide relevant statistics on offences relating to the misuse of cyberspace for terrorist purposes (including possibly: cases recorded, investigated, brought to court, convictions, victims etc.)**

In the Republic of Cyprus no offences related to the misuse of cyberspace for terrorist purposes have been observed.

16. **Where possible, please describe briefly the profile of offenders typically involved in the misuse of cyberspace for terrorist purposes (professional background, gender, age, nationality), and possible typical organisational characteristics, including transnational links and links to other forms of organised crime.**

Since no offences related to the misuse of cyberspace for terrorist purposes have been observed in the Republic of Cyprus, there is no profile of such offenders.

Czech Republic

A.   National policy

1.   Is there a national policy regarding the analysis, detection, prosecution and prevention of cybercrime in general and the misuse of cyberspace for terrorist purposes in particular? If yes, please briefly describe it.

The Government of the Czech Republic, with the aim of maximising the potential of the modern information and communication technologies, decided to find a new definition of its objectives in the area of the so-called information society and in the area of telecommunications - and to formulate a new state strategy for the future.

Contrary to the previous approach, where the two concepts were elaborated separately (see the documents "State Information Policy: Toward Information Society" and "National Telecommunication Policy"), the Government decided to respect their close interconnection and the general trend towards the convergence of both areas, and to create one common strategic document, entitled "State Information and Communication Policy: e-Czech Republic 2006". The name of the document itself also reflects the transformation of the former *telecommunications* branch into the *electronic communications* branch.

The four main areas of the activity of the Government of the Czech Republic were set out:
–   available and secure communication services;
–   information education;
–   modern public services on-line;
–   dynamic environment for the electronic enterprises.

With the goal of strengthening information security in the sphere of the communication and information infrastructure of the Czech Republic and in compliance with Section 4 (1b) of Act No. 365/2000 Coll., on public administration information systems, strategic documents were drafted in the sphere of the protection of public administration information systems of the Czech Republic, explicitly mentioning also the possible threat of a terrorist attack. These are in particular:

–   "National Strategy of Information Security of the Czech Republic", which sets tasks in the sphere of building trustworthy information and communication systems in the setting of the Czech Republic.
–   "Concept of Transfer of Classified Information by the Czech Republic's Public Administration Communication Infrastructure" which responds to the constantly increasing requirements for transfer of certain, especially classified, information determined by legal regulations. The document proposes a solution via the integration of the information systems into a universally usable secure public administration communication system

> providing access to the networks of other countries of the European Union.

- "Proposed Protection Levels for the Information Systems Necessary for the Functioning of the Critical Infrastructure of the Czech Republic".
- Amendment to Act No. 101/2000 Coll., on personal data protection and on changing some laws, as amended by later regulations (439/2004 Coll.), Section 13 (2), which says that the administrator or processor is obliged to process and document the adopted and realised technical and organisational measures for ensuring personal data protection in compliance with the law and other legal regulations.
- "Updated Strategy for Combating Organised Crime", elaborated by the Ministry of the Interior and approved by a resolution of the Government of the Czech Republic of 23 October 2000 No. 1044.
- "Strategy of the Fight against Information Technology Crime", subsequently elaborated by the Ministry of the Interior and approved by the Minister of the Interior on 5 June 2001. This document is based on the outcome of police work in this area.

Both qualitative and quantitative analyses of these forms of crime indicate their apparent dangerous character for society, as there is not only a danger of material damage in individual cases, but also the danger of consequences in the form of a threat to the unstable and uncontrolled environment of the information and communication dimension of society, which could lead to the development of modern society being hindered. Since information and communication technologies are increasingly being interlocked with individual areas of human activities, insecurity in these structures could lead to the social and economic system itself being destabilised.

The Strategy also represents a reaction to the task set out for the Minister of the Interior in the Updated Strategy of Combating Organised Crime approved by the Government of the Czech Republic in October 2000. The Minister of the Interior was charged (on the basis of the Schedule of Measures forming the annex to the relevant Government Resolution) "to continuously and in a strategic way address combating organised crime activities in the area of information technologies." The Strategy presented here is, however, of a more complex nature because information technology-related crime is not limited to organised crime activities.

The key starting point of the strategy is the opinion that the approach of the Government to this type of criminality should be: systematic; balanced in putting differentiated emphasis on each aspect of such crimes according to their danger to society; diversified in a desirable way amongst the ministries and within the ministries; and, at the same time, coordinated through intensive co-operation between all the departments of the state bodies involved and through the Government co-operating with non-governmental organisations and with foreign countries.

The most important objectives of the above-mentioned document are:

– To ensure conditions for the further development of the structures directly engaged in the detection of computer crime (high-tech crime), including material and personal development of specialised police units.

– To increase and support co-operation between the law enforcement agencies, intelligence services and NGOs involved in the fight against various aspects of computer crime (high-tech crime).

– To elaborate principles for the protection of state, and some strategically important non-state, information systems.

– To elaborate a project for an alert system in the area of computer crime (high-tech crime).

– To elaborate a project in the area of educating the personnel of law enforcement bodies, with special regard to the clarification of criminal activity in the area of computer crime (high-tech crime).

– To develop and to set up forensic standards for seeking and verifying electronic data during criminal investigations and criminal procedures.

– To support independent research, public relations and statistics activities in the area of the fight against computer crime (high-tech crime).

– To promote public awareness campaigns, focused on recommended behaviour in cyberspace.

– To monitor the respective activities of the international platforms in the area of the fight against computer crime (high-tech crime). To participate in the relevant conferences and workshops.

This agenda must be understood as being interconnected with other parallel intra-community activities in order to ensure appropriate relations between the personal and technical capacities concerned. This especially applies to activities within the framework of the Security Research of the Ministry of the Interior for the years 2007-2010.

B. Legal framework

2. Does your national legislation criminalise the misuse of cyberspace for terrorist purposes, and
a. are these offences specifically defined with regard to the terrorist nature or technical means of committing the crime, or
b. is the misuse covered by other, non-specific criminal offences? How are these offences defined and which sanctions (criminal, administrative, civil) are attached?

In the Czech Republic, the respective acts are punishable as criminal offences within the framework of criminal law according to Act No. 140/1961 Coll., Criminal Code (hereinafter "Criminal Code").

The Criminal Code contains the constituent elements of a terrorist attack through which the implementation of the Framework Decision on combating terrorism was ensured. In the view of the Czech Republic, the described examples of behaviour might be prosecuted on the basis of this section. The constituent elements apply not only to a person committing an actual terrorist act, but also to a person who threatens to commit a terrorist act or who provides financial, material or other support (i.e. propagation, approval of or *apologie* of terrorist acts) to such an act. Imprisonment of five to fifteen years (under specific circumstances, even the exceptional sanction of life imprisonment) and, eventually, the forfeiture of property may also be imposed for these acts.

Furthermore, the Criminal Code contains provisions concerning public provocation to commit a crime and approving a crime. However, these crimes are of a general nature - they refer to all types of criminal behaviour, not only to terrorist offences.

Under Section 164 of the Criminal Code providing for the crime of instigation, anyone who publicly incites other persons to commit a crime or not to fulfil *en masse* an important duty imposed by law, shall be sentenced to imprisonment for a term of up to two years. This crime may be committed orally, in writing or in any other way possible.

Under Section 165 providing for the crime of approving of a crime, anyone who publicly approves a crime or publicly praises the perpetrator of a crime shall be sentenced to imprisonment for a term of up to one year.

Furthermore, if the above-mentioned examples of conduct are intended to support racially- or ethnically-motivated terrorism, they may be punished as the crime of incitement of national and racial hatred (Section 198a of the Criminal Code). The constituent elements consist in a person publicly inciting hatred of another nation or race or calling for the restriction of the rights and freedoms of other nationals or members of a particular race and may be punished.

At constitutional level, freedom of expression is provided for in Article 17 of the Charter of Fundamental Rights and Freedoms of the Czech Republic. According to its paragraph 4, it is possible to limit the freedom of expression and the right to information by a law adopted by Parliament, if it is necessary in a democratic society for the protection of the rights and freedoms of others, state security, public security or the protection of public health and morals.

As far as the legislative process is concerned, no serious problems were encountered as regards the adoption of anti-terrorism legislation with respect to the freedom of expression in the Czech Republic.[1]

---

[1] Following 11 September 2001, several cases of the *apologie* of terrorism (verbal, printed or posted on the Internet) have been recorded, usually associated with extremist groups (extreme left/right wing groups and fundamentalists). Some of these incidents have been examined by the authorities to determine whether a crime has been committed under Section 164 of the Criminal Code (incitement) or

It has been possible to prosecute all the relevant cases (except cases involving the distribution of bomb- or explosives-making expertise) as criminal offences. Since there are no doubts that this is a criminal offence, the police have not registered any serious problems (except for lengthy procedures) with the prosecution of suspected criminals who are considered to have committed their crimes in the Czech Republic.

The Criminal Code does not provide specific regulations covering the transmission of bomb- or explosives-making expertise, preparation of attacks, hostage-taking or other actions related to the commission of a terrorist offence. However, such conduct may be punished according to its general provisions, namely the provisions on participation in a crime might be used in this relation. Section 10 of the Criminal Code provides that a participant in a completed crime or an attempted crime is a person who intentionally organises or directs the commission of a crime (the organiser), instigated another person to commit a crime (the instigator) or grants another person assistance in committing a crime, particularly by providing the means for committing such crime, removing obstacles, giving advice, strengthening the person's intent, or promising assistance after the commission of the crime (an assistant). The criminal liability and liability to punishment of a participant are governed by the provisions on the offender's criminal liability and liability to punishment, unless the Criminal Code provides otherwise.

Furthermore, the outlined behaviour could be considered as preparation of a crime under Section 7 of the Criminal Code. This section provides that conduct which threatens society and which consists in the organising of an especially serious crime (indeed, this category covers terrorist offences), the acquisition or adaptation of means or tools for the purpose of committing a crime or associating, assembling, instigating or giving assistance for such purpose, or other intentional creation of conditions for the commission of a crime shall be considered as preparation of a crime, even if such a crime is not attempted or committed. Preparation of a crime is punishable within the sentencing guidelines for the crime which was prepared unless the Special Part of the Criminal Code provides otherwise.

Section 165 (advocating a crime). However, nobody has been convicted of a terrorism-related crime.

The Police of the Czech Republic often face problems when the authorities are unable to prosecute activities that are considered as being dangerous to society (for example cases involving terrorist attacks being described "in a positive way") but these activities are difficult to prosecute as a criminal offence. The authors of such texts usually "react" to an official article concerning a particular terrorist attack. Their "comments" are published on "problematic" webpages. The comments are written in a sophisticated way, so the authorities are unable to prosecute these activities as a criminal offence. Theoretically, these activities could be prosecuted as minor offences, but in reality it is not possible because in such cases the police are not entitled to obtain the relevant telecommunications data.

The police monitor web pages and other sources which provide readers with such information or expertise. However providing information and expertise on explosives-making is not defined as a criminal offence.

3. Do you plan to introduce new legislation to counter terrorist misuse of cyberspace? What are the basic concepts of these legislative initiatives?

The legislative and other measures adopted by other countries against religiously-motivated hate crime are constantly monitored by the authorities. Especially the possibility of a more precise qualification of the activity, that could be considered as verbal approval of a terrorist attack, promotion of terrorism and incitement to terrorism, is being analysed.

The Czech Republic considers the above-mentioned legal regulation on the penalties for the propagation, *apologie* and glorification of terrorist attacks to be sufficient and there are currently no plans to amend this regulation.

With respect to the above, the Czech Republic holds the view that the current legislation is sufficient and no further specific legislation is required.

However, some *lacunae* may be identified as an outcome of the Security Research of the Ministry of the Interior for the years 2007-2010.

4. What are the existing national practices in the field of detecting, monitoring and closing down websites used for terrorist purposes?

– Act No. 365/2000 Coll., information systems of the public administration, stipulates the conditions and limits of the transmission of data within the public administration. This Act does not have a direct impact on the prosecution of possible misuses of information or their dissemination by terrorists via the Internet.
– Act No. 127/2005 Coll., on electronic communications, and amendment of some relevant acts, stipulates new conditions for access to commercial services via electronic communications. This act does not stipulate the responsibility of the subject who provides the service for the content of the information transmitted.
– The limitation of access to the public electronic communications service is possible only on the grounds of a special act (Act. No. 241/2000 Coll., economic measures during a crisis situation).

5. Does your national legislation provide criteria for establishing jurisdiction over such offences? What are those criteria?

See the reply to question 4.

6. Does your national legal system establish ancillary offences related to the misuse of cyberspace?

Yes, for example the following sections of the Penal Code:
152: Infringement of copyright;
176: Forgery of official documents;
239: Violation of the privacy of transmitted messages;
250: Fraud;
257: Damaging another's property;
257a: Damaging or misusing data carrier records;
260: Support and propagation of movements aimed at suppressing citizens' rights and freedoms.

7. What kind of national procedures do you have for submitting an application on the activities of Internet-providers and/or hosting companies, to deprive a user from a domain name or to cancel his/her/its registration or licence?

For the purpose of administering the domain *.cz, a Special-Interest Association of Legal Entities, CZ.NIC (http://www.nic.cz/), was established, in accordance with the provisions of Section 20f *et seq.* of the Civil Code by a Foundation Contract dated 21 May 1998. From the Rules for the registration of Domain Names in the *.cz domain:

14. Rights and duties of the cz.nic association

14.1. The CZ.NIC Association undertakes to register a Domain Name under the conditions specified by these Rules and to maintain that registration under the set conditions.

14.2. The CZ.NIC Association undertakes to keep an entry on a registered Domain Name in the Central Register and the CZ Zone under the conditions specified by these Rules.

14.3. The CZ.NIC Association undertakes to develop all possible efforts as may reasonably be required to secure the failure-free and problem-free operation of the Central Register and the primary name server.

14.4. The CZ.NIC Association, based on its decision, is authorised to cancel registration of a Domain Name, providing:
14.4.1. Data kept in connection with a Domain Name in the Central Register is false or misleading;
14.4.2. The facts based on which a Domain Name was registered have changed. For example, the Holder ceased to exist without any legal successor or died without inheritors;
14.4.3. No approval of the Rules of Registration is granted according to the Rules of Registration;

14.4.4. Such a right derives from other provisions of the Rules of Registration.

14.5. The CZ.NIC Association will cancel the Delegation of a Domain Name or registration of a Domain Name if it is requested by an executable judicial verdict or an award of an arbitration court. The CZ.NIC Association will transfer a Domain Name to a third person if it is requested by an executable judicial verdict or an award of an arbitration court.

14.6. The CZ.NIC Association is authorised to take all the measures that will be ordered by a preliminary measure, including limitation of the right to transfer a Domain Name.

14.7. As regards the pursuit of the CZ.NIC Association according to items 14.5 and/or 14.6, the CZ.NIC Association is not obligated to return any previously paid amounts.

15. Damage liability

15.1. The Holder acknowledges that a Domain Name, its registration, or its use may infringe on third persons´ rights to other Domain Names, trade marks, brand names, names, business companies or legal regulations concerning unfair competition, protection of personality, etc. By filing an application for registration of a Domain Name, the Holder confirms that they are aware of the potential infringement on the specified rights and legal regulations and he/she has developed all the possible efforts that may reasonably be required from him/her to make sure that his/her registered Domain Name does not infringe on those rights and legal regulations.

15.2. The Holder is liable for damages caused to the CZ.NIC Association by providing the CZ.NIC Association with wrong or misleading data or by using his/her Domain Name in a way that contravenes the Rules of Registration or infringes on third persons´ rights.

15.3. The CZ.NIC Association does not check the correctness of an application for registration of a Domain Name in terms of rights or rightful interests of third persons.

15.4. The Holder acknowledges that registration of a Domain Name does not constitute protection from third parties' objections against registration or using a given Domain Name.

15.5. The CZ.NIC Association is liable neither for using or misusing a registered Domain Name, nor the manner of using a Domain Name. The CZ.NIC Association, therefore, is not liable for infringement on rights to trade marks, brand names, names or business firms of third persons arising from the registration or use of a Domain Name.

15.6. The CZ.NIC Association is not responsible for the functionality of name servers allocated to a Domain Name.

15.7. All the liabilities for all damages caused by the action or inaction of the CZ.NIC Association to the Holder in connection with one Domain Name is limited to an amount of CZK 250,000.

17. Solving disputes

17.1. The Holder is obliged to develop all the possible efforts he/she may reasonably be required to develop to peacefully settle disputes concerning Domain Names or their registrations, which may arise between the Holder and other persons.

17.2. If the parties in dispute do not solve a dispute peacefully, they are completely free to solve their dispute in the framework of valid legal regulations, which is to say, through arbitration or general courts.

17.3. If requested by all the parties in dispute, the CZ.NIC Association will act as a mediator in peacefully solving their dispute.

17.4. If a Holder and the CZ.NIC Association do not settle a mutual dispute concerning a Domain Name, any of the parties may submit the dispute for decision to an arbitrary court of the Economic Chamber of the Czech Republic and the Agrarian Chamber of the Czech Republic. The arbitration will be executed by three arbitrators in Prague, in the Czech language, in accordance with an order of the specified arbitration court. The arbitration award is final and binding for the contracting parties.

8. **What non-legislative measures do your have in your country to prevent and counter terrorist misuse of cyberspace, including self-regulatory measures?**

Some organisational activities are being prepared within the scope of the Security Research of the Ministry of the Interior for the years 2007-2010 (establishing of the CERT.cz, educational campaigns for public officials and the wider public, etc.).

C. International co-operation

9. Please describe the general framework for international co-operation regarding the misuse of cyberspace for terrorist purposes.

The Czech Republic fully supports the idea of better co-operation between Council of Europe member states in the sphere of the fight against cybernetic threats.

The Czech Republic welcomes any activities that would enhance the fight against terrorism. The initiative "Check the Web", kicked-off by the Federal Republic of Germany, is a good example of how to deal with the current problem of the misuse of the Internet by terrorists and how to coordinate and enhance the effectiveness of police work in this area.

The initiative of France to create platforms for reporting the presence of illicit content on the Internet is currently being discussed.

10. What are the existing practices and experiences with regard to international co-operation, in particular in relation to the procedures described in question 4?

According to the Council of Europe Cybercrime Convention, the police of the Czech Republic act as the direct international co-operation contact point. Since November 2004, the criminal police of the Czech Republic also act as the 24/7 contact point for international communication. In the course of 2005, there were 42 urgent cases requiring international co-operation (especially regarding phishing attacks – fake pages or advertisements from banks, etc.).

D. Institutional framework

11. Please list the institutions that are competent for countering terrorist misuse of cyberspace.

During 1999, a specialised group for the fight against computer crime (high-tech crime) was created within the Office of the Service of the Criminal Police of the Police Presidium. This group is now called the "Information Crime Group" ("Skupina informační kriminality", SIK). The activity of the Group is especially focused on:
- detection and clarification of intellectual property crime (with the use of information technologies);
- detection and documentation of computer crime (high-tech crime), and initiation of criminal proceedings in the respective area;
- developing conditions for the police of the Czech Republic to fight these forms of crime;

- co-ordination of the regional units of the Criminal Police and Investigation Service and the provision of methodical support for such units;
- active steps in the area of educational activities for police officers at the regional and district levels and also within the framework of the special units of the police of the Czech Republic;
- co-operation with bodies involved in the fight against computer crime (high-tech crime) outside the Police;
- analysing the reasons and conditions leading to the commission of computer crime (high-tech crime) and submitting proposals for its reduction;
- serving as a national contact point for the computer crime (high-tech crime) agenda.

Between 1996 and 1998, workplaces were established in all of the regional Criminal Police branches for forensic technical expertise. This step was necessary because of the increase in the number of relevant cases, which was interconnected with the ever-increasing occurrence of the criminal misuse of information technologies.

This phenomenon is also investigated by the Police's Unit for Combating Organised Crime.

The Forensic Institute Prague was the first place in the Czech Republic to deal with the agenda of computer crime (high-tech crime) in terms of securing evidence via forensic research. A workplace was established between 1990 and 1993 and was recently transformed into the Computer Expertise Department of the Forensic Institute.

The Police Academy of the Czech Republic is, in the context of its research activity, responsible for dealing with criminological issues in the detection, investigation and prevention of computer crime (high-tech crime). Within the framework of this activity the Police Academy also publishes expert journals and produces research studies related to the issue of computer crime (high-tech crime).

Other institutions worth mentioning in this context are specialised academic and private facilities which provide certain types of "service" or specific know-how to the security community of the Czech Republic (e.g. the activity of court experts). It is important to establish links between all of the respective scientific areas involved in the analysis of cybernetic threats (especially the legal and social science specialists).

12. **Are there any partnerships between the public and private sectors (Internet-service providers, hosting companies, etc.) to counter terrorist misuse of cyberspace?**

It is important to state clearly that the fight against the numerous aspects of the cybernetic threats in the Czech Republic cannot be effectively won without the active participation of high-profile experts from the non-public sphere (especially academic).

A number of the academic and private research facilities already existing in the Czech Republic are engaged in the fight against computer crime (high-tech crime). Co-operation between such platforms with their public counterparts can be helpful for all the parties involved.

Some private and academic bodies are currently involved in research projects co-ordinated by the Ministry of the Interior (for the period 2007-2010). Some other similar projects are currently in progress (or are being prepared) by the police of the Czech Republic and by the intelligence services of the Czech Republic.

The most suitable systematic solution to the current situation in this area could be the establishment of a specialised "Centre for the Fight against Cybernetic Threats". Such a body would gather highly developed technical capacities together with qualified experts from various areas of specialisation (IT studies, sociology, psychology, law studies, forensics, security studies) that relate to the issue of securing the cybernetic security of the State.

Aside from difficulties related to personnel, it is apparent that what is typical for the security community in the Czech Republic is (in most cases) the lack of specialised equipment (specialised and certified software, modern specialised hardware, etc.).

Only a small number of the members of the police (and of the intelligence services) are educated in the area of information and communication technologies in general. However, they can hardly acquire such knowledge, for various reasons (especially because of its specific nature), in an institution that does not fully reflect the needs of law enforcement authorities. Police educational capacities are far from coping with this problem either.

E. **Statistical information**

13. **Please provide relevant statistics on offences relating to the misuse of cyberspace for terrorist purposes (including possibly: cases recorded, investigated, brought to court, convictions, victims etc.).**

No such cases have been reported.

14. Where possible, please describe briefly the profile of offenders typically involved in the misuse of cyberspace for terrorist purposes (professional background, gender, age, nationality), and possible typical organisational characteristics, including transnational links and links to other forms of organised crime.

The Ministry of the Interior is currently studying such topics within the framework of its research project. The results will not be available until the end of 2008.

The current (2007) level of danger in the Czech Republic related to cybercrime can be described in the following way:

- The number of incidents, motivated by an increase in the "prestige" within the community of hackers (for example defacement) is decreasing. Among those on the increase (or which are generally supposed to be) are especially hidden profit-motivated incidents.
- The number of high-tech specialists that are ready to be hired by criminals is also on the increase.
- An increase in the distribution of harmful or illegal content (computer programs, movies, music, prohibited forms of pornography and extremist propaganda) via the Internet has been reported.
- Cases of the misuse of phone lines for the unauthorised re-dialling of Internet end-users are still being recorded.
- An increase has been reported in the misuse of Internet sales.
- There were cases recorded of "sophisticated" misuse of Internet banking.
- One new phenomenon seems to be "phishing" (various forms of unauthorised gathering of sensitive data).
- The number of misused or forged credit cards and cheques, elaborated (originally issued) abroad, is steadily increasing. Also, the so-called "skimming" of credit cards is frequent.

All the above-mentioned activities are of a very latent nature. It is difficult to collect enough evidence to commence a trial in such cases.

Denmark

A. National policy

1. Is there a national policy regarding the analysis, detection, prosecution and prevention of cybercrime in general and the misuse of cyberspace for terrorist purposes in particular? If yes, please briefly describe it.

Though not laid down in a national policy, the distribution of responsibility regarding analysis, detection, prosecution and prevention of the misuse of cyberspace for terrorist purposes in Denmark is clear. The Danish Security and Intelligence Service carries out the analysis, detection and prevention of such crimes. Prosecution remains the responsibility of the Danish Prosecution Service.

Furthermore, close co-operation on data analysis and IP-based investigations has been established between the Danish Security and Intelligence Service and the National High Tech Crime Centre of the Danish National Commissioner of Police on this type of case.

B. Legal framework

2. Does your national legislation criminalise the misuse of cyberspace for terrorist purposes, and
a. are these offences specifically defined with regard to terrorist nature or technical means of committing the crime or
b. is the misuse covered by other, non-specific criminal offences? How are these offences defined and which sanctions (criminal, administrative, civil) are attached?

The Convention on Cybercrime was ratified by Denmark on 21 July 2005 and entered into force on 1 October 2005. The misuse of cyberspace is punishable in accordance with various provisions of the Danish Criminal Code. Some offences are explicitly described as computer-related offences, for instance:

- *Illegal access and illegal interception* (Articles 2 and 3 of the Convention) may give rise to criminal liability pursuant to section 263 (2) of the Danish Criminal Code. According to the said provision, any person who unlawfully obtains access to another person's information system shall be liable to a fine or to imprisonment for a term not exceeding one year and six months. According to section 263 (3), the penalty may be increased to imprisonment for a term not exceeding six years if the act is committed with the intent to procure or make oneself acquainted with information about a firm's trade secrets, in the case of offences of a more systematic or organised nature, or in other particularly aggravating circumstances.
- *Misuse of devices* (Article 6 of the Convention) may be punishable according to section 263 a or 301 a of the Criminal Code. According to

section 263 a, any person who, in an unlawful manner, commercially sells or widely disseminates a password or other means of access to an information system, which is not accessible to the public and to which access is secured by a password or other special access restrictions, shall be liable to a fine or to imprisonment for a term not exceeding one year and six months. According to section 301 a, any person who unlawfully obtains or passes on passwords or other means of access to information systems, to which access is reserved for paying users and secured by a password or other special access restrictions, shall be liable to a fine or to imprisonment for a term not exceeding one year and six months.

– *Computer-related fraud* (Article 8 in the Convention) may be punishable according to section 279 a of the Criminal Code. According to the said provision, any person who for the purpose of obtaining for him/herself or for others an unlawful gain, unlawfully changes, adds or erases information or programs for the use of electronic data processing, or who in any other manner attempts to affect the results of such data processing, shall be guilty of computer fraud. The penalty may be imprisonment for a term not exceeding one year and six months, cf. section 285 (1). If the offence is of a particularly aggravated nature, the penalty may be increased to imprisonment for a term not exceeding eight years, cf. section 286 (2). If the offence is of minor importance the penalty shall be a fine, cf. section 287 (1).

Other types of misuse of cyberspace are covered by non-specific criminal law provisions, for instance:

– *Data interference and system interference* (Articles 4 and 5 of the Convention) may give rise to criminal liability pursuant to section 291 and/or section 293 (2) of the Criminal Code. According to Article 291 (1), any person who destroys, damages or removes objects belonging to others shall be liable to a fine or to imprisonment for a term not exceeding one year and six months. According to section 293 (2), any person who unlawfully prevents any other person completely or in part, from using or disposing of objects shall be liable to a fine or imprisonment for a term not exceeding one year.

– *Computer-related forgery* (Article 7 of the Convention) may be punishable according to section 171 of the Criminal Code. According to the said provision, any person who, with the intent to deceive in any matter involving legal consequences, makes use of a false document shall be guilty of forgery of documents. A document is a written or electronic manifestation bearing the name or the issuer and appearing to be intended to serve as evidence. The penalty may be a fine or imprisonment for a term not exceeding two years. If the offence is of a particularly serious nature, or if a large number of offences have been committed, the penalty may be increased to imprisonment for a term not exceeding six years.

3. **Do you plan to introduce new legislation to counter terrorist misuse of cyberspace? What are the basic concepts of these legislative initiatives?**

The Danish Government does not plan to introduce new legislation to counter terrorist misuse of cyberspace.

4. **What are the existing national practices in the field of detecting, monitoring and closing down websites used for illicit, in particular, terrorist purposes and what kind of national procedures allow the blocking of access to websites or pages considered illicit?**

A project involving the Danish Security and Intelligence Service, the National Commissioner of Police and academia has been launched in order to enhance monitoring of websites in relation to terrorism systematically.

Websites used for illicit terrorist purposes can be closed on the basis of a court order.

5. **What are the existing national practices in the field of interception of, or infiltration to, the electronic correspondence (e.g. e-mail, forum, instantaneous message service, voice over IP-skype, etc).**

The interception of communications by the police is regulated by Part 71 of the Administration of Justice Act.

The first condition for the interception of communications is that there must be certain grounds for assuming that messages to or from a suspect are conveyed by the communication in question.

Secondly, it is a condition for interception of communications that the interference is assumed to be of decisive importance to the investigation.

The third and last condition for interception of communications is a requirement as to the nature of the crime, particularly that the investigation concerns an offence with a maximum penalty exceeding six years or contravention of certain enumerated provisions of the Criminal Code, for example section 263 (2) (*Illegal access and illegal interception*) and Parts 12 and 13 (*Offences against the independence and safety of the State, offences against the Constitution and the supreme authorities of the State, terrorism, etc.*).

Any interception of communications must take place on the basis of a court order.

6. Does your national legislation provide criteria for establishing jurisdiction over the misuse of cyberspace for terrorist purposes? What are those criteria?

According to part 2 of the Criminal Code, acts committed within the territory of the Danish state shall be subject to Danish criminal jurisdiction. Acts committed outside the territory of the Danish state by a Danish national or by a person resident in the Danish state shall be subject to Danish criminal jurisdiction if the act committed is punishable both under Danish law and the law in force in the territory where the act is committed.

Where the punishable nature of an act depends on or is influenced by an actual or intended consequence, the act shall be deemed to have been committed where the consequence has taken effect or was intended to take effect.

Acts committed outside the territory of the Danish state shall also come within Danish criminal jurisdiction irrespective of the nationality of the perpetrator, where the act violates the independence, security, Constitution or public authorities of the Danish state, official duties toward the state or such interests, the legal protection of which depends on a personal connection with the Danish state; or where the act is covered by an international convention in pursuance of which Denmark is under an obligation to start legal proceedings.

7. Does your national legal system establish additional offences related to attempts at, or complicity in, the commission of the misuse of cyberspace for terrorist purposes (ancillary offences)?

Acts which aim at the promotion or accomplishment of an offence shall be punished as an attempt when the offence is not completed, cf. section 21 (1) of the Criminal Code.

The penalty in respect of an offence shall apply to any person who has contributed to the execution of the wrongful act by instigation, advice or action, cf. section 23 (1) of the Criminal Code.

8. What kind of national procedures do you have for submitting an application on the activities of Internet-providers and/or hosting companies or other entities, to deprive a user from a domain name or to cancel his/her/its registration or licence?

DK Hostmaster is the administrator of domain names ending in .dk. The rules for DK Hostmaster's assignment, registration and administration of domain names under the .dk domain are set out in the general conditions for the assignment, registration and administration of domain names under the .dk top level domain.

According to section 8(3)(5) of these conditions a domain name may be suspended or deleted if it is actively being used in connection with manifestly illegal acts or omissions. The provision concerns the content of the website, not the name of it. This provision can be used to suspend, for example, websites which support terrorism.

The domain name can only be suspended for significant safety or social reasons and if these reasons go against letting a suspension or deletion await a decision from the Complaints Board for Domain Names, the court of law or other public authorities.

9. **What non-legislative measures do you have in your country to prevent and counter terrorist misuse of cyberspace, including self-regulatory measures?**

The Danish Security and Intelligence Service has set up a special Centre for Prevention in the Preventive Security Department. This Centre is responsible for the initiation and implementation of a number of specific projects aiming at preventing radicalisation and terrorism. In this respect, several of the projects focus on the role of the Internet.

C. International co-operation

10. **Please describe your country's general framework for international co-operation regarding the misuse of cyberspace for terrorist purposes.**

The Danish Security and Intelligence Service participates in several international working groups regarding the misuse of cyberspace for terrorist purposes.

11. **What are the existing practices and experiences with regard to international co-operation, in particular in relation to the procedures described in question 4?**

The Danish Security and Intelligence Service has had positive experiences with regard to international co-operation regarding terrorist activities involving the use of cyberspace. The international co-operation channels and networks are well established and effective.

D. Institutional framework

12. **Please list the institutions that are competent for countering terrorist misuse of cyberspace.**

The Danish Security and Intelligence Service and the Danish Defence Intelligence Service are responsible for countering terrorist misuse of cyberspace.

13. **In order to counter terrorist misuse of cyberspace are there any partnerships between the public and private sectors or legal obligations for operators of electronic communication (Internet-service providers. hosting companies, etc.) as well as persons providing the public with access to systems which allow on-line communication via access to the network (cybercafe, WiFi hotspot)?**

In 2004, the Danish Security and Intelligence Service set up a contact group on Information security. The contact group has been involved in the work of the Service with respect to general as well as specific threat and risk assessments within IT in relation to terrorism.

14. **Are there any hotlines regulated by the public or private sectors permitting denouncement of those websites which could be of a terrorist character / nature?**

There are no hotlines regulated by the public or private sectors permitting denouncement of those websites which could be of a terrorist character/nature.

E. Statistical information

15. **Please provide relevant statistics on offences relating to the misuse of cyberspace for terrorist purposes (including possibly: cases recorded, investigated, brought to court, convictions, victims etc.).**

There are no statistics on offences relating to the misuse of cyberspace for terrorist purposes available in Denmark.

16. **Where possible, please describe briefly the profile of offenders typically involved in the misuse of cyberspace for terrorist purposes (professional background, gender, age, nationality), and possible typical organisational characteristics, including trans-national links and links to other forms of organised crime.**

On the basis of the available Danish data, it is not possible to describe the typical profile of offenders involved in the misuse of cyberspace for terrorist purposes.

Estonia

A.   National policy

1.   Is there a national policy regarding the analysis, detection, prosecution and prevention of cybercrime in general and the misuse of cyberspace for terrorist purposes in particular? If yes, please briefly describe it.

Following the wide-ranging cyber attacks experienced by Estonia in spring 2007, the Government is taking steps in order to have its cyber security strategy ready for the end of 2007. This strategy will, among other things, define the critical infrastructure to be protected, systematise Estonia's security measures and its measures to counter cyber attacks and produce a clear division of tasks among governmental institutions. It will also include further guidelines for co-operation with the private sector, as private companies operate most of the critical infrastructure.

Estonia was the first EU member state to suffer massive, coordinated cyber attacks, in April and May this year. Therefore Estonia has a special interest in developing a more rigid policy against cybercrime. The Estonian Parliament is currently discussing revisions of the Penal Code whereby cybercrime committed with the purpose of forcing the State or an international organisation to perform an act or to omit to perform an act, or to seriously interfere with or destroy the political, constitutional, economic or social structure of the state would be punishable by five to twenty years' imprisonment, or life imprisonment.

Until now, the fight against terrorism is based on the Fundamentals of Counter-Terrorism in Estonia (Anti-Terrorism Action Plan) that was approved by the Government in August 2006. The Fundamentals of Counter-Terrorism in Estonia sets goals for the fight against terrorism to be conducted through the prevention, combating and detection of terrorism and by responding to emergencies.

B.   Legal framework

**2.   Does your national legislation criminalise the misuse of cyberspace for terrorist purposes, and
a. are these offences specifically defined with regard to the terrorist nature or technical means of committing the crime (e.g. cyberterrorism), or
b. is the misuse covered by other, non-specific criminal offences?
How are these offences defined and which sanctions (criminal, administrative, civil) are attached?**

At present cybercrime is not included in the definition of acts of terrorism in the Penal Code of Estonia. However, a proposal to this effect has been submitted to the Parliament. Attacks against computer systems are currently covered by other crimes, such as:

§ 206. Computer sabotage

(1) Unlawful replacement, deletion, damaging or blocking of data or programs in a computer, if significant damage is thereby caused, or unlawful entry of data or programs in a computer, if significant damage is thereby caused, is punishable by a pecuniary punishment or up to one year of imprisonment.

(2) The same act, if committed with the intention to interfere with the work of a computer or telecommunications system, is punishable by a pecuniary punishment or up to 3 years' imprisonment.

§ 206[1]. Unlawful removal and alteration of means of identification of terminal equipment

(1) Unlawful removal or alteration, for commercial purposes, of the means of identification of terminal equipment used in an electronic communication network is punishable by a pecuniary punishment or up to 3 years' imprisonment.

(2) The same act, if committed by a legal person, is punishable by a pecuniary punishment.

§ 207. Damaging of connection to computer network

Damaging or obstructing a connection to a computer network or computer system is punishable by a pecuniary punishment.

§ 208. Spreading of computer viruses

(1) Spreading of a computer virus is punishable by a pecuniary punishment or up to one year of imprisonment.

(2) The same act, if committed:
1) at least twice, or
2) in a manner which causes significant damage,
is punishable by a pecuniary punishment or up to 3 years' imprisonment.

§ 213. Computer-related fraud

A person who receives proprietary benefits through unlawful entry, replacement, deletion or blocking of computer programs or data or other unlawful interference with a data processing operation and thereby influences the result of the data processing operation shall be punished by a pecuniary punishment or up to 5 years' imprisonment.

§ 284. Handing over protection codes

Unlawfully handing over the protection codes of a computer, computer system or computer network, if committed for the purpose of personal gain and in a manner which causes significant damage or results in other serious consequences is punishable by a pecuniary punishment or up to 3 years' imprisonment.

The offence related to the dissemination of illegal content is defined as follows:

§ 237². Preparation of and incitement to acts of terrorism

(1) Organisation of training or recruiting persons for the commission of a criminal offence provided in § 237 of this Code, or preparation for such criminal offence in another manner as well as public incitement for the commission of such criminal offence is punishable by 2 to 10 years' imprisonment.

(2) The same act, if committed by a legal person, is punishable by a pecuniary punishment or compulsory dissolution.

3. Do you plan to introduce new legislation to counter terrorist misuse of cyberspace? What are the basic concepts of these legislative initiatives?

Yes, according to a new legislative initiative, computer sabotage and damaging connections to computer networks will be explicitly included in the definition of an act of terrorism.

4. What are the existing national practices in the field of detecting, monitoring and closing down websites used for terrorist purposes?

The Security Police Board is responsible for the prevention of terrorism and is also responsible for detecting and monitoring websites used for terrorist purposes. There is no censorship and Internet Service Providers have self-regulation for closing down websites, for example if the website incites people to commit crimes. A website with illegal content shall be closed or restricted upon a court order.

5. Does your national legislation provide criteria for establishing jurisdiction over such offences? What are those criteria?

There are no specific rules for establishing jurisdiction over offences connected to terrorist misuse of cyberspace. The general rules of jurisdiction are applied as follows:

The penal law of Estonia applies to:
- acts committed within the territory of Estonia;
- acts committed on board or against ships or aircraft registered in Estonia, regardless of the location of the ship or aircraft at the time of commission of the offence or the penal law of the country where the offence is committed;
- an act committed outside the territory of Estonia if such act constitutes a criminal offence pursuant to the penal law of Estonia and is punishable

at the place of commission of the act, or if no penal power is applicable at the place of commission of the act and if:

a)   the act is committed against a citizen of Estonia or a legal person registered in Estonia;

b)   the offender is a citizen of Estonia at the time of commission of the act or becomes a citizen of Estonia after the commission of the act, or if the offender is an alien who has been detained in Estonia and is not extradited;

–   an act committed outside the territory of Estonia if such act constitutes a criminal offence pursuant to the penal law of Estonia and the offender is a member of the Defence Forces performing his or her duties.

–   regardless of the law of the place of commission of an act, the penal law of Estonia shall apply to an act committed outside the territory of Estonia if the punishability of the act arises from an international agreement binding on Estonia.

–   regardless of the law of the place of commission of an act, the penal law of Estonia applies to acts committed outside the territory of Estonia if according to the penal law of Estonia the act is a criminal offence in the first degree and if such act:

a)   causes damage to the life or health of the population of Estonia;

b)   interferes with the exercise of state authority or the defence capability of Estonia, or

c)   causes damage to the environment.

6.   Does your national legal system establish ancillary offences related to the misuse of cyberspace?

The general ancillary offences are those of acting as an accomplice and attempt. There are no special ancillary offences related to the misuse of cyberspace. A further ancillary offence related to acts of terrorism is the preparation of acts of terrorism (see the answer to question 2).

7.   What kind of national procedures do you have for submitting an application on the activities of Internet-providers and/or hosting companies, to deprive a user from a domain name or to cancel his/her/its registration or licence?

There is no specific legislation on this question. It is regulated by the state owned academic Internet Service Providers' "ee.net", which has developed the registration rules of domain names that are liable for every domain name holder. General provisions on court proceedings apply and upon a court order, different restricting measures can be taken.

8. **What non-legislative measures do you have in your country to prevent and counter terrorist misuse of cyberspace, including self-regulatory measures?**

The Security Police Board collects and analyses information for the prevention of terrorism as well as for the prevention and countering of terrorist misuse of cyberspace.

C. International co-operation

9. **Please describe the general framework for international co-operation regarding the misuse of cyberspace for terrorist purposes.**

Security authorities and law enforcement agencies exchange information with their counterparts in foreign countries according to the existing exchange of information framework. Estonia is taking part in the European Union project, "Check the Web": Council Conclusions on co-operation to combat terrorist use of the Internet.

10. **What are the existing practices and experiences with regard to international co-operation, in particular in relation to the procedures described in question 4?**

Estonia has no special experience of international co-operation in the detecting, monitoring and closing down websites.

D. Institutional framework

11. **Please list the institutions that are competent for countering terrorist misuse of cyberspace.**

The Security Police Board.

12. **Are there any partnerships between the public and private sectors (Internet-service providers, hosting companies, etc.) to counter terrorist misuse of cyberspace?**

There are no formalised partnership agreements or memoranda of understanding, but the law enforcement authorities and Internet Service Providers co-operate closely to counter terrorist misuse of cyberspace.

E. Statistical information

13. Please provide relevant statistics on offences relating to the misuse of cyberspace for terrorist purposes (including possibly: cases recorded, investigated, brought to court, convictions, victims etc.).

There are no such statistics yet.

14. Where possible, please describe briefly the profile of offenders typically involved in the misuse of cyberspace for terrorist purposes (professional background, gender, age, nationality), and possible typical organisational characteristics, including transnational links and links to other forms of organised crime.

This question is still being analysed by the competent authorities.

Finland

A. National policy

1. Is there a national policy regarding the analysis, detection, prosecution and prevention of cybercrime in general and the misuse of cyberspace for terrorist purposes in particular? If yes, please briefly describe it.

Even if it has been estimated that Finland does not face any direct threat of terrorist violence on its own territory, it is clear that no country is safe from the terrorist threat. The Finnish Internal Security Programme was drawn up as an inter-ministerial effort under the lead of the Ministry of the Interior in 2004. The Internal Security Programme outlines the goals for internal security, including in the event of a terrorist attack, as well as the measures and resources to achieve them. The Programme focuses especially on the improvement of co-operation between public authorities, with the aim of increasing the effectiveness of internal security measures and improving the quality of services. In terms of its goals and measures to achieve them, the Internal Security Programme also applies to cybercrime.

B. Legal framework

2. Does your national legislation criminalise the misuse of cyberspace for terrorist purposes, and
a. are these offences specifically defined with regard to the terrorist nature or technical means of committing the crime, or
b. is the misuse covered by other, non-specific criminal offences?
How are these offences defined and which sanctions (criminal, administrative, civil) are attached?

Terrorist offences

Finland's penal legislation does not contain any specific penal provisions concerning the misuse of cyberspace for terrorist purposes. Chapter 34a of the Penal Code (39/1889) criminalises terrorist offences. Depending on the manner in which such offences are committed, the Internet may also be exploited to commit them.

Chapter 34a, section 1, of the Penal Code criminalises offences made with terrorist intent. This section provides for a more severe punishment for the types of offences referred to if they are committed with terrorist intent. Of these offences, unlawful threats or aggravated damage to property may be committed both in the traditional manner and in cyberspace. A person who makes him/herself guilty of an unlawful threat with terrorist intent may be sentenced to imprisonment for at least four months and at most three years. A person guilty of causing aggravated damage to property with terrorist intent may be sentenced to imprisonment for at least four months or at most six years.

Section 2 of Chapter 34a on terrorist offences criminalises the preparation of an offence to be committed with terrorist intent. Of the manners of committing this offence that are mentioned in this section, acquiring formulas or diagrams for the production of equipment or materials for the preparation or a nuclear explosive, a chemical or biological weapon or a toxin weapon may in practice also take place in cyberspace. The punishment for such preparation may be a fine or imprisonment for at most three years.

Section 4 of Chapter 34a criminalises the promotion of the activity of a terrorist group. Nearly all manners of committing this offence mentioned in the section are practicable also in cyberspace or by misusing cyberspace. The promotion of the activity of a terrorist group may be punishable by imprisonment for at least four months and at most eight years.

Section 5 of Chapter 34a criminalises the financing of terrorism. Cyberspace may also be exploited for collecting funds for terrorist financing. The punishment provided for the financing of terrorism is imprisonment for at least four months and at most eight years.

A legal person, too, may be sentenced to liability for terrorist offences. The corporate fine imposed on a legal person ranges from 850 to 850 000 Euros.

According to the Penal Code's provisions on participation, cyberspace may also be used for incitement to a terrorist offence or for abetting it (Sections 5 and 6 of Chapter 5). In some cases, participation in the planning of a punishable act with a common intent may lead to a person being sentenced for complicity in an offence under Chapter 5, Section 3, of the Penal Code.

If an act has not been committed with terrorist intent or if the conditions of punishability prescribed in Chapter 34a of the Penal Code are not met (e.g. training is not provided to a terrorist group), the act may constitute incitement to or abetting the offences mentioned for example in Chapter 34a, Section 1(1). Moreover, Chapter 17, Section 1, of the Code criminalises public incitement to an offence.

There is no case-law on, for instance, incitement or abetting in cases where the commission of an offence has been directed through the Internet. It should be noted that the applicability of a significant number of the relevant provisions of the Penal Code require the commission of a terrorist offence or a comparable offence or at least an attempt thereof. In such cases it must be proved that the activity carried out through the Internet has influenced the commission of the offence or the attempt thereof in some way. There must be concrete case-specific evidence that, for example, the perpetrator has, by means of the Internet, managed to create an intent to commit an offence or given instructions promoting the commission of an offence. Also public incitement to an offence is required to cause a danger of the offence or a punishable attempt thereof being committed or to otherwise clearly endanger public order or security.

As for the content of the provisions of Chapter 5, Section 1 of Chapter 17, and Chapter 34a of the Penal Code and the punishments provided for therein, please see the English translation of the Finnish Penal Code at http://www.finlex.fi/en/laki/kaannokset/1889/en18890039.pdf

Cyber offences

Finland ratified the Council of Europe Convention on Cybercrime on 24 May 2007. In this connection, a number of the Penal Code's provisions on cyber offences were amended by an Act (540/2007) that took effect on 1 September 2007. There are no updated English translations of the amended provisions yet.

In Finland, cyber offences are criminalised to a great extent. The provisions concerning these offences do not specifically mention the commission thereof with terrorist intent. The following cyber offences are covered by the Penal Code:
- Chapter 34 on endangerment criminalises the endangerment of data processing, which may be punishable by a fine or imprisonment for two years.
- Chapter 35 on criminal damage criminalises the causing of damage to data recorded on an information device or other recording. This offence may be punishable by a fine or imprisonment for at most one year. If the criminal damage causes particularly serious economic loss or it has been committed in the context of organised crime, it constitutes aggravated criminal damage and may be punishable by imprisonment for at least four months and at most four years.
- Chapter 38 on data and communications offences criminalises interference with telecommunications, which may be punishable by a fine or imprisonment for two years. If the perpetrator makes use of his/her special position of trust or hinders or interferes with the radio transmission of distress signals or such other telecommunications or radio transmissions that are made in order to protect human life, the act is deemed to constitute aggravated interference, for which the punishment may be imprisonment for four months or at most four years.
- Chapter 38 criminalises interference with an information system. This offence may be punishable by a fine or imprisonment for at most two years. The act may be deemed to constitute aggravated interference with an information system (imprisonment for at least four months or at most four years), if it causes particularly severe damage or is committed in a particularly methodical manner.
- Chapter 38 criminalises computer break-in, which may be punishable by a fine or imprisonment for at most one year. The act may be deemed to constitute aggravated computer break-in, if it is committed as part of the activities of an organised criminal group or is committed in a

particularly methodical manner. In such cases the punishment is a fine or imprisonment for at most two years.

Also a legal person may be sentenced to criminal liability for most cyber offences.

An offence criminalised in the Penal Code may be sanctioned by a penal sanction provided for by the Code, by forfeiture and possibly by damages governed by civil law.

3. **Do you plan to introduce new legislation to counter terrorist misuse of cyberspace? What are the basic concepts of these legislative initiatives?**

The ratification of the 2005 Council of Europe Convention on the Prevention of Terrorism is currently underway in Finland. The Government Bill concerning its ratification was submitted to the Parliament in September 2007 and the ratification process is due to be completed by the end of 2007. The provisions on public provocation in Article 5 of the Convention are particularly relevant with regard to terrorist use of the Internet.

4. **What are the existing national practices in the field of detecting, monitoring and closing down websites used for terrorist purposes?**

When detected, websites used for terrorist purposes in Finland would immediately be monitored with a view to a criminal investigation and possible prosecution. Where such websites and/or the users are located outside Finland, the relevant information is shared with the competent authorities according to national legislation on information sharing and data protection.

5. **Does your national legislation provide criteria for establishing jurisdiction over such offences? What are those criteria?**

Because the terrorist offences referred to in Chapter 34a of the Finnish Penal Code are international offences, they may be adjudicated in Finland irrespective of the scene of the crime and its law.

As a rule, Finnish law is, however, applied to offences committed in the territory of Finland or on board Finnish vessels or aircraft. An offence is deemed to have been committed in Finland both if it has, in fact, been committed in Finland or if a consequence thereof manifests itself in Finland. Thus, for example a cyber offence committed abroad but with effects manifesting themselves in Finland may fall under the jurisdiction of Finland.

Finnish law is also applicable to an offence committed abroad, if it is an offence directed at Finland. An offence directed at Finland refers to an offence of treason or high treason or an act that violates or endangers the national, military or economic rights or interests of Finland or has been directed at a Finnish authority.

In other cases, the punishability under Finnish law of an offence committed outside Finland may depend, for instance, on the nationality of the victim or the perpetrator and involve dual punishment.

For the content of the provisions of Chapter 1 of the Penal Code, please see the English translation of the Penal Code at: http://www.finlex.fi/en/laki/kaannokset/1889/en18890039.pdf.

6. Does your national legal system establish ancillary offences related to the misuse of cyberspace?

The question of abetting the commission of offences was covered above under question 2.

7. What kind of national procedures do you have for submitting an application on the activities of Internet-providers and/or hosting companies, to deprive a user from a domain name or to cancel his/her/its registration or licence?

The communications legislation of Finland does not contain specific provisions concerning the misuse of cyberspace for terrorist purposes.

According to Section 131 (1) of the Communications Market Act (393/2003) "if a communications network or equipment item causes danger or interference to a communications network, equipment, communications network user or another person, the telecommunications operator or the keeper of another communications network or equipment shall take measures immediately to rectify the situation and, if necessary, isolate the communications network or equipment from the public communications network".

According to Section 3 (3) of the Regulation on Information Security and Functionality of Internet Access Services (13/2005) "prior to connecting the customer subscription, the telecommunications operator shall inform the customer about the general information security risks and risks related to the specific subscription type, and about the available methods to ensure information security". Section 5 (3) of the Regulation also provides that "the telecommunications operator shall disconnect a customer subscription or its service from the public communications network, if the subscription essentially endangers information security or availability of the communications service. Disconnection and reconnection of the subscription shall be carried out in accordance with the predefined processes and guidelines of the operator. The special circumstances related to the subscription type may be taken into consideration while the measures are carried out."

Communications Market Act in English:
http://www.finlex.fi/en/laki/kaannokset/2003/en20030393.pdf
Regulation 13/2005 of the Finnish Communications Regulatory Authority in English:
http://www.ficora.fi/attachments/englanti/1156489108776/Files/CurrentFile/FI CORA132005M.pdf

Recommendation on Application of the Regulation 13/2005 in English:
http://www.ficora.fi/attachments/englanti/1156489127183/Files/CurrentFile/S MS13.pdf

8. **What non-legislative measures do your have in your country to prevent and counter terrorist misuse of cyberspace, including self-regulatory measures?**

-

C. **International co-operation**

9. **Please describe the general framework for international co-operation regarding the misuse of cyberspace for terrorist purposes.**

The misuse of cyberspace for terrorist purposes has been recognised as part of the terrorist threat in a number of international fora, including the United Nations, the European Union, the Council of Europe and the OSCE.

The Security Police participates in exchanges of information and co-operation in the relevant bilateral and multilateral frameworks.

10. **What are the existing practices and experiences with regard to international co-operation, in particular in relation to the procedures described in question 4?**

-

D. **Institutional framework**

11. **Please list the institutions that are competent for countering terrorist misuse of cyberspace.**

In the Finnish system for administering criminal justice, the police authorities are responsible for preventing, investigating and uncovering offences; public prosecutors are responsible for prosecuting suspects, and the general courts (district courts as the first instance; courts of appeals and the Supreme Court as appellate courts) for sentencing defendants in criminal cases.

12. Are there any partnerships between the public and private sectors (Internet-service providers, hosting companies, etc.) to counter terrorist misuse of cyberspace?

The National Board of Economic Defence (NBED) is a network of committees consisting of the leading experts from both the public administration and the business world. Its tasks are to analyse threats against the country's security of supply and to plan measures to control these threats. At present, the public-private-partnership in the NBED is unique in the world.

The partnership between the public and private sectors is most conspicuous in NBED's pool organisation. The pools are bodies managed by the business world and responsible for operative preparedness. Their task is to monitor, study, plan and prepare measures for improving security of supply in their own branches, in co-operation with companies. One of the NBED sectors is the IT Society. Representatives of ministries, government agencies, private economy, and various organisations are members of these sectors.

E. Statistical information

13. Please provide relevant statistics on offences relating to the misuse of cyberspace for terrorist purposes (including possibly: cases recorded, investigated, brought to court, convictions, victims etc.).

In Finland, no criminal charges have been brought and no sentences have been passed for the terrorist offences referred to in Chapter 34a of the Penal Code. Nor have there been charges or sentences for cyber offences committed with terrorist intent.

14. Where possible, please describe briefly the profile of offenders typically involved in the misuse of cyberspace for terrorist purposes (professional background, gender, age, nationality), and possible typical organisational characteristics, including trans-national links and links to other forms of organised crime.

No cases have been detected in Finland so far.

Germany

A. National policy

1. Is there a national policy regarding the analysis, detection, prosecution and prevention of cybercrime in general and the misuse of cyberspace for terrorist purposes in particular? If yes, please briefly describe it.

German anti-terror policy is determined by five important goals: (1) Breaking up terrorist networks by intensifying investigative efforts in order to increase the pressure on offenders; (2) Preventing terrorist threats; (3) Expanding international co-operation; (4) Protecting the population, taking preventive measures and reducing overall vulnerability; (5) Abolishing the causes of terrorism.

This policy aims to comprehensively prevent and combat terrorist activities, including the misuse of cyberspace for terrorist purposes. In particular, in January 2007 a Joint Internet Monitoring Centre was established in Berlin, which focuses on Islamist terrorism. The BfV (Federal Office for the Protection of the Consitution, lead service), the BKA (Federal Office for Criminal Investigation) and the BND (Federal Intelligence Service), as well as other national security authorities, co-operate within the framework of the centre.

This takes into account the fact that the Internet has a dual significance in terms of combating terrorism: on the one hand, monitoring Internet use by terrorists may lead to the gathering and assessment of information. But on the other hand, the use of the Internet by terrorists may cause direct threats as well.

Furthermore, taking into account the all-hazard approach in protecting information infrastructure, such as the Internet, there is no distinction made in Germany as a matter of principle between the types of danger in taking action against potential misuse. The focus is on maintaining procedures and processes independently of whether the threat is of a terrorist or other criminal nature.

Combating cybercrime with police measures is, as a matter of principle, undertaken by the *Länder* in Germany. The Federal Criminal Police Office (BKA) supports investigations in the *Länder;* it has an independent unit of experts who serve as special investigators.

The Federal Office for Information Security has preventive competence for Internet security in Germany. In this way, the Computer Emergency Response Team (CERT) warns all user groups (authorities, consumers, companies) specifically of dangers posed by the Internet.

B.   Legal framework

2.   Does your national legislation criminalise the misuse of cyberspace for terrorist purposes, and
a. are these offences specifically defined with regard to the terrorist nature or technical means of committing the crime, or
b. is the misuse covered by other, non-specific criminal offences? How are these offences defined and which sanctions (criminal, administrative, civil) are attached?

German penal law criminalises certain forms of misuse of the Internet for terrorist purposes. The relevant provisions of the law relating to crimes against the state as well as other crimes included in the Criminal Code (StGB) may be applicable. Sections 129a and 129b of the Criminal Code, which deal with the formation of terrorist groups domestically and abroad, are primarily relevant to the area of law relating to crimes against the state.

The following criminal offences are primarily relevant in terms of an attack on or the misuse of computer systems:
–   Section 202a of the Criminal Code (data espionage);
–   Section 303a of the Criminal Code (alteration of data);
–   Section 303b of the Criminal Code (computer sabotage);
–   Section 263a of the Criminal Code (computer fraud);
–   Section 269 of the Criminal Code (falsification of legally relevant data).

This does not require the existence of "terrorist intent"; however pursuant to Section 46 of the Criminal Code such an intent may be considered for the sentence.

Additional provisions were created to implement the Council of Europe Convention on Cybercrime of 23 November 2001 (ETS No. 185). Specifically, these provide for the following:
–   separate criminal offence of data interception in a new criminal provision, Section 202b of the Criminal Code;
–   an amendment to Section 303b of the Criminal Code which extends its paragraph 1 to all data processing that is of substantial significance "to another" and includes as criminal conduct the entry and communication of data;
–   the extension of criminal liability for preparatory activities to additional cybercrime offences by establishing a new criminal offence in Section 202c of the Criminal Code, which criminalises the preparation of a criminal offence pursuant to Section 202a or 202b of the Criminal Code.

Likewise, these provisions do not contain any special elements of qualification or aggravation in the case of terrorist activities.

Germany does not consider it necessary to establish further-reaching offences for cybercrime.

Finally, other criminal offences may also be applicable to cases of misuse of the Internet. These include, for example, public incitement to crime (Section 111 of the Criminal Code). According to that provision, those who publicly, in a meeting or through the dissemination of writings, including audio and visual media, data storage media, illustrations and other images, incite an unlawful act, are subject to punishment. This may take place via the Internet.

Also potentially relevant is the criminal offence of rewarding and publicly approving a crime (Section 140 No. 2 of the Criminal Code). Pursuant thereto, those who publicly, in a meeting or through the dissemination of writings, and in a manner that is capable of disturbing the public peace, approve of certain criminal offences detailed therein, after they have been committed or attempted, are subject to punishment. This may occur via the Internet as well.

Furthermore, punishment could be imposed for giving instructions for certain criminal offences (Section 130a of the Criminal Code). Such instructions could be published on the Internet.

3. **Do you plan to introduce new legislation to counter terrorist misuse of cyberspace? What are the basic concepts of these legislative initiatives?**

The coalition agreement between the political forces forming the Federal Government provides for an assessment as to whether and to what extent amendments are necessary in the criminal law relating to the fight against terrorism. That assessment has thus far not been concluded.

Concerning the above-mentioned criminal offences in Sections 111, 140 No. 2 and 130a of the Criminal Code, no legislative measures are planned.

4. **What are the existing national practices in the field of detecting, monitoring and closing down websites used for terrorist purposes?**

Procedures to find, track and monitor websites are wire and phone tapping, source information, forums, Google etc. Guidelines or methodologies for conducting research do not yet exist, but their development is in process. Furthermore, relevant websites are stored in the archives. Monitoring is carried out both on a regular/systematic basis and through ongoing investigations by intelligence services. Systems to ensure full and appropriate analysis and investigation started in January 2007, when the Joint Internet Monitoring Centre was established in Berlin. Furthermore, all known Internet addresses are saved in a specially developed portal. The websites are supplied with additional information provided by the respective pre-evaluation staff. The results taken from the Internet, translations and assessments are saved in a special system in the portal; from there, they can be retrieved by all staff members as well as by various other security authorities. Various Internet tools, such as website monitoring systems and various search engines, form part of this system as well.

Germany's legal system provides mechanisms to close down Internet websites. In the case of criminal offences, it is possible to close down websites on the basis of court orders. In addition, websites that are harmful to young people may be placed on an index of banned sites. Regardless of the legal situation, German providers can be approached on a "good will" basis and asked to close their websites down.

One hurdle is that many of the websites that are being monitored are located on servers abroad. In that case it is not possible to take any legal action from within Germany. A decision whether to monitor or disrupt depends on individual evaluations as the cases arises.

5.   Does your national legislation provide criteria for establishing jurisdiction over such offences? What are those criteria?

The general German law concerning the applicability of criminal law (jurisdiction) applies also to criminal offences in connection with the misuse of the Internet for terrorist purposes.

Section 3 of the Criminal Code provides that German criminal law applies to offences committed on German territory. For offences committed outside the country, German criminal law applies in the cases of Sections 5 and 6 of the Criminal Code for the offences listed there, independently of the law of the place of the offence, and pursuant to Section 7 subsection 1 and subsection 2 No. 1 of the Criminal Code, if the offence was committed by or against a German national or the perpetrator was a German at the time of the offence or became a German thereafter.

If the perpetrator was a foreigner at the time of an act committed abroad, German criminal law applies if the perpetrator was found to be in Germany and, although extradition would be permissible for such an offence, is not extradited because a request for extradition within a reasonable period of time is not made, is rejected, or the extradition is not practicable (§ 7 (2) No. 2 of the Criminal Code). In cases involving section 7 of the Criminal Code, it is a prerequisite that the act be threatened with punishment at the place of the act or that the place of commission is not subject to any criminal jurisdiction.

Section 9 of the Criminal Code governs the question of where an offence is committed. Pursuant to Section 9 subsection 1 of the Criminal Code, an act is committed at any place where the perpetrator acted or, in case of an omission, should have acted, or at which the result, which is an element of the offence, occurs or should occur according to the understanding of the perpetrator.

6. Does your national legal system establish ancillary offences related to the misuse of cyberspace?

Punishability for participation in the misuse of the Internet for terrorist purposes is, in principle, based upon the generally applicable provisions of German criminal law. As such, those who intentionally incite others to intentionally commit a criminal offence may be punished in the same way as the perpetrators (Section 26 of the Criminal Code). Furthermore, those who intentionally provide aid to another with a view to that person intentionally committing an unlawful act may be punished as an accessory (section 27 of the Criminal Code).

The Criminal Code also provides that those who attempt to induce or incite another to commit a serious criminal offence (i.e. an unlawful act punishable by at least one year's imprisonment) will be subject to punishment (Section 30 subsection 1 of the Criminal Code). Those who declare willingness, accept an offer from another or agree with another to commit or incite the commission of a serious criminal offence are also subject to punishment (Section 30 subsection 2 of the Criminal Code). Depending on the circumstances of the specific case, these offences may also be committed by using the Internet.

7. What kind of national procedures do you have for submitting an application on the activities of Internet-providers and/or hosting companies, to deprive a user from a domain name or to cancel his/her/its registration or licence?

Internet providers and/or hosting companies are not concerned with the registration of domain names. The domain name registration service is separate from the provision of the Internet service. A domain name can only be withdrawn from its user if the domain name is held illegally, which means violating the rights of another person or company. The use of Internet services (access or hosting) is based on service contracts governed by civil law. There are no national procedures to interrupt the contractual relationship between service providers and users.

On the other hand, of course, there are procedures to block or prevent the use of illegal websites. This can be ordered by law enforcement authorities to Internet and/or hosting providers. These blocking orders must be followed by service providers even if, as Internet intermediaries, they cannot be held liable for the illegal action itself.

8.   **What non-legislative measures do your have in your country to prevent and counter terrorist misuse of cyberspace, including self-regulatory measures?**

There are no specific non-legislative or self-regulating measures to prevent and counter terrorist misuse of cyberspace in Germany. However, there are general measures which include terrorist misuse. Since 1999, there has been a community programme at the European level to counter illegal or dangerous content (especially but not only for the better protection of (children and) minors using the Internet). At the moment this programme is ongoing as Safer-Internet-Plus 2005-2008. It will probably be continued for a further period until 2013. The central activities of this measure are the establishment of national hotlines and awareness-nodes including their co-operation at the European level (INHOPE, INSAFE). Private and national German institutions are participating in these activities with outstanding projects.

C.   **International co-operation**

9.   **Please describe the general framework for international co-operation regarding the misuse of cyberspace for terrorist purposes.**

At the level of the European Union, Germany has, within the scope of its Council Presidency, successfully initiated the "Check the web" project to intensify co-operation, including the division of tasks among the member states, in monitoring and assessing the use of the Internet by international terrorists. For that purpose, Europol has opened an information portal, which may be used by all member states for exchanges of information.

This portal has succeeded in making considerable progress in the co-operation among the member states: It supplies a platform which allows member states to make their information available to one another and thus pool all the knowledge of the European Union. Co-operation among the member states, with a focus on the division of tasks, is being expanded on that basis.

Regular expert meetings have been initiated as well. They serve to promote exchanges of experiences with regard to the analysis of relevant Internet appearances and the technical questions of Internet monitoring, as well as for the targeted coordination of concrete co-operation projects.

Apart from this the rules of international legal co-operation also apply in such cases.

10. What are the existing practices and experiences with regard to international co-operation, in particular in relation to the procedures described in question 4?

The "Check the web" project has met with a great deal of positive response at the European Union level. The member states recognise the need for a division of tasks in monitoring the Internet in a way that conserves resources. The project includes a comprehensive exchange of information among the member states. Operative activities, such as blocking and closing down Internet sites, are discussed at regular expert meetings - in addition to other topics such as the analysis of Internet content.

Initiatives taken within the framework of the European Union's Community Programme to combat illegal and harmful content on the Internet should also be mentioned in this connection. These initiatives first began in 1999 under the Internet Action Plan and are currently being continued under the Safer Internet Plus programme. Within this context, member states have set up hotlines that allow users to lodge complaints about illegal or harmful content on the Internet. In Germany, the complaint service jointly operated by *Freiwillige Selbstkontrolle Multimedia* (Association for the Voluntary Self-Monitoring of Multimedia) and the *Eco* Internet association, as well as the project *jugendschutz.net* ("protection of minors"), represent two such hotlines.

D. Institutional framework

11. Please list the institutions that are competent for countering terrorist misuse of cyberspace.

In Germany, the agencies responsible for monitoring of websites are the BKA, the *Bundesnachrichtendienst* (BND), the Bundesamt für Verfassungsschutz (BfV), and the *Landesämter für Verfassungsschutz* (state offices for the protection of the constitution - LfV).

12. Are there any partnerships between the public and private sectors (Internet-service providers, hosting companies, etc.) to counter terrorist misuse of cyberspace?

There are no permanent partnerships between the public and the private sector; rather, the private sector is approached on a case-by-case basis (as described under question 4.).

E. Statistical information

13. Please provide relevant statistics on offences relating to the misuse of cyberspace for terrorist purposes (including possibly: cases recorded, investigated, brought to court, convictions, victims etc.).

Germany does not have such statistics available.

14. Where possible, please describe briefly the profile of offenders typically involved in the misuse of cyberspace for terrorist purposes (professional background, gender, age, nationality), and possible typical organisational characteristics, including trans-national links and links to other forms of organised crime.

In the German view, no generalised statements may be made with regard to typical offender profiles in connection with the misuse of the Internet or other data networks for terrorist purposes.

Hungary

A. National policy

1. Is there a national policy regarding the analysis, detection, prosecution and prevention of cybercrime in general and the misuse of cyberspace for terrorist purposes in particular? If yes, please briefly describe it.

There is no national policy regarding the misuse, analysis, detection, prosecution and prevention of cybercrime in general and the misuse of cyberspace for terrorist purposes, but Hungary's Criminal Code includes the necessary articles.

B. Legal framework

2. Does your national legislation criminalise the misuse of cyberspace for terrorist purposes, and
a. are these offences specifically defined with regard to the terrorist nature or technical means of committing the crime, or
b. is the misuse covered by other, non-specific criminal offences? How are these offences defined and which sanctions (criminal, administrative, civil) are attached?

Both a. and b. are present in Hungarian Criminal Law, if the act meets certain criteria. Misuse of cyberspace may be considered in Hungarian criminal law as a preparatory act to a terrorist offence[1] but breaching

---

[1] *Preparation: Section 18.of the Criminal Code*
(1) If it is expressly prescribed by law, any person who provides for the perpetration of a crime the conditions required therefore or facilitating that, who invites, offers for, undertakes its perpetration, or agrees on joint perpetration, shall be punishable for preparation.
Terrorist offence: Section 261.
(1) Any person who commits a violent crime against one of the persons referred to in Subsection (9) or commits a crime that endangers the public or involves the use of a firearm in order to:
a) coerce a government agency, another state or an international body into doing, not doing or countenancing something;
b) intimidate the general public;
c) conspire to change or disrupt the constitutional, economic or social order of another state, or to disrupt the operation of an international organisation;
is guilty of a felony punishable by imprisonment between ten to fifteen years, or life imprisonment.
(2) Any person who seizes considerable assets or property for the purpose defined in Paragraph a) and makes demands to government agencies or non-governmental organisations in exchange for refraining from harming or injuring said assets and property or for returning them shall be punishable according to Subsection (1).
(3) The punishment of any person who:
a) abandons commission of the criminal act defined under Subsections (1) and (2) before any grave consequences are able to materialise; and

computer systems and computer data[2] in general (i.e. without terrorist purpose) is punishable, too.

3.   Do you plan to introduce new legislation to counter terrorist misuse of cyberspace? What are the basic concepts of these legislative initiatives?

It is under consideration.

4.   What are the existing national practices in the field of detecting, monitoring and closing down websites used for illicit, in particular, terrorist purposes and what kind of national procedures allow the blocking of access to websites or pages considered illicit?

The Hungarian law does not permit the closing down of websites directly by the Police. The Police indicate the reported websites to the content service provider with reference to the Electronic Commercial Law and ask for the removal of the illicit content. So far there have been no cases of the misuse of cyberspace for terrorist purposes.

---

b) confesses his conduct to the authorities;
in such a manner as to co-operate with the authorities to prevent or mitigate the consequences of such criminal act, apprehend other co-actors, and prevent other criminal acts may be reduced without limitation.
(4) Any person engaged in plotting or making preparations for any of the criminal acts defined under Subsections (1) and (2) is guilty of a felony punishable by imprisonment between five to ten years.
[2] *Section 300/C. of the Criminal Code*
(1) Any person who gains unauthorised entry to a computer system or network by compromising or defrauding the integrity of the computer protection system or device, or overrides or infringes his user privileges, is guilty of misdemeanour punishable by imprisonment for up to one year, community service work, or a fine.
(2) Any person who:
a) without permission alters, damages or deletes data stored, processed or transmitted in a computer system or network or denies access to the legitimate users;
b) without permission adds, transmits, alters, damages, deletes any data, or uses any other means to disrupt use of the computer system or network is guilty of misdemeanour punishable by imprisonment for up to two years, community service work, or a fine.
(3) Any person who, for financial gain or advantage:
a) alters, damages or deletes data stored, processed or transmitted in a computer system or network or denies access to the legitimate users;
b) adds, transmits, alters, damages, deletes data or uses any other means to disrupt use of the computer system or network;
is guilty of felony punishable by imprisonment for up to three years.
(4) The punishment for the criminal act defined in Subsection (3) shall be:
a) imprisonment between one to five years if it causes considerable damage;
b) imprisonment between two to eight years if it causes substantial damage;
c) imprisonment between five to ten years if it causes particularly substantial damage.

5. **What are the existing national practices in the field of interception of, or infiltration to, the electronic correspondence (e.g. e-mail, forum, instantaneous message service, voice over IP-skype, etc).**

The existing national policy does not permit the infiltration of electronic correspondence – except for interception to be authorised by a judicial permit.

6. **Does your national legislation provide criteria for establishing jurisdiction over the misuse of cyberspace for terrorist purposes? What are those criteria?**

There are no special criteria.

7. **Does your national legal system establish additional offences related to attempts at, or complicity in, the commission of the misuse of cyberspace for terrorist purposes (ancillary offences)?**

See the answer to question 2.

8. **What kind of national procedures do you have for submitting an application on the activities of Internet-providers and/or hosting companies or other entities, to deprive a user from a domain name or to cancel his/her/its registration or licence?**

Anybody whose rightful interests as protected by law have been violated by any activity interfering with the Electronic Communications Act or any civil organisation protecting consumers' rights may report it to the National Communications Authority which shall use the following sanctions (proportionally and gradually):
- prohibit the activity;
- seize the device used for the activity;
- suspend the right to provide the service.

The service provider is also entitled to give notice to the subscriber if the service is used for illicit purposes.

With regard to the content, Hungarian legislation follows the Electronic Commerce Directive (2000/31/EC): the intermediary service provider is not liable for the content of the information disclosed unless being aware that it violates the rights of a third party.

9. **What non-legislative measures do you have in your country to prevent and counter terrorist misuse of cyberspace, including self-regulatory measures?**

There are no specific anti-terrorist self-regulatory measures. The self-regulatory codes of service providers aim at filtering illicit content in general.

The delegation and withdrawal of domains are regulated by a civil organisation (Internet Service Providers' Council).

C.   International co-operation

10. Please describe your country's general framework for international co-operation regarding the misuse of cyberspace for terrorist purposes.

Hungary is a member of the EU's "Check the Web" Project.

11. What are the existing practices and experiences with regard to international co-operation, in particular in relation to the procedures described in question 4?

Hungary has no practice or experience with regard to international co-operation but officials regularly attend "Check the Web" conferences.

D.   Institutional framework

12. Please list the institutions that are competent for countering terrorist misuse of cyberspace.

The counter-terrorist institution competent for terrorist misuse of cyberspace is the National Bureau of Investigation's High-Tech Crime Department.

13. In order to counter terrorist misuse of cyberspace are there any partnerships between the public and private sectors or legal obligations for operators of electronic communication (Internet-service providers, hosting companies, etc.) as well as persons providing the public with access to systems which allow on-line communication via access to the network (cybercafe, WiFi hotspot)?

The Electronic Communications Act obliges service providers to co-operate with authorities in order to collect information and evidence in secret, in extraordinary periods and for military purposes.

14. Are there any hotlines regulated by the public or private sectors permitting denouncement of those websites which could be of a terrorist character / nature?

The Hungarian Association of Content Industry runs a hotline service with the support of the Hungarian Government and the EU in order to suppress illicit or harmful content on the web. This hotline is a member of the international "INHOPE Association" – it receives notices or complaints which are forwarded to the Police, to the service provider or to another (foreign) hotline. Its address is www.internethotline.hu.

E. Statistical information

15. **Please provide relevant statistics on offences relating to the misuse of cyberspace for terrorist purposes (including possibly: cases recorded, investigated, brought to court, convictions, victims etc.).**

There have not been any cases in Hungary so far.

16. **Where possible, please describe briefly the profile of offenders typically involved in the misuse of cyberspace for terrorist purposes (professional background, gender, age, nationality), and possible typical organisational characteristics, including transnational links and links to other forms of organised crime.**

Profiles cannot be provided since there have not been any cases in Hungary so far.

Latvia

A. National policy

1. Is there a national policy regarding the analysis, detection, prosecution and prevention of cybercrime in general and the misuse of cyberspace for terrorist purposes in particular? If yes, please briefly describe it.

The national policy of the Republic of Latvia is in conformity with the European Convention on the Suppression of Terrorism, the International Convention for the Suppression of the Financing of Terrorism, and the Protocol amending the European Convention on the Suppression of Terrorism. Furthermore, the Republic of Latvia has signed the Council of Europe Convention on the Prevention of Terrorism. The ratification of the said Convention is in process.

B. Legal framework

**2. Does your national legislation criminalise the misuse of cyberspace for terrorist purposes, and
a. are these offences specifically defined with regard to the terrorist nature or technical means of committing the crime, or
b. is the misuse covered by other, non-specific criminal offences? How are these offences defined and which sanctions (criminal, administrative, civil) are attached?**

Section 241 of the Criminal Law criminalises the arbitrary accessing of automated data processing systems, further criminalising the arbitrary accessing of automated data processing systems where this is directed against the state information system.

Section 243 of the Criminal Law criminalises interference in the operation of automated data processing systems and unlawful actions with the information included in such systems. Again criminal liability applies if such interference is directed against the state information system.

Section 244 of the Criminal Law criminalises unlawful operations with devices influencing the resources of automated data processing systems.

It must be noted that liability for the acts mentioned above applies not only in accordance with the provisions set out in the Council of Europe's Convention on Cybercrime and Council Framework Decision on attacks against information systems, but in all cases where such devices have been used as tools for committing any of the criminal offences established in the Special Part of the Criminal Law.

3. Do you plan to introduce new legislation to counter terrorist misuse of cyberspace? What are the basic concepts of these legislative initiatives?

There are no plans for new legislation to counter terrorist misuse of cyberspace to be introduced, as the existing legislation in force is fully sufficient.

4. What are the existing national practices in the field of detecting, monitoring and closing down websites used for terrorist purposes?

So far no security incidents have been detected in .lv domains, thus it is not possible to give comments on a presumable action. A domain can be closed by virtue of a court judgment and in accordance with the laws and regulations in force in the Republic of Latvia.

At the same time it must be noted that owners of web pages are not liable for the content of web pages in their possession.

5. Does your national legislation provide criteria for establishing jurisdiction over such offences? What are those criteria?

The criteria for establishing jurisdiction over terrorist misuse of cyberspace are the same as for any other criminal offence, and fully conform to the requirements of the Council of Europe Convention on Cybercrime. The traditional criteria of jurisdiction (territorial, *in rem* and *in personam*) are applied.

6. Does your national legal system establish ancillary offences related to the misuse of cyberspace?

See the answer to question 2.

In addition to that, Sections 19 and 20 of the General Part of the Criminal Law define participation and joint participation and are applied to all the criminal offences established in the Special Part of the Criminal law.

7. What kind of national procedures do you have for submitting an application on the activities of Internet-providers and/or hosting companies, to deprive a user from a domain name or to cancel his/her/its registration or licence?

The Regulations on the requirements for holders of higher level.lv domain names set out the requirements as well as the system for the control of the implementation of those requirements. The Public Utilities Commission carries out the control referred to above.

8. **What non-legislative measures do your have in your country to prevent and counter terrorist misuse of cyberspace, including self-regulatory measures?**

The DDIRV (Incident Response Unit for Computer Security) was established to provide quality recommendations and consultations for IT administrators in Latvia in case of security incidents.

The basic service provided by the DDIRV (i.e. recommendations in the event of a computer security incident) is available to both registered and unregistered clients, but only IT administrators of state and municipal institutions can voluntarily register for additional benefits like pre-emptive information about threats that might affect their systems.

The DDIRV was established as a department in the State Information Network Agency (VITA)

C. **International co-operation**

9. **Please describe the general framework for international co-operation regarding the misuse of cyberspace for terrorist purposes.**

The general framework for international co-operation regarding the misuse of cyberspace for terrorist purposes is governed in accordance with Part C of the Criminal Procedure Law on International Co-operation in the Criminal Legal Field, as with any other criminal offence.

10. **What are the existing practices and experiences with regard to international co-operation, in particular in relation to the procedures described in question 4?**

International co-operation takes place in accordance with the bilateral agreements concluded by the Republic of Latvia and other states.

D. **Institutional framework**

11. **Please list the institutions that are competent for countering terrorist misuse of cyberspace.**

The governmental and security authorities of the Republic of Latvia are competent for countering terrorist misuse of cyberspace.

12. **Are there any partnerships between the public and private sectors (Internet-service providers, hosting companies, etc.) to counter terrorist misuse of cyberspace?**

-

E.   Statistical information

13. Please provide relevant statistics on offences relating to the misuse of cyberspace for terrorist purposes (including possibly: cases recorded, investigated, brought to court, convictions, victims etc.).

In 2005 no criminal procedures were initiated in accordance with Section 88 (Terrorism), Section 177[1] (Fraud in Automated Data Processing System), Section 241 (Arbitrary Accessing of Automated Data Processing Systems), Section 243 (Interference in the Operation of Automated Data Processing Systems and Unlawful Actions with the Information included in Such Systems) and Section 244 (Unlawful Operations with Automated Data Processing System Resource Influencing Devices).

One criminal proceeding was initiated in 2006 in accordance with Section 177[1] (Fraud in Automated Data Processing System). The case was accordingly heard by court and three persons were sentenced. The sentence came into effect in January 2007.

14. Where possible, please describe briefly the profile of offenders typically involved in the misuse of cyberspace for terrorist purposes (professional background, gender, age, nationality), and possible typical organisational characteristics, including trans-national links and links to other forms of organised crime.

The Republic of Latvia has no information on the profile of offenders typically involved in the misuse of cyberspace for terrorist purposes.

Lithuania

A.   National policy

1.   Is there a national policy regarding the analysis, detection, prosecution and prevention of cybercrime in general and the misuse of cyberspace for terrorist purposes in particular? If yes, please briefly describe it.

National policy for fighting criminal acts of international terrorism as well as crimes conducted in cyberspace is formed by the general programmes for the fight against crime, the Law on Essentials of National Security of the Republic of Lithuania, the Strategy on National Security approved by the *Seimas* of the Republic of Lithuania, and international acts of law.

In 2006 the Government of the Republic of Lithuania approved the National Strategy on State Institutions Information Systems Electronic Information Security until 2008. One of its goals is to establish an effective system for combating criminal acts in cyberspace.

In addition, the Government has approved the National Programme against Terrorism for the period 2008-2016. The aforesaid inter-institutional programme focuses on the prevention of and protection against terrorism. One of the Programme's objectives is to enhance the fight against the use of the Internet and cyberspace to commit acts of a terrorist nature.

B.   Legal framework

2.   Does your national legislation criminalise the misuse of cyberspace for terrorist purposes, and
a. are these offences specifically defined with regard to the terrorist nature or technical means of committing the crime, or
b. is the misuse covered by other, non-specific criminal offences? How are these offences defined and which sanctions (criminal, administrative, civil) are attached?

a. The misuse of cyberspace for terrorist purposes is criminalised. According to the Criminal Code of the Republic of Lithuania (which defines criminal liability for particular criminal acts it provides for) in some cases the use of cyberspace may be regarded as a means to achieve criminal goals. This principle is applied also in respect of criminal acts of a terrorist nature.

Articles 7, 250 and 250[1] of the Criminal Code apply:

Article 7 Criminal Liability for Crimes provided in International Agreements

Persons shall be criminally liable under this Code regardless of their citizenship, their place of residence, the place of commission of the crime and whether the committed act is punishable under the laws of the place where the crime was committed, if they commit the following crimes the liability for which is provided on the grounds of international agreements:

1) crimes against humanity and war crimes (Articles 99 to 113)
2) trafficking in human beings (Article 147)
3) sale, purchase of a child (Article 157)
4) making, possession or sale of counterfeit money or securities (Article 213)
5) legalisation of criminally gained money or assets (Article 216)
6) act of terrorism (Article 250)
7) unlawful seizure of aircrafts, ships or steady-state platform in continental shelf (Article 251)
8) hostage taking (Article 252)
9) unlawful handling of radioactive materials (Articles 256 and 257)
10) crimes related to disposal of narcotic drugs, psychotropic, poisonous or highly active substances (Articles 259 to 269).

Amendments of the article:
No. IX-1495, 2003-04-10, Žin., 2003, No. 38-1733 (2003-03-24)

Article 250 Act of Terror

1.   Any person who placed explosives in the place of residence or work, or in a public place intending to cause explosion, caused explosion or set fire, shall be punished by imprisonment of up to ten years.

2.   Any person who committed the acts indicated in the part 1 thereof resulting in health impairment of the victim or destruction or damage of means of transport or building, or equipment inside of the building, shall be punished by imprisonment from three to twelve years.

3.   Any person, who bombed, set afire a building or equipment or destroyed it in some other way which resulted in danger to lives or health of many people, or in spreading of radioactive, biological or chemical hazardous substances, preparations or micro-organisms, shall be punished by imprisonment from five to fifteen years.

4.   Any person who committed the acts provided for in the part 3 thereof against an object of strategic importance thus causing serious consequences, shall be punished by imprisonment from ten to twenty years or by life imprisonment.

5.   Any person who formed a group of accomplices or an organised group for conducting acts provided for herein or participated in the activities of such a group, or financed it, or provided it with material or

any other support, shall be punished by imprisonment from four to ten years.

6. Any person who formed a terrorist group which by the acts provided herein is aimed at threatening people or demanding illegitimately the State, its institution or international organisation to perform certain acts or refrain from performing them, or participated in the activities of such group or financed it or provided it with material or any other support, shall be punished by imprisonment from ten to twenty years.

7. Legal persons shall also be liable for the acts indicated herein.

Amendments of the article:
No. IX-1495, 2003-04-10, Žin., 2003, No. 38-1733 (2003-03-24)

Article 250(1). Inciting Terrorism

1. Any person who by public oral or written statements or using mass media encouraged or incited an act of terror or other crimes related to terrorism or despised the victims of terror,
Shall be punished by a fine or freedom limitation, or detention, or imprisonment of up to three years.

2. Legal persons shall also be liable for the acts indicated herein.

Amendments of the article:
No. IX-2570, 2004-11-11, Žin., 2004, No. 171-6318 (2004-11-26)

b. Section XXX "Crimes against Informatics" (Articles 196–198 of the Criminal Code) establishes criminal liability for some types of cybercrime (unlawful destruction, appropriation, dissemination of computer data, etc.).

Criminal sanctions are applied for the above-mentioned illegal actions.

3. Do you plan to introduce new legislation to counter terrorist misuse of cyberspace? What are the basic concepts of these legislative initiatives?

There are no drafts of legal acts foreseen at present, but the relevant laws and other legislation in force are analysed periodically.

4. What are the existing national practices in the field of detecting, monitoring and closing down websites used for terrorist purposes?

In 2003 the Government of the Republic of Lithuania approved the Procedure on the Control of Forbidden Information on Public Use Computer

Networks and the Distribution of Restricted Public Information (hereinafter referred to as the "Procedure"). Its aim is to provide: regulations for the control of forbidden information (the publication and/or distribution of such information is prohibited by the Laws of the Republic of Lithuania) on public use computer networks; regulations for the distribution of restricted public information on these networks; and control over the implementation of the above-mentioned regulations.

According to the Procedure, the Police Department under the Ministry of the Interior ensures the proper operation of a special phone number and mailbox for relevant persons to report violations of the Procedure. The Lithuanian Criminal Police Bureau and other law enforcement institutions must carry out the investigations within their competence in the manner prescribed by law. Violations of the Procedure are reported to the information provider hosting service or to the network service provider. Where the information provider hosting service and/or the network service provider have been informed that illicit information is stored in their server, they must terminate access to this information, if the termination procedure is technically possible. The individuals having violated the Procedure are liable under the Laws of the Republic of Lithuania.

5. Does your national legislation provide criteria for establishing jurisdiction over such offences? What are those criteria?

Article 250 of the Criminal Code of the Republic of Lithuania establishes criminal liability for acts of terror, including support of any kind to a person or group conducting a terrorist act. If such support is provided using cyberspace or the terrorist activity is incited, prepared, conducted or financed using cyberspace and technical means then the questions of criminal liability and international jurisdiction are decided upon in accordance with Article 7 of the Criminal Code of the Republic of Lithuania which defines the liability of persons for the crimes provided for in international acts. On the grounds of point 6 of the above-mentioned Article, criminal liability is applied regardless of the nationality and place of residence of the person, the scene of the crime and the penalisation of the crime according to the law of place where the crime was committed.

6. Does your national legal system establish ancillary offences related to the misuse of cyberspace?

As was already mentioned in the answer to question 2, criminal liability originates from the use of cyberspace to commit any of the criminal acts provided for in the Criminal Code.

7. **What kind of national procedures do you have for submitting an application on the activities of Internet-providers and/or hosting companies, to deprive a user from a domain name or to cancel his/her/its registration or licence?**

The academic network LITNET is the Lithuanian DNS (Domain Name System) provider for the domain name .lt. A user can be deprived of or have his/her DNS cancelled by the provider on the basis of a court decision or on the grounds of violation of contract, according to the provider rules described in the document "Procedural regulation of the .lt domain".

8. **What non-legislative measures do your have in your country to prevent and counter terrorist misuse of cyberspace, including self-regulatory measures?**

The Computer Emergency Response Team (CERT-RRT), established by a decision of the Lithuanian Government, has been active since 1 October 2006 (http://cert.rrt.lt). The purpose of the CERT-RRT is to provide the capability to deal with network and information security incidents in the Lithuanian public electronic networks, to coordinate the management of incidents within Lithuania, and to prevent them.

C. **International co-operation**

9. **Please describe the general framework for international co-operation regarding the misuse of cyberspace for terrorist purposes.**

In the case of the detection of the misuse of cyberspace by terrorists in other EU countries, the police would provide this information to the countries concerned via the Europol Secure Network; where non-EU countries are involved, the Interpol I-24/7 network would be used. General, strategic and operational intelligence in this field is usually provided by Europol (monthly reports, TE-SAT report, CTTF projects).

10. **What are the existing practices and experiences with regard to international co-operation, in particular in relation to the procedures described in question 4?**

International co-operation on cases concerning all kinds of criminal acts is conducted on the basis of international multilateral and bilateral agreements, EU acts of law and national legal acts on the implementation thereof. The Republic of Lithuania has ratified all the international conventions regulating international co-operation in criminal matters. The services of the European Police Bureau (Europol), the EU institution for judicial co-operation (Eurojust), the European Judicial Network, and Interpol are used for the purposes of international co-operation. A prosecutor from the Prosecutor General's Office has been appointed as the European national correspondent on terrorism-related matters. The procedure for exchanging information with Eurojust and Europol was set up by a regulation of 14 December 2004 and by an order of the Prosecutor General of 19 June 2006.

D. Institutional framework

11. Please list the institutions that are competent for countering terrorist misuse of cyberspace.

Main institution:	State Security Department
Related institutions:	Police Department under the Ministry of the Interior;
	Criminal Police Bureau;
	Prosecutor General's Office.

12. Are there any partnerships between the public and private sectors (Internet-service providers, hosting companies, etc.) to counter terrorist misuse of cyberspace?

There are currently no institutional arrangements for partnerships between the public and private sectors.

E. Statistical information

13. Please provide relevant statistics on offences relating to the misuse of cyberspace for terrorist purposes (including possibly: cases recorded, investigated, brought to court, convictions, victims etc.).

There is no information available, because there have been no relevant cases.

14. Where possible, please describe briefly the profile of offenders typically involved in the misuse of cyberspace for terrorist purposes (professional background, gender, age, nationality), and possible typical organisational characteristics, including trans-national links and links to other forms of organised crime.

There is no information available, because there have been no relevant cases.

Luxembourg

A. National policy

1. Is there a national policy regarding the analysis, detection, prosecution and prevention of cybercrime in general and the misuse of cyberspace for terrorist purposes in particular? If yes, please briefly describe it.

Under a scheme of deployment of existing human and material resources to match the scale of the problem as observed in Luxembourg, a unit of the Grand-Ducal Criminal Investigation Department (Police Judiciaire), the "new technologies section", was specially assigned the task of cybercrime prevention. This unit's principal activity consists in fighting this type of crime and supporting other police units less specialised in this respect. Some degree of prevention can also be achieved in so far as – once the police become acquainted with a new modus operandi – a public information campaign is carried out. However, as this unit's activities are focused essentially on prosecution, it would not be correct to speak of an actual national policy on prevention.

The misuse of cyberspace for terrorist purposes is not subject to specific control but is part of the general measures against terrorism in Luxembourg. The Criminal Investigation Department's anti-terrorist unit – in charge of the whole Grand Ducal police force's action against terrorism – is also vested with authority for surveillance of the use of cyberspace, without it being possible to speak of proactive investigations in this field, as this concept is unknown in Luxembourg's criminal procedure.

B. Legal framework

2. Does your national legislation criminalise the misuse of cyberspace for terrorist purposes, and
a. are these offences specifically defined with regard to the terrorist nature or technical means of committing the crime, or
b. is the misuse covered by other, non-specific criminal offences? How are these offences defined and which sanctions (criminal, administrative, civil) are attached?

Acts of terrorism and membership of a terrorist group constitute criminal offences under the terms of the law of 12 August 2003 punishing terrorism and the financing thereof, as this statute incorporated Articles 135-1 to 135-8 into the Luxembourg Penal Code. These offences are defined in general terms in so far as the technical or material resources used for committing them are immaterial. These provisions define an act of terrorism as an offence which, owing to its nature or context, can be seriously damaging to a country or an international organisation or body, and has been deliberately committed in order to:

- gravely intimidate a population,
- improperly compel the public authorities or an international organisation or body to perform or refrain from any act, or
- severely destabilise or destroy the fundamental political, constitutional, economic or social structures a country or an international organisation or body.

A further requirement is that this "basic offence" should be punishable by a prison sentence or heavier custodial penalty of at least three years' maximum duration.

In addition, Luxembourg's criminal law contemplates certain other offences in the data processing field (Articles 509-1 to 509-7 of the Penal Code). Some of these offences – such as tampering with a computer system – are liable to penalties that fulfil the criteria of the basic offence under the antiterrorist provisions, and may thus be regarded as acts of terrorism.

The provisions criminalising terrorist acts are formulated as follows:

Chapter III-1.- On terrorism.
(L. 12 August 2003)

Article 135-1. (L. 12 August 2003)

Any crime or offence punishable by a maximum term of imprisonment of three years or more, or by a heavier penalty, shall constitute an act of terrorism where its nature or context is such that it may do serious harm to a country or an international organisation or body and has been deliberately committed in order to:
- gravely intimidate a population,
- improperly compel the public authorities or an international organisation or body to perform or refrain from any act, or
- severely destabilise or destroy the fundamental political, constitutional, economic or social structures a country or an international organisation or body.

Article 135-2. (L. 12 August 2003)

Perpetrators of an act of terrorism as provided above shall be punished by fifteen to twenty years' imprisonment.

They shall be imprisoned for life where the act has caused one or more fatalities.

Article 135-3. (L. 12 August 2003)

A terrorist group is constituted by an organised association of more than two persons lastingly established in order to commit, in a concerted manner, one or more of the acts of terrorism referred to in Articles 135-1 and 135-2.

Article 135-4. (L. 12 August 2003)

(1) Anyone who intentionally and wittingly is an active member of a terrorist group shall be punished by one to eight years' imprisonment and a fine of 2 500 to 12 500 euros, or by one of these penalties alone, even if not intending to commit an offence within that group or to associate with it as principal or accomplice.

(2) Anyone who participates in preparing or carrying out any lawful activity of the aforesaid terrorist group in the knowledge that his or her participation furthers its aims as defined above shall be punished by one to eight years' imprisonment and/or a fine of 2 500 to 12 500 euros.

(3) Anyone who participates in any decision-making in connection with the activities of a terrorist group in the knowledge that his or her participation furthers its aims as defined above shall be punished by five to ten years' imprisonment and/or a fine of 12 500 to 25 000 euros.

(4) Any leader of a terrorist group shall be punished by ten to fifteen years' imprisonment and/or a fine of 25 000 to 50 000 euros.

(5) Where acts referred to in paragraphs 1 to 4 above occur within the national territory, the culprits shall be prosecuted in accordance with the law of Luxembourg irrespective of where the terrorist group is based or engages in its activities.

Article 135-5. (L. 12 August 2003)

It constitutes an act of financing terrorism to provide or to raise by any means whatsoever, whether directly or indirectly, illegally and intentionally, funds, assets or wealth of any kind with the intention or in the knowledge that they will be wholly or partially used to commit one or more of the offences provided for in Articles 135-1 to 135-4 and 442-1, even if they have not actually been used to commit one of these offences.

Article 135-6. (L. 12 August 2003)

Persons who have committed an act of financing terrorism as provided above shall incur the same penalties as are prescribed by Articles 135-1 to 135-4 and 442-1, and according to the distinctions drawn therein.

Article 135-7. (L. 12 August 2003)

Exemption from punishment shall apply to persons who, before any attempt to commit offences defined in Articles 135-1, 135-2, 135-5 and 135-6 and before any proceedings have been instituted, disclose to the authorities that acts are afoot to prepare for the commission of offences defined under the aforementioned provisions, or the identities of the perpetrators of such acts.

In the same cases, the severe prison sentences applicable shall be reduced in the proportions determined by Article 52 and according to the scale prescribed therein for persons who, after proceedings are instituted, disclose to the authorities the identities of hitherto unidentified culprits.

Article 135-8. (L. 12 August 2003)

Exemption from punishment shall apply to persons guilty of participating in a terrorist group who, before any attempt to commit acts of terrorism for which the group exists and before any proceedings have been instituted, disclose to the authorities the existence of that group and the names of its principal or subordinate leaders.

Common provision in respect of this title.

Article 136.

Exemption from the penalties for offences of conspiracy punishable under the terms of this title and for the offences prescribed in Article 111 shall apply to culprits who, before any attack and before any proceedings are instituted, inform the authorities of such conspiracies or offences, and of the perpetrators thereof or accomplices therein.

In addition, the definitions of offences relating to computer crimes under the Penal Code provide as follows:

Section VII.4 – On offences in the field of data processing.
(L. 15 July 1993)

Article 509-1. (L. 14 August 2000)

Anyone who has fraudulently gained or maintained access to all or part of an automated data processing or transmission system shall be punished by two months to two years of imprisonment and/or a fine of 500 to 25 000 euros.

When this access results in the deletion or alteration of data contained in the system, or in impairment of its operation, the term of imprisonment shall be four months to two years and the fine 1 250 to 25 000 euros.

Article 509-2. (L. 15 July 1993)

Anyone who deliberately or in contempt of the rights of others has impeded or tampered with the operation of an automated data processing or transmission system shall be punished by three months to three years of imprisonment and/or a fine of 1 250 to 12 500 euros.

Article 509-3. (L. 14 August 2000)

Anyone who deliberately or in contempt of the rights of others has directly or indirectly fed data into an automated processing or transmission system or deleted or altered the data which it contains or the methods of processing or transmitting such data shall be punished by three months to three years of imprisonment and/or a fine of 1 250 to 12 500 euros.

Article 509-4. (L. 10 November 2006)

Where, in the cases contemplated in Articles 509-1 to 509-3, money or monetary value has been transferred so as to cause a third party a loss of possession with the aim of securing an economic advantage to the person committing the offence or to any other person, the penalty incurred shall be four months to five years of imprisonment and a fine of 1 250 to 30 000 euros.

The same penalties shall apply to persons who have produced, received, procured, held, sold or transferred to a third party software intended to make an offence referred to in the foregoing sub-paragraph materially possible.

Article 509-5. Repealed (L. 14 August 2000).

Article 509-6. (L. 15 July 1993)

An attempt to commit the offences provided for in Articles 509-1 to 509-5 shall be punishable by the same penalties as an actual offence.

Article 509-7. (L. 15 July 1993)

Anyone who has participated in an association or conspiracy formed for the preparation, effected by one or more material acts, of one or more offences prescribed by Articles 509-1 to 509-5 shall incur the penalties prescribed for the actual offence or for the most severely punished of the potential offences.

3. **Do you plan to introduce new legislation to counter terrorist misuse of cyberspace? What are the basic concepts of these legislative initiatives?**

At the present stage it is not planned to adopt new statutory provisions, particularly because the cases met with in practice have not revealed any legislative deficiencies.

4. **What are the existing national practices in the field of detecting, monitoring and closing down websites used for illicit, in particular, terrorist purposes and what kind of national procedures allow the blocking of access to websites or pages considered illicit?**

As regards the detection and monitoring aspect, reference is made to the reply to question 1.

It is possible to close down websites based in Luxembourg if the publications posted on them constitute criminal offences. Closure is the measure designed to put an end to the offence. Closure is thus possible during the phase of court investigation on the investigating judge's order.

If the site is located abroad, a request for judicial assistance must be made by Luxembourg, and the outcome depends on the decisions taken by the competent authorities of the requested country.

Where Luxembourg is the requested country, it suffices that the offence charged also constitutes an offence under the law of Luxembourg.

5. **What are the existing national practices in the field of interception of, or infiltration to, the electronic correspondence (e.g. e-mail, forum, instantaneous message service, voice over IP-skype, etc).**

National practices are determined by law (Code of Criminal Investigation), the relevant excerpt from which is reproduced below, at the end of this reply. From a statutory standpoint, Luxembourg has an instrument suited to present-day technical possibilities. It is self-evident that in practice, the police – and the State intelligence service as the case may be – are faced with the same technical problems as the corresponding departments of other states, in particular the rapid development of technology, efficient encoding tools, etc.

Section VIII. - Special surveillance measures.

Article 88-1. (L. 26 November 1982)

The investigating judge may, as an exceptional measure and by a decision expressly substantiated according to the facts of the case and with reference to the conditions stated below, order the use of technical devices for surveillance and monitoring of all forms of communication, if:

a) the criminal proceedings concern an act of particular gravity carrying a maximum criminal sentence of two years or more of imprisonment, and if

b) established facts bring the person subject to surveillance under suspicion either of having committed or participated in the offence, or of receiving or sending information intended for or originating from the person charged with or suspected of the offence; and if

c) the ordinary methods of investigation prove ineffective owing to the nature of the facts and the special circumstances of the case.

The measures ordered shall be lifted once they are no longer necessary. They shall cease automatically one month after the date of the order. They are nevertheless subject to extensions of one month each, although the total duration may not exceed one year, by reasoned order of the investigating judge, approved by the presiding judge of the chamber of the court of appeal who is to rule within two days after receiving the order, the state counsel general's submissions having been heard.

These measures cannot be ordered in respect of a person charged after his or her first interview with the investigating judge, and any such measures ordered earlier shall automatically cease to operate at that date.

These measures cannot be ordered in respect of a person who is bound by professional secrecy within the meaning of Article 458 of the Penal Code, unless personally suspected of having committed or abetted the offence.

The state counsel general may in all cases object to the orders of the investigating judge. The objection shall be made within two days after the date of the order. It shall be brought before the presiding judge of the chamber of the court of appeal who is to rule within two days after receiving the order, the state counsel general's submissions having been heard.

Article 88-2. (L. 30 May 2005)

Decisions by which the investigating judge or the presiding judge of the chamber of the court of appeal have ordered surveillance and monitoring of telecommunications and postal correspondence shall be notified to the operators of the post and telecommunications services who shall carry them out forthwith.

(L. 30 May 2005) These decisions and the action taken on them shall be recorded in a special register kept by each operator of post and telecommunications services.

(L. 30 May 2005) Recorded telecommunications and correspondence, together with data or information obtained by the use of other technical surveillance and monitoring devices under Article 88-1, shall be handed over, with seals affixed and in return for a receipt, to the investigating judge who shall draw up a record of their delivery. The judge shall have copies made of all correspondence which may serve as prosecution or defence evidence, and file the copies, the recordings and all other data and information received. The judge shall send back any written correspondence whose seizure is not deemed expedient to the postal service providers, who shall deliver them promptly to the addressees.

(L. 7 July 1989) Where the measures of surveillance and monitoring of communications ordered under Article 88-1 have had no result, the copies, recordings and all other data and information on file shall be destroyed by the investigating judge not later than twelve months after the order to discontinue the surveillance measures. Where the investigating judge considers that these copies or recordings, or the data or information received, may be of use for further investigation, he/she shall direct that they be kept on file by an order reasoned according to the facts of the case. The state counsel general and the person whose correspondence or telecommunications have been placed under surveillance, notified in accordance with sub-paragraph 6 below, may challenge the relevant order subject to the conditions stated in the last indent of Article 88-1. When the measures for surveillance and monitoring of communications ordered under Article 88-1 have led to a decision which has acquired *res judicata* force to discharge, acquit or convict the person charged, the copies and recordings together with all other data and information shall be destroyed by the state counsel general or the state prosecutor within one month after the date on which the court decision acquires res judicata force.

(L. 30 May 2005) Communications with persons bound by professional secrecy within the meaning of Article 458 of the Penal Code, not suspected of having personally committed or abetted the offence, cannot be used. Recordings and transcriptions of them shall be destroyed forthwith by the investigating judge.

(L. 7 July 1989) A person whose correspondence or telecommunications have been placed under surveillance shall be informed of the measure ordered not later than twelve months after the termination of the aforesaid measure.

(L. 26 November 1982) After the first interview with the investigating judge, the person charged and the defence counsel may receive disclosure of the telecommunications recorded, the correspondence and all other data and information placed in the file.

(L. 26 November 1982) The person charged and the defence counsel are entitled to have the recordings reproduced in the presence of a judicial police officer (Police Judiciaire).

Article 88-3. (L. 26 November 1982)

The President of the Government may, with the assent of a commission consisting of the presiding judges of the Supreme Court of Justice, the Administrative Court and the Luxembourg District Court, order the surveillance and monitoring, using appropriate technical devices, of all forms of communication for the purpose of detecting breaches of the State's external security which one or more culprits are attempting to commit or have committed or attempted to commit, if the ordinary methods of investigation prove ineffective owing to the nature of the facts and the special circumstances of the case.

(L. 7 November 1996; L. 8 June 1999; L. 15 June 2004) In urgent cases, the President of the Government may on his/her own authority order the surveillance and monitoring referred to in the foregoing sub-paragraph, but shall diligently consult the commission provided for therein, which shall decide whether or not the surveillance and monitoring should be maintained.

Surveillance and monitoring shall cease immediately the required information has been obtained, and not later than three months after the date on which the measures were ordered.

Surveillance and monitoring may, with the assent of the commission, be ordered by the President of the Government for a further period of three months. The decision of the President of the Government shall be renewable at intervals of three months on the same terms.

Should any member of the commission be unavailable, the presiding judge of the Supreme of Court of Justice shall be replaced by a member of the Court of Cassation and the presiding judges of the Administrative Court and of the Luxembourg District Court by a member of the Council of State's litigation board.

Article 88-4. (L. 30 May 2005)

Decisions whereby the President of the Government has ordered surveillance and monitoring of telecommunications and correspondence shall be notified to the post and telecommunications service operators, who shall carry them out forthwith.

(L. 26 November 1982) Surveillance and monitoring of telecommunications shall be performed by the intelligence service instituted by the law of 30 July 1960 concerning the guarding of secrets affecting the external security of the State.

(L. 26 November 1982) Communications with persons bound by professional secrecy within the meaning of Article 458 of the Penal Code and not personally suspected of attempting to commit or of having committed or attempted to commit the offence as principal or accomplice may not be used. Recordings and transcriptions of such communications shall be immediately destroyed by the head of the intelligence service.

(L. 30 May 2005) Correspondence shall be handed over with seals affixed and in return for a receipt to the intelligence service. The head of the intelligence service shall have photocopies made of correspondence which may serve as prosecution or defence evidence and shall send back any written correspondence whose retention is not deemed expedient to the post and telecommunications service operators, who shall have it delivered to the addressee.

(L. 26 November 1982) Where the measures of surveillance and monitoring of communications implemented under Article 88-3 have had no result, the copies, recordings and all other data and information obtained shall be destroyed by the head of the intelligence service.

Where these copies, recordings, data or information may be of use for further investigation, destruction shall take place by the time prosecution becomes subject to limitation.

6.   Does your national legislation provide criteria for establishing jurisdiction over the misuse of cyberspace for terrorist purposes? What are those criteria?

Jurisdiction is apportioned by Luxembourg's judicial organisation in two judicial districts, Luxembourg and Diekirch. However, where terrorism and money laundering are concerned, the legislator (Article 26 (2) of the Code of Criminal Investigation) has consolidated judicial authority around the judicial district of Luxembourg. The criterion for establishing jurisdiction is thus the nature of the offence irrespective of the seriousness of the acts or the territorial aspects.

7.   Does your national legal system establish additional offences related to attempts at, or complicity in, the commission of the misuse of cyberspace for terrorist purposes (ancillary offences)?

The definition of an act of terrorism is such that there is no need for the "basic" offences to have actually had their effects, since Article 135-1 of the

Penal Code provides that: "Any crime or offence punishable by a maximum term of imprisonment of three years or more, or by a heavier penalty, shall constitute an act of terrorism where its nature or context is such that it may do serious harm to a country or an international organisation or body (...)". Suffice it that they could have done serious harm.

Moreover, as regards the basic offences proper, the general rules of attempting to commit are applicable. In Luxembourg, an attempt to commit a crime is still punishable, as is an attempt to commit a lesser offence where the legislation so provides.

The rules on complicity are prescribed by Articles 66 to 68 of the Penal Code which provide as follows:

Article 66.

The following are punishable as perpetrators of a crime or lesser offence:
Those who carried it out or directly co-operated in carrying it out;
Those who, by any act whatsoever, have rendered such assistance in carrying out the act that without it the crime or offence could not have been committed;
Those who by means of gifts, promises, threats, abuse of authority or power, culpable machinations or deceit, have offered direct incitement to that crime or offence;
(L. 8 June 2004) Those who, whether through statements made in meetings or in public places, or through placards or posters, or through writings whether or not printed and sold or distributed, have offered direct incitement to commit the crime or offence, subject to the last two provisions of Article 22 of the law of 8 June 2004 on freedom of expression in the media.

Article 67.

The following are punishable as accomplices in a crime or lesser offence:
Those who issued instructions to commit it;
Those who obtained weapons, instruments or any other means employed for the crime or offence, knowing that they were to be so employed;
Those who, except in the case prescribed by paragraph 3 of Article 66, have wittingly aided or abetted the culprit or culprits of the crime or offence in the acts by which it was prepared or facilitated, or the acts by which it was committed.

Article 68.

Persons who, being acquainted with the criminal behaviour of the malefactors engaging in extortion or violence detrimental to the security of the State, in breach of the peace or against persons or property, have habitually afforded them a place of abode, refuge or assembly, shall be punished as their accomplices.

8. **What kind of national procedures do you have for submitting an application on the activities of Internet-providers and/or hosting companies or other entities, to deprive a user from a domain name or to cancel his/her/its registration or licence?**

In Luxembourg, management of the geographic first level domain LU is handled as a public service by the *Réseau Téléinformatique de l'Education Nationale et de la Recherche* (RESTENA) (remote processing network for national education and research).

This service commenced at the time when Luxembourg's first physical connection to the Internet was made and authority for first level domain was assigned to RESTENA by the Internet Assigned Numbers Authority (IANA) in March 1992.[1]

Access to the WHOIS service of RESTENA DNS-LU is allowed for any person wishing to obtain information on a domain name stored in the LU database. RESTENA DNS-LU supplies the data therein solely for purposes of consultation, and RESTENA DNS-LU does not guarantee their accuracy. This information cannot be used in full or even in part for compilation, distribution or any other purpose without the prior written permission of RESTENA DNS-LU.[2]

Apart from this service intended for every individual, the standard procedures for gathering information in police or judicial investigations may be applied.

Deprivation of the use of a domain name and cancellation of registration are matters governed by civil law in most instances. A judicial ruling will be implemented by RESTENA which has no independent power to rule in disputes between two individuals claiming the same right of ownership for a domain name.

Use of a domain name may, however, also be a criminal law matter, particularly as regards infringement of the legislation on intellectual property and protected trademarks or where the use of a domain name would be

---

[1] Le système des noms de domaine d'Internet, Antoine Barthel, Théo Duhautpas, Marc Hensel RESTENA, http://www.dns.lu/Pdfs/News_paper1999.pdf.
[2] http://www.dns.lu/en/EN-LUChercher.html.

immoral. In this case, cancellation of a domain name would also depend on a judicial ruling. In some circumstances, cancellation during the judicial investigation would be conceivable to put an end to the offence. Here, the decision would rest with the investigating authorities.

9. What non-legislative measures do you have in your country to prevent and counter terrorist misuse of cyberspace, including self-regulatory measures?

The state authorities only hold powers vested in them by law. In that sense, all measures are legislative measures in one way or another. In the absence of further particulars as to the exact purport of this question, it is not possible to give a more detailed reply.

C. International co-operation

10. Please describe your country's general framework for international co-operation regarding the misuse of cyberspace for terrorist purposes.

The general provisions on international co-operation are applicable to cyberterrorism, in particular the Council of Europe Convention on Mutual Assistance in Criminal Matters of 20 April 1959, the Council of Europe Convention on Extradition of 13 December 1957 and the relevant European Union instruments. In relation to other countries, monitoring is usually implemented on the basis of a search warrant issued by an investigating magistrate. That said, on the basis of a reasoned order, special means of surveillance may be designated by an investigating judge, allowing an Internet screening operation which targets a given login to be set up. This procedure is also applicable for combating terrorist movements that misuse cyberspace for their own ends.

11. What are the existing practices and experiences with regard to international co-operation, in particular in relation to the procedures described in question 4?

The law enforcement authorities do not perform any proactive monitoring of the Internet. Only on finding an offence covered by the specific provisions of the Penal Code on terrorism can the investigating judge to whom the case is referred issue an order requiring the access provider or the host of the incriminated site to take blocking and/or closure measures. As regards experiences of collaboration with foreign police departments in this field, the cases dealt with in this way principally concerned national investigations focused on the storage or dissemination of child pornography, whereas it has not yet been possible to acquire experience in measures to block sites preaching terrorism.

D. Institutional framework

12. Please list the institutions that are competent for countering terrorist misuse of cyberspace.

The competent institutions are the judicial authorities (prosecution department and investigating judges) and the Grand-Ducal Police Force. Within the police they are, more specifically, the judicial police department (Police Judiciaire) and in particular the Anti-Terrorist Unit of the General Crime Section in collaboration with the New Technologies Section for the technical side.

13. In order to counter terrorist misuse of cyberspace are there any partnerships between the public and private sectors or legal obligations for operators of electronic communication (Internet-service providers, hosting companies, etc.) as well as persons providing the public with access to systems which allow on-line communication via access to the network (cybercafe, WiFi hotspot)?

At present there is no specific legal obligation as regards the use of cyberspace. Among the "ordinary" obligations in force in this respect, mention should be made of the law of 30 May 2005 requiring providers in the communications sector to retain a certain number of pieces of information (see excerpt below).

There is no formal partnership between the public and the private sectors, although the relevant police departments keep up excellent relations with the service providers and their co-operation is good on the whole.

> **Law of 30 May 2005**
> **– on the specific arrangements to protect the individual as regards the processing of personal data in the electronic communications sector, and**
> **– amending Articles 88-2 and 88-4 of the Code of Criminal Investigation**
>
> **Article 5.** Data on traffic
>
> (1) (a) To meet the needs of detecting, determining and prosecuting criminal offences, and for the sole purpose of allowing information to be made available as required to the judicial authorities, all service providers or operators processing data which relate to traffic are obliged to retain such data for a period of 12 months. A Grand-Ducal regulation shall determine the categories of traffic data which may be of use in detecting, determining and prosecuting criminal offences.

(b) After the period of retention prescribed in sub-paragraph (a) above, the service provider or operator shall delete or render anonymous the traffic data concerning the subscribers and users.

(…)

Article 9. Location data other than traffic data

(1)   (a) To meet the needs of detecting, determining and prosecuting criminal offences, and for the sole purpose of allowing information to be made available as required to the judicial authorities, all service providers or operators processing location data other than traffic data are obliged to retain such data for a period of 12 months. For the purposes of this paragraph, a single indication of location shall be required for each communication or call. A Grand-Ducal regulation shall determine the categories of location data other than traffic data which may be of use in detecting, determining and prosecuting criminal offences.

14. **Are there any hotlines regulated by the public or private sectors permitting denouncement of those websites which could be of a terrorist character / nature?**

No.

E.   **Statistical information**

15. **Please provide relevant statistics on offences relating to the misuse of cyberspace for terrorist purposes (including possibly: cases recorded, investigated, brought to court, convictions, victims etc.).**

No offence relating to misuse of cyberspace for terrorist purposes has been detected in Luxembourg to date.

16. **Where possible, please describe briefly the profile of offenders typically involved in the misuse of cyberspace for terrorist purposes (professional background, gender, age, nationality), and possible typical organisational characteristics, including transnational links and links to other forms of organised crime.**

As Luxembourg has not as yet been confronted with this type of offence, it is impossible to establish a criminal profile as envisaged by this question.

Moldova

A. National policy

1. Is there a national policy regarding the analysis, detection, prosecution and prevention of cybercrime in general and the misuse of cyberspace for terrorist purposes in particular? If yes, please briefly describe it.

Moldovan national policy is orientated to detect, prevent and prosecute the misuse of cyberspace for terrorist purposes. The legislative acts that define national policy in this domain are: the Law on Informatics and State Informational Resources, the National Telecommunications Agency's Regulation, Chapter XI of the Criminal Code and certain articles of the Law on combating extremist activities.

Furthermore, it should be mentioned that the Moldovan anti-cyberterrorist policy is currently in the process of being elaborated. There are draft laws that will be adopted in the future.

B. Legal framework

2. Does your national legislation criminalise the misuse of cyberspace for terrorist purposes, and
a. are these offences specifically defined with regard to the terrorist nature or technical means of committing the crime, or
b. is the misuse covered by other, non-specific criminal offences? How are these offences defined and which sanctions (criminal, administrative, civil) are attached?

Moldovan national legislation criminalises the misuse of cyberspace.

a. The above-mentioned offences are not defined with regard to their terrorist nature; they are considered as offences in the fields of information technology and telecommunications.

b. For example, according to Articles 7 and 8 of the Law on combating extremist activities (No. 54-XV of 21.02.2003), in Moldova the use of any telecommunications network for extremist or terrorist purposes is prohibited.

Offences involving the use of cyberspace for criminal purposes or attacks on information technology systems through telecommunications networks are punished either by a fine or by deprivation of liberty (one to five years, depending on the case).

3. **Do you plan to introduce new legislation to counter terrorist misuse of cyberspace? What are the basic concepts of these legislative initiatives?**

On 27 April 2006 an interdepartmental working group was created, including representatives from the General Prosecutor's Office, the Ministry of Justice, the Ministry of the Interior, the Ministry of Information Technology Development, and the Security and Intelligence Service. This working group elaborated the following draft legislatives acts: Conception of information technology security of the Republic of Moldova, Law on information, Law on combating fraud with electronic communication, Amendment of Chapter XI of the Criminal Code "Offences in the field of information technology and telecommunications".

The basic concept of these legislative initiatives is: detection, prevention and prosecution of cybercrimes and misuse of cyberspace for terrorist purposes.

4. **What are the existing national practices in the field of detecting, monitoring and closing down websites used for terrorist purposes?**

There have been no cases in Moldova involving the detecting and closing down of websites used for terrorist purposes.

5. **Does your national legislation provide criteria for establishing jurisdiction over such offences? What are those criteria?**

Article 12 of Criminal Code stipulates the criteria for establishing jurisdiction over such offences. The place of commission of a crime is the place where the damaging action was committed.

6. **Does your national legal system establish ancillary offences related to the misuse of cyberspace?**

Moldovan national legislation establishes ancillary offences related to the misuse of cyberspace. Moldovan legislation is related to the place of commission of a transnational crime; the misuse of cyberspace falls within this category (Article 12 of the Criminal Code).

7. **What kind of national procedures do you have for submitting an application on the activities of Internet-providers and/or hosting companies, to deprive a user from a domain name or to cancel his/her/its registration or licence?**

According to Chapter V of the Usage of .md domain name Regulations (28.08.2000), the "use of sub-domain, including links to other sites on activities prohibited by national legislation and international conventions" is prohibited. In the event of a violation of this Regulation, the National

Registration Authority deprives such a user of the used name and cancels his/her/its registration.

8. What non-legislative measures do your have in your country to prevent and counter terrorist misuse of cyberspace, including self-regulatory measures?

Moldova has no non-legislative tools to prevent the misuse of cyberspace.

C. International co-operation

9. Please describe the general framework for international co-operation regarding the misuse of cyberspace for terrorist purposes.

The Republic of Moldova has the necessary general framework for international co-operation regarding the misuse of cyberspace for terrorist purposes: Law on legal international assistance in criminal matters No. 371-XVI of 01.12.2006, the Criminal Procedure Code and other legislative acts.

10. What are the existing practices and experiences with regard to international co-operation, in particular in relation to the procedures described in question 4?

Moldova has no such practice or experience.

D. Institutional framework

11. Please list the institutions that are competent for countering terrorist misuse of cyberspace.

The institutions competent for countering the terrorist misuse of cyberspace are the Ministry of the Interior, the Ministry of Information Technology, the Development, Security and Intelligence Service, the Centre for Combating Economic Crimes and Corruption, and the National Agency for the Regulation of Telecommunications.

12. Are there any partnerships between the public and private sectors (Internet-service providers, hosting companies, etc.) to counter terrorist misuse of cyberspace?

In Moldova there are no partnerships between the public and private sectors to counter terrorist misuse of cyberspace.

E. Statistical information

13. Please provide relevant statistics on offences relating to the misuse of cyberspace for terrorist purposes (including possibly: cases recorded, investigated, brought to court, convictions, victims etc.).

There have been no such cases.

14. Where possible, please describe briefly the profile of offenders typically involved in the misuse of cyberspace for terrorist purposes (professional background, gender, age, nationality), and possible typical organisational characteristics, including trans-national links and links to other forms of organised crime.

No information is available.

Norway

A. National policy

1. Is there a national policy regarding the analysis, detection, prosecution and prevention of cybercrime in general and the misuse of cyberspace for terrorist purposes in particular? If yes, please briefly describe it.

Norway does not have a comprehensive national policy regarding the analysis, detection, prosecution and prevention of cybercrime. However, the Norwegian authorities give high priority to the detection of serious cybercrime. For that purpose, a technology centre with the capacity to intercept and monitor activity on the Internet has been established within the National Criminal Investigation Service.

B. Legal framework

2. Does your national legislation criminalise the misuse of cyberspace for terrorist purposes, and
a. are these offences specifically defined with regard to the terrorist nature or technical means of committing the crime, or
b. is the misuse covered by other, non-specific criminal offences? How are these offences defined and which sanctions (criminal, administrative, civil) are attached?

The Convention on Cybercrime was ratified by Norway on 30 June 2006, and entered into force on 1 October 2006. According to Norwegian legislation, the misuse of cyberspace is a criminal offence. Some offences are explicitly described as computer-related offences, as for instance:
–   Illegal interception (Article 3 of the Convention) may give rise to criminal liability pursuant to Section 145, second paragraph, of the General Civil Penal Code (Act of 22 May 1902 No. 10, hereinafter "the Penal Code"). According to the said provision, a person who unlawfully obtains data or software which are stored or transferred by electronic or other technical means, shall be liable to a fine or to imprisonment for a term not exceeding six months, or both.
–   Misuse of devices (Article 6 of the Convention) may be punishable according to Section 145 b of the Penal Code. The said provision makes it a criminal offence to unlawfully make available to other persons passwords or other data that may provide access to a data system. The penalty may be either a fine or imprisonment for a term not exceeding six months, or both.

Other types of misuse of cyberspace are covered by non-specific criminal law provisions, as for instance:
–   Data interference and system interference (Articles 4 and 5 of the Convention) may give rise to liability pursuant to Section 291 of the Penal Code. The said provision imposes criminal liability on any person

who unlawfully destroys, damages, renders useless or wastes an object that wholly or partly belongs to another; that person shall be liable to a fine or imprisonment for a term not exceeding one year. The term "object" is interpreted broadly by the Supreme Court, to cover also stored data.

- *Computer-related forgery* (Article 7 of the Convention) may be punishable according to Section 182, first paragraph, of the Penal Code. The said provision makes it a criminal offence to use as genuine or unfalsified any document that is forged or falsified with unlawful intent. The penalty may be either a fine or imprisonment for a term not exceeding two years, but not exceeding four years if the document is a Norwegian or foreign official document.

3. **Do you plan to introduce new legislation to counter terrorist misuse of cyberspace? What are the basic concepts of these legislative initiatives?**

The Ministry of Justice and the Police are currently drafting a new penal code. This work will presumably result in penal provisions on computer-related offences. A Norwegian Official Report on the issue (NOU 2007:2) will serve as a background document.

4. **What are the existing national practices in the field of detecting, monitoring and closing down websites used for illicit, in particular, terrorist purposes and what kind of national procedures allow the blocking of access to websites or pages considered illicit?**

Illegal acts on the Internet may be detected by the use of extraordinary police methods, for instance communications surveillance. The closing down of websites has to take place in co-operation with the service providers. In order for law enforcement authorities to close down websites, a court order is required.

5. **What are the existing national practices in the field of interception of, or infiltration to, the electronic correspondence (e.g. e-mail, forum, instantaneous message service, voice over IP-skype, etc).**

According to Section 216 a of the Criminal Procedure Act (Act of 22 May 1981 No. 25), a court may make an order permitting the police to carry out communications surveillance when a person is with just cause suspected of an act or of attempting to commit an act that is punishable by imprisonment for a term of 10 years or more or that contravenes certain enumerated provisions. Communications surveillance may consist of audio surveillance of conversations or other communications conducted to or from for example specific computers or other apparatus for electronic communication. Section 216 b permits the court to make an order permitting the police to carry out other controls of communication apparatus when a person is with just cause suspected of committing an act or attempting to commit an act that is punishable by imprisonment for a term of five years or more or that contravenes certain enumerated provisions. The control may be exercised, for instance, by discontinuing or interrupting the transmission of conversations or other communications or by closing down the communication apparatus. If there is a great risk that the investigation will be impaired by delay, an order from the prosecuting authority may take the place of a court order (cf. Section 216 d).

6. Does your national legislation provide criteria for establishing jurisdiction over the misuse of cyberspace for terrorist purposes? What are those criteria?

According to Section 12, first paragraph, of the Penal Code, Norwegian criminal law is applicable to acts committed in the realm (cf. item 1) and to certain acts committed abroad by any Norwegian national or any person domiciled in Norway (cf. item 3). Among the penal provisions mentioned in item 3 are Section 145, second paragraph, and Section 145 b. Furthermore, Norwegian criminal law is applicable to certain acts committed abroad by a foreigner (cf. item 4). This provision enables the Norwegian authorities to prosecute cybercrime when the act constitutes a criminal offence both in Norway and in the state where the act is committed and the offender is resident in the realm or is staying therein.

Section 12, second paragraph, states that in cases in which the criminality of an act depends on or is influenced by any actual or intended effect, the act shall be regarded as committed also where such effect has occurred or is intended to be produced. This provision may be of particular importance in respect of cybercrime.

7. Does your national legal system establish additional offences related to attempts at, or complicity in, the commission of the misuse of cyberspace for terrorist purposes (ancillary offences)?

An attempt to commit a criminal act shall be subject to criminal liability, cf. section 49 of the Penal Code. Any person who aids and abets such criminal acts as mentioned above may be liable to criminal liability pursuant to Section 145, fourth paragraph, Section 145 b, third paragraph, Section 291, second paragraph, and Section 182, first paragraph. As a general remark, it must be emphasised that under Norwegian law criminal liability as an accomplice does not depend on a criminal act actually being committed. If the said criminal act is merely attempted, an accomplice is subject to criminal liability for aiding and abetting the attempt. Even if the said criminal act is not attempted, the person can be held criminally liable for attempted aiding and abetting.

8. **What kind of national procedures do you have for submitting an application on the activities of Internet-providers and/or hosting companies or other entities, to deprive a user from a domain name or to cancel his/her/its registration or licence?**

A user can be deprived of a domain name following a court decision. The registry for the .no domain is responsible for the implementation of such decisions. The registry may also withdraw an assigned domain name when it is obvious that the assignment is in conflict with the domain name policy.

9. **What non-legislative measures do you have in your country to prevent and counter terrorist misuse of cyberspace, including self-regulatory measures?**

Law enforcement authorities may use information from open sources for intelligence purposes.

C. International co-operation

10. **Please describe your country's general framework for international co-operation regarding the misuse of cyberspace for terrorist purposes.**

International police co-operation is essential to effectively combat terrorism. In addition to participation in international organisations and operative co-operation, importance is attached to the exchange of police experience and information, outreach activities and networking. As mentioned in section 3, the Ministry of Justice and the Police are currently preparing a new penal code. This work will presumably result in penal provisions on terrorist acts, implementing obligations stemming from international instruments in the terrorism field.

11. **What are the existing practices and experiences with regard to international co-operation, in particular in relation to the procedures described in question 4?**

There is no information available at this moment.

D. Institutional framework

12. **Please list the institutions that are competent for countering terrorist misuse of cyberspace.**

The Police Security Service, partly in co-operation with the National Criminal Investigation Service, is responsible for countering terrorist misuse of cyberspace.

13. **In order to counter terrorist misuse of cyberspace are there any partnerships between the public and private sectors or legal obligations for operators of electronic communication (Internet-service providers, hosting companies, etc.) as well as persons providing the public with access to systems which allow on-line communication via access to the network (cybercafe, WiFi hotspot)?**

According to the Norwegian E-Commerce Act, operators of electronic communications are legally obliged to block access to stored information on servers following a court decision or an administrative decision.

The Norwegian authorities have established close co-operation with the owners of the major networks.

14. **Are there any hotlines regulated by the public or private sectors permitting denouncement of those websites which could be of a terrorist character / nature?**

A hotline to the National Criminal Investigation Service has been established. However, this hotline is primarily used to report child pornography.

E. **Statistical information**

15. **Please provide relevant statistics on offences relating to the misuse of cyberspace for terrorist purposes (including possibly: cases recorded, investigated, brought to court, convictions, victims etc.).**

No statistics are available at the moment.

16. **Where possible, please describe briefly the profile of offenders typically involved in the misuse of cyberspace for terrorist purposes (professional background, gender, age, nationality), and possible typical organisational characteristics, including trans-national links and links to other forms of organised crime.**

No statistics are available at the moment.

Portugal

A. National policy

1. Is there a national policy regarding the analysis, detection, prosecution and prevention of cybercrime in general and the misuse of cyberspace for terrorist purpose in particular? If yes, please briefly describe it.

There is no national policy *strictu sensu*. The actions taken follow the criteria of need and opportunity.

B. Legal framework

2. Does your national legislation criminalise the misuse of cyberspace for terrorist purposes, and
a. are these offences specifically defined with regard to the terrorist nature or technical means of committing the crime (e.g. cyberterrorism), or
b. is the misuse covered by other, non-specific criminal offences? How are these offences defined and which sanctions (criminal, administrative, civil) are attached?

2.a. The misuse of cyberspace when associated with terrorist acts has special criminal provisions in Portuguese law (Law No. 52/2003, Articles 2 No. 1 b) and 4 No. 1)).

2.b. The Portuguese Law on Cybercrime (Law No. 109/91, 17 August 1991), foresees both criminal and administrative sanctions for the misuse of cyberspace (Articles 4 to 18).

3. Do you plan to introduce new legislation to counter terrorist misuse of cyberspace? What are the basic concepts of these legislative initiatives?

The ratification of the Cybercrime Convention of the Council of Europe will necessarily bring with it initiatives to amend legislation.

4. What are the existing national practices in the field of detecting, monitoring and closing down websites used for terrorist purposes?

Websites are scanned in search of terrorist content. If terrorist content is detected on a website, the website is monitored and, if appropriate, the competent authorities are notified to proceed to close it down.

5. **Does your national legislation provide criteria for establishing jurisdiction over such offences? What are those criteria?**

According to the Crime Investigation Law (Law No. 21/2000), cybercrime is within the Judiciary Police's scope of jurisdiction.

6. **Does your national legal system establish ancillary offences related to the misuse of cyberspace?**

The Portuguese Penal Code establishes other criminal sanctions for the misuse of cyberspace (Article 221 of the Penal Code). Also the above-mentioned Law on Cybercrime (see 2b.) foresees both criminal and administrative sanctions for the misuse of cyberspace (Articles 4 to 18).

7. **What kind of national procedures do you have for submitting an application on the activities of Internet-providers and/or hosting companies, to deprive a user from a domain name or cancel his/hers/its registration or licence?**

In the case of a citizen's individual complaint or *ex oficio* in cases involving child pornography, terrorism and other public criminal offences to human dignity, ICP/ANACOM, the Administrative Authority for this matter (Law No. 7/2004 of 7 January 2004, Articles 7, 9, 16, 17 and 18), will deprive the users from the targeted domain, blocking its access and informing the competent foreign authorities when the ISP is placed abroad.

8. **What non-legislative measures do you have in your country to prevent and counter terrorist misuse of cyberspace, including self-regulatory measures?**

See the answer to question 4.

C. **International co-operation**

9. **Please describe the general framework for international co-operation regarding the misuse of cyberspace for terrorist purposes.**

and

10. **What are the existing practices and experiences with regard to international co-operation, in particular in relation to the procedures described in question 4?**

International co-operation takes place within the scope of Interpol and Europol.

D. Institutional frame work

11. Please list the institutions that are competent for countering terrorist misuse of cyberspace.

ANACOM (National Communications Authority) as the Administrative Authority; the Judiciary Police as the Police Criminal Authority; and the Public Prosecutors Office as the Judicial Authority responsible for the direction of the criminal investigation.

12. Are there any partnerships between the public and private sectors (Internet-service providers, hosting companies, etc.) to counter terrorist misuse of cyberspace?

There is a partnership with a Portuguese scientific foundation (Fundação para a Computação Científica Nacional – *Foundation for National Scientific Computing*) which is responsible for an Internet site (http://linhaalerta.internetsegura.pt) that enables the reception of complaints related to the criminal use of cyberspace, including terrorist-related misuse. This service, integrated in the European programme "Safer Internet Plus", proceeds to a preliminary screening of the reported content, establishing whether it should be directed to the Portuguese Judiciary Police or to the competent authorities abroad.

E. Statistical information

13. Please provide relevant statistics on offences relating to the misuse of cyberspace for terrorist purposes (including possibly: cases recorded, investigated, brought to court, convictions, victims etc.).

There is no record of such offences.

14. Where possible, please describe briefly the profile of offenders typically involved in the misuse of cyberspace for terrorist purposes (professional background, gender, age, nationality), and possible typical organisational characteristics, including transnational links and links to other forms of organised crime.

-

Romania

A. National policy

1. Is there a national policy regarding the analysis, detection, prosecution and prevention of cybercrime in general and the misuse of cyberspace for terrorist purposes in particular? If yes, please briefly describe it.

As a part of the national policy for preventing and suppressing cybercrime, the following have been adopted:
- Government Decision No. 2.074 of 24 November 2004 approving the National Strategy for the Prevention of Crime (2005 to 2007);
- Government Decision No. 2.209 of 9 December 2004 approving the National Strategy on Suppressing Organised Crime (2004 to 2007);

These two normative acts include provisions on preventing and suppressing cybercrime and on the setting-up of a portal to receive online notices on cybercrime.
- The Supreme Council of National Defence Decision No. 36/2002 approving the National Strategy for the Prevention and Suppression of Terrorism.

B. Legal framework

2. Does your national legislation criminalise the misuse of cyberspace for terrorist purposes, and
a. are these offences specifically defined with regard to the terrorist nature or technical means of committing the crime, or
b. is the misuse covered by other, non-specific criminal offences? How are these offences defined and which sanctions (criminal, administrative, civil) are attached?

Romanian national legislation does not specifically criminalise the misuse of cyberspace for terrorist purposes.

The general legal framework in this field is represented by the following normative acts:
- Law No. 161/2003/Title III – Preventing and Suppressing Cybercrime, subsequently amended and supplemented;
- Law No. 365/2002 on E-Commerce, republished;
- Law No. 656/2002 to Prevent and Punish Money Laundering, and Setting Forth Measures to Prevent and Suppress the Financing of Terrorist Acts, subsequently amended and supplemented;
- Law No. 535/2004 to Prevent and Suppress Terrorism.

The general framework for the prevention and suppression of cybercrime is set forth in Title III of Law No. 161/2003 on Certain Measures to Ensure

Transparency in the Exercise of Public Dignity, of Public Office and in the Business Environment, and to Prevent and Punish Corruption.

This Title provides definitions, sets forth the general measures to prevent cybercrime, the authorities that are competent in this field, as well as the offences and the transgressions of the legal provisions.

Thus, according to Article 39, "*The Ministry of Justice, the Ministry of the Interior and of Administrative Reform, the Ministry of Communication and Information Technology, the Romanian Intelligence Service and the Foreign Intelligence Service shall create and permanently update databases with respect to cybercrime*". Also, these authorities carry out special training and improvement programmes for the personnel working in the field of prevention and suppression of cybercrime.

The above law includes a distinct chapter containing procedural provisions.

Article 54 provides that "*In urgent and justified situations, where solid data or evidence point to the preparation or commission of an offence through computer systems, immediate preservation of electronic data or of data referring to informational traffic, which are in danger to be destroyed or altered, may be ordered, for the purpose of producing evidence or of identifying the perpetrators in cases of emergency.*"

Law No. 161/2003 provides also, in its Article 57, that "*access to a computer system, as well as interception and recording of communications taking place through computer systems may be done when they are useful for finding the truth, and when establishing the factual situation or identifying the perpetrators would be impossible based on any other evidence.*"

In justified cases, to prevent, detect or eliminate threats to national security, *the State agencies having competences in the field of national security may intercept and record communications, according to Law No. 535/2004 to Prevent and Suppress Terrorism, based on an authorisation (warrant) issued by a judge.*

According to the national legislation in this field, the word "communications", includes "*signals sent through wire, radio, optical fibre or any other electromagnetic means, including satellite communications, fixed networks (with circuit or packet switching, including the Internet) and land mobile networks, systems for the conveyance of electricity, to the extent that they are used in order to send signals, networks used for transmitting audiovisual communication and TV cable networks, regardless of the type of information that they convey* " (G.O. No. 34/2002, Article 2 (a)).

Law No. 656/2002 to Prevent and Punish Money Laundering, and Setting Forth Measures to Prevent and Suppress the Financing of Terrorist Acts provides, in its Article 27, that whenever solid clues indicate the commission of the offence of money laundering or of financing of terrorist acts, the following measures may be ordained for the purpose of gathering evidence or identifying the perpetrator:

a) placing bank accounts and related accounts under surveillance;
b) placing under surveillance, intercepting or recording communications;
c) access to computer systems.

The measures b) and c) may be ordained by a judge, under Article 91^1-91^6 of the Criminal Procedure Code, which is applicable accordingly.

Article 16 paras.(1) to (3) of Law No. 365/2002 on E-Commerce, as republished and as subsequently amended and supplemented, provides the following:

"(1) Service providers are bound to inform at once the competent public authorities about any apparently illegal activities pursued, or about any apparently illegal information provided by, the recipients of their services.

(2) Service providers are bound to immediately provide to the authorities in para. (1), at their request, information that would allow for the identification of the recipients of their services with whom the providers concluded contracts for permanent storage of data.

(3) Service providers are bound to interrupt, either temporarily or permanently, the transmission over a communications network or the hosting of data provided by a recipient of that service, in particular by removing the data or by blocking access to them, access to a communications network or the provision of any other information society service, should such measures be ordained by the public authority defined in Article 17 para. (2) (*i.e. – the National Authority for Regulation of Communications*); this public authority may act *ex officio* or based on a complaint or notice lodged by a concerned person."

According to this law, the service provider is any natural or legal person who makes available to a determinate or indeterminate number of persons an information society service.

Where any of the offences provided in Law No. 535/2004 (Chapter IV) – which is the framework law on preventing and suppressing terrorism – is committed using computer systems and the constitutive elements of any of the offences in Law No. 161/2003 are also met, there may be a concurrence of offences.

3. **Do you plan to introduce new legislation to counter terrorist misuse of cyberspace? What are the basic concepts of these legislative initiatives?**

There is no information in this respect.

4. **What are the existing national practices in the field of detecting, monitoring and closing down websites used for illicit, in particular, terrorist purposes and what kind of national procedures allow the blocking of access to websites or pages considered illicit?**

There is no information in this respect.

5. **What are the existing national practices in the field of interception of, or infiltration to, the electronic correspondence (e.g. e-mail, forum, instantaneous message service, voice over IP-skype, etc).**

Article 57 on access to computer systems of Law No. 161/2003, read with Article 91[1] on the Conditions and Cases of Interception and Recording of Conversations or Communications Taking Place over the Telephone or by Any Other Electronic Means of Communication in the Criminal Procedure Code, is the legal framework regarding the interception of computer systems communications.

6. **Does your national legislation provide criteria for establishing jurisdiction over the misuse of cyberspace for terrorist purposes? What are those criteria?**

There are no special criteria relating to substantive or territorial jurisdiction, other than those provided in the Criminal Procedure Code or in special laws.

7. **Does your national legal system establish additional offences related to attempts at, or complicity in, the commission of the misuse of cyberspace for terrorist purposes (ancillary offences)?**

The general provisions that criminalise attempt (Article 20-22) or criminal participation (Article 23-31) are provided in the Criminal Code.

8. **What kind of national procedures do you have for submitting an application on the activities of Internet-providers and/or hosting companies or other entities, to deprive a user from a domain name or to cancel his/her/its registration or licence?**

There are common provisions in the Criminal Procedure Code, regarding the liability of legal persons (Article 479[1]-479[15]).

9. **What non-legislative measures do you have in your country to prevent and counter terrorist misuse of cyberspace, including self-regulatory measures?**

There is no information in this respect.

C. **International co-operation**

10. **Please describe your country's general framework for international co-operation regarding the misuse of cyberspace for terrorist purposes.**

-   Law No. 64 of 24 March 2004 ratifying the Council of Europe Convention on Cybercrime, adopted in Budapest on 23 November 2001;
-   Law No. 19 of 28 February 1997 ratifying the European Convention on the Suppression of Terrorism;
-   Law No. 411 of 9 November 2006 ratifying the Council of Europe Convention on the Prevention of Terrorism, adopted in Warsaw on 16 May 2005.

11. **What are the existing practices and experiences with regard to international co-operation, in particular in relation to the procedures described in question 4?**

There is no information in this respect

D. **Institutional framework**

12. **Please list the institutions that are competent for countering terrorist misuse of cyberspace.**

-   The Directorate for Investigating Offences of Organised Crime and Terrorism (Law No. 508/2004, as subsequently amended and supplemented);
-   The Romanian Intelligence Service (Law No. 14/1992, as subsequently amended and supplemented; Law No. 535/2004);
-   The Public Ministry (Law No. 304/2004, as republished and as subsequently amended and supplemented; the Criminal Procedure Code);
-   the Ministry of Justice (Law No. 161/2003, as subsequently amended and supplemented; G.D. No. 83/2005, as subsequently amended and supplemented);
-   The Ministry of the Interior and of Administrative Reform (Law No. 161/2003, as subsequently amended and supplemented; G.E.O. No. 30/2007)

- the Foreign Intelligence Service (Law No. 161/2003, as subsequently amended and supplemented; Law No. 1/1998, as republished and as subsequently amended and supplemented);
- The Ministry of Communications and Information Technology (Law No. 161/2003, as subsequently amended and supplemented; G.D. No. 744/2003 as subsequently amended and supplemented).

- **In order to counter terrorist misuse of cyberspace are there any partnerships between the public and private sectors or legal obligations for operators of electronic communication (Internet-service providers, hosting companies, etc.) as well as persons providing the public with access to systems which allow on-line communication via access to the network (cybercafe, WiFi hotspot)?**

There is no information available.

14. **Are there any hotlines regulated by the public or private sectors permitting denouncement of those websites which could be of a terrorist character / nature?**

There is no information available.

E. **Statistical information**

15. **Please provide relevant statistics on offences relating to the misuse of cyberspace for terrorist purposes (including possibly: cases recorded, investigated, brought to court, convictions, victims etc.).**

There is no information available.

16. **Where possible, please describe briefly the profile of offenders typically involved in the misuse of cyberspace for terrorist purposes (professional background, gender, age, nationality), and possible typical organisational characteristics, including trans-national links and links to other forms of organised crime.**

There is no information available.

Russian Federation

A. National policy

1. Is there a national policy regarding the analysis, detection, prosecution and prevention of cybercrime in general and the misuse of cyberspace for terrorist purposes in particular? If yes, please briefly describe it.

The Russian Federation's National Cybercrime Policy is defined in the Federal Laws on Communications and on Information, Information Technology and Information Protection, and in the Information Security Doctrine of the Russian Federation. The relevant *corpora delicti* are provided for in Articles 272-274 of Russia's Penal Code. National policy to counter the misuse of cyberspace for terrorist purposes is part of the Russian Federation's national counter-terrorism policy (the federal counter-terrorism and counter-extremism laws) and at present is not governed separately.

Russia has a coherent system of government bodies dealing with the set of tasks to ensure information security, including countering cybercrime, particularly cyberterrorism. This system comprises federal legislative and executive bodies: first and foremost the law enforcement agencies, the state authority bodies of the subjects of the Federation, research and educational institutions, and relevant public and commercial organisations.

In 1998, a specialised directorate within the Ministry of the Interior was established to counter cybercrime. It now has regional units functioning in all the subjects of the Russian Federation. Thanks to the action taken by these bodies, the IT-related crime situation has been stabilised. About 14 000 such crimes were registered in 2007 and there is definitely evidence to suggest that the number of cybercrimes will decrease further.

B. Legal framework

2. Does your national legislation criminalise the misuse of cyberspace for terrorist purposes, and
a. are these offences specifically defined with regard to terrorist nature or technical means of committing the crime or
b. is the misuse covered by other, non-specific criminal offences? How are these offences defined and which sanctions (criminal, administrative, civil) are attached?

The Russian Federation's criminal legislation does not contain the misuse of cyberspace for terrorist purposes as a separate *corpus delicti* or qualifying feature, however such acts may, depending on the circumstances, be qualified by the totality of crimes of a terrorist nature (Article 205 of the Russian Penal Code "Terrorist Acts", Article 205.1 "Assistance for Terrorist Activity", Article 208 "Organisation of, or Participation in Illegal Armed Units") and in the field of computer information (Article 272 of the Penal Code "Illicit Access to Computer Information", Article 373 "Creation, Use or Distribution of Harmful Computer Programs", and Article 274 "Violation of the Operating Rules for Computers, Computer Systems or Networks").

The *corpora delicti* of some offences of a terrorist nature that may be committed using cyberspace are provided for in the Russian Federation's Code of Administrative Violations (Articles 20.3, 20.27 and 20.28).

Where misuse of the Internet cannot be fully qualified as a crime under Article 205.2 of the Russian Penal Code (for example, the collection of donations or ideological brainwashing of users, but without incitement to commit terrorist acts) the provision on "instigating hatred or enmity as well as degrading human dignity" contained in Article 282 of the Penal Code can be invoked to bring persons involved in the creation and administering of such websites to justice.

Depending on the circumstances, the misuse of cyberspace for terrorist purposes may also be qualified under Article 205.2 "Public Exhortations to Engage in Terrorist Activities or Public Justification of Terrorism."

3. **Do you plan to introduce new legislation to counter terrorist misuse of cyberspace? What are the basic concepts of these legislative initiatives?**

The current legal framework in the Russian Federation for countering terrorism and extremism, particularly in the information sphere, is provided by the federal laws on counter-terrorism (6 March 2006) and on information, information technology and information protection, which prohibits the dissemination of information advocating war, fomenting national, racial or religious hatred and enmity, as well as other information whose dissemination entails criminal or administrative liability (Article 10, para 6).

Federal laws may also provide for the compulsory identification of persons and entities that use the information and telecommunications network in carrying out their entrepreneurial activity. Furthermore, recipients of electronic messages within Russia are entitled to carry out checks to establish the sender's identity, and must do so where required by federal laws or by a mutual agreement of the parties.

Legal norms aimed at counteracting the dissemination of extremist or terrorist information and establishing liability for such activities are also contained in the Federal Laws on Counteracting Extremist Activities, of 25 July 2007, and on Communications, of 7 July 2003, in the Code of Administrative Violations and in the Penal Code of the Russian Federation.

Discussion is under way in the Russian Federation on the advisability of modifying or amending Mass Media Law No. 2 2124-1 of 27 December

1991, to equate Internet sites with mass media. Supporters of the bill think that regarding websites as media would allow for the effective use of the existing norms to curb public exhortations to terrorist activity by applying them analogously to cyberspace. A draft federal law to amend the Mass Media Law is now undergoing interagency approval.

4. **What are the existing national practices in the field of detecting, monitoring and closing down websites used for illicit, in particular, terrorist purposes and what kind of national procedures allow the blocking of access to websites or pages considered illicit?**

The monitoring of the Internet to identify terrorist websites is done by the authorities responsible for combating terrorism. The use of such websites may be banned by a court decision. Also, information on such resources or their illegal functioning may be sent to the technical support provider for the site, proposing that it be banned. As a rule, the relevant contracts provide for a possible ban on websites which contravene the laws of the Russian Federation.

Within its scope of authority, the Ministry of the Interior of Russia monitors the Internet for sites used for illicit, including terrorist, purposes. Upon the identification of such websites hosted by domestic service providers, the Ministry's bodies carry out investigative activities to establish the identity of persons involved in setting up and administering the website, and bring them to justice. If, on completion of those activities, it has not been possible to establish the perpetrator's identity, notices of the need to block the particular sites are sent to the communications operators under Law No. 144-ФЗ of 12 August 1995, on Investigative Activities and Law No. 126-ФЗ of 7 July 2003, on Communications.

Where the Internet sites with illicit content which are identified are hosted on foreign servers, in order to have them suppressed, the Ministry of the Interior sends information to the law enforcement bodies of the relevant states via Interpol channels and the international 24/7 network of national points of contact.

5. **What are the existing national practices in the field of interception of, or infiltration to, the electronic correspondence (e.g. e-mail, forum, instantaneous message service, voice over IP-skype, etc).**

Under Russian legislation, such investigative activities belong to a category limiting the constitutional rights of citizens. Hence, the Russian Federation Criminal Procedure Code stipulates that they are to be carried out solely by a court decision as part of the investigation of a serious or a particularly serious crime.

Electronic correspondence may only be intercepted under the Federal Law on Investigative Activities; Article 8 of this Law provides for the compulsory receipt of a court decision on "interception."

6. Does your national legislation provide criteria for establishing jurisdiction over the misuse of cyberspace for terrorist purposes? What are those criteria?

The usual principle of defining jurisdiction operates in the laws of the Russian Federation: it is first established whether a particular act can be regarded as a crime or offence, then the territory where it was committed is determined, after which this act is deemed to come under the jurisdiction of the respective country. The procedure for defining jurisdiction is laid down in Articles 11 and 12 of the Penal Code.

Article 11 of the Penal Code establishes the territorial principle defining jurisdiction, that is a person having committed a crime on the territory of the Russian Federation shall be held liable under Russian law. The jurisdiction also extends to crimes committed within its territorial sea or airspace, on its continental shelf or in its exclusive economic zone.

A person having committed a crime in the open water or air space outside the Russian Federation against a ship or an aircraft registered in the Russian Federation shall be held criminally liable under the Penal Code of the Russian Federation, unless this is otherwise provided for by a relevant international treaty. The Russian Federation's jurisdiction also covers crimes committed against naval ships or military aircraft, regardless of their location.

Where a diplomatic official of foreign state, or another citizen who enjoys immunity, commits a crime in the Russian Federation, the issue of criminal liability is resolved in accordance with the rules of international law.

The effect of criminal law with regard to persons having committed crimes outside of the Russian Federation is determined pursuant to Article 12 of the Penal Code.

This Article stipulates that Russian citizens, as well as stateless persons permanently resident in the Russian Federation, who have committed a crime outside the Russian Federation against interests protected by the Penal Code of the Russian Federation shall be held criminally liable under this Code unless there is a related decision by a foreign court of law in respect of these persons. Members of Russian army units stationed outside of the Russian Federation are held criminally liable for crimes committed on the territory of a foreign state under the Penal Code, unless an international treaty to which the Russian Federation is a party provides otherwise.

Foreign citizens and stateless persons not permanently resident in the Russian Federation having committed a crime outside of the Russian Federation are to be held criminally liable under the Penal Code of the Russian Federation in cases where the crime is directed against national interests of the Russian Federation or a citizen of the Russian Federation or a stateless person permanently resident in the Russian Federation, as well as in the cases provided for by international treaties to which the Russian Federation is a party if the foreign citizens or stateless persons not permanently resident in the Russian Federation have not been convicted in a foreign state and criminal proceedings are being instituted against them on the territory of the Russian Federation.

The criteria for establishing jurisdiction in preventing the misuse of cyberspace for terrorist purposes are provided for in Article 4 of the Russian Federation Constitution and in Chapter 2 of the Russian Penal Code and are universal with respect to fighting against all offences.

7. **Does your national legal system establish additional offences related to attempts at, or complicity in, the commission of the misuse of cyberspace for terrorist purposes (ancillary offences)?**

The Penal Code of the Russian Federation provides for the institution of legal proceedings against citizens for committing a variety of illicit acts, including those where information technologies or cyberspace act as a tool or the place of the crime. This also applies fully to illicit acts of a terrorist nature. In this connection persons involved in the misuse of cyberspace for terrorist purposes, upon committing accompanying crimes (illicit access to computer information, slander and so on) may be prosecuted in accordance with the nature of the illicit act identified.

8. **What kind of national procedures do you have for submitting an application on the activities of Internet-providers and/or hosting companies or other entities, to deprive a user from a domain name or to cancel his/her/its registration or licence?**

The Coordination Centre of the National Internet Domain has currently approved the Rules for the Registration of Domain Names in the .ru domain (decision No. 2 P2- 2.1,4.1/06 of 24 April 2006). The registration of a domain name is effected on the basis of an application by a user (any person may apply in this capacity) and the terms of use of the domain name are determined by a contract.

One of the grounds for denying the registration of a domain name is the use in the domain name of words contrary to public interest or to the principles of humanity and morality (words of indecent content, exhortations of an antihuman nature insulting human dignity or religious feelings).

Registration is effected by a legal entity, an accredited coordinator, for a period of one year with the possibility of annual re-registration. There are no provisions for the annulment of the registration of a domain name for the use of the domain for illicit activities.

In addition, it is possible to block registration upon proof of the institution of legal proceedings over a domain name. Administration rights may be terminated on the basis of a judgment having become *res judicata*: (1) prohibiting the administrator from using in the domain name a designation in which the plaintiff has rights; (2) declaring the administration of the domain to be in violation of the plaintiff's rights; (3) otherwise obliging the administrator to give up the domain name. A judgment establishing the fact of a domain name being used for illicit activities is not indicated among those grounds either.

Under Article 37 of the Federal Law on Communications, a licensing authority has the right to suspend a license in the event of the identification of a violation that may harm the rights, lawful interests, human life or health as well as state government needs, including presidential or government communications, national defence needs, state security and law and order. If the license holder fails to remove the circumstances that caused the suspension within the specified period of time, the license may be annulled.

9. **What non-legislative measures do you have in your country to prevent and counter terrorist misuse of cyberspace, including self-regulatory measures?**

To prevent the use of cyberspace for terrorist purposes, the Ministry of the Interior maintains regular contacts with the service provider companies, some of which independently control the websites they host. Educational work is furthermore conducted among the population through the media.

C. International co-operation

10. **Please describe your country's general framework for international co-operation regarding the misuse of cyberspace for terrorist purposes.**

The problem of countering terrorist activities on the Internet is seen by Russia as a fundamental element of international information security (IIS). Russia initiated the consideration of this problem in the UN format. A study of the set of IIS-related problems is currently under way within the Shanghai Co-operation Organization and in 2009 work will be resumed at the level of a UN group of government experts.

11. **What are the existing practices and experiences with regard to international co-operation, in particular in relation to the procedures described in question 4?**

In order to suppress Internet sites with illicit content identified by the Ministry of the Interior as being hosted by foreign service providers, information is sent to the law enforcement agencies of the respective states via Interpol channels and the permanently functioning international network of national points of contact.

In the course of bilateral co-operation with the security services and law enforcement agencies of foreign states, data is transmitted to partners on the presence of sites of a terrorist nature in their national segments of the Internet.

D. Institutional framework

12. **Please list the institutions that are competent for countering terrorist misuse of cyberspace.**

In the Russian Federation matters related to combating the misuse of cyberspace lie within the remit of the Federal Security Service, Foreign Intelligence Service and the Ministry of the Interior, as well as of the Prosecutor General's Office as regards the identification, documenting, preventing and investigating of crimes. Furthermore, some aspects of this issue are the prerogative of the Ministry of Information and Communications and the Cultural Heritage Protection Agency, including the licensing of communications operators providing Internet access and monitoring and oversight in the area of mass communications.

13. **In order to counter terrorist misuse of cyberspace are there any partnerships between the public and private sectors or legal obligations for operators of electronic communication (Internet-service providers. hosting companies, etc.) as well as persons providing the public with access to systems which allow on-line communication via access to the network (cybercafe, WiFi hotspot)?**

To counter the misuse of cyberspace, the Ministry of the Interior interacts with the relevant public and commercial entities on a regular basis, among them the Documental Telecommunications Association, the Information Protection Association, and a number of other organisations as well as communication operator companies.

Co-operation between the law enforcement agencies and communication operators is set out in the Rules for Interaction by Communication Operators with Authorised Government Agencies Engaged in Investigative Activities, as approved by Government Resolution No. 538 of 27 August 2005. These

Rules include provisions obliging operator companies to keep information on subscribers (users) and the services provided to them for three years.

Russian law does not currently provide for the liability of officials of communication operators and hosting companies for providing communication services and websites or registering domain names for *mala fide* users. At the same time, where firms do not comply with the well-grounded orders of law enforcement agencies to block sites used for the support of terrorist activities or other illicit acts their licenses may be suspended by court decisions.

Under the Federal Law on Information, Information Technology and Information Protection, in cases where disseminating certain information is limited or prohibited by federal laws, a person rendering information storage/access services (Internet provider) does not incur civil law liability for disseminating such information provided the person could not have known about the illegality of disseminating that information.

Under Article 13 of the Federal Counter-Extremism Law, information materials, including those disseminated through information and telecommunications networks, may be recognised as extremist by a court decision.

Pursuant to the above-mentioned normative legal acts, communications operators must take action to discontinue the dissemination of such information.

Article 64.3 of the Federal Law on Communications stipulates that an operator must suspend the provision of communications services to legal entities and persons on the basis of a substantiated decision in writing taken by a senior official of the agency in charge of investigative activities or responsible for the security of the Russian Federation, in the cases determined by federal laws.

Under Article 17.3 of the Federal Law on Information, Information Technology and Information Protection, in cases where disseminating certain information is limited or prohibited by federal laws, a person does not incur civil law liability for disseminating such information where he or she renders services involving:
1) either the transmission of information provided by another person on the condition that it is transmitted it without changes or corrections; or
2) the storage of information and provision of access to it on the condition that the person could not have known about the illegality of disseminating the information.

14. **Are there any hotlines regulated by the public or private sectors permitting denouncement of those websites which could be of a terrorist character / nature?**

To inform the public about the activities of its bodies, as well as to obtain information from citizens about crimes, particularly in the area of information technologies, the Russian Ministry of the Interior has set up a website on the Internet. On this resource any user may leave a message about a crime which has been committed, is being planned or prepared. The information is sent immediately to the relevant Ministry subdivision for verification.

There is also a Federal Security Service (FSB) hotline: 914-22-22; e-mail address: fsb@fsb.ru.

E. Statistical information

15. **Please provide relevant statistics on offences relating to the misuse of cyberspace for terrorist purposes (including possibly: cases recorded, investigated, brought to court, convictions, victims etc.).**

In the first half of 2007, the bodies of the Ministry of the Interior suppressed, from the Russian segment of the Internet, 69 websites used by criminals to spread propaganda materials of an extremist nature.

Furthermore, the Ministry of the Interior Directorate in the Samara Region instituted a criminal proceeding involving elements of a crime stipulated in Article 282 of the Russian Penal Code, regarding the posting on an Internet site of exhortations to commit terrorist acts.

The limited number of criminal proceedings results from the objective difficulty of establishing the identity of persons involved in creating and administering the websites used for disseminating extremist propaganda materials.

The FSB of Russia has identified about 400 instances of misuse of open telecommunications networks for extremist or terrorist purposes this year. In 2006, about 900 such instances were identified. The agency has put a stop to about 100 of the instances; investigative activities are continuing.

16. **Where possible, please describe briefly the profile of offenders typically involved in the misuse of cyberspace for terrorist purposes (professional background, gender, age, nationality), and possible typical organisational characteristics, including transnational links and links to other forms of organised crime.**

According to the operational data of the Russian Ministry of the Interior, the citizens involved in IT-related crimes, including those linked to the misuse of cyberspace, may be described as follows: by age: 27% are aged under 20, 55% are aged 20-35, 18% are over 35; by their level of education: 57% are citizens with higher or incomplete higher education, 20% are students of educational institutions, and 23% are citizens with specialised secondary education.

Most offenders are men. Women feature extremely rarely among criminals.

Regarding the criminal links of the figures in question, it should be noted that there is a growing tendency for criminals to organise themselves into groups, which is particularly characteristic of such illicit acts as computer fraud, often associated with illegal access to the information/telecommunications resources of banking entities and major communications operators.

Slovak Republic

A. National policy

1. Is there a national policy regarding the analysis, detection, prosecution and prevention of cybercrime in general and the misuse of cyberspace for terrorist purpose in particular? If yes, please briefly describe it.

There is no specific national policy in respect of the misuse of cyberspace for terrorist purposes.

As far as the fight against terrorism in general is concerned, the Slovak Republic has adopted a National Action Plan (NAP) for the fight against terrorism. The objective of this document is to continue creating favourable conditions for the consistent fulfilment and implementation of several international treaties and commitments such as the UN Security Council resolutions, the directives and framework decisions of the European Union institutions, decrees issued by international institutions and by specific countries where sanctions are declared against individuals and groups suspected of terrorism and of supporting terrorism. The NAP creates conditions for the solution of basic problems in the area of coordination and co-operation of different key subjects in the fight against terrorism and in this way, it enables the removal or elimination of original reasons, criminogenic factors and potential perpetrators of terrorist criminal acts.

B. Legal framework

2. Does your national legislation criminalise the misuse of cyberspace for terrorist purposes, and
a. are these offences specifically defined with regard to the terrorist nature or technical means of committing the crime (e.g. cyberterrorism), or
b. is the misuse covered by other, non-specific criminal offences? How are these offences defined and which sanctions (criminal, administrative, civil) are attached?

The legal order of the Slovak Republic criminalises misuse of cyberspace for terrorist purposes within the framework of the criminal offence of terrorism. There is no specifically defined offence for this type of criminal conduct.

The general criminal offence of "Terrorism" is defined in Article 419 of the Criminal Code as:

"(1) Any person who, with the intention to destabilise or destroy constitutional, political, economic or social order of a state or order of international organisation, or to force the government of a state or an international organisation in order to do or to omit to do something, threatens to commit or commits a crime against the life or health of

245

persons, their personal liberty or property, or without any authorisation produces, obtains, owns, possesses, transports, supplies or in some other way uses explosive, nuclear, biological or chemical weapons, or carries out illicit research into or development of such arms or other arms prohibited by law or international treaty, shall be liable to a term of imprisonment of twenty to twenty-five years or a life imprisonment sentence.

(2) The offender shall be liable to life imprisonment if he/she commits the crime referred to in paragraph 1
a) and thereby causes the death of persons,
b) against a protected person,
c) against the armed forces or armed corps,
d) as a member of dangerous group, or
e) during a crisis situation."

The non-specific criminal offences which can be applied in that respect are the following: preparation of an offence; conspiracy in a committed or an attempted criminal offence of terrorism; establishing, contriving and supporting a terrorist group; instigating and condoning a criminal offence of terrorism.

For the wording of all the relevant criminal law provisions related to the fight against terrorism, please see the national legislation of the Slovak Republic published on the CODEXTER website.[1]

3. Do you plan to introduce new legislation to counter terrorist misuse of cyberspace? What are the basic concepts of these legislative initiatives?

The legislative procedure for the amendment of the Criminal Code is currently underway. This amendment will facilitate the criminal prosecution of misuse of cyberspace through the proper implementation and application of the provisions of the Council of Europe Convention on the Prevention of Terrorism (Articles 5, 6, 7 and 9). Misuse of cyberspace for criminal purposes is defined as "public" for that purpose.

4. What are the existing national practices in the field of detecting, monitoring and closing down websites used for illicit, in particular, terrorist purposes and what kind of national procedures allow the blocking of access to websites or pages considered illicit?

A new special unit for cybercrime has been established within the Presidium of the Police Force. This unit provides technical and methodical assistance to the other units of the police force by detecting any crime committed through cyberspace.

---

[1] http://www.coe.int/gmt.

5. **What are the existing national practices in the field of interception of, or infiltration to, the electronic correspondence (e.g. e-mail, forum, instantaneous message service, voice over IP-skype, etc.)**

National practices in the field of the interception of electronic correspondence are the same as practices relating to the interception of telecommunications devices.

Interception is initiated by the police authorities, which submit a request for interception to the prosecutor. The fundamental prerequisites for interception are specified in the Code of Criminal Procedure. Interception is only allowed on the basis of an order issued by the competent judge and is conducted by a special police unit.

6. **Does your national legislation provide criteria for establishing jurisdiction over the misuse of cyberspace for terrorist purposes? What are those criteria?**

The legal order of the Slovak Republic specifies that the jurisdiction of the Slovak Criminal Code in relation to this kind of criminal conduct is the same as in respect of any other criminal offence. The applicable criteria are the following: the principle of territoriality, the principle of personality, the principle *aut dedere aut judicare* and jurisdiction based on international treaties.

7. **Does your national legal system establish additional offences related to attempts at, or complicity in, the commission of the misuse of cyberspace for terrorist purposes (ancillary offences)?**

Additional offences related the misuse of cyberspace for terrorist purposes are established in respect of the criminal offence of terrorism. There is no specific regulation in that respect.

8. **What kind of national procedures do you have for submitting an application on the activities of Internet-providers and/or hosting companies, to deprive a user from a domain name or cancel his/hers/its registration or licence?**

See the reply to question 9.

National procedures are regulated in detail in Act No. 610/2003 Coll. on e-communications and in the Code of Criminal Procedure.

9. What non-legislative measures do you have in your country to prevent and counter terrorist misuse of cyberspace, including self-regulatory measures?

Where there is intelligence that the content of a website or that any activity connected with the use of cyberspace gives grounds to suspect the commission of a criminal offence, the police may carry out an investigation aimed at finding the Internet providers, hosting companies and/or other persons connected with the crime. The police may also request that the Internet providers cancel the illicit website. The cancelling of a license is not allowed; however, within the criminal procedure the court can issue a sentence to ban the activity.

C. International co-operation

10. Please describe the general framework for international co-operation regarding the misuse of cyberspace for terrorist purposes.

Within criminal proceedings, all relevant multi- and bilateral international instruments related to police and judicial co-operation are applicable.

At the pre-trial stage, the main communication channels used are those of Interpol and Europol.

11. What are the existing practices and experiences with regard to international cooperation, in particular in relation to the procedures described in question 4?

No specific practices or experiences have been identified in this respect.

The Presidium of the Police Force is actively involved in the "Check the web" project. The participation of the Slovak authorities in this project is welcomed and considered very useful.

D. Institutional frame work

12. Please list the institutions that are competent for countering terrorist misuse of cyberspace.

See the reply to question 4.

13. In order to counter terrorist misuse of cyberspace are they any partnerships between the public and private sectors or legal obligations for operators of electronic communication?

N/A

14. Are there any hotlines regulated by the public or private sectors permitting denouncement of those websites which could be of terrorist character / nature?

N/A

E. Statistical information

15. Please provide relevant statistics on offences relating to the misuse of cyberspace for terrorist purposes (including possibly: cases recorded, investigated, brought to court, convictions, victims etc.).

No statistical data is available.

16. Where possible, please describe briefly the profile of offenders typically involved in the misuse of cyberspace for terrorist purposes (professional background, gender, age, nationality), and possible typical organisational characteristics, including trans-national links and links to other forms of organised crime.

N/A.

Spain

A. National policy

1. **Is there a national policy regarding the analysis, detection, prosecution and prevention of cybercrime in general and the misuse of cyberspace for terrorist purposes in particular? If yes, please briefly describe it.**

In Spain, there is the political intention to fight cybercrime, as can be inferred from the creation of special bodies within the National Police Force, such as the Investigation Unit on Information Technology Crime, or within the Spanish *Guardia Civil*, the Counter-Technological Crime Task Force whose technical measures are more and more innovative.

B. Legal framework

2. **Does your national legislation criminalise the misuse of cyberspace for terrorist purposes, and**
a. are these offences specifically defined with regard to the terrorist nature or technical means of committing the crime (e.g. cyberterrorism), or
b. is the misuse covered by other, non-specific criminal offences? How are these offences defined and which sanctions (criminal, administrative, civil) are attached?

National legislation does not specifically criminalise the misuse of cyberspace for terrorist purposes.

This offence is partially covered by the results of the cyber-action, if it kills or causes bodily injuries (Articles 138-142 of the Criminal Code) or, by the use of explosives or by means of a similar destructive power, causes the destruction of ports, airports, buildings, explosives or chemicals in storage, the sinking of a ship, explosions on industrial sites, etc. (Article 346 of the Criminal Code). These provisions do not exclude the possibility of the explosion or similar action being caused by a cyber attack.

On the other hand, there are several provisions that specifically criminalise these offences if they are committed while belonging to or helping a terrorist group (Articles 572 and 573 of the Criminal Code).

Where a computer system is attacked, hacked into or brought down with the objective of gaining access to , revealing or changing personal data, Article 197 of the Criminal Code applies. Damage to electronic data, electronic documents or programs is specifically punished in Article 264 as "qualified damages".

Finally, there is a general provision that aggravates any crime committed while belonging to, or helping, a terrorist group (Article 574 of the Criminal Code).

3. Do you plan to introduce new legislation to counter terrorist misuse of cyberspace? What are the basic concepts of these legislative initiatives?

The new draft Criminal Code, which is pending in the national parliament, contains important innovations on fighting cybercrime.

4. What are the existing national practices in the field of detecting, monitoring and closing down websites used for terrorist purposes?

The Spanish Police Forces constantly monitor all the places (blogs, websites, etc.) which are used or are likely to be used by terrorists and connected people. Monitoring activities are carried out in response to police investigations, information from citizens or other sources.

5. Does your national legislation provide criteria for establishing jurisdiction over such offences? What are those criteria?

There are no specific rules to establish jurisdiction over cybercrime, so the general rules are applied.

6. Does your national legal system establish ancillary offences related to the misuse of cyberspace?

No specific ancillary offences related to the misuse of cyberspace are contemplated. Article 197 of the Spanish Criminal Code protects privacy and punishes the penetration of e-mails or databases.

7. What kind of national procedures do you have for submitting an application on the activities of Internet-providers and/or hosting companies, to deprive a user from a domain name or to cancel his/her/its registration or licence?

In relation to the second level domain name ".es", there is an administrative procedure managed by a government corporation called RED.es; this public body would obey a court order related to the deprivation of a second level .es domain name.

8. **What non-legislative measures do your have in your country to prevent and counter terrorist misuse of cyberspace, including self-regulatory measures?**

-

C. **International co-operation**

9. **Please describe the general framework for international co-operation regarding the misuse of cyberspace for terrorist purposes.**

Cyberterrorism is a global threat; for this reason it is absolutely necessary to coordinate the efforts of the different countries in order to control the activity of terrorist groups on the Internet. In particular, European law enforcement agencies are developing mechanisms to coordinate the fight against the use of Internet for terrorist purposes.

10. **What are the existing practices and experiences with regard to international cooperation in particular in relation to the procedures described in question 4?**

For several years, Spain has been maintaining contacts with police forces from other countries. As a result, Spain regularly attends international meetings where different projects and subprojects are carried out.

D. **Institutional framework**

11. **Please list the institutions that are competent for countering terrorist misuse of cyberspace.**

The fight against terrorism, which includes all forms of terrorism and of course the fight against the misuse of cyberspace, represents undoubtedly one of the top priorities of the Spanish government, which has over the years developed different institutional measures to fight this phenomenon:
–   The Ministry of Home Affairs directs police activities against terrorism. Under the Minister, the Secretary of State for Security directs and coordinates the activities of the Directorate General of the National Police and the Civil Guard. The National Police includes the Intelligence General Headquarters which is responsible for fighting terrorism. There are also law enforcement agencies reporting to the governments of certain autonomous regions, which in certain cases have competence in the fight against terrorism. The Secretary of State for Security coordinates the activities of the state law enforcement agencies and those of the autonomous police with competence in the fight against terrorism, e.g. the Police of the Autonomous Communities of Catalonia and the Basque Country.

- Under the Ministry of Defence, the National Centre of Intelligence (CNI) is the public body which provides the President of the Government with information, analyses and proposals to prevent and avoid any danger, threat or aggression against the independence or territorial integrity of Spain, against national interests and against the stability of the state of law or its institutions.
- The Ministry for Foreign Affairs and Co-operation deals with terrorist issues through the Directorate General of International Affairs on Terrorism, Disarmament and Non Proliferation.
- The Ministry of Economy has competence for the basic measures that involve countering terrorist funding.
- The Ministry of Justice promotes the legislative policy of the Government relative to the fight against terrorism.
- There are various coordination institutions such as the Government Commission for Intelligence Affairs, the Government Commission for Crisis Situations and the National Centre for Anti-terrorist Coordination (CNCA)1.

12. Are there any partnerships between the public and private sectors (Internet-service providers, hosting companies, etc.) to counter terrorist misuse of cyberspace?

There is close collaboration between national police forces. Due to this co-operation, there is a fluid exchange of experiences and information, which includes the sharing of technical training. Likewise, the authorities are in touch with universities and businesses, both public or private, to whom they turn when necessary (to obtain information, for training courses for police staff, etc.) or in a judicial framework.

The private sector is of crucial relevance to the fight against the terrorist use of the Internet. Generally private companies are aware of their key role in this matter and maintain positive relationship with the police forces. This co-operation is reflected in the organisation of training courses as well as co-operation with investigations conducted by the police forces.

E. Statistical information

13. Please provide relevant statistics on offences relating to the misuse of cyberspace for terrorist purposes (including possibly: cases recorded, investigated, brought to court, convictions, victims etc.).

There are no statistics on offences relating to the misuse of cyberspace for terrorist purposes.

14. Where possible, please describe briefly the profile of offenders typically involved in the misuse of cyberspace for terrorist purposes (professional background, gender, age, nationality), and possible typical organisational characteristics, including transnational links and links to other forms of organised crime.

Currently it is not possible to talk about a cybernetic terrorist profile. However, it is possible to say that it is mainly young males with technical knowledge who use cyberspace for terrorist purposes (an increase in the production and distribution of digital publications concerning subjects such as intrusions, communication security, etc. has been observed; these are produced regularly by the technical divisions of terrorist organisations or linked to them).

Regarding the frequent use of the Internet by these groups or persons, it mostly consists in: communications, obtaining information for the committing of terrorist attacks, propaganda and spreading of terrorist activity hand books. No attacks by terrorist groups against Spanish servers concerning the denial of Internet services have been detected, although attacks consisting in the disfiguration of web pages have been detected.

Sweden

A. National policy

1. **Is there a national policy regarding the analysis, detection, prosecution and prevention of cybercrime in general and the misuse of cyberspace for terrorist purposes in particular? If yes, please briefly describe it.**

There is no separate national policy for cybercrime or cyberterrorism.

At the heart of Swedish counter-terrorism policy is the principle that threats can be combated legitimately only by using methods that belong to an open, democratic and legally secure society and that respect fundamental freedoms and rights. Sweden is working both nationally and internationally to gain as much support as possible for this principle. Since international terrorism represents a threat to the safety of us all, Sweden considers it highly important to take part actively and constructively in the international co-operation that is essential for combating terrorism. The rule of law and openness are key principles for all counter-terrorist activities.

B. Legal framework

2. **Does your national legislation criminalise the misuse of cyberspace for terrorist purposes, and**
   a. are these offences specifically defined with regard to the terrorist nature or technical means of committing the crime, or
   b. is the misuse covered by other, non-specific criminal offences? How are these offences defined and which sanctions (criminal, administrative, civil) are attached?

Misuse of cyberspace for terrorist purposes is criminalised under Swedish penal law.

Swedish penal law does not contain special provisions on cyberterrorism. The same rules are applicable to the misuse of cyberspace for terrorist purposes as to other acts of terrorism. It is the terrorist motive of an act which qualifies it as a terrorist offence.

Since 2003 there is a special law on criminal responsibility for terrorist offences. This law contains a list of certain actions that may lead to penalties under the Swedish Penal Code or other statutes. Under special circumstances these offences are to be considered terrorist offences instead.

This is the case if the offence might seriously damage a state or an intergovernmental organisation. The offence must also be undertaken for certain, specific purposes, such as serious intimidation of a population or a group of population or compelling a government to take a certain decision.

Under these circumstances, the acts that constitute terrorist offences are, for example, murder, kidnapping, sabotage, hijacking, spreading poison or a contagious substance and unlawful handling of chemical weapons. The penalty for terrorist offences is imprisonment for a maximum of ten years, or for life.

Acts that were committed before the entry into force of the Act on Criminal Responsibility for Terrorist Offences, or that are not punishable under this Act for other reasons, are punishable under the provisions of the Swedish Penal Code concerning murder and other crimes against life and health, or provisions concerning offences involving public danger such as arson, devastation endangering the public and spreading poison or a contagious substance or under the penal provisions of other acts. The maximum penalty for such crimes is life imprisonment.

In order to fulfil the obligations of the EU Council Framework Decision on attacks against information systems, new legislation on extended criminal liability for breach of data secrecy entered into force on 1 June 2007. According to the new legislation it is punishable to unlawfully block computer data or unlawfully seriously disturb or obstruct the use of such data. Attempts and preparation to commit such crimes as well as complicity in such crimes are also punishable. Their criminalisation means for example that so-called denial-of-service attacks have become punishable. The maximum penalty is imprisonment for two years.

3.   Do you plan to introduce new legislation to counter terrorist misuse of cyberspace? What are the basic concepts of these legislative initiatives?

Work on the ratification of the Convention on the Prevention of Terrorism and of the Convention on Cybercrime is ongoing within the Swedish Ministry of Justice. It is too early yet to tell whether the ratifications will call for any amendments of Swedish law.

4.   What are the existing national practices in the field of detecting, monitoring and closing down websites used for terrorist purposes?

The Swedish National Security Service monitors, on a regular basis, websites that might contain terror-related messages. The activities include monitoring the development, considering possible threats and preventing future criminality. If a crime is detected, the Security Service, as a public authority, can initiate a preliminary investigation. However, the Security Service is not authorised to take any measures in order to shut the website down, other than notifying the provider of the website about its content. According to national law, the provider then has the responsibility, under certain conditions, to remove the message from the website. Failure to act on such a notification might lead to sentencing according to the same law.

There are no legal measures to prevent inappropriate information from being posted on a website.

5. Does your national legislation provide criteria for establishing jurisdiction over such offences? What are those criteria?

The general provisions on jurisdiction for Swedish courts in criminal matters in the Swedish Penal Code also apply for crimes committed on the Internet.

Where a crime has been committed in Sweden, it can always be adjudged by a Swedish court. This also applies when it is uncertain where the crime was committed but grounds exist for assuming that it was committed within Sweden. This ground for jurisdiction can be of special interest for crimes committed on the Internet, since in these cases it can often be difficult to trace the computer used by the perpetrator, but there might be circumstances (e.g. the domicile of the perpetrator) indicating that the message was sent from Sweden. Swedish legislation provides for a wide jurisdiction over crimes committed abroad, especially for terrorist offences which are subject to universal jurisdiction and do not presuppose dual criminality.

The use of the Internet raises specific questions, *inter alia*, the question of the location of a committed crime. According to Swedish law a crime is deemed to have been committed where the criminal act was perpetrated and also where the crime was completed or, in the case of an attempt, where the intended crime would have been completed.

6. Does your national legal system establish ancillary offences related to the misuse of cyberspace?

Attempt, preparation or conspiracy to commit a terrorist offence or failure to disclose such an offence is punishable under the Swedish Penal law. These provisions are applicable to the misuse of cyberspace.

7. What kind of national procedures do you have for submitting an application on the activities of Internet-providers and/or hosting companies, to deprive a user from a domain name or to cancel his/her/its registration or licence?

The Swedish authorities are not tasked with deciding on matters of registration of a domain name. This is a matter for private companies. Registration and revocation of domain names are therefore regulated by contract law.

8. **What non-legislative measures do your have in your country to prevent and counter terrorist misuse of cyberspace, including self-regulatory measures?**

The Security Service may, in its crime prevention efforts, establish contacts with individuals, in order to point out that a certain kind of behaviour carries a high level of risk, even though it is not necessary criminal. Such contacts are always on a voluntary basis.

C. International co-operation

9. **Please describe the general framework for international co-operation regarding the misuse of cyberspace for terrorist purposes.**

The general framework for international judicial co-operation regarding the misuse of cyberspace is more or less identical to that regarding national judicial actions against criminal activities of this kind. Measures available nationally, including coercive measures, are also available when assisting other states in their prosecution. Moreover, in many cases assistance may be granted when there is no dual criminality or where the requesting authority requests a procedure which is different from the normal procedures under Swedish law. Generally, there are no special rules for giving assistance in matters regarding the misuse of cyberspace. General rules are applicable to such assistance.

10. **What are the existing practices and experiences with regard to international co-operation, in particular in relation to the procedures described in question 4?**

The experience of giving or asking for judicial assistance in this area is very limited. According to information from Swedish prosecutors, this has never occurred.

D. Institutional framework

11. **Please list the institutions that are competent for countering terrorist misuse of cyberspace.**

Preventing and obstructing the planning and implementation of terrorist acts are measures that come under the responsibility of the Swedish Police Service. The main responsibility for combating terrorism lies with the Security Service.

In 2004, the Security Service established a Counter Terrorism Co-operation Council. The Council includes representatives of the Military Intelligence and Security Service, the National Defence Radio Establishment, the Swedish Defence Research Agency, the Swedish Emergency Management Agency, the Swedish Coast Guard, the Swedish Customs Service, the Swedish Prosecution Authority, the Swedish National Economic Crimes Bureau, the Swedish Migration Board and the National Criminal Police.

12. Are there any partnerships between the public and private sectors (Internet-service providers, hosting companies, etc.) to counter terrorist misuse of cyberspace?

The Security Service does not co-operate on counter-terrorism with the private sector on a regular basis. Occasionally, such co-operation might occur on a voluntary basis. The Security Service also receives information from the public.

E. Statistical information

13. Please provide relevant statistics on offences relating to the misuse of cyberspace for terrorist purposes (including possibly: cases recorded, investigated, brought to court, convictions, victims etc.).

and

14. Where possible, please describe briefly the profile of offenders typically involved in the misuse of cyberspace for terrorist purposes (professional background, gender, age, nationality), and possible typical organisational characteristics, including trans-national links and links to other forms of organised crime.

No relevant information can be reported at the moment.

Switzerland

A.   National policy

1.   Is there a national policy regarding the analysis, detection, prosecution and prevention of cybercrime in general and the misuse of cyberspace for terrorist purposes in particular? If yes, please briefly describe it.

Against a background of various parliamentary initiatives and with a general view to reviewing the opportunities for abuse offered by the Internet, in 2001 the Department of Justice set up a committee of experts on cybercrime to consider what legal, organisational and technical measures were needed to prevent and take action against Internet-based offences, with particular reference to determining where criminal liability lay, and, if appropriate, to propose rules on civil liability and the protection of intellectual property. The committee reported in June 2003.[1] In October 2004, the Federal Council produced a report setting out preliminary draft changes to the Swiss Criminal Code and the military Criminal Code concerning the criminal liability of service providers and the powers of the Confederation to prosecute offences committed via the electronic media (cybercrime).

The Federal Council report on the 2003-2007 legislative programme shows that protecting security in Switzerland is a important objective, as part of the major policy of "strengthening Switzerland in the world". There is growing support for a change in security policy in which autonomous defence is reinforced by co-operation. This reorientation implies closer bilateral co-operation with selected partners and improved European and Euro-Atlantic co-operation on security matters. A comprehensive approach to security also entails efforts to counter the causes of and prevent future conflicts, for example by combating poverty.

In the course of the 2003-2007 Parliament, the Federal Council's strategy for optimising international co-operation, prevention and internal judicial and policing arrangements has involved, among other things, the negotiation of Schengen and Dublin association agreements, as part of the "bilateral II" package, the ratification of new UN agreements on organised crime and countering the spread of cybercrime.[2] The strategy necessitates more international co-operation, changes to Swiss legislation and closer collaboration with the cantons. Similarly, efforts to prevent violence call for certain improvements, particularly measures against racism, hooliganism and incitement to violence. Efforts to combat cybercrime through criminal

---

[1] Report of the committee of experts on cybercrime, Federal Department of Justice and Police, Berne, June 2003,
http://www.bj.admin.ch/bj/fr/home/themen/kriminalitaet/gesetzgebung/netzwerkkriminalitaet.html.
[2] Federal Council report on the 2003-2007 parliament, p. 72, available in PDF format at http://www.ch.ch/behoerden/00215/00329/00350/index.html?.

proceedings need to be strengthened by means of organisational measures, closer co-operation with Interpol and the application of international instruments. More specifically, the Federal Council intends to introduce criminal liability for those who circulate material on the Internet whose content is subject to prosecution and grant the relevant federal departments new powers of co-operation.

Switzerland is active in the Partnership for Peace and the Euro-Atlantic Partnership Council in a number of fields, including efforts to combat terrorist financing. With regard to conventions on terrorism, Switzerland's policy is to "depoliticise" terrorist offences.

B. Legal framework

2. Does your national legislation criminalise the misuse of cyberspace for terrorist purposes, and
a. are these offences specifically defined with regard to the terrorist nature or technical means of committing the crime, or
b. is the misuse covered by other, non-specific criminal offences? How are these offences defined and which sanctions (criminal, administrative, civil) are attached?

Under Swiss law the misuse of cyberspace for terrorist purposes is a criminal offence. There is no specific offence in Swiss law of misuse of cyberspace for terrorist purposes or even of cybercrime in general and terrorism (other than Article 260bis: preparing criminal activities; Article 260ter: organised crime and Article 260quinquies: terrorist financing). Such misuse is covered by other, more general, provisions of Swiss law.

Misuse of cyberspace for terrorist purposes is currently covered by the general provisions of the Swiss Criminal Code of 21 December 1937, for example, Article 25 for web hosts and access providers when the offence is not a media offence; the criminal law provisions on the media (Articles 28 and 322bis – in principle, only the perpetrators of media offences are criminally liable, web hosts and access providers are only liable if the perpetrator cannot be identified or brought before a Swiss court), and certain special provisions of the Criminal Code that may also be applied to cyberterrorism. The latter cover, firstly, computer crime, in the sense of terrorist attacks on the Internet network, such as Article 143: removal of data; Article 143bis: unauthorised access to a computer system; Article 144bis: data contamination, including the manufacture and dissemination of computer viruses; Article 147: fraudulent use of a computer; Article 150.4: service obtained by fraud; Article 150bis: manufacture and marketing of equipment for the illicit decoding of encrypted services; Article 181: constraint, such as that resulting from the dispatch of e-mails that are unsolicited or in very large numbers or denial of service attack; Article 239.1: interference with services of general interest, such as serious damage to the communications network,[3] and, secondly, the use of the Internet to commit terrorist acts, such as Article 135: depiction of violence; Article 146: fraud, for example using a website; Article 226.3: manufacturing, concealing or transporting explosives or toxic gases; Article 259: public incitement to crime or violence; Article 260ter: organised crime; Article 260quater: threatening public safety through the use of arms; Article 260quinquies: terrorist financing; Article 261bis: racial discrimination; 265-278: offences against the state or national defence; Article 305bis: money laundering, for example, using e-banking via Internet;[4] Article 305ter: failure to exercise vigilance in connection with financial transactions and duty to communicate relevant information. These offences carry criminal penalties, in accordance with the relevant provisions.

With regard to whether knowledge of specific Internet content is sufficient for activities covered by Article 322bis to be deemed intentional, it is neither possible nor reasonable to expect access providers themselves to carry out the necessary checks. Information from third parties on such content must be specific and come from a reliable source. Access providers can only be held to have known that content was unlawful if the relevant information came from a prosecution authority. Mere statements by individuals or general press releases are not normally sufficient to demonstrate relevant knowledge of intention.

In the case of media content-related offences that are not covered by the special provisions of media criminal law, access providers are subject to the general rules on participation, whereby they may be guilty of complicity (Article 25 of the Criminal Code) with a predicate offence if they fail to take the necessary steps despite being aware that the Internet content was unlawful. Information supplied by a criminal prosecution authority to an access provider about specific network content must be considered adequate for this purpose. Communications from private persons will not normally meet the required conditions. In contrast, and as in the case of media law, additional detailed and specific information from other sources is necessary for hosting service providers.

Certain general administrative standards, such as the federal Telecommunications Act of 30 April 1997 and its subsidiary order on telecommunication services of 9 March 2007 and the federal Radio and Television Act of 24 March 2006 may also be applicable to the fields of cybercrime and, at least in part, cyberterrorism (though in the latter case they are more difficult to apply).

---

[3] Assessment of the situation in and threats to Switzerland in the light of the terrorist attacks of 11 September 2001, Federal Council report to Parliament of 26 June 2002, p. 1709, http://www.admin.ch/ch/f/ff/2003/1674.pdf.
[4] Assessment of the situation in and threats to Switzerland in the light of the terrorist attacks of 11 September 2001, Federal Council report to parliament of 26 June 2002, p. 1711, http://www.admin.ch/ch/f/ff/2003/1674.pdf.

The federal legislation of 21 March 1997 on measures to protect internal security is critical. When propaganda material whose content constitutes a serious and specific incitement to violence against persons or objects is disseminated, paragraph 5 of Article 13a of the legislation authorises the federal justice office to order the removal of the site concerned, if the material appears on a Swiss server, and to recommend Swiss providers to block the site concerned, if the material is not on a Swiss server. According to the Federal Council report to Parliament of 26 June 2002 assessing the situation in and threats to Switzerland in the light of the terrorist attacks of 11 September 2001, restrictive measures against terrorist group propaganda networks and logistical activities in Switzerland, such as bans on fund raising, are only justified if the public interest outweighs any private interests concerned and the measures taken are not disproportionate.

The perpetrators of Internet offences for terrorist purposes may also be found to be civilly liable for their actions. The law of obligations and the special rules on civil liability are applicable, since there are currently no specific civil provisions relating to Internet services.

3. Do you plan to introduce new legislation to counter terrorist misuse of cyberspace? What are the basic concepts of these legislative initiatives?

Work is currently under way on new or modified provisions on cybercrime that might, in part, apply to cyberterrorism. In December 2004, the Federal Justice and Police Department launched consultations on two draft laws that would amend the Criminal Code and the Military Criminal Code of 13 June 1927 concerning the criminal liability of Internet providers for unlawful content on the Internet and the powers of the Confederation to prosecute offences committed through the electronic media.

In the case of the first draft, the proposed new regulations would include all cybercrime and would therefore not be confined, as in the case of media criminal law, to media offences. In contrast to the media law, the proposed new Article 322bis of the Criminal Code provides for the criminal liability of hosting service providers even if the content provider cannot be identified, or if the latter cannot be brought before a Swiss court. Again in contrast to the media law, it excludes criminal liability for negligence. Hosting service providers will therefore be liable as co-perpetrators, instigators or accomplices, if they intentionally permit unlawful information on their servers.

Under the second draft, the new regulations would authorise the Confederation to undertake investigations during the first phase of a procedure, without infringing cantons' powers to conduct criminal prosecutions.

4. What are the existing national practices in the field of detecting, monitoring and closing down websites used for illicit, in particular, terrorist purposes and what kind of national procedures allow the blocking of access to websites or pages considered illicit?

In Switzerland, it is not necessary to seek authorisation to open a website as this would be incompatible with the ban on censorship (Article 17.2 of the Constitution). The same applies to the supply of memory capacity for third parties to provide information to the general public. There is not even a general legal obligation to check content, which would probably be inappropriate and disproportionate.

Opinions differ in Switzerland as to whether "monitoring" constitutes justifiable censorship (Article 36 of the Constitution).[5] In January 2003, a Department to co-ordinate the fight against Internet crime (SCOCI), with surveillance responsibilities, was set up in the Federal Police Office. It is the central point of contact for persons wishing to report suspicious Internet sites. It examines any criminal content of messages entering, collects data, co-ordinates with any proceedings under way and transmits information received to the relevant prosecution authorities in Switzerland and abroad. The SCOCI also looks for unlawful content on the Internet and undertakes detailed assessments of Internet crime.[6] The monitoring, clearing and analytical functions are undertaken by three operational units of the federal police. Monitoring and the new analytical function are incorporated into an Analysis and Prevention Department (SAP) and the clearing function is performed by the Federal Judicial Police (PJF). The committee of experts on cybercrime considers that "monitoring" is compatible with the federal Constitution.[7]

The central body for recording and analysis in relation to information security (MELANI), made up of persons from the fields of computer system and Internet security and the protection of national and vital infrastructure, identifies threats and risks as soon as possible, to permit the immediate introduction of defence measures and prevent the use of high risk technologies.[8]

The Analysis and Prevention Department (SAP) has responsibilities relating to the preventive protection of the State and at federal level also undertakes analyses and assessments of the internal security situation. It works closely

---

[5] http://www.ofj.admin.ch.
[6] http://www.ofj.admin.ch/fedpol/fr/home/themen/kriminalitaet/cybercrime.html; http://www.cybercrime.admin.ch/f/koord.htm.
[7] http://www.ofj.admin.ch/etc/medialib/data/kriminalitaet/gestzgebung/netzwerkkrimina litaet.Par.0007.File.tmp/ber-netzwerkkrim-f.pdf, p. 82.
[8] http://www.efd.admin.ch/dokumentation/zahlen/00579/00700/00824/index.html?lan g=fr, MELANI second six-monthly report for 2006, Information security situation in Switzerland and internationally, accessible in PDF format at http://www.melani.admin.ch/index.html?lang=fr.

with cantonal police authorities and the Federal Judicial Police, and with other departments in Switzerland and abroad.[9] The SAP and its external intelligence service (RS) co-operate closely with foreign counterparts in gathering information on terrorism.[10]

Various practices are used in Switzerland to identify, monitor and close websites used for unlawful purposes, particularly terrorism.

For identification and monitoring purposes, certain cantons have set up computer crime groups within their police forces.

The following measures are considered to be reasonable, in the current legal and technical circumstances:[11]

- Access providers who receive detailed and specific information from the law enforcement authorities on content of a criminal nature must block access to these sites. The relevant measures include blocking the IP address, if the offending material is stored on a site with its own IP address, and the offending URL in the proxy server.[12]

- Hosting service providers with detailed and specific information (not necessarily originating from enforcement authorities) about offending material on one of their servers must make sure that this information is no longer accessible or is wiped out. If the information does not come from law enforcement authorities they must themselves carry out any necessary additional investigations, if appropriate by calling on a prosecuting authority or another qualified professional third party. The same applies if they receive information through a contractual relationship with a content provider that creates doubts about the legality of the use of their facilities.

From the standpoint of criminal liability, access providers with specific information from criminal proceedings about presumed unlawful content circulating on the Internet are asked to block it if this is reasonable. It is neither feasible nor reasonable to undertake active and individual searches for offending material on the Internet, because such material changes and increases daily. Such steps are therefore not required. Hosting service providers are required to look for detailed and specific information about unlawful web content and newsgroups. If they find it they must remove it or

---

[9] http://www.fedpol.admin.ch/fedpol/fr/home/fedpol/organisation/dienst_fuer_analyse .html.

[10] Assessment of the situation in and threats to Switzerland in the light of the terrorist attacks of 11 September 2001, Federal Council report to parliament of 26 June 2002, p. 1712, http://www.admin.ch/ch/f/ff/2003/1674.pdf.

[11] http://www.ejpd.admin.ch/etc/medialib/data/kriminalitaet/internetkriminalitaet.Par.0 002.File.tmp/Avis%20de%20la%20Police%20fédérale.pdf p. 12.

[12] http://www.ejpd.admin.ch/etc/medialib/data/kriminalitaet/internetkriminalitaet.Par.0 002.File.tmp/Avis%20de%20la%20Police%20fédérale.pdf p. 12.

block access to it. Since web hosts have much closer relations with content providers than do access providers, they are required to monitor, at least on a sample basis, suspect content providers. Such surveillance is particularly important in the case of files on FTP servers that allow data to be stored freely, to the extent that these files can be read by traditional software.

Internet service providers are not obliged to report offending attitudes or content to the police authorities. Nevertheless, the general rules governing the reporting of offences apply. In the case of offences that are investigated following complaints, providers may be informed of the penalties they are liable to incur or the persons concerned may be informed of the infringement of their rights.

In the case of criminal investigations not concerning providers, the general duties arising from the law of criminal procedure apply, including the duty to give evidence and to hand over documents or computer-derived information. In the case of communications such as e-mail, private chat services and Internet telephony that are protected by telecommunications confidentiality, the competent authorities may order steps to be taken, under the applicable criminal procedure. These include:

–   Information on the Internet traffic of users who are clients of Internet service providers, who must supply this on a real-time basis where possible. In so far as the technology allows, therefore, this involves direct surveillance. "The authority that orders surveillance must compensate the provider appropriately".

–   Personal data on each user concerning the traffic and bills stored in log files. This data must be made available to the competent authorities for at least six months.

In Switzerland, the following procedures may be used to block access to websites or pages considered to be unlawful:

–   The web server IP address is blocked by the provider at the router. This measure blocks all the material on the server and not just the offending content. It is therefore an impracticable solution for major providers offering thousands of different pages but is more suitable for unlawful pages with their own server or name for which a particular domain name or IP address only offers the same sorts of content (such as material produced by racists or violent extremists). This applies fairly frequently to racist or extremist content, since these content providers wish to take advantage of easy-to-remember domain names, such as stormfront.org. The police now recommend the blocking (among other measures) of this type of website. A variant of this approach is to exclude certain domain names at the DSN (domain name server).

- "The provider uses a proxy server. All WWW consultations (for example Port 80) enter into the basic configuration of the web browser via this proxy. The latter then allows consultations to be registered and the temporary storage of data requested, as well as their blocking. Clients must configure their web browsers accordingly. If they fail to do so, the proxy server is missed out and communication is established directly with the site being sought. Most providers use such proxy servers, but with a view to greater efficiency. There are also proxies for servers other than http, for example FTP".

- "The provider uses a transparent proxy, with the result that clients automatically use the proxy server, whether or not they wish to. It is possible to install a blocking mechanism in the proxy, applicable to individual pages. In principle, this constitutes an open firewall that can divert and if necessary filter certain services".

In the world of Internet, there are problems with national approaches to blocking access to unlawful server content. Swiss clients can choose foreign servers with no blocking mechanism. Moreover, certain on-line service providers, such as AOL, claim to offer Internet access throughout Europe via the same network. With such a network arrangement, it would be impossible to block access that only applied to Switzerland.

5. What are the existing national practices in the field of interception of, or infiltration to, the electronic correspondence (e.g. e-mail, forum, instantaneous message service, voice over IP-skype, etc).

The special duties section of the federal environment, transport, energy and communications department can intercept e-mail exchanges between suspects, at the request of the prosecuting authorities.

6. Does your national legislation provide criteria for establishing jurisdiction over the misuse of cyberspace for terrorist purposes? What are those criteria?

In Switzerland, responsibility for criminal prosecutions is shared between the confederation and the cantons. In the majority of cases such prosecutions are a cantonal responsibility. Federal jurisdiction is thus the exception (Article 123.2 of the Constitution).[13] The Confederation does not currently have special surveillance rights with regard to cybercrime. With particular reference to cyberterrorism, subject to certain conditions, Article 337 of the Criminal Code makes offences relating to organised crime, terrorist financing and economic crime subject to federal jurisdiction.

---

[13] http://www.ejpd.admin.ch/etc/medialib/data/kriminalitaet/gesetzgebung/netzwerkri minalitaet.Par.0004.File.tmp/ber-genesis-f.pdf, p. 7.

7. **Does your national legal system establish additional offences related to attempts at, or complicity in, the commission of the misuse of cyberspace for terrorist purposes (ancillary offences)?**

There are no specific provisions in Switzerland on misuse of cyberspace for terrorist purposes so neither is there any legislation on attempts at, or complicity in, the commission of such an offence. The relevant legislation therefore comprises the general provisions of the Criminal Code on attempted offences (Articles 22 and 23) and complicity (Article 25) and the special provisions of the Code on attempted offences and complicity that might apply to cyberterrorism, such as Article 260bis, on preparations to commit an offence. Similarly, as noted above, in the case of media offences Articles 28 and 322bis establish different levels of liability for network providers.

8. **What kind of national procedures do you have for submitting an application on the activities of Internet-providers and/or hosting companies or other entities, to deprive a user from a domain name or to cancel his/her/its registration or licence?**

When a licence holder has accepted certain conditions for the use of a website, the site editor may invoke the right to withdraw that licence automatically, if the conditions are not met.

9. **What non-legislative measures do you have in your country to prevent and counter terrorist misuse of cyberspace, including self-regulatory measures?**

The non-legislative measures in Switzerland to prevent and counter terrorist misuse of cyberspace include the technical practices for identifying, monitoring and blocking websites or pages considered to be unlawful. In addition, there is encouragement to service providers to collaborate more closely, both nationally and internationally. Such collaboration makes it possible to put greater pressure on providers in other countries not to tolerate such content. Such collaboration would be based on various general conditions and provider codes of conduct. Several providers have also installed a direct telephone line to report such content. So far, these lines have generally be restricted to their own servers.

C. International co-operation

10. Please describe your country's general framework for international co-operation regarding the misuse of cyberspace for terrorist purposes.

There are three elements to Swiss co-operation beyond its frontiers: international, European and bilateral co-operation.[14]

At the international level, Switzerland is a founder member of the International Criminal Police Organization (INTERPOL), which circulates information from police forces throughout the world, operates data bases and gives operational support to member states. Within Europe, it has reached a co-operation agreement (24 September 2004, entry into force 1 March 2006) with the European Police Office (Europol). It has also signed the Schengen Agreement, which was approved by the Swiss people on 5 June 2005. This will enable Switzerland to intensify police co-operation with several European countries. From the police standpoint, the main element of the agreement is the second generation Schengen Information System (SIS II). Switzerland has signed bilateral co-operation agreements with several neighbouring states, leading to the establishment of police and customs co-operation centres in Geneva and Chiasso. It has also signed new agreements on combating organised crime with Slovenia, Latvia, the Czech Republic, Romania, Albania and "the former Yugoslav Republic of Macedonia".

The Federal Council also decided on 29 September 2006 to start negotiations on a co-operation agreement with Eurojust, the Community institution that promotes the co-ordination of criminal investigations and proceedings between member states and facilitates the implementation of international mutual legal assistance and of extradition requests.[15]

11. What are the existing practices and experiences with regard to international co-operation, in particular in relation to the procedures described in question 4?

As stated under question 10, the SCOCI contributes to closer international co-operation in the fields of cybercrime and cyberterrorism. It is active internationally as well as nationally in the fields of monitoring, clearing and analysis.[16]

---

[14] 2005 report of the Federal Police Office on Swiss internal security; http://www.fedpol.admin.ch/etc/medialib/data/sicherheit/bericht_innere_sicherheit Par.0039.File.tmp./BISS_2005_f.pdf, p. 82.

[15] http://www.ejpd.admin.ch/ejpd/fr/home/dokumentation/mi/2006/2006-09-293.html.

[16] www.cybercrime.admin.ch.

In conjunction with the SCOCI, MELANI produces and publishes six-monthly reports on "Information security: the situation in Switzerland and internationally". These reports identify the main trends in the information and communication technologies (ICT) sector, noting any particular incidents or events that have occurred, offer technical explanations of the current forms of pirating, describe the current situation in Switzerland and abroad, identify the main developments in the field of prevention and summarise the key activities of the main state and private bodies concerned.

D. Institutional framework

12. Please list the institutions that are competent for countering terrorist misuse of cyberspace.

–   Certain cantons have already set up specialised police units to combat cybercrime.[17]

–   In June 2000, the Conference of Swiss cantonal police commanders (CCPCS) established an inter-cantonal working group to combat the misuse of information and communication technologies (BEMIK). The group submitted recommendations to the CCPCS in January 2001.

–   The SCOCI, established in the Federal Police Office (fedpol) in 2003, examines any criminal content of messages entering, saves data, co-ordinates with any proceedings under way and transmits information received to the relevant prosecution authorities in Switzerland and abroad. The department also looks for unlawful content on the Internet and undertakes detailed assessments of Internet crime.[18] The monitoring, clearing and analytical functions are undertaken by three operational units of the federal police. Monitoring and the new analytical function are incorporated into an analysis and prevention unit and the clearing function is performed by the federal judicial police.

13. In order to counter terrorist misuse of cyberspace are there any partnerships between the public and private sectors or legal obligations for operators of electronic communication (Internet-service providers, hosting companies, etc.) as well as persons providing the public with access to systems which allow on-line communication via access to the network (cybercafe, WiFi hotspot)?

-

---

[17]   Strategic analysis report of October 2001 of the federal police office's analysis and prevention department: "The hidden face of the information revolution", http://www.mihaly.ch/lois/textes/cybercriminalite.pdf p. 14.
[18]   http://www.ofj.admin.ch/fedpol/fr/home/themen/kriminalitaet/cybercrime.html; http://www.cybercrime.admin.ch/f/koord.htm.

14. Are there any hotlines regulated by the public or private sectors permitting denouncement of those websites which could be of a terrorist character / nature?

The SCOCI is the central point for persons wishing to report suspicious Internet sites.

E. Statistical information

15. Please provide relevant statistics on offences relating to the misuse of cyberspace for terrorist purposes (including possibly: cases recorded, investigated, brought to court, convictions, victims etc.).

The SCOCI recorded as many reports in 2006 as in previous years, with an average of 500 to 600 communications a month. The Federal Police Office's 2006 report on Switzerland's internal security said that communications concerning unlawful pornography were down on the previous year and were more often linked to chat forums while communications on economic crime had risen, particularly in the case of money laundering linked to phishing.

Cyberterrorism cases in Switzerland

Publication on a forum of a video of Al-Zawahiri. On 23 December 2005, an Internet forum published a video message showing Aiman al-Zawahiri, Al-Qaeda's number two, making threats against western countries. The forum was managed by a Dutch woman of Moroccan origin living in Guin, in Fribourg, a committed Salafist whose Tunisian husband had died in a suicide attack in Afghanistan and who was known to the authorities. In September 2004, she had placed photos on her site of the decapitation of a hostage in Iraq. In February 2005 the Federal Criminal Police had searched several homes of persons belonging to militant Islamic groups. The woman was one of five suspects arrested. After her release, she openly threatened the criminal prosecution authorities. She left Switzerland in 2006 to return to Belgium. She was banned from re-entering the country. In 2006, the Federal Investigating Judges' Office completed its criminal investigation into the activities of the manager of the forum www.islamic-minbar, namely the husband of the Dutch woman referred to above. The Internet forums that were open in 2004 and 2005 have been deactivated. In 2006, pages with similar names but no longer hosted in Switzerland, were again in operation. The couple were charged with support for a criminal organisation, public incitement to crime and violence and scenes of violence and were found guilty by the Federal Criminal Court on 21 June 2007.

The central computer of the University of Geneva hosts Islamic propaganda. On 29 October 2005, a newspaper reported that an unknown person was using the University of Geneva computer network to store and disseminate

Islamic propaganda whose source was clearly Al-Qaida. In particular, films showed the Jordanian terrorist Abu Musab al-Zarqawi committing acts of violence. The perpetrators were a 27 year-old Moroccan who had been living in Geneva for years without a residence permit and an Algerian asylum seeker aged 41 who had entered the country illegally. They had apparently transferred propaganda videos onto servers in a number of countries, in each case using the Internet access of four students who were officially registered at the university. For example, they had downloaded two video recordings of suicide attacks in Iraq and then published them on other sites. The case was detected by Evan Kohlmann, an American expert of cyberterrorism, who has been patrolling Islamic Internet sites for years and who runs an independent office in New York called Globalterroralert. To obtain access data – user names and passwords – for the accounts they used, the two intruders had watched authorised users over their shoulders while they logged on.[19]

16. **Where possible, please describe briefly the profile of offenders typically involved in the misuse of cyberspace for terrorist purposes (professional background, gender, age, nationality), and possible typical organisational characteristics, including transnational links and links to other forms of organised crime.**

Script kiddies or kiddiots. These complete beginners look for codes on the Internet and change them slightly to launch new forms of virus.

Virus authors. After they have acquired certain code writing skills, they write viruses in their spare time, which they either publish on the Internet or send by e-mail to launch attacks.

Occasional pirates. These abandon virus writing and the initial excitement this affords in favour of greater risks. Virus programmers are fully-fledged computer pirates who become immersed in cybercrime. However, they still have an "official" job. Most of the individuals who turn to computer piracy in their spare time work in the information technology sector.

Professional pirates. The full-time cybercriminals earn their living by stealing credit card information from their victims or hacking into the websites of banks for the purposes of theft or blackmail.

Phishers. These require more highly developed skills than pirates. Among other things, phishers counterfeit the websites of well-know banks. They then steal the passwords of users' accounts when the latter enter them on the counterfeit sites, in the mistaken belief that they are browsing the real ones.

Cybercriminals for hire. These more recently emerged figures in the world of cybercrime offer their services to organised crime at a high price.

---

[19] MELANI second six-monthly report for 2005, Information security situation in Switzerland and internationally,
http://www.news-service.admin.ch/NSBSubscriber/message/fr/attachments/4554/780
7/2409/MELANI_rapport_semestriel_05_02.pdf p. 14.

"The former Yugoslav Republic of Macedonia"

Cyberterrorism is a new category which is not legally regulated in this country. As a result, there is no general national policy aimed at the analysis, detection, prosecution and prevention of cybercrime and the misuse of cyberspace for terrorist purposes. However, there are specific criminal acts in the area of computer crime which are defined in the Criminal Code ("Official Gazette of the Republic of Macedonia" (hereafter "OGRM") Nos. 37/96, 80/99, 4/02, 43/03, 19/04, 81/05, 60/06 and 73/06). The Criminal Code does not provide for a special offence which would sanction these criminal acts, but they are contained in different criminal offences covered by the Code.

In particular, the adoption of the Law on amendment and supplement of the Criminal Code (OGRM No. 19/04) introduced into the criminal law system several criminal offences in the field of computer crime which were not previously included in any legal regulation. Thus, this country joined the other countries in their attempt to oppose the different forms and types of abuse of computer and IT systems.

As a result, there are no relevant national statistics on violations related to the misuse of cyberspace for terrorist purposes, nor is there a profile of the perpetrators involved in the realisation of these criminal acts, nor of their organisational features, transnational connections or links with other forms of organised crime.

In national criminal legal theory, there is no generally accepted definition of computer crime to cover the different forms and types of abuse of computer or IT systems, especially cyberterrorism.

National criminal legislation does not include criminal acts in the field of computer crime, which are defined in view of their terrorist character or the technical means used to commit the crime; the issue of cyberterrorism is not addressed either. However these criminal acts may be used by individuals or terrorist organisations to achieve specific terrorist aims or to perpetrate other criminal acts which are provided for in the Criminal Code.

Terrorism as a criminal act against the state is provided for under Article 313 of the Criminal Code prescribing at least four years' imprisonment for persons endangering the constitutional order or national security, causing or seriously threatening to cause an explosion, fire, flood or other socially dangerous action or an act of violence, creating a feeling of insecurity or fear in citizens.

The Internet can also be used to publish threats to cause an explosion, fire, flood or to carry out any other generally dangerous action or an act of violence, for instance on the webpage of a specific terrorist organisation, or by hacking into a webpage of a state authority, or in another manner, thus creating a feeling of insecurity or fear in citizens.

This means of committing the criminal act of "terrorism", i.e. via the misuse of computer and IT systems or unauthorised access to a web page of a state body or another institution which in fact means the misuse of cyber (virtual) space for terrorist purposes, is still not criminalised in national criminal legal theory.

Article 394a of the Criminal Code provides for the criminal act "terrorist organisation" as an act against the public order. A terrorist organisation is defined as a group, gang or another criminal organisation created to perpetrate criminal acts: murder, bodily harm, abduction of individuals, destruction of public facilities, transport systems, infrastructure, IT systems and other public structures, hijacking of planes or other means of public transport, manufacture and trafficking of nuclear arms, biological or chemical weapons, other types of weapons and dangerous materials, releasing dangerous radioactive or poisonous substances and other dangerous substances or causing fires or explosions, destroying water or electricity supply stations or other natural resources with the aim of creating a sense of insecurity or fear in citizens or endangering the constitutional order of the country or the interests of an international organisation or foreign country.

Paragraph 3 of this Article prescribes a sentence of four to ten years' imprisonment for persons publicly calling upon, instigating or supporting the creation of a terrorist organisation, including where this is done via the Internet as a publicly accessible system linking computer networks around the world i.e. the global data network to which everyone has access.

Criminal acts in the field of computer crime are mostly committed with the aim of gaining, either for the perpetrator or for another person, an illegal property benefit or of causing damage to a third party. However in some cases they can be used for terrorist purposes. i.e. to endanger the constitutional order or national security.

The national legal system distinguishes several types of criminal acts in the field of computer crime which in some cases can be used for terrorist purposes. The aim of these criminal acts is the protection of the security of computer data, i.e. IT systems. These are the following criminal acts:
1. Prevention of an access to a public information system – Article 149-a
2. Damaging and unauthorised entry into computer system – Article 251
3. Making and uploading computer viruses – Article 251a
4. Computer fraud – Article 251b
5. Computer forgery – Article 379a

As a part of the criminal acts against the freedoms and rights of citizens, Article 149-a of the Criminal Code defines as a criminal act the "Prevention of access to a public IT system" which sanctions the unauthorised prevention or limitation of a person's access to a public IT system. The subject of this criminal act is the public IT system: in the sense that an individual, without authorisation, and contrary to the regulations determined by law, prevents or limits access to a public IT system.

As a part of the criminal acts against property, there are three criminal acts provided for in the field of computer crime, namely: "Damaging and unauthorised entry into a computer system" – Article 251; "Creating and uploading computer viruses" – Article 251a; and "Computer fraud" – Article 251b.

"Damaging and unauthorised entry into a computer system", provided for under Article 251 of the Criminal Code, is perpetrated when a person, without authorisation, erases, amends, damages, hides or in another way renders useless IT data, programs or appliances for computer systems maintenance, other data, programs or computer communications.

It may also be committed when a person enters another person's computer or system without authorisation in order to use his/her data or programs in order to obtain illegal property or other benefit for him/herself or for another person or to cause damage to property or other damage or to transfer computer data which were not intended for him/her or to which he/she had access without authorisation.

Paragraph 3 of this Article provides for a qualified form of this act where a person or a member of a group commits these acts against computer systems, data or programs which are protected by special protection measures or are used in the work of state bodies, public enterprises or public facilities and international communications.

Paragraph 6 of this Article furthermore provides that if a person, without authorisation, prepares, obtains, sells, maintains or makes available to another person special appliances, means, computer programs or data aimed at or appropriate for committing the acts set out in paragraphs 1 and 2, he/she will be punished with a fine or a sentence of up to one year's imprisonment.

The objects used or intended to be used to commit this criminal act, such as special appliances, computer programs or data, will be seized upon a court decision to apply the measure "seizure of objects". "Creating and uploading computer viruses" is a criminal act which is perpetrated when a person makes, or copies from another person, a computer virus with the intention of infecting a third party's computer or computer network, for which the person will be sanctioned with a fine or a sentence of one year's imprisonment.

Another form of this criminal act is provided for in item 2 of Article 251a where there is a prison sentence of between six months and three years for a perpetrator who by committing this act, i.e. using a computer virus, causes damage to another computer, data system or program.

Two more criminal acts in the field of computer crime are provided in the Criminal Code. Article 251b establishes as a criminal act "Computer fraud", which is included in the criminal acts against property, and "Computer forgery" is provided for in Article 379a, Chapter 32 of the Criminal Code entitled "Criminal acts against legal traffic".

These criminal acts are related to property, meaning that the intention of the perpetrators of these criminal acts is to obtain for themselves, or for a third party, illegal property benefit or, in some cases, to harm somebody else, and in this sense, they cannot be treated as criminal acts relating to the endangering of the constitutional order or national security or creating a sense of insecurity and fear in citizens.

The measure "seizure of objects" is applied to both of these criminal acts which means that the objects which were used or were intended to be used to commit the acts, such as: special appliances, means, computer programs or data, will be seized upon a court decision on the seizure of objects.

Article 146 of the Law on Criminal Procedure (OGRM Nos. 15/97, 44/02, 74/04 and 15/05) provides for the special investigative measures which are applied, by a warrant from the competent court or a public prosecutor, in relation to criminal acts for which the prescribed sentence is at least four years' imprisonment and for criminal acts for which there is a sentence of up to five years' imprisonment where there is reasonable doubt that they have been perpetrated by an organised group, gang or other criminal association.

These special investigative measures are applied in order to provide the data and evidence necessary to ensure the success of the criminal procedure, which cannot be obtained in any other way or which would have proved difficult to obtain otherwise.

Where there is reasonable doubt that one of the above-mentioned criminal acts in the field of computer crime has been committed, a warrant may be obtained to apply some of the following special investigative measures:
–   interception of communications and search of homes or other premises or means of transport in order to create the conditions for the interception of communications, according to the terms and procedures specified by law;
–   inspection and search of computer systems, seizure of computer systems or parts thereof or of computer storage databases; and
–   covert monitoring, surveillance and visual-audio recording of persons and objects with technical means.

In order for criminal acts in the field of computer crime to be prevented or detected or to provide evidence and data in relation to them, depending on the type and the form of the act, there may be another special investigative measure applied in accordance with the Law on Criminal Procedure.

According to its competences set out in the Law on Internal Affairs (OGRM Nos. 19/95, 55/97, 38/2002, 33/2003, 19/2004 and 51/2005), the Administration for Security and Counter-Intelligence performs tasks relating to protection against espionage, terrorism and other activities aimed at endangering or destroying democratic institutions determined by the Constitution with violent means, as well as protection against serious forms of organised crime.

In this connection, the Administration for Security and Counter-Intelligence is competent to act against the perpetrators of criminal acts which endanger the constitutional order or national security, including the commission of the criminal act of "terrorism", and therefore also "cyberterrorism".

Bearing in mind that it is impossible today for the country and its citizens to function without the use of computers, modern information technology and the use of the Internet, it is becoming more than clear that these means may be used to commit specific illegal actions in order to obtain illegal property or in some cases for terrorist aims, i.e. to endanger the constitutional order or national security.

Due to the fact that many activities are carried out electronically, and that the threat from cyberterrorism is real and very serious, the Government must make efforts to cover these issues by legislation as soon as possible so that it can act preventively against the different types of illegal actions involving the use of computers and information technology which may pose a threat to the constitutional order and national security.

Turkey

A. National policy

1. Is there a national policy regarding the analysis, detection, prosecution and prevention of cybercrime in general and the misuse of cyberspace for terrorist purposes in particular? If yes, please briefly describe it.

While bringing many facilities and innovations to social life, the development of technology has lead to the occurrence of some new types of crime which may cause unprecedented levels of damage since it is vulnerable to misuse as well. Along with harmonising the organisational structures of the jurisprudence and its relative units in order to protect public and individual rights and to establish security in this field, it is also essential to provide specially qualified personnel and the necessary technological infrastructure.

The Turkish National Police initiated a new structure in the Cybercrimes and IT Division at the beginning of 2006 so as to put the above-mentioned articles into practice. Within the context of an efficient fight against cybercrime, it is a prerequisite to provide a sound database which creates crime profiles with the common and different aspects of crime types and practice types by analysing these crimes accurately. The Statistics and Strategic Analysis Bureau established for this purpose is engaged in carrying out surveys on cybercrime and creating the above-mentioned database; determining strategies in order to develop efficient means of combating cybercrime; establishing coordination between other relevant units; co-operating with banks, the Interbank Card Centre (ICC) and other authorities; and conducting activities so as to raise public awareness.

Moreover, Anti-Terrorism Law (ATL) No. 3713 was amended by Law No. 5532 on 29 June 2006. According to the amendment made to Article 4 of the Anti-Terrorism Law, if the crimes referred in Articles 243 and 244 of Turkish Criminal Law No. 5237 (entered into force on 01/06/2005) regarding cybercrime are committed for the purposes of a terrorist act, this type of cybercrime is defined as a terrorist crime. The misuse of cyberspace for terrorist acts is also a crime in the Turkish Penal System. Search and seizure requests are also carried out by judicial authorities.

Widespread use of the Internet since the early 1990s has brought about the problem of misuse of the Internet for terrorist purposes. In this respect, terrorist organisations have been increasingly using the Internet, particularly for communication and propaganda activities.

With the aim of spreading its views through the Internet, PKK/KONGRA-GEL has established various websites, hired from different service providers all over the world, under its own name as well as other names, such as:
www.kongra-gel.com,   www.pkkonline.com,   www.hpg-online.com,
www.teyrebaz.com,   www.pajk-online.com,   www.emkine.dk,

www.sexwebun.com,   www.abdullah-ocalan.com,   www.rojaciwan.com,
www.rojname.com,   www.dengeciwan.com,   www.coldhackers.com,
www.gerillaonline.com, www.zazaki.de, www.turkiyegercegi.com.

In line with the relevant provisions of Press Law No. 5187, as well as of
Code on Criminal Procedure No. 5271, such websites are closed down and
filtered by court decisions. Nevertheless, they continue to be accessible
outside Turkey through Internet service providers all over the world.

B.   Legal framework

2.   **Does your national legislation criminalise the misuse of
cyberspace for terrorist purposes, and
a. are these offences specifically defined with regard to the
terrorist nature or technical means of committing the crime, or
b. is the misuse covered by other, non-specific criminal offences?
How are these offences defined and which sanctions (criminal,
administrative, civil) are attached?**

There is no specific definition of a cyberterrorism offence in Turkish Law.
However, Article 4 of Anti-Terrorism Law No. 3713, which was amended by
Law No. 5532 on 29 June 2006, provides that if the offences regulated under
Articles 243 and 243 of the Turkish Penal Code are committed within the
framework of the activities of a terrorist organisation, these offences shall be
deemed as terrorist offences and punishments regarding these offences will
be increased by one half.

The relevant articles are as follows:

*Article 3. Offences committed for terrorist purposes: (Amended:
29/06/2006 – Law No. 5532)*

Article 4. In applying this Law offences defined in:

*a) 79, 80, 81, 82, 84, 86, 87, 96, 106, 107, 108, 109, 112, 113, 114,
115, 116, 117, 118, 142, 148, 149, 151, 152, 170, 172, 173, 174, 185,
188, 199, 200, 202, 204, 210, 213, 214, 215, 223, 224, 243, 244, 265,
294, 300, 316, 317, 318 , 319 and paragraph 2 of Article 310*

b) ...

*are terrorist offences if they are committed for terrorist purposes as
described in Article 1.*

Turkish Penal Code:

Accessing a Data Processing System
Article 243

(1) Any person who unlawfully accesses, partially or fully, a data processing system, or remains within such system, shall be subject to a penalty of imprisonment for a term of up to one year or a judicial fine.

(2) Where the act defined in the aforementioned section is committed in relation to a system which is only accessible with the payment of a fee then the penalty to be imposed shall be decreased by up to one half.

(3) Where any data within any such system is deleted or altered as a result of this act then the penalty to be imposed shall be a term of imprisonment of six months to two years.

Preventing the Functioning of a System and Deletion, Alteration or Corrupting of Data
Article 244

(1) Any person who prevents the functioning of a data processing system or renders such useless shall be subject to a penalty of imprisonment for a term of one to five years.

(2) Any person who deletes, alters, corrupts or bars access to data, or introduces data into a system or sends existing data to another place shall be subject to a penalty of imprisonment for a term of six months to three years.

(3) Where this offence is committed in relation to a data processing system of a public institution or establishment, bank or credit institution then the penalty to be imposed shall be increased by one half.

(4) Where a person obtains an unjust benefit for him/herself or another by committing the acts defined in the aforementioned sections, and such acts do not constitute a separate offence, he/she shall be subject to a penalty of imprisonment from two years to six years and a judicial fine of up to five thousand days shall be imposed

Special security measures, such as confiscation or banning of activities, may be applied against legal persons who have benefited from the commission of the above-mentioned offences.

3. Do you plan to introduce new legislation to counter terrorist misuse of cyberspace? What are the basic concepts of these legislative initiatives?

The "Draft law on the regulation of the information network services and offences regarding information technology" was prepared by the Ministry of

Justice, taking into consideration the Council of Europe Convention on Cybercrime (ETS No. 185), and sent to the Prime Ministry on 28/12/2006.

4. What are the existing national practices in the field of detecting, monitoring and closing down websites used for terrorist purposes?

Where such websites are detected by the law enforcement authorities, they are closed down and filtered by court decisions.

5. Does your national legislation provide criteria for establishing jurisdiction over such offences? What are those criteria?

The principle of territoriality is accepted by the Turkish Penal Code, however *lacunae* are filled by the principles of personality (Articles 10 and 11 of the Turkish Penal Code), universality (Article 12/3 of the Turkish Penal Code) and protection (Article 13 of Turkish Penal Code).

Jurisdiction regarding offences committed abroad is regulated under Article 8 of the Turkish Penal Code.

The relevant articles are as follows:

Jurisdiction
Time

Article 7

(1) *No person shall be subject to a penalty or security measure for any act which did not constitute a criminal offence under the law in force at the time it was committed. No one shall be subject to a penalty or security measure for an act which does not constitute an offence according to the law which came into force after the commission of the offence. Where such a penalty or security measure has been imposed its enforcement and the legal consequences of such shall be automatically set aside.*

(2) *If there is a difference between the law in force at the time a criminal offence was committed and a provision subsequently brought into force, then the law which is more favourable to the offender is applied and enforced.*

(3) *The Enforcement Code provisions shall be applied immediately, except insofar as those provisions relate to suspended prison sentences, conditional release, and repeat offending.*

(4) *Temporary and Provisional laws are to continue to apply to criminal offences which were committed during the period those laws were in force.*

Territorial Jurisdiction
Article 8

(1) Turkish law shall apply to all criminal offences committed in Turkey. Where a criminal act is partially, or fully, committed in Turkey or the result of a criminal act occurs in Turkey the offence shall be presumed to have been committed in Turkey.

(2) If the criminal offence is committed:
  a) within Turkish territory, airspace or in Turkish territorial waters;
  b) on the open sea or in the space extending directly above these waters and in, or by using, Turkish sea and air vessels;
  c) in, or by using, Turkish military sea or air vehicles;
  d) on or against fixed platforms erected on the continental shelf or in the economic zone of Turkey
  then this offence is presumed to have been committed in Turkey.

Conviction in a Foreign Country
Article 9

(1) Any person who is convicted in a foreign country for an offence committed in Turkey shall be subject to retrial in Turkey.

Offences Committed During the Performance of a Duty
Article 10

(1) Any person who is employed as a public officer or is charged with a particular duty by the Turkish State and who, in the course of that employment or duty, commits a criminal offence shall be tried in Turkey, despite having been convicted in a foreign country in respect of his acts.

Offences Committed by Citizens
Article 11

(1) If a Turkish citizen commits an offence in a foreign country that would amount to an offence under Turkish law and that offence is subject to a penalty of imprisonment where the minimum limit is greater than one year, and he is present in Turkey, and upon satisfying the conditions that he has not been convicted for the same offence in a foreign country and a prosecution is possible in Turkey, he shall be subject to a penalty under Turkish law, except in regard as to the offences defined in Article 13.

(2) Where the aforementioned offence is subject to a penalty of imprisonment, the minimum limit of which is less than one year, then criminal proceedings shall only be initiated upon the making of a complaint by a victim or a foreign government. In such a case

the complaint must be made within six months of the date the citizen entered Turkey.

Offences Committed by Non-Citizens
Article 12

(1) Where a non-citizen commits an offence (other than one defined in Article 13), to the detriment of Turkey, in a foreign country, that would amount to an offence under Turkish law and that offence is subject to a penalty of imprisonment where the minimum limit is greater than 1 year, and he is present in Turkey, he shall be subject to penalty under Turkish law. Criminal proceedings shall only be brought upon a request by the Minister of Justice.

(2) Where the aforementioned offence is committed to the detriment of a Turkish citizen or to the detriment of a legal personality established under Turkish civil law and the offender is present in Turkey and there has been no conviction in a foreign country for the same offence then, upon the making of a complaint by the victim, he shall be subject to penalty under Turkish law.

(3) If the victim is a non-citizen the offender shall be subject to criminal proceedings, upon the request of the Minister of Justice, provided the following conditions are fulfilled:
   a) the offence is subject to a penalty of imprisonment under Turkish law where the minimum limit of imprisonment is not less than 3 years; and
   b) there is no extradition agreement; or the government of the country in which the crime has been committed, or the State of which the offender is a national, has refused to grant extradition.

(4) In relation to offences to which section one is applicable, if a non-citizen is convicted or acquitted in a foreign Court or has any criminal proceedings or penalty against him stayed or set aside respectively by such Court or the offence becomes one which cannot be the subject of a prosecution in a foreign Court then, upon the request of the Minister of Justice, criminal proceedings shall be brought in Turkey.

Miscellaneous Offences
Article 13

(1) Turkish law shall apply to the following offences committed in a foreign country whether or not committed by a citizen or non-citizen of Turkey:
   a) Offences defined in Chapter I, Volume II;
   b) Offences defined in Parts 3-8, Chapter IV, Volume II;

c)   *Torture (Articles 94-95);*

d)   *Intentional Pollution of the Environment (Article 181);*

e)   *Production and Trade of Narcotics or Psychotropic Substances (Article 188); Facilitating the use of Narcotics or Psychotropic Substances (Article 190);*

f)   *Counterfeiting Money (Article 197), Manufacturing and Trading of Instruments used in the Production of Money and valuable Seals (Article 200); Counterfeiting a Seal (Article 202);*

g)   *Prostitution (Article 227);*

h)   *Bribery (Article 252); and*

i)   *Seizing control or hijacking of air, sea or rail transport vehicles (Article 223, sections 2 and 3) and offences relating to the damaging of such vehicles (Article 152).*

(2)   *Except for offences defined in parts 3, 5, 6 and 7 of Chapter IV, Volume II, the conducting of criminal proceedings in Turkey for crimes within the scope of section one shall be subject to a request of the Ministry of Justice.*

(3)   *Even where a conviction or acquittal pursuant to the offences listed in section one subsections (a) and (b) have occurred in a foreign country, criminal proceedings in Turkey shall be conducted upon the request of the Ministry of Justice.*

6.   Does your national legal system establish ancillary offences related to the misuse of cyberspace?

"Ancillary offences", such as attempts to commit or participation in an offence, are covered in the general provisions of the Turkish Penal Code. "Attempt", a term of which affects criminal responsibility, is provided for in Article 35 of the Turkish Penal Code.

The provisions of the Turkish Penal Code regarding attempt, jointly committed offences, incitement, involvement and assistance are as follows:

Attempt
Article 35

(1)   *Any person who begins to directly act, with the appropriate means and with the intention of committing an offence, but has been unable to complete such offence due to circumstances beyond his control, shall be culpable for the attempt.*

(2)   *In a case of attempt, depending upon the seriousness of the damage and danger that accrued, the offender shall be sentenced to a penalty of imprisonment for a term of thirteen to twenty years where the offence committed requires a penalty of aggravated life*

imprisonment, or to a penalty of imprisonment for a term of nine years to fifteen years where the offence committed requires a penalty of life imprisonment. Otherwise the penalty shall be reduced by one-quarter to three-quarters.

Principal Involvement
Article 37

(1) Any person who jointly performs an act prescribed by law as an offence shall be culpable as the offender of that act.

(2) Any person who uses another as an instrument for the commission of an offence shall remain culpable as the offender. The penalty for a person who uses another as an instrument who lacks the capacity of acting with fault shall be increased by one-third to one-half.

Incitement
Article 38

(1) A person who incites another to commit an offence shall be subject to the penalty appropriate to the offence that is committed.

(2) Where there is incitement to offend by using influence arising from a direct-descendent or direct-antecedent relationship, the penalty of the instigator shall be increased by one-third to one half. Where there is incitement of a minor, a direct-descendant or direct-antecedent relationship is not necessary for the application of this section.

(3) Where the identity of the instigator is not known and if the offender plays a role in the identification of the instigator, or other accomplice, he shall be sentenced to a penalty of imprisonment for a term of twenty to twenty-five years if the offence committed requires aggravated life imprisonment and to a term of imprisonment of fifteen years to twenty years if the offence committed requires life imprisonment. Otherwise the penalty to be imposed may be reduced of one-third.

Assistance
Article 39

(1) A person who assists another with the commission of an offence shall be sentenced to a penalty of imprisonment for a term of fifteen years to twenty years if the offence committed requires aggravated life imprisonment, and to a term of ten to fifteen years imprisonment if the offence committed requires life imprisonment. Otherwise the penalty to be imposed shall be reduced by one-half.

However, in this case, the penalty to be imposed shall not exceed eight years.

(2)   A person remains culpable as an assistant if he:

a)   encourages the commission of an offence, or reinforces the decision to commit an offence, or promises that he will assist after the commission of an act.

b)   provides counsel as to how an offence is to be committed, or provides the means used for the commission of the offence.

c)   facilitate the execution of an offence by providing assistance before or after the commission of the offence.

7.   **What kind of national procedures do you have for submitting an application on the activities of Internet-providers and/or hosting companies, to deprive a user from a domain name or to cancel his/her/its registration or licence?**

-

8.   **What non-legislative measures do your have in your country to prevent and counter terrorist misuse of cyberspace, including self-regulatory measures?**

-

C.   **International co-operation**

9.   **Please describe the general framework for international co-operation regarding the misuse of cyberspace for terrorist purposes.**

Turkey fulfils legal assistance requests on the basis of the bilateral and multilateral agreements to which it is a party and also in accordance with the general principles of domestic law.

The main international conventions to which Turkey is party are:
–   European Convention on Mutual Assistance in Criminal Matters, which was ratified on 24 June 1969 by Law 1034 of 18 March 1968 and entered into force on 22 September 1969.
–   Additional Protocol to European Convention on Mutual Assistance in Criminal Matters, which was ratified on 29 March 1990 by Law 3363 of 18 May 1987 and entered into force on 27 June 1990.
–   European Convention on the Suppression of Terrorism, which was ratified on 19 May 1981 and entered into force on 20 August 1981.

Turkey has ratified 12 United Nations anti-terrorism conventions, including the 1999 International Convention for the Suppression of the Financing of Terrorism (Terrorist Financing Convention) which was adopted by Law 4738 on 10 January 2002 and ratified by Decree of the Council of Ministers 3801 of 1 March 2002.

However, Turkey is not a party to the European Convention on Cybercrime.

Under Article 90 of the Constitution "International agreements duly put into effect bear the force of law."

Turkey does not refuse requests for legal assistance for any reasons other than those stipulated in the agreements to which Turkey is a party. It is required, for example, that the request is not related to political crimes or military offences, that it does not infringe on the sovereignty, security, public order and other essential interests of Turkey, that it does not seek an arrest or the execution of a conviction, and that meeting the request would not be a violation of human rights. These limits are specified in the provisions of the conventions to which Turkey is a party.

While there are no specific provisions regarding international co-operation on the misuse of cyberspace for terrorist purposes, Turkey carries out mutual legal assistance within the framework of the European Convention on Mutual Assistance in Criminal Matters.

In the event of a legal assistance request relating to the misuse of cyberspace for terrorist purposes in matters such as procurement of information and documents, the hearing of witnesses and the accused and the taking of statements are carried out by Turkish judicial authorities within the scope of the European Convention on Mutual Legal Assistance in Criminal Matters and the dual criminality principle is not sought.

Under Article 3 of the European Convention on Mutual Assistance in Criminal Matters, "The requested Party shall execute in the manner provided for by its law any letters rogatory relating to a criminal matter and addressed to it by the judicial authorities of the requesting Party for the purpose of procuring evidence or transmitting Articles to be produced in evidence, records or documents". Thus, the powers of competent authorities in Turkey to obtain documents and information from any natural or legal person, including compulsory measures, may be used to answer a mutual legal assistance request providing that the request for mutual legal assistance is consistent with the international agreements to which Turkey is a party.

The central authority coordinating mutual legal assistance in Turkey is the Ministry of Justice.

A simple method applies to meeting mutual legal assistance requests. After the Ministry of Justice determines whether the request is consistent with the bilateral and multilateral conventions to which Turkey is a party and with Turkey's domestic legislation, the approved request is conveyed to the relevant competent authority in order to meet the request. The competent authorities for mutual legal assistance requests are the public prosecutors and courts, depending on the nature of the request and the stage of investigation.

The principle of dual criminality is only sought in requests regarding seizure and search as Turkey has a declaration on Article 5 of the European Convention on Mutual Assistance in Criminal Matters.

10. What are the existing practices and experiences with regard to international co-operation, in particular in relation to the procedures described in question 4?

So far, there is no existing noteworthy practice or experience with regard to international co-operation.

E. Statistical information

13. Please provide relevant statistics on offences relating to the misuse of cyberspace for terrorist purposes (including possibly: cases recorded, investigated, brought to court, convictions, victims etc.).

and

14. Where possible, please describe briefly the profile of offenders typically involved in the misuse of cyberspace for terrorist purposes (professional background, gender, age, nationality), and possible typical organisational characteristics, including transnational links and links to other forms of organised crime.

There is no statistical information as the provisions regarding cybercrime and the amendment of Article 4 of the Anti-Terrorism Law are too recent.

United Kingdom

A. National policy

1. Is there a national policy regarding the analysis, detection, prosecution and prevention of cybercrime in general and the misuse of cyberspace for terrorist purposes in particular? If yes, please briefly describe it.

The United Kingdom monitors the Internet in the context of its strategy to reduce the risk from terrorism by tackling the radicalisation of individuals, disrupting terrorists and their operations, reducing the vulnerability of the UK and UK interests overseas and preparing for the consequences of a terrorist attack. Internet monitoring is particularly relevant with respect to the first two of these objectives. This activity, and all other activities to prevent criminal and other types of cybercrime, are carried out under a range of legal provisions notably the Regulation of Investigatory Powers Act 2000 and adhering to relevant EU legislation and conventions.

The United Kingdom takes a flexible intelligence-led approach which leads to specific monitoring of themes, groups or websites according to national requirements and priorities.

B. Legal framework

2. Does your national legislation criminalise the misuse of cyberspace for terrorist purposes, and
a. are these offences specifically defined with regard to the terrorist nature or technical means of committing the crime, or
b. is the misuse covered by other, non-specific criminal offences? How are these offences defined and which sanctions (criminal, administrative, civil) are attached?

It is UK practice to criminalise specific actions rather than the medium through which the actions are committed. There are therefore a number of terrorist-related actions which could take place in cyberspace which are unlawful in the UK, such as the dissemination of terrorist publications or the encouragement of terrorism, but the illegality of these is not limited to their taking place in cyberspace.

3. Do you plan to introduce new legislation to counter terrorist misuse of cyberspace? What are the basic concepts of these legislative initiatives?

No new legislation is planned to specifically counter terrorist misuse of cyberspace.

4.   What are the existing national practices in the field of detecting, monitoring and closing down websites used for illicit, in particular, terrorist purposes and what kind of national procedures allow the blocking of access to web sites or pages considered illicit?

Detecting and monitoring is carried out by a range of organisations and competent authorities according to their functions and legal remits within the framework of the UK's counter-terrorism (and criminal etc) strategy and legislation. There is UK legislation to act against those who are operating or participating in websites illegally.

5.   What are the existing national practices in the field of interception of, or infiltration to, the electronic correspondence (e.g. e-mail, forum, instantaneous message service, voice over IP-skype, etc).

The Regulation of Investigatory Powers Act 2000 provides a comprehensive regime governing the interception of communications and certain bodies are given statutory powers to intercept communications as set out on the face of the statute. The system is described in the annual Interception Commissioners Report.

6.   Does your national legislation provide criteria for establishing jurisdiction over the misuse of cyberspace for terrorist purposes? What are those criteria?

The Terrorism Act 2006 provides that anyone doing anything outside the UK which would be an offence in the UK under certain sections of anti terrorist legislation (including the encouragement of terrorism and the dissemination of terrorist publications) will be guilty in the UK of those offences.

7.   Does your national legal system establish additional offences related to attempts at, or complicity in, the commission of the misuse of cyberspace for terrorist purposes (ancillary offences)?

Conspiracy to commit, attempting to commit, and aiding and abetting the commission of any criminal offence are also criminal offences under UK law.

8.   What kind of national procedures do you have for submitting an application on the activities of Internet-providers and/or hosting companies or other entities, to deprive a user from a domain name or to cancel his/her/its registration or licence?

Nominet, the UK's registry for Internet domain names, has a number of relevant documents:

1. Standard terms for registrars
(http://www.nominet.org.uk/registrars/ra/racontract/). For example, clause
3.2.3 states that it is a breach of contract if a registrar asks to make an
update to a domain name record that has not been requested by the
registrant. This includes cancelling a domain name without the registrant's
permission.

2. Good practice terms http://www.nominet.org.uk/registrars/ra/gpt/ provide
general guidance on what is expected from a UK registrar. In general,
registrars have to provide basic information about the services they offer,
and transparency about charges (i.e. no surprise charges if a registrant
wants to move registrar).

There are also statutory complaints schemes run by for example the Office
of the Telecommunication Ombudsman.

**9.   What non-legislative measures do you have in your country to
prevent and counter terrorist misuse of cyberspace, including self-
regulatory measures?**

The government's policy in relation to the development of the Internet is not
to place general monitoring obligations on those who provide Internet
services, host websites etc., but rather to allow self-regulation.

ISPs may be liable to prosecution if they are aware that a website contains
illegal material, but fail to take appropriate action.

In practice there are excellent working relationships with the Internet
industry, and they have developed strong working practices and guidelines
relating to services they offer and content they host. Where a UK ISP is
advised – usually by law enforcement – that they are hosting material which
is illegal, they have an excellent record in removing it.

C.   International co-operation

**10. Please describe your country's general framework for international
co-operation regarding the misuse of cyberspace for terrorist
purposes.**

and

**11. What are the existing practices and experiences with regard to
international co-operation, in particular in relation to the
procedures described in question 4?**

The United Kingdom shares information from monitored sites with European
partners including Europol and Sitcen/SIAC. This is flexible intelligence-led

and changes frequently, also depending on the use to which the information will be put.

D. Institutional framework

12. Please list the institutions that are competent for countering terrorist misuse of cyberspace.

A number of institutions have a role to play in countering terrorist misuse of cyberspace. The police and the Crown Prosecution Service have responsibility for, respectively, investigating and prosecuting criminal acts, including those involving the terrorist misuse of cyberspace.

13. In order to counter terrorist misuse of cyberspace are there any partnerships between the public and private sectors or legal obligations for operators of electronic communication (Internet-service providers, hosting companies, etc.) as well as persons providing the public with access to systems which allow on-line communication via access to the network (cybercafe, WiFi hotspot)?

There are no formal partnerships or legal obligations.

14. Are there any hotlines regulated by the public or private sectors permitting denouncement of those web sites which could be of a terrorist character / nature?

There is an anti-terrorist hotline run by the Metropolitan Police Service.

E. Statistical information

15. Please provide relevant statistics on offences relating to the misuse of cyberspace for terrorist purposes (including possibly: cases recorded, investigated, brought to court, convictions, victims etc.).

Statistical information is not collated according to the medium used but by the offence itself.

16. Where possible, please describe briefly the profile of offenders typically involved in the misuse of cyberspace for terrorist purposes (professional background, gender, age, nationality), and possible typical organisational characteristics, including trans-national links and links to other forms of organised crime.

Information unavailable.

Mexico

The Mexican Government recognises the necessity to strengthen its institutional capacity to fight organised crime in relation to the use of information and communication technology, such as the Internet.

Even though Mexico does not have a national programme related to cybercrime, it has established a Special Unit on Cybernetic Policy under the authority of the Federal Public Security Secretary. The Unit is responsible for preventing cybercrime, as well as for the prevention of, and responding to, complaints about crimes committed against minors using computer equipment. This Unit also carries out "anti-hacker patrol operations", by using the Internet to detect offenders who commit fraud, interference or organise their criminal activity via the Internet.

In relation to the misuse of cyberspace for terrorist purposes, Mexico still does not have a specialised police force.

The 2007-2012 National Development Plan limits itself – in Objective 14 on "Ensuring border security, as well as the integrity and respect for human rights of both the inhabitants of border areas, and migrants" – to establishing the following:

> *Strategy 14.1. [...]*
>
> *Strategy 14.2. Create channels for the exchange of information and strategies in relation to border security.*
> *Work together with countries both to the North and to the South to refine the mechanisms for exchanging information in order to ensure the proper control of people's movement from one country to another, in order to protect migrants' rights and, at the same time, to prevent international crime and terrorism.*

United States of America

The responses provided below focus on the use of the United States' federal criminal law enforcement authorities as the key to combating misuse of the Internet for criminal and terrorist purposes. Therefore, the responses do not seek to address every action the United States might take at the national level with regard to cybercrime or cyberterrorism, but rather those actions and policies that are most commonly employed by federal prosecutors and law enforcement agencies. Furthermore, the United States has attempted to provide responses from national experience that can be readily adopted by other states through full implementation of the Council of Europe's Convention on Cybercrime.

A. National Policy

1. Is there a national policy regarding the analysis, detection, prosecution and prevention of cybercrime in general and the misuse of cyberspace for terrorist purposes in particular? If yes, please briefly describe it.

In 2003, the President of the United States signed the National Strategy to Secure Cyberspace. The National Strategy's strategic objectives are to (1) prevent cyber attacks against America's critical infrastructures; (2) reduce national vulnerability to cyber attacks; and (3) minimise damage and recovery time from cyber attacks that do occur. As explained in the National Strategy, the United States Department of Justice and the Federal Bureau of Investigation lead the national effort to investigate and prosecute cybercrime.

The United States has enacted criminal laws that allow for the investigation and prosecution of a wide range of cybercrimes, whether committed by individuals, organised criminal groups, institutions, or terrorists. Law enforcement agencies at the federal, state and local levels investigate cybercrimes and other criminal offences that target or involve computers and computer networks. The United States works closely with other nations to counter cybercrime, through institutions such as the 24/7 emergency contact network, multilateral treaties such as the Convention on Cybercrime, and bilateral mutual legal assistance and extradition treaties. The United States is a strong proponent of the Convention on Cybercrime and urges all Council of Europe member states and other interested parties who have not done so to implement it as a key step to combat transnational cybercrime and misuse of cyberspace for terrorist purposes.

B. Legal Framework

2. Does your national legislation criminalise the misuse of cyberspace for terrorist purposes, and
a. are these offences specifically defined with regard to the terrorist nature or technical means of committing the crime, or
b. is the misuse covered by other, non-specific criminal offences? How are these offences defined and which sanctions (criminal, administrative, civil) are attached?

a. The United States has enacted its cybercrime laws to focus on the acts committed (such as hacking, distributed denial of service attacks, furthering a fraud through the use of a computer), rather than the identity of the perpetrator. Although U.S. cybercrime laws take into account potential results from terrorist acts, those laws do not require proof of terrorist intent.

b. The United States has enacted specific criminal offences related to terrorism (such as providing material support to terrorists or financing terrorism), but cybercrimes are investigated and prosecuted as described in the answer to question 2.a.

The United States has enacted criminal laws that allow for the investigation and prosecution of a wide range of cybercrimes, whether committed by individuals, organised criminal groups, institutions or terrorists. The United States has also enacted criminal laws that allow for the investigation and prosecution of certain criminal offences related to terrorism (such as providing material support to terrorists or financing terrorism). Furthermore, under U.S. law, the same set of facts may give rise to multiple charges, provided that each charge alleges some different element. Thus a person who commits a cybercrime for the purpose of, for example, providing material support to a terrorist organisation may be guilty of multiple offences arising out of the same conduct.

Individuals convicted of violating the key United States federal cybercrime statute, Title 18 U.S. Code, Section 1030 (Fraud and related activity in connection with computers), may, depending on the circumstances, be sentenced to imprisonment for a term of years (or for life, if the offender knowingly or recklessly caused or attempted to cause death for certain violations), ordered to serve a term of supervised release, ordered to pay restitution to victims, and/or ordered to pay a fine. In addition, criminal and civil asset forfeiture statutes may be used to seize and forfeit to the government proceeds and property used in, or derived from, the criminal activity.

Individuals convicted of violating terrorism criminal statutes enumerated in Title 18 U.S. Code, Chapter 113B, are subject to similar criminal penalties. U.S. law provides for increased criminal penalties for certain terrorism-related offences. Some violations of Title 18 U.S. Code, Section 1030 (Fraud and related activity in connection with computers), are included within the enumerated list of "federal crimes of terrorism," contained in Title 18 U.S. Code, Section 2332b (Acts of terrorism transcending national boundaries).

3. Do you plan to introduce new legislation to counter terrorist misuse of cyberspace? What are the basic concepts of these legislative initiatives?

There are no indications that the executive branch of the U.S. government plans to propose any such legislation. It should be noted, however, that any legislation enacted on this topic would have to be consistent with the freedom of speech protections contained in the First Amendment of the U.S. Constitution.

4. What are the existing national practices in the field of detecting, monitoring and closing down websites used for terrorist purposes?

In the United States, federal, state and local law enforcement agencies may, during the course of a criminal investigation and consistent with U.S. law, read and gather information from publicly-available websites that promote violations of U.S. law, such as violent crimes, money laundering or material support for terrorists. Similarly, the United States Government will, consistent with U.S. law, read and review publicly-available websites that promote violence or terrorism against United States citizens.

5. Does your national legislation provide criteria for establishing jurisdiction over such offences? What are those criteria?

The cybercrime offences contained in Title 18 of the United States code can, depending on the offence, have both domestic and extra-territorial application. Both domestically and extra-territorially, this jurisdiction is very broad and based on factors such as whether the offence affects interstate or foreign commerce, the identity of the victim or intended victim, and where the offence is committed.

Under Title 18 of the United States Code, Section 1030 (Fraud and related activity in connection with computers), jurisdiction is generally based on whether the affected computer is a "protected computer" as defined in Section 1030(e)(2). Examples of a "protected computer" include a computer which is used in interstate or foreign commerce, a computer exclusively for the use of a financial institution or the United States Government or a computer used by a non-U.S. bank or non-U.S. government agency.

6. Does your national legal system establish ancillary offences related to the misuse of cyberspace?

Under United States criminal law, individuals may be convicted of a criminal offence, including a cybercrime or terrorism offence, if they commit the offence themselves, or if they aid, abet, counsel, command, induce or procure another to commit the offence. An individual may also be convicted of attempting to commit, or conspiring to commit, a cybercrime offence. In addition, criminal liability based on attempt and conspiracy applies to most terrorism offences.

7. What kind of national procedures do you have for submitting an application on the activities of Internet-providers and/or hosting companies, to deprive a user from a domain name or to cancel his/her/its registration or licence?

Under United States criminal law, any property used to commit a criminal offence, or derived from the proceeds of criminal activity, may be subject to criminal and civil seizure and forfeiture. In certain circumstances, a domain name could be subject to criminal forfeiture. For example, in one criminal prosecution brought by the United States Department of Justice, the domain name for a notorious international, online criminal marketplace was criminally forfeited to the United States government.

8. What non-legislative measures do your have in your country to prevent and counter terrorist misuse of cyberspace, including self-regulatory measures?

The United States Government sponsors a number of education and awareness programmes designed to counter cybercrime in general, regardless of the identity or intentions of the perpetrators. For example, the Federal Bureau of Investigation website provides information and resources related to protecting computers from the effects of cybercrime: http://www.fbi.gov/cyberinvest/protect_online.htm. In addition, the United States Government sponsors numerous training programmes, domestically and internationally, focused on preventing, countering, investigating and prosecuting cybercrime and protecting individuals from a wide range of cyber threats.

The United States Government actively participates in international organisations that address the issues of cybercrime and cyberterrorism, including the G8, the Council of Europe, the Organization for Security and Co-operation in Europe, the Organization of American States, and numerous others.

C. International co-operation

9. Please describe the general framework for international co-operation regarding the misuse of cyberspace for terrorist purposes.

The United States is strongly committed to promoting international co-operation in the battle against cybercrime, and firmly believes there is already an adequate international framework for co-operation and mutual legal assistance on the issues of cybercrime and cyberterrorism. The existing international framework includes, inter alia: (1) bilateral mutual legal assistance and extradition treaties; (2) international treaties such as the Convention on Cybercrime; (3) multilateral organisations such as the Council of Europe and the United Nations; and (4) law enforcement contact networks such as the 24/7 emergency contact network.

The United States supports the recognition of the Convention on Cybercrime as the one international standard for fighting cybercrime. The United States believes that the investigative and international co-operation tools set forth in the Convention on Cybercrime are precisely the tools needed to identify and prosecute criminals and terrorists for their misuse of, and attacks on, computers and computer networks.

10. What are the existing practices and experiences with regard to international co-operation, in particular in relation to the procedures described in question 4?

The international co-operation framework and mechanisms described in the answer to question 9 can be employed to deal with a wide range of criminal or terrorist conduct.

As to international co-operation relating to detecting, monitoring, and closing down websites used for terrorist purposes (question 4), the United States does receive foreign requests for such assistance. It processes them in the same way as other requests (prioritising them according to urgency, etc).

D. Institutional Framework

11. Please list the institutions that are competent to countering terrorist misuse of cyberspace.

The Federal Bureau of Investigation and the United States Secret Service are the two principal U.S. law enforcement agencies responsible for investigating cybercrime.

The Federal Bureau of Investigation has primary responsibility for investigating terrorism crimes that occur in or affect the United States. Two of the top three priorities for the FBI are protecting the United States from terrorist attack and protecting the United States against cyber-based attacks and high-technology crimes.

The United States Department of Justice has responsibility for prosecuting both cybercrimes (e.g. hacking and distributed denial of service attacks) and terrorism crimes (e.g. providing material support to terrorists).

The United States Department of Homeland Security has responsibility for safeguarding the United States' critical infrastructure, including the telecommunications infrastructure and the Internet.

12. Are there any partnerships between the public and private sectors (Internet-service providers, hosting companies, etc.) to counter terrorist misuse of cyberspace?

The United States Department of Justice, the Federal Bureau of Investigation, the U.S. Secret Service and the Department of Homeland Security have many formal and informal relationships with public and private sector entities, some of which address the misuse of cyberspace.

E. Statistical Information

13. Please provide relevant statistics on offences relating to the misuse of cyberspace for terrorist purposes (including possibly: cases recorded, investigated, brought to court, convictions, victims etc.).

The United States does not collect statistics according to these categories.

14. Where possible, please describe briefly the profile of offenders typically involved in the misuse of cyberspace for terrorist purposes (professional background, gender, age, nationality), and possible typical organisational characteristics, including transnational links and links to other forms of organised crime.

The United States does not collect statistics according to these categories.

Selected Council of Europe reference texts

Council of Europe Convention on the Prevention of Terrorism (CETS No. 196)[1]

The member States of the Council of Europe and the other Signatories hereto,

Considering that the aim of the Council of Europe is to achieve greater unity between its members;

Recognising the value of reinforcing co-operation with the other Parties to this Convention;

Wishing to take effective measures to prevent terrorism and to counter, in particular, public provocation to commit terrorist offences and recruitment and training for terrorism;

Aware of the grave concern caused by the increase in terrorist offences and the growing terrorist threat;

Aware of the precarious situation faced by those who suffer from terrorism, and in this connection reaffirming their profound solidarity with the victims of terrorism and their families;

Recognising that terrorist offences and the offences set forth in this Convention, by whoever perpetrated, are under no circumstances justifiable by considerations of a political, philosophical, ideological, racial, ethnic, religious or other similar nature, and recalling the obligation of all Parties to prevent such offences and, if not prevented, to prosecute and ensure that they are punishable by penalties which take into account their grave nature;

Recalling the need to strengthen the fight against terrorism and reaffirming that all measures taken to prevent or suppress terrorist offences have to respect the rule of law and democratic values, human rights and fundamental freedoms as well as other provisions of international law, including, where applicable, international humanitarian law;

Recognising that this Convention is not intended to affect established principles relating to freedom of expression and freedom of association;

Recalling that acts of terrorism have the purpose by their nature or context to seriously intimidate a population or unduly compel a government or an international organisation to perform or abstain from performing any act or seriously destabilise or destroy the fundamental

---

[1] The state of signatures and ratifications of this Convention can be consulted at http://conventions.coe.int/.

political, constitutional, economic or social structures of a country or an international organisation;

Have agreed as follows:

Article 1 – Terminology

1   For the purposes of this Convention, "terrorist offence" means any of the offences within the scope of and as defined in one of the treaties listed in the Appendix.

2   On depositing its instrument of ratification, acceptance, approval or accession, a State or the European Community which is not a party to a treaty listed in the Appendix may declare that, in the application of this Convention to the Party concerned, that treaty shall be deemed not to be included in the Appendix. This declaration shall cease to have effect as soon as the treaty enters into force for the Party having made such a declaration, which shall notify the Secretary General of the Council of Europe of this entry into force.

Article 2 – Purpose

The purpose of the present Convention is to enhance the efforts of Parties in preventing terrorism and its negative effects on the full enjoyment of human rights, in particular the right to life, both by measures to be taken at national level and through international co-operation, with due regard to the existing applicable multilateral or bilateral treaties or agreements between the Parties.

Article 3 – National prevention policies

1   Each Party shall take appropriate measures, particularly in the field of training of law enforcement authorities and other bodies, and in the fields of education, culture, information, media and public awareness raising, with a view to preventing terrorist offences and their negative effects while respecting human rights obligations as set forth in, where applicable to that Party, the Convention for the Protection of Human Rights and Fundamental Freedoms, the International Covenant on Civil and Political Rights, and other obligations under international law.

2   Each Party shall take such measures as may be necessary to improve and develop the co-operation among national authorities with a view to preventing terrorist offences and their negative effects by, *inter alia*:

a   exchanging information;

b   improving the physical protection of persons and facilities;

c   enhancing training and co-ordination plans for civil emergencies.

3   Each Party shall promote tolerance by encouraging inter-religious and cross-cultural dialogue involving, where appropriate, non-governmental organisations and other elements of civil society with a view to preventing tensions that might contribute to the commission of terrorist offences.

4   Each Party shall endeavour to promote public awareness regarding the existence, causes and gravity of and the threat posed by terrorist offences and the offences set forth in this Convention and consider encouraging the public to provide factual, specific help to its competent authorities that may contribute to preventing terrorist offences and offences set forth in this Convention.

Article 4 – International co-operation on prevention

Parties shall, as appropriate and with due regard to their capabilities, assist and support each other with a view to enhancing their capacity to prevent the commission of terrorist offences, including through exchange of information and best practices, as well as through training and other joint efforts of a preventive character.

Article 5 – Public provocation to commit a terrorist offence

1   For the purposes of this Convention, "public provocation to commit a terrorist offence" means the distribution, or otherwise making available, of a message to the public, with the intent to incite the commission of a terrorist offence, where such conduct, whether or not directly advocating terrorist offences, causes a danger that one or more such offences may be committed.

2   Each Party shall adopt such measures as may be necessary to establish public provocation to commit a terrorist offence, as defined in paragraph 1, when committed unlawfully and intentionally, as a criminal offence under its domestic law.

Article 6 – Recruitment for terrorism

1   For the purposes of this Convention, "recruitment for terrorism" means to solicit another person to commit or participate in the commission of a terrorist offence, or to join an association or group, for the purpose of contributing to the commission of one or more terrorist offences by the association or the group.

2   Each Party shall adopt such measures as may be necessary to establish recruitment for terrorism, as defined in paragraph 1, when

committed unlawfully and intentionally, as a criminal offence under its domestic law.

Article 7 – Training for terrorism

1   For the purposes of this Convention, "training for terrorism" means to provide instruction in the making or use of explosives, firearms or other weapons or noxious or hazardous substances, or in other specific methods or techniques, for the purpose of carrying out or contributing to the commission of a terrorist offence, knowing that the skills provided are intended to be used for this purpose.

2   Each Party shall adopt such measures as may be necessary to establish training for terrorism, as defined in paragraph 1, when committed unlawfully and intentionally, as a criminal offence under its domestic law.

Article 8 – Irrelevance of the commission of a terrorist offence

For an act to constitute an offence as set forth in Articles 5 to 7 of this Convention, it shall not be necessary that a terrorist offence be actually committed.

Article 9 – Ancillary offences

1   Each Party shall adopt such measures as may be necessary to establish as a criminal offence under its domestic law:

a   Participating as an accomplice in an offence as set forth in Articles 5 to 7 of this Convention;

b   Organising or directing others to commit an offence as set forth in Articles 5 to 7 of this Convention;

c   Contributing to the commission of one or more offences as set forth in Articles 5 to 7 of this Convention by a group of persons acting with a common purpose. Such contribution shall be intentional and shall either:

   i   be made with the aim of furthering the criminal activity or criminal purpose of the group, where such activity or purpose involves the commission of an offence as set forth in Articles 5 to 7 of this Convention; or

   ii   be made in the knowledge of the intention of the group to commit an offence as set forth in Articles 5 to 7 of this Convention.

2   Each Party shall also adopt such measures as may be necessary to establish as a criminal offence under, and in accordance with, its domestic law the attempt to commit an offence as set forth in Articles 6 and 7 of this Convention.

Article 10 – Liability of legal entities

1   Each Party shall adopt such measures as may be necessary, in accordance with its legal principles, to establish the liability of legal entities for participation in the offences set forth in Articles 5 to 7 and 9 of this Convention.

2   Subject to the legal principles of the Party, the liability of legal entities may be criminal, civil or administrative.

3   Such liability shall be without prejudice to the criminal liability of the natural persons who have committed the offences.

Article 11 – Sanctions and measures

1   Each Party shall adopt such measures as may be necessary to make the offences set forth in Articles 5 to 7 and 9 of this Convention punishable by effective, proportionate and dissuasive penalties.

2   Previous final convictions pronounced in foreign States for offences set forth in the present Convention may, to the extent permitted by domestic law, be taken into account for the purpose of determining the sentence in accordance with domestic law.

3   Each Party shall ensure that legal entities held liable in accordance with Article 10 are subject to effective, proportionate and dissuasive criminal or non-criminal sanctions, including monetary sanctions.

Article 12 – Conditions and safeguards

1   Each Party shall ensure that the establishment, implementation and application of the criminalisation under Articles 5 to 7 and 9 of this Convention are carried out while respecting human rights obligations, in particular the right to freedom of expression, freedom of association and freedom of religion, as set forth in, where applicable to that Party, the Convention for the Protection of Human Rights and Fundamental Freedoms, the International Covenant on Civil and Political Rights, and other obligations under international law.

2   The establishment, implementation and application of the criminalisation under Articles 5 to 7 and 9 of this Convention should furthermore be subject to the principle of proportionality, with respect to the legitimate aims pursued and to their necessity in a democratic

society, and should exclude any form of arbitrariness or discriminatory or racist treatment.

Article 13 – Protection, compensation and support for victims of terrorism

Each Party shall adopt such measures as may be necessary to protect and support the victims of terrorism that has been committed within its own territory. These measures may include, through the appropriate national schemes and subject to domestic legislation, *inter alia*, financial assistance and compensation for victims of terrorism and their close family members.

Article 14 – Jurisdiction

1   Each Party shall take such measures as may be necessary to establish its jurisdiction over the offences set forth in this Convention:

    a   when the offence is committed in the territory of that Party;

    b   when the offence is committed on board a ship flying the flag of that Party, or on board an aircraft registered under the laws of that Party;

    c   when the offence is committed by a national of that Party.

2   Each Party may also establish its jurisdiction over the offences set forth in this Convention:

    a   when the offence was directed towards or resulted in the carrying out of an offence referred to in Article 1 of this Convention, in the territory of or against a national of that Party;

    b   when the offence was directed towards or resulted in the carrying out of an offence referred to in Article 1 of this Convention, against a State or government facility of that Party abroad, including diplomatic or consular premises of that Party;

    c   when the offence was directed towards or resulted in an offence referred to in Article 1 of this Convention, committed in an attempt to compel that Party to do or abstain from doing any act;

    d   when the offence is committed by a stateless person who has his or her habitual residence in the territory of that Party;

    e   when the offence is committed on board an aircraft which is operated by the Government of that Party.

3   Each Party shall take such measures as may be necessary to establish its jurisdiction over the offences set forth in this Convention in the case where the alleged offender is present in its territory and it does not extradite him or her to a Party whose jurisdiction is based on a rule of jurisdiction existing equally in the law of the requested Party.

4   This Convention does not exclude any criminal jurisdiction exercised in accordance with national law.

5   When more than one Party claims jurisdiction over an alleged offence set forth in this Convention, the Parties involved shall, where appropriate, consult with a view to determining the most appropriate jurisdiction for prosecution.

Article 15 – Duty to investigate

1   Upon receiving information that a person who has committed or who is alleged to have committed an offence set forth in this Convention may be present in its territory, the Party concerned shall take such measures as may be necessary under its domestic law to investigate the facts contained in the information.

2   Upon being satisfied that the circumstances so warrant, the Party in whose territory the offender or alleged offender is present shall take the appropriate measures under its domestic law so as to ensure that person's presence for the purpose of prosecution or extradition.

3   Any person in respect of whom the measures referred to in paragraph 2 are being taken shall be entitled to:

a   communicate without delay with the nearest appropriate representative of the State of which that person is a national or which is otherwise entitled to protect that person's rights or, if that person is a stateless person, the State in the territory of which that person habitually resides;

b   be visited by a representative of that State;

c   be informed of that person's rights under subparagraphs a. and b.

4   The rights referred to in paragraph 3 shall be exercised in conformity with the laws and regulations of the Party in the territory of which the offender or alleged offender is present, subject to the provision that the said laws and regulations must enable full effect to be given to the purposes for which the rights accorded under paragraph 3 are intended.

5   The provisions of paragraphs 3 and 4 shall be without prejudice to the right of any Party having a claim of jurisdiction in accordance with

Article 14, paragraphs 1.c and 2.d to invite the International Committee of the Red Cross to communicate with and visit the alleged offender.

Article 16 – Non application of the Convention

This Convention shall not apply where any of the offences established in accordance with Articles 5 to 7 and 9 is committed within a single State, the alleged offender is a national of that State and is present in the territory of that State, and no other State has a basis under Article 14, paragraph 1 or 2 of this Convention, to exercise jurisdiction, it being understood that the provisions of Articles 17 and 20 to 22 of this Convention shall, as appropriate, apply in those cases.

Article 17 – International co-operation in criminal matters

1   Parties shall afford one another the greatest measure of assistance in connection with criminal investigations or criminal or extradition proceedings in respect of the offences set forth in Articles 5 to 7 and 9 of this Convention, including assistance in obtaining evidence in their possession necessary for the proceedings.

2   Parties shall carry out their obligations under paragraph 1 in conformity with any treaties or other agreements on mutual legal assistance that may exist between them. In the absence of such treaties or agreements, Parties shall afford one another assistance in accordance with their domestic law.

3   Parties shall co-operate with each other to the fullest extent possible under relevant law, treaties, agreements and arrangements of the requested Party with respect to criminal investigations or proceedings in relation to the offences for which a legal entity may be held liable in accordance with Article 10 of this Convention in the requesting Party.

4   Each Party may give consideration to establishing additional mechanisms to share with other Parties information or evidence needed to establish criminal, civil or administrative liability pursuant to Article 10.

Article 18 – Extradite or prosecute

1   The Party in the territory of which the alleged offender is present shall, when it has jurisdiction in accordance with Article 14, if it does not extradite that person, be obliged, without exception whatsoever and whether or not the offence was committed in its territory, to submit the case without undue delay to its competent authorities for the purpose of prosecution, through proceedings in accordance with the laws of that Party. Those authorities shall take their decision in the same manner as

in the case of any other offence of a serious nature under the law of that Party.

2   Whenever a Party is permitted under its domestic law to extradite or otherwise surrender one of its nationals only upon the condition that the person will be returned to that Party to serve the sentence imposed as a result of the trial or proceeding for which the extradition or surrender of the person was sought, and this Party and the Party seeking the extradition of the person agree with this option and other terms they may deem appropriate, such a conditional extradition or surrender shall be sufficient to discharge the obligation set forth in paragraph 1.

Article 19 – Extradition

1   The offences set forth in Articles 5 to 7 and 9 of this Convention shall be deemed to be included as extraditable offences in any extradition treaty existing between any of the Parties before the entry into force of this Convention. Parties undertake to include such offences as extraditable offences in every extradition treaty to be subsequently concluded between them.

2   When a Party which makes extradition conditional on the existence of a treaty receives a request for extradition from another Party with which it has no extradition treaty, the requested Party may, if it so decides, consider this Convention as a legal basis for extradition in respect of the offences set forth in Articles 5 to 7 and 9 of this Convention. Extradition shall be subject to the other conditions provided by the law of the requested Party.

3   Parties which do not make extradition conditional on the existence of a treaty shall recognise the offences set forth in Articles 5 to 7 and 9 of this Convention as extraditable offences between themselves, subject to the conditions provided by the law of the requested Party.

4   Where necessary, the offences set forth in Articles 5 to 7 and 9 of this Convention shall be treated, for the purposes of extradition between Parties, as if they had been committed not only in the place in which they occurred but also in the territory of the Parties that have established jurisdiction in accordance with Article 14.

5   The provisions of all extradition treaties and agreements concluded between Parties in respect of offences set forth in Articles 5 to 7 and 9 of this Convention shall be deemed to be modified as between Parties to the extent that they are incompatible with this Convention.

Article 20 – Exclusion of the political exception clause

1   None of the offences referred to in Articles 5 to 7 and 9 of this Convention, shall be regarded, for the purposes of extradition or mutual legal assistance, as a political offence, an offence connected with a political offence, or as an offence inspired by political motives. Accordingly, a request for extradition or for mutual legal assistance based on such an offence may not be refused on the sole ground that it concerns a political offence or an offence connected with a political offence or an offence inspired by political motives.

2   Without prejudice to the application of Articles 19 to 23 of the Vienna Convention on the Law of Treaties of 23 May 1969 to the other Articles of this Convention, any State or the European Community may, at the time of signature or when depositing its instrument of ratification, acceptance, approval or accession of the Convention, declare that it reserves the right to not apply paragraph 1 of this Article as far as extradition in respect of an offence set forth in this Convention is concerned. The Party undertakes to apply this reservation on a case-by-case basis, through a duly reasoned decision.

3   Any Party may wholly or partly withdraw a reservation it has made in accordance with paragraph 2 by means of a declaration addressed to the Secretary General of the Council of Europe which shall become effective as from the date of its receipt.

4   A Party which has made a reservation in accordance with paragraph 2 of this Article may not claim the application of paragraph 1 of this Article by any other Party; it may, however, if its reservation is partial or conditional, claim the application of this Article in so far as it has itself accepted it.

5   The reservation shall be valid for a period of three years from the day of the entry into force of this Convention in respect of the Party concerned. However, such reservation may be renewed for periods of the same duration.

6   Twelve months before the date of expiry of the reservation, the Secretary General of the Council of Europe shall give notice of that expiry to the Party concerned. No later than three months before expiry, the Party shall notify the Secretary General of the Council of Europe that it is upholding, amending or withdrawing its reservation. Where a Party notifies the Secretary General of the Council of Europe that it is upholding its reservation, it shall provide an explanation of the grounds justifying its continuance. In the absence of notification by the Party concerned, the Secretary General of the Council of Europe shall inform that Party that its reservation is considered to have been extended automatically for a period of six months. Failure by the Party concerned

to notify its intention to uphold or modify its reservation before the expiry of that period shall cause the reservation to lapse.

7   Where a Party does not extradite a person in application of this reservation, after receiving an extradition request from another Party, it shall submit the case, without exception whatsoever and without undue delay, to its competent authorities for the purpose of prosecution, unless the requesting Party and the requested Party agree otherwise. The competent authorities, for the purpose of prosecution in the requested Party, shall take their decision in the same manner as in the case of any offence of a grave nature under the law of that Party. The requested Party shall communicate, without undue delay, the final outcome of the proceedings to the requesting Party and to the Secretary General of the Council of Europe, who shall forward it to the Consultation of the Parties provided for in Article 30.

8   The decision to refuse the extradition request on the basis of this reservation shall be forwarded promptly to the requesting Party. If within a reasonable time no judicial decision on the merits has been taken in the requested Party according to paragraph 7, the requesting Party may communicate this fact to the Secretary General of the Council of Europe, who shall submit the matter to the Consultation of the Parties provided for in Article 30. This Consultation shall consider the matter and issue an opinion on the conformity of the refusal with the Convention and shall submit it to the Committee of Ministers for the purpose of issuing a declaration thereon. When performing its functions under this paragraph, the Committee of Ministers shall meet in its composition restricted to the States Parties.

Article 21 – Discrimination clause

1   Nothing in this Convention shall be interpreted as imposing an obligation to extradite or to afford mutual legal assistance, if the requested Party has substantial grounds for believing that the request for extradition for offences set forth in Articles 5 to 7 and 9 or for mutual legal assistance with respect to such offences has been made for the purpose of prosecuting or punishing a person on account of that person's race, religion, nationality, ethnic origin or political opinion or that compliance with the request would cause prejudice to that person's position for any of these reasons.

2   Nothing in this Convention shall be interpreted as imposing an obligation to extradite if the person who is the subject of the extradition request risks being exposed to torture or to inhuman or degrading treatment or punishment.

3   Nothing in this Convention shall be interpreted either as imposing an obligation to extradite if the person who is the subject of the extradition

request risks being exposed to the death penalty or, where the law of the requested Party does not allow for life imprisonment, to life imprisonment without the possibility of parole, unless under applicable extradition treaties the requested Party is under the obligation to extradite if the requesting Party gives such assurance as the requested Party considers sufficient that the death penalty will not be imposed or, where imposed, will not be carried out, or that the person concerned will not be subject to life imprisonment without the possibility of parole.

Article 22 – Spontaneous information

1   Without prejudice to their own investigations or proceedings, the competent authorities of a Party may, without prior request, forward to the competent authorities of another Party information obtained within the framework of their own investigations, when they consider that the disclosure of such information might assist the Party receiving the information in initiating or carrying out investigations or proceedings, or might lead to a request by that Party under this Convention.

2   The Party providing the information may, pursuant to its national law, impose conditions on the use of such information by the Party receiving the information.

3   The Party receiving the information shall be bound by those conditions.

4   However, any Party may, at any time, by means of a declaration addressed to the Secretary General of the Council of Europe, declare that it reserves the right not to be bound by the conditions imposed by the Party providing the information under paragraph 2 above, unless it receives prior notice of the nature of the information to be provided and agrees to its transmission.

Article 23 – Signature and entry into force

1   This Convention shall be open for signature by the member States of the Council of Europe, the European Community and by non-member States which have participated in its elaboration.

2   This Convention is subject to ratification, acceptance or approval. Instruments of ratification, acceptance or approval shall be deposited with the Secretary General of the Council of Europe.

3   This Convention shall enter into force on the first day of the month following the expiration of a period of three months after the date on which six Signatories, including at least four member States of the Council of Europe, have expressed their consent to be bound by the Convention in accordance with the provisions of paragraph 2.

4   In respect of any Signatory which subsequently expresses its consent to be bound by it, the Convention shall enter into force on the first day of the month following the expiration of a period of three months after the date of the expression of its consent to be bound by the Convention in accordance with the provisions of paragraph 2.

Article 24 – Accession to the Convention

1   After the entry into force of this Convention, the Committee of Ministers of the Council of Europe, after consulting with and obtaining the unanimous consent of the Parties to the Convention, may invite any State which is not a member of the Council of Europe and which has not participated in its elaboration to accede to this convention. The decision shall be taken by the majority provided for in Article 20.d of the Statute of the Council of Europe and by the unanimous vote of the representatives of the Parties entitled to sit on the Committee of Ministers.

2   In respect of any State acceding to the convention under paragraph 1 above, the Convention shall enter into force on the first day of the month following the expiration of a period of three months after the date of deposit of the instrument of accession with the Secretary General of the Council of Europe.

Article 25 – Territorial application

1   Any State or the European Community may, at the time of signature or when depositing its instrument of ratification, acceptance, approval or accession, specify the territory or territories to which this Convention shall apply.

2   Any Party may, at any later date, by a declaration addressed to the Secretary General of the Council of Europe, extend the application of this Convention to any other territory specified in the declaration. In respect of such territory the Convention shall enter into force on the first day of the month following the expiration of a period of three months after the date of receipt of the declaration by the Secretary General.

3   Any declaration made under the two preceding paragraphs may, in respect of any territory specified in such declaration, be withdrawn by a notification addressed to the Secretary General of the Council of Europe. The withdrawal shall become effective on the first day of the month following the expiration of a period of three months after the date of receipt of such notification by the Secretary General.

Article 26 – Effects of the Convention

1   The present Convention supplements applicable multilateral or bilateral treaties or agreements between the Parties, including the provisions of the following Council of Europe treaties:

–   European Convention on Extradition, opened for signature, in Paris, on 13 December 1957 (ETS No. 24);

–   European Convention on Mutual Assistance in Criminal Matters, opened for signature, in Strasbourg, on 20 April 1959 (ETS No. 30);

–   European Convention on the Suppression of Terrorism, opened for signature, in Strasbourg, on 27 January 1977 (ETS No. 90);

–   Additional Protocol to the European Convention on Mutual Assistance in Criminal Matters, opened for signature in Strasbourg on 17 March 1978 (ETS No. 99);

–   Second Additional Protocol to the European Convention on Mutual Assistance in Criminal Matters, opened for signature in Strasbourg on 8 November 2001 (ETS No. 182);

–   Protocol amending the European Convention on the Suppression of Terrorism, opened for signature in Strasbourg on 15 May 2003 (ETS No. 190).

2   If two or more Parties have already concluded an agreement or treaty on the matters dealt with in this Convention or have otherwise established their relations on such matters, or should they in future do so, they shall also be entitled to apply that agreement or treaty or to regulate those relations accordingly. However, where Parties establish their relations in respect of the matters dealt with in the present Convention other than as regulated therein, they shall do so in a manner that is not inconsistent with the Convention's objectives and principles.

3   Parties which are members of the European Union shall, in their mutual relations, apply Community and European Union rules in so far as there are Community or European Union rules governing the particular subject concerned and applicable to the specific case, without prejudice to the object and purpose of the present Convention and without prejudice to its full application with other Parties.

4   Nothing in this Convention shall affect other rights, obligations and responsibilities of a Party and individuals under international law, including international humanitarian law.

5   The activities of armed forces during an armed conflict, as those terms are understood under international humanitarian law, which are governed by that law, are not governed by this Convention, and the activities undertaken by military forces of a Party in the exercise of their official duties, inasmuch as they are governed by other rules of international law, are not governed by this Convention.

Article 27 – Amendments to the Convention

1   Amendments to this Convention may be proposed by any Party, the Committee of Ministers of the Council of Europe or the Consultation of the Parties.

2   Any proposal for amendment shall be communicated by the Secretary General of the Council of Europe to the Parties.

3   Moreover, any amendment proposed by a Party or the Committee of Ministers shall be communicated to the Consultation of the Parties, which shall submit to the Committee of Ministers its opinion on the proposed amendment.

4   The Committee of Ministers shall consider the proposed amendment and any opinion submitted by the Consultation of the Parties and may approve the amendment.

5   The text of any amendment approved by the Committee of Ministers in accordance with paragraph 4 shall be forwarded to the Parties for acceptance.

6   Any amendment approved in accordance with paragraph 4 shall come into force on the thirtieth day after all Parties have informed the Secretary General of their acceptance thereof.

Article 28 – Revision of the Appendix

1   In order to update the list of treaties in the Appendix, amendments may be proposed by any Party or by the Committee of Ministers. These proposals for amendment shall only concern universal treaties concluded within the United Nations system dealing specifically with international terrorism and having entered into force. They shall be communicated by the Secretary General of the Council of Europe to the Parties.

2   After having consulted the non-member Parties, the Committee of Ministers may adopt a proposed amendment by the majority provided for in Article 20.d of the Statute of the Council of Europe. The amendment shall enter into force following the expiry of a period of one year after the date on which it has been forwarded to the Parties. During this period, any Party may notify the Secretary General of the Council of Europe of any objection to the entry into force of the amendment in respect of that Party.

3   If one third of the Parties notifies the Secretary General of the Council of Europe of an objection to the entry into force of the amendment, the amendment shall not enter into force.

4   If less than one third of the Parties notifies an objection, the amendment shall enter into force for those Parties which have not notified an objection.

5   Once an amendment has entered into force in accordance with paragraph 2 and a Party has notified an objection to it, this amendment shall come into force in respect of the Party concerned on the first day of the month following the date on which it notifies the Secretary General of the Council of Europe of its acceptance.

Article 29 – Settlement of disputes

In the event of a dispute between Parties as to the interpretation or application of this Convention, they shall seek a settlement of the dispute through negotiation or any other peaceful means of their choice, including submission of the dispute to an arbitral tribunal whose decisions shall be binding upon the Parties to the dispute, or to the International Court of Justice, as agreed upon by the Parties concerned.

Article 30 – Consultation of the Parties

1   The Parties shall consult periodically with a view to:

a   making proposals to facilitate or improve the effective use and implementation of this Convention, including the identification of any problems and the effects of any declaration made under this Convention;

b   formulating its opinion on the conformity of a refusal to extradite which is referred to them in accordance with Article 20, paragraph 8;

c   making proposals for the amendment of this Convention in accordance with Article 27;

d   formulating their opinion on any proposal for the amendment of this Convention which is referred to them in accordance with Article 27, paragraph 3;

e   expressing an opinion on any question concerning the application of this Convention and facilitating the exchange of information on significant legal, policy or technological developments.

2   The Consultation of the Parties shall be convened by the Secretary General of the Council of Europe whenever he finds it necessary and in any case when a majority of the Parties or the Committee of Ministers request its convocation.

3   The Parties shall be assisted by the Secretariat of the Council of Europe in carrying out their functions pursuant to this Article.

Article 31 – Denunciation

1   Any Party may, at any time, denounce this Convention by means of a notification addressed to the Secretary General of the Council of Europe.

2   Such denunciation shall become effective on the first day of the month following the expiration of a period of three months after the date of receipt of the notification by the Secretary General.

Article 32 – Notification

The Secretary General of the Council of Europe shall notify the member States of the Council of Europe, the European Community, the non-member States which have participated in the elaboration of this Convention as well as any State which has acceded to, or has been invited to accede to, this Convention of:

a   any signature;

b   the deposit of any instrument of ratification, acceptance, approval or accession;

c   any date of entry into force of this Convention in accordance with Article 23;

d   any declaration made under Article 1, paragraph 2, 22, paragraph 4, and 25;

e   any other act, notification or communication relating to this Convention.

In witness whereof the undersigned, being duly authorised thereto, have signed this Convention.

Done at Warsaw, this 16th day of May 2005, in English and in French, both texts being equally authentic, in a single copy which shall be deposited in the archives of the Council of Europe. The Secretary General of the Council of Europe shall transmit certified copies to each member State of the Council of Europe, to the European Community, to the non-member States which have participated in the elaboration of this Convention, and to any State invited to accede to it.

Appendix

1   Convention for the Suppression of Unlawful Seizure of Aircraft, signed at The Hague on 16 December 1970;

2   Convention for the Suppression of Unlawful Acts Against the Safety of Civil Aviation, concluded at Montreal on 23 September 1971;

3   Convention on the Prevention and Punishment of Crimes Against Internationally Protected Persons, Including Diplomatic Agents, adopted in New York on 14 December 1973;

4   International Convention Against the Taking of Hostages, adopted in New York on 17 December 1979;

5   Convention on the Physical Protection of Nuclear Material, adopted in Vienna on 3 March 1980;

6   Protocol for the Suppression of Unlawful Acts of Violence at Airports Serving International Civil Aviation, done at Montreal on 24 February 1988;

7   Convention for the Suppression of Unlawful Acts Against the Safety of Maritime Navigation, done at Rome on 10 March 1988;

8   Protocol for the Suppression of Unlawful Acts Against the Safety of Fixed Platforms Located on the Continental Shelf, done at Rome on 10 March 1988;

9   International Convention for the Suppression of Terrorist Bombings, adopted in New York on 15 December 1997;

10   International Convention for the Suppression of the Financing of Terrorism, adopted in New York on 9 December 1999.

Explanatory Report

I.   The Council of Europe Convention on the Prevention of Terrorism (hereafter referred to as "the Convention") and its Explanatory Report were adopted by the Committee of Ministers of the Council of Europe at its 925th meeting. The Convention was then opened for signature by the member States of the Council of Europe, the European Community and non-member States which participated in its elaboration on 16 May 2005 on the occasion of the Third Summit of Heads of State and Government of the Council of Europe.

II.   The text of this Explanatory Report does not constitute an instrument providing an authoritative interpretation of the Convention, although it may serve to facilitate the application of the provisions contained therein.

Introduction

1.   The Council of Europe's response to the terrorist attacks of unprecedented violence committed in the United States of America on 11 September 2001 was both firm and immediate.

2.   At its 109th Session on 8 November 2001, the Committee of Ministers "agreed to take steps rapidly to increase the effectiveness of the existing international instruments within the Council of Europe on the fight against terrorism by, *inter alia*, setting up a Multidisciplinary Group on International Action against Terrorism (GMT)".

3.   Among the tasks given to the GMT was reviewing the implementation of and examining the possibility of updating existing Council of Europe international instruments relating to the fight against terrorism, in particular the European Convention on the Suppression of Terrorism, in view also of a possible opening of that Convention to non-member States, and the other relevant instruments.

4.   As a result of this work, on 13 February 2003, the Committee of Ministers approved a Protocol amending the European Convention on the Suppression of Terrorism (ETS No. 190) which was opened for signature on 15 May 2003.

5.   In the course of the discussions of the GMT concerning the preparation of the Protocol, the question of the drafting of a comprehensive convention on terrorism in the Council of Europe was raised several times. However, the GMT did not formally take a stand on this question because it considered this issue to be beyond its remit.

6.   The issue was re-launched by the Parliamentary Assembly in its Recommendation 1550 (2002) on combating terrorism and respect for human rights and, later on, in its Opinion No. 242 (2003) concerning the

above-mentioned protocol, where the Assembly expressed its belief "that it would be appropriate, in due course, to consider the possibility of drawing up a comprehensive Council of Europe convention on terrorism, taking into account the work carried out by the United Nations". Furthermore, in January 2004, the Parliamentary Assembly adopted Recommendation 1644 (2004) on terrorism: a threat to democracies, where it invited the Committee of Ministers to begin work without delay on the elaboration of a comprehensive Council of Europe convention on terrorism, based on the normative *acquis* of the legal instruments and other texts of the United Nations, the Council of Europe and the European Union.

7.   In May 2003, the Committee of Ministers stressed the necessity of reinforcing international co-operation in the fight against terrorism and supporting the efforts of the United Nations in this field. In this context, the Ministers noted with interest the proposal of the Parliamentary Assembly to draft a comprehensive convention on terrorism under the aegis of the Council of Europe.

8.   In June 2003, the Committee of Ministers agreed to return to the discussion of the initial proposal to prepare a comprehensive convention on terrorism under the auspices of the Council of Europe on the basis of the conclusions of the 25th Conference of European Ministers of Justice (Sofia, 9 and 10 October 2003) on the theme of the fight against terrorism and of the proposals of the Committee of Experts on Terrorism (CODEXTER), a new governmental committee of experts set up following the expiry of the terms of reference of the GMT.

9.   At the 25th Conference of the European Ministers of Justice, the Ministers invited the CODEXTER to provide the Committee of Ministers with an opinion on the added value of a possible comprehensive Council of Europe convention on terrorism, or of some elements of such a convention, which would contribute significantly to the United Nations' efforts in this field.

10. In pursuance of this request, at its first meeting (Strasbourg, 27-30 October 2003), the CODEXTER commissioned the preparation of an independent expert report on possible gaps in international instruments against terrorism and on the "possible added value" of a comprehensive Council of Europe convention in relation to existing universal and European instruments of relevance to the fight against terrorism. The general conclusion of the report was that a comprehensive Council of Europe convention on terrorism would provide considerable added value with respect to existing European and universal counter-terrorism instruments.

11. The CODEXTER considered this report at its second meeting (Strasbourg, 29 March-1 April 2004), but could not reach a consensus on the question of whether or not the Council of Europe should elaborate a comprehensive convention on terrorism. However, it agreed that an instrument, or instruments, with limited scope, dealing with the prevention of

terrorism and covering existing lacunae in international law or action, would bring added value, and agreed to propose to the Committee of Ministers to instruct the CODEXTER to undertake work in this direction.

12. At its 114th Session (12 and 13 May 2004), the Committee of Ministers took note of the CODEXTER's work and agreed to give instructions for the elaboration of one or more instruments (which could be legally binding or not) with specific scope dealing with lacunae in existing international law or action on the fight against terrorism, such as those identified by the CODEXTER in its report. On this basis, in May 2004, the Committee of Ministers instructed the Secretariat to prepare proposals for follow-up to the 114th Session concerning the Council of Europe's contribution to international action against terrorism.

13. On 11 June 2004, the Committee of Ministers adopted revised specific terms of reference for the CODEXTER, pursuant to which the CODEXTER was instructed, *inter alia*, to "elaborate proposals for one or more instruments (which could be legally binding or not) with specific scope dealing with existing lacunae in international law or action on the fight against terrorism, such as those identified by the CODEXTER in its second meeting report."

14. The CODEXTER held a further six meetings, from July 2004 to February 2005 (its third to eighth meetings), concerning the preparation of a draft Convention on the prevention of terrorism. It was chaired by Ms Gertraude Kabelka (Austria), with Mr Zdzislaw Galicki (Poland) and Mr Martin Sørby (Norway) as vice-chairs.

15. From the outset, the CODEXTER agreed on the need to strengthen legal action against terrorism while ensuring respect for human rights and fundamental values, and on the necessity of including provisions on appropriate safeguards and conditions securing these aims.

16. Two of the Council of Europe texts adopted after the setting up of the GMT were particularly significant for the work of the CODEXTER, namely: the above-mentioned Recommendation 1550 (2002) and the Guidelines on Human Rights and the Fight against Terrorism, adopted by the Committee of Ministers on 11 July 2002.

17. It should be recalled that at its first meeting in October 2003, the CODEXTER had decided to set up the working group CODEXTER-Apologie to analyse the conclusions of an independent expert report on "*apologie du terrorisme*" and "incitement to terrorism" as criminal offences in the national legislation of member and observer States of the Council of Europe, which was prepared on the basis of relevant legislation and case-law in member and observer States, and the case-law of the European Court of Human Rights. From the survey on the situation in member States it appeared that a majority of them did not have a specific offence regarding "*apologie du*

terrorisme". The working group was instructed to present proposals for follow-up, particularly in the context of the ongoing discussions relating to the preparation of new international instruments on terrorism.

18. The CODEXTER-Apologie, which was chaired by Mr David Touvet (France), reached a series of conclusions which the CODEXTER endorsed at its second meeting in March/April 2004, recognising the existence, at this stage, of lacunae in international law as far as the handling of "*apologie du terrorisme*" and/or "incitement to terrorism" was concerned. It further agreed to include this issue in the framework of its reflection on the possible elaboration of international instruments.

19. At the third meeting of the CODEXTER, the working group CODEXTER-Apologie produced preliminary draft provisions for a possible instrument on public provocation to commit acts of terrorism. These draft provisions, along with further substantial input from a number of delegations, were subsequently used by the Bureau of the CODEXTER in the elaboration of the draft instrument on the prevention of terrorism presented at the fourth meeting of the CODEXTER.

20. The CODEXTER adopted the draft Convention on first reading at its sixth meeting in December 2004 and then submitted it to the Committee of Ministers which authorised consultation of the Parliamentary Assembly and of the Commissioner for Human Rights of the Council of Europe.

21. At its seventh meeting, early in February 2005, the CODEXTER revised the draft in the light of the above-mentioned opinions and adopted the text on second reading, notwithstanding some issues which required further consideration. At this meeting, the CODEXTER also decided to make the drafts public and to invite interested organisations to submit comments.

22. At its eighth meeting at the end of February 2005, the CODEXTER finalised the draft Convention and approved the present explanatory report. The CODEXTER submitted both texts to the Committee of Ministers, asking it to adopt the Convention and open it for signature, and to authorise the publication of the explanatory report.

23. At the 925th meeting of the Ministers' Deputies on 3 May 2005, the Committee of Ministers adopted the Convention and decided to open it for signature by the member States of the Council of Europe, the European Community and non-member States that had participated in its elaboration on the occasion of the 3rd Summit of Heads of State and Government of the Council of Europe.

General considerations

24. The purpose of the Convention is to enhance the efforts of Parties in preventing terrorism and its negative effects on the full enjoyment of human

rights and in particular the right to life, both by measures to be taken at national level and through international co-operation, with due regard to the existing applicable multilateral or bilateral treaties or arrangements between the Parties, as explicitly stated in Article 2.

25. The title of the Convention does not presuppose that the Convention is exhaustive in providing for all the means that may contribute to the prevention of terrorism. Clearly, it only provides some means and concentrates on policy and legal measures. In this respect, the present Convention joins other international standards in the overall objective of preventing and fighting terrorism.

26. The Convention purports to achieve this objective, on the one hand, by establishing as criminal offences certain acts that may lead to the commission of terrorist offences, namely: public provocation, recruitment and training and, on the other hand, by reinforcing co-operation on prevention both internally, in the context of the definition of national prevention policies, and internationally through a number of measures, *inter alia*, by means of supplementing and, where necessary, modifying existing extradition and mutual assistance arrangements concluded between Parties and providing for additional means, such as spontaneous information, together with obligations relating to law enforcement, such as the duty to investigate, obligations relating to sanctions and measures, the liability of legal entities in addition to that of individuals, and the obligation to prosecute where extradition is refused.

27. It was felt that the climate of mutual confidence among likeminded States, namely the member and observer States of the Council of Europe, based on their democratic nature and their respect for human rights, safeguarded by the institutions set up under the Convention for the Protection of Human Rights and Fundamental Freedoms of 4 November 1950 (hereafter "ECHR") and other applicable international instruments, justified moving forward with the criminalisation of certain kinds of behaviour which until now had not been dealt with at international level, supplemented by provisions to strengthen international judicial co-operation.

28. The Committee carefully considered the possibility of including an explicit article on declarations and reservations regarding specific provisions in the Convention. Some countries made proposals related to problems where they saw a need for declarations and reservations concerning the application of the International Convention for the Suppression of the Financing of Terrorism to the criminalisation provisions of the Convention; the criminalisation requirements set out in Articles 5 and 9 and problems connected with Article 14, paragraph 1.c. The Committee concluded that it was better to leave those issues to be resolved in accordance with international law, in particular the regime set out in the Vienna Convention on the Law of Treaties.

29. The Convention, starting with the Preamble, contains several provisions concerning the protection of human rights and fundamental freedoms, both in respect of internal and international co-operation on the one hand and as an integral part of the new criminalisation provisions (in the form of conditions and safeguards) on the other hand, not overlooking, in the given context, the situation of victims (see paragraph 31 *infra*).

30. This is a crucial aspect of the Convention, given that it deals with issues which are on the border between the legitimate exercise of freedoms, such as freedom of expression, association or religion, and criminal behaviour.

31. It also contains a provision regarding the protection and compensation of victims of terrorism and a provision emphasising that the human rights that must be respected are not only the rights of those accused or convicted of terrorist offences, but also the rights of the victims, or potential victims, of those offences (see Article 17 of the ECHR).

32. The Convention does not define new terrorist offences in addition to those included in the existing conventions against terrorism. In this respect, it refers to the treaties listed in the Appendix. However, it creates three new offences which may lead to the terrorist offences as defined in those treaties.

33. These new offences are: public provocation to commit a terrorist offence (Article 5), recruitment for terrorism (Article 6) and training for terrorism (Article 7). They are coupled with a provision on accessory (ancillary) offences (Article 9) providing for the criminalisation of complicity (such as aiding and abetting) in the commission of all of the three aforementioned offences and, in addition, of attempts to commit an offence under Articles 6 and 7 (recruitment and training).

34. One of the characteristics of the new crimes introduced by the Convention is that they do not require that a terrorist offence, within the meaning of Article 1, that is: any of the offences within the scope of and as defined in one of the international treaties against terrorism listed in the Appendix, actually be committed. This is explicitly stated by the Convention in Article 8 based on an equivalent provision in the International Convention for the Suppression of the Financing of Terrorism. Consequently, the place where such an offence would be committed is also irrelevant for the purposes of establishing the commission of any of the offences set forth in Articles 5 to 7 and 9.

35. In addition, these offences must be committed unlawfully and intentionally, as is explicitly stated for each and every one of them.

36. Concerning international co-operation, the Convention builds on the latest trends reflected by treaties such as the Protocol amending the European Convention on the Suppression of Terrorism, the Second Additional Protocol to the European Convention on Mutual Assistance in

Criminal Matters (ETS No. 182) and the United Nations Convention against Transnational Organized Crime.

37. Where extradition and mutual assistance are concerned, it modifies the agreements concluded between member States of the Council of Europe, including the European Convention on Extradition of 13 December 1957 (ETS No. 24) and its additional protocols of 15 October 1975 and 17 March 1978 (ETS Nos. 86 and 98), the European Convention on Mutual Assistance in Criminal Matters of 20 April 1959 (ETS No. 30) and its additional protocols of 17 March 1978 and 8 November 2001 (ETS Nos. 99 and 182) and the European Convention on the Suppression of Terrorism (ETS No. 90) and its amending Protocol, in particular by making the offences set forth in the Convention extraditable, and imposing an obligation to provide mutual legal assistance with respect to them.

38. At the same time, in Article 21 safeguards are provided with respect to extradition and mutual legal assistance that make clear that this Convention does not derogate from important traditional grounds for refusal of co-operation under applicable treaties and laws; for example, refusal of extradition where the person will be subjected to torture or to inhuman or degrading treatment or punishment, or to the death penalty, or refusal of either extradition or mutual legal assistance where the person will be prosecuted for political or other impermissible purposes. Where the person is not extradited for these or other reasons, the Party in which he or she is found has the obligation to submit the case for domestic prosecution pursuant to Article 18.

39. The obligations which Parties undertake by adhering to the Convention are closely linked with the special climate of mutual confidence among likeminded States, which is based on their collective recognition of the rule of law and the protection of human rights. For that reason, in spite of the fact that terrorism is a global problem, it was thought necessary to restrict the circle of Parties to the member and observer States of the Council of Europe and to the European Community, although the Committee of Ministers may invite other States to become Parties to the Convention.

40. It goes without saying that the Convention does not affect the other rights, obligations and responsibilities of Parties and individuals in accordance with other international undertakings to which the Parties to the Convention are Parties.

Specific commentaries on the Articles of the Convention

Preamble

41. At the outset, it should be recalled that the preambular paragraphs are not part of the operative provisions of the Convention and therefore by their nature, do not bestow rights or impose obligations on Parties. However, the

preambular paragraphs are intended to set a general framework and facilitate the understanding of the operative provisions of the Convention.

42. Against the background of the *grave concern caused by the increase in terrorist offences and the growing terrorist threat and aware of the precarious situation faced by those who suffer from terrorism*, the preamble states the objective pursued by the Parties which is to *take effective measures to prevent terrorism and to counter, in particular, public provocation to commit terrorist offences and recruitment and training for terrorism*.

43. The preamble further excludes any justification of terrorist offences and the offences set forth in the Convention, while also recalling that all measures taken in the fight against terrorism must respect the rule of law and democratic values, human rights and fundamental freedoms as well as other provisions of international law, including, where applicable, international humanitarian law.

44. The preamble recognises that the Convention is not intended to affect established principles relating to freedom of expression and freedom of association.

45. The eighth preambular paragraph is rather intended to cover established legal principles relating to freedom of expression and freedom of association as expressed in international and/or national law.

46. Finally, this provision recalls that terrorist offences are characterised by so-called terrorist motivation, stating that acts of terrorism "have the purpose by their nature or context to seriously intimidate a population or unduly compel a government or an international organisation to perform or abstain from performing any act or seriously destabilise or destroy the fundamental political, constitutional, economic or social structures of a country or an international organisation." Terrorist motivation is not a substantial element in addition to the requirements laid down in the operative part for the offences set forth in this Convention.

Article 1 – Terminology

47. This article provides that for the purposes of the Convention, the term "terrorist offence" is taken to mean any of the offences within the scope of and as defined in one of the treaties listed in the Appendix.

48. When the CODEXTER considered this article, it bore in mind Parliamentary Assembly Recommendation 1550 (2002) which requested that the Council of Europe consider using the definition of terrorism adopted by the European Union in the European Council Common Position of 27 December 2001 on the application of specific measures to combat

terrorism (2001/931/CFSP).[2] The CODEXTER decided not to do so, given that the European Union definition had been agreed upon "for the purpose of the Common Position" and because it had not received the mandate to draft a comprehensive convention on terrorism but rather a limited scope specific instrument for the prevention of terrorism.

49. In paragraph 1, the offences are defined by reference to the treaties in the Appendix. The reference to the offences "within the scope and as defined" in the conventions listed in the Appendix indicates that, in addition to the definitions of crimes, there may be other provisions in these conventions that affect their scope of application. This reference covers both principal and ancillary offences. Nevertheless, when establishing the offences in their national law, Parties should bear in mind the purpose of the Convention and the principle of proportionality as set forth in Article 2 and Article 12, paragraph 2 respectively. The purpose of the Convention is to prevent terrorism and its negative effects on the full enjoyment of human rights and in particular the right to life. To this end, it obliges Parties to criminalise conduct that has the potential to lead to terrorist offences, but it does not aim at, and create a legal basis for, the criminalisation of conduct which has only a theoretical connection to such offences. Thus, the Convention does not address hypothetical chains of events, such as "provoking an attempt to finance a threat".

50. It should be recalled that the Appendix contains the same list of treaties as in Article 1, paragraph 1 of the European Convention on the Suppression of Terrorism as revised by its amending Protocol.

51. Paragraph 2 is based on similar provisions in other international treaties against terrorism, including the International Convention for the Suppression of the Financing of Terrorism (Article 2, paragraph 2).

52. Its purpose is to deal with the situation where a Party to the present Convention is not a party to a treaty listed in the Appendix, taking into account the consequences that this could cause for the Party concerned in terms of the treaty obligations incumbent upon it.

53. Parties are therefore given the possibility to exclude from the Appendix any of the treaties to which they are not a party. This would be done by means of a declaration at the time of expressing the consent to be bound by the Convention. Such a declaration would cease to have effect once the treaty in question entered into force for the declaring Party. The latter is required to inform the Secretary General of the Council of Europe, as depository of the Convention, of this fact.

---

[2] In the European Union context, this definition was subsequently agreed upon for the purpose of the approximation of the legislation of the European Union member states in the Framework Decision of the Council of 13 June 2002 (2002/475/JAI, JO L 164 of 13.6.2002, p. 3).

Article 2 – Purpose

54. This article states explicitly the purpose of the Convention which is to enhance the efforts of Parties in preventing terrorism and dealing with its effects, both by measures to be taken at national level and through international co-operation, with due regard to the existing applicable multilateral or bilateral treaties or arrangements between the Parties.

55. Reference is made to the negative effects of terrorism on human rights, the right to life being expressly stressed for the reason that terrorist acts mostly result in the loss of human life.

Article 3 – National prevention policies

56. This article is closely connected with Article 12 in so far as they both draw on the same reference texts. However, there are clear differences between the two Articles. While the former deals with prevention policies, the latter comprises safeguards pertaining to the criminalisation obligations established in Articles 5 to 7 and 9.

57. The article is also connected with Article 4. While Article 3 aims at improving co-operation at domestic level, Article 4 is designed to foster co-operation at international level.

58. Article 3 refers to national prevention policies and particularly includes four aspects connected with the prevention of terrorism: a. training, education, culture, information, media and public awareness (paragraph 1); b. co-operation between public authorities (paragraph 2); c. promotion of tolerance (paragraph 3); and d. co-operation of the citizens with the public authorities (paragraph 4). The entire Article is worded in such a way as to make sure that it must not be understood as providing an exhaustive list of possible and appropriate measures.

59. Paragraph 1 requires Parties to take appropriate measures (in particular in the fields of law enforcement training, information and media, public education and awareness raising) for the purposes of preventing the commission of terrorist offences.

60. Reference to training is made in this paragraph because it covers a wider field than the domestic co-operation provided for in paragraph 2.

61. The term "other bodies" is taken to mean bodies other than law-enforcement or judicial authorities at various levels (central, regional, local), civil protection, etc.

62. Each Party is to determine the extent and manner of implementation, in a manner consistent with its system of government, and its laws and procedures applicable to these fields.

63. In carrying out prevention measures, Parties are to ensure respect for human rights, and a number of international human rights instruments that provide relevant human rights standards are listed.

64. The term "where applicable" is intended to exclude the application of those treaties to which a Party to this Convention is not a Party. This is due to the fact that the Convention is open to non-member States of the Council of Europe which therefore would not be Parties to the ECHR.

65. Thus, such non-member States of the Council of Europe which become Parties to this Convention would be required to implement this paragraph pursuant to obligations they have undertaken with respect to the 1966 International Covenant on Civil and Political Rights (ICCPR), other applicable human rights instruments to which they are party, customary law, and their respective domestic laws.

66. Paragraph 2 focuses on specific measures that Parties are called upon to take for the purposes of enhancing co-operation between public authorities as a means of better preventing terrorist offences and their effects. A number of concrete examples of such measures are given to illustrate the point, some concern prevention as such, for instance through better protection of persons and/or facilities, others the readiness to deal with the effects of terrorist attacks by focusing on the civil emergencies they generate and the challenges they pose.

67. Paragraph 3 calls upon Parties to encourage inter-religious and cross-cultural dialogue with a view to reducing tensions and, in this manner, helping to prevent terrorist offences.

68. Here again, considerable flexibility is left to Parties to determine the precise extent and manner in which they implement this paragraph, in order to ensure consistency with their systems of government, including their laws and procedures applicable in the given context.

69. The term "tensions" is used broadly and covers any factor contributing to the rise of terrorism. Thus, these tensions may be of an ethnic, religious or other nature. They may also include situations of injustice for a variety of reasons.

70. As has been stated above, paragraph 4 deals with co-operation between citizens and public authorities for the purposes of the prevention of terrorism.

71. It starts by calling upon Parties to promote public awareness about the terrorist threat. The notion of public awareness is also included in paragraph 1 of this article, but contrary to that paragraph, where it is used in general terms, in this paragraph it is used specifically in relation to citizens.

72. This provision then goes on to invite the Parties to consider encouraging the public to provide specific, factual help to public authorities with a view to preventing the commission of the offences set forth in the Convention.

73. The wording of this paragraph is based on the United Nations Convention against Transnational Organized Crime, adopted in Palermo on 15 December 2000 (Article 31, paragraph 5) and on Resolution A/RES/55/25 adopted by the United Nations General Assembly on 15 November 2000 which, in its operative paragraph 6, calls upon all States to recognise the links between transnational organised criminal activities and terrorist offences, taking into account the relevant General Assembly resolutions, and to apply the United Nations Convention against Transnational Organized Crime in combating all forms of criminal activity, as provided therein.

Article 4 – International co-operation on prevention

74. This article deals with international co-operation and aims at enhancing the capacity of Parties to prevent terrorism. It calls upon Parties to assist and support each other in this respect and provides a series of possible means to this end, including exchanges of information and best practice, training and joint efforts, such as joint teams for analysis and investigation.

75. This provision is to be implemented subject to the capabilities of Parties and where deemed by them to be appropriate.

Articles 5 to 7 – criminalisation provisions – common aspects

76. Articles 5 to 7 provide the core provisions of the Convention, which require Parties to establish criminal offences concerning "*public provocation to commit terrorist offences*" (Article 5), "*recruitment for terrorism*" (Article 6) and "*training for terrorism*" (Article 7), coupled with a series of accessory crimes (Article 9).

77. These offences should not be considered as terrorist offences in the sense of Article 1, that is the offences established by the international conventions included in the Appendix.

78. They are criminal offences of a serious nature related to terrorist offences as they have the potential to lead to the commission of the offences established by the above-mentioned international conventions. However, they do not require that a terrorist offence be committed. The absence of such a requirement is affirmed by Article 8.

79. By the same token, the place where the terrorist offence might be committed is irrelevant for the purposes of the application of this Convention.

80. The offences set forth in Articles 5 to 7 have several elements in common: they must be committed unlawfully and intentionally.

81. The requirement of unlawfulness reflects the insight that the conduct described may be legal or justified not only in cases where classical legal defences are applicable but also where other principles or interests lead to the exclusion of criminal liability, for example for law enforcement purposes.

82. The expression "unlawfully" derives its meaning from the context in which it is used. Thus, without restricting how Parties may implement the concept in their domestic law, it may refer to conduct undertaken without authority (whether legislative, executive, administrative, judicial, contractual or consensual) or conduct that is otherwise not covered by established legal defences or relevant principles under domestic law.

83. The Convention, therefore, leaves unaffected conduct undertaken pursuant to lawful government authority.

84. Furthermore, the offences must be committed "intentionally" for criminal liability to apply. In certain cases an additional specific intentional element forms part of the offence.

85. The drafters of the Convention agreed that the exact meaning of "intentionally" should be left to interpretation under national law.

Article 5 – Public provocation to commit a terrorist offence

86. This article resulted from thorough discussions and deep considerations, first by a working party of the CODEXTER, the CODEXTER-Apologie, which was called upon to carry out a survey of the situation in member and observer States and to consider an independent expert report prepared on this basis.

87. The CODEXTER-Apologie concluded in favour of focusing on public expressions of support for terrorist offences and/or groups; causality links – direct or indirect – with the perpetration of a terrorist offence; and temporal connections – *ex ante* or *ex post* – with the perpetration of a terrorist offence.

88. The Committee therefore focused on the recruitment of terrorists and the creation of new terrorist groups; the instigation of ethnic and religious tensions which can provide a basis for terrorism; the dissemination of "hate speech" and the promotion of ideologies favourable to terrorism, while paying particular attention to the case-law of the European Court of Human Rights concerning the application of Article 10, paragraph 2 of the ECHR,

and to the experience of States in the implementation of their national provisions on "*apologie du terrorisme*" and/or "incitement to terrorism" in order to carefully analyse the potential risk of a restriction of fundamental freedoms.

89. Freedom of expression is one of the essential foundations of a democratic society and applies, according to the case-law of the European Court of Human Rights (see, for example, the *Lingens v. Austria* judgment of 8 July 1986, HUDOC REF 000000108), not only to ideas and information that are favourably received or regarded as inoffensive but also to those that "offend, shock or disturb".

90. However, in contrast to certain fundamental rights which are absolute rights and therefore admit no restrictions, such as the prohibition of torture and inhuman and degrading treatment or punishment (Article 3 of the ECHR), interference with, or restrictions on freedom of expression may be allowed in highly specific circumstances. Article 10, paragraph 2 of the ECHR lays down the conditions under which restrictions on, or interference with, the exercise of freedom of expression are admissible under the ECHR, while Article 15 of the ECHR provides for possible derogations in time of emergency.

91. Thus, for instance, incitement to racial hatred cannot be considered admissible on the grounds of the right to freedom of expression (see Article 9, paragraph 2 of the Convention on the Elimination of All Forms of Racial Discrimination of 21 December 1965). The same goes for incitement to violent terrorist offences, and the Court has already held that certain restrictions on messages that might constitute an indirect incitement to violent terrorist offences are in keeping with the ECHR (see *Hogefeld v. Germany*, 20 January 2000, HUDOC REF 00005340).

92. The question is where the boundary lies between indirect incitement to commit terrorist offences and the legitimate voicing of criticism, and this is the question that the CODEXTER addressed.

93. The current provision is construed on the basis of the Additional Protocol to the Cybercrime Convention concerning the criminalisation of acts of a racist and xenophobic nature committed through computer systems (ETS No. 189, Article 3).

94. In the present Convention, Article 5, paragraph 1 defines public provocation to commit a terrorist offence as "the distribution, or otherwise making available, of a message to the public, with the intent to incite the commission of a terrorist offence, where such conduct, whether or not directly advocating terrorist offences, causes a danger that one or more such offences may be committed."

95.   When drafting this provision, the CODEXTER bore in mind the opinions of the Parliamentary Assembly (Opinion No. 255 (2005), paragraph 3.vii and following), and of the Commissioner for Human Rights of the Council of Europe (document BcommDH (2005) 1, paragraph 30 *in fine*) which suggested that such a provision could cover "the dissemination of messages praising the perpetrator of an attack, the denigration of victims, calls for funding for terrorist organisations or other similar behaviour" which could constitute indirect provocation to terrorist violence.

96.   This provision uses a generic formula as opposed to a more *casuistic* one and requires Parties to criminalise the distributing or otherwise making available of a message to the public advocating terrorist offences. Whether this is done directly or indirectly is irrelevant for the application of this provision.

97.   Direct provocation does not raise any particular problems in so far as it is already a criminal offence, in one form or another, in most legal systems. The aim of making indirect provocation a criminal offence is to remedy the existing lacunae in international law or action by adding provisions in this area.

98.   The provision allows Parties a certain amount of discretion with respect to the definition of the offence and its implementation. For instance, presenting a terrorist offence as necessary and justified may constitute the offence of indirect incitement.

99.   However, its application requires that two conditions be met: first, there has to be a specific intent to incite the commission of a terrorist offence, which is supplemented with the requirements in paragraph 2 (see below) that provocation be committed unlawfully and intentionally.

100. Second, the result of such an act must be to cause a danger that such an offence might be committed. When considering whether such danger is caused, the nature of the author and of the addressee of the message, as well as the context in which the offence is committed shall be taken into account in the sense established by the case-law of the European Court of Human Rights. The significance and the credible nature of the danger should be considered when applying this provision in accordance with the requirements of domestic law.

101. As far as provocation of the offences set forth in the International Convention for the Suppression of the Financing of Terrorism is concerned, it should be stressed that such offences may play an important role in the chain of events that leads to the commission of violent terrorist offences. While the prospect of violent crime in such cases is fairly remote from the act of provocation, it is what ultimately justifies the criminalisation of public provocation to commit the offence of terrorist financing.

102. The term "distribution" refers to the active dissemination of a message advocating terrorism, while the expression "making available" refers to providing that message in a way that is easily accessible to the public, for instance, by placing it on the Internet or by creating or compiling hyperlinks in order to facilitate access to it.

103. The term "to the public" makes it clear that private communications fall outside the scope of this provision.

104. In order to make a message available to the public, a variety of means and techniques may be used. For instance, printed publications or speeches delivered at places accessible to others, the use of mass media or electronic facilities, in particular the Internet, which provides for the dissemination of messages by e-mail or for possibilities such as the exchange of materials in chat rooms, newsgroups or discussion fora.

105. Further guidance is provided by the case-law of the European Court of Human Rights. In this connection, reference should be made to the Collection of relevant case law of the European Court of Human Rights prepared for the CODEXTER (document CODEXTER (2004)19).

Article 6 – Recruitment for terrorism

106. This article requires Parties to criminalise the recruitment of possible future terrorists, understood as solicitation to carry out terrorist offences whether individually or collectively, whether directly committing, participating in or contributing to the commission of such offences.

107. For the purposes of paragraph 1, a Party may choose to interpret the terms "association or group" to mean "proscribed" organisations or groups in accordance with its national law and Parties can so declare in accordance with the general principles of international law.

108. Solicitation can take place by various means, for instance, via the Internet or directly by addressing a person.

109. For the completion of the act, it is not necessary that the addressee actually participate in the commission of a terrorist offence or that he or she join a group for that purpose. Nevertheless, for the crime to be completed, it is necessary that the recruiter successfully approach the addressee.

110. If the execution of the crime is commenced but not completed (for example, the person is not persuaded to be recruited, or the recruiter is apprehended by law enforcement authorities before successfully recruiting the person), the conduct is still punishable as an attempt to recruit under Article 9, paragraph 2.

111. A Party is free to use the term "solicit" in its domestic implementing laws or different terminology for purposes of clarity under its national legal system.

112. What is important is that implementation of Article 6 and Article 9, paragraph 2 together results in the criminalisation of the completed, as well as commenced but not completed, recruitment conduct described above, and as has already been said, the solicitation effectively takes place regardless of whether the addressees of the solicitation actually participate in the commission of a terrorist offence or join an association or group for that purpose.

113. Paragraph 1 requires that the recruiter intends that the person or persons he or she recruits commit or contribute to the commission of a terrorist offence or join an association or group for that purpose.

Article 7 – Training for terrorism

114. The CODEXTER considered that this provision was closely connected with the provision of the International Convention for the Suppression of the Financing of Terrorism, listed in the Appendix to the Convention. While the latter criminalises the provision of financial resources to terrorists or for terrorist purposes, this provision criminalises the provision of know-how.

115. Thus, this article requires Parties to criminalise the supplying of know-how for the purpose of carrying out or contributing to the commission of a terrorist offence. This is defined as providing instruction in methods or techniques that are suitable for use for terrorist purposes, including in the making or use of explosives, firearms and noxious or hazardous substances.

116. This provision does not criminalise the fact of receiving such know-how or the trainee.

117. The Convention does not contain a definition of weapons, firearms and explosives, or noxious or hazardous substances, which are generic terms. They are characterised by existing international treaties and national legislation.

118. Thus, the term "explosive" could be defined according to the International Convention for the Suppression of Terrorist Bombings, Article 1, paragraph 3.a as *"an explosive or incendiary weapon or device that is designed, or has the capability, to cause death, serious bodily injury or substantial material damage."*

119. The term "firearm" could be understood within the meaning of Appendix I to the European Convention on the Control of the Acquisition and Possession of Firearms by Individuals (ETS No. 101).

120. The term "other weapons" could be understood in the sense of "lethal weapon" as defined by the International Convention for the Suppression of Terrorist Bombings, Article 1, paragraph 3.b which characterises it as "*a weapon or device that is designed, or has the capability, to cause death, serious bodily injury or substantial material damage through the release, dissemination or impact of toxic chemicals, biological agents or toxins or similar substances or radiation or radioactive material.*"

121. As concerns the term "noxious or hazardous substances", more specific references can be found, for instance, in the International Maritime Organisation (IMO) Protocol on Preparedness, Response and Co-operation to Pollution Incidents by Hazardous and Noxious Substances, 2000 (HNS Protocol, Article 1, paragraph 5) which defines them by reference to lists of substances included in various IMO conventions and codes. These include oils; other liquid substances defined as noxious or dangerous; liquefied gases; liquid substances with a flashpoint not exceeding 60°C; dangerous, hazardous and harmful materials and substances carried in packaged form; and solid bulk materials defined as possessing chemical hazards.

122. For such conduct to be criminally liable, it is necessary that the trainer know that the skills provided are intended to be used for the commission of or the contribution to commit a terrorist offence. This requirement of knowledge is complemented with the two additional requirements of unlawfulness and intention stated in paragraph 2, as explained above in the paragraphs relating to the common aspects of Articles 5 to 7 (see paragraphs 76 to 85).

Article 8 – Irrelevance of the commission of a terrorist offence

123. When deciding on the title of this article, the Committee based itself on the French version of the text, namely: "*Indifférence du résultat*". Both language versions convey the same message, that is: for an act to constitute an offence as set forth in Articles 5 to 7 of this Convention, it shall not be necessary that a terrorist offence be actually committed. The same holds true for the accessory crimes set forth in Article 9.

124. This article is based on an equivalent provision in Article 2, paragraph 3 of the International Convention for the Suppression of the Financing of Terrorism.

125. It should be recalled that the negotiators had a number of common understandings flowing from the obligation set forth in Articles 5 to 7 to punish public provocation, recruitment and training, even where no terrorist offence is ultimately committed.

126. For instance, it was understood that since no terrorist offence need be carried out at all for the conduct in Articles 5 to 7 to be punishable, it is consequently not necessary that the provocation, recruitment or training be

aimed at the commission of a terrorist offence in the territory of the Party concerned.

127. Rather, each Party has the obligation to punish the crimes set forth in Articles 5 to 7 and 9, irrespective of whether it may have been envisaged that the ultimate terrorist offence would be committed in that Party or elsewhere.

Article 9 – Ancillary offences

128. This article is based on similar provisions in existing international conventions against terrorism, including, most recently, the International Convention for the Suppression of Terrorist Bombings (Article 2, paragraphs 2 and 3) and the International Convention for the Suppression of the Financing of Terrorism (Article 2, paragraphs 4 and 5).

129. Its purpose is to establish additional offences related to attempts at or complicity in the commission of the offences defined in this Convention.

130. As with all the offences established in the Convention, attempt and participation as an accomplice must be committed intentionally. The term "participation as accomplice" comprises the concept of "aiding and abetting".

131. While paragraph 1 refers to the accessory crimes in relation to the offences established in Articles 5 to 7, paragraph 2 limits the criminalisation of attempt to the offences established in Articles 6 to 7, and excludes it in relation to public provocation to commit terrorist offences.

132. Paragraph 1 requires Parties to establish as a criminal offence the participation as an accomplice in the commission of any of the offences under Articles 5 to 7. Liability for such complicity arises where the person who commits a crime established in the Convention is aided by another person who also intends that the crime be committed. For example, although public provocation to commit a terrorist offence through the Internet requires the assistance of service providers as a conduit, a service provider that does not have criminal intent cannot incur liability under this provision.

133. With respect to paragraph 2 on attempt, the offence covered by Article 5 or elements thereof were considered to be conceptually difficult to attempt. Moreover, unlike in paragraph 1, the offence must be established not only under but also in accordance with national law. In so far as the mental elements required for attempt are furnished by domestic law, the notion of attempt may differ from country to country.

Article 10 – Liability of legal entities

134. This article deals with the liability of legal entities or persons and is based on a similar provision of the United Nations Transnational Organized

Crime Convention (Article 10), although it uses the term "entity" instead of "persons" as it was considered to have a wider scope.

135. It is consistent with the current legal trend to recognise the liability of legal entities. It is intended to impose liability on corporations, associations and similar legal persons for the criminal actions undertaken for the benefit of that legal person.

136. Under paragraph 1, Parties are required to establish the liability of legal entities in accordance with their legal principles.

137. Liability under this article may be criminal, civil or administrative. Each Party has the flexibility to choose to provide for any or all of these forms of liability, in accordance with the legal principles of each Party, as long as it meets the criteria of Article 11, paragraph 3, that the sanction, whether criminal or not, should be "effective, proportionate and dissuasive" and should include monetary sanctions.

138. Paragraph 3 clarifies that corporate liability does not exclude individual liability.

Article 11 – Sanctions and measures

139. This article deals with the punishment of the offences set forth in the Convention and is consistent with the general trend in international criminal law. Thus, similar provisions are to be found, for instance, in the United Nations Convention against Corruption (Article 26), the United Nations Convention against Transnational Organized Crime, (Article 10) and the International Convention for the Suppression of the Financing of Terrorism (Articles 4, paragraph 2 and 5, paragraph 3).

140. Paragraph 1 requires that the penalties be effective, proportionate and dissuasive. While paragraph 2 invites Parties to consider previous convictions in other States for the purposes of determining the sentence and, where this is possible according to domestic law, of determining recidivism.

141. Paragraph 3 relates to Article 10 more specifically as it deals with the sanctions to be imposed upon legal entities whose liability is established in accordance with Article 10 and shall also be subject to sanctions that are effective, proportionate and dissuasive. Such sanctions can be of a criminal or non criminal nature, that is: administrative or civil. Parties are compelled, under this paragraph, to provide for the possibility of imposing monetary sanctions on legal persons.

142. This article leaves open the possibility of other sanctions or measures reflecting the seriousness of the offence, for example, measures could include an injunction or forfeiture. It leaves Parties the discretionary power to

create a system of criminal offences and sanctions that is compatible with their existing national legal systems.

Article 12 – Conditions and safeguards

143. This is one of the key provisions of the Convention by which the negotiators purport to enhance the efficiency of the fight against terrorism while ensuring the protection of human rights and fundamental freedoms.

144. The formulation of this article is similar to that of Article 3 in relation to the human rights obligations and standards that are referred to therein.

145. This article requires Parties to ensure respect for human rights in establishing and applying the offences set forth in Articles 5 to 7 and 9.

146. A number of international human rights instruments are listed that provide relevant human rights standards to which Parties to the Convention must adhere as they represent obligations arising from international law. The list is not exhaustive.

147. These instruments include the ECHR and its additional Protocols Nos. 1, 4, 6, 7, 12 and 13 (ETS Nos. 005, 009, 046, 114, 117, 177 and 187), in respect of European States that are Parties to them.

148. They also include other applicable human rights instruments in respect of States in other regions of the world (for example, the 1969 American Convention on Human Rights and the 1981 African Charter on Human Rights and Peoples' Rights) which are Parties to these instruments, as well as the ICCPR and other universal human rights instruments. In addition, similar protection is provided under the laws of most States.

149. As in Article 3, the term "where applicable" is used here to indicate that, because the Convention is open to non-member States of the Council of Europe, the human rights framework in the ECHR would not be applicable to non-member States which are Parties to the present Convention. Rather, non-member States of the Council of Europe will implement this paragraph pursuant to obligations they have undertaken with respect to the ICCPR, other applicable human rights instruments to which they are party, customary law, and their respective domestic laws.

150. An additional safeguard is provided by paragraph 2 which requires that the establishment, implementation and application of the criminalisation under Articles 5 to 7 and 9 "be subject to the principle of proportionality, with respect to the legitimate aims pursued and to their necessity in a democratic society" while excluding "any form of arbitrariness or discriminatory or racist treatment".

151. The principle of proportionality shall be implemented by each Party in accordance with the relevant principles of its domestic law. For European countries, this will be derived from the principles of the ECHR, its applicable case-law, and national legislation and case-law. This principle requires that the power or procedure shall be proportional to the nature and circumstances of the offence.

152. For non-member States, the principle of proportionality is applied through constitutional or other domestic legal norms applied for the purposes of fixing an appropriate range of potential punishments in light of the conduct aimed at, and of imposing an appropriate sentence in an individual criminal prosecution. The exclusion of arbitrary, discriminatory or racist treatment is similarly to be carried out through the application of relevant constitutional or other domestic legal norms.

Article 13 – Protection, compensation and support of victims of terrorism

153. This article is consistent with recent developments in international law and the growing concern for the victims of terrorism as reflected, for instance, in the European Convention on Compensation of Victims of Violent Crimes (ETS No. 116, Article 2), the Council of Europe Guidelines on Human Rights and the Fight against Terrorism (Guideline No. XVII) and the additional Guidelines on the protection of victims of terrorism (principle No. 1) at regional level, or at universal level in United Nations Security Council resolutions, including Resolution 1566 (2004) of 8 October 2004; and in the International Convention for the Suppression of the Financing of Terrorism (Article 8, paragraph 4).

154. Furthermore, this issue forms part of the Council of Europe's priority activities against terrorism, as requested by the 25th Conference of European Ministers of Justice in October 2003 (see Resolution No. 1 on combating terrorism). The CODEXTER therefore pursues work in this area with a view to promoting exchanges of information and best practice among member States.

155. More specifically, this provision requires Parties to adopt measures to protect and support the victims of terrorism that has been committed within their own territory. These measures which are subject to domestic legislation may include, for instance, financial assistance and compensation for victims of terrorism and their close family members, in the framework of national schemes.

156. The CODEXTER was also provided with the opinion of the Commissioner for Human Rights, who considered that the protection afforded to victims might also include many other aspects, such as emergency and long-term assistance, psychological support, effective access to the law and the courts (in particular access to criminal

procedures), access to information and the protection of victims' private and family lives, dignity and security, particularly when they co-operate with the courts.

Article 14 – Jurisdiction

157. This article establishes a series of criteria under which Parties are obliged to establish jurisdiction over the offences set forth in the Convention and is based on similar provisions to be found in most international conventions against terrorism, as well as in the Cybercrime Convention (ETS No. 185).

158. Paragraph 1.a is based upon the principle of territoriality. Each Party is required to establish jurisdiction for the offences set forth in the Convention that are committed in its territory. This is notwithstanding what has been said in relation to Articles 5 to 7 regarding the irrelevance of the place where a terrorist offence, as defined in Article 1, may be committed as a result of the commission of any of the offences set forth in Articles 5 to 7 and 9.

159. Paragraph 1.b is based upon a variant of the principle of territoriality. It requires each Party to establish criminal jurisdiction over offences committed upon ships flying its flag or aircraft registered under its laws.

160. This obligation is already implemented as a general matter in the laws of many States, since such ships and aircraft are frequently considered to be an extension of the territory of the State. This type of jurisdiction is most useful where the ship or aircraft is not located in its territory at the time of the commission of the crime, as a result of which paragraph 1.a would not be available as a basis to assert jurisdiction. If the crime is committed on a ship or aircraft that is beyond the territory of the flag Party, there may be no other State that would be able to exercise jurisdiction. In addition, if a crime is committed aboard a ship or aircraft which is merely passing through the waters or airspace of another State, the latter State may face significant practical impediments to the exercise of its jurisdiction, and it is therefore useful for the State of registry to also have jurisdiction.

161. Paragraph 1.c is based upon the principle of nationality. The nationality theory is most frequently applied by States applying the civil law tradition. It provides that nationals of a State are obliged to comply with its domestic law even when they are outside its territory. Under this provision, if a national commits an offence abroad, the Party is obliged to have the ability to prosecute him or her if the act is also an offence under the law of the Party in which it was committed or the act has been committed outside the territorial jurisdiction of any Party.

162. Paragraph 2 provides a second set of criteria on the basis of which Parties have the possibility, at their discretion, of establishing their jurisdiction over the offences set forth in the Convention.

163. This provision incorporates the latest trends in international criminal law and is based on similar provisions in the International Convention for the Suppression of the Financing of Terrorism (Article 7, paragraph 2) and the International Convention for the Suppression of Terrorist Bombings (Article 6, paragraph 2).

164. Thus, paragraph 2.a covers cases where the offence is directed towards the commission of an offence *in the territory of or against a national of that Party*.

165. Paragraph 2.b covers the case of offences against the governmental premises of a Party abroad, including its embassies and consulates.

166. Paragraph 2.c covers cases where an offence is committed *to compel that Party to do or abstain from doing any act*.

167. Paragraph 2d. contains a traditional criterion for jurisdiction and covers cases where the offence is committed by a *stateless person who has his or her habitual residence in the territory of that Party*.

168. The criterion in paragraph 2.e is closely related to the one in paragraph 1.b with the specific feature that the aircraft on which the offence is committed must be operated by the Government of that Party.

169. Paragraph 3 establishes an additional criterion for jurisdiction which is of a mandatory nature and is related to cases falling under the principle of *aut dedere aut judicare* established in Article 18 by requiring a Party to establish its jurisdiction where the alleged offender is present in its territory and it does not extradite that person to any of the Parties whose jurisdiction is based on a rule of jurisdiction existing equally in the law of the requested Party.

170. Finally, it should be noted that the bases of jurisdiction set forth in paragraph 1 are not exclusive. Paragraph 4 permits Parties to establish, in conformity with their domestic law, other types of criminal jurisdiction as well.

171. Paragraph 5 covers conflicts of jurisdiction, where more than one Party claims jurisdiction over an alleged offence set forth in this Convention and invites the Parties involved to consult with a view to determining the most appropriate jurisdiction for prosecution.

172. It is based on an identical provision in the Cybercrime Convention (Article 22, paragraph 5) which is most relevant in this case. In the case of crimes committed by use of computer systems or through the Internet, for instance public provocation to commit a terrorist offence, there will be occasions in which more than one Party has jurisdiction over some or all of the participants in the crime.

173. Thus, in order to avoid duplication of effort, unnecessary inconvenience for witnesses, or competition among law enforcement officials of the Parties concerned, or to otherwise facilitate the efficiency and fairness of the proceedings, the affected Parties are to consult in order to determine the proper venue for prosecution. In some cases, it will be most effective for the Parties concerned to choose a single venue for prosecution; in others, it may be best for one Party to prosecute some participants, while one or more other Parties pursue others. Either result is permitted under this paragraph. Finally, the obligation to consult is not absolute, but is to take place "where appropriate." Thus, for example, if one of the Parties knows that consultation is not necessary (for example, it has received confirmation that the other Party is not planning to take action), or if a Party is of the view that consultation may impair its investigation or proceedings, it may delay or decline consultation.

Article 15 – Duty to investigate

174. This article is based on similar provisions in most international treaties against terrorism, including the International Convention for the Suppression of the Financing of Terrorism (Article 9) and the International Convention for the Suppression of Terrorist Bombings (Article 7).

175. Paragraph 1 calls upon a Party to investigate the information provided to it that a person who has committed or who is alleged to have committed an offence set forth in this Convention may be present in its territory.

176. The term "information" in this paragraph is not to be understood necessarily as having the same meaning as the same term used in Article 22, paragraph 1, since the information may come from various sources.

177. It is up to national legislation to define the conditions that the information will have to satisfy in terms of reliability in the context of legal proceedings or for the purposes of law enforcement.

178. Once such conditions are met, by virtue of paragraph 2, the Party in whose territory the offender or alleged offender is present is called upon to take the appropriate measures under its domestic law so as to ensure that person's presence for the purposes of prosecution or extradition. In relation to such measures, paragraph 3 provides for a set of rights relating to the Vienna Convention on Consular Relations (see Article 36, paragraph 1) which are self-explanatory and shall be exercised in conformity with the laws of the Party unless they do not enable full effect to be given to the purposes for which the rights are intended (paragraph 4) and without prejudice to the right of any Party having a claim of jurisdiction in accordance with Article 14, paragraphs 1.c and 2.d to invite the International Committee of the Red Cross to communicate with and visit the alleged offender.

Article 16 – Non application of the Convention

179. This article provides for the non-application of the Convention in cases of a purely national nature, that is: where the offence is committed within a single State, the alleged offender is a national of that State and is present in the territory of that State, and no other State has jurisdiction.

180. It is based on a similar provision in the International Convention for the Suppression of the Financing of Terrorism (Article 3) and the International Convention for the Suppression of Terrorist Bombings (Article 3).

181. This provision does not modify the regime established by the Convention, particularly in so far as the establishment of criminal offences in pursuance of Articles 5 to 7 and 9 should comply with the conditions and safeguards provided for in Article 12.

182. Neither does it exclude or limit the possibility for Parties to criminalise the acts provided for in the Convention, even when the conditions of this article are met, that is when only "national" elements are present.

183. This provision has the primary effect of excluding the application of the provisions on extradition or mutual assistance and is closely connected with the provision on jurisdiction, Article 14. The application of this provision is complicated by the fact that some of the offences may be committed through the Internet.

Article 17 – International co-operation in criminal matters

184. This article deals with mutual assistance, within the meaning of the European Convention on Mutual Assistance in Criminal Matters and bilateral mutual assistance treaties in force between Parties, in criminal investigations and related proceedings concerning the offences set forth in the Convention.

185. Paragraph 1 is based on the International Convention for the Suppression of the Financing of Terrorism (Article 12, paragraph 1) and requires Parties to provide each other mutual assistance in the investigation of and in the legal proceedings relating to the offences set forth in the Convention.

186. Parties are called upon to implement the obligations arising from paragraph 1 in conformity with applicable treaties or arrangements on mutual legal assistance and, where such treaties or arrangements do not exist, in accordance with their domestic law (paragraph 2).

187. Paragraph 3 is based on the United Nations Convention against Transnational Organized Crime (Article 18, paragraph 2) and specifies the

requirements in paragraphs 1 in relation to legal entities, consistently with the provisions of Article 10.

188. Finally, paragraph 4, which is based on the International Convention for the Suppression of the Financing of Terrorism (Article 12, paragraph 4) and the United Nations Transnational Organized Crime Convention (Article 18, paragraph 30) invites Parties to establish additional co-operation mechanisms for the purposes of sharing information and evidence in the prosecution of the offences set forth in the Convention.

Article 18 – Extradite or prosecute

189. This article is based on a similar provision in the International Convention for the Suppression of Terrorist Bombings (Article 8) and the International Convention for the Suppression of the Financing of Terrorism (Article 10). It establishes an obligation on the requested Party to submit the case to its competent authorities for the purpose of prosecution if it refuses extradition (*aut dedere aut judicare*).

190. This obligation is subject to conditions similar to those laid down in paragraph 1 of Article 14: the suspected offender must have been found in the territory of the requested Party, which must have received a request for extradition from a Party whose jurisdiction is based on a rule of jurisdiction existing equally in its own law.

191. The case must be submitted to the prosecuting authority without exception and without undue delay. Investigation and prosecution follow the rules of law and procedure in force in the requested Party for offences of a comparably serious nature. The same goes for the judicial decision concerning the case.

192. The Convention does not provide an indication of what is meant by "offence of a serious nature". It will be up to national authorities to characterise such an offence. However, recent international treaties provide standards in this respect. For instance, the United Nations Convention against Transnational Organized Crime defines – for the purpose of that Convention – "serious crimes" as "conduct constituting an offence punishable by a maximum deprivation of liberty of at least four years or a more serious penalty."

193. Paragraph 2 covers cases where a "Party extradites or otherwise surrenders one of its nationals only upon the condition that the person will be returned to that Party to serve the sentence imposed as a result of the trial or proceeding for which the extradition or surrender of the person was sought."

194. It provides that the requirements of paragraph 1 are met where the requesting and the requested Party agree with such conditional extradition or surrender.

Article 19 – Extradition

195. This article is based on similar provisions in the International Convention for the Suppression of Terrorist Bombings (Article 9) and in the International Convention for the Suppression of the Financing of Terrorism (Article 11).

196. Paragraph 1 provides for the automatic inclusion, as an extraditable offence, of any of the offences set forth in the Convention into any existing extradition treaty concluded between Parties. Moreover, Parties undertake to include such offences in every extradition treaty they may conclude.

197. Furthermore, paragraph 2 introduces the possibility for a Party which makes extradition conditional on the existence of a treaty, and receives a request for extradition from another Party with which it has no extradition treaty, to consider the Convention as a legal basis for extradition in relation to any of the offences set forth in the Convention. Such a decision is at the discretion of the requested Party, which may subject its decision to extradite to conditions provided by national law, for example that the person subject to extradition will not be exposed to the death penalty (see Article 21).

198. As for Parties which do not make extradition conditional on the existence of a treaty, paragraph 3 requires them to recognise the offences set forth in the Convention as extraditable offences between themselves, subject to the conditions provided by the law of the requested Party.

199. Paragraph 4 is related to the Convention's provisions on jurisdiction (Article 14) and aims at facilitating international co-operation by providing that, for the purposes of extradition between the Parties, the offences set forth in the Convention be treated as if they had been committed in the territory of the Parties that have established jurisdiction in accordance with Article 14.

200. Paragraph 5 is related to Article 26, paragraph 2 as it provides that the provisions of all extradition treaties and arrangements between Parties with regard to offences set forth in the Convention shall be deemed to be modified between Parties to the extent that they are incompatible with this Convention.

201. In this connection, the term "arrangements" is intended to cover extradition procedures which are not enshrined in a formal treaty, such as those existing between Ireland and the United Kingdom. For that reason, the term "*accords*" in the French text is not to be understood as designating a formal international instrument.

202. One of the consequences of this paragraph is the modification of Article 3, paragraph 1 of the European Convention on Extradition. For States

which are Parties to both the present Convention and the European Convention on Extradition, Article 3, paragraph 1 of the latter is modified, in so far as it is incompatible with the new obligations arising from the former. The same applies to similar provisions contained in bilateral treaties and arrangements which are applicable between Parties to this Convention.

Article 20 – Exclusion of the political exception clause

203. This article is based on similar provisions in the International Convention for the Suppression of Terrorist Bombings (Article 11) and the International Convention for the Suppression of the Financing of Terrorism (Article 14) and was later incorporated in the Protocol amending the European Convention on the Suppression of Terrorism.

204. It aims at facilitating international co-operation by excluding the political character of the offences set forth in the Convention for the purposes of extradition or mutual legal assistance.

205. Accordingly, a request for extradition or for mutual legal assistance based on such an offence may not be refused on the sole ground that it concerns a political offence or an offence connected with a political offence or an offence inspired by political motives.

206. Thus, it modifies the consequences of existing extradition and mutual legal assistance agreements and arrangements with regard to the evaluation of the nature of these offences. It eliminates the possibility for the requested Party to invoke the political nature of the offence in order to oppose an extradition or mutual legal assistance request.

207. It does not, however, create an obligation to extradite, as the Convention is not an extradition treaty as such. The legal basis for extradition remains the extradition treaty, arrangement or law concerned. Nevertheless, under Article 19 of the Convention, a Party may use the Convention as a legal basis for extradition at its discretion.

208. The terms "political offence" and "offence connected with a political offence" were taken from Article 3, paragraph 1 of the European Convention on Extradition, which is modified to the effect that Parties to the present Convention may no longer consider as "political" any of the offences set forth in the Convention.

209. The term "offence inspired by political motives" is intended to supplement the list of cases in which the political nature of an offence cannot be invoked. Reference to the political motives of an act of terrorism is made in Resolution (74) 3 on international terrorism, adopted by the Committee of Ministers of the Council of Europe on 24 January 1974.

210. In paragraph 2, the term "Without prejudice to the application of (...) the Vienna Convention on the Law of Treaties (...) to the other articles in the Convention" indicates that reservations to other articles of the Convention would still be subject to the general regime of the Vienna Convention on the Law of Treaties.

211. This paragraph allows Parties to make reservations in respect of the application of paragraph 1 of this Article. The Convention thus recognises that a Party might be impeded, for instance for legal or constitutional reasons, from fully accepting the obligations arising from paragraph 1, whereby certain offences cannot be regarded as political for the purposes of extradition. However, this possibility has been made subject to a number of conditions.

212. If a Party avails itself of this possibility of making a reservation it can subsequently refuse extradition in respect of the offences set forth in the Convention. However, it is under the obligation to apply the reservation on a case-by-case basis and to give reasons for its decision. However, the requested Party remains free to grant or to refuse extradition, subject to the conditions referred to in the other paragraphs of this article.

213. The notion of "duly reasoned decision" should be taken to mean an adequate, clear and detailed written statement explaining the factual and legal reasons for refusing the extradition request.

214. Paragraph 3 provides for the withdrawal of reservations made in pursuance of paragraph 2 and of partial or conditional reservations.

215. Paragraph 4 in particular lays down the rule of reciprocity in respect of the application of paragraph 1 by a Party having availed itself of a reservation. This provision repeats the provisions contained in Article 26, paragraph 3 of the European Convention on Extradition. The rule of reciprocity applies equally to reservations not provided for in this Article.

216. Paragraphs 5 and 6 deal with the temporal validity of reservations. Paragraph 5 provides that reservations have a limited validity of three years from the date of entry into force of the Convention. After this deadline they will lapse, unless they are expressly renewed. Paragraph 6 provides a procedure for the automatic lapsing of non-renewed reservations. Where a Party upholds its reservation, it shall provide an explanation of the grounds justifying its continuance. Paragraphs 5 and 6 reflect provisions of the Criminal Law Convention on Corruption of 27 January 1999 (ETS No. 173, Article 38, paragraphs 1 and 2). They have been added with a view to ensuring that reservations are regularly reviewed by the Parties which have entered them.

217. If extradition is refused on the grounds of a reservation made in accordance with paragraph 2, Articles 14, 15 and, 18 apply. This is explicitly

stated in paragraph 7, which reflects and reinforces the principle of *aut dedere aut judicare* by a duty to forward the decision promptly to the requesting Party, as provided in paragraph 8.

218. In paragraph 7, an obligation for the requested Party to submit the case to the competent authorities for the purpose of prosecution arises as a result of the refusal of the extradition request made by the requesting Party. Nevertheless, the requesting and the requested Party may agree that the case will not be submitted to the competent authorities of the requested Party for prosecution. For instance, where the requesting or the requested Party consider that there is not sufficient evidence to bring a case in the requested Party, it might be more appropriate to pursue their investigations until the case is ready for prosecution. Thus, the strict application of the maxima *aut dedere aut judicare* is balanced with a degree of flexibility which reflects the necessity for full co-operation between the requesting and the requested Parties for the successful prosecution of such cases.

219. Where the requested Party submits the case to its competent authorities for the purpose of prosecution, the latter are required to consider and decide on the case in the same manner as any offence of a serious nature under the law of that Party. The requested Party is required to communicate the final outcome of the proceedings to the requesting Party and to the Secretary General of the Council of Europe, who shall forward it to the Consultation of the Parties provided in Article 30 for information.

220. Where a requesting Party considers that a requested reserving Party has disregarded the conditions of paragraphs 2 and/or 7 because, for instance, no judicial decision on the merits has been taken within a reasonable time in the requested Party in accordance with paragraph 7, it has the possibility of bringing the matter before the Consultation of the Parties pursuant to paragraph 8. The Consultation of the Parties is competent to consider the matter and issue an opinion on the conformity of the refusal with the Convention. This opinion is submitted to the Committee of Ministers for the purpose of issuing a declaration thereon. When performing its functions under this paragraph, the Committee of Ministers shall meet in its composition restricted to the Parties to the Convention.

221. The notion of "without undue delay" used in paragraph 7 and "within a reasonable time" in paragraph 8 shall be understood as synonyms. They are flexible concepts which, in the words of the European Court of Human Rights must be assessed in the light of the particular circumstances of the case and having regard to the criteria laid down in the case-law of the Court, in particular the complexity of the case, the conduct of the subject of the extradition request and of the relevant authorities (see, among many other judgments: Pélissier and Sassi v. France of 25 March 1999, [GC], No. 25444/94, ECHR 1999-II, and Philis v. Greece (No. 2) of 27 June 1997, Reports of Judgments and Decisions 1997-IV, p. 1083, § 35) (see Zannouti v. France of 31 July 2001, in French only).

Article 21 – Discrimination clause

222. This article is based on a similar provision in the International Convention for the Suppression of the Financing of Terrorism (Article 15) and concerns the grounds for refusing extradition and mutual legal assistance.

223. It is intended to emphasise the aim of the Convention, which is to assist Parties in the prevention of terrorism which constitutes an attack on the fundamental rights to life and liberty of persons. While Articles 17 to 20 are international co-operation tools to strengthen the ability of law enforcement to act effectively, this article ensures that the Convention complies with the requirements of the protection of human rights and fundamental freedoms as they are enshrined in the ECHR or other applicable international instruments. This is all the more important because of the very nature of the offences set forth in the Convention.

224. In this connection, it should be recalled that the Convention does not seek to determine the grounds on which extradition or mutual assistance may be refused, other than by reference to the exception regarding political offences.

225. This article is intended to make this clear by reference to certain existing grounds on which extradition or mutual assistance may be refused. The Article is not, however, intended to be exhaustive as to the possible grounds for refusal.

226. One of the purposes of this Article is to safeguard the traditional right of asylum and the principle of non-refoulement. Although the prosecution, punishment or discrimination of a person on account of his or her race, religion, nationality or political opinion is unlikely to occur in the member States of the Council of Europe which, at the time of the adoption of this Convention, have all, with the exception of one State which has recently joined the Organisation, ratified the ECHR, it was considered appropriate to insert this traditional provision (paragraph 1) in this Convention also, particularly in view of the opening of the Convention to non-member States (see Article 23 below). It is already contained in Article 3, paragraph 2 of the European Convention on Extradition.

227. If a requested Party has substantial grounds for believing that the real purpose of an extradition or mutual assistance request, made for one of the offences set forth in the Convention, is to enable the requesting Party to prosecute or punish the person concerned for the political opinions he or she holds, the requested Party may refuse to grant extradition.

228. The same applies where the requested Party has substantial grounds for believing that the person's position may be prejudiced for political

reasons, or for any of the other reasons mentioned in this Article. This would be the case, for instance, if the person to be extradited would, in the requesting Party, be deprived of the rights of defence guaranteed by the ECHR.

229. Two additional paragraphs have been added to this Article, bearing in mind, in particular, Parliamentary Assembly Recommendation 1550 (2002) on Combating terrorism and respect for human rights (paragraph 7.i) and the Guidelines on Human Rights and the Fight against Terrorism (Guidelines IV, X, XIII and XV) adopted by the Committee of Ministers on 11 July 2002. These had also been added to the equivalent provision in the European Convention on the Suppression of Terrorism by means of its amending Protocol.

230. These paragraphs explicitly recognise that Parties have no obligation to extradite and can indeed refuse extradition on the ground that the subject of the extradition request risks being exposed to torture or to inhuman or degrading treatment or punishment (paragraph 2) or, in certain circumstances, where the person in question risks being exposed to the death penalty or to life imprisonment without the possibility of parole (paragraph 3).

231. In paragraph 2, the reference to inhuman or degrading treatment as a ground for refusal represents an addition to the formula used in the European Convention on the Suppression of Terrorism as revised by its amending Protocol and was requested by the Parliamentary Assembly and the Commissioner for Human Rights of the Council of Europe in their respective opinions on the draft of this Convention. Furthermore, it was consistent with the Council of Europe Guidelines on Human Rights and the Fight against Terrorism, Guideline IV of which provides for the absolute prohibition of torture and inhuman or degrading treatment or punishment in all circumstances, and in particular during the arrest, questioning and detention of a person suspected or convicted of terrorist activities, irrespective of the nature of the acts that the person is suspected of or for which he/she was convicted.

232. As stated above, these grounds for refusal already exist independently of the Convention. For instance, the possibility of refusing extradition where there is a risk of the death penalty being carried out is provided in Article 11 of the European Convention on Extradition, and Article 3 of the United Nations Convention against Torture governs the issue of non-extradition where there is a danger of torture. Nevertheless, like the GMT before it, the CODEXTER considered it necessary to state them explicitly, in order to stress the necessity to reconcile an efficient fight against terrorism with respect for fundamental rights, particularly in view of the opening of the Convention to non-member States.

233. It is obvious that a Party applying this Article should provide the requesting Party with reasons for its refusal to grant the extradition request. It is by virtue of the same principle that Article 18, paragraph 2 of the European Convention on Extradition provides that "reasons shall be given for any complete or partial rejection" and that Article 19 of the European Convention on Mutual Assistance in Criminal Matters states that "reasons shall be given for any refusal of mutual assistance".

234. If extradition is refused on human rights grounds, Article 18 of the Convention applies and the requested Party must submit the case to its competent authorities for the purpose of prosecution.

Article 22 – Spontaneous information

235. This article is based on a similar provision in the Second Additional Protocol to the European Convention on Mutual Assistance in Criminal Matters (Article 11), which in turn is based on other international treaties, the Convention on Laundering, Search, Seizure and Confiscation of the Proceeds from Crime (ETS No. 141, Article 10) concerning paragraph 1 and the Convention on Mutual Assistance in Criminal Matters between the member States of the European Union (Article 6) concerning paragraphs 2 and 3.

236. It extends to mutual assistance in general following the trend in other fields of criminality, for instance money laundering, organised crime, cybercrime and corruption. Thus, it recognises the possibility for Parties, without prior request, to forward to each other information about investigations or proceedings which might contribute to the common aim of responding to crime.

237. It should be noted that this provision introduces a possibility; it does not place obligations on Parties. Moreover, it expressly provides that the relevant exchanges are to be carried out within the limits of national law.

238. The competent authorities in the "sending" Party are those authorities who deal with the case in which the information came up; the competent authorities in the "receiving" Party are the authorities who are likely to use the information forwarded or who have the powers to do so.

239. In accordance with paragraph 2, conditions may be attached to the use of information provided under this article, and paragraph 3 provides that, if that should be the case, the receiving Party is bound by those conditions.

240. In reality, the sending Party only binds the receiving Party to the extent that the receiving Party accepts the unsolicited information. By accepting the information, it also accepts to be bound by the conditions attached to the transmission of that information. In this sense, Article 9 creates a "take it or leave it" situation.

241. The conditions attached to the use of the information may, for example, be a condition that the information transmitted will not be used or re-transmitted by the authorities of the receiving Party for investigations or proceedings, as specified by the sending Party.

242. Some Parties might have difficulties in not accepting the information once it has been transmitted, for example where their national law puts a positive duty upon authorities who have access to such information. Paragraph 4 therefore opens the possibility for Parties to declare that information must not be transmitted without their prior consent. Should the sending Party attach conditions to the use of such information, if the receiving Party agrees to the conditions, it must honour them.

Articles 23 to 32 – the final clauses

243. With some exceptions, the provisions contained in Articles 23 to 32 are, for the most part, based on the "Model final clauses for conventions and agreements concluded within the Council of Europe" approved by the Committee of Ministers at the 315th meeting of the Deputies in February 1980.

244. As most of Articles 23 to 32 either use the standard language of the model clauses or are based on long-standing treaty-making practice at the Council of Europe, they do not call for specific comments.

245. However, certain modifications of the standard model clauses or some new provisions require some explanation. It is noted in this context that the model clauses have been adopted as a non-binding set of provisions. As the Introduction to the model clauses points out, "these model final clauses are only intended to facilitate the task of committees of experts and avoid textual divergences which would not have any real justification. The model is in no way binding and different clauses may be adapted to fit particular cases."

Article 23 – Signature and entry into force

246. This article provides the conditions for signature and entry into force of the Convention.

247. Paragraph 1 has been drafted following several precedents established in other conventions elaborated within the framework of the Council of Europe, for instance, the Convention on the Transfer of Sentenced Persons (ETS No. 112) and the Convention on Laundering, Search, Seizure and Confiscation of the Proceeds from Crime or, more recently, the Cybercrime Convention, which allow for signature, before their entry into force, not only by the member States of the Council of Europe, but also by non-member States which have participated in their elaboration. Similarly, this paragraph foresees the possibility for the European Community to sign the Convention,

thus following the trends in other draft conventions of the Council of Europe, including the draft conventions on laundering, search, seizure and confiscation of the proceeds from crime and on the financing of terrorism (see Article 49) and on action against trafficking in human beings (see Article 42).

248. In this connection, it should be noted that from the outset, the Council of Europe wished to provide for the signature of the Convention both by member States and by the non-member States that have participated in its elaboration, that is, those States which have Observer status with the Council of Europe, as these had been included in the specific terms of reference given to the CODEXTER, similar to those provided earlier on to the GMT in relation to the updating of the European Convention on the Suppression of Terrorism by its amending Protocol.

249. The provision is intended to enable the maximum number of interested States, not just members of the Council of Europe, to become Parties as soon as possible. Here, the provision is intended to apply to five non-member States: the Holy See, Canada, Japan, the United States of America and Mexico, which actively participated in the elaboration of the Convention.

250. Once the Convention has entered into force, in accordance with paragraph 3, other non-member States not covered by this provision may be invited to accede to the Convention in conformity with Article 24, paragraph 1.

251. Paragraph 3 sets the number of ratifications, acceptances or approvals required for the Convention's entry into force at six. This figure reflects the belief that a slightly larger group of Parties is needed to successfully begin addressing the challenge posed by the offences set forth in the Convention. The number is not so high, however, so as not to delay unnecessarily the Convention's entry into force. Among the six initial Signatories, at least four must be members of the Council of Europe, but the two others could belong to the non-member States that participated in the Convention's elaboration or the European Community. This provision would of course also allow for the Convention to enter into force based on expressions of consent to be bound by six Council of Europe member States.

Article 24 – Accession to the Convention

252. This article regulates the accession by non-member States other than those which have participated in the elaboration of the Convention and are therefore covered by the provisions of Article 23, paragraph 1.

253. It has been drafted on precedents established in other Council of Europe conventions, but with an additional express element. The procedure is established in paragraph 1.

254. In accordance with long-standing practice, the Committee of Ministers decides, on its own initiative or upon request, to invite a non-member State, which has not participated in the elaboration of a convention, to accede to that convention after having consulted all the Parties, whether they are member States or not.

255. This implies that if any Party objects to the non-member State's accession, the Committee of Ministers would normally not invite it to join the convention. However, under the usual formulation, the Committee of Ministers could, at least in theory, invite such a non-member State to accede to a convention even if a non-member Party objected to its accession. This means that no right of veto is usually granted to non-member Parties in the process of extending Council of Europe treaties to other non-member States.

256. However, an express requirement that the Committee of Ministers consult with and obtain the unanimous consent of all Parties – not just member States of the Council of Europe – before inviting a non-member State to accede to the Convention, has been inserted in paragraph 1. This new practice was established with the Cybercrime Convention which contains an identical provision (Article 37).

257. As indicated above, such a requirement is consistent with usual practice and recognises that all Parties to the Convention should be able to determine with which non-member States they are to enter into treaty relations.

258. Nevertheless, the formal decision to invite a non-member State to accede will be taken, in accordance with usual practice, by the representatives of the States Parties entitled to sit on the Committee of Ministers. This decision requires the two-thirds majority provided for in Article 20.d of the Statute of the Council of Europe and the unanimous vote of the representatives of the States Parties entitled to sit on the Committee.

259. Paragraph 2 states the date of entry into force of the Convention for the acceding State in a similar fashion to Article 23, paragraph 4.

Article 25 – Territorial application

260. It should be noted that during discussions within the GMT on a similar provision in the Protocol amending the European Convention on the Suppression of Terrorism, the proposal was put forward to modify this territorial clause by replacing the words "shall apply" by "shall or shall not apply". Ultimately, the GMT decided to retain the original formula of the final clause in order to conform with the long-standing practice of the Council of Europe aiming at ensuring the uniform application of European treaties upon the territory of each Party (the scope of the standard territorial clause being limited to overseas territories and territories with a special status).

261. It was stated that the wording of this provision would not, however, constitute an obstacle for Parties claiming not to have control over their entire national territory to make unilateral statements declaring that they would not be able to ensure the application of the treaty in a certain territory. Any such declarations would not be considered as territorial declarations, but statements of factual character, prompted by exceptional circumstances making full compliance with a treaty temporarily impossible.

Article 26 – Effects of the Convention

262. This article merits particular attention as it regulates the effects of the Convention on other treaties, and on rights, obligations and responsibilities assumed under international law. It is based on similar provisions in existing treaties, namely the Cybercrime Convention (Article 39) for paragraphs 1, 2 and, notwithstanding certain specifications, 3, and the International Convention for the Suppression of Terrorist Bombings (Article 19, paragraph 2) for paragraph 4.

263. Paragraphs 1 and 2 address the Convention's relationship with other international agreements or arrangements. The subject of how conventions of the Council of Europe should relate to one another or to other, bilateral or multilateral, treaties concluded outside the Council of Europe is not dealt with by the model clauses referred to above.

264. The usual approach taken in Council of Europe conventions in the criminal law area (for example, Agreement on Illicit Traffic by Sea (ETS No. 156)) is to provide that: 1. new conventions do not affect the rights and undertakings derived from existing international multilateral conventions concerning special matters; 2. Parties to a new convention may conclude bilateral or multilateral agreements with one another on the matters dealt with by the convention for the purposes of supplementing or strengthening its provisions or facilitating the application of the principles embodied in it; and 3. if two or more Parties to the new convention have already concluded an agreement or treaty in respect of a subject which is dealt with in the convention or otherwise have established their relations in respect of that subject, they shall be entitled to apply that agreement or treaty or regulate those relations accordingly, in lieu of the new convention, provided this facilitates international co-operation.

265. Inasmuch as the Convention is generally intended to supplement and not supplant multilateral and bilateral agreements and arrangements between Parties, the drafters did not believe that a possibly limiting reference to "special matters" was particularly instructive and were concerned that it could lead to unnecessary confusion. Instead, paragraph 1 simply indicates that the present Convention supplements other applicable treaties or arrangements between Parties and it mentions, in particular, a series of Council of Europe conventions dealing with international co-operation and terrorism.

266. Therefore, regarding general matters, such agreements or arrangements should in principle be applied by the Parties to this Convention. Regarding specific matters only dealt with by this Convention, the rule of interpretation *lex specialis derogat legi generali* provides that the Parties should give precedence to the rules contained in the Convention and, where such specificity exists, this Convention, as *lex specialis*, should provide a rule of first resort over provisions in more general mutual assistance agreements.

267. Similarly, the drafters considered language making the application of existing or future agreements contingent on whether they "strengthen" or "facilitate" co-operation as possibly problematic, because, under the approach established in the provisions on international co-operation, the presumption is that Parties will apply relevant international agreements and arrangements.

268. For example, where there is an existing mutual assistance treaty or arrangement as a basis for co-operation, the present Convention would only supplement, where necessary, the existing rules.

269. Consistent with the Convention's supplementary nature in this respect and, in particular, its approach to international co-operation, paragraph 2 provides that Parties are also free to apply agreements that are already in force or that may come into force in the future. The precedent for such an articulation is found in the Convention on the Transfer of Sentenced Persons.

270. Certainly it is expected that the application of other international agreements (many of which offer proven, longstanding formulas for international assistance) will in fact promote international co-operation. Consistent with the terms of the present Convention, Parties may also agree to apply such other agreements in lieu. As the present Convention generally provides for minimum obligations, paragraph 2 recognises that Parties are free to assume obligations that are more specific in addition to those already set out in the Convention, when establishing their relations concerning matters dealt with therein. However, this is not an absolute right: Parties must respect the objective and purpose of the Convention.

271. Furthermore, in determining the Convention's relationship with other international agreements, the relevant provisions in the Vienna Convention on the Law of Treaties apply.

272. Paragraph 3 relates to the mutual relations between the Parties to the Convention which are members of the European Union. In relation to this paragraph, upon the adoption of the Convention, the European Community and the member States of the European Union, made the following declaration:

"The European Community/European Union and its Member States reaffirm that their objective in requesting the inclusion of a "disconnection clause" is to take account of the institutional structure of the Union when acceding to international conventions, in particular in case of transfer of sovereign powers from the Member States to the Community.

This clause is not aimed at reducing the rights or increasing the obligations of a non-European Union Party vis-à-vis the European Community/European Union and its Member States, inasmuch as the latter are also parties to this Convention.

The disconnection clause is necessary for those parts of the Convention which fall within the competence of the Community/Union, in order to indicate that European Union Member States cannot invoke and apply the rights and obligations deriving from the Convention directly among themselves (or between themselves and the European Community/Union). This does not detract from the fact that the Convention applies fully between the European Community/European Union and its Member States on the one hand, and the other Parties to the Convention, on the other; the Community and the European Union Members States will be bound by the Convention and will apply it like any Party to the Convention, if necessary, through Community/Union legislation. They will thus guarantee the full respect of the Convention's provisions vis-à-vis non-European Union Parties."

As an instrument made in connection with the conclusion of a treaty, within the meaning of Article 31, para. 2(b) of the Vienna Convention on the Law of Treaties, this declaration forms part of the "context" of the Convention.

273. The European Community would be in a position to provide, for the sole purpose of transparency, necessary information about the division of competence between the Community and its Member States in the area covered by the present Convention, inasmuch as this does not lead to additional obligations placed on the Community.

274. While the Convention provides a level of harmonisation, it does not purport to address all outstanding issues relating to fight against terrorism, even from a preventive perspective. Therefore, paragraph 4 was inserted to make plain that the Convention only affects what it addresses. Other rights, restrictions, obligations and responsibilities that may exist but that are not dealt with by the Convention are left unaffected. Precedent for such a "savings clause" may be found in other international agreements, such as the International Convention for the Suppression of the Financing of Terrorism.

275. In this connection, this paragraph mentions in particular international humanitarian law given the specific nature of the subject of the Convention.

276. The wording of paragraph 4 is based on similar provisions in recent international texts, including the Inter-American Convention against Terrorism (Article 15, paragraph 2) and United Nations Security Council Resolution 1566 (2004) which contains similar language (preambular paragraph 6).

277. It should be noted that obligations under international refugee law include the responsibility to ensure that the institution of asylum is not abused by persons who are responsible for terrorist acts.

278. Refugee status may only be granted to those who fulfil the criteria as set out in Article 1.A.2. of the 1951 Convention relating to the Status of Refugees, that is "a well-founded fear of being persecuted for reasons of race, religion, nationality, membership of a particular social group or political opinion". In many cases, persons responsible for terrorist acts may not fear persecution for a motive provided for in the 1951 Convention but rather may be fleeing legitimate prosecution for criminal acts they have committed.

279. According to Article 1.F. of the 1951 Convention, persons who would otherwise meet the refugee criteria of Article 1.A.2. shall be excluded from international refugee protection if there are serious reasons for considering that they have committed a crime against peace, a war crime, a crime against humanity, or a serious non-political crime outside the country of refuge prior to admission to that country as a refugee, or have been guilty of acts contrary to the purposes and principles of the United Nations.

280. While indications of an applicant's involvement in acts prohibited under the present Convention would make it necessary to examine the applicability of Article 1.F. of the 1951 Convention, international refugee law requires an assessment of the context and circumstances of the individual case in a fair and efficient procedure before a decision is taken.

281. Paragraph 5 of Article 26, which is based on Article 19, paragraph 2 of the International Convention for the Suppression of Terrorist Bombings, is an additional saving clause which provides for the application of international humanitarian law and not the present Convention in relation to activities of armed forces during an armed conflict. As for activities undertaken by military forces of a Party in the exercise of their official duties, reference is made to paragraph 82 above, which states that the Convention leaves unaffected conduct in pursuance of lawful instructions or government authority.

282. Paragraph 5 does not legitimise the behaviour covered by Articles 5 to 7 of this Convention when carried out by armed forces during an armed conflict or by military forces of a Party in the exercise of their official

duties, and is thus consistent with other international treaties against terrorism such as the International Convention for the Suppression of Terrorist Bombings which states in its preamble that "Noting that the activities of military forces of States are governed by rules of international law outside the framework of this Convention and that the exclusion of certain actions from the coverage of this Convention does not condone or make lawful otherwise unlawful acts, or preclude prosecution under other laws."

Articles 27 and 28 – Amendment procedures

283. Amendments of the Convention are regulated by Articles 27 and 28 which are based on a similar provision in the Protocol amending the European Convention on the Suppression of Terrorism which the GMT provided in order to solve the problem of possible future amendments to the convention. Two procedures are provided for: a general procedure for amendments concerning the Convention other than those concerning the Appendix and a simplified procedure for the revision of the Appendix allowing for new conventions to be added to this list. In this connection, it should be recalled that the Appendix contains the same list of treaties as Article 1, paragraph 1 of the European Convention on the Suppression of Terrorism as revised by its amending Protocol.

Article 27 – Amendments to the Convention

284. This provision concerns amendments to the Convention other than those relating to the Appendix. It aims to simplify the amendment procedure by replacing the negotiation of a protocol with an accelerated procedure.

285. Paragraph 1 provides that amendments may be proposed by any Party, the Committee of Ministers or the Consultation of the Parties provided for in Article 30, in accordance with standard Council of Europe treaty-making procedures.

286. This procedure provides therefore for a form of consultation that the Committee of Ministers should carry out before proceeding to the formal adoption of any amendment. This is the mandatory consultation of the Parties to the Convention including non-member Parties. This consultation is justified in so far as non-member Parties are concerned because they do not sit in the Committee of Ministers and therefore it is necessary to provide them with some form of participation in the adoption procedure. This procedure takes place in the framework of the Consultation of the Parties which gives an opinion in pursuance of Article 30.

287. The Committee of Ministers may then adopt the proposed amendment. Although it is not explicitly mentioned, it is understood that the Committee of Ministers would adopt the amendment in accordance with the majority provided for in Article 20.d of the Statute of the Council of Europe, that is a

two-thirds majority of the representatives casting a vote and of a majority of the representatives entitled to sit on the Committee (paragraph 4).

288. The amendment would then be submitted to the Parties for acceptance (paragraph 5).

289. Once accepted by all the Parties, the amendment enters into force on the thirtieth day following notification of acceptance by the last Party (paragraph 6).

290. In accordance with standard Council of Europe practice and in keeping with the role of the Secretary General as depositary of Council of Europe conventions, the Secretary General receives proposed amendments (paragraph 1), communicates them to the Parties for information (paragraph 2) and for acceptance once adopted by the Committee of Ministers (paragraph 5) and receives notification of acceptance by the Parties and notifies them of the entry into force of the amendments (paragraph 6).

Article 28 – Revision of the Appendix

291. Article 28 introduces a new simplified amendment procedure for updating the list of treaties in the Appendix to the Convention.

292. This procedure represents a development in Council of Europe conventions inaugurated by the Protocol amending the European Convention on the Suppression of Terrorism (Article 13) which was inspired by existing anti-terrorist conventions, such as the International Convention for the Suppression of the Financing of Terrorism of 9 December 1999 (Article 23). The novelty lies in the fact that this simplified procedure concerns an appendix which is not of a purely technical nature, as it was the case, for instance, with the appendices to the Bern Convention on the Conservation of European Wildlife and Natural Habitats (ETS No. 104) or to the Protocol of Amendment to the European Convention for the Protection of Vertebrate Animals used for Experimental and other Scientific Purposes (ETS No. 170).

293. Paragraph 1 provides for a number of substantive conditions that have to be met in order to have recourse to this procedure. Firstly, the amendment can only concern the list of treaties in Article 1, paragraph 1. Secondly, such amendments can only concern treaties concluded within the United Nations System – these terms cover the United Nations Organisation and its Specialised Agencies, dealing specifically with international terrorism and having entered into force.

294. In line with Article 27, amendments may be proposed by any Party or by the Committee of Ministers and are communicated by the Secretary General of the Council of Europe to the Parties (paragraph 1). However, contrary to

Article 27, the Consultation of the Parties is not entitled to make such proposals for amendments.

295. The forms of consultation and adoption by the Committee of Ministers of a proposed amendment provided for in the general amendment procedure of Article 27 are provided in Article 28 also, for the simplified procedure in paragraph 2.

296. However, contrary to the general procedure under Article 27, in the simplified procedure an amendment, once adopted by the Committee of Ministers, enters into force after the expiry of a period of one year from the date on which it was communicated to the Parties by the Secretary General (paragraph 2), provided that one third or more of the Parties do not notify an objection to the entry into force of the amendment to the Secretary General (paragraph 3), in which case the amendment would not enter into force.

297. Any objection from a Party shall be without prejudice to the other Parties' tacit acceptance and where less than one-third of the Parties object to the entry into force of the amendment, the proposed amendment enters into force for those Parties which have not objected (paragraph 4).

298. Acceptance by all the Parties is therefore not required for the entry into force of the amendment.

299. For those Parties which have objected, the amendment comes into force on the first day of the month following the date on which they have notified the Secretary General of the Council of Europe of their subsequent acceptance (paragraph 5).

Article 29 – Settlement of disputes

300. Article 29 concerns the settlement, by means of negotiation, arbitration or other peaceful means, of those disputes over the interpretation or application of the Convention. The current provision is similar to the one found in the Cybercrime Convention (Article 45, paragraph 2).

301. It provides, *inter alia,* for the setting up of an arbitration tribunal along the lines of Article 47, paragraph 2 of the European Convention for the Protection of Animals during International Transport of 13 December 1968 where this system of arbitration was for the first time introduced. Alternatively, the Parties may also agree to submit their dispute to the International Court of Justice. Whatever procedure is chosen to settle the dispute, it should be agreed upon by the Parties.

302. Further guidance is provided by the European Convention on the Peaceful Settlement of Disputes (ETS No. 23, Article 1).

Article 30 – Consultation of the Parties

303. This article provides for the setting up of a conventional committee, the Consultation of the Parties responsible for a number of conventional follow-up tasks and providing for the participation of all Parties.

304. Such a procedure was believed necessary by the drafters of the Convention to ensure that all Parties to the Convention, including Parties non-member of the Council of Europe, could be involved – on an equal footing – in any follow-up mechanism.

305. When drafting this provision, the negotiators wanted to devise as simple and flexible a mechanism as possible, pending the entry into force of the Protocol amending the European Convention on the Suppression of Terrorism which itself provides for another specific follow-up committee, the COSTER (Conference of States Parties against Terrorism).

306. Beyond its purely conventional functions in relation to the revised European Convention on the Suppression of Terrorism, the COSTER has a broader role in the Council of Europe's anti-terrorist legal activities. It is called upon to act as a forum for exchanges of information on legal and policy developments and, at the request of the Committee of Ministers, to examine additional legal measures with regard to terrorism adopted within the Council of Europe and could well discharge the role of the Consultation of the Parties with its membership restricted to representatives of the Parties to the present Convention.

307. The flexibility of the follow-up mechanism established by the present Convention is reflected by the fact that there is no temporal requirement for its convocation. It will be convened by the Secretary General of the Council of Europe (paragraph 2) as appropriate and periodically (paragraph 1).

308. However, it can only be convened at the request of the majority of the Parties or at the request of the Committee of Ministers (paragraph 1).

309. With respect to this Convention, the Consultation of the Parties has the traditional follow-up competencies and plays a role in respect of :

a. the effective implementation of the Convention, by making proposals to facilitate or improve the effective use and implementation of this Convention, including the identification of any problems thereof, as well as the effects of any declaration made under this Convention;

b. the amendment of the Convention, by making proposals for amendment in accordance with Article 27, paragraph 1 and formulating its opinion on any proposal for amendment of this Convention which is referred to it in accordance with Article 27, paragraph 3;

c.   a general advisory role in respect of the Convention by expressing an opinion on any question concerning the application of this Convention;

d.   serving as a *clearing house* and facilitating the exchange of information on significant legal, policy or technological developments in relation to the application of the provisions of the Convention.

Article 31 – Denunciation

310. This provision aims at allowing any Party to denounce this Convention. The sole requirement is that the denunciation be notified to the Secretary General of the Council in his or her role as depository of the Convention.

311. This denunciation takes effect three months after it has been received, that is, as from the reception of the notification by the Secretary General.

Article 32 – Notification

312. This provision, which is a standard final clause in Council of Europe treaties, concerns notifications to Parties. It goes without saying that the Secretary General must inform Parties also of any other acts, notifications and communications within the meaning of Article 77 of the Vienna Convention on the Law of Treaties relating to the Convention and not expressly provided for by this article.

European Convention on Cybercrime (ETS No. 185)[1]

Preamble

The member States of the Council of Europe and the other States signatory hereto,

Considering that the aim of the Council of Europe is to achieve a greater unity between its members;

Recognising the value of fostering co-operation with the other States parties to this Convention;

Convinced of the need to pursue, as a matter of priority, a common criminal policy aimed at the protection of society against cybercrime, inter alia, by adopting appropriate legislation and fostering international co-operation;

Conscious of the profound changes brought about by the digitalisation, convergence and continuing globalisation of computer networks;

Concerned by the risk that computer networks and electronic information may also be used for committing criminal offences and that evidence relating to such offences may be stored and transferred by these networks;

Recognising the need for co-operation between States and private industry in combating cybercrime and the need to protect legitimate interests in the use and development of information technologies;

Believing that an effective fight against cybercrime requires increased, rapid and well-functioning international co-operation in criminal matters;

Convinced that the present Convention is necessary to deter action directed against the confidentiality, integrity and availability of computer systems, networks and computer data as well as the misuse of such systems, networks and data by providing for the criminalisation of such conduct, as described in this Convention, and the adoption of powers sufficient for effectively combating such criminal offences, by facilitating their detection, investigation and prosecution at both the domestic and international levels and by providing arrangements for fast and reliable international co-operation;

Mindful of the need to ensure a proper balance between the interests of law enforcement and respect for fundamental human rights as enshrined in the 1950 Council of Europe Convention for the Protection of Human

---

[1] The state of signatures and ratifications of this Convention can be consulted at http://conventions.coe.int/.

Rights and Fundamental Freedoms, the 1966 United Nations International Covenant on Civil and Political Rights and other applicable international human rights treaties, which reaffirm the right of everyone to hold opinions without interference, as well as the right to freedom of expression, including the freedom to seek, receive, and impart information and ideas of all kinds, regardless of frontiers, and the rights concerning the respect for privacy;

Mindful also of the right to the protection of personal data, as conferred, for example, by the 1981 Council of Europe Convention for the Protection of Individuals with regard to Automatic Processing of Personal Data;

Considering the 1989 United Nations Convention on the Rights of the Child and the 1999 International Labour Organization Worst Forms of Child Labour Convention;

Taking into account the existing Council of Europe conventions on co-operation in the penal field, as well as similar treaties which exist between Council of Europe member States and other States, and stressing that the present Convention is intended to supplement those conventions in order to make criminal investigations and proceedings concerning criminal offences related to computer systems and data more effective and to enable the collection of evidence in electronic form of a criminal offence;

Welcoming recent developments which further advance international understanding and co-operation in combating cybercrime, including action taken by the United Nations, the OECD, the European Union and the G8;

Recalling Committee of Ministers Recommendations No. R (85) 10 concerning the practical application of the European Convention on Mutual Assistance in Criminal Matters in respect of letters rogatory for the interception of telecommunications, No. R (88) 2 on piracy in the field of copyright and neighbouring rights, No. R (87) 15 regulating the use of personal data in the police sector, No. R (95) 4 on the protection of personal data in the area of telecommunication services, with particular reference to telephone services, as well as No. R (89) 9 on computer-related crime providing guidelines for national legislatures concerning the definition of certain computer crimes and No. R (95) 13 concerning problems of criminal procedural law connected with information technology;

Having regard to Resolution No. 1 adopted by the European Ministers of Justice at their 21st Conference (Prague, 10 and 11 June 1997), which recommended that the Committee of Ministers support the work on cybercrime carried out by the European Committee on Crime Problems (CDPC) in order to bring domestic criminal law provisions closer to each other and enable the use of effective means of investigation into such offences, as well as to Resolution No. 3 adopted at the 23rd Conference of the European Ministers of Justice (London, 8 and 9 June 2000), which encouraged the negotiating parties to pursue their efforts with a view to finding appropriate solutions to enable the largest possible number of States to become parties to the Convention and acknowledged the need for a swift and efficient system of international co-operation, which duly takes into account the specific requirements of the fight against cybercrime;

Having also regard to the Action Plan adopted by the Heads of State and Government of the Council of Europe on the occasion of their Second Summit (Strasbourg, 10 and 11 October 1997), to seek common responses to the development of the new information technologies based on the standards and values of the Council of Europe;

Have agreed as follows:

Chapter I – Use of terms

Article 1 – Definitions

For the purposes of this Convention:

a   "computer system" means any device or a group of interconnected or related devices, one or more of which, pursuant to a program, performs automatic processing of data;

b   "computer data" means any representation of facts, information or concepts in a form suitable for processing in a computer system, including a program suitable to cause a computer system to perform a function;

c   "service provider" means:

    i   any public or private entity that provides to users of its service the ability to communicate by means of a computer system, and

    ii   any other entity that processes or stores computer data on behalf of such communication service or users of such service;

d   "traffic data" means any computer data relating to a communication by means of a computer system, generated by a computer system that formed a part in the chain of communication, indicating the communication's origin, destination, route, time, date, size, duration, or type of underlying service.

Chapter II – Measures to be taken at the national level

Section 1 – Substantive criminal law

Title 1 – Offences against the confidentiality, integrity and availability of computer data and systems

Article 2 – Illegal access

Each Party shall adopt such legislative and other measures as may be necessary to establish as criminal offences under its domestic law, when committed intentionally, the access to the whole or any part of a computer system without right. A Party may require that the offence be committed by infringing security measures, with the intent of obtaining computer data or other dishonest intent, or in relation to a computer system that is connected to another computer system.

Article 3 – Illegal interception

Each Party shall adopt such legislative and other measures as may be necessary to establish as criminal offences under its domestic law, when committed intentionally, the interception without right, made by technical means, of non-public transmissions of computer data to, from or within a computer system, including electromagnetic emissions from a computer system carrying such computer data. A Party may require that the offence be committed with dishonest intent, or in relation to a computer system that is connected to another computer system.

Article 4 – Data interference

1   Each Party shall adopt such legislative and other measures as may be necessary to establish as criminal offences under its domestic law, when committed intentionally, the damaging, deletion, deterioration, alteration or suppression of computer data without right.

2   A Party may reserve the right to require that the conduct described in paragraph 1 result in serious harm.

Article 5 – System interference

Each Party shall adopt such legislative and other measures as may be necessary to establish as criminal offences under its domestic law, when committed intentionally, the serious hindering without right of the functioning of a computer system by inputting, transmitting, damaging, deleting, deteriorating, altering or suppressing computer data.

Article 6 – Misuse of devices

1   Each Party shall adopt such legislative and other measures as may be necessary to establish as criminal offences under its domestic law, when committed intentionally and without right:

   a   the production, sale, procurement for use, import, distribution or otherwise making available of:

      i   a device, including a computer program, designed or adapted primarily for the purpose of committing any of the offences established in accordance with the above Articles 2 through 5;

      ii   a computer password, access code, or similar data by which the whole or any part of a computer system is capable of being accessed,

         with intent that it be used for the purpose of committing any of the offences established in Articles 2 through 5; and

   b   the possession of an item referred to in paragraphs a.i or ii above, with intent that it be used for the purpose of committing any of the offences established in Articles 2 through 5. A Party may require by law that a number of such items be possessed before criminal liability attaches.

2   This article shall not be interpreted as imposing criminal liability where the production, sale, procurement for use, import, distribution or otherwise making available or possession referred to in paragraph 1 of this article is not for the purpose of committing an offence established in accordance with Articles 2 through 5 of this Convention, such as for the authorised testing or protection of a computer system.

3   Each Party may reserve the right not to apply paragraph 1 of this article, provided that the reservation does not concern the sale, distribution or otherwise making available of the items referred to in paragraph 1 a.ii of this article.

Title 2 – Computer-related offences

Article 7 – Computer-related forgery

Each Party shall adopt such legislative and other measures as may be necessary to establish as criminal offences under its domestic law, when committed intentionally and without right, the input, alteration, deletion, or suppression of computer data, resulting in inauthentic data with the intent that it be considered or acted upon for legal purposes as if it were authentic, regardless whether or not the data is directly readable and intelligible. A Party may require an intent to defraud, or similar dishonest intent, before criminal liability attaches.

Article 8 – Computer-related fraud

Each Party shall adopt such legislative and other measures as may be necessary to establish as criminal offences under its domestic law, when committed intentionally and without right, the causing of a loss of property to another person by:

a   any input, alteration, deletion or suppression of computer data;

b   any interference with the functioning of a computer system,

with fraudulent or dishonest intent of procuring, without right, an economic benefit for oneself or for another person.

Title 3 – Content-related offences

Article 9 – Offences related to child pornography

1   Each Party shall adopt such legislative and other measures as may be necessary to establish as criminal offences under its domestic law, when committed intentionally and without right, the following conduct:

a   producing child pornography for the purpose of its distribution through a computer system;

b   offering or making available child pornography through a computer system;

c   distributing or transmitting child pornography through a computer system;

d   procuring child pornography through a computer system for oneself or for another person;

e   possessing child pornography in a computer system or on a computer-data storage medium.

2   For the purpose of paragraph 1 above, the term "child pornography" shall include pornographic material that visually depicts:

a   a minor engaged in sexually explicit conduct;

b   a person appearing to be a minor engaged in sexually explicit conduct;

c   realistic images representing a minor engaged in sexually explicit conduct.

3   For the purpose of paragraph 2 above, the term "minor" shall include all persons under 18 years of age. A Party may, however, require a lower age-limit, which shall be not less than 16 years.

4   Each Party may reserve the right not to apply, in whole or in part, paragraphs 1, sub-paragraphs d. and e, and 2, sub-paragraphs b. and c.

Title 4 – Offences related to infringements of copyright and related rights

Article 10 – Offences related to infringements of copyright and related rights

1   Each Party shall adopt such legislative and other measures as may be necessary to establish as criminal offences under its domestic law the infringement of copyright, as defined under the law of that Party, pursuant to the obligations it has undertaken under the Paris Act of 24 July 1971 revising the Bern Convention for the Protection of Literary and Artistic Works, the Agreement on Trade-Related Aspects of Intellectual Property Rights and the WIPO Copyright Treaty, with the exception of any moral rights conferred by such conventions, where such acts are committed wilfully, on a commercial scale and by means of a computer system.

2   Each Party shall adopt such legislative and other measures as may be necessary to establish as criminal offences under its domestic law the infringement of related rights, as defined under the law of that Party, pursuant to the obligations it has undertaken under the International Convention for the Protection of Performers, Producers of Phonograms and Broadcasting Organisations (Rome Convention), the Agreement on Trade-Related Aspects of Intellectual Property Rights and the WIPO Performances and Phonograms Treaty, with the exception of any moral rights conferred by such conventions, where such acts are committed wilfully, on a commercial scale and by means of a computer system.

3   A Party may reserve the right not to impose criminal liability under paragraphs 1 and 2 of this article in limited circumstances, provided that other effective remedies are available and that such reservation does not derogate from the Party's international obligations set forth in the international instruments referred to in paragraphs 1 and 2 of this article.

Title 5 – Ancillary liability and sanctions

Article 11 – Attempt and aiding or abetting

1   Each Party shall adopt such legislative and other measures as may be necessary to establish as criminal offences under its domestic law, when committed intentionally, aiding or abetting the commission of any of the offences established in accordance with Articles 2 through 10 of the present Convention with intent that such offence be committed.

2   Each Party shall adopt such legislative and other measures as may be necessary to establish as criminal offences under its domestic law, when committed intentionally, an attempt to commit any of the offences established in accordance with Articles 3 through 5, 7, 8, and 9.1.a and c. of this Convention.

3   Each Party may reserve the right not to apply, in whole or in part, paragraph 2 of this article.

Article 12 – Corporate liability

1   Each Party shall adopt such legislative and other measures as may be necessary to ensure that legal persons can be held liable for a criminal offence established in accordance with this Convention, committed for their benefit by any natural person, acting either individually or as part of an organ of the legal person, who has a leading position within it, based on:

a   a power of representation of the legal person;

b   an authority to take decisions on behalf of the legal person;

c   an authority to exercise control within the legal person.

2   In addition to the cases already provided for in paragraph 1 of this article, each Party shall take the measures necessary to ensure that a legal person can be held liable where the lack of supervision or control by a natural person referred to in paragraph 1 has made possible the commission of a criminal offence established in accordance with this Convention for the benefit of that legal person by a natural person acting under its authority.

3   Subject to the legal principles of the Party, the liability of a legal person may be criminal, civil or administrative.

4   Such liability shall be without prejudice to the criminal liability of the natural persons who have committed the offence.

Article 13 – Sanctions and measures

1   Each Party shall adopt such legislative and other measures as may be necessary to ensure that the criminal offences established in accordance with Articles 2 through 11 are punishable by effective, proportionate and dissuasive sanctions, which include deprivation of liberty.

2   Each Party shall ensure that legal persons held liable in accordance with Article 12 shall be subject to effective, proportionate and dissuasive criminal or non-criminal sanctions or measures, including monetary sanctions.

Section 2 – Procedural law

Title 1 – Common provisions

Article 14 – Scope of procedural provisions

1   Each Party shall adopt such legislative and other measures as may be necessary to establish the powers and procedures provided for in this section for the purpose of specific criminal investigations or proceedings.

2   Except as specifically provided otherwise in Article 21, each Party shall apply the powers and procedures referred to in paragraph 1 of this article to:

a   the criminal offences established in accordance with Articles 2 through 11 of this Convention;

b   other criminal offences committed by means of a computer system; and

c   the collection of evidence in electronic form of a criminal offence.

3   a   Each Party may reserve the right to apply the measures referred to in Article 20 only to offences or categories of offences specified in the reservation, provided that the range of such offences or categories of offences is not more restricted than the range of offences to which it applies the measures referred to in Article 21. Each Party shall consider restricting such a reservation to enable the broadest application of the measure referred to in Article 20.

b   Where a Party, due to limitations in its legislation in force at the time of the adoption of the present Convention, is not able to apply the measures referred to in Articles 20 and 21 to communications being transmitted within a computer system of a service provider, which system:

i   is being operated for the benefit of a closed group of users, and

ii   does not employ public communications networks and is not connected with another computer system, whether public or private,

that Party may reserve the right not to apply these measures to such communications. Each Party shall consider restricting such a reservation to enable the broadest application of the measures referred to in Articles 20 and 21.

Article 15 – Conditions and safeguards

1   Each Party shall ensure that the establishment, implementation and application of the powers and procedures provided for in this Section are subject to conditions and safeguards provided for under its domestic law, which shall provide for the adequate protection of human rights and liberties, including rights arising pursuant to obligations it has undertaken under the 1950 Council of Europe Convention for the Protection of Human Rights and Fundamental Freedoms, the 1966 United Nations International Covenant on Civil and Political Rights, and other applicable international human rights instruments, and which shall incorporate the principle of proportionality.

2   Such conditions and safeguards shall, as appropriate in view of the nature of the procedure or power concerned, inter alia, include judicial or other independent supervision, grounds justifying application, and limitation of the scope and the duration of such power or procedure.

3   To the extent that it is consistent with the public interest, in particular the sound administration of justice, each Party shall consider the impact of the powers and procedures in this section upon the rights, responsibilities and legitimate interests of third parties.

Title 2 – Expedited preservation of stored computer data

Article 16 – Expedited preservation of stored computer data

1   Each Party shall adopt such legislative and other measures as may be necessary to enable its competent authorities to order or similarly obtain the expeditious preservation of specified computer data, including traffic data, that has been stored by means of a computer system, in particular where there are grounds to believe that the computer data is particularly vulnerable to loss or modification.

2   Where a Party gives effect to paragraph 1 above by means of an order to a person to preserve specified stored computer data in the person's possession or control, the Party shall adopt such legislative and other

measures as may be necessary to oblige that person to preserve and maintain the integrity of that computer data for a period of time as long as necessary, up to a maximum of ninety days, to enable the competent authorities to seek its disclosure. A Party may provide for such an order to be subsequently renewed.

3   Each Party shall adopt such legislative and other measures as may be necessary to oblige the custodian or other person who is to preserve the computer data to keep confidential the undertaking of such procedures for the period of time provided for by its domestic law.

4   The powers and procedures referred to in this article shall be subject to Articles 14 and 15.

Article 17 – Expedited preservation and partial disclosure of traffic data

1   Each Party shall adopt, in respect of traffic data that is to be preserved under Article 16, such legislative and other measures as may be necessary to:

a   ensure that such expeditious preservation of traffic data is available regardless of whether one or more service providers were involved in the transmission of that communication; and

b   ensure the expeditious disclosure to the Party's competent authority, or a person designated by that authority, of a sufficient amount of traffic data to enable the Party to identify the service providers and the path through which the communication was transmitted.

2   The powers and procedures referred to in this article shall be subject to Articles 14 and 15.

Title 3 – Production order

Article 18 – Production order

1   Each Party shall adopt such legislative and other measures as may be necessary to empower its competent authorities to order:

a   a person in its territory to submit specified computer data in that person's possession or control, which is stored in a computer system or a computer-data storage medium; and

b   a service provider offering its services in the territory of the Party to submit subscriber information relating to such services in that service provider's possession or control.

2   The powers and procedures referred to in this article shall be subject to Articles 14 and 15.

3   For the purpose of this article, the term "subscriber information" means any information contained in the form of computer data or any other form that is held by a service provider, relating to subscribers of its services other than traffic or content data and by which can be established:

   a   the type of communication service used, the technical provisions taken thereto and the period of service;

   b   the subscriber's identity, postal or geographic address, telephone and other access number, billing and payment information, available on the basis of the service agreement or arrangement;

   c   any other information on the site of the installation of communication equipment, available on the basis of the service agreement or arrangement.

Title 4 – Search and seizure of stored computer data

Article 19 – Search and seizure of stored computer data

1   Each Party shall adopt such legislative and other measures as may be necessary to empower its competent authorities to search or similarly access:

   a   a computer system or part of it and computer data stored therein; and

   b   a computer-data storage medium in which computer data may be stored

   in its territory.

2   Each Party shall adopt such legislative and other measures as may be necessary to ensure that where its authorities search or similarly access a specific computer system or part of it, pursuant to paragraph 1.a, and have grounds to believe that the data sought is stored in another computer system or part of it in its territory, and such data is lawfully accessible from or available to the initial system, the authorities shall be able to expeditiously extend the search or similar accessing to the other system.

3   Each Party shall adopt such legislative and other measures as may be necessary to empower its competent authorities to seize or similarly secure computer data accessed according to paragraphs 1 or 2. These measures shall include the power to:

a   seize or similarly secure a computer system or part of it or a computer-data storage medium;

b   make and retain a copy of those computer data;

c   maintain the integrity of the relevant stored computer data;

d   render inaccessible or remove those computer data in the accessed computer system.

4   Each Party shall adopt such legislative and other measures as may be necessary to empower its competent authorities to order any person who has knowledge about the functioning of the computer system or measures applied to protect the computer data therein to provide, as is reasonable, the necessary information, to enable the undertaking of the measures referred to in paragraphs 1 and 2.

5   The powers and procedures referred to in this article shall be subject to Articles 14 and 15.

Title 5 – Real-time collection of computer data

Article 20 – Real-time collection of traffic data

1   Each Party shall adopt such legislative and other measures as may be necessary to empower its competent authorities to:

a   collect or record through the application of technical means on the territory of that Party, and

b   compel a service provider, within its existing technical capability:

   i   to collect or record through the application of technical means on the territory of that Party; or

   ii   to co-operate and assist the competent authorities in the collection or recording of,

   traffic data, in real-time, associated with specified communications in its territory transmitted by means of a computer system.

2   Where a Party, due to the established principles of its domestic legal system, cannot adopt the measures referred to in paragraph 1.a, it may instead adopt legislative and other measures as may be necessary to ensure the real-time collection or recording of traffic data associated with specified communications transmitted in its territory, through the application of technical means on that territory.

3   Each Party shall adopt such legislative and other measures as may be necessary to oblige a service provider to keep confidential the fact of the execution of any power provided for in this article and any information relating to it.

4   The powers and procedures referred to in this article shall be subject to Articles 14 and 15.

Article 21 – Interception of content data

1   Each Party shall adopt such legislative and other measures as may be necessary, in relation to a range of serious offences to be determined by domestic law, to empower its competent authorities to:

   a   collect or record through the application of technical means on the territory of that Party, and

   b   compel a service provider, within its existing technical capability:

      i   to collect or record through the application of technical means on the territory of that Party, or

      ii   to co-operate and assist the competent authorities in the collection or recording of,

   content data, in real-time, of specified communications in its territory transmitted by means of a computer system.

2   Where a Party, due to the established principles of its domestic legal system, cannot adopt the measures referred to in paragraph 1.a, it may instead adopt legislative and other measures as may be necessary to ensure the real-time collection or recording of content data on specified communications in its territory through the application of technical means on that territory.

3   Each Party shall adopt such legislative and other measures as may be necessary to oblige a service provider to keep confidential the fact of the execution of any power provided for in this article and any information relating to it.

4   The powers and procedures referred to in this article shall be subject to Articles 14 and 15.

Section 3 – Jurisdiction

Article 22 – Jurisdiction

1   Each Party shall adopt such legislative and other measures as may be necessary to establish jurisdiction over any offence established in accordance with Articles 2 through 11 of this Convention, when the offence is committed:

   a   in its territory; or

   b   on board a ship flying the flag of that Party; or

   c   on board an aircraft registered under the laws of that Party; or

   d   by one of its nationals, if the offence is punishable under criminal law where it was committed or if the offence is committed outside the territorial jurisdiction of any State.

2   Each Party may reserve the right not to apply or to apply only in specific cases or conditions the jurisdiction rules laid down in paragraphs 1.b through 1.d of this article or any part thereof.

3   Each Party shall adopt such measures as may be necessary to establish jurisdiction over the offences referred to in Article 24, paragraph 1, of this Convention, in cases where an alleged offender is present in its territory and it does not extradite him or her to another Party, solely on the basis of his or her nationality, after a request for extradition.

4   This Convention does not exclude any criminal jurisdiction exercised by a Party in accordance with its domestic law.

5   When more than one Party claims jurisdiction over an alleged offence established in accordance with this Convention, the Parties involved shall, where appropriate, consult with a view to determining the most appropriate jurisdiction for prosecution.

Chapter III – International co-operation

Section 1 – General principles

Title 1 – General principles relating to international co-operation

Article 23 – General principles relating to international co-operation

The Parties shall co-operate with each other, in accordance with the provisions of this chapter, and through the application of relevant international instruments on international co-operation in criminal matters, arrangements agreed on the basis of uniform or reciprocal legislation, and domestic laws, to the widest extent possible for the purposes of investigations or proceedings concerning criminal offences related to computer systems and data, or for the collection of evidence in electronic form of a criminal offence.

Title 2 – Principles relating to extradition

Article 24 – Extradition

1   a   This article applies to extradition between Parties for the criminal offences established in accordance with Articles 2 through 11 of this Convention, provided that they are punishable under the laws of both Parties concerned by deprivation of liberty for a maximum period of at least one year, or by a more severe penalty.

     b   Where a different minimum penalty is to be applied under an arrangement agreed on the basis of uniform or reciprocal legislation or an extradition treaty, including the European Convention on Extradition (ETS No. 24), applicable between two or more parties, the minimum penalty provided for under such arrangement or treaty shall apply.

2   The criminal offences described in paragraph 1 of this article shall be deemed to be included as extraditable offences in any extradition treaty existing between or among the Parties. The Parties undertake to include such offences as extraditable offences in any extradition treaty to be concluded between or among them.

3   If a Party that makes extradition conditional on the existence of a treaty receives a request for extradition from another Party with which it does not have an extradition treaty, it may consider this Convention as the legal basis for extradition with respect to any criminal offence referred to in paragraph 1 of this article.

4   Parties that do not make extradition conditional on the existence of a treaty shall recognise the criminal offences referred to in paragraph 1 of this article as extraditable offences between themselves.

5   Extradition shall be subject to the conditions provided for by the law of the requested Party or by applicable extradition treaties, including the grounds on which the requested Party may refuse extradition.

6   If extradition for a criminal offence referred to in paragraph 1 of this article is refused solely on the basis of the nationality of the person sought, or because the requested Party deems that it has jurisdiction over the offence, the requested Party shall submit the case at the request of the requesting Party to its competent authorities for the purpose of

prosecution and shall report the final outcome to the requesting Party in due course. Those authorities shall take their decision and conduct their investigations and proceedings in the same manner as for any other offence of a comparable nature under the law of that Party.

7   a   Each Party shall, at the time of signature or when depositing its instrument of ratification, acceptance, approval or accession, communicate to the Secretary General of the Council of Europe the name and address of each authority responsible for making or receiving requests for extradition or provisional arrest in the absence of a treaty.

    b   The Secretary General of the Council of Europe shall set up and keep updated a register of authorities so designated by the Parties. Each Party shall ensure that the details held on the register are correct at all times.

Title 3 – General principles relating to mutual assistance

Article 25 – General principles relating to mutual assistance

1   The Parties shall afford one another mutual assistance to the widest extent possible for the purpose of investigations or proceedings concerning criminal offences related to computer systems and data, or for the collection of evidence in electronic form of a criminal offence.

2   Each Party shall also adopt such legislative and other measures as may be necessary to carry out the obligations set forth in Articles 27 through 35.

3   Each Party may, in urgent circumstances, make requests for mutual assistance or communications related thereto by expedited means of communication, including fax or e-mail, to the extent that such means provide appropriate levels of security and authentication (including the use of encryption, where necessary), with formal confirmation to follow, where required by the requested Party. The requested Party shall accept and respond to the request by any such expedited means of communication.

4   Except as otherwise specifically provided in articles in this chapter, mutual assistance shall be subject to the conditions provided for by the law of the requested Party or by applicable mutual assistance treaties, including the grounds on which the requested Party may refuse co-operation. The requested Party shall not exercise the right to refuse mutual assistance in relation to the offences referred to in Articles 2 through 11 solely on the ground that the request concerns an offence which it considers a fiscal offence.

5   Where, in accordance with the provisions of this chapter, the requested Party is permitted to make mutual assistance conditional upon the existence of dual criminality, that condition shall be deemed fulfilled, irrespective of whether its laws place the offence within the same category of offence or denominate the offence by the same terminology as the requesting Party, if the conduct underlying the offence for which assistance is sought is a criminal offence under its laws.

Article 26 – Spontaneous information

1   A Party may, within the limits of its domestic law and without prior request, forward to another Party information obtained within the framework of its own investigations when it considers that the disclosure of such information might assist the receiving Party in initiating or carrying out investigations or proceedings concerning criminal offences established in accordance with this Convention or might lead to a request for co-operation by that Party under this chapter.

2   Prior to providing such information, the providing Party may request that it be kept confidential or only used subject to conditions. If the receiving Party cannot comply with such request, it shall notify the providing Party, which shall then determine whether the information should nevertheless be provided. If the receiving Party accepts the information subject to the conditions, it shall be bound by them.

Title 4 – Procedures pertaining to mutual assistance requests
in the absence of applicable international agreements

Article 27 – Procedures pertaining to mutual assistance requests in the absence of applicable international agreements

1   Where there is no mutual assistance treaty or arrangement on the basis of uniform or reciprocal legislation in force between the requesting and requested Parties, the provisions of paragraphs 2 through 9 of this article shall apply. The provisions of this article shall not apply where such treaty, arrangement or legislation exists, unless the Parties concerned agree to apply any or all of the remainder of this article in lieu thereof.

2   a   Each Party shall designate a central authority or authorities responsible for sending and answering requests for mutual assistance, the execution of such requests or their transmission to the authorities competent for their execution.

     b   The central authorities shall communicate directly with each other;

     c   Each Party shall, at the time of signature or when depositing its instrument of ratification, acceptance, approval or accession, communicate to the Secretary General of the Council of Europe the names and addresses of the authorities designated in pursuance of this paragraph;

d   The Secretary General of the Council of Europe shall set up and keep updated a register of central authorities designated by the Parties. Each Party shall ensure that the details held on the register are correct at all times.

3   Mutual assistance requests under this article shall be executed in accordance with the procedures specified by the requesting Party, except where incompatible with the law of the requested Party.

4   The requested Party may, in addition to the grounds for refusal established in Article 25, paragraph 4, refuse assistance if:

a   the request concerns an offence which the requested Party considers a political offence or an offence connected with a political offence, or

b   it considers that execution of the request is likely to prejudice its sovereignty, security, ordre public or other essential interests.

5   The requested Party may postpone action on a request if such action would prejudice criminal investigations or proceedings conducted by its authorities.

6   Before refusing or postponing assistance, the requested Party shall, where appropriate after having consulted with the requesting Party, consider whether the request may be granted partially or subject to such conditions as it deems necessary.

7   The requested Party shall promptly inform the requesting Party of the outcome of the execution of a request for assistance. Reasons shall be given for any refusal or postponement of the request. The requested Party shall also inform the requesting Party of any reasons that render impossible the execution of the request or are likely to delay it significantly.

8   The requesting Party may request that the requested Party keep confidential the fact of any request made under this chapter as well as its subject, except to the extent necessary for its execution. If the requested Party cannot comply with the request for confidentiality, it shall promptly inform the requesting Party, which shall then determine whether the request should nevertheless be executed.

9   a   In the event of urgency, requests for mutual assistance or communications related thereto may be sent directly by judicial authorities of the requesting Party to such authorities of the

requested Party. In any such cases, a copy shall be sent at the same time to the central authority of the requested Party through the central authority of the requesting Party.

b   Any request or communication under this paragraph may be made through the International Criminal Police Organisation (Interpol).

c   Where a request is made pursuant to sub-paragraph a. of this article and the authority is not competent to deal with the request, it shall refer the request to the competent national authority and inform directly the requesting Party that it has done so.

d   Requests or communications made under this paragraph that do not involve coercive action may be directly transmitted by the competent authorities of the requesting Party to the competent authorities of the requested Party.

e   Each Party may, at the time of signature or when depositing its instrument of ratification, acceptance, approval or accession, inform the Secretary General of the Council of Europe that, for reasons of efficiency, requests made under this paragraph are to be addressed to its central authority.

Article 28 – Confidentiality and limitation on use

1   When there is no mutual assistance treaty or arrangement on the basis of uniform or reciprocal legislation in force between the requesting and the requested Parties, the provisions of this article shall apply. The provisions of this article shall not apply where such treaty, arrangement or legislation exists, unless the Parties concerned agree to apply any or all of the remainder of this article in lieu thereof.

2   The requested Party may make the supply of information or material in response to a request dependent on the condition that it is:

a   kept confidential where the request for mutual legal assistance could not be complied with in the absence of such condition, or

b   not used for investigations or proceedings other than those stated in the request.

3   If the requesting Party cannot comply with a condition referred to in paragraph 2, it shall promptly inform the other Party, which shall then determine whether the information should nevertheless be provided. When the requesting Party accepts the condition, it shall be bound by it.

4   Any Party that supplies information or material subject to a condition referred to in paragraph 2 may require the other Party to explain, in relation to that condition, the use made of such information or material.

Section 2 – Specific provisions

Title 1 – Mutual assistance regarding provisional measures

Article 29 – Expedited preservation of stored computer data

1   A Party may request another Party to order or otherwise obtain the expeditious preservation of data stored by means of a computer system, located within the territory of that other Party and in respect of which the requesting Party intends to submit a request for mutual assistance for the search or similar access, seizure or similar securing, or disclosure of the data.

2   A request for preservation made under paragraph 1 shall specify:

a   the authority seeking the preservation;

b   the offence that is the subject of a criminal investigation or proceedings and a brief summary of the related facts;

c   the stored computer data to be preserved and its relationship to the offence;

d   any available information identifying the custodian of the stored computer data or the location of the computer system;

e   the necessity of the preservation; and

f   that the Party intends to submit a request for mutual assistance for the search or similar access, seizure or similar securing, or disclosure of the stored computer data.

3   Upon receiving the request from another Party, the requested Party shall take all appropriate measures to preserve expeditiously the specified data in accordance with its domestic law. For the purposes of responding to a request, dual criminality shall not be required as a condition to providing such preservation.

4   A Party that requires dual criminality as a condition for responding to a request for mutual assistance for the search or similar access, seizure or similar securing, or disclosure of stored data may, in respect of offences other than those established in accordance with Articles 2 through 11 of this Convention, reserve the right to refuse the request for preservation

under this article in cases where it has reasons to believe that at the time of disclosure the condition of dual criminality cannot be fulfilled.

5   In addition, a request for preservation may only be refused if:

a   the request concerns an offence which the requested Party considers a political offence or an offence connected with a political offence, or

b   the requested Party considers that execution of the request is likely to prejudice its sovereignty, security, ordre public or other essential interests.

6   Where the requested Party believes that preservation will not ensure the future availability of the data or will threaten the confidentiality of or otherwise prejudice the requesting Party's investigation, it shall promptly so inform the requesting Party, which shall then determine whether the request should nevertheless be executed.

7   Any preservation effected in response to the request referred to in paragraph 1 shall be for a period not less than sixty days, in order to enable the requesting Party to submit a request for the search or similar access, seizure or similar securing, or disclosure of the data. Following the receipt of such a request, the data shall continue to be preserved pending a decision on that request.

Article 30 – Expedited disclosure of preserved traffic data

1   Where, in the course of the execution of a request made pursuant to Article 29 to preserve traffic data concerning a specific communication, the requested Party discovers that a service provider in another State was involved in the transmission of the communication, the requested Party shall expeditiously disclose to the requesting Party a sufficient amount of traffic data to identify that service provider and the path through which the communication was transmitted.

2   Disclosure of traffic data under paragraph 1 may only be withheld if:

a   the request concerns an offence which the requested Party considers a political offence or an offence connected with a political offence; or

b   the requested Party considers that execution of the request is likely to prejudice its sovereignty, security, ordre public or other essential interests.

Title 2 – Mutual assistance regarding investigative powers

Article 31 – Mutual assistance regarding accessing of stored computer data

1   A Party may request another Party to search or similarly access, seize or similarly secure, and disclose data stored by means of a computer system located within the territory of the requested Party, including data that has been preserved pursuant to Article 29.

2   The requested Party shall respond to the request through the application of international instruments, arrangements and laws referred to in Article 23, and in accordance with other relevant provisions of this chapter.

3   The request shall be responded to on an expedited basis where:

a   there are grounds to believe that relevant data is particularly vulnerable to loss or modification; or

b   the instruments, arrangements and laws referred to in paragraph 2 otherwise provide for expedited co-operation.

Article 32 – Trans-border access to stored computer data with consent or where publicly available

A Party may, without the authorisation of another Party:

a   access publicly available (open source) stored computer data, regardless of where the data is located geographically; or

b   access or receive, through a computer system in its territory, stored computer data located in another Party, if the Party obtains the lawful and voluntary consent of the person who has the lawful authority to disclose the data to the Party through that computer system.

Article 33 – Mutual assistance in the real-time collection of traffic data

1   The Parties shall provide mutual assistance to each other in the real-time collection of traffic data associated with specified communications in their territory transmitted by means of a computer system. Subject to the provisions of paragraph 2, this assistance shall be governed by the conditions and procedures provided for under domestic law.

2   Each Party shall provide such assistance at least with respect to criminal offences for which real-time collection of traffic data would be available in a similar domestic case.

Article 34 – Mutual assistance regarding the interception of content data

The Parties shall provide mutual assistance to each other in the real-time collection or recording of content data of specified communications transmitted by means of a computer system to the extent permitted under their applicable treaties and domestic laws.

Title 3 – 24/7 Network

Article 35 – 24/7 Network

1   Each Party shall designate a point of contact available on a twenty-four hour, seven-day-a-week basis, in order to ensure the provision of immediate assistance for the purpose of investigations or proceedings concerning criminal offences related to computer systems and data, or for the collection of evidence in electronic form of a criminal offence. Such assistance shall include facilitating, or, if permitted by its domestic law and practice, directly carrying out the following measures:

   a   the provision of technical advice;

   b   the preservation of data pursuant to Articles 29 and 30;

   c   the collection of evidence, the provision of legal information, and locating of suspects.

2   a   A Party's point of contact shall have the capacity to carry out communications with the point of contact of another Party on an expedited basis.

   b   If the point of contact designated by a Party is not part of that Party's authority or authorities responsible for international mutual assistance or extradition, the point of contact shall ensure that it is able to co-ordinate with such authority or authorities on an expedited basis.

3   Each Party shall ensure that trained and equipped personnel are available, in order to facilitate the operation of the network.

Chapter IV – Final provisions

Article 36 – Signature and entry into force

1   This Convention shall be open for signature by the member States of the Council of Europe and by non-member States which have participated in its elaboration.

2   This Convention is subject to ratification, acceptance or approval. Instruments of ratification, acceptance or approval shall be deposited with the Secretary General of the Council of Europe.

3   This Convention shall enter into force on the first day of the month following the expiration of a period of three months after the date on which five States, including at least three member States of the Council of Europe, have expressed their consent to be bound by the Convention in accordance with the provisions of paragraphs 1 and 2.

4   In respect of any signatory State which subsequently expresses its consent to be bound by it, the Convention shall enter into force on the first day of the month following the expiration of a period of three months after the date of the expression of its consent to be bound by the Convention in accordance with the provisions of paragraphs 1 and 2.

Article 37 – Accession to the Convention

1   After the entry into force of this Convention, the Committee of Ministers of the Council of Europe, after consulting with and obtaining the unanimous consent of the Contracting States to the Convention, may invite any State which is not a member of the Council and which has not participated in its elaboration to accede to this Convention. The decision shall be taken by the majority provided for in Article 20.d. of the Statute of the Council of Europe and by the unanimous vote of the representatives of the Contracting States entitled to sit on the Committee of Ministers.

2   In respect of any State acceding to the Convention under paragraph 1 above, the Convention shall enter into force on the first day of the month following the expiration of a period of three months after the date of deposit of the instrument of accession with the Secretary General of the Council of Europe.

Article 38 – Territorial application

1   Any State may, at the time of signature or when depositing its instrument of ratification, acceptance, approval or accession, specify the territory or territories to which this Convention shall apply.

2   Any State may, at any later date, by a declaration addressed to the Secretary General of the Council of Europe, extend the application of this Convention to any other territory specified in the declaration. In respect of such territory the Convention shall enter into force on the first day of the month following the expiration of a period of three months after the date of receipt of the declaration by the Secretary General.

3   Any declaration made under the two preceding paragraphs may, in respect of any territory specified in such declaration, be withdrawn by a notification addressed to the Secretary General of the Council of Europe. The withdrawal shall become effective on the first day of the month following the expiration of a period of three months after the date of receipt of such notification by the Secretary General.

Article 39 – Effects of the Convention

1   The purpose of the present Convention is to supplement applicable multilateral or bilateral treaties or arrangements as between the Parties, including the provisions of:

–   the European Convention on Extradition, opened for signature in Paris, on 13 December 1957 (ETS No. 24);

–   the European Convention on Mutual Assistance in Criminal Matters, opened for signature in Strasbourg, on 20 April 1959 (ETS No. 30);

–   the Additional Protocol to the European Convention on Mutual Assistance in Criminal Matters, opened for signature in Strasbourg, on 17 March 1978 (ETS No. 99).

2   If two or more Parties have already concluded an agreement or treaty on the matters dealt with in this Convention or have otherwise established their relations on such matters, or should they in future do so, they shall also be entitled to apply that agreement or treaty or to regulate those relations accordingly. However, where Parties establish their relations in respect of the matters dealt with in the present Convention other than as regulated therein, they shall do so in a manner that is not inconsistent with the Convention's objectives and principles.

3   Nothing in this Convention shall affect other rights, restrictions, obligations and responsibilities of a Party.

Article 40 – Declarations

By a written notification addressed to the Secretary General of the Council of Europe, any State may, at the time of signature or when depositing its instrument of ratification, acceptance, approval or accession, declare that it avails itself of the possibility of requiring additional elements as provided for under Articles 2, 3, 6 paragraph 1.b, 7, 9 paragraph 3, and 27, paragraph 9.e.

Article 41 – Federal clause

1   A federal State may reserve the right to assume obligations under Chapter II of this Convention consistent with its fundamental principles governing the relationship between its central government and constituent States or other similar territorial entities provided that it is still able to co-operate under Chapter III.

2   When making a reservation under paragraph 1, a federal State may not apply the terms of such reservation to exclude or substantially diminish its obligations to provide for measures set forth in Chapter II. Overall, it shall provide for a broad and effective law enforcement capability with respect to those measures.

3   With regard to the provisions of this Convention, the application of which comes under the jurisdiction of constituent States or other similar territorial entities, that are not obliged by the constitutional system of the federation to take legislative measures, the federal government shall inform the competent authorities of such States of the said provisions with its favourable opinion, encouraging them to take appropriate action to give them effect.

Article 42 – Reservations

By a written notification addressed to the Secretary General of the Council of Europe, any State may, at the time of signature or when depositing its instrument of ratification, acceptance, approval or accession, declare that it avails itself of the reservation(s) provided for in Article 4, paragraph 2, Article 6, paragraph 3, Article 9, paragraph 4, Article 10, paragraph 3, Article 11, paragraph 3, Article 14, paragraph 3, Article 22, paragraph 2, Article 29, paragraph 4, and Article 41, paragraph 1. No other reservation may be made.

Article 43 – Status and withdrawal of reservations

1   A Party that has made a reservation in accordance with Article 42 may wholly or partially withdraw it by means of a notification addressed to the Secretary General of the Council of Europe. Such withdrawal shall take effect on the date of receipt of such notification by the Secretary General. If the notification states that the withdrawal of a reservation is to take effect on a date specified therein, and such date is later than the date on which the notification is received by the Secretary General, the withdrawal shall take effect on such a later date.

2   A Party that has made a reservation as referred to in Article 42 shall withdraw such reservation, in whole or in part, as soon as circumstances so permit.

3   The Secretary General of the Council of Europe may periodically enquire with Parties that have made one or more reservations as referred to in Article 42 as to the prospects for withdrawing such reservation(s).

Article 44 – Amendments

1   Amendments to this Convention may be proposed by any Party, and shall be communicated by the Secretary General of the Council of Europe to the member States of the Council of Europe, to the non-member States which have participated in the elaboration of this Convention as well as to any State which has acceded to, or has been invited to accede to, this Convention in accordance with the provisions of Article 37.

2   Any amendment proposed by a Party shall be communicated to the European Committee on Crime Problems (CDPC), which shall submit to the Committee of Ministers its opinion on that proposed amendment.

3   The Committee of Ministers shall consider the proposed amendment and the opinion submitted by the CDPC and, following consultation with the non-member States Parties to this Convention, may adopt the amendment.

4   The text of any amendment adopted by the Committee of Ministers in accordance with paragraph 3 of this article shall be forwarded to the Parties for acceptance.

5   Any amendment adopted in accordance with paragraph 3 of this article shall come into force on the thirtieth day after all Parties have informed the Secretary General of their acceptance thereof.

Article 45 – Settlement of disputes

1   The European Committee on Crime Problems (CDPC) shall be kept informed regarding the interpretation and application of this Convention.

2   In case of a dispute between Parties as to the interpretation or application of this Convention, they shall seek a settlement of the dispute through negotiation or any other peaceful means of their choice, including submission of the dispute to the CDPC, to an arbitral tribunal whose decisions shall be binding upon the Parties, or to the International Court of Justice, as agreed upon by the Parties concerned.

Article 46 – Consultations of the Parties

1   The Parties shall, as appropriate, consult periodically with a view to facilitating:

    a   the effective use and implementation of this Convention, including the identification of any problems thereof, as well as the effects of any declaration or reservation made under this Convention;

    b   the exchange of information on significant legal, policy or technological developments pertaining to cybercrime and the collection of evidence in electronic form;

    c   consideration of possible supplementation or amendment of the Convention.

2   The European Committee on Crime Problems (CDPC) shall be kept periodically informed regarding the result of consultations referred to in paragraph 1.

3   The CDPC shall, as appropriate, facilitate the consultations referred to in paragraph 1 and take the measures necessary to assist the Parties in their efforts to supplement or amend the Convention. At the latest three years after the present Convention enters into force, the European Committee on Crime Problems (CDPC) shall, in co-operation with the Parties, conduct a review of all of the Convention's provisions and, if necessary, recommend any appropriate amendments.

4   Except where assumed by the Council of Europe, expenses incurred in carrying out the provisions of paragraph 1 shall be borne by the Parties in the manner to be determined by them.

5   The Parties shall be assisted by the Secretariat of the Council of Europe in carrying out their functions pursuant to this article.

Article 47 – Denunciation

1   Any Party may, at any time, denounce this Convention by means of a notification addressed to the Secretary General of the Council of Europe.

2   Such denunciation shall become effective on the first day of the month following the expiration of a period of three months after the date of receipt of the notification by the Secretary General.

Article 48 – Notification

The Secretary General of the Council of Europe shall notify the member States of the Council of Europe, the non-member States which have participated in the elaboration of this Convention as well as any State which has acceded to, or has been invited to accede to, this Convention of:

a   any signature;

b   the deposit of any instrument of ratification, acceptance, approval or accession;

c   any date of entry into force of this Convention in accordance with Articles 36 and 37;

d   any declaration made under Article 40 or reservation made in accordance with Article 42;

e   any other act, notification or communication relating to this Convention.

In witness whereof the undersigned, being duly authorised thereto, have signed this Convention.

Done at Budapest, this 23rd day of November 2001, in English and in French, both texts being equally authentic, in a single copy which shall be deposited in the archives of the Council of Europe. The Secretary General of the Council of Europe shall transmit certified copies to each member State of the Council of Europe, to the non-member States which have participated in the elaboration of this Convention, and to any State invited to accede to it.

Explanatory Report

I.   The Convention and its Explanatory Report have been adopted by the Committee of Ministers of the Council of Europe at its 109th Session (8 November 2001) and the Convention has been opened for signature in Budapest, on 23 November 2001, on the issue of the International Conference on Cybercrime.

II.   The text of this explanatory report does not constitute an instrument providing an authoritative interpretation of the Convention, although it might be of such a nature as to facilitate the application of the provisions contained therein.

I. Introduction

1.   The revolution in information technologies has changed society fundamentally and will probably continue to do so in the foreseeable future. Many tasks have become easier to handle. Where originally only some specific sectors of society had rationalised their working procedures with the help of information technology, now hardly any sector of society has remained unaffected. Information technology has in one way or the other pervaded almost every aspect of human activities.

2.   A conspicuous feature of information technology is the impact it has had and will have on the evolution of telecommunications technology. Classical telephony, involving the transmission of human voice, has been overtaken by the exchange of vast amounts of data, comprising voice, text, music and static and moving pictures. This exchange no longer occurs only between human beings, but also between human beings and computers, and between computers themselves. Circuit-switched connections have been replaced by packet-switched networks. It is no longer relevant whether a direct connection can be established; it suffices that data is entered into a network with a destination address or made available for anyone who wants to access it.

3.   The pervasive use of electronic mail and the accessing through the Internet of numerous websites are examples of these developments. They have changed our society profoundly.

4.   The ease of accessibility and searchability of information contained in computer systems, combined with the practically unlimited possibilities for its exchange and dissemination, regardless of geographical distances, has lead to an explosive growth in the amount of information available and the knowledge that can be drawn there from.

5.   These developments have given rise to an unprecedented economic and social changes, but they also have a dark side: the emergence of new types of crime as well as the commission of traditional crimes by means of

new technologies. Moreover, the consequences of criminal behaviour can be more far-reaching than before because they are not restricted by geographical limitations or national boundaries. The recent spread of detrimental computer viruses all over the world has provided proof of this reality. Technical measures to protect computer systems need to be implemented concomitantly with legal measures to prevent and deter criminal behaviour.

6.   The new technologies challenge existing legal concepts. Information and communications flow more easily around the world. Borders are no longer boundaries to this flow. Criminals are increasingly located in places other than where their acts produce their effects. However, domestic laws are generally confined to a specific territory. Thus solutions to the problems posed must be addressed by international law, necessitating the adoption of adequate international legal instruments. The present Convention aims to meet this challenge, with due respect to human rights in the new Information Society.

II. The preparatory work

7.   By decision CDPC/103/211196, the European Committee on Crime Problems (CDPC) decided in November 1996 to set up a committee of experts to deal with cybercrime. The CDPC based its decision on the following rationale:

8.   "The fast developments in the field of information technology have a direct bearing on all sections of modern society. The integration of telecommunication and information systems, enabling the storage and transmission, regardless of distance, of all kinds of communication opens a whole range of new possibilities. These developments were boosted by the emergence of information super-highways and networks, including the Internet, through which virtually anybody will be able to have access to any electronic information service irrespective of where in the world he is located. By connecting to communication and information services users create a kind of common space, called "cyber-space", which is used for legitimate purposes but may also be the subject of misuse. These "cyber-space offences" are either committed against the integrity, availability, and confidentiality of computer systems and telecommunication networks or they consist of the use of such networks of their services to commit traditional offences. The transborder character of such offences, e.g. when committed through the Internet, is in conflict with the territoriality of national law enforcement authorities.

9.   The criminal law must therefore keep abreast of these technological developments which offer highly sophisticated opportunities for misusing facilities of the cyber-space and causing damage to legitimate interests. Given the cross-border nature of information networks, a concerted international effort is needed to deal with such misuse. Whilst

Recommendation No. (89) 9 resulted in the approximation of national concepts regarding certain forms of computer misuse, only a binding international instrument can ensure the necessary efficiency in the fight against these new phenomena. In the framework of such an instrument, in addition to measures of international co-operation, questions of substantive and procedural law, as well as matters that are closely connected with the use of information technology, should be addressed."

10. In addition, the CDPC took into account the Report, prepared – at its request – by Professor H.W.K. Kaspersen, which concluded that " ... it should be looked to another legal instrument with more engagement than a Recommendation, such as a Convention. Such a Convention should not only deal with criminal substantive law matters, but also with criminal procedural questions as well as with international criminal law procedures and agreements."[2] A similar conclusion emerged already from the Report attached to Recommendation No. R (89) 9[3] concerning substantive law and from Recommendation No. R (95) 13[4] concerning problems of procedural law connected with information technology.

11. The new committee's specific terms of reference were as follows:

i. "Examine, in the light of Recommendations No. R (89) 9 on computer-related crime and No. R (95) 13 concerning problems of criminal procedural law connected with information technology, in particular the following subjects:

ii. cyber-space offences, in particular those committed through the use of telecommunication networks, e.g. the Internet, such as illegal money transactions, offering illegal services, violation of copyright, as well as those which violate human dignity and the protection of minors;

iii. other substantive criminal law issues where a common approach may be necessary for the purposes of international co-operation such as definitions, sanctions and responsibility of the actors in cyber-space, including Internet service providers;

iv. the use, including the possibility of transborder use, and the applicability of coercive powers in a technological environment, e.g. interception of telecommunications and electronic surveillance of information networks, e.g. via the Internet, search and seizure in

---

[2] Implementation of Recommendation No. R (89) 9 on computer-related crime, Report prepared by Professor Dr. H.W.K. Kaspersen (doc. CDPC (97) 5 and PC-CY (97) 5, page 106).
[3] See Computer-related crime, Report by the European Committee on Crime Problems, page 86.
[4] See Problems of criminal procedural law connected with information technology, Recommendation No. R (95) 13, principle No. 17.

information-processing systems (including Internet sites), rendering illegal material inaccessible and requiring service providers to comply with special obligations, taking into account the problems caused by particular measures of information security, e.g. encryption;

v. the question of jurisdiction in relation to information technology offences, e.g. to determine the place where the offence was committed (locus delicti) and which law should accordingly apply, including the problem of ne bis idem in the case of multiple jurisdictions and the question how to solve positive jurisdiction conflicts and how to avoid negative jurisdiction conflicts;

vi. questions of international co-operation in the investigation of cyber-space offences, in close co-operation with the Committee of Experts on the Operation of European Conventions in the Penal Field (PC-OC).

The Committee should draft a binding legal instrument, as far as possible, on items i) – v), with particular emphasis on international questions and, if appropriate, accessory recommendations regarding specific issues. The Committee may make suggestions on other issues in the light of technological developments."

12. Further to the CDPC's decision, the Committee of Ministers set up the new committee, called "the Committee of Experts on Crime in Cyber-space (PC-CY)" by decision No. CM/Del/Dec(97)583, taken at the 583rd meeting of the Ministers' Deputies (held on 4 February 1997). The Committee PC-CY started its work in April 1997 and undertook negotiations on a draft international convention on cybercrime. Under its original terms of reference, the Committee was due to finish its work by 31 December 1999. Since by that time the Committee was not yet in a position to fully conclude its negotiations on certain issues in the draft Convention, its terms of reference were extended by decision No. CM/Del/Dec(99)679 of the Ministers' Deputies until 31 December 2000. The European Ministers of Justice expressed their support twice concerning the negotiations: by Resolution No. 1, adopted at their 21st Conference (Prague, June 1997), which recommended the Committee of Ministers to support the work carried out by the CDPC on cybercrime in order to bring domestic criminal law provisions closer to each other and enable the use of effective means of investigation concerning such offences, as well as by Resolution No. 3, adopted at the 23rd Conference of the European Ministers of Justice (London, June 2000), which encouraged the negotiating parties to pursue their efforts with a view to finding appropriate solutions so as to enable the largest possible number of States to become parties to the Convention and acknowledged the need for a swift and efficient system of international co-operation, which duly takes into account the specific requirements of the fight against cybercrime. The member States of the European Union expressed their support to the work of the PC-CY through a Joint Position, adopted in May 1999.

13. Between April 1997 and December 2000, the Committee PC-CY held 10 meetings in plenary and 15 meetings of its open-ended Drafting Group. Following the expiry of its extended terms of reference, the experts held, under the aegis of the CDPC, three more meetings to finalise the draft Explanatory Memorandum and review the draft Convention in the light of the opinion of the Parliamentary Assembly. The Assembly was requested by the Committee of Ministers in October 2000 to give an opinion on the draft Convention, which it adopted at the second part of its plenary session in April 2001.

14. Following a decision taken by the Committee PC-CY, an early version of the draft Convention was declassified and released in April 2000, followed by subsequent drafts released after each plenary meeting, in order to enable the negotiating States to consult with all interested parties. This consultation process proved useful.

15. The revised and finalised draft Convention and its Explanatory Memorandum were submitted for approval to the CDPC at its 50th plenary session in June 2001, following which the text of the draft Convention was submitted to the Committee of Ministers for adoption and opening for signature.

III. The Convention

16. The Convention aims principally at (1) harmonising the domestic criminal substantive law elements of offences and connected provisions in the area of cybercrime (2) providing for domestic criminal procedural law powers necessary for the investigation and prosecution of such offences as well as other offences committed by means of a computer system or evidence in relation to which is in electronic form (3) setting up a fast and effective regime of international co-operation.

17. The Convention, accordingly, contains four chapters: (I) Use of terms; (II) Measures to be taken at domestic level – substantive law and procedural law; (III) International co-operation; (IV) Final clauses.

18. Section 1 of Chapter II (substantive law issues) covers both criminalisation provisions and other connected provisions in the area of computer- or computer-related crime: it first defines 9 offences grouped in 4 different categories, then deals with ancillary liability and sanctions. The following offences are defined by the Convention: illegal access, illegal interception, data interference, system interference, misuse of devices, computer-related forgery, computer-related fraud, offences related to child pornography and offences related to copyright and neighbouring rights.

19. Section 2 of Chapter II (procedural law issues) – the scope of which goes beyond the offences defined in Section 1 in that it applies to any offence committed by means of a computer system or the evidence of which

is in electronic form – determines first the common conditions and safeguards, applicable to all procedural powers in this Chapter. It then sets out the following procedural powers: expedited preservation of stored data; expedited preservation and partial disclosure of traffic data; production order; search and seizure of computer data; real-time collection of traffic data; interception of content data. Chapter II ends with the jurisdiction provisions.

20. Chapter III contains the provisions concerning traditional and computer crime-related mutual assistance as well as extradition rules. It covers traditional mutual assistance in two situations: where no legal basis (treaty, reciprocal legislation, etc.) exists between parties – in which case its provisions apply – and where such a basis exists – in which case the existing arrangements also apply to assistance under this Convention. Computer- or computer-related crime specific assistance applies to both situations and covers, subject to extra-conditions, the same range of procedural powers as defined in Chapter II. In addition, Chapter III contains a provision on a specific type of transborder access to stored computer data which does not require mutual assistance (with consent or where publicly available) and provides for the setting up of a 24/7 network for ensuring speedy assistance among the Parties.

21. Finally, Chapter IV contains the final clauses, which – with certain exceptions – repeat the standard provisions in Council of Europe treaties.

Commentary on the articles of the Convention

Chapter I – Use of terms

Introduction to the definitions at Article 1

22. It was understood by the drafters that under this Convention Parties would not be obliged to copy *verbatim* into their domestic laws the four concepts defined in Article 1, provided that these laws cover such concepts in a manner consistent with the principles of the Convention and offer an equivalent framework for its implementation.

Article 1 (a) – Computer system

23. A computer system under the Convention is a device consisting of hardware and software developed for automatic processing of digital data. It may include input, output, and storage facilities. It may stand alone or be connected in a network with other similar devices "Automatic" means without direct human intervention, "processing of data" means that data in the computer system is operated by executing a computer program. A "computer program" is a set of instructions that can be executed by the computer to achieve the intended result. A computer can run different programs. A computer system usually consists of different devices, to be distinguished as the processor or central processing unit, and peripherals. A "peripheral" is a

device that performs certain specific functions in interaction with the processing unit, such as a printer, video screen, CD reader/writer or other storage device.

24. A network is an interconnection between two or more computer systems. The connections may be earthbound (e.g., wire or cable), wireless (e.g., radio, infrared, or satellite), or both. A network may be geographically limited to a small area (local area networks) or may span a large area (wide area networks), and such networks may themselves be interconnected. The Internet is a global network consisting of many interconnected networks, all using the same protocols. Other types of networks exist, whether or not connected to the Internet, able to communicate computer data among computer systems. Computer systems may be connected to the network as endpoints or as a means to assist in communication on the network. What is essential is that data is exchanged over the network.

Article 1 (b) – Computer data

25. The definition of computer data builds upon the ISO-definition of data. This definition contains the terms "suitable for processing". This means that data is put in such a form that it can be directly processed by the computer system. In order to make clear that data in this Convention has to be understood as data in electronic or other directly processable form, the notion " computer data" is introduced. Computer data that is automatically processed may be the target of one of the criminal offences defined in this Convention as well as the object of the application of one of the investigative measures defined by this Convention.

Article 1 (c) – Service provider

26. The term "service provider" encompasses a broad category of persons that play a particular role with regard to communication or processing of data on computer systems (cf. also comments on Section 2). Under (i) of the definition, it is made clear that both public and private entities which provide users the ability to communicate with one another are covered. Therefore, it is irrelevant whether the users form a closed group or whether the provider offers its services to the public, whether free of charge or for a fee. The closed group can be e.g. the employees of a private enterprise to whom the service is offered by a corporate network.

27. Under (ii) of the definition, it is made clear that the term "service provider" also extends to those entities that store or otherwise process data on behalf of the persons mentioned under (i). Further, the term includes those entities that store or otherwise process data on behalf of the users of the services of those mentioned under (i). For example, under this definition, a service provider includes both services that provide hosting and caching services as well as services that provide a connection to a network. However, a mere provider of content (such as a person who contracts with a

web hosting company to host his website) is not intended to be covered by this definition if such content provider does not also offer communication or related data processing services.

Article 1 (d) – Traffic data

28. For the purposes of this Convention traffic data as defined in Article 1, under subparagraph d., is a category of computer data that is subject to a specific legal regime. This data is generated by computers in the chain of communication in order to route a communication from its origin to its destination. It is therefore auxiliary to the communication itself.

29. In case of an investigation of a criminal offence committed in relation to a computer system, traffic data is needed to trace the source of a communication as a starting point for collecting further evidence or as part of the evidence of the offence. Traffic data might last only ephemerally, which makes it necessary to order its expeditious preservation. Consequently, its rapid disclosure may be necessary to discern the communication's route in order to collect further evidence before it is deleted or to identify a suspect. The ordinary procedure for the collection and disclosure of computer data might therefore be insufficient. Moreover, the collection of this data is regarded in principle to be less intrusive since as such it doesn't reveal the content of the communication which is regarded to be more sensitive.

30. The definition lists exhaustively the categories of traffic data that are treated by a specific regime in this Convention: the origin of a communication, its destination, route, time (GMT), date, size, duration and type of underlying service. Not all of these categories will always be technically available, capable of being produced by a service provider, or necessary for a particular criminal investigation. The "origin" refers to a telephone number, Internet Protocol (IP) address, or similar identification of a communications facility to which a service provider renders services. The "destination" refers to a comparable indication of a communications facility to which communications are transmitted. The term "type of underlying service" refers to the type of service that is being used within the network, e.g., file transfer, electronic mail, or instant messaging.

31. The definition leaves to national legislatures the ability to introduce differentiation in the legal protection of traffic data in accordance with its sensitivity. In this context, Article 15 obliges the Parties to provide for conditions and safeguards that are adequate for protection of human rights and liberties. This implies, *inter alia*, that the substantive criteria and the procedure to apply an investigative power may vary according to the sensitivity of the data.

Chapter II – Measures to be taken at the national level

32. Chapter II (Articles 2-22) contains three sections: substantive criminal law (Articles 2-13), procedural law (Articles 14-21) and jurisdiction (Article 22).

Section 1 – Substantive criminal law

33. The purpose of Section 1 of the Convention (Articles 2-13) is to improve the means to prevent and suppress computer- or computer-related crime by establishing a common minimum standard of relevant offences. This kind of harmonisation alleviates the fight against such crimes on the national and on the international level as well. Correspondence in domestic law may prevent abuses from being shifted to a Party with a previous lower standard. As a consequence, the exchange of useful common experiences in the practical handling of cases may be enhanced, too. International co-operation (esp. extradition and mutual legal assistance) is facilitated e.g. regarding requirements of double criminality.

34. The list of offences included represents a minimum consensus not excluding extensions in domestic law. To a great extent it is based on the guidelines developed in connection with Recommendation No. R (89) 9 of the Council of Europe on computer-related crime and on the work of other public and private international organisations (OECD, UN, AIDP), but taking into account more modern experiences with abuses of expanding telecommunication networks.

35. The section is divided into five titles. Title 1 includes the core of computer-related offences, offences against the confidentiality, integrity and availability of computer data and systems, representing the basic threats, as identified in the discussions on computer and data security to which electronic data processing and communicating systems are exposed. The heading describes the type of crimes which are covered, that is the unauthorised access to and illicit tampering with systems, programmes or data. Titles 2-4 include other types of 'computer-related offences', which play a greater role in practice and where computer and telecommunication systems are used as a means to attack certain legal interests which mostly are protected already by criminal law against attacks using traditional means. The Title 2 offences (computer-related fraud and forgery) have been added by following suggestions in the guidelines of the Council of Europe Recommendation No. R (89) 9. Title 3 covers the 'content-related offences of unlawful production or distribution of child pornography by use of computer systems as one of the most dangerous *modi operandi* in recent times. The committee drafting the Convention discussed the possibility of including other content-related offences, such as the distribution of racist propaganda through computer systems. However, the committee was not in a position to reach consensus on the criminalisation of such conduct. While there was significant support in favour of including this as a criminal offence,

some delegations expressed strong concern about including such a provision on freedom of expression grounds. Noting the complexity of the issue, it was decided that the committee would refer to the European Committee on Crime Problems (CDPC) the issue of drawing up an additional Protocol to the present Convention.

Title 4 sets out 'offences related to infringements of copyright and related rights'. This was included in the Convention because copyright infringements are one of the most widespread forms of computer- or computer-related crime and its escalation is causing international concern. Finally, Title 5 includes additional provisions on attempt, aiding and abetting and sanctions and measures, and, in compliance with recent international instruments, on corporate liability.

36. Although the substantive law provisions relate to offences using information technology, the Convention uses technology-neutral language so that the substantive criminal law offences may be applied to both current and future technologies involved.

37. The drafters of the Convention understood that Parties may exclude petty or insignificant misconduct from implementation of the offences defined in Articles 2-10.

38. A specificity of the offences included is the express requirement that the conduct involved is done "without right". It reflects the insight that the conduct described is not always punishable per se, but may be legal or justified not only in cases where classical legal defences are applicable, like consent, self defence or necessity, but where other principles or interests lead to the exclusion of criminal liability. The expression 'without right' derives its meaning from the context in which it is used. Thus, without restricting how Parties may implement the concept in their domestic law, it may refer to conduct undertaken without authority (whether legislative, executive, administrative, judicial, contractual or consensual) or conduct that is otherwise not covered by established legal defences, excuses, justifications or relevant principles under domestic law. The Convention, therefore, leaves unaffected conduct undertaken pursuant to lawful government authority (for example, where the Party's government acts to maintain public order, protect national security or investigate criminal offences). Furthermore, legitimate and common activities inherent in the design of networks, or legitimate and common operating or commercial practices should not be criminalised. Specific examples of such exceptions from criminalisation are provided in relation to specific offences in the corresponding text of the Explanatory Memorandum below. It is left to the Parties to determine how such exemptions are implemented within their domestic legal systems (under criminal law or otherwise).

39. All the offences contained in the Convention must be committed "intentionally" for criminal liability to apply. In certain cases an additional

specific intentional element forms part of the offence. For instance, in Article 8 on computer-related fraud, the intent to procure an economic benefit is a constituent element of the offence. The drafters of the Convention agreed that the exact meaning of 'intentionally' should be left to national interpretation.

40. Certain articles in the section allow the addition of qualifying circumstances when implementing the Convention in domestic law. In other instances even the possibility of a reservation is granted (cf. Articles 40 and 42). These different ways of a more restrictive approach in criminalisation reflect different assessments of the dangerousness of the behaviour involved or of the need to use criminal law as a countermeasure. This approach provides flexibility to governments and parliaments in determining their criminal policy in this area.

41. Laws establishing these offences should be drafted with as much clarity and specificity as possible, in order to provide adequate foreseeability of the type of conduct that will result in a criminal sanction.

42. In the course of the drafting process, the drafters considered the advisability of criminalising conduct other than those defined at Articles 2-11, including the so-called cyber-squatting, i.e. the fact of registering a domain-name which is identical either to the name of an entity that already exists and is usually well-known or to the trade-name or trademark of a product or company. Cyber-squatters have no intent to make an active use of the domain-name and seek to obtain a financial advantage by forcing the entity concerned, even though indirectly, to pay for the transfer of the ownership over the domain-name. At present this conduct is considered as a trademark-related issue. As trademark violations are not governed by this Convention, the drafters did not consider it appropriate to deal with the issue of criminalisation of such conduct.

Title 1 – Offences against the confidentiality, integrity and availability of computer data and systems

43. The criminal offences defined under (Articles 2-6) are intended to protect the confidentiality, integrity and availability of computer systems or data and not to criminalise legitimate and common activities inherent in the design of networks, or legitimate and common operating or commercial practices.

Illegal access (Article 2)

44. "Illegal access" covers the basic offence of dangerous threats to and attacks against the security (i.e. the confidentiality, integrity and availability) of computer systems and data. The need for protection reflects the interests of organisations and individuals to manage, operate and control their systems in an undisturbed and uninhibited manner. The mere unauthorised

intrusion, i.e. "hacking", "cracking" or "computer trespass" should in principle be illegal in itself. It may lead to impediments to legitimate users of systems and data and may cause alteration or destruction with high costs for reconstruction. Such intrusions may give access to confidential data (including passwords, information about the targeted system) and secrets, to the use of the system without payment or even encourage hackers to commit more dangerous forms of computer-related offences, like computer-related fraud or forgery.

45. The most effective means of preventing unauthorised access is, of course, the introduction and development of effective security measures. However, a comprehensive response has to include also the threat and use of criminal law measures. A criminal prohibition of unauthorised access is able to give additional protection to the system and the data as such and at an early stage against the dangers described above.

46. "Access" comprises the entering of the whole or any part of a computer system (hardware, components, stored data of the system installed, directories, traffic and content-related data). However, it does not include the mere sending of an e-mail message or file to that system. "Access" includes the entering of another computer system, where it is connected via public telecommunication networks, or to a computer system on the same network, such as a LAN (local area network) or Intranet within an organisation. The method of communication (e.g. from a distance, including via wireless links or at a close range) does not matter.

47. The act must also be committed 'without right'. In addition to the explanation given above on this expression, it means that there is no criminalisation of the access authorised by the owner or other right holder of the system or part of it (such as for the purpose of authorised testing or protection of the computer system concerned). Moreover, there is no criminalisation for accessing a computer system that permits free and open access by the public, as such access is "with right."

48. The application of specific technical tools may result in an access under Article 2, such as the access of a web page, directly or through hypertext links, including deep-links or the application of 'cookies' or 'bots' to locate and retrieve information on behalf of communication. The application of such tools per se is not 'without right'. The maintenance of a public website implies consent by the website-owner that it can be accessed by any other web-user. The application of standard tools provided for in the commonly applied communication protocols and programs, is not in itself 'without right', in particular where the rightholder of the accessed system can be considered to have accepted its application, e.g. in the case of 'cookies' by not rejecting the initial instalment or not removing it.

49. Many national legislations already contain provisions on "hacking" offences, but the scope and constituent elements vary considerably. The

broad approach of criminalisation in the first sentence of Article 2 is not undisputed. Opposition stems from situations where no dangers were created by the mere intrusion or where even acts of hacking have led to the detection of loopholes and weaknesses of the security of systems. This has led in a range of countries to a narrower approach requiring additional qualifying circumstances which is also the approach adopted by Recommendation No. R (89) 9 and the proposal of the OECD Working Party in 1985.

50. Parties can take the wide approach and criminalise mere hacking in accordance with the first sentence of Article 2. Alternatively, Parties can attach any or all of the qualifying elements listed in the second sentence: infringing security measures, special intent to obtain computer data, other dishonest intent that justifies criminal culpability, or the requirement that the offence is committed in relation to a computer system that is connected remotely to another computer system. The last option allows Parties to exclude the situation where a person physically accesses a stand-alone computer without any use of another computer system. They may restrict the offence to illegal access to networked computer systems (including public networks provided by telecommunication services and private networks, such as Intranets or Extranets).

Illegal interception (Article 3)

51. This provision aims to protect the right of privacy of data communication. The offence represents the same violation of the privacy of communications as traditional tapping and recording of oral telephone conversations between persons. The right to privacy of correspondence is enshrined in Article 8 of the European Convention on Human Rights. The offence established under Article 3 applies this principle to all forms of electronic data transfer, whether by telephone, fax, e-mail or file transfer.

52. The text of the provision has been mainly taken from the offence of 'unauthorised interception' contained in Recommendation No. R (89) 9. In the present Convention it has been made clear that the communications involved concern "transmissions of computer data" as well as electromagnetic radiation, under the circumstances as explained below.

53. Interception by 'technical means' relates to listening to, monitoring or surveillance of the content of communications, to the procuring of the content of data either directly, through access and use of the computer system, or indirectly, through the use of electronic eavesdropping or tapping devices. Interception may also involve recording. Technical means includes technical devices fixed to transmission lines as well as devices to collect and record wireless communications. They may include the use of software, passwords and codes. The requirement of using technical means is a restrictive qualification to avoid over-criminalisation.

54. The offence applies to 'non-public' transmissions of computer data. The term 'non-public' qualifies the nature of the transmission (communication) process and not the nature of the data transmitted. The data communicated may be publicly available information, but the parties wish to communicate confidentially. Or data may be kept secret for commercial purposes until the service is paid, as in Pay-TV. Therefore, the term 'non-public' does not *per se* exclude communications via public networks. Communications of employees, whether or not for business purposes, which constitute "non-public transmissions of computer data" are also protected against interception without right under Article 3 (see e.g. ECHR judgment in Halford v. UK case, 25 June 1997, 20605/92).

55. The communication in the form of transmission of computer data can take place inside a single computer system (flowing from CPU to screen or printer, for example), between two computer systems belonging to the same person, two computers communicating with one another, or a computer and a person (e.g. through the keyboard). Nonetheless, Parties may require as an additional element that the communication be transmitted between computer systems remotely connected.

56. It should be noted that the fact that the notion of 'computer system' may also encompass radio connections does not mean that a Party is under an obligation to criminalise the interception of any radio transmission which, even though 'non-public', takes place in a relatively open and easily accessible manner and therefore can be intercepted, for example by radio amateurs.

57. The creation of an offence in relation to 'electromagnetic emissions' will ensure a more comprehensive scope. Electromagnetic emissions may be emitted by a computer during its operation. Such emissions are not considered as 'data' according to the definition provided in Article 1. However, data can be reconstructed from such emissions. Therefore, the interception of data from electromagnetic emissions from a computer system is included as an offence under this provision.

58. For criminal liability to attach, the illegal interception must be committed "intentionally", and "without right". The act is justified, for example, if the intercepting person has the right to do so, if he acts on the instructions or by authorisation of the participants of the transmission (including authorised testing or protection activities agreed to by the participants), or if surveillance is lawfully authorised in the interests of national security or the detection of offences by investigating authorities. It was also understood that the use of common commercial practices, such as employing 'cookies', is not intended to be criminalised as such, as not being an interception "without right". With respect to non-public communications of employees protected under Article 3 (see above paragraph 54), domestic law may provide a ground for legitimate interception of such communications. Under Article 3, interception in such circumstances would be considered as undertaken "with right".

59. In some countries, interception may be closely related to the offence of unauthorised access to a computer system. In order to ensure consistency of the prohibition and application of the law, countries that require dishonest intent, or that the offence be committed in relation to a computer system that is connected to another computer system in accordance with Article 2, may also require similar qualifying elements to attach criminal liability in this article. These elements should be interpreted and applied in conjunction with the other elements of the offence, such as "intentionally" and "without right".

Data interference (Article 4)

60. The aim of this provision is to provide computer data and computer programs with protection similar to that enjoyed by corporeal objects against intentional infliction of damage. The protected legal interest here is the integrity and the proper functioning or use of stored computer data or computer programs.

61. In paragraph 1, 'damaging' and 'deteriorating' as overlapping acts relate in particular to a negative alteration of the integrity or of information content of data and programmes. 'Deletion' of data is the equivalent of the destruction of a corporeal thing. It destroys them and makes them unrecognisable. Suppressing of computer data means any action that prevents or terminates the availability of the data to the person who has access to the computer or the data carrier on which it was stored. The term 'alteration' means the modification of existing data. The input of malicious codes, such as viruses and Trojan horses is, therefore, covered under this paragraph, as is the resulting modification of the data.

62. The above acts are only punishable if committed "without right". Common activities inherent in the design of networks or common operating or commercial practices, such as, for example, for the testing or protection of the security of a computer system authorised by the owner or operator, or the reconfiguration of a computer's operating system that takes place when the operator of a system acquires new software (e.g., software permitting access to the Internet that disables similar, previously installed programs), are with right and therefore are not criminalised by this article. The modification of traffic data for the purpose of facilitating anonymous communications (e.g., the activities of anonymous remailer systems), or the modification of data for the purpose of secure communications (e.g. encryption), should in principle be considered a legitimate protection of privacy and, therefore, be considered as being undertaken with right. However, Parties may wish to criminalise certain abuses related to anonymous communications, such as where the packet header information is altered in order to conceal the identity of the perpetrator in committing a crime.

63. In addition, the offender must have acted "intentionally".

64. Paragraph 2 allows Parties to enter a reservation concerning the offence in that they may require that the conduct result in serious harm. The interpretation of what constitutes such serious harm is left to domestic legislation, but Parties should notify the Secretary General of the Council of Europe of their interpretation if use is made of this reservation possibility.

System interference (Article 5)

65. This is referred to in Recommendation No. (89) 9 as computer sabotage. The provision aims at criminalising the intentional hindering of the lawful use of computer systems including telecommunications facilities by using or influencing computer data. The protected legal interest is the interest of operators and users of computer or telecommunication systems being able to have them function properly. The text is formulated in a neutral way so that all kinds of functions can be protected by it.

66. The term "hindering" refers to actions that interfere with the proper functioning of the computer system. Such hindering must take place by inputting, transmitting, damaging, deleting, altering or suppressing computer data.

67. The hindering must furthermore be "serious" in order to give rise to criminal sanction. Each Party shall determine for itself what criteria must be fulfilled in order for the hindering to be considered "serious." For example, a Party may require a minimum amount of damage to be caused in order for the hindering to be considered serious. The drafters considered as "serious" the sending of data to a particular system in such a form, size or frequency that it has a significant detrimental effect on the ability of the owner or operator to use the system, or to communicate with other systems (e.g., by means of programs that generate "denial of service" attacks, malicious codes such as viruses that prevent or substantially slow the operation of the system, or programs that send huge quantities of electronic mail to a recipient in order to block the communications functions of the system).

68. The hindering must be "without right". Common activities inherent in the design of networks, or common operational or commercial practices are with right. These include, for example, the testing of the security of a computer system, or its protection, authorised by its owner or operator, or the reconfiguration of a computer's operating system that takes place when the operator of a system installs new software that disables similar, previously installed programs. Therefore, such conduct is not criminalised by this article, even if it causes serious hindering.

69. The sending of unsolicited e-mail, for commercial or other purposes, may cause nuisance to its recipient, in particular when such messages are sent in large quantities or with a high frequency ("spamming"). In the opinion of the drafters, such conduct should only be criminalised where the

communication is intentionally and seriously hindered. Nevertheless, Parties may have a different approach to hindrance under their law, e.g. by making particular acts of interference administrative offences or otherwise subject to sanction. The text leaves it to the Parties to determine the extent to which the functioning of the system should be hindered – partially or totally, temporarily or permanently – to reach the threshold of harm that justifies sanction, administrative or criminal, under their law.

70. The offence must be committed intentionally, that is the perpetrator must have the intent to seriously hinder.

Misuse of devices (Article 6)

71. This provision establishes as a separate and independent criminal offence the intentional commission of specific illegal acts regarding certain devices or access data to be misused for the purpose of committing the above-described offences against the confidentiality, the integrity and availability of computer systems or data. As the commission of these offences often requires the possession of means of access ("hacker tools") or other tools, there is a strong incentive to acquire them for criminal purposes which may then lead to the creation of a kind of black market in their production and distribution. To combat such dangers more effectively, the criminal law should prohibit specific potentially dangerous acts at the source, preceding the commission of offences under Articles 2-5. In this respect the provision builds upon recent developments inside the Council of Europe (European Convention on the legal protection of services based on, or consisting of, conditional access – ETS No. 178) and the European Union (Directive 98/84/EC of the European Parliament and of the Council of 20 November 1998 on the legal protection of services based on, or consisting of, conditional access) and relevant provisions in some countries. A similar approach has already been taken in the 1929 Geneva Convention on currency counterfeiting.

72. Paragraph 1(a)1 criminalises the production, sale, procurement for use, import, distribution or otherwise making available of a device, including a computer programme, designed or adapted primarily for the purpose of committing any of the offences established in Articles 2-5 of the present Convention. 'Distribution' refers to the active act of forwarding data to others, while 'making available' refers to the placing online devices for the use of others. This term also intends to cover the creation or compilation of hyperlinks in order to facilitate access to such devices. The inclusion of a 'computer program' refers to programs that are for example designed to alter or even destroy data or interfere with the operation of systems, such as virus programs, or programs designed or adapted to gain access to computer systems.

73. The drafters debated at length whether the devices should be restricted to those which are designed exclusively or specifically for committing

offences, thereby excluding dual-use devices. This was considered to be too narrow. It could lead to insurmountable difficulties of proof in criminal proceedings, rendering the provision practically inapplicable or only applicable in rare instances. The alternative to include all devices even if they are legally produced and distributed, was also rejected. Only the subjective element of the intent of committing a computer offence would then be decisive for imposing a punishment, an approach which in the area of money counterfeiting also has not been adopted. As a reasonable compromise the Convention restricts its scope to cases where the devices are objectively designed, or adapted, primarily for the purpose of committing an offence. This alone will usually exclude dual-use devices.

74. Paragraph 1(a)2 criminalises the production, sale, procurement for use, import, distribution or otherwise making available of a computer password, access code or similar data by which the whole or any part of a computer system is capable of being accessed.

75. Paragraph 1(b) creates the offence of possessing the items set out in paragraph 1(a)1 or 1(a)2. Parties are permitted, by the last phrase of paragraph 1(b), to require by law that a number of such items be possessed. The number of items possessed goes directly to proving criminal intent. It is up to each Party to decide the number of items required before criminal liability attaches.

76. The offence requires that it be committed intentionally and without right. In order to avoid the danger of overcriminalisation where devices are produced and put on the market for legitimate purposes, e.g. to counter-attacks against computer systems, further elements are added to restrict the offence. Apart from the general intent requirement, there must be the specific (i.e. direct) intent that the device is used for the purpose of committing any of the offences established in Articles 2-5 of the Convention.

77. Paragraph 2 sets out clearly that those tools created for the authorised testing or the protection of a computer system are not covered by the provision. This concept is already contained in the expression 'without right'. For example, test-devices ('cracking-devices') and network analysis devices designed by industry to control the reliability of their information technology products or to test system security are produced for legitimate purposes, and would be considered to be 'with right'.

78. Due to different assessments of the need to apply the offence of "Misuse of Devices" to all of the different kinds of computer offences in Articles 2-5, paragraph 3 allows, on the basis of a reservation (cf. Article 42), to restrict the offence in domestic law. Each Party is, however, obliged to criminalise at least the sale, distribution or making available of a computer password or access data as described in paragraph 1(a)2.

Title 2 – Computer-related offences

79. Articles 7-10 relate to ordinary crimes that are frequently committed through the use of a computer system. Most States already have criminalised these ordinary crimes, and their existing laws may or may not be sufficiently broad to extend to situations involving computer networks (for example, existing child pornography laws of some States may not extend to electronic images). Therefore, in the course of implementing these articles, States must examine their existing laws to determine whether they apply to situations in which computer systems or networks are involved. If existing offences already cover such conduct, there is no requirement to amend existing offences or enact new ones.

80. "Computer-related forgery" and "Computer-related fraud" deal with certain computer-related offences, i.e. computer-related forgery and computer-related fraud as two specific kinds of manipulation of computer systems or computer data. Their inclusion acknowledges the fact that in many countries certain traditional legal interests are not sufficiently protected against new forms of interference and attacks.

Computer-related forgery (Article 7)

81. The purpose of this article is to create a parallel offence to the forgery of tangible documents. It aims at filling gaps in criminal law related to traditional forgery, which requires visual readability of statements, or declarations embodied in a document and which does not apply to electronically stored data. Manipulations of such data with evidentiary value may have the same serious consequences as traditional acts of forgery if a third party is thereby misled. Computer-related forgery involves unauthorised creating or altering stored data so that they acquire a different evidentiary value in the course of legal transactions, which relies on the authenticity of information contained in the data, is subject to a deception. The protected legal interest is the security and reliability of electronic data which may have consequences for legal relations.

82. It should be noted that national concepts of forgery vary greatly. One concept is based on the authenticity as to the author of the document, and others are based on the truthfulness of the statement contained in the document. However, it was agreed that the deception as to authenticity refers at minimum to the issuer of the data, regardless of the correctness or veracity of the contents of the data. Parties may go further and include under the term "authentic" the genuineness of the data.

83. This provision covers data which is the equivalent of a public or private document, which has legal effects. The unauthorised "input" of correct or incorrect data brings about a situation that corresponds to the making of a false document. Subsequent alterations (modifications, variations, partial changes), deletions (removal of data from a data medium) and suppression

(holding back, concealment of data) correspond in general to the falsification of a genuine document.

84. The term "for legal purposes" refers also to legal transactions and documents which are legally relevant.

85. The final sentence of the provision allows Parties, when implementing the offence in domestic law, to require in addition an intent to defraud, or similar dishonest intent, before criminal liability attaches.

Computer-related fraud (Article 8)

86. With the arrival of the technological revolution the opportunities for committing economic crimes such as fraud, including credit card fraud, have multiplied. Assets represented or administered in computer systems (electronic funds, deposit money) have become the target of manipulations like traditional forms of property. These crimes consist mainly of input manipulations, where incorrect data is fed into the computer, or by programme manipulations and other interferences with the course of data processing. The aim of this article is to criminalise any undue manipulation in the course of data processing with the intention to effect an illegal transfer of property.

87. To ensure that all possible relevant manipulations are covered, the constituent elements of 'input', 'alteration', 'deletion' or 'suppression' in Article 8(a) are supplemented by the general act of 'interference with the functioning of a computer programme or system' in Article 8(b). The elements of 'input, alteration, deletion or suppression' have the same meaning as in the previous articles. Article 8(b) covers acts such as hardware manipulations, acts suppressing printouts and acts affecting recording or flow of data, or the sequence in which programs are run.

88. The computer fraud manipulations are criminalised if they produce a direct economic or possessory loss of another person's property and the perpetrator acted with the intent of procuring an unlawful economic gain for himself or for another person. The term 'loss of property', being a broad notion, includes loss of money, tangibles and intangibles with an economic value.

89. The offence must be committed "without right", and the economic benefit must be obtained without right. Of course, legitimate common commercial practices, which are intended to procure an economic benefit, are not meant to be included in the offence established by this article because they are conducted with right. For example, activities carried out pursuant to a valid contract between the affected persons are with right (e.g. disabling a website as entitled pursuant to the terms of the contract).

90. The offence has to be committed "intentionally". The general intent element refers to the computer manipulation or interference causing loss of property to another. The offence also requires a specific fraudulent or other dishonest intent to gain an economic or other benefit for oneself or another. Thus, for example, commercial practices with respect to market competition that may cause an economic detriment to a person and benefit to another, but are not carried out with fraudulent or dishonest intent, are not meant to be included in the offence established by this article. For example, the use of information gathering programs to comparison shop on the Internet ("bots"), even if not authorised by a site visited by the "bot" is not intended to be criminalised.

Title 3 – Content-related offences

Offences related to child pornography (Article 9)

91. Article 9 on child pornography seeks to strengthen protective measures for children, including their protection against sexual exploitation, by modernising criminal law provisions to more effectively circumscribe the use of computer systems in the commission of sexual offences against children.

92. This provision responds to the preoccupation of Heads of State and Government of the Council of Europe, expressed at their 2nd Summit (Strasbourg, 10-11 October 1997) in their Action Plan (item III.4) and corresponds to an international trend that seeks to ban child pornography, as evidenced by the recent adoption of the Optional Protocol to the UN Convention on the rights of the child, on the sale of children, child prostitution and child pornography and the recent European Commission initiative on combating sexual exploitation of children and child pornography (COM2000/854).

93. This provision criminalises various aspects of the electronic production, possession and distribution of child pornography. Most States already criminalise the traditional production and physical distribution of child pornography, but with the ever-increasing use of the Internet as the primary instrument for trading such material, it was strongly felt that specific provisions in an international legal instrument were essential to combat this new form of sexual exploitation and endangerment of children. It is widely believed that such material and on-line practices, such as the exchange of ideas, fantasies and advice among paedophiles, play a role in supporting, encouraging or facilitating sexual offences against children.

94. Paragraph 1(a) criminalises the production of child pornography for the purpose of distribution through a computer system. This provision was felt necessary to combat the dangers described above at their source.

95. Paragraph 1(b) criminalises the 'offering' of child pornography through a computer system. 'Offering' is intended to cover soliciting others to obtain

child pornography. It implies that the person offering the material can actually provide it. 'Making available' is intended to cover the placing of child pornography on line for the use of others e.g. by means of creating child pornography sites. This paragraph also intends to cover the creation or compilation of hyperlinks to child pornography sites in order to facilitate access to child pornography.

96. Paragraph 1(c) criminalises the distribution or transmission of child pornography through a computer system. 'Distribution' is the active dissemination of the material. Sending child pornography through a computer system to another person would be addressed by the offence of 'transmitting' child pornography.

97. The term 'procuring for oneself or for another' in paragraph 1(d) means actively obtaining child pornography, e.g. by downloading it.

98. The possession of child pornography in a computer system or on a data carrier, such as a diskette or CD-Rom, is criminalised in paragraph 1(e). The possession of child pornography stimulates demand for such material. An effective way to curtail the production of child pornography is to attach criminal consequences to the conduct of each participant in the chain from production to possession.

99. The term 'pornographic material' in paragraph 2 is governed by national standards pertaining to the classification of materials as obscene, inconsistent with public morals or similarly corrupt. Therefore, material having an artistic, medical, scientific or similar merit may be considered not to be pornographic. The visual depiction includes data stored on computer diskette or on other electronic means of storage, which are capable of conversion into a visual image.

100. A 'sexually explicit conduct' covers at least real or simulated: a) sexual intercourse, including genital-genital, oral-genital, anal-genital or oral-anal, between minors, or between an adult and a minor, of the same or opposite sex; b) bestiality; c) masturbation; d) sadistic or masochistic abuse in a sexual context; or e) lascivious exhibition of the genitals or the pubic area of a minor. It is not relevant whether the conduct depicted is real or simulated.

101. The three types of material defined in paragraph 2 for the purposes of committing the offences contained in paragraph 1 cover depictions of sexual abuse of a real child (2a), pornographic images which depict a person appearing to be a minor engaged in sexually explicit conduct (2b), and finally images, which, although 'realistic', do not in fact involve a real child engaged in sexually explicit conduct (2c). This latter scenario includes pictures which are altered, such as morphed images of natural persons, or even generated entirely by the computer.

102. In the three cases covered by paragraph 2, the protected legal interests are slightly different. Paragraph 2(a) focuses more directly on the protection against child abuse. Paragraphs 2(b) and 2(c) aim at providing protection against behaviour that, while not necessarily creating harm to the 'child' depicted in the material, as there might not be a real child, might be used to encourage or seduce children into participating in such acts, and hence form part of a subculture favouring child abuse.

103. The term 'without right' does not exclude legal defences, excuses or similar relevant principles that relieve a person of responsibility under specific circumstances. Accordingly, the term 'without right' allows a Party to take into account fundamental rights, such as freedom of thought, expression and privacy. In addition, a Party may provide a defence in respect of conduct related to "pornographic material" having an artistic, medical, scientific or similar merit. In relation to paragraph 2(b), the reference to 'without right' could also allow, for example, that a Party may provide that a person is relieved of criminal responsibility if it is established that the person depicted is not a minor in the sense of this provision.

104. Paragraph 3 defines the term 'minor' in relation to child pornography in general as all persons under 18 years, in accordance with the definition of a 'child' in the UN Convention on the Rights of the Child (Article 1). It was considered an important policy matter to set a uniform international standard regarding age. It should be noted that the age refers to the use of (real or fictitious) children as sexual objects, and is separate from the age of consent for sexual relations.

Nevertheless, recognising that certain States require a lower age-limit in national legislation regarding child pornography, the last phrase of paragraph 3 allows Parties to require a different age-limit, provided it is not less than 16 years.

105. This article lists different types of illicit acts related to child pornography which, as in Articles 2-8, Parties are obligated to criminalise if committed "intentionally." Under this standard, a person is not liable unless he has an intent to offer, make available, distribute, transmit, produce or possess child pornography. Parties may adopt a more specific standard (see, for example, applicable European Community law in relation to service provider liability), in which case that standard would govern. For example, liability may be imposed if there is "knowledge and control" over the information which is transmitted or stored. It is not sufficient, for example, that a service provider served as a conduit for, or hosted a website or newsroom containing such material, without the required intent under domestic law in the particular case. Moreover, a service provider is not required to monitor conduct to avoid criminal liability.

106. Paragraph 4 permits Parties to make reservations regarding paragraph 1(d) and (e), and paragraph 2(b) and (c). The right not to apply these

sections of the provision may be made in part or in whole. Any such reservation should be declared to the Secretary General of the Council of Europe at the time of signature or when depositing the Party's instruments of ratification, acceptance, approval or accession, in accordance with Article 42.

Title 4 – Offences related to infringements of copyright and related rights

Offences related to infringements of copyright and related rights (Article 10)

107. Infringements of intellectual property rights, in particular of copyright, are among the most commonly committed offences on the Internet, which cause concern both to copyright holders and those who work professionally with computer networks. The reproduction and dissemination on the Internet of protected works, without the approval of the copyright holder, are extremely frequent. Such protected works include literary, photographic, musical, audio-visual and other works. The ease with which unauthorised copies may be made due to digital technology and the scale of reproduction and dissemination in the context of electronic networks made it necessary to include provisions on criminal law sanctions and enhance international co-operation in this field.

108. Each Party is obliged to criminalise wilful infringements of copyright and related rights, sometimes referred to as neighbouring rights, arising from the agreements listed in the article, when such infringements have been committed by means of a computer system and on a commercial scale". Paragraph 1 provides for criminal sanctions against infringements of copyright by means of a computer system. Infringement of copyright is already an offence in almost all States. Paragraph 2 deals with the infringement of related rights by means of a computer system.

109. Infringement of both copyright and related rights is as defined under the law of each Party and pursuant to the obligations the Party has undertaken in respect of certain international instruments. While each Party is required to establish as criminal offences those infringements, the precise manner in which such infringements are defined under domestic law may vary from State to State. However, criminalisation obligations under the Convention do not cover intellectual property infringements other than those explicitly addressed in Article 10 and thus exclude patent or trademark-related violations.

110. With regard to paragraph 1, the agreements referred to are the Paris Act of 24 July 1971 of the Bern Convention for the Protection of Literary and Artistic Works, the Agreement on Trade-Related Aspects of Intellectual Property Rights (TRIPS), and the World Intellectual Property Organisation (WIPO) Copyright Treaty. With regard to paragraph 2, the international

instruments cited are the International Convention for the Protection of Performers, Producers of Phonograms and Broadcasting Organisations (Rome Convention), the Agreement on Trade-Related Aspects of Intellectual Property Rights (TRIPS) and the World Intellectual Property Organisation (WIPO) Performances and Phonograms Treaty. The use of the term "pursuant to the obligations it has undertaken" in both paragraphs makes it clear that a Contracting Party to the current Convention is not bound to apply agreements cited to which it is not a Party; moreover, if a Party has made a reservation or declaration permitted under one of the agreements, that reservation may limit the extent of its obligation under the present Convention.

111. The WIPO Copyright Treaty and the WIPO Performances and Phonograms Treaty had not entered into force at the time of concluding the present Convention. These treaties are nevertheless important as they significantly update the international protection for intellectual property (especially with regard to the new right of 'making available' of protected material 'on demand' over the Internet) and improve the means to fight violations of intellectual property rights worldwide. However it is understood that the infringements of rights established by these treaties need not be criminalised under the present Convention until these treaties have entered into force with respect to a Party.

112. The obligation to criminalise infringements of copyright and related rights pursuant to obligations undertaken in international instruments does not extend to any moral rights conferred by the named instruments (such as in Article 6bis of the Bern Convention and in Article 5 of the WIPO Copyright Treaty).

113. Copyright and related rights offences must be committed "wilfully" for criminal liability to apply. In contrast to all the other substantive law provisions of this Convention, the term "wilfully" is used instead of "intentionally" in both paragraphs 1 and 2, as this is the term employed in the TRIPS Agreement (Article 61), governing the obligation to criminalise copyright violations.

114. The provisions are intended to provide for criminal sanctions against infringements 'on a commercial scale' and by means of a computer system. This is in line with Article 61 of the TRIPS Agreement which requires criminal sanctions in copyright matters only in the case of "piracy on a commercial scale". However, Parties may wish to go beyond the threshold of "commercial scale" and criminalise other types of copyright infringement as well.

115. The term "without right" has been omitted from the text of this article as redundant, since the term "infringement" already denotes use of the copyrighted material without authorisation. The absence of the term "without right" does not a contrario exclude application of criminal law defences,

justifications and principles governing the exclusion of criminal liability associated with the term "without right" elsewhere in the Convention.

116. Paragraph 3 allows Parties not to impose criminal liability under paragraphs 1 and 2 in "limited circumstances" (e.g. parallel imports, rental rights), as long as other effective remedies, including civil and/or administrative measures, are available. This provision essentially allows Parties a limited exemption from the obligation to impose criminal liability, provided that they do not derogate from obligations under Article 61 of the TRIPS Agreement, which is the minimum pre-existing criminalisation requirement.

117. This article shall in no way be interpreted to extend the protection granted to authors, film producers, performers, producers of phonograms, broadcasting organisations or other right holders to persons that do not meet the criteria for eligibility under domestic law or international agreement.

Title 5 – Ancillary liability and sanctions

Attempt and aiding or abetting (Article 11)

118. The purpose of this article is to establish additional offences related to attempt and aiding or abetting the commission of the offences defined in the Convention. As discussed further below, it is not required that a Party criminalise the attempt to commit each offence established in the Convention.

119. Paragraph 1 requires Parties to establish as criminal offences aiding or abetting the commission of any of the offences under Articles 2-10. Liability arises for aiding or abetting where the person who commits a crime established in the Convention is aided by another person who also intends that the crime be committed. For example, although the transmission of harmful content data or malicious code through the Internet requires the assistance of service providers as a conduit, a service provider that does not have the criminal intent cannot incur liability under this section. Thus, there is no duty on a service provider to actively monitor content to avoid criminal liability under this provision.

120. With respect to paragraph 2 on attempt, some offences defined in the Convention, or elements of these offences, were considered to be conceptually difficult to attempt (for example, the elements of offering or making available of child pornography). Moreover, some legal systems limit the offences for which the attempt is punished. Accordingly, it is only required that the attempt be criminalised with respect to offences established in accordance with Articles 3, 4, 5, 7, 8, 9(1)(a) and 9(1)(c).

121. As with all the offences established in accordance with the Convention, attempt and aiding or abetting must be committed intentionally.

122. Paragraph 3 was added to address the difficulties Parties may have with paragraph 2, given the widely varying concepts in different legislations and despite the effort in paragraph 2 to exempt certain aspects from the provision on attempt. A Party may declare that it reserves the right not to apply paragraph 2 in part or in whole. This means that any Party making a reservation as to that provision will have no obligation to criminalise attempt at all, or may select the offences or parts of offences to which it will attach criminal sanctions in relation to attempt. The reservation aims at enabling the widest possible ratification of the Convention while permitting Parties to preserve some of their fundamental legal concepts.

Corporate liability (Article 12)

123. Article 12 deals with the liability of legal persons. It is consistent with the current legal trend to recognise corporate liability. It is intended to impose liability on corporations, associations and similar legal persons for the criminal actions undertaken by a person in a leading position within such legal person, where undertaken for the benefit of that legal person. Article 12 also contemplates liability where such a leading person fails to supervise or control an employee or an agent of the legal person, where such failure facilitates the commission by that employee or agent of one of the offences established in the Convention.

124. Under paragraph 1, four conditions need to be met for liability to attach. First, one of the offences described in the Convention must have been committed. Second, the offence must have been committed for the benefit of the legal person. Third, a person who has a leading position must have committed the offence (including aiding and abetting). The term "person who has a leading position" refers to a natural person who has a high position in the organisation, such as a director. Fourth, the person who has a leading position must have acted on the basis of one of these powers – a power of representation or an authority to take decisions or to exercise control – which demonstrate that such a physical person acted within the scope of his or her authority to engage the liability of the legal person. In sum, paragraph 1 obligates Parties to have the ability to impose liability on the legal person only for offences committed by such leading persons.

125. In addition, paragraph 2 obligates Parties to have the ability to impose liability upon a legal person where the crime is committed not by the leading person described in paragraph 1, but by another person acting under the legal person's authority, i.e., one of its employees or agents acting within the scope of their authority. The conditions that must be fulfilled before liability can attach are that (1) an offence has been committed by such an employee or agent of the legal person, (2) the offence has been committed for the benefit of the legal person; and (3) the commission of the offence has been made possible by the leading person having failed to supervise the employee or agent. In this context, failure to supervise should be interpreted

to include failure to take appropriate and reasonable measures to prevent employees or agents from committing criminal activities on behalf of the legal person. Such appropriate and reasonable measures could be determined by various factors, such as the type of the business, its size, the standards or the established business best practices, etc. This should not be interpreted as requiring a general surveillance regime over employee communications (see also paragraph 54). A service provider does not incur liability by virtue of the fact that a crime was committed on its system by a customer, user or other third person, because the term "acting under its authority" applies exclusively to employees and agents acting within the scope of their authority.

126. Liability under this Article may be criminal, civil or administrative. Each Party has the flexibility to choose to provide for any or all of these forms of liability, in accordance with the legal principles of each Party, as long as it meets the criteria of Article 13, paragraph 2, that the sanction or measure be "effective, proportionate and dissuasive" and includes monetary sanctions.

127. Paragraph 4 clarifies that corporate liability does not exclude individual liability.

Sanctions and measures (Article 13)

128. This article is closely related to Articles 2-11, which define various computer- or computer-related crimes that should be made punishable under criminal law. In accordance with the obligations imposed by those articles, this provision obliges the Contracting Parties to draw consequences from the serious nature of these offences by providing for criminal sanctions that are 'effective, proportionate and dissuasive' and, in the case of natural persons, include the possibility of imposing prison sentences.

129. Legal persons whose liability is to be established in accordance with Article 12 shall also be subject to sanctions that are 'effective, proportionate and dissuasive', which can be criminal, administrative or civil in nature. Contracting Parties are compelled, under paragraph 2, to provide for the possibility of imposing monetary sanctions on legal persons.

130. The article leaves open the possibility of other sanctions or measures reflecting the seriousness of the offences, for example, measures could include injunction or forfeiture. It leaves to the Parties the discretionary power to create a system of criminal offences and sanctions that is compatible with their existing national legal systems.

Section 2 – Procedural law

131. The articles in this Section describe certain procedural measures to be taken at the national level for the purpose of criminal investigation of the offences established in Section 1, other criminal offences committed by

means of a computer system and the collection of evidence in electronic form of a criminal offence. In accordance with Article 39, paragraph 3, nothing in the Convention requires or invites a Party to establish powers or procedures other than those contained in this Convention, nor precludes a Party from doing so.

132. The technological revolution, which encompasses the "electronic highway" where numerous forms of communication and services are interrelated and interconnected through the sharing of common transmission media and carriers, has altered the sphere of criminal law and criminal procedure. The ever-expanding network of communications opens new doors for criminal activity in respect of both traditional offences and new technological crimes. Not only must substantive criminal law keep abreast of these new abuses, but so must criminal procedural law and investigative techniques. Equally, safeguards should also be adapted or developed to keep abreast of the new technological environment and new procedural powers.

133. One of the major challenges in combating crime in the networked environment is the difficulty in identifying the perpetrator and assessing the extent and impact of the criminal act. A further problem is caused by the volatility of electronic data, which may be altered, moved or deleted in seconds. For example, a user who is in control of the data may use the computer system to erase the data that is the subject of a criminal investigation, thereby destroying the evidence. Speed and, sometimes, secrecy are often vital for the success of an investigation.

134. The Convention adapts traditional procedural measures, such as search and seizure, to the new technological environment. Additionally, new measures have been created, such as expedited preservation of data, in order to ensure that traditional measures of collection, such as search and seizure, remain effective in the volatile technological environment. As data in the new technological environment is not always static, but may be flowing in the process of communication, other traditional collection procedures relevant to telecommunications, such as real-time collection of traffic data and interception of content data, have also been adapted in order to permit the collection of electronic data that is in the process of communication. Some of these measures are set out in Council of Europe Recommendation No. R (95) 13 on problems of criminal procedural law connected with information technology.

135. All the provisions referred to in this Section aim at permitting the obtaining or collection of data for the purpose of specific criminal investigations or proceedings. The drafters of the present Convention discussed whether the Convention should impose an obligation for service providers to routinely collect and retain traffic data for a certain fixed period of time, but did not include any such obligation due to lack of consensus.

136. The procedures in general refer to all types of data, including three specific types of computer data (traffic data, content data and subscriber data), which may exist in two forms (stored or in the process of communication). Definitions of some of these terms are provided in Articles 1 and 18. The applicability of a procedure to a particular type or form of electronic data depends on the nature and form of the data and the nature of the procedure, as specifically described in each article.

137. In adapting traditional procedural laws to the new technological environment, the question of appropriate terminology arises in the provisions of this section. The options included maintaining traditional language ('search' and 'seize'), using new and more technologically oriented computer terms ('access' and 'copy'), as adopted in texts of other international fora on the subject (such as the G8 High Tech Crime Subgroup), or employing a compromise of mixed language ('search or similarly access', and 'seize or similarly secure'). As there is a need to reflect the evolution of concepts in the electronic environment, as well as identify and maintain their traditional roots, the flexible approach of allowing States to use either the old notions of "search and seizure" or the new notions of "access and copying" is employed.

138. All the articles in the Section refer to "competent authorities" and the powers they shall be granted for the purposes of specific criminal investigations or proceedings. In certain countries, only judges have the power to order or authorise the collection or production of evidence, while in other countries prosecutors or other law enforcement officers are entrusted with the same or similar powers. Therefore, 'competent authority' refers to a judicial, administrative or other law enforcement authority that is empowered by domestic law to order, authorise or undertake the execution of procedural measures for the purpose of collection or production of evidence with respect to specific criminal investigations or proceedings.

Title 1 – Common provisions

139. The Section begins with two provisions of a general nature that apply to all the articles relating to procedural law.

Scope of procedural provisions (Article 14)

140. Each State Party is obligated to adopt such legislative and other measures as may be necessary, in accordance with its domestic law and legal framework, to establish the powers and procedures described in this Section for the purpose of "specific criminal investigations or proceedings."

141. Subject to two exceptions, each Party shall apply the powers and procedures established in accordance with this Section to: (i) criminal offences established in accordance with Section 1 of the Convention; (ii) other criminal offences committed by means of a computer system; and

(iii) the collection of evidence in electronic form of a criminal offence. Thus, for the purpose of specific criminal investigations or proceedings, the powers and procedures referred to in this Section shall be applied to offences established in accordance with the Convention, to other criminal offences committed by means of a computer system, and to the collection of evidence in electronic form of a criminal offence. This ensures that evidence in electronic form of any criminal offence can be obtained or collected by means of the powers and procedures set out in this Section. It ensures an equivalent or parallel capability for the obtaining or collection of computer data as exists under traditional powers and procedures for non-electronic data. The Convention makes it explicit that Parties should incorporate into their laws the possibility that information contained in digital or other electronic form can be used as evidence before a court in criminal proceedings, irrespective of the nature of the criminal offence that is prosecuted.

142. There are two exceptions to this scope of application. First, Article 21 provides that the power to intercept content data shall be limited to a range of serious offences to be determined by domestic law. Many States limit the power of interception of oral communications or telecommunications to a range of serious offences, in recognition of the privacy of oral communications and telecommunications and the intrusiveness of this investigative measure. Likewise, this Convention only requires Parties to establish interception powers and procedures in relation to content data of specified computer communications in respect of a range of serious offences to be determined by domestic law.

143. Second, a Party may reserve the right to apply the measures in Article 20 (real-time collection of traffic data) only to offences or categories of offences specified in the reservation, provided that the range of such offences or categories is not more restricted than the range of offences to which it applies the interception measures referred to in Article 21. Some States consider the collection of traffic data as being equivalent to the collection of content data in terms of privacy and intrusiveness. The right of reservation would permit these States to limit the application of the measures to collect traffic data, in real-time, to the same range of offences to which it applies the powers and procedures of real-time interception of content data. Many States, however, do not consider the interception of content data and the collection of traffic data to be equivalent in terms of privacy interests and degree of intrusiveness, as the collection of traffic data alone does not collect or disclose the content of the communication. As the real-time collection of traffic data can be very important in tracing the source or destination of computer communications (thus, assisting in identifying criminals), the Convention invites Parties that exercise the right of reservation to limit their reservation so as to enable the broadest application of the powers and procedures provided to collect, in real-time, traffic data.

144. Paragraph (b) provides a reservation for countries which, due to existing limitations in their domestic law at the time of the Convention's adoption, cannot intercept communications on computer systems operated for the benefit of a closed group of users and which do not use public communications networks nor are they connected with other computer systems. The term "closed group of users" refers, for example, to a set of users that is limited by association to the service provider, such as the employees of a company for which the company provides the ability to communicate amongst themselves using a computer network. The term "not connected with other computer systems" means that, at the time an order under Articles 20 or 21 would be issued, the system on which communications are being transmitted does not have a physical or logical connection to another computer network. The term "does not employ public communications networks" excludes systems that use public computer networks (including the Internet), public telephone networks or other public telecommunications facilities in transmitting communications, whether or not such use is apparent to the users.

Conditions and safeguards (Article 15)

145. The establishment, implementation and application of the powers and procedures provided for in this Section of the Convention shall be subject to the conditions and safeguards provided for under the domestic law of each Party. Although Parties are obligated to introduce certain procedural law provisions into their domestic law, the modalities of establishing and implementing these powers and procedures into their legal system, and the application of the powers and procedures in specific cases, are left to the domestic law and procedures of each Party. These domestic laws and procedures, as more specifically described below, shall include conditions or safeguards, which may be provided constitutionally, legislatively, judicially or otherwise. The modalities should include the addition of certain elements as conditions or safeguards that balance the requirements of law enforcement with the protection of human rights and liberties. As the Convention applies to Parties of many different legal systems and cultures, it is not possible to specify in detail the applicable conditions and safeguards for each power or procedure. Parties shall ensure that these conditions and safeguards provide for the adequate protection of human rights and liberties. There are some common standards or minimum safeguards to which Parties to the Convention must adhere. These include standards or minimum safeguards arising pursuant to obligations that a Party has undertaken under applicable international human rights instruments. These instruments include the 1950 European Convention for the Protection of Human Rights and Fundamental Freedoms and its additional Protocols Nos. 1, 4, 6, 7 and 12 (ETS Nos. 005,[5] 009, 046, 114, 117 and 177), in respect of European States that

---

[5] The text of the Convention had been amended according to the provisions of Protocol No. 3 (ETS No. 45), which entered into force on 21 September 1970, of Protocol No. 5 (ETS No. 55), which entered into force on 20 December 1971 and of

are Parties to them. It also includes other applicable human rights instruments in respect of States in other regions of the world (e.g. the 1969 American Convention on Human Rights and the 1981 African Charter on Human Rights and Peoples' Rights) which are Parties to these instruments, as well as the more universally ratified 1966 International Covenant on Civil and Political Rights. In addition, there are similar protections provided under the laws of most States.

146. Another safeguard in the convention is that the powers and procedures shall "incorporate the principle of proportionality." Proportionality shall be implemented by each Party in accordance with relevant principles of its domestic law. For European countries, this will be derived from the principles of the 1950 Council of Europe Convention for the Protection of Human Rights and Fundamental Freedoms, its applicable jurisprudence and national legislation and jurisprudence, that the power or procedure shall be proportional to the nature and circumstances of the offence. Other States will apply related principles of their law, such as limitations on overbreadth of production orders and reasonableness requirements for searches and seizures. Also, the explicit limitation in Article 21 that the obligations regarding interception measures are with respect to a range of serious offences, determined by domestic law, is an explicit example of the application of the proportionality principle.

147. Without limiting the types of conditions and safeguards that could be applicable, the Convention requires specifically that such conditions and safeguards include, as appropriate in view of the nature of the power or procedure, judicial or other independent supervision, grounds justifying the application of the power or procedure and the limitation on the scope or the duration thereof. National legislatures will have to determine, in applying binding international obligations and established domestic principles, which of the powers and procedures are sufficiently intrusive in nature to require implementation of particular conditions and safeguards. As stated in Paragraph 215, Parties should clearly apply conditions and safeguards such as these with respect to interception, given its intrusiveness. At the same time, for example, such safeguards need not apply equally to preservation. Other safeguards that should be addressed under domestic law include the right against self-incrimination, and legal privileges and specificity of individuals or places which are the object of the application of the measure.

Protocol No. 8 (ETS No. 118), which entered into force on 1 January 1990, and comprised also the text of Protocol No. 2 (ETS No. 44) which, in accordance with Article 5, paragraph 3 thereof, had been an integral part of the Convention since its entry into force on 21 September 1970. All provisions which had been amended or added by these Protocols are replaced by Protocol No. 11 (ETS No. 155), as from the date of its entry into force on 1 November 1998. As from that date, Protocol No. 9 (ETS No. 140), which entered into force on 1 October 1994, is repealed and Protocol No. 10 (ETS No. 146) has lost its purpose.

148. With respect to the matters discussed in paragraph 3, of primary importance is consideration of the "public interest", in particular the interests of "the sound administration of justice". To the extent consistent with the public interest, Parties should consider other factors, such as the impact of the power or procedure on "the rights, responsibilities and legitimate interests" of third parties, including service providers, incurred as a result of the enforcement measures, and whether appropriate means can be taken to mitigate such impact. In sum, initial consideration is given to the sound administration of justice and other public interests (e.g. public safety and public health and other interests, including the interests of victims and the respect for private life). To the extent consistent with the public interest, consideration would ordinarily also be given to such issues as minimising disruption of consumer services, protection from liability for disclosure or facilitating disclosure under this Chapter, or protection of proprietary interests.

Title 2 – Expedited preservation of stored computer data

149. The measures in Articles 16 and 17 apply to stored data that has already been collected and retained by data-holders, such as service providers. They do not apply to the real-time collection and retention of future traffic data or to real-time access to the content of communications. These issues are addressed in Title 5.

150. The measures described in the articles operate only where computer data already exists and is currently being stored. For many reasons, computer data relevant for criminal investigations may not exist or no longer be stored. For example, accurate data may not have been collected and retained, or if collected was not maintained. Data protection laws may have affirmatively required the destruction of important data before anyone realised its significance for criminal proceedings. Sometimes there may be no business reason for the collection and retention of data, such as where customers pay a flat rate for services or the services are free. Articles 16 and 17 do not address these problems.

151. "Data preservation" must be distinguished from "data retention". While sharing similar meanings in common language, they have distinctive meanings in relation to computer usage. To preserve data means to keep data, which already exists in a stored form, protected from anything that would cause its current quality or condition to change or deteriorate. To retain data means to keep data, which is currently being generated, in one's possession into the future. Data retention connotes the accumulation of data in the present and the keeping or possession of it into a future time period. Data retention is the process of storing data. Data preservation, on the other hand, is the activity that keeps that stored data secure and safe.

152. Articles 16 and 17 refer only to data preservation, and not data retention. They do not mandate the collection and retention of all, or even

some, data collected by a service provider or other entity in the course of its activities. The preservation measures apply to computer data that "has been stored by means of a computer system", which presupposes that the data already exists, has already been collected and is stored. Furthermore, as indicated in Article 14, all of the powers and procedures required to be established in Section 2 of the Convention are 'for the purpose of specific criminal investigations or proceedings', which limits the application of the measures to an investigation in a particular case. Additionally, where a Party gives effect to preservation measures by means of an order, this order is in relation to "specified stored computer data in the person's possession or control" (paragraph 2). The articles, therefore, provide only for the power to require preservation of existing stored data, pending subsequent disclosure of the data pursuant to other legal powers, in relation to specific criminal investigations or proceedings.

153. The obligation to ensure preservation of data is not intended to require Parties to restrict the offering or use of services that do not routinely collect and retain certain types of data, such as traffic or subscriber data, as part of their legitimate business practices. Neither does it require them to implement new technical capabilities in order to do so, e.g. to preserve ephemeral data, which may be present on the system for such a brief period that it could not be reasonably preserved in response to a request or an order.

154. Some States have laws that require that certain types of data, such as personal data, held by particular types of holders must not be retained and must be deleted if there is no longer a business purpose for the retention of the data. In the European Union, the general principle is implemented by Directive 95/46/EC and, in the particular context of the telecommunications sector, Directive 97/66/EC. These directives establish the obligation to delete data as soon as its storage is no longer necessary. However, member States may adopt legislation to provide for exemptions when necessary for the purpose of the prevention, investigation or prosecution of criminal offences. These directives do not prevent member States of the European Union from establishing powers and procedures under their domestic law to preserve specified data for specific investigations.

155. Data preservation is for most countries an entirely new legal power or procedure in domestic law. It is an important new investigative tool in addressing computer and computer-related crime, especially crimes committed through the Internet. First, because of the volatility of computer data, the data is easily subject to manipulation or change. Thus, valuable evidence of a crime can be easily lost through careless handling and storage practices, intentional manipulation or deletion designed to destroy evidence or routine deletion of data that is no longer required to be retained. One method of preserving its integrity is for competent authorities to search or similarly access and seize or similarly secure the data. However, where the custodian of the data is trustworthy, such as a reputable business, the integrity of the data can be secured more quickly by means of an order to

preserve the data. For legitimate businesses, a preservation order may also be less disruptive to its normal activities and reputation than the execution of a search and seizure of its premises. Second, computer and computer-related crimes are committed to a great extent as a result of the transmission of communications through the computer system. These communications may contain illegal content, such as child pornography, computer viruses or other instructions that cause interference with data or the proper functioning of the computer system, or evidence of the commission of other crimes, such as drug trafficking or fraud. Determining the source or destination of these past communications can assist in identifying the identity of the perpetrators. In order to trace these communications so as to determine their source or destination, traffic data regarding these past communications is required (see further explanation on the importance of traffic data below under Article 17). Third, where these communications contain illegal content or evidence of criminal activity and copies of such communications are retained by service providers, such as e-mail, the preservation of these communications is important in order to ensure that critical evidence is not lost. Obtaining copies of these past communications (e.g., stored e-mail that has been sent or received) can reveal evidence of criminality.

156. The power of expedited preservation of computer data is intended to address these problems. Parties are therefore required to introduce a power to order the preservation of specified computer data as a provisional measure, whereby data will be preserved for a period of time as long as necessary, up to a maximum of 90 days. A Party may provide for subsequent renewal of the order. This does not mean that the data is disclosed to law enforcement authorities at the time of preservation. For this to happen, an additional measure of disclosure or a search has to be ordered. With respect to disclosure to law enforcement of preserved data, see paragraphs 152 and 160.

157. It is also important that preservation measures exists at the national level in order to enable Parties to assist one another at the international level with expedited preservation of stored data located in their territory. This will help to ensure that critical data is not lost during often time-consuming traditional mutual legal assistance procedures that enable the requested Party to actually obtain the data and disclose it to the requesting Party.

Expedited preservation of stored computer data (Article 16)

158. Article 16 aims at ensuring that national competent authorities are able to order or similarly obtain the expedited preservation of specified stored computer-data in connection with a specific criminal investigation or proceeding.

159. 'Preservation' requires that data, which already exists in a stored form, be protected from anything that would cause its current quality or condition to change or deteriorate. It requires that it be kept safe from modification,

deterioration or deletion. Preservation does not necessarily mean that the data be 'frozen' (i.e. rendered inaccessible) and that it, or copies thereof, cannot be used by legitimate users. The person to whom the order is addressed may, depending on the exact specifications of the order, still access the data. The article does not specify how data should be preserved. It is left to each Party to determine the appropriate manner of preservation and whether, in some appropriate cases, preservation of the data should also entail its 'freezing'.

160. The reference to 'order or similarly obtain' is intended to allow the use of other legal methods of achieving preservation than merely by means of a judicial or administrative order or directive (e.g. from police or prosecutor). In some States, preservation orders do not exist in their procedural law, and data can only be preserved and obtained through search and seizure or production order. Flexibility is intended by the use of the phrase 'or otherwise obtain' to permit these States to implement this article by the use of these means. However, it is recommended that States consider the establishment of powers and procedures to actually order the recipient of the order to preserve the data, as quick action by this person can result in the more expeditious implementation of the preservation measures in particular cases.

161. The power to order or similarly obtain the expeditious preservation of specified computer data applies to any type of stored computer data. This can include any type of data that is specified in the order to be preserved. It can include, for example, business, health, personal or other records. The measures are to be established by Parties for use "in particular where there are grounds to believe that the computer data is particularly vulnerable to loss or modification." This can include situations where the data is subject to a short period of retention, such as where there is a business policy to delete the data after a certain period of time or the data is ordinarily deleted when the storage medium is used to record other data. It can also refer to the nature of the custodian of the data or the insecure manner in which the data is stored. However, if the custodian were untrustworthy, it would be more secure to effect preservation by means of search and seizure, rather than by means of an order that could be disobeyed. A specific reference to "traffic data" is made in paragraph 1 in order to signal the provisions particular applicability to this type of data, which if collected and retained by a service provider, is usually held for only a short period of time. The reference to "traffic data" also provides a link between the measures in Articles 16 and 17.

162. Paragraph 2 specifies that where a Party gives effect to preservation by means of an order, the order to preserve is in relation to "specified stored computer data in the person's possession or control". Thus, the stored data may actually be in the possession of the person or it may be stored elsewhere but subject to the control of this person. The person who receives the order is obliged "to preserve and maintain the integrity of that computer data for a period of time as long as necessary, up to a maximum of 90 days,

to enable the competent authorities to seek its disclosure." The domestic law of a Party should specify a maximum period of time for which data, subject to an order, must be preserved, and the order should specify the exact period of time that the specified data is to be preserved. The period of time should be as long as necessary, up to a maximum of 90 days, to permit the competent authorities to undertake other legal measures, such as search and seizure, or similar access or securing, or the issuance of a production order, to obtain the disclosure of the data. A Party may provide for subsequent renewal of the production order. In this context, reference should be made to Article 29, which concerns a mutual assistance request to obtain the expeditious preservation of data stored by means of a computer system. That article specifies that preservation effected in response to a mutual assistance request "shall be for a period not less than 60 days in order to enable the requesting Party to submit a request for the search or similar access, seizure or similar securing, or disclosure of the data."

163. Paragraph 3 imposes an obligation of confidentiality regarding the undertaking of preservation procedures on the custodian of the data to be preserved, or on the person ordered to preserve the data, for a period of time as established in domestic law. This requires Parties to introduce confidentiality measures in respect of expedited preservation of stored data, and a time limit in respect of the period of confidentiality. This measure accommodates the needs of law enforcement so that the suspect of the investigation is not made aware of the investigation, as well as the right of individuals to privacy. For law enforcement authorities, the expedited preservation of data forms part of initial investigations and, therefore, covertness may be important at this stage. Preservation is a preliminary measure pending the taking of other legal measures to obtain the data or its disclosure. Confidentiality is required in order that other persons do not attempt to tamper with or delete the data. For the person to whom the order is addressed, the data subject or other persons who may be mentioned or identified in the data, there is a clear time limit to the length of the measure. The dual obligations to keep the data safe and secure and to maintain confidentiality of the fact that the preservation measure has been undertaken helps to protect the privacy of the data subject or other persons who may be mentioned or identified in that data.

164. In addition to the limitations set out above, the powers and procedures referred to in Article 16 are also subject to the conditions and safeguards provided in Articles 14 and 15.

Expedited preservation and partial disclosure of traffic data (Article 17)

165. This article establishes specific obligations in relation to the preservation of traffic data under Article 16 and provides for expeditious disclosure of some traffic data so as to identify that other service providers were involved in the transmission of specified communications. "Traffic data" is defined in Article 1.

166. Obtaining stored traffic data that is associated with past communications may be critical in determining the source or destination of a past communication, which is crucial to identifying the persons who, for example, have distributed child pornography, distributed fraudulent misrepresentations as part of a fraudulent scheme, distributed computer viruses, attempted or successfully accessed illegally computer systems, or transmitted communications to a computer system that have interfered either with data in the system or with the proper functioning of the system. However, this data is frequently stored for only short periods of time, as laws designed to protect privacy may prohibit or market forces may discourage the long-term storage of such data. Therefore, it is important that preservation measures be undertaken to secure the integrity of this data (see discussion related to preservation, above).

167. Often more than one service provider may be involved in the transmission of a communication. Each service provider may possess some traffic data related to the transmission of the specified communication, which either has been generated and retained by that service provider in relation to the passage of the communication through its system or has been provided from other service providers. Sometimes traffic data, or at least some types of traffic data, are shared among the service providers involved in the transmission of the communication for commercial, security, or technical purposes. In such a case, any one of the service providers may possess the crucial traffic data that is needed to determine the source or destination of the communication. Often, however, no single service provider possesses enough of the crucial traffic data to be able to determine the actual source or destination of the communication. Each possesses one part of the puzzle, and each of these parts needs to be examined in order to identify the source or destination.

168. Article 17 ensures that where one or more service providers were involved in the transmission of a communication, expeditious preservation of traffic data can be effected among all of the service providers. The article does not specify the means by which this may be achieved, leaving it to domestic law to determine a means that is consistent with its legal and economic system. One means to achieve expeditious preservation would be for competent authorities to serve expeditiously a separate preservation order on each service provider. Nevertheless, obtaining a series of separate orders can be unduly time consuming. A preferred alternative could be to obtain a single order, the scope of which however would apply to all service providers that were identified subsequently as being involved in the transmission of the specific communication. This comprehensive order could be served sequentially on each service provider identified. Other possible alternatives could involve the participation of service providers. For example, requiring a service provider that was served with an order to notify the next service provider in the chain of the existence and terms of the preservation order. This notice could, depending on domestic law, have the effect of

either permitting the other service provider to preserve voluntarily the relevant traffic data, despite any obligations to delete it, or mandating the preservation of the relevant traffic data. The second service provider could similarly notify the next service provider in the chain.

169. As traffic data is not disclosed to law enforcement authorities upon service of a preservation order to a service provider (but only obtained or disclosed subsequently upon the taking of other legal measures), these authorities will not know whether the service provider possesses all of the crucial traffic data or whether there were other service providers involved in the chain of transmitting the communication. Therefore, this article requires that the service provider, which receives a preservation order or similar measure, disclose expeditiously to the competent authorities, or other designated person, a sufficient amount of traffic data to enable the competent authorities to identify any other service providers and the path through which the communication was transmitted. The competent authorities should specify clearly the type of traffic data that is required to be disclosed. Receipt of this information would enable the competent authorities to determine whether to take preservation measures with respect to the other service providers. In this way, the investigating authorities can trace the communication back to its origin, or forward to its destination, and identify the perpetrator or perpetrators of the specific crime being investigated. The measures in this article are also subject to the limitations, conditions and safeguards provided in Articles 14 and 15.

Title 3 – Production order

Production order (Article 18)

170. Paragraph 1 of this article calls for Parties to enable their competent authorities to compel a person in its territory to provide specified stored computer data, or a service provider offering its services in the territory of the Party to submit subscriber information. The data in question are stored or existing data, and do not include data that has not yet come into existence such as traffic data or content data related to future communications. Instead of requiring States to apply systematically coercive measures in relation to third parties, such as search and seizure of data, it is essential that States have within their domestic law alternative investigative powers that provide a less intrusive means of obtaining information relevant to criminal investigations.

171. A "production order" provides a flexible measure which law enforcement can apply in many cases, especially instead of measures that are more intrusive or more onerous. The implementation of such a procedural mechanism will also be beneficial to third party custodians of data, such as ISPs, who are often prepared to assist law enforcement authorities on a voluntary basis by providing data under their control, but who prefer an

appropriate legal basis for such assistance, relieving them of any contractual or non-contractual liability.

172. The production order refers to computer data or subscriber information that are in the possession or control of a person or a service provider. The measure is applicable only to the extent that the person or service provider maintains such data or information. Some service providers, for example, do not keep records regarding the subscribers to their services.

173. Under paragraph 1(a), a Party shall ensure that its competent law enforcement authorities have the power to order a person in its territory to submit specified computer data stored in a computer system, or data storage medium that is in that person's possession or control. The term "possession or control" refers to physical possession of the data concerned in the ordering Party's territory, and situations in which the data to be produced is outside of the person's physical possession but the person can nonetheless freely control production of the data from within the ordering Party's territory (for example, subject to applicable privileges, a person who is served with a production order for information stored in his or her account by means of a remote online storage service, must produce such information). At the same time, a mere technical ability to access remotely stored data (e.g. the ability of a user to access through a network link remotely stored data not within his or her legitimate control) does not necessarily constitute "control" within the meaning of this provision. In some States, the concept denominated under law as "possession" covers physical and constructive possession with sufficient breadth to meet this "possession or control" requirement.

Under paragraph 1(b), a Party shall also provide for the power to order a service provider offering services in its territory to "submit subscriber information in the service provider's possession or control". As in paragraph 1(a), the term "possession or control" refers to subscriber information in the service provider's physical possession and to remotely stored subscriber information under the service provider's control (for example at a remote data storage facility provided by another company). The term "relating to such service" means that the power is to be available for the purpose of obtaining subscriber information relating to services offered in the ordering Party's territory.

174. The conditions and safeguards referred to in paragraph 2 of the article, depending on the domestic law of each Party, may exclude privileged data or information. A Party may wish to prescribe different terms, different competent authorities and different safeguards concerning the submission of particular types of computer data or subscriber information held by particular categories of persons or service providers. For example, with respect to some types of data, such as publicly available subscriber information, a Party might permit law enforcement agents to issue such an order where in other situations a court order could be required. On the other hand, in some situations a Party might require, or be mandated by human rights safeguards

to require that a production order be issued only by judicial authorities in order to be able to obtain certain types of data. Parties may wish to limit the disclosure of this data for law enforcement purposes to situations where a production order to disclose such information has been issued by judicial authorities. The proportionality principle also provides some flexibility in relation to the application of the measure, for instance in many States in order to exclude its application in minor cases.

175. A further consideration for Parties is the possible inclusion of measures concerning confidentiality. The provision does not contain a specific reference to confidentiality, in order to maintain the parallel with the non-electronic world where confidentiality is not imposed in general regarding production orders. However, in the electronic, particularly on-line, world a production order can sometimes be employed as a preliminary measure in the investigation, preceding further measures such as search and seizure or real-time interception of other data. Confidentiality could be essential for the success of the investigation.

176. With respect to the modalities of production, Parties could establish obligations that the specified computer data or subscriber information must be produced in the manner specified in the order. This could include reference to a time period within which disclosure must be made, or to form, such as that the data or information be provided in "plain text", on-line or on a paper print-out or on a diskette.

177. "Subscriber information" is defined in paragraph 3. In principle, it refers to any information held by the administration of a service provider relating to a subscriber to its services. Subscriber information may be contained in the form of computer data or any other form, such as paper records. As subscriber information includes forms of data other than just computer data, a special provision has been included in the article to address this type of information. "Subscriber" is intended to include a broad range of service provider clients, from persons holding paid subscriptions, to those paying on a per-use basis, to those receiving free services. It also includes information concerning persons entitled to use the subscriber's account.

178. In the course of a criminal investigation, subscriber information may be needed primarily in two specific situations. First, subscriber information is needed to identify which services and related technical measures have been used or are being used by a subscriber, such as the type of telephone service used (e.g., mobile), type of other associated services used (e.g., call forwarding, voice-mail, etc.), telephone number or other technical address (e.g., e-mail address). Second, when a technical address is known, subscriber information is needed in order to assist in establishing the identity of the person concerned. Other subscriber information, such as commercial information about billing and payment records of the subscriber may also be relevant to criminal investigations, especially where the crime under investigation involves computer fraud or other economic crimes.

179. Therefore, subscriber information includes various types of information about the use of a service and the user of that service. With respect to the use of the service, the term means any information, other than traffic or content data, by which can be established the type of communication service used, the technical provisions related thereto, and the period of time during which the person subscribed to the service. The term 'technical provisions' includes all measures taken to enable a subscriber to enjoy the communication service offered. Such provisions include the reservation of a technical number or address (telephone number, website address or domain name, e-mail address, etc.), as well as the provision and registration of communication equipment used by the subscriber, such as telephone devices, call centres or LANs (local area networks).

180. Subscriber information is not limited to information directly related to the use of the communication service. It also means any information, other than traffic data or content data, by which can be established the user's identity, postal or geographic address, telephone and other access number, and billing and payment information, which is available on the basis of the service agreement or arrangement between the subscriber and the service provider. It also means any other information, other than traffic data or content data, concerning the site or location where the communication equipment is installed, which is available on the basis of the service agreement or arrangement. This latter information may only be relevant in practical terms where the equipment is not portable, but knowledge as to the portability or purported location of the equipment (on the basis of the information provided according to the service agreement or arrangement) can be instrumental to an investigation.

181. However, this article should not be understood as to impose an obligation on service providers to keep records of their subscribers, nor would it require service providers to ensure the correctness of such information. Thus, a service provider is not obliged to register identity information of users of so-called prepaid cards for mobile telephone services. Nor is it obliged to verify the identity of the subscribers or to resist the use of pseudonyms by users of its services.

182. As the powers and procedures in this Section are for the purpose of specific criminal investigations or proceedings (Article 14), production orders are to be used in individual cases concerning, usually, particular subscribers. For example, on the basis of the provision of a particular name mentioned in the production order, a particular associated telephone number or e-mail address may be requested. On the basis of a particular telephone number or e-mail address, the name and address of the subscriber concerned may be ordered. The provision does not authorise Parties to issue a legal order to disclose indiscriminate amounts of the service provider's subscriber information about groups of subscribers e.g. for the purpose of data-mining.

183. The reference to a "service agreement or arrangement" should be interpreted in a broad sense and includes any kind of relationship on the basis of which a client uses the provider's services.

Title 4 – Search and seizure of stored computer data

Search and seizure of stored computer data (Article 19)

184. This article aims at modernising and harmonising domestic laws on search and seizure of stored computer data for the purposes of obtaining evidence with respect to specific criminal investigations or proceedings. Any domestic criminal procedural law includes powers for search and seizure of tangible objects. However, in a number of jurisdictions stored computer data per se will not be considered as a tangible object and therefore cannot be secured on behalf of criminal investigations and proceedings in a parallel manner as tangible objects, other than by securing the data medium upon which it is stored. The aim of Article 19 of this Convention is to establish an equivalent power relating to stored data.

185. In the traditional search environment concerning documents or records, a search involves gathering evidence that has been recorded or registered in the past in tangible form, such as ink on paper. The investigators search or inspect such recorded data, and seize or physically take away the tangible record. The gathering of data takes place during the period of the search and in respect of data that exists at that time. The precondition for obtaining legal authority to undertake a search is the existence of grounds to believe, as prescribed by domestic law and human rights safeguards, that such data exists in a particular location and will afford evidence of a specific criminal offence.

186. With respect to the search for evidence, in particular computer data, in the new technological environment, many of the characteristics of a traditional search remain. For example, the gathering of the data occurs during the period of the search and in respect of data that exists at that time. The preconditions for obtaining legal authority to undertake a search remain the same. The degree of belief required for obtaining legal authorisation to search is not any different whether the data is in tangible form or in electronic form. Likewise, the belief and the search are in respect of data that already exists and that will afford evidence of a specific offence.

187. However, with respect to the search of computer data, additional procedural provisions are necessary in order to ensure that computer data can be obtained in a manner that is equally effective as a search and seizure of a tangible data carrier. There are several reasons for this: first, the data is in intangible form, such as in an electromagnetic form. Second, while the data may be read with the use of computer equipment, it cannot be seized and taken away in the same sense as can a paper record. The physical medium on which the intangible data is stored (e.g., the computer hard-drive

or a diskette) must be seized and taken away, or a copy of the data must be made in either tangible form (e.g., computer print-out) or intangible form, on a physical medium (e.g., diskette), before the tangible medium containing the copy can be seized and taken away. In the latter two situations, where such copies of the data are made, a copy of the data remains in the computer system or storage device. Domestic law should provide for a power to make such copies. Third, due to the connectivity of computer systems, data may not be stored in the particular computer that is searched, but such data may be readily accessible to that system. It could be stored in an associated data storage device that is connected directly to the computer, or connected to the computer indirectly through communication systems, such as the Internet. This may or may not require new laws to permit an extension of the search to where the data is actually stored (or the retrieval of the data from that site to the computer being searched), or the use traditional search powers in a more co-ordinated and expeditious manner at both locations.

188. Paragraph 1 requires Parties to empower law enforcement authorities to access and search computer data, which is contained either within a computer system or part of it (such as a connected data storage device), or on an independent data storage medium (such as a CD-ROM or diskette). As the definition of "computer system" in Article 1 refers to "any device or a group of inter-connected or related devices", paragraph 1 concerns the search of a computer system and its related components that can be considered together as forming one distinct computer system (e.g., a PC together with a printer and related storage devices, or a local area network). Sometimes data that is physically stored in another system or storage device can be legally accessed through the searched computer system by establishing a connection with other distinct computer systems. This situation, involving linkages with other computer systems by means of telecommunication networks within the same territory (e.g., wide area network or Internet), is addressed at paragraph 2.

189. Although search and seizure of a "computer-data storage medium in which computer data may be stored" (paragraph 1 (b)) may be undertaken by use of traditional search powers, often the execution of a computer search requires both the search of the computer system and any related computer-data storage medium (e.g., diskettes) in the immediate vicinity of the computer system. Due to this relationship, a comprehensive legal authority is provided in paragraph 1 to encompass both situations.

190. Article 19 applies to stored computer data. In this respect, the question arises whether an unopened e-mail message waiting in the mailbox of an ISP until the addressee will download it to his or her computer system, has to be considered as stored computer data or as data in transfer. Under the law of some Parties, that e-mail message is part of a communication and therefore its content can only be obtained by applying the power of interception, whereas other legal systems consider such message as stored

data to which Article 19 applies. Therefore, Parties should review their laws with respect to this issue to determine what is appropriate within their domestic legal systems.

191. Reference is made to the term 'search or similarly access'. The use of the traditional word 'search' conveys the idea of the exercise of coercive power by the State, and indicates that the power referred to in this article is analogous to traditional search. 'Search' means to seek, read, inspect or review data. It includes the notions of searching for data and searching of (examining) data. On the other hand, the word 'access' has a neutral meaning, but it reflects more accurately computer terminology. Both terms are used in order to marry the traditional concepts with modern terminology.

192. The reference to 'in its territory' is a reminder that this provision, as all the articles in this Section, concern only measures that are required to be taken at the national level.

193. Paragraph 2 allows the investigating authorities to extend their search or similar access to another computer system or part of it if they have grounds to believe that the data required is stored in that other computer system. The other computer system or part of it must, however, also be 'in its territory'.

194. The Convention does not prescribe how an extension of a search is to be permitted or undertaken. This is left to domestic law. Some examples of possible conditions are: empowering the judicial or other authority which authorised the computer search of a specific computer system, to authorise the extension of the search or similar access to a connected system if he or she has grounds to believe (to the degree required by national law and human rights safeguards) that the connected computer system may contain the specific data that is being sought; empowering the investigative authorities to extend an authorised search or similar access of a specific computer system to a connected computer system where there are similar grounds to believe that the specific data being sought is stored in the other computer system; or exercising search or similar access powers at both locations in a co-ordinated and expeditious manner. In all cases the data to be searched must be lawfully accessible from or available to the initial computer system.

195. This article does not address 'transborder search and seizure', whereby States could search and seize data in the territory of other States without having to go through the usual channels of mutual legal assistance. This issue is discussed below at the Chapter on international co-operation.

196. Paragraph 3 addresses the issues of empowering competent authorities to seize or similarly secure computer data that has been searched or similarly accessed under paragraphs 1 or 2. This includes the power of seizure of computer hardware and computer-data storage media. In certain

cases, for instance when data is stored in unique operating systems such that it cannot be copied, it is unavoidable that the data carrier as a whole has to be seized. This may also be necessary when the data carrier has to be examined in order to retrieve from it older data which was overwritten but which has, nevertheless, left traces on the data carrier.

197. In this Convention, 'seize' means to take away the physical medium upon which data or information is recorded, or to make and retain a copy of such data or information. 'Seize' includes the use or seizure of programmes needed to access the data being seized. As well as using the traditional term 'seize', the term 'similarly secure' is included to reflect other means by which intangible data is removed, rendered inaccessible or its control is otherwise taken over in the computer environment. Since the measures relate to stored intangible data, additional measures are required by competent authorities to secure the data; that is, 'maintain the integrity of the data', or maintain the 'chain of custody' of the data, meaning that the data which is copied or removed be retained in the State in which they were found at the time of the seizure and remain unchanged during the time of criminal proceedings. The term refers to taking control over or the taking away of data.

198. The rendering inaccessible of data can include encrypting the data or otherwise technologically denying anyone access to that data. This measure could usefully be applied in situations where danger or social harm is involved, such as virus programs or instructions on how to make viruses or bombs, or where the data or their content are illegal, such as child pornography. The term 'removal' is intended to express the idea that while the data is removed or rendered inaccessible, it is not destroyed, but continues to exist. The suspect is temporarily deprived of the data, but it can be returned following the outcome of the criminal investigation or proceedings.

199. Thus, seize or similarly secure data has two functions: 1) to gather evidence, such as by copying the data, or 2) to confiscate data, such as by copying the data and subsequently rendering the original version of the data inaccessible or by removing it. The seizure does not imply a final deletion of the seized data.

200. Paragraph 4 introduces a coercive measure to facilitate the search and seizure of computer data. It addresses the practical problem that it may be difficult to access and identify the data sought as evidence, given the quantity of data that can be processed and stored, the deployment of security measures, as well as the nature of computer operations. It recognises that system administrators, who have particular knowledge of the computer system, may need to be consulted concerning the technical modalities about how best the search should be conducted. This provision, therefore, allows law enforcement to compel a system administrator to assist, as is reasonable, the undertaking of the search and seizure.

201. This power is not only of benefit to the investigating authorities. Without such co-operation, investigative authorities could remain on the searched premises and prevent access to the computer system for long periods of time while undertaking the search. This could be an economic burden on legitimate businesses or customers and subscribers that are denied access to data during this time. A means to order the co-operation of knowledgeable persons would help in making searches more effective and cost efficient, both for law enforcement and innocent individuals affected. Legally compelling a system administrator to assist may also relieve the administrator of any contractual or other obligations not to disclose the data.

202. The information that can be ordered to be provided is that which is necessary to enable the undertaking of the search and seizure, or the similarly accessing or securing. The provision of this information, however, is restricted to that which is "reasonable". In some circumstances, reasonable provision may include disclosing a password or other security measure to the investigating authorities. However, in other circumstances, this may not be reasonable; for example, where the disclosure of the password or other security measure would unreasonably threaten the privacy of other users or other data that is not authorised to be searched. In such case, the provision of the "necessary information" could be the disclosure, in a form that is intelligible and readable, of the actual data that is being sought by the competent authorities.

203. Under paragraph 5 of this article, the measures are subject to conditions and safeguards provided for under domestic law on the basis of Article 15 of this Convention. Such conditions may include provisions relating to the engagement and financial compensation of witnesses and experts.

204. The drafters discussed further in the frame of paragraph 5 if interested parties should be notified of the undertaking of a search procedure In the on-line world it may be less apparent that data has been searched and seized (copied) than that a seizure in the off-line world took place, where seized objects will be physically missing. The laws of some Parties do not provide for an obligation to notify in the case of a traditional search. For the Convention to require notification in respect of a computer search would create a discrepancy in the laws of these Parties. On the other hand, some Parties may consider notification as an essential feature of the measure, in order to maintain the distinction between computer search of stored data (which is generally not intended to be a surreptitious measure) and interception of flowing data (which is a surreptitious measure, see Articles 20 and 21). The issue of notification, therefore, is left to be determined by domestic law. If Parties consider a system of mandatory notification of persons concerned, it should be borne in mind that such notification may prejudice the investigation. If such a risk exists, postponement of the notification should be considered.

Title 5 – Real-time collection of computer data

205. Articles 20 and 21 provide for the real-time collection of traffic data and the real-time interception of content data associated with specified communications transmitted by a computer system. The provisions address the real-time collection and real-time interception of such data by competent authorities, as well as their collection or interception by service providers. Obligations of confidentiality are also addressed.

206. Interception of telecommunications usually refers to traditional telecommunications networks. These networks can include cable infrastructures, whether wire or optical cable, as well as inter-connections with wireless networks, including mobile telephone systems and microwave transmission systems. Today, mobile communications are facilitated also by a system of special satellite networks. Computer networks may also consist of an independent fixed cable infrastructure, but are more frequently operated as a virtual network by connections made through telecommunication infrastructures, thus permitting the creation of computer networks or linkages of networks that are global in nature. The distinction between telecommunications and computer communications, and the distinctiveness between their infrastructures, is blurring with the convergence of telecommunication and information technologies. Thus, the definition of 'computer system' in Article 1 does not restrict the manner by which the devices or group of devices may be inter-connected. Articles 20 and 21, therefore, apply to specified communications transmitted by means of a computer system, which could include transmission of the communication through telecommunication networks before it is received by another computer system.

207. Articles 20 and 21 do not make a distinction between a publicly or a privately owned telecommunication or computer system or to the use of systems and communication services offered to the public or to closed user groups or private parties. The definition of 'service provider' in Article 1 refers to public and private entities that provide to users of their services the ability to communicate by means of a computer system.

208. This Title governs the collection of evidence contained in currently generated communications, which are collected at the time of the communication (i.e., 'real time'). The data are intangible in form (e.g., in the form of transmissions of voice or electronic impulses). The flow of the data is not significantly interfered with by the collection, and the communication reaches its intended recipient. Instead of a physical seizure of the data, a recording (i.e., a copy) is made of the data being communicated. The collection of this evidence takes place during a certain period of time. A legal authority to permit the collection is sought in respect of a future event (i.e., a future transmission of data).

209. The type of data that can be collected is of two types: traffic data and content data. 'Traffic data' is defined in Article 1 d to mean any computer data relating to a communication made by means of a computer system, which is generated by the computer system and which formed a part in the chain of communication, indicating the communication's origin, destination, route, time, date, size and duration or the type of service. 'Content data' is not defined in the Convention but refers to the communication content of the communication; i.e., the meaning or purport of the communication, or the message or information being conveyed by the communication (other than traffic data).

210. In many States, a distinction is made between the real-time interception of content data and real-time collection of traffic data in terms of both the legal prerequisites required to authorise such investigative measure and the offences in respect of which this measure can be employed. While recognising that both types of data may have associated privacy interests, many States consider that the privacy interests in respect of content data are greater due to the nature of the communication content or message. Greater limitations may be imposed with respect to the real-time collection of content data than traffic data. To assist in recognising this distinction for these States, the Convention, while operationally acknowledging that the data is collected or recorded in both situations, refers normatively in the titles of the articles to the collection of traffic data as 'real-time collection' and the collection of content data as 'real-time interception'.

211. In some States existing legislation makes no distinction between the collection of traffic data and the interception of content data, either because no distinction has been made in the law regarding differences in privacy interests or the technological collection techniques for both measures are very similar. Thus, the legal prerequisites required to authorise the undertaking of the measures, and the offences in respect of which the measures can be employed, are the same. This situation is also recognised in the Convention by the common operational use of the term 'collect or record' in the actual text of both Articles 20 and 21.

212. With respect to the real-time interception of content data, the law often prescribes that the measure is only available in relation to the investigation of serious offences or categories of serious offences. These offences are identified in domestic law as serious for this purpose often by being named in a list of applicable offences or by being included in this category by reference to a certain maximum sentence of incarceration that is applicable to the offence. Therefore, with respect to the interception of content data, Article 21 specifically provides that Parties are only required to establish the measure 'in relation to a range of serious offences to be determined by domestic law'.

213. Article 20, concerning the collection of traffic data, on the other hand, is not so limited and in principle applies to any criminal offence covered by the

Convention. However, Article 14, paragraph 3, provides that a Party may reserve the right to apply the measure only to offences or categories of offences specified in the reservation, provided that the range of offences or categories of offences is not more restricted than the range of offences to which it applies the measure of interception of content data. Nevertheless, where such a reservation is taken, the Party shall consider restricting such reservation so as to enable the broadest range of application of the measure of collection of traffic data.

214. For some States, the offences established in the Convention would normally not be considered serious enough to permit interception of content data or, in some cases, even the collection of traffic data. Nevertheless, such techniques are often crucial for the investigation of some of the offences established in the Convention, such as those involving illegal access to computer systems, and distribution of viruses and child pornography. The source of the intrusion or distribution, for example, cannot be determined in some cases without real-time collection of traffic data. In some cases, the nature of the communication cannot be discovered without real-time interception of content data. These offences, by their nature or the means of transmission, involve the use of computer technologies. The use of technological means should, therefore, be permitted to investigate these offences. However, due to the sensitivities surrounding the issue of interception of content data, the Convention leaves the scope of this measure to be determined by domestic law. As some countries legally assimilate the collection of traffic data with the interception of content data, a reservation possibility is permitted to restrict the applicability of the former measure, but not to an extent greater than a Party restricts the measure of real-time interception of content data. Nevertheless, Parties should consider applying the two measures to the offences established by the Convention in Section 1 of Chapter II, in order to provide an effective means for the investigation of these computer offences and computer-related offences.

215. The conditions and safeguards regarding the powers and procedures related to real-time interception of content data and real-time collection of traffic data are subject to Articles 14 and 15. As interception of content data is a very intrusive measure on private life, stringent safeguards are required to ensure an appropriate balance between the interests of justice and the fundamental rights of the individual. In the area of interception, the present Convention itself does not set out specific safeguards other than limiting authorisation of interception of content data to investigations into serious criminal offences as defined in domestic law. Nevertheless, the following important conditions and safeguards in this area, applied in domestic laws, are: judicial or other independent supervision; specificity as to the communications or persons to be intercepted; necessity, subsidiarity and proportionality (e.g. legal predicates justifying the taking of the measure; other less intrusive measures not effective); limitation on the duration of interception; right of redress. Many of these safeguards reflect the European Convention on Human Rights and its subsequent case-law (see judgments

in Klass,[6] Kruslin,[7] Huvig,[8] Malone,[9] Halford,[10] Lambert[11] cases). Some of these safeguards are applicable also to the collection of traffic data in real-time.

Real-time collection of traffic data (Article 20)

216. Often, historical traffic data may no longer be available or it may not be relevant as the intruder has changed the route of communication. Therefore, the real-time collection of traffic data is an important investigative measure. Article 20 addresses the subject of real-time collection and recording of traffic data for the purpose of specific criminal investigations or proceedings.

217. Traditionally, the collection of traffic data in respect of telecommunications (e.g., telephone conversations) has been a useful investigative tool to determine the source or destination (e.g., telephone numbers) and related data (e.g., time, date and duration) of various types of illegal communications (e.g., criminal threats and harassment, criminal conspiracy, fraudulent misrepresentations) and of communications affording evidence of past or future crimes (e.g., drug trafficking, murder, economic crimes, etc.).

218. Computer communications can constitute or afford evidence of the same types of criminality. However, given that computer technology is capable of transmitting vast quantities of data, including written text, visual images and sound, it also has greater potential for committing crimes involving distribution of illegal content (e.g., child pornography). Likewise, as computers can store vast quantities of data, often of a private nature, the potential for harm, whether economic, social or personal, can be significant if the integrity of this data is interfered with. Furthermore, as the science of computer technology is founded upon the processing of data, both as an end product and as part of its operational function (e.g., execution of computer programs), any interference with this data can have disastrous effects on the proper operation of computer systems. When an illegal distribution of child pornography, illegal access to a computer system or interference with the proper functioning of the computer system or the integrity of data, is committed, particularly from a distance such as through the Internet, it is necessary and crucial to trace the route of the communications back from the victim to the perpetrator. Therefore, the ability to collect traffic data in respect of computer communications is just as, if not more, important as it is in respect of purely traditional telecommunications. This investigative technique can correlate the time, date and source and destination of the

---

[6] ECHR Judgment in the case of Klass and others v. Germany, A28, 06/09/1978.

[7] ECHR Judgment in the case of Kruslin v. France, 176-A, 24/04/1990.

[8] ECHR Judgment in the case of Huvig v. France, 176-B, 24/04/1990.

[9] ECHR Judgment in the case of Malone v. United Kingdom, A82, 02/08/1984.

[10] ECHR Judgment in the case of Halford v. United Kingdom, Reports 1997 – III, 25/06/1997.

[11] ECHR Judgment in the case of Lambert v. France, Reports 1998 – V, 24/08/1998.

suspect's communications with the time of the intrusions into the systems of victims, identify other victims or show links with associates.

219. Under this article, the traffic data concerned must be associated with specified communications in the territory of the Party. The specified 'communications' are in the plural, as traffic data in respect of several communications may need to be collected in order to determine the human source or destination (for example, in a household where several different persons have the use of the same telecommunications facilities, it may be necessary to correlate several communications with the individuals' opportunity to use the computer system). The communications in respect of which the traffic data may be collected or recorded, however, must be specified. Thus, the Convention does not require or authorise the general or indiscriminate surveillance and collection of large amounts of traffic data. It does not authorise the situation of 'fishing expeditions' where criminal activities are hopefully sought to be discovered, as opposed to specific instances of criminality being investigated. The judicial or other order authorising the collection must specify the communications to which the collection of traffic data relates.

220. Subject to paragraph 2, Parties are obliged, under paragraph 1(a) to ensure that their competent authorities have the capacity to collect or record traffic data by technical means. The article does not specify technologically how the collection is to be undertaken, and no obligations in technical terms are defined.

221. In addition, under paragraph 1(b), Parties are obliged to ensure that their competent authorities have the power to compel a service provider to collect or record traffic data or to co-operate and assist the competent authorities in the collection or recording of such data. This obligation regarding service providers is applicable only to the extent that the collection or recording, or co-operation and assistance, is within the existing technical capability of the service provider. The article does not obligate service providers to ensure that they have the technical capability to undertake collections, recordings, co-operation or assistance. It does not require them to acquire or develop new equipment, hire expert support or engage in costly re-configuration of their systems. However, if their systems and personnel have the existing technical capability to provide such collection, recording, co-operation or assistance, the article would require them to take the necessary measures to engage such capability. For example, the system may be configured in such a manner, or computer programs may already be possessed by the service provider, which would permit such measures to be taken, but they are not ordinarily executed or used in the normal course of the service provider's operation. The article would require the service provider to engage or turn-on these features, as required by law.

222. As this is a measure to be carried out at national level, the measures are applied to the collection or recording of specified communications in the

territory of the Party. Thus, in practical terms, the obligations are generally applicable where the service provider has some physical infrastructure or equipment on that territory capable of undertaking the measures, although this need not be the location of its main operations or headquarters. For the purposes of this Convention, it is understood that a communication is in a Party's territory if one of the communicating parties (human beings or computers) is located in the territory or if the computer or telecommunication equipment through which the communication passes is located on the territory.

223. In general, the two possibilities for collecting traffic data in paragraph 1(a) and (b) are not alternatives. Except as provided in paragraph 2, a Party must ensure that both measures can be carried out. This is necessary because if a service provider does not have the technical ability to assume the collection or recording of traffic data (1(b)), then a Party must have the possibility for its law enforcement authorities to undertake themselves the task (1(a)). Likewise, an obligation under paragraph 1(b)(ii) to co-operate and assist the competent authorities in the collection or recording of traffic data is senseless if the competent authorities are not empowered to collect or record themselves the traffic data. Additionally, in the situation of some local area networks (LANs), where no service provider may be involved, the only way for collection or recording to be carried out would be for the investigating authorities to do it themselves. Both measures in paragraphs 1 (a) and (b) do not have to be used each time, but the availability of both methods is required by the article.

224. This dual obligation, however, posed difficulties for certain States in which the law enforcement authorities were only able to intercept data in telecommunication systems through the assistance of a service provider, or not surreptitiously without at least the knowledge of the service provider. For this reason, paragraph 2 accommodates such a situation. Where a Party, due to the 'established principles of its domestic legal system', cannot adopt the measures referred to in paragraph 1 (a), it may instead adopt a different approach, such as only compelling service providers to provide the necessary technical facilities, to ensure the real-time collection of traffic data by law enforcement authorities. In such case, all of the other limitations regarding territory, specificity of communications and use of technical means still apply.

225. Like real-time interception of content data, real-time collection of traffic data is only effective if undertaken without the knowledge of the persons being investigated. Interception is surreptitious and must be carried out in such a manner that the communicating parties will not perceive the operation. Service providers and their employees knowing about the interception must, therefore, be under an obligation of secrecy in order for the procedure to be undertaken effectively.

226. Paragraph 3 obligates Parties to adopt such legislative or other measures as may be necessary to oblige a service provider to keep confidential the fact of and any information about the execution of any of the measures provided in this article concerning the real-time collection of traffic data. This provision not only ensures the confidentiality of the investigation, but it also relieves the service provider of any contractual or other legal obligations to notify subscribers that data about them is being collected. Paragraph 3 may be effected by the creation of explicit obligations in the law. On the other hand, a Party may be able to ensure the confidentiality of the measure on the basis of other domestic legal provisions, such as the power to prosecute for obstruction of justice those persons who aid the criminals by telling them about the measure. Although a specific confidentiality requirement (with effective sanction in case of a breach) is a preferred procedure, the use of obstruction of justice offences can be an alternative means to prevent inappropriate disclosure and, therefore, also suffices to implement this paragraph. Where explicit obligations of confidentiality are created, these shall be subject to the conditions and safeguards as provided in Articles 14 and 15. These safeguards or conditions should impose reasonable time periods for the duration of the obligation, given the surreptitious nature of the investigative measure.

227. As noted above, the privacy interest is generally considered to be less with respect to the collection of traffic data than interception of content data. Traffic data about time, duration and size of communication reveals little personal information about a person or his or her thoughts. However, a stronger privacy issue may exist in regard to data about the source or destination of a communication (e.g. the visited websites). The collection of this data may, in some situations, permit the compilation of a profile of a person's interests, associates and social context. Accordingly, Parties should bear such considerations in mind when establishing the appropriate safeguards and legal prerequisites for undertaking such measures, pursuant to Articles 14 and 15.

Interception of content data (Article 21)

228. Traditionally, the collection of content data in respect of telecommunications (e.g., telephone conversations) has been a useful investigative tool to determine that the communication is of an illegal nature (e.g., the communication constitutes a criminal threat or harassment, a criminal conspiracy or fraudulent misrepresentations) and to collect evidence of past or future crimes (e.g., drug trafficking, murder, economic crimes, etc.). Computer communications can constitute or afford evidence of the same types of criminality. However, given that computer technology is capable of transmitting vast quantities of data, including written text, visual images and sound, it has greater potential for committing crimes involving distribution of illegal content (e.g., child pornography). Many of the computer crimes involve the transmission or communication of data as part of their commission; for example, communications sent to effect an illegal access of

a computer system or the distribution of computer viruses. It is not possible to determine in real-time the harmful and illegal nature of these communications without intercepting the content of the message. Without the ability to determine and prevent the occurrence of criminality in progress, law enforcement would merely be left with investigating past and completed crimes where the damage has already occurred. Therefore, the real-time interception of content data of computer communications is just as, if not more, important as is the real-time interception of telecommunications.

229. 'Content data' refers to the communication content of the communication; i.e., the meaning or purport of the communication, or the message or information being conveyed by the communication. It is everything transmitted as part of the communication that is not traffic data.

230. Most of the elements of this article are identical to those of Article 20. Therefore, the comments, above, concerning the collection or recording of traffic data, obligations to co-operate and assist, and obligations of confidentiality apply equally to the interception of content data. Due to the higher privacy interest associated with content data, the investigative measure is restricted to 'a range of serious offences to be determined by domestic law'.

231. Also, as set forth in the comments above on Article 20, the conditions and safeguards applicable to real-time interception of content data may be more stringent than those applicable to the real-time collection of traffic data, or to the search and seizure or similar accessing or securing of stored data.

Section 3 – Jurisdiction

Jurisdiction (Article 22)

232. This Article establishes a series of criteria under which Contracting Parties are obliged to establish jurisdiction over the criminal offences enumerated in Articles 2-11 of the Convention.

233. Paragraph 1 *littera a* is based upon the principle of territoriality. Each Party is required to punish the commission of crimes established in this Convention that are committed in its territory. For example, a Party would assert territorial jurisdiction if both the person attacking a computer system and the victim system are located within its territory, and where the computer system attacked is within its territory, even if the attacker is not.

234. Consideration was given to including a provision requiring each Party to establish jurisdiction over offences involving satellites registered in its name. The drafters decided that such a provision was unnecessary since unlawful communications involving satellites will invariably originate from and/or be received on earth. As such, one of the bases for a Party's jurisdiction set forth in paragraph 1(a) – (c) will be available if the transmission originates or

terminates in one of the locations specified therein. Further, to the extent the offence involving a satellite communication is committed by a Party's national outside the territorial jurisdiction of any State, there will be a jurisdictional basis under paragraph 1(d). Finally, the drafters questioned whether registration was an appropriate basis for asserting criminal jurisdiction since in many cases there would be no meaningful nexus between the offence committed and the State of registry because a satellite serves as a mere conduit for a transmission.

235. Paragraph 1, *litterae b* and *c* are based upon a variant of the principle of territoriality. These *litterae* require each Party to establish criminal jurisdiction over offences committed upon ships flying its flag or aircraft registered under its laws. This obligation is already implemented as a general matter in the laws of many States, since such ships and aircraft are frequently considered to be an extension of the territory of the State. This type of jurisdiction is most useful where the ship or aircraft is not located in its territory at the time of the commission of the crime, as a result of which paragraph 1, *littera a* would not be available as a basis to assert jurisdiction. If the crime is committed on a ship or aircraft that is beyond the territory of the flag Party, there may be no other State that would be able to exercise jurisdiction barring this requirement. In addition, if a crime is committed aboard a ship or aircraft which is merely passing through the waters or airspace of another State, the latter State may face significant practical impediments to the exercise of its jurisdiction, and it is therefore useful for the State of registry to also have jurisdiction.

236. Paragraph 1, *littera d* is based upon the principle of nationality. The nationality theory is most frequently applied by States applying the civil law tradition. It provides that nationals of a State are obliged to comply with the domestic law even when they are outside its territory. Under *littera d*, if a national commits an offence abroad, the Party is obliged to have the ability to prosecute it if the conduct is also an offence under the law of the State in which it was committed or the conduct has taken place outside the territorial jurisdiction of any State.

237. Paragraph 2 allows Parties to enter a reservation to the jurisdiction grounds laid down in paragraph 1, *litterae b, c,* and *d*. However, no reservation is permitted with respect to the establishment of territorial jurisdiction under *littera a*, or with respect to the obligation to establish jurisdiction in cases falling under the principle of *"aut dedere aut judicare"* (extradite or prosecute) under paragraph 3, i.e. where that Party has refused to extradite the alleged offender on the basis of his nationality and the offender is present on its territory. Jurisdiction established on the basis of paragraph 3 is necessary to ensure that those Parties that refuse to extradite a national have the legal ability to undertake investigations and proceedings domestically instead, if sought by the Party that requested extradition pursuant to the requirements of "Extradition", Article 24, paragraph 6 of this Convention.

238. The bases of jurisdiction set forth in paragraph 1 are not the exclusive. Paragraph 4 of this article permits the Parties to establish, in conformity with their domestic law, other types of criminal jurisdiction as well.

239. In the case of crimes committed by use of computer systems, there will be occasions in which more than one Party has jurisdiction over some or all of the participants in the crime. For example, many virus attacks, frauds and copyright violations committed through use of the Internet target victims located in many States. In order to avoid duplication of effort, unnecessary inconvenience for witnesses, or competition among law enforcement officials of the States concerned, or to otherwise facilitate the efficiency or fairness of the proceedings, the affected Parties are to consult in order to determine the proper venue for prosecution. In some cases, it will be most effective for the States concerned to choose a single venue for prosecution; in others, it may be best for one State to prosecute some participants, while one or more other States pursue others. Either result is permitted under this paragraph. Finally, the obligation to consult is not absolute, but is to take place "where appropriate." Thus, for example, if one of the Parties knows that consultation is not necessary (e.g., it has received confirmation that the other Party is not planning to take action), or if a Party is of the view that consultation may impair its investigation or proceeding, it may delay or decline consultation.

Chapter III – International co-operation

240. Chapter III contains a number of provisions relating to extradition and mutual legal assistance among the Parties.

Section 1 – General principles

Title 1 – General principles relating to international co-operation

General principles relating to international co-operation (Article 23)

241. Article 23 sets forth three general principles with respect to international co-operation under Chapter III.

242. Initially, the article makes clear that international co-operation is to be provided among Parties "to the widest extent possible." This principle requires Parties to provide extensive co-operation to each other, and to minimise impediments to the smooth and rapid flow of information and evidence internationally.

243. Second, the general scope of the obligation to co-operate is set forth in Article 23: co-operation is to be extended to all criminal offences related to computer systems and data (i.e. the offences covered by Article 14, paragraph 2, *litterae a-b*), as well as to the collection of evidence in electronic form of a criminal offence. This means that either where the crime

is committed by use of a computer system, or where an ordinary crime not committed by use of a computer system (e.g., a murder) involves electronic evidence, the terms of Chapter III are applicable. However, it should be noted that Articles 24 (Extradition), 33 (Mutual assistance regarding the real time collection of traffic data) and 34 (Mutual assistance regarding the interception of content data) permit the Parties to provide for a different scope of application of these measures.

244. Finally, co-operation is to be carried out both "in accordance with the provisions of this Chapter" and "through application of relevant international agreements on international co-operation in criminal matters, arrangements agreed to on the basis of uniform or reciprocal legislation, and domestic laws." The latter clause establishes the general principle that the provisions of Chapter III do not supersede the provisions of international agreements on mutual legal assistance and extradition, reciprocal arrangements as between the parties thereto (described in greater detail in the discussion of Article 27 below), or relevant provisions of domestic law pertaining to international co-operation. This basic principle is explicitly reinforced in Articles 24 (Extradition), 25 (General principles relating to mutual assistance), 26 (Spontaneous information), 27 (Procedures pertaining to mutual assistance requests in the absence of applicable international agreements), 28 (Confidentiality and limitation on use), 31 (Mutual assistance regarding accessing of stored computer data), 33 (Mutual assistance regarding the real-time collection of traffic data) and 34 (Mutual assistance regarding the interception of content data).

Title 2 – Principles relating to extradition

Extradition (Article 24)

245. Paragraph 1 specifies that the obligation to extradite applies only to offences established in accordance with Articles 2-11 of the Convention that are punishable under the laws of both Parties concerned by deprivation of liberty for a maximum period of at least one year or by a more severe penalty. The drafters decided to insert a threshold penalty because, under the Convention, Parties may punish some of the offences with a relatively short maximum period of incarceration (e.g., Article 2 – illegal access – and Article 4 – data interference). Given this, the drafters did not believe it appropriate to require that each of the offences established in Articles 2-11 be considered per se extraditable. Accordingly, agreement was reached on a general requirement that an offence is to be considered extraditable if – as in Article 2 of the European Convention on Extradition (ETS No. 24) – the maximum punishment that could be imposed for the offence for which extradition was sought was at least one year's imprisonment. The determination of whether an offence is extraditable does not hinge on the actual penalty imposed in the particular case at hand, but instead on the maximum period that may legally be imposed for a violation of the offence for which extradition is sought.

246. At the same time, in accordance with the general principle that international co-operation under Chapter III should be carried out pursuant to instruments in force between the Parties, Paragraph 1 also provides that where a treaty on extradition or an arrangement on the basis of uniform or reciprocal legislation is in force between two or more Parties (see description of this term in discussion of Article 27 below) which provides for a different threshold for extradition, the threshold provided for in such treaty or arrangement shall apply. For example, many extradition treaties between European countries and non-European countries provide that an offence is extraditable only if the maximum punishment is greater than one year's imprisonment or there is a more severe penalty. In such cases, international extradition practitioners will continue to apply the normal threshold under their treaty practice in order to determine whether an offence is extraditable. Even under the European Convention on Extradition (ETS No. 24), reservations may specify a different minimum penalty for extradition. Among Parties to that Convention, when extradition is sought from a Party that has entered such a reservation, the penalty provided for in the reservation shall be applied in determining whether the offence is extraditable.

247. Paragraph 2 provides that the offences described in paragraph 1 are to be deemed extraditable offences in any extradition treaty between or among the Parties, and are to be included in future treaties they may negotiate among themselves. This does not mean that extradition must be granted on every occasion on which a request is made but rather that the possibility of granting extradition of persons for such offences must be available. Under paragraph 5, Parties are able to provide for other requirements for extradition.

248. Under paragraph 3, a Party that would not grant extradition, either because it has no extradition treaty with the requesting Party or because the existing treaties would not cover a request made in respect of the offences established in accordance with this Convention, may use the Convention itself as a basis for surrendering the person requested, although it is not obligated to do so.

249. Where a Party, instead of relying on extradition treaties, utilises a general statutory scheme to carry out extradition, paragraph 4 requires it to include the offences described in paragraph 1 among those for which extradition is available.

250. Paragraph 5 provides that the requested Party need not extradite if it is not satisfied that all of the terms and conditions provided for by the applicable treaty or law have been fulfilled. It is thus another example of the principle that co-operation shall be carried out pursuant to the terms of applicable international instruments in force between the Parties, reciprocal arrangements, or domestic law. For example, conditions and restrictions set forth in the European Convention on Extradition (ETS No. 24) and its

Additional Protocols (ETS Nos. 86 and 98) will apply to Parties to those agreements, and extradition may be refused on such bases (e.g., Article 3 of the European Convention on Extradition provides that extradition shall be refused if the offence is considered political in nature, or if the request is considered to have been made for the purpose of prosecuting or punishing a person on account of, *inter alia*, race, religion, nationality or political opinion).

251. Paragraph 6 applies the principle "*aut dedere aut judicare*" (extradite or prosecute). Since many States refuse extradition of their nationals, offenders who are found in the Party of which they are a national may avoid responsibility for a crime committed in another Party unless local authorities are obliged to take action. Under paragraph 6, if another Party has sought extradition of the offender, and extradition has been refused on the grounds that the offender is a national of the requested Party, the requested Party must, upon request of the requesting Party, submit the case to its authorities for the purpose of prosecution. If the Party whose extradition request has been refused does not request submission of the case for local investigation and prosecution, there is no obligation on the requested Party to take action. Moreover, if no extradition request has been made, or if extradition has been denied on grounds other than nationality, this paragraph establishes no obligation on the requested Party to submit the case for domestic prosecution. In addition, paragraph 6 requires the local investigation and prosecution to be carried out with diligence; it must be treated as seriously "as in the case of any other offence of a comparable nature" in the Party submitting the case. That Party shall report the outcome of its investigation and proceedings to the Party that had made the request.

252. In order that each Party know to whom its requests for provisional arrest or extradition should be directed, paragraph 7 requires Parties to communicate to the Secretary General of the Council of Europe the name and address of its authorities responsible for making or receiving requests for extradition or provisional arrest in the absence of a treaty. This provision has been limited to situations in which there is no extradition treaty in force between the Parties concerned because if a bilateral or multilateral extradition treaty is in force between the Parties (such as ETS No. 24), the Parties will know to whom extradition and provisional arrest requests are to be directed without the necessity of a registration requirement. The communication to the Secretary General must be made at the time of signature or when depositing the Party's instrument of ratification, acceptance, approval or accession. It should be noted that designation of an authority does not exclude the possibility of using the diplomatic channel.

Title 3 – General principles relating to mutual assistance

General principles relating to mutual assistance (Article 25)

253. The general principles governing the obligation to provide mutual assistance are set forth in paragraph 1. Co-operation is to be provided "to

the widest extent possible." Thus, as in Article 23 ("General principals relating to international co-operation"), mutual assistance is in principle to be extensive, and impediments thereto strictly limited. Second, as in Article 23, the obligation to co-operate applies in principle to both criminal offences related to computer systems and data (i.e. the offences covered by Article 14, paragraph 2, *litterae a-b*), and to the collection of evidence in electronic form of a criminal offence. It was agreed to impose an obligation to co-operate as to this broad class of crimes because there is the same need for streamlined mechanisms of international co-operation as to both of these categories. However, Articles 34 and 35 permit the Parties to provide for a different scope of application of these measures.

254. Other provisions of this Chapter will clarify that the obligation to provide mutual assistance is generally to be carried out pursuant to the terms of applicable mutual legal assistance treaties, laws and arrangements. Under paragraph 2, each Party is required to have a legal basis to carry out the specific forms of co-operation described in the remainder of the Chapter, if its treaties, laws and arrangements do not already contain such provisions. The availability of such mechanisms, particularly those in Articles 29 through 35 (Specific provisions – Titles 1, 2, 3), is vital for effective co-operation in computer related criminal matters.

255. Some Parties will not require any implementing legislation in order to apply the provisions referred to in paragraph 2, since provisions of international treaties that establish detailed mutual assistance regimes are considered to be self-executing in nature. It is expected that Parties will either be able to treat these provisions as self executing, already have sufficient flexibility under existing mutual assistance legislation to carry out the mutual assistance measures established under this Chapter, or will be able to rapidly enact any legislation required to do so.

256. Computer data is highly volatile. By a few keystrokes or by operation of automatic programs, it may be deleted, rendering it impossible to trace a crime to its perpetrator or destroying critical proof of guilt. Some forms of computer data are stored for only short periods of time before being deleted. In other cases, significant harm to persons or property may take place if evidence is not gathered rapidly. In such urgent cases, not only the request, but the response as well should be made in an expedited manner. The objective of paragraph 3 is therefore to facilitate acceleration of the process of obtaining mutual assistance so that critical information or evidence is not lost because it has been deleted before a request for assistance could be prepared, transmitted and responded to. Paragraph 3 does so by (1) empowering the Parties to make urgent requests for co-operation through expedited means of communications, rather than through traditional, much slower transmission of written, sealed documents through diplomatic pouches or mail delivery systems; and (2) requiring the requested Party to use expedited means to respond to requests in such circumstances. Each Party is required to have the ability to apply this measure if its mutual

assistance treaties, laws or arrangement do not already so provide. The listing of fax and e-mail is indicative in nature; any other expedited means of communication may be used as would be appropriate in the particular circumstances at hand. As technology advances, further expedited means of communicating will be developed that may be used to request mutual assistance. With respect to the authenticity and security requirement contained in the paragraph, the Parties may decide among themselves how to ensure the authenticity of the communications and whether there is a need for special security protections (including encryption) that may be necessary in a particularly sensitive case. Finally, the paragraph also permits the requested Party to require a formal confirmation sent through traditional channels to follow the expedited transmission, if it so chooses.

257. Paragraph 4 sets forth the principle that mutual assistance is subject to the terms of applicable mutual assistance treaties (MLATs) and domestic laws. These regimes provide safeguards for the rights of persons located in the requested Party that may become the subject of a request for mutual assistance. For example, an intrusive measure, such as search and seizure, is not executed on behalf of a requesting Party, unless the requested Party's fundamental requirements for such measure applicable in a domestic case have been satisfied. Parties also may ensure protection of rights of persons in relation to the items seized and provided through mutual legal assistance.

258. However, paragraph 4 does not apply if "otherwise specifically provided in this Chapter." This clause is designed to signal that the Convention contains several significant exceptions to the general principle. The first such exception has been seen in paragraph 2 of this article, which obliges each Party to provide for the forms of co-operation set forth in the remaining articles of the Chapter (such as preservation, real time collection of data, search and seizure, and maintenance of a 24/7 network), regardless of whether or not its MLATs, equivalent arrangements or mutual assistance laws currently provide for such measures. Another exception is found in Article 27 which is always to be applied to the execution of requests in lieu of the requested Party's domestic law governing international co-operation in the absence of an MLAT or equivalent arrangement between the requesting and requested Parties. Article 27 provides a system of conditions and grounds for refusal. Another exception, specifically provided for in this paragraph, is that co-operation may not be denied, at least as far as the offences established in Articles 2-11 of the Convention are concerned, on the grounds that the requested Party considers the request to involve a "fiscal" offence. Finally, Article 29 is an exception in that it provides that preservation may not be denied on dual criminality grounds, although the possibility of a reservation is provided for in this respect.

259. Paragraph 5 is essentially a definition of dual criminality for purposes of mutual assistance under this Chapter. Where the requested Party is permitted to require dual criminality as a condition to the providing of assistance (for example, where a requested Party has reserved its right to

require dual criminality with respect to the preservation of data under Article 29, paragraph 4 "Expedited preservation of stored computer data"), dual criminality shall be deemed present if the conduct underlying the offence for which assistance is sought is also a criminal offence under the requested Party's laws, even if its laws place the offence within a different category of offence or use different terminology in denominating the offence. This provision was believed necessary in order to ensure that requested Parties do not adopt too rigid a test when applying dual criminality. Given differences in national legal systems, variations in terminology and categorisation of criminal conduct are bound to arise. If the conduct constitutes a criminal violation under both systems, such technical differences should not impede assistance. Rather, in matters in which the dual criminality standard is applicable, it should be applied in a flexible manner that will facilitate the granting of assistance.

Spontaneous information (Article 26)

260. This article is derived from provisions in earlier Council of Europe instruments, such as Article 10 of the Convention on the Laundering, Search, Seizure and Confiscation of the Proceeds from Crime (ETS No. 141) and Article 28 of the Criminal Law Convention on Corruption (ETS No. 173). More and more frequently, a Party possesses valuable information that it believes may assist another Party in a criminal investigation or proceeding, and which the Party conducting the investigation or proceeding is not aware exists. In such cases, no request for mutual assistance will be forthcoming. Paragraph 1 empowers the State in possession of the information to forward it to the other State without a prior request. The provision was thought useful because, under the laws of some States, such a positive grant of legal authority is needed in order to provide assistance in the absence of a request. A Party is not obligated to spontaneously forward information to another Party; it may exercise its discretion in light of the circumstances of the case at hand. Moreover, the spontaneous disclosure of information does not preclude the disclosing Party, if it has jurisdiction, from investigating or instituting proceedings in relation to the facts disclosed.

261. Paragraph 2 addresses the fact that in some circumstances, a Party will only forward information spontaneously if sensitive information will be kept confidential or other conditions can be imposed on the use of information. In particular, confidentiality will be an important consideration in cases in which important interests of the providing State may be endangered should the information be made public, e.g., where there is a need to protect the identity of a means of collecting the information or the fact that a criminal group is being investigated. If advance inquiry reveals that the receiving Party cannot comply with a condition sought by the providing Party (for example, where it cannot comply with a condition of confidentiality because the information is needed as evidence at a public trial), the receiving Party shall advise the providing Party, which then has the option of not providing the information. If the receiving Party agrees to the condition, however, it must honour it. It is

foreseen that conditions imposed under this article would be consistent with those that could be imposed by the providing Party pursuant to a request for mutual assistance from the receiving Party.

Title 4 – Procedures pertaining to mutual assistance requests in the absence of applicable international agreements

Procedures pertaining to mutual assistance requests in the absence of applicable international agreements (Article 27)

262. Article 27 obliges the Parties to apply certain mutual assistance procedures and conditions where there is no mutual assistance treaty or arrangement on the basis of uniform or reciprocal legislation in force between the requesting and requested Parties. The Article thus reinforces the general principle that mutual assistance should be carried out through application of relevant treaties and similar arrangements for mutual assistance. The drafters rejected the creation of a separate general regime of mutual assistance in this Convention that would be applied in lieu of other applicable instruments and arrangements, agreeing instead that it would be more practical to rely on existing MLAT regimes as a general matter, thereby permitting mutual assistance practitioners to use the instruments and arrangements they are the most familiar with and avoiding confusion that may result from the establishment of competing regimes. As previously stated, only with respect to mechanisms particularly necessary for rapid effective co-operation in computer related criminal matters, such as those in Articles 29-35 (Specific provisions – Title 1, 2, 3), is each Party required to establish a legal basis to enable the carrying out of such forms of co-operation if its current mutual assistance treaties, arrangements or laws do not already do so.

263. Accordingly, most forms of mutual assistance under this Chapter will continue to be carried out pursuant to the European Convention on Mutual Assistance in Criminal Matters (ETS No. 30) and its Protocol (ETS No. 99) among the Parties to those instruments. Alternatively, Parties to this Convention that have bilateral MLATs in force between them, or other multilateral agreements governing mutual assistance in criminal cases (such as between member States of the European Union), shall continue to apply their terms, supplemented by the computer- or computer-related crime-specific mechanisms described in the remainder of Chapter III, unless they agree to apply any or all of the provisions of this Article in lieu thereof. Mutual assistance may also be based on arrangements agreed on the basis of uniform or reciprocal legislation, such as the system of co-operation developed among the Nordic countries, which is also admitted by the European Convention on Mutual Assistance in Criminal Matters (Article 25, paragraph 4), and among members of the Commonwealth. Finally, the reference to mutual assistance treaties or arrangements on the basis of uniform or reciprocal legislation is not limited to those instruments in force at

the time of entry into force of the present Convention, but also covers instruments that may be adopted in the future.

264. Article 27 (Procedures pertaining to mutual assistance requests in the absence of applicable international agreements), paragraphs 2-10, provide a number of rules for providing mutual assistance in the absence of an MLAT or arrangement on the basis of uniform or reciprocal legislation, including establishment of central authorities, imposing of conditions, grounds for and procedures in cases of postponement or refusal, confidentiality of requests, and direct communications. With respect to such expressly covered issues, in the absence of a mutual assistance agreement or arrangement on the basis of uniform or reciprocal legislation, the provisions of this Article are to be applied in lieu of otherwise applicable domestic laws governing mutual assistance. At the same time, Article 27 does not provide rules for other issues typically dealt with in domestic legislation governing international mutual assistance. For example, there are no provisions dealing with the form and contents of requests, taking of witness testimony in the requested or requesting Parties, the providing of official or business records, transfer of witnesses in custody, or assistance in confiscation matters. With respect to such issues, Article 25, paragraph 4 provides that absent a specific provision in this Chapter, the law of the requested Party shall govern specific modalities of providing that type of assistance.

265. Paragraph 2 requires the establishment of a central authority or authorities responsible for sending and answering requests for assistance. The institution of central authorities is a common feature of modern instruments dealing with mutual assistance in criminal matters, and it is particularly helpful in ensuring the kind of rapid reaction that is so useful in combating computer- or computer-related crime. Initially, direct transmission between such authorities is speedier and more efficient than transmission through diplomatic channels. In addition, the establishment of an active central authority serves an important function in ensuring that both incoming and outgoing requests are diligently pursued, that advice is provided to foreign law enforcement partners on how best to satisfy legal requirements in the requested Party, and that particularly urgent or sensitive requests are dealt with properly.

266. Parties are encouraged as a matter of efficiency to designate a single central authority for the purpose of mutual assistance; it would generally be most efficient for the authority designated for such purpose under a Party's MLATs, or domestic law to also serve as the central authority when this article is applicable. However, a Party has the flexibility to designate more than one central authority where this is appropriate under its system of mutual assistance. Where more than one central authority is established, the Party that has done so should ensure that each authority interprets the provisions of the Convention in the same way, and that both incoming and outgoing requests are treated rapidly and efficiently. Each Party is to advise the Secretary General of the Council of Europe of the names and addresses

(including e-mail and fax numbers) of the authority or authorities designated to receive and respond to mutual assistance requests under this article, and Parties are obliged to ensure that the designation is kept up-to-date.

267. A major objective of a State requesting mutual assistance often is to ensure that its domestic laws governing the admissibility of evidence are fulfilled, and it can use the evidence before its courts as a result. To ensure that such evidentiary requirements can be met, paragraph 3 obliges the requested Party to execute requests in accordance with the procedures specified by the requesting Party, unless to do so would be incompatible with its law. It is emphasised that this paragraph relates only to the obligation to respect technical procedural requirements, not to fundamental procedural protections. Thus, for example, a requesting Party cannot require the requested Party to execute a search and seizure that would not meet the requested Party's fundamental legal requirements for this measure. In light of the limited nature of the obligation, it was agreed that the mere fact that the requested Party's legal system knows no such procedure is not a sufficient ground to refuse to apply the procedure requested by the requesting Party; instead, the procedure must be incompatible with the requested Party's legal principles. For example, under the law of the requesting Party, it may be a procedural requirement that a statement of a witness be given under oath. Even if the requested Party does not domestically have the requirement that statements be given under oath, it should honour the requesting Party's request.

268. Paragraph 4 provides for the possibility of refusing requests for mutual assistance requests brought under this Article. Assistance may be refused on the grounds provided for in Article 25, paragraph 4 (i.e. grounds provided for in the law of the requested Party), including prejudice to the sovereignty of the State, security, ordre public or other essential interests, and where the offence is considered by the requested Party to be a political offence or an offence connected with a political offence. In order to promote the overriding principle of providing the widest measure of co-operation (see Articles 23, 25), grounds for refusal established by a requested Party should be narrow and exercised with restraint. They may not be so expansive as to create the potential for assistance to be categorically denied, or subjected to onerous conditions, with respect to broad categories of evidence or information.

269. In line with this approach, it was understood that apart from those grounds set out in Article 28, refusal of assistance on data protection grounds may be invoked only in exceptional cases. Such a situation could arise if, upon balancing the important interests involved in the particular case (on the one hand, public interests, including the sound administration of justice and, on the other hand, privacy interests), furnishing the specific data sought by the requesting Party would raise difficulties so fundamental as to be considered by the requested Party to fall within the essential interests ground of refusal. A broad, categorical, or systematic application of data protection principles to refuse co-operation is therefore precluded. Thus, the

fact the Parties concerned have different systems of protecting the privacy of data (such as that the requesting Party does not have the equivalent of a specialised data protection authority) or have different means of protecting personal data (such as that the requesting Party uses means other than the process of deletion to protect the privacy or the accuracy of the personal data received by law enforcement authorities), do not as such constitute grounds for refusal. Before invoking "essential interests" as a basis for refusing co-operation, the requested Party should instead attempt to place conditions which would allow the transfer of the data. (see Article 27, paragraph 6 and paragraph 271 of this report).

270. Paragraphs 5 permits the requested Party to postpone, rather than refuse, assistance where immediate action on the request would be prejudicial to investigations or proceedings in the requested Party. For example, where the requesting Party has sought to obtain evidence or witness testimony for purposes of investigation or trial, and the same evidence or witness are needed for use at a trial that is about to commence in the requested Party, the requested Party would be justified in postponing the providing of assistance.

271. Paragraph 6 provides that where the assistance sought would otherwise be refused or postponed, the requested Party may instead provide assistance subject to conditions. If the conditions are not agreeable to the requesting Party, the requested Party may modify them, or it may exercise its right to refuse or postpone assistance. Since the requested Party has an obligation to provide the widest possible measure of assistance, it was agreed that both grounds for refusal and conditions should be exercised with restraint.

272. Paragraph 7 obliges the requested Party to keep the requesting Party informed of the outcome of the request, and requires reasons to be given in the case of refusal or postponement of assistance. The providing of reasons can, *inter alia*, assist the requesting Party to understand how the requested Party interprets the requirements of this article, provide a basis for consultation in order to improve the future efficiency of mutual assistance, and provide to the requesting Party previously unknown factual information about the availability or condition of witnesses or evidence.

273. There are times when a Party makes a request in a particularly sensitive case, or in a case in which there could be disastrous consequences if the facts underlying the request were to be made public prematurely. Paragraph 8 accordingly permits the requesting Party to request that the fact and content of the request be kept confidential. Confidentiality may not be sought, however, to the extent that it would undermine the requested Party's ability to obtain the evidence or information sought, e.g., where the information will need to be disclosed in order to obtain a court order needed to effect assistance, or where private persons possessing evidence will need to be made aware of the request in order for it

to be successfully executed. If the requested Party cannot comply with the request for confidentiality, it shall notify the requesting Party, which then has the option of withdrawing or modifying the request.

274. Central authorities designated in accordance with paragraph 2 shall communicate directly with one another. However, in case of urgency, requests for mutual legal assistance may be sent directly by judges and prosecutors of the requesting Party to the judges and prosecutors of the requested Party. The judge or prosecutor following this procedure must also address a copy of the request made to his own central authority with a view to its transmission to the central authority of the requested Party. Under *littera b*, requests may be channelled through Interpol. Authorities of the requested Party that receive a request falling outside their field of competence, are, pursuant to *littera c*, under a two-fold obligation. First, they must transfer the request to the competent authority of the requested Party. Second, they must inform the authorities of the requesting Party of the transfer made. Under *littera d*, requests may also be transmitted directly without the intervention of central authorities even if there is no urgency, as long as the authority of the requested Party is able to comply with the request without making use of coercive action. Finally, *littera e* enables a Party to inform the others, through the Secretary General of the Council of Europe, that, for reasons of efficiency, direct communications are to be addressed to the central authority.

Confidentiality and limitation on use (Article 28)

275. This provision specifically provides for limitations on use of information or material, in order to enable the requested Party, in cases in which such information or material is particularly sensitive, to ensure that its use is limited to that for which assistance is granted, or to ensure that it is not disseminated beyond law enforcement officials of the requesting Party. These restrictions provide safeguards that are available for, *inter alia*, data protection purposes.

276. As in the case of Article 27, Article 28 only applies where there is no mutual assistance treaty, or arrangement on the basis of uniform or reciprocal legislation in force between the requesting and requested Parties. Where such treaty or arrangement is in force, its provisions on confidentiality and use limitations shall apply in lieu of the provisions of this article, unless the Parties thereto agree otherwise. This avoids overlap with existing bilateral and multilateral mutual legal assistance treaties (MLATs) and similar arrangements, thereby enabling practitioners to continue to operate under the normal well-understood regime rather than seeking to apply two competing, possibly contradictory, instruments.

277. Paragraph 2 allows the requested Party, when responding to a request for mutual assistance, to impose two types of conditions. First, it may request that the information or material furnished be kept confidential where

the request could not be complied with in the absence of such condition, such as where the identity of a confidential informant is involved. It is not appropriate to require absolute confidentiality in cases in which the requested Party is obligated to provide the requested assistance, as this would, in many cases, thwart the ability of the requesting Party to successfully investigate or prosecute crime, e.g. by using the evidence in a public trial (including compulsory disclosure).

278. Second, the requested Party may make furnishing of the information or material dependent on the condition that it not be used for investigations or proceedings other than those stated in the request. In order for this condition to apply, it must be expressly invoked by the requested Party, otherwise, there is no such limitation on use by the requesting Party. In cases in which it is invoked, this condition will ensure that the information and material may only be used for the purposes foreseen in the request, thereby ruling out use of the material for other purposes without the consent of the requested Party. Two exceptions to the ability to limit use were recognised by the negotiators and are implicit in the terms of the paragraph. First, under fundamental legal principles of many States, if material furnished is evidence exculpatory to an accused person, it must be disclosed to the defence or a judicial authority. In addition, most material furnished under mutual assistance regimes is intended for use at trial, normally a public proceeding (including compulsory disclosure). Once such disclosure takes place, the material has essentially passed into the public domain. In these situations, it is not possible to ensure confidentiality to the investigation or proceeding for which mutual assistance was sought.

279. Paragraph 3 provides that if the Party to which the information is forwarded cannot comply with the condition imposed, it shall notify the providing Party, which then has the option of not providing the information. If the receiving Party agrees to the condition, however, it must honour it.

280. Paragraph 4 provides that the requesting Party may be required to explain the use made of the information or material it has received under conditions described in paragraph 2, in order that the requested Party may ascertain whether such condition has been complied with. It was agreed that the requested Party may not call for an overly burdensome accounting e.g., of each time the material or information furnished was accessed.

Section 2 – Specific provisions

281. The aim of the present Section is to provide for specific mechanisms in order to take effective and concerted international action in cases involving computer-related offences and evidence in electronic form.

Title 1 – Mutual assistance regarding provisional measures

Expedited preservation of stored computer data (Article 29)

282. This article provides for a mechanism at the international level equivalent to that provided for in Article 16 for use at the domestic level. Paragraph 1 of this article authorises a Party to make a request for, and paragraph 3 requires each Party to have the legal ability to obtain, the expeditious preservation of data stored in the territory of the requested Party by means of a computer system, in order that the data not be altered, removed or deleted during the period of time required to prepare, transmit and execute a request for mutual assistance to obtain the data. Preservation is a limited, provisional measure intended to take place much more rapidly than the execution of a traditional mutual assistance. As has been previously discussed, computer data is highly volatile. With a few keystrokes, or by operation of automatic programs, it may be deleted, altered or moved, rendering it impossible to trace a crime to its perpetrator or destroying critical proof of guilt. Some forms of computer data are stored for only short periods of time before being deleted. Thus, it was agreed that a mechanism was required in order to ensure the availability of such data pending the lengthier and more involved process of executing a formal mutual assistance request, which may take weeks or months.

283. While much more rapid than ordinary mutual assistance practice, this measure is at the same time less intrusive. The mutual assistance officials of the requested Party are not required to obtain possession of the data from its custodian. The preferred procedure is for the requested Party to ensure that the custodian (frequently a service provider or other third party) preserve (i.e., not delete) the data pending the issuance of process requiring it to be turned over to law enforcement officials at a later stage. This procedure has the advantage of being both rapid and protective of the privacy of the person whom the data concerns, as it will not be disclosed to or examined by any government official until the criteria for full disclosure pursuant to normal mutual assistance regimes have been fulfilled. At the same time, a requested Party is permitted to use other procedures for ensuring the rapid preservation of data, including the expedited issuance and execution of a production order or search warrant for the data. The key requirement is to have an extremely rapid process in place to prevent the data from being irretrievably lost.

284. Paragraph 2 sets forth the contents of a request for preservation pursuant to this article. Bearing in mind that this is a provisional measure and that a request will need to be prepared and transmitted rapidly, the information provided will be summary and include only the minimum information required to enable preservation of the data. In addition to specifying the authority that is seeking preservation and the offence for which the measure is sought, the request must provide a summary of the facts, information sufficient to identify the data to be preserved and its

location, and a showing that the data is relevant to the investigation or prosecution of the offence concerned and that preservation is necessary. Finally, the requesting Party must undertake to subsequently submit a request for mutual assistance so that it may obtain production of the data.

285. Paragraph 3 sets forth the principle that dual criminality shall not be required as a condition to providing preservation. In general, application of the principle of dual criminality is counterproductive in the context of preservation. First, as a matter of modern mutual assistance practice, there is a trend to eliminate the dual criminality requirement for all but the most intrusive procedural measures, such as search and seizure or interception. Preservation as foreseen by the drafters, however, is not particularly intrusive, since the custodian merely maintains possession of data lawfully in its possession, and the data is not disclosed to or examined by officials of the requested Party until after execution of a formal mutual assistance request seeking disclosure of the data. Second, as a practical matter, it often takes so long to provide the clarifications necessary to conclusively establish the existence of dual criminality that the data would be deleted, removed or altered in the meantime. For example, at the early stages of an investigation, the requesting Party may be aware that there has been an intrusion into a computer in its territory, but may not until later have a good understanding of the nature and extent of damage. If the requested Party were to delay preserving traffic data that would trace the source of the intrusion pending conclusive establishment of dual criminality, the critical data would often be routinely deleted by service providers holding it for only hours or days after the transmission has been made. Even if thereafter the requesting Party were able to establish dual criminality, the crucial traffic data could not be recovered and the perpetrator of the crime would never be identified.

286. Accordingly, the general rule is that Parties must dispense with any dual criminality requirement for the purpose of preservation. However, a limited reservation is available under paragraph 4. If a Party requires dual criminality as a condition for responding to a request for mutual assistance for production of the data, and if it has reason to believe that, at the time of disclosure, dual criminality will not be satisfied, it may reserve the right to require dual criminality as a precondition to preservation. With respect to offences established in accordance with Articles 2 through 11, it is assumed that the condition of dual criminality is automatically met between the Parties, subject to any reservations they may have entered to these offences where permitted by the Convention. Therefore, Parties may impose this requirement only in relation to offences other than those defined in the Convention.

287. Otherwise, under paragraph 5, the requested Party may only refuse a request for preservation where its execution will prejudice its sovereignty, security, *ordre public* or other essential interests, or where it considers the offence to be a political offence or an offence connected with a political offence. Due to the centrality of this measure to the effective investigation

and prosecution of computer- or computer-related crime, it was agreed that the assertion of any other basis for refusing a request for preservation is precluded.

288. At times, the requested Party will realise that the custodian of the data is likely to take action that will threaten the confidentiality of, or otherwise prejudice, the requesting Party's investigation (for example, where the data to be preserved is held by a service provider controlled by a criminal group, or by the target of the investigation himself). In such situations, under paragraph 6, the requesting Party must be notified promptly, so that it may assess whether to take the risk posed by carrying through with the request for preservation, or to seek a more intrusive but safer form of mutual assistance, such as production or search and seizure.

289. Finally, paragraph 7 obliges each Party to ensure that data preserved pursuant to this Article will be held for at least 60 days pending receipt of a formal mutual assistance request seeking the disclosure of the data, and continue to be held following receipt of the request.

Expedited disclosure of preserved traffic data (Article 30)

290. This article provides the international equivalent of the power established for domestic use in Article 17. Frequently, at the request of a Party in which a crime was committed, a requested Party will preserve traffic data regarding a transmission that has travelled through its computers, in order to trace the transmission to its source and identify the perpetrator of the crime, or locate critical evidence. In doing so, the requested Party may discover that the traffic data found in its territory reveals that the transmission had been routed from a service provider in a third State, or from a provider in the requesting State itself. In such cases, the requested Party must expeditiously provide to the requesting Party a sufficient amount of the traffic data to enable identification of the service provider in, and path of the communication from, the other State. If the transmission came from a third State, this information will enable the requesting Party to make a request for preservation and expedited mutual assistance to that other State in order to trace the transmission to its ultimate source. If the transmission had looped back to the requesting Party, it will be able to obtain preservation and disclosure of further traffic data through domestic processes.

291. Under paragraph 2, the requested Party may only refuse to disclose the traffic data, where disclosure is likely to prejudice its sovereignty, security, *ordre public* or other essential interests, or where it considers the offence to be a political offence or an offence connected with a political offence. As in Article 29 (Expedited preservation of stored computer data), because this type of information is so crucial to identification of those who have committed crimes within the scope of this Convention or locating of critical evidence, grounds for refusal are to be strictly limited, and it was agreed that the assertion of any other basis for refusing assistance is precluded.

Title 2 – Mutual assistance regarding investigative powers

Mutual assistance regarding accessing of stored computer data (Article 31)

292. Each Party must have the ability to, for the benefit of another Party, search or similarly access, seize or similarly secure, and disclose data stored by means of a computer system located within its territory – just as under Article 19 (Search and seizure of stored computer data) it must have the ability to do so for domestic purposes. Paragraph 1 authorises a Party to request this type of mutual assistance, and paragraph 2 requires the requested Party to be able to provide it. Paragraph 2 also follows the principle that the terms and conditions for providing such co-operation should be those set forth in applicable treaties, arrangements and domestic laws governing mutual legal assistance in criminal matters. Under paragraph 3, such a request must be responded to on an expedited basis where (1) there are grounds to believe that relevant data is particularly vulnerable to loss or modification, or (2) otherwise where such treaties, arrangements or laws so provide.

Transborder access to stored computer data with consent or where publicly available (Article 32)

293. The issue of when a Party is permitted to unilaterally access computer data stored in another Party without seeking mutual assistance was a question that the drafters of the Convention discussed at length. There was detailed consideration of instances in which it may be acceptable for States to act unilaterally and those in which it may not. The drafters ultimately determined that it was not yet possible to prepare a comprehensive, legally binding regime regulating this area. In part, this was due to a lack of concrete experience with such situations to date; and, in part, this was due to an understanding that the proper solution often turned on the precise circumstances of the individual case, thereby making it difficult to formulate general rules. Ultimately, the drafters decided to only set forth in Article 32 of the Convention situations in which all agreed that unilateral action is permissible. They agreed not to regulate other situations until such time as further experience has been gathered and further discussions may be held in light thereof. In this regard, Article 39, paragraph 3 provides that other situations are neither authorised, nor precluded.

294. Article 32 (Trans-border access to stored computer data with consent or where publicly available) addresses two situations: first, where the data being accessed is publicly available, and second, where the Party has accessed or received data located outside of its territory through a computer system in its territory, and it has obtained the lawful and voluntary consent of the person who has lawful authority to disclose the data to the Party through that system. Who is a person that is "lawfully authorised" to disclose data

may vary depending on the circumstances, the nature of the person and the applicable law concerned. For example, a person's e-mail may be stored in another country by a service provider, or a person may intentionally store data in another country. These persons may retrieve the data and, provided that they have the lawful authority, they may voluntarily disclose the data to law enforcement officials or permit such officials to access the data, as provided in the Article.

Mutual assistance regarding the real-time collection of traffic data (Article 33)

295. In many cases, investigators cannot ensure that they are able to trace a communication to its source by following the trail through records of prior transmissions, as key traffic data may have been automatically deleted by a service provider in the chain of transmission before it could be preserved. It is therefore critical for investigators in each Party to have the ability to obtain traffic data in real time regarding communications passing through a computer system in other Parties. Accordingly, under Article 33 (Mutual assistance regarding the real-time collection of traffic data), each Party is under the obligation to collect traffic data in real time for another Party. While this Article requires the Parties to co-operate on these matters, here, as elsewhere, deference is given to existing modalities of mutual assistance. Thus, the terms and conditions by which such co-operation is to be provided are generally those set forth in applicable treaties, arrangements and laws governing mutual legal assistance in criminal matters.

296. In many countries, mutual assistance is provided broadly with respect to the real time collection of traffic data, because such collection is viewed as being less intrusive than either interception of content data, or search and seizure. However, a number of States take a narrower approach. Accordingly, in the same way as the Parties may enter a reservation under Article 14 (Scope of procedural provisions), paragraph 3, with respect to the scope of the equivalent domestic measure, paragraph 2 permits Parties to limit the scope of application of this measure to a more narrow range of offences than provided for in Article 23 (General principles relating to international co-operation). One caveat is provided: in no event may the range of offences be more narrow than the range of offences for which such measure is available in an equivalent domestic case. Indeed, because real time collection of traffic data is at times the only way of ascertaining the identity of the perpetrator of a crime, and because of the lesser intrusiveness of the measure, the use of the term "at least" in paragraph 2 is designed to encourage Parties to permit as broad assistance as possible, i.e., even in the absence of dual criminality.

Mutual assistance regarding the interception of content data (Article 34)

297. Because of the high degree of intrusiveness of interception, the obligation to provide mutual assistance for interception of content data is restricted. The assistance is to be provided to the extent permitted by the Parties' applicable treaties and laws. As the provision of co-operation for interception of content is an emerging area of mutual assistance practice, it was decided to defer to existing mutual assistance regimes and domestic laws regarding the scope and limitation on the obligation to assist. In this regard, reference is made to the comments on Articles 14, 15 and 21 as well as to No. R (85) 10 concerning the practical application of the European Convention on Mutual Assistance in Criminal Matters in respect of letters rogatory for the interception of telecommunications.

Title 3 – 24/7 Network

24/7 Network (Article 35)

298. As has been previously discussed, effective combating of crimes committed by use of computer systems and effective collection of evidence in electronic form requires very rapid response. Moreover, with a few keystrokes, action may be taken in one part of the world that instantly has consequences many thousands of kilometres and many time zones away. For this reason, existing police co-operation and mutual assistance modalities require supplemental channels to address the challenges of the computer age effectively. The channel established in this Article is based upon the experience gained from an already functioning network created under the auspices of the G8 group of nations. Under this Article, each Party has the obligation to designate a point of contact available 24 hours per day, 7 days per week in order to ensure immediate assistance in investigations and proceedings within the scope of this Chapter, in particular as defined under Article 35, paragraph 1, *litterae a)-c)*. It was agreed that establishment of this network is among the most important means provided by this Convention of ensuring that Parties can respond effectively to the law enforcement challenges posed by computer- or computer-related crime.

299. Each Party's 24/7 point of contact is to either facilitate or directly carry out, *inter alia*, the providing of technical advice, preservation of data, collection of evidence, giving of legal information, and locating of suspects. The term "legal information" in Paragraph 1 means advice to another Party that is seeking co-operation of any legal prerequisites required for providing informal or formal co-operation.

300. Each Party is at liberty to determine where to locate the point of contact within its law enforcement structure. Some Parties may wish to house the 24/7 contact within its central authority for mutual assistance, some may believe that the best location is with a police unit specialised in fighting

computer- or computer-related crime, yet other choices may be appropriate for a particular Party, given its governmental structure and legal system. Since the 24/7 contact is to provide both technical advice for stopping or tracing an attack, as well as such international co-operation duties as locating of suspects, there is no one correct answer, and it is anticipated that the structure of the network will evolve over time. In designating the national point of contact, due consideration should be given to the need to communicate with points of contacts using other languages.

301. Paragraph 2 provides that among the critical tasks to be carried out by the 24/7 contact is the ability to facilitate the rapid execution of those functions it does not carry out directly itself. For example, if a Party's 24/7 contact is part of a police unit, it must have the ability to co-ordinate expeditiously with other relevant components within its government, such as the central authority for international extradition or mutual assistance, in order that appropriate action may be taken at any hour of the day or night. Moreover, paragraph 2 requires each Party's 24/7 contact to have the capacity to carry out communications with other members of the network on an expedited basis.

302. Paragraph 3 requires each point of contact in the network to have proper equipment. Up-to-date telephone, fax and computer equipment will be essential to the smooth operation of the network, and other forms of communication and analytical equipment will need to be part of the system as technology advances. Paragraph 3 also requires that personnel participating as part of a Party's team for the network be properly trained regarding computer- or computer-related crime and how to respond to it effectively.

Chapter IV – Final provisions

303. With some exceptions, the provisions contained in this Chapter are, for the most part, based on the 'Model final clauses for conventions and agreements concluded within the Council of Europe' which were approved by the Committee of Ministers at the 315th meeting of the Deputies in February 1980. As most of the Articles 36 through 48 either use the standard language of the model clauses or are based on long-standing treaty-making practice at the Council of Europe, they do not call for specific comments. However, certain modifications of the standard model clauses or some new provisions require some explanation. It is noted in this context that the model clauses have been adopted as a non-binding set of provisions. As the Introduction to the Model Clauses pointed out "these model final clauses are only intended to facilitate the task of committees of experts and avoid textual divergences which would not have any real justification. The model is in no way binding and different clauses may be adapted to fit particular cases."

Signature and entry into force (Article 36)

304. Article 36, paragraph 1, has been drafted following several precedents established in other conventions elaborated within the framework of the Council of Europe, for instance, the Convention on the Transfer of Sentenced Persons (ETS No. 112) and the Convention on Laundering, Search, Seizure and Confiscation of the Proceeds from Crime (ETS No. 141), which allow for signature, before their entry into force, not only by the member States of the Council of Europe, but also by non-member States which have participated in their elaboration. The provision is intended to enable the maximum number of interested States, not just members of the Council of Europe, to become Parties as soon as possible. Here, the provision is intended to apply to four non-member States, Canada, Japan, South Africa and the United States of America, which actively participated in the elaboration of the Convention. Once the Convention enters into force, in accordance with paragraph 3, other non-member States not covered by this provision may be invited to accede to the Convention in conformity with Article 37, paragraph 1.

305. Article 36, paragraph 3 sets the number of ratifications, acceptances or approvals required for the Convention's entry into force at 5. This figure is higher than the usual threshold (3) in Council of Europe treaties and reflects the belief that a slightly larger group of States is needed to successfully begin addressing the challenge of international computer- or computer-related crime. The number is not so high, however, so as not to delay unnecessarily the Convention's entry into force. Among the five initial States, at least three must be Council of Europe members, but the two others could come from the four non-member States that participated in the Convention's elaboration. This provision would of course also allow for the Convention to enter into force based on expressions of consent to be bound by five Council of Europe member States.

Accession to the Convention (Article 37)

306. Article 37 has also been drafted on precedents established in other Council of Europe conventions, but with an additional express element. Under long-standing practice, the Committee of Ministers decides, on its own initiative or upon request, to invite a non-member State, which has not participated in the elaboration of a convention, to accede to the convention after having consulted all contracting Parties, whether member States or not. This implies that if any contracting Party objects to the non-member State's accession, the Committee of Ministers would usually not invite it to join the convention. However, under the usual formulation, the Committee of Ministers could – in theory – invite such a non-member State to accede to a convention even if a non-member State Party objected to its accession. This means that – in theory – no right of veto is usually granted to non-member States Parties in the process of extending Council of Europe treaties to other non-member States. However, an express requirement that the Committee

of Ministers consult with and obtain the unanimous consent of all Contracting States – not just members of the Council of Europe – before inviting a non-member State to accede to the Convention has been inserted. As indicated above, such a requirement is consistent with practice and recognises that all Contracting States to the Convention should be able to determine with which non-member States they are to enter into treaty relations. Nevertheless, the formal decision to invite a non-member State to accede will be taken, in accordance with usual practice, by the representatives of the contracting Parties entitled to sit on the Committee of Ministers. This decision requires the two-thirds majority provided for in Article 20.d of the Statute of the Council of Europe and the unanimous vote of the representatives of the contracting Parties entitled to sit on the Committee.

307. Federal States seeking to accede to the Convention, which intend to make a declaration under Article 41, are required to submit in advance a draft of the statement referred to in Article 41, paragraph 3, so that the Parties will be in a position to evaluate how the application of the federal clause would affect the prospective Party's implementation of the Convention.(see paragraph 320).

Effects of the Convention (Article 39)

308. Article 39, paragraphs 1 and 2 address the Convention's relationship to other international agreements or arrangements. The subject of how conventions of the Council of Europe should relate to one another or to other treaties, bilateral or multilateral, concluded outside the Council of Europe is not dealt with by the Model Clauses referred to above. The usual approach utilised in Council of Europe conventions in the criminal law area (e.g., Agreement on Illicit Traffic by Sea (ETS No. 156)) is to provide that: (1) new conventions do not affect the rights and undertakings derived from existing international multilateral conventions concerning special matters; (2) Parties to a new convention may conclude bilateral or multilateral agreements with one another on the matters dealt with by the convention for the purposes of supplementing or strengthening its provisions or facilitating the application of the principles embodied in it; and (3) if two or more Parties to the new convention have already concluded an agreement or treaty in respect of a subject which is dealt with in the convention or otherwise have established their relations in respect of that subject, they shall be entitled to apply that agreement or treaty or to regulate those relations accordingly, in lieu of the new convention, provided this facilitates international co-operation.

309. Inasmuch as the Convention generally is intended to supplement and not supplant multilateral and bilateral agreements and arrangements between Parties, the drafters did not believe that a possibly limiting reference to "special matters" was particularly instructive and were concerned that it could lead to unnecessary confusion. Instead, paragraph 1 of Article 39 simply indicates that the present Convention supplements other applicable treaties or arrangements as between Parties and it mentions in

particular three Council of Europe treaties as non-exhaustive examples: the 1957 European Convention on Extradition (ETS No. 24), the 1959 European Convention on Criminal Matters (ETS No. 30) and its 1978 Additional Protocol (ETS No. 99). Therefore, regarding general matters, such agreements or arrangements should in principle be applied by the Parties to the Convention on cybercrime. Regarding specific matters only dealt with by this Convention, the rule of interpretation *lex specialis derogat legi generali* provides that the Parties should give precedence to the rules contained in the Convention. An example is Article 30, which provides for the expedited disclosure of preserved traffic data when necessary to identify the path of a specified communication. In this specific area, the Convention, as *lex specialis*, should provide a rule of first resort over provisions in more general mutual assistance agreements.

310. Similarly, the drafters considered language making the application of existing or future agreements contingent on whether they "strengthen" or "facilitate" co-operation as possibly problematic, because, under the approach established in the international co-operation Chapter, the presumption is that Parties will apply relevant international agreements and arrangements.

311. Where there is an existing mutual assistance treaty or arrangement as a basis for co-operation, the present Convention would only supplement, where necessary, the existing rules. For example, this Convention would provide for the transmission of mutual assistance requests by expedited means of communications (see Article 25, paragraph 3) if such a possibility does not exist under the original treaty or arrangement.

312. Consistent with the Convention's supplementary nature and, in particular, its approach to international co-operation, paragraph 2 provides that Parties are also free to apply agreements that already are or that may in the future come into force. Precedent for such an articulation is found in the Transfer of Sentenced Persons Convention (ETS No. 112). Certainly, in the context of international co-operation, it is expected that application of other international agreements (many of which offer proven, longstanding formulas for international assistance) will in fact promote co-operation. Consistent with the terms of the present Convention, Parties may also agree to apply its international co-operation provisions in lieu of such other agreements (see Article 27(1)). In such instances the relevant co-operation provisions set forth in Article 27 would supersede the relevant rules in such other agreements. As the present Convention generally provides for minimum obligations, Article 39, paragraph 2 recognises that Parties are free to assume obligations that are more specific in addition to those already set out in the Convention, when establishing their relations concerning matters dealt with therein. However, this is not an absolute right: Parties must respect the objectives and principles of the Convention when so doing and therefore cannot accept obligations that would defeat its purpose.

313. Further, in determining the Convention's relationship to other international agreements, the drafters also concurred that Parties may look for additional guidance to relevant provisions in the Vienna Convention on the Law of Treaties.

314. While the Convention provides a much-needed level of harmonisation, it does not purport to address all outstanding issues relating to computer- or computer-related crime. Therefore, paragraph 3 was inserted to make plain that the Convention only affects what it addresses. Left unaffected are other rights, restrictions, obligations and responsibilities that may exist but that are not dealt with by the Convention. Precedent for such a "savings clause" may be found in other international agreements (e.g., UN Terrorist Financing Convention).

Declarations (Article 40)

315. Article 40 refers to certain articles, mostly in respect of the offences established by the Convention in the substantive law section, where Parties are permitted to include certain specified additional elements which modify the scope of the provisions. Such additional elements aim at accommodating certain conceptual or legal differences, which in a treaty of global ambition are more justified than they perhaps might be in a purely Council of Europe context. Declarations are considered acceptable interpretations of Convention provisions and should be distinguished from reservations, which permit a Party to exclude or to modify the legal effect of certain obligations set forth in the Convention. Since it is important for Parties to the Convention to know which, if any, additional elements have been attached by other Parties, there is an obligation to declare them to the Secretary General of the Council of Europe at the time of signature or when depositing an instrument of ratification, acceptance, approval or accession. Such notification is particularly important concerning the definition of offences, as the condition of dual criminality will have to be met by the Parties when applying certain procedural powers. No numerical limit was felt necessary in respect of declarations.

Federal clause (Article 41)

316. Consistent with the goal of enabling the largest possible number of States to become Parties, Article 41 allows for a reservation which is intended to accommodate the difficulties federal States may face as a result of their characteristic distribution of power between central and regional authorities. Precedents exist outside the criminal law area for federal declarations or reservations to other international agreements.[12] Here,

---

[12] E.g. Convention relating to the Status of Refugees of 28 July 1951, Art. 34; Convention relating to the Status of Stateless Persons of 28 September 1954, Art. 37; Convention on the Recognition and Enforcement of Foreign Arbitral Awards

Article 41 recognises that minor variations in coverage may occur as a result of well-established domestic law and practice of a Party which is a federal State. Such variations must be based on its Constitution or other fundamental principles concerning the division of powers in criminal justice matters between the central government and the constituent States or territorial entities of a federal State. There was agreement among the drafters of the Convention that the operation of the federal clause would only lead to minor variations in the application of the Convention.

317. For example, in the United States, under its Constitution and fundamental principles of federalism, federal criminal legislation generally regulates conduct based on its effects on interstate or foreign commerce, while matters of minimal or purely local concern are traditionally regulated by the constituent States. This approach to federalism still provides for broad coverage of illegal conduct encompassed by this Convention under US federal criminal law, but recognises that the constituent States would continue to regulate conduct that has only minor impact or is purely local in character. In some instances, within that narrow category of conduct regulated by State but not federal law, a constituent State may not provide for a measure that would otherwise fall within the scope of this Convention. For example, an attack on a stand-alone personal computer, or network of computers linked together in a single building, may only be criminal if provided for under the law of the State in which the attack took place; however the attack would be a federal offence if access to the computer took place through the Internet, since the use of the Internet provides the effect on interstate or foreign commerce necessary to invoke federal law. The implementation of this Convention through United States federal law, or through the law of another federal State under similar circumstances, would be in conformity with the requirements of Article 41.

318. The scope of application of the federal clause has been restricted to the provisions of Chapter II (substantive criminal law, procedural law and jurisdiction). Federal States making use of this provision would still be under the obligation to co-operate with the other Parties under Chapter III, even where the constituent State or other similar territorial entity in which a fugitive or evidence is located does not criminalise conduct or does not have procedures required under the Convention.

319. In addition, paragraph 2 of Article 41 provides that a federal State, when making a reservation under paragraph 1 of this article, may not apply the terms of such reservation to exclude or substantially diminish its obligations to provide for measures set forth in Chapter II. Overall, it shall provide for a broad and effective law enforcement capability with respect to those measures. In respect of provisions the implementation of which come within the legislative jurisdiction of the constituent States or other similar territorial

---

of 10 June 1958, Art. 11; Convention for the Protection of World Cultural and Natural Heritage of 16 November 1972, Art. 34.

entities, the federal government shall refer the provisions to the authorities of these entities with a favourable endorsement, encouraging them to take appropriate action to give them effect.

Reservations (Article 42)

320. Article 42 provides for a number of reservation possibilities. This approach stems from the fact that the Convention covers an area of criminal law and criminal procedural law which is relatively new to many States. In addition, the global nature of the Convention, which will be open to member and non-member States of the Council of Europe, makes having such reservation possibilities necessary. These reservation possibilities aim at enabling the largest number of States to become Parties to the Convention, while permitting such States to maintain certain approaches and concepts consistent with their domestic law. At the same time, the drafters endeavoured to restrict the possibilities for making reservations in order to secure to the largest possible extent the uniform application of the Convention by the Parties. Thus, no other reservations may be made than those enumerated. In addition, reservations may only be made by a Party at the time of signature or upon deposit of its instrument of ratification, acceptance, approval or accession.

321. Recognising that for some Parties certain reservations were essential to avoid conflict with their constitutional or fundamental legal principles, Article 43 imposes no specific time limit for the withdrawal of reservations. Instead, they should be withdrawn as soon as circumstances so permit.

322. In order to maintain some pressure on the Parties and to make them at least consider withdrawing their reservations, the Convention authorises the Secretary General of the Council of Europe to periodically enquire about the prospects for withdrawal. This possibility of enquiry is current practice under several Council of Europe instruments. The Parties are thus given an opportunity to indicate whether they still need to maintain their reservations in respect of certain provisions and to withdraw, subsequently, those which no longer prove necessary. It is hoped that over time Parties will be able to remove as many of their reservations as possible so as promote the Convention's uniform implementation.

Amendments (Article 44)

323. Article 44 takes its precedent from the Convention on Laundering, Search, Seizure and Confiscation of the Proceeds from Crime (ETS No. 141), where it was introduced as an innovation in respect of criminal law conventions elaborated within the framework of the Council of Europe. The amendment procedure is mostly thought to be for relatively minor changes of a procedural and technical character. The drafters considered that major changes to the Convention could be made in the form of additional protocols.

324. The Parties themselves can examine the need for amendments or protocols under the consultation procedure provided for in Article 46. The European Committee on Crime Problems (CDPC) will in this regard be kept periodically informed and required to take the necessary measures to assist the Parties in their efforts to amend or supplement the Convention.

325. In accordance with paragraph 5, any amendment adopted would come into force only when all Parties have informed the Secretary General of their acceptance. This requirement seeks to ensure that the Convention will evolve in a uniform manner.

Settlement of disputes (Article 45)

326. Article 45, paragraph 1, provides that the European Committee on Crime Problems (CDPC) should be kept informed about the interpretation and application of the provisions of the Convention. Paragraph 2 imposes an obligation on the Parties to seek a peaceful settlement of any dispute concerning the interpretation or the application of the Convention. Any procedure for solving disputes should be agreed upon by the Parties concerned. Three possible mechanisms for dispute-resolution are suggested by this provision: the European Committee on Crime Problems (CDPC) itself, an arbitral tribunal or the International Court of Justice.

Consultations of the Parties (Article 46)

327. Article 46 creates a framework for the Parties to consult regarding implementation of the Convention, the effect of significant legal, policy or technological developments pertaining to the subject of computer- or computer-related crime and the collection of evidence in electronic form, and the possibility of supplementing or amending the Convention. The consultations shall in particular examine issues that have arisen in the use and implementation of the Convention, including the effects of declarations and reservations made under Articles 40 and 42.

328. The procedure is flexible and it is left to the Parties to decide how and when to convene if they so wish. Such a procedure was believed necessary by the drafters of the Convention to ensure that all Parties to the Convention, including non-member States of the Council of Europe, could be involved – on an equal footing basis – in any follow-up mechanism, while preserving the competences of the European Committee on Crime Problems (CDPC). The latter shall not only be kept regularly informed of the consultations taking place among the Parties, but also facilitate those and take the necessary measures to assist the Parties in their efforts to supplement or amend the Convention. Given the needs of effective prevention and prosecution of cybercrime and the associated privacy issues, the potential impact on business activities, and other relevant factors, the views of interested parties,

including law enforcement, non-governmental and private sector organisations, may be useful to these consultations (see also paragraph 14).

329. Paragraph 3 provides for a review of the Convention's operation after 3 years of its entry into force, at which time appropriate amendments may be recommended. The CDPC shall conduct such review with the assistance of the Parties.

330. Paragraph 4 indicates that except where assumed by the Council of Europe it will be for the Parties themselves to finance any consultations carried out in accordance with paragraph 1 of Article 46. However, apart from the European Committee on Crime Problems (CDPC), the Council of Europe Secretariat shall assist the Parties in their efforts under the Convention.

**Parliamentary Assembly Recommendation 1706 (2005)[1]
on media and terrorism**

1.   The Parliamentary Assembly of the Council of Europe believes that terrorism should not affect the importance of freedom of expression and information in the media as one of the essential foundations of democratic society. This freedom carries with it the right of the public to be informed on matters of public concern, including terrorist acts and threats, as well as the response by the state and international organisations to these threats and acts.

2.   Terrorist acts are acts which are intended to create terror, fear or chaos among the public. The spread of public terror, fear and feelings of chaos depends largely on the images and messages being carried by media reports about the terrorist acts and threats. The omnipresence of the mass media at global level frequently exaggerates these effects out of proportion.

3.   The Assembly recalls its Resolution 1271 (2002) and Recommendation 1550 (2002) on combating terrorism and respect for human rights and reaffirms that the fight against terrorism must not be used as a pretext to restrict the fundamental rights and freedoms guaranteed under the European Convention on Human Rights and related legal texts of the Council of Europe. In this respect, it supports the Committee of Ministers' Guidelines on Human Rights and the Fight against Terrorism of 11 July 2002.

4.   Referring to the Committee of Ministers' Declaration of 2 March 2005 on freedom of expression and information in the media in the context of the fight against terrorism, the Assembly emphasises that Article 15 of the European Convention on Human Rights cannot be invoked in cases of terrorism in order to restrict this freedom beyond the existing limitations of Article 10, paragraph 2 of the Convention, because terrorist action can neither be regarded as war in a legal sense, nor can it threaten the life of a democratic nation.

5.   The Assembly considers it necessary for the public and media to be aware of the fact that terrorists direct their action towards the public and thus utilise the media in order to have the strongest possible impact. This is even more important because terrorists have learned how to use information technologies in order to disseminate their own audiovisual recordings, electronic messages or websites on the Internet, which compels states and the media to react accordingly.

---

[1] *Assembly debate* on 20 June 2005 (17th Sitting) (see Doc. 10557, report of the Committee on Culture, Science and Education, rapporteur: Mr Jarab).
Text adopted by the Assembly on 20 June 2005 (17th Sitting).

6.   With due regard to the privacy and human dignity of victims of terrorist acts and their families, the Assembly stresses the importance of fully informing the public about terrorist acts, particularly the suffering caused by these acts as well as the socio-cultural and political context of such acts. Informed public debate about concrete acts of terrorism can lead to forming adequate political responses to it and to preventing others from joining terrorist groups.

7.   The Assembly trusts in the ability of the European political system and culture and in its citizens, politicians and journalists to avoid sensationalist media reports related to terrorism.

8.   The Assembly invites media professionals:

    i.   to develop, through their professional organisations, a code of conduct for journalists, photographers and editors dealing with terrorist acts and threats, in order to keep the public informed without contributing unduly to the impact of terrorism;

    ii.   to organise training courses for media professionals aimed at increasing awareness of the sensitive nature of media reports on terrorism;

    iii.   to co-operate between themselves, for instance through their professional organisations, in order to avoid a race for sensationalist news and images which plays into the hands of terrorists;

    iv.   to avoid acting in the interests of terrorists by adding to the feeling of public fear which terrorist acts can create or by offering terrorists a platform for publicity;

    v.   to refrain from publishing shocking pictures or disseminating images of terrorist acts which violate the privacy and human dignity of victims or contribute to increase the terrorising effect of such acts on the public as well as on the victims and their families;

    vi.   to avoid aggravating, through their news and comments, the societal tensions underlying terrorism, and in particular to refrain from disseminating any kind of hate speech.

9.   The Assembly asks all its member and observer delegations to take account of this recommendation in their national work and to hold a debate on this issue in their respective national parliaments.

10. The Assembly recommends that the Committee of Ministers ask member and observer states:

i.   to inform the public and the media regularly about government strategies and action towards combating terrorism as well as its causes;

ii.   to abstain from prohibiting or even restricting unduly the dissemination of information and opinions in the media about terrorism as well as about the reaction by state authorities to terrorist acts and threats under the pretext of fighting terrorism;

iii.   to inform, upon their request, media dealing with terrorism about the specific security situation in each context, in order to avoid journalists investigating terrorism being unnecessarily exposed to dangers caused by terrorists or the anti-terrorist action of state authorities;

iv.   to include media literacy in their school curricula, in order to encourage a critical and informed consumption of media content and raise citizens' awareness of the horror of terrorist acts as early as possible;

v.   to co-operate through their law enforcement authorities and police in order to prevent the dissemination of illegal messages and images by terrorists on the Internet;

vi.   to apply the Additional Protocol to the Convention on Cybercrime concerning the criminalisation of acts of a racist and xenophobic nature committed through computer systems to terrorist content in so far as the latter advocates, promotes or incites hatred or violence against any individual or group of individuals based on race, colour, descent or national or ethnic origin, as well as religion if used as a pretext for any of these factors.

11. The Assembly asks the Committee of Ministers to:

i.   to monitor the treatment of terrorism in European media in particular with regard to its Declaration on freedom of expression and information in the media in the context of the fight against terrorism;

ii.   to prepare, under the guidance and in close co-operation with media professionals and their professional organisations, and with UNESCO and other organisations working in the same field, a handbook for journalists reporting about terrorist acts and violence;

iii.   to initiate work towards an additional protocol to the Convention on Cybercrime setting up a framework for security co-operation between member and observer states for the prevention of cyberterrorism, in the form of large-scale attacks on and through computer systems which threaten a state's national security, public safety or economic well-being.

Parliamentary Assembly Resolution 1565 (2007)[1]
How to prevent cybercrime against state institutions in member and observer states?

1.   The Parliamentary Assembly recalls its Opinion No. 226 (2001) on the draft convention on cybercrime in which it considered the fight against cybercrime to be a crucially important challenge in view of the obstacles which this form of crime may pose to the development of new technologies and, more generally, to legal and economic security.

2.   The Assembly considers that cybercrime is a real threat to democratic stability and national security, and raises fundamental issues as regards the respect for human rights and the rule of law. Thus, this issue should be treated as a matter of top priority.

3.   Politically-motivated attacks against military or government websites of a number of Council of Europe member and observer states are increasingly frequent and sophisticated. Indeed, for the first time, criminal cyber attacks have targeted a state as a whole, attempting to paralyse the functioning of infrastructure vital to the Republic of Estonia. A few attacks have also been noted in other countries at the same time.

4.   This shows that cybercrime is a dangerous reality which has to be taken seriously at the highest level and that it represents a real threat to states whose technology-based infrastructures can be paralysed or even destroyed. This threat can emanate from private individuals, organised groups or states.

5.   As all states are vulnerable in the face of this danger; it is of utmost importance that an efficient protection and reaction system be developed at international level.

6.   The Assembly recalls that the Convention on Cybercrime (ETS No. 185, hereinafter "the convention"), contains extensive legislative provisions to counter cyber attacks against critical infrastructure. This treaty – the only binding one on this subject to date – has received widespread international support and therefore, in order to fight such crime effectively, all member states of the Council of Europe should urgently sign and ratify it and, more importantly, fully implement its provisions.

7.   The Assembly also recalls that the Council of Europe Convention on the Prevention of Terrorism (CETS No. 196) offers an additional instrument in

---

[1] *Assembly debate* on 28 June 2007 (25th Sitting) (see Doc. 11325, report of the Committee on Legal Affairs and Human Rights, rapporteur: Mr Sasi; Doc. 11335, opinion of the Political Affairs Committee, rapporteur: Mr Agramunt; and Doc. 11333, opinion of the Committee on Economic Affairs and Development, rapporteur: Mrs Lilliehöök). *Text adopted by the Assembly* on 28 June 2007 (25th Sitting).

the fight against cyberterrorism, as well as against the use of the Internet for terrorist purposes.

8.   The Assembly deplores the fact that a large number of member and observer states have not yet ratified these important conventions.

9.   The Assembly notes that the fight against cybercrime requires urgent international co-operation between governments, the private sector and non-governmental organisations, as cybercriminals rely on their ability to operate across borders and to exploit differences in national law. The lack of co-operation by the member states exposes them to considerable danger.

10.   The Assembly recalls that the convention is an open treaty and therefore invites non-member states to accede to it as soon as possible to reinforce international co-operation on this important subject.

11.   In this context, the Assembly welcomes the various initiatives taken in order to enhance international co-operation and co-ordination in the fight against cybercrime, *inter alia*, the 24/7 points of contact and the "Check the Web" programme, and strongly encourages member states to continue to reinforce their efforts, to strengthen international co-operation and to support concrete, co-ordinated measures for more efficient protection.

12.   In so doing, the Assembly emphasises that measures to fight and prevent cybercrime must be based on laws that fully respect human rights and civil liberties.

13.   Furthermore, the relevant laws need to be standardised, or at least compatible with one another, to permit the required level of international co-operation.

14.   Cyber attacks are not only a legal challenge; countries should develop policies and strategies to effectively protect their critical infrastructures, an undertaking which entails providing the necessary human, financial and technical resources for that purpose. In doing so, they should involve private actors, including computer, networking and software industries.

15.   The Assembly consequently invites member and observer states to:

   15.1 consider the question of fighting against and preventing cybercrimes as a matter of priority;

   15.2 sign and ratify the Council of Europe Convention on the Prevention of Terrorism and the Convention on Cybercrime and its Additional Protocol concerning the Criminalisation of Acts of a Racist and Xenophobic Nature committed through Computer Systems (ETS No. 189) without delay, and fully implement them as soon as possible;

15.3 evaluate their respective legal frameworks to assess whether they provide appropriate sanctions for cybercrime, in particular provisions for cases of computer-based terrorist attacks, and to amend their legislation if necessary, while fully respecting individual freedoms, in particular freedom of expression and information;

15.4 ensure that their relevant legislation is compatible with that of other states in order to facilitate international co-operation and exchange of information;

15.5 develop a framework for facilitating urgent political consultations and exchange of information, at all necessary levels of the countries concerned, in situations of extensive cyber attacks;

15.6 develop policies and strategies, on the basis of relevant technical studies, to effectively protect their critical infrastructures and to provide the necessary human, financial and technical resources for that purpose;

15.7 associate the private sector more closely, notably by building public-private partnerships for more effective and cross-sector international co-operation against cybercrime;

15.8 take effective national measures to prevent cybercrime activities;

15.9 give every assistance to the Government of Estonia in ensuring that a full and exhaustive investigation of the recent cyber attacks in that country is undertaken so as to inform future international efforts to combat cybercrime.

16. While considering that the convention should be regularly examined in the light of technological advances and new challenges, the Assembly awaits eagerly the findings of the Committee of Experts on Terrorism (CODEXTER) – which is currently examining the question of whether gaps in existing instruments (including the Convention on Cybercrime) require the development of additional instruments – before addressing its recommendations to the Committee of Ministers. The Assembly resolves to return to this matter as soon as possible.

Further publications

"*Apologie du terrorisme*" and "Incitement to terrorism" (2004)
English edition only

The fight against terrorism must never lead to a curtailing of the values and freedoms terrorists intend to destroy: the rule of law and freedom of thought and expression must never be sacrificed in this struggle.

This report analyses the situation in member and observer States of the Council of Europe and their different legal approaches to the phenomenon of the public expression of praise, justification and other forms of support for terrorism and terrorists, referred to in this publication as "apologie du terrorisme" and "incitement to terrorism".

ISBN: 92-871-5468-6, €19 / US$29

The fight against terrorism – Council of Europe standards (4th edition) (2007)

The Council of Europe has been dedicated, since 1949, to upholding human rights, the rule of law and pluralist democracy. Terrorism repudiates these three fundamental values and the Council of Europe is determined to combat it.

The Council of Europe has drafted a number of international legal instruments and standards which reflects the importance it attaches to combating terrorism and illustrate the underlying message of the Organisation, which is that it is possible to fight efficiently against terrorism while upholding the basic values that are the common heritage of the European continent.

The updated, enriched fourth edition of this book contains these texts and is intended to provide a handy, comprehensive document.

ISBN: 978-92-871-6277-9, €53 / US$80

Terrorism: special investigation techniques (2005)
English edition only

In order to combat terrorism and serious crime, law enforcement authorities have had to adapt their investigative means and develop special investigation techniques. Since there is a risk that they may infringe individual rights, special investigation techniques must be subject to control.

This publication contains an analytical report, which examines special investigation techniques in relation to law enforcement and prosecution, the control of their implementation, human rights and international co-operation and also contains a survey of national practice.

ISBN: 92-871-5655-7, €39 / US$59

Human rights and the fight against terrorism – The Council of Europe Guidelines (2005)

The Council of Europe believes that an effective fight against terrorism fully respecting human rights is possible.

This publication contains the Guidelines on Human Rights and the fight against terrorism, the first international instrument in this area, and the Guidelines on the protection of victims of terrorist acts, together with the reference and supporting texts and relevant case-law of the European Court of Human Rights.

ISBN:92-871-5694-8, €8 / US$12

Terrorism: protection of witnesses and collaborators of justice (2006)
English edition only

In order to combat terrorism, States often rely on the testimony of people who are closely connected to terrorist groups and who are more vulnerable than others to the use of intimidation against them or against people close to them. This may endanger the success of prosecutions often based on long and complicated investigations. Strengthening international co-operation in this field is also a useful means to ensure the protection of those persons whose protection would prove difficult on a merely national basis, given the conditions in the country where they are located. This publication contains the recently adopted standards in this field and a summary of relevant case-law from European Court of Human Rights, as well as a survey of national laws and practice in Council of Europe member and observer states and an analytical report.

ISBN 92-871-5811-8, 500 pages, €39 / US$59

Victims – Support and assistance (2nd edition) (2007)

True justice depends not only an states' ability to prosecute the perpetrators of a crime, but also on their capacity to restore the situation of victims. For over fifty years, the Council of Europe has contributed to building a common legal area based on the respect of human rights, democracy and the rule of law. The fight against crime has been at the heart of these efforts.

Since the 1980s, the Council of Europe has integrated the victims' perspective in its work in this field and has produced and updated a set of legal instruments to assist states in dealing with victims' needs.

This book brings together these standards and is intended to provide a handy, comprehensive reference document.

ISBN: 978-92-871-6377-6, 264 pages, €23 / US$35

Dirty money – The evolution of international measures to counter money laundering and the financing of terrorism

Dirty Money has been restructured so as to fully reflect the high priority which has been afforded by the international community since September 2001 to the financing of terrorism. It includes coverage of relevant initiatives taken in this latter sphere by the United Nations, the FATF, the Council of Europe, the Organization of American States and other institutions and groupings and places them in context.

The book is, as with the previous editions, designed for a wide audience. It will be of particular value for government officials and regulators with responsibility for money laundering and terrorist finance issues, for their counterparts in banks, non-bank financial institutions, as well as members of professions such as lawyers and accountants, to whom many of the counter-measures in question have now been applied. Finally, scholars and university students will continue to find Dirty Money a valuable tool for both research and teaching.

ISBN: 92-871-5467-8, 350 pages, €28 / US$42

For further publications see: www.coe.int/gmt

Sales agents for publications of the Council of Europe
Agents de vente des publications du Conseil de l'Europe

Council of Europe Publishing/Editions du Conseil de l'Europe
F-67075 Strasbourg Cedex
Tel.: +33 (0)3 88 41 25 81 – Fax: +33 (0)3 88 41 39 10 – E-mail: publishing@coe.int – Website: http://book.coe.int